Critical Thinking, Thoughtful Writing

A Rhetoric with Readings

Critical Thinking, Thoughtful Writing: A Rhetoric with Readings, Fifth Edition

John Chaffee

Senior Publisher: Lyn Uhl

Executive Editor: Monica Eckman

Acquisitions Editor: Margaret Leslie

Senior Development Editor: Leslie Taggart

Development Editor: Cheri Dellelo

Assistant Editor: Amy Haines

Senior Editorial Assistant: Elizabeth Ramsey

Media Editor: Janine Tangney

Executive Marketing Manager:
Stacey Purviance

Marketing Communications Manager:
Courtney Morris

Content Project Manager: Corinna Dibble

Senior Art Director: Jill Ort

Senior Print Buyer: Betsy Donaghey

Senior Rights Acquisition Specialist, Image:
Jen Meyer Dare

Rights Acquisition Specialist, Text:
Shalice Shah-Caldwell

Production Service:
S4Carlisle Publishing Services

Text Designer: Nesbitt Graphics

Cover Designer: Nesbitt Graphics

Cover Image: Jupiter Images

Compositor: S4Carlisle Publishing Services

Source for Image on page xxxi: © 2010
Gary Bates/Jupiterimages Corporation

Source for Image on page xxxii: © 2010
Photos.com/Jupiterimages Corporation

For product information and technology assistance, contact us at
Cengage Learning Customer & Sales Support, 1-800-354-9706

For permission to use material from this text or product,
submit all requests online at **www.cengage.com/permissions**.
Further permissions questions can be emailed to
permissionrequest@cengage.com.

Library of Congress Control Number: 2010938170

ISBN-13: 978-0-495-89978-5
ISBN-10: 0-495-89978-X

Wadsworth
20 Channel Center Street
Boston, MA 02210
USA

Cengage Learning is a leading provider of customized learning solutions with office locations around the globe, including Singapore, the United Kingdom, Australia, Mexico, Brazil and Japan. Locate your local office at **international.cengage.com/region**

Cengage Learning products are represented in Canada by Nelson Education, Ltd.

For your course and learning solutions, visit **www.cengage.com**.

Purchase any of our products at your local college store or at our preferred online store **www.cengagebrain.com**.

Printed in the United States of America
3 4 5 6 7 15 14 13 12 11

For Jessie and Joshua

Brief Contents

Contents

Thinking Critically About Visuals
Learn to think critically about what you see on page 14.

New Media & Thoughtful Writing
Learn to think critically about new media on page 10.

New Media & Thoughtful Writing

Learn to think critically about new media on pages 58.

© Argus/Shutterstock.com

CHAPTER 4

Thinking: Becoming More Creative and Visually Aware 93

© Brenda Ann Kenneally/Corbis

Thinking Critically About Visuals

Learn to think critically about what you see on page 104.

Thinking Critically About New Media

Learn to think critically about new media on pages 108.

© Argus/Shutterstock.com

New Media & Thoughtful Writing
Learn to think critically about new media on pages 188.

© Argus/Shutterstock.com

PART 2 **Thinking and Writing to Shape Our World** **203**

CHAPTER 7 **Writing to Describe and Narrate: Exploring Perceptions** **205**

© 2010 Radius Images/Jupiterimages Corporation

Thinking Critically About Visuals
Learn to think critically about what you see on page 209.

Thinking Critically About New Media
Learn to think critically about new media on page 210.

© Argus/Shutterstock.com

CHAPTER 8 **Writing to Classify and Define: Exploring Concepts** **235**

Thinking Critically About Visuals

Learn to think critically about what you see on page 246.

Source: AP Photo/Peter Kramer

Thinking Critically About New Media

Learn to think critically about new media on page 244.

© Argus/Shutterstock.com

CHAPTER 9

Writing to Compare and Evaluate: Exploring Perspectives and Relationships   291

Thinking Critically About Visuals

Learn to think critically about what you see on page 301.

AP Photo/Esteban Felix

Thinking Critically About New Media

Learn to think critically about new media on page 292.

CHAPTER 10   Writing to Speculate: Exploring Cause and Effect   343

Thinking Critically About Visuals

Learn to think critically about what you see on page 350.

Thinking Critically About New Media

Learn to think critically about new media on page 352.

Pete Souza/The White House/PSG/Newscom

Thinking Critically About Visuals
Learn to think critically about what you see on page 411.

© Argus/Shutterstock.com

Thinking Critically About New Media
Learn to think critically about new media on page 396.

© Lucas Oleniuk/The Toronto Star/ zReportage.com

Thinking Critically About Visuals
Learn to think critically about what you see on page 455.

© Argus/Shutterstock.com

Thinking Critically About New Media
Learn to think critically about new media on page 456.

© Library of Congress

Thinking Critically About Visuals
Learn to think critically about what you see on page 480.

Thinking Critically About New Media

Learn to think critically about new media on page 484.

© Argus/Shutterstock.com

CHAPTER 14   Writing About Investigations: Thinking About Research   539

Thinking Critically About Visuals
Learn to think critically about what you see on page 549.

Thinking Critically About New Media
Learn to think critically about new media on page 546.

APPENDIX   MLA and APA Documentation Styles   585

Readings

FIFTH EDITION

Critical Thinking, Thoughtful Writing

A Rhetoric with Readings

John Chaffee, PhD

Director, Center for Philosophy
and Critical Thinking
City University of New York

Christine McMahon
Barbara Stout

English Department, Montgomery College

WADSWORTH
CENGAGE Learning™

Australia • Brazil • Japan • Korea • Mexico • Singapore • Spain • United Kingdom • United States

Thinking-Writing Activities

Preface

Leo Tolstoy eloquently observed that "the relations of word to thought, and the creation of new concepts, is a complex, delicate, and enigmatic process unfolding in our soul." Writers and teachers of writing have long recognized intricate relationships between the extraordinary human processes of thought and language. This insight, which helps beginning college students become thoughtful writers, informs the comprehensive approach of *Critical Thinking, Thoughtful Writing: A Rhetoric with Readings,* Fifth Edition. The synergy between what experts in the thinking process (philosophers and psychologists, for example) understand about learning can be powerfully integrated with the critical thinking process as understood by teachers of writing and composition, especially in an age of increasingly complex channels of information and media.

Critical Thinking, Thoughtful Writing: A Rhetoric with Readings, Fifth Edition, presents an integrated approach to teaching the thinking, writing, and reading skills—of both verbal and visual texts—that first-year composition students need in order to successfully meet the challenges of academic work as well as the professional workplace. As students develop higher-order thinking abilities, they learn to articulate their ideas through writing and the creation of multimodal texts. And as they develop their abilities to navigate the writing process, students learn to think coherently, precisely, and creatively. This approach integrates the development of thinking skills with composing skills so they not only reinforce each other but also become inseparable.

This book stimulates and guides students to think deeply and beyond superficialities, to refuse to be satisfied with the first idea they have, to look objectively at multiple perspectives on complex issues, and to formulate their own informed conclusions. It encourages students to develop an interest in research and in delving into possibilities rather than settling for easy answers. It challenges students to be independent in their thinking and courageous in their convictions. And it shows them how to organize information, interpret different perspectives, solve challenging problems, analyze complex issues, and communicate their ideas clearly.

Advantages of a Critical Thinking Framework

The critical thinking framework of this text helps instructors and students in the following ways:

- **By providing an intellectual and thematic framework** that helps writing teachers place rhetorical concerns in a meaningful context. *Critical Thinking,*

Thoughtful Writing challenges and guides students to think and write about important topics that build on their cognitive activities and critical explorations. This process enables students to improve both the technical aspects of their writing (coherence, organization, detail, grammar, and mechanics) and the quality of their writing (depth, insight, sophistication).

- **By leading students to understand the reciprocal relationship** between the process of thinking and the process of writing. The text stimulates students to explore their own composing processes, gradually mastering the forms of thought and critical thinking that are the hallmark of mature and thoughtful writing.

- **By helping students to appreciate that reading is a thinking activity** rather than a series of decoding skills. This understanding accelerates and enhances reading development. Students are better able to understand and develop the interrelated thinking abilities that the reading process comprises, including problem solving, forming and applying concepts, and relating ideas to larger conceptual frameworks.

Content and Organization

Movement from the Personal to the Social

The book moves logically from introducing creative and critical thinking to explaining how these tools can be used in different kinds of writing. Part One helps students understand themselves as thinkers and writers; the Writing Projects in this section ask them to write from their own experiences and observations. Part Two explores important thinking patterns and language issues; here, the Writing Projects ask them to incorporate ideas and perspectives from others into their expository writing. Part Three uses an increasing number of sources as students work with problem solving, argumentation, and research. This logical progression pulls students beyond their personal experiences and pushes them to think and write about challenging issues and concepts, while seeing how social issues are connected with their own lives. The practical strategies will help students address writing assignments in other academic classes and in the workplace.

Four Integrated Elements to Each Chapter

1. **Critical Thinking Focus** examines the thinking skill central to each chapter. Examples of critical thinking skills are thinking about thinking, creative thinking, decision-making, evaluating perspectives, causal reasoning, conceptualizing, constructing knowledge, problem solving, and developing reasoned arguments.

2. **Writing Focus** provides strategies and Thinking-Writing Activities that draw upon the chapter's critical thinking skill.

3. **Reading Focus** comprises 45 professional readings (essays, articles, or book chapters) and 14 student essays, on themes including creativity, decision making, politics and culture, gender, language, problem solving, and arguments on timely and provocative topics. Each chapter offers three or more pieces of professional writing (such as essays, investigative reporting, and editorials, as well as some imaginative genres) and at least one student essay. The readings reflect the critical thinking focus in each chapter and provide the basis for assignments that initiate students' writing.

4. **Writing Project** builds on the reading themes and skills developed through the chapter's activities. These carefully structured projects move systematically through stages toward a finished project, providing guidance for each stage of the writing process. Each chapter includes at least one student example of the completed Writing Project.

Special Features

Practical Critical Thinking Strategies for Writing and for Evaluating Images This book introduces the process of thinking critically as a practical and powerful approach to writing, to critically evaluating electronic and visual media, and to life in general. For example, in learning a thoughtful approach for making decisions, students apply the decision-making process to revising drafts as well as to making important decisions in other areas of their lives. By developing their problem-solving abilities, students become able both to compose a problem-solving essay and to be more effective in solving problems beyond the classroom.

Comprehensive Thinking-Writing Model The Thinking-Writing Model introduced in Chapter 1 (pages 6–8) and reinforced throughout the book provides a clear graphic representation of the writing process and of the connections between critical thinking and thoughtful writing, as well as creative thinking and inventive writing.

Creative Thinking to Enrich the Writing Process The book shows that creative thought can and should be an integral part of academic writing. All aspects of the writing process can be approached creatively, including topic selection, generating ideas and drafting, using specific details, and writing introductions and conclusions. In learning to think creatively, students discover strategies to make their writing more inventive, while also infusing creative energy into other areas of their lives.

Emphasis on Collaboration The value of collaboration in thinking and writing is emphasized throughout, with this special icon highlighting Thinking-Writing Activities and other material specifically designed for collaboration and peer review. Critical thinking is emphasized in the active exploration of ideas, listening to others, and carefully evaluating opinions and arguments, and provides a context for collaborative learning. Students learn to examine their own opinions more analytically and relate these opinions to the world at large. They learn to assess alternative points of view in dialogue with others, contributing to their development into a community of concerned thinkers and writers.

Cross-Disciplinary Approach Recognizing that first-year composition courses prepare students to write in all of their courses and after college, this book presents examples, selections, and assignments from sociology, psychology, linguistics, history, business, cultural studies, economics, and the natural and hard sciences.

Critical Thinking as a Tool for Living The book views learning to think, write, and read as integral dimensions of an individual's personal growth and transformation. It aims to help students grow. While learning how to think and write, students are encouraged to apply these critical and creative thinking skills to all facets of their lives, enabling them to make enlightened decisions, solve challenging problems, analyze complex issues, communicate effectively, nurture creative talents, and become more thoughtful and socially aware citizens.

New to the Fifth Edition

The fifth edition of *Critical Thinking, Thoughtful Writing* makes even clearer the connections between active reading, critical thinking, and thoughtful writing. New chapters, features, and content include the following:

- **NEW: Focus on New Media.** Either a "Thinking Critically About New Media" or a "New Media & Thoughtful Writing" feature now appears in each chapter, giving students the opportunity to explore, critically analyze, and write about the unique challenges (e.g., Internet hoaxes, scams, and urban legends online) and opportunities (e.g., blogging as a form or journaling) posed by new media.

- **NEW: Readings.** The fifth edition has a number of new readings by a variety of noteworthy authors (e.g., Daniel Pink, Nicholas Carr, Peter Singer, and Michael Pollan) covering timely and provocative topics, including the pros and cons of food science, the effect of Google on our ability to attend, and the concept of health care rationing. In addition, a new casebook in Chapter 9 includes four new essays exploring the role of perspectives and relationships in the coverage of the January 2010 earthquake in Haiti.

- **NEW: More Writing Exercises.** New "Questions for Writing Thoughtfully" appear at the end of each reading to emphasize and reinforce the focus on writing.

- **NEW: Emphasis on Visual Rhetoric.** Each chapter now includes a feature, "Thinking Critically About Visuals," that engages students in comparing and evaluating images drawn from current events and popular culture. In addition, the majority of the photos in the two four-color inserts (in Chapter 4 and Chapter 13) have been updated. These challenge students to see how the "evidence" of seemingly objective photojournalism can tell startlingly different stories about the same phenomenon, as well as evaluate how effective combinations of text and image can create compelling persuasive messages. Additional discussion of how images (from photojournalism to advertising) are created, how to interpret their messages, and how to incorporate them within students' own work appears in Chapters 4, 9, 10, 13, and 14.

Supplements

Book Companion Website Visit the book companion website to access valuable course resources. Students will find an extensive library of interactive exercises and animations that cover grammar, diction, mechanics, punctuation, research, and writing concepts, as well as a complete library of student papers and a section on avoiding plagiarism. The site also offers a downloadable Instructor's Manual.

Online Instructor's Manual Available for download on the book companion site, the Instructor's Manual introduces instructors not only to the text, but to Critical Thinking as a course. Features include sample syllabi, writing inventory template; chapter-by-chapter teaching suggestions; Test of Critical Thinking Abilities; bibliography of additional readings, films, and videos for use with the text; and classroom handouts.

The Authors

Critical Thinking, Thoughtful Writing is the result of collaboration of three authors. John Chaffee is Director of the Center for Philosophy and Critical Thinking, and Professor of Philosophy at The City University of New York. His best-selling textbook *Thinking Critically,* going into its tenth edition, presents a comprehensive, language-based approach to learning that helped define the field of critical thinking. His introduction to philosophy text, *The Philosopher's Way,* has been acclaimed as a genuinely innovative contribution to the field. Barbara Stout and Christine McMahon, both former English professors at Montgomery College, used *Thinking Critically* in their composition courses for seven years, which made them ideally suited to adapt its critical thinking approach to the teaching of writing, resulting in the first edition of this text.

Acknowledgments

The following reviewers offered wise insights to and suggestions for the manuscript in this or earlier editions: Belinda Adams, Navarro College; Sonya Alvarado, Eastern Michigan University; Catherine Amdahl, Harrisburg Area Community College; Sonya Alvarado, Eastern Michigan University; Kathryn Bartle Angus, California State University, Fullerton; Jeanelle Barrett, Tarleton State University; Sally M. Baynton, San Antonio College; Larry Beason, University of South Alabama; Bruce Beckum, Colorado Mountain College; Patricia Bizzel, College of the Holy Cross; Bradley W. Bleck, Spokane Falls Community College; Paul Bodmer, Bismarck State College; Stephanie Byrd, Cleveland State University; Linda Caine, Prairie State College; Jamie Carey, Cerritos College; Christine Caver, University of Texas, San Antonio; Frankie Chadwick, University of Arkansas at Little Rock; William Church, Missouri Western State College; Gina Claywell, Murray State University; Huey Crisp, University of Arkansas at Little Rock; Sarah Dangelantonio, Franklin Pierce College; Lisette Davies Ward, Santa Barbara City College; Charlie Davis, Boise State University; Damian Doyle, University of Colorado at Boulder; Thomas Fink, LaGuardia College; Adam Fischer, Bowie State University; Kim Grewe, Wor-Wic Community College; Judith A. Hinman, College of the Redwoods; Mark Hoffman, Borough of Manhattan Community College, CUNY; Martha M. Holder, Wytheville Community College; Elizabeth Hooper, University of Texas, San Antonio; Margaret Hosty, Tarrant County College; Frederick T. Janzow, Southeast Missouri State University; Margaret Johnson, Idaho State University; John H. Jones, Jacksonville State University; Dipo Kalejaiye, Prince George's Community College; John Kinkade, University of Southern Indiana; Chikako D. Kumamoto, College of DuPage; Anna M. Lang, University of Indianapolis; Shirley Wilson Logan, University of Maryland; Lewis Long, Irvine Valley College; Cheryl R. Lyda, Idaho State University; Linda McHenry, Fort Hays State University; Mary Kate McMaster, Anna Maria College; Paul J. Morris, II, Pittsburgh State University; Andrea Muldoon, University of Wisconsin—Stout; Joan Mullin, University of Toledo; Robbi Nester, Irvine Valley College; Lisa Nicholas, University of Southern Indiana; Elizabeth A. Nist, Anoka-Ramsey Community College; John Regan, Boston University; Shirley Roberts, Brookhaven College; Jeffrey Roessner, Mercyhurst College; Denise Rogers, University of Louisiana at Lafayette; Kenneth Rosenauer, Missouri Western State College; Nicholas Schevera, College of Lake County; Isaiah Smithson, Southern Illinois University; Byrin Stay, Mount St. Mary's College; Judith L. Steele, Mid-America Christian University; Kay Stokes, Hanover College; Leslie Stoupas, Colorado Mountain College; John T. Stovall, National-Louis University; Michael Thomas, College of the Redwoods; William Vaughn, Central Missouri State University; Elizabeth Wahlquist, Brigham Young University; Jane Armstrong Woodman, Northern Arizona University.

John Chaffee would also like to thank Christine McMahon and Barbara Stout for the dedication and expertise they brought to the unique project of extending his work in critical thinking to the field of composition. Their approaches to teaching writing and their active involvement in the composition field have contributed significantly to a text that is practical, effective, and adaptable to a variety of instructional contexts.

As has been the case for the last several decades, John has been privileged to work with a stellar team of individuals at Cengage Learning who are exemplary professionals and also valued friends. Lyn Uhl, Publisher, has been steadfast in her personal and professional support of *Critical Thinking, Thoughtful Writing,* and John is deeply grateful. His thanks also go to the Executive Editor Monica Eckman for her efforts on behalf of the book. Margaret Leslie, Acquisitions Editor, provided wise guidance and crucial decisions in overseeing this revision of *Critical Thinking, Thoughtful Writing:* her steady hand at the helm and insightful suggestions at key junctures were essential. His heartfelt thanks go to Leslie Taggart, who in her role as Senior Development Editor provided the comprehensive direction and creative vision for this splendid edition that will be crucial for its success. It was a special pleasure working with the Development Editor Cheri Dellelo. Cheri was the invaluable core of the revision, instrumental in shaping every element of this new edition with a conscientious attention to detail and unwavering commitment to excellence. John is appreciative of the excellent support provided by the Assistant Editor Amy Haines, and also the Editorial Assistant Elizabeth Ramsey. Thanks also go to Janine Tangney in her role as Associate Media Editor. He is indebted to the Marketing staff for their talented and innovative efforts on behalf of *Critical Thinking, Thoughtful Writing*; Marketing Manager Melissa Holt; Marketing Director Jason Sakos; and Marketing Coordinator Ryan Ahern. He extends special appreciation to the Production team, for their dedicated and talented efforts on behalf of the book: Corinna Dibble, and S4Carlisle Publishing Services.

A special acknowledgment goes to Joyce Neff at Old Dominion University for her superb work in writing the earlier editions of the Instructor's Resource Manual. John is particularly indebted to the members of the English Department at LaGuardia College for their creative collaboration in linking the writing and critical thinking programs, a process that was initially supported with funding from the National Endowment for the Humanities.

John's children, Jessie and Joshua, and his wife, Heide Lange, have provided ongoing love, support, and guidance that have enhanced this book and brought purpose and meaning to his life. He would also like to remember his parents, Charlotte Hess and Hubert Chaffee who taught him lasting lessons about the most important things in life.

Critical Thinking, Thoughtful Writing

A Rhetoric with Readings

PART 1

Tools for Thinking, Reading, and Writing

Writing, reading, and creating text and images are how our minds explore and explain our world. The use of language and images is what makes us human; it is how we argue, how we tell stories, how we learn, how we creatively and politically express ourselves. To write is to use language thoughtfully, with a sense of audience and purpose. When you write, you pay close attention to the words that you choose, the structure of your paragraphs, the images you create. You contemplate your subject, search for exactly the right word to describe an observation, draw together different pieces of evidence to persuade a reader to think as you do. Writing helps you make sense of yourself and your world by illuminating your thought processes; writing is your mind in motion, working to clarify and understand. Learning to read critically helps you to become more aware of the strategies available to thoughtful writers. Reading texts and critically viewing images engage your mind with other conversations and open up additional perspectives.

Thinking clearly and critically about your reading strategies and your writing process will greatly enhance your ability to express yourself in all areas of your life. Part One of this book sharpens your awareness of the relationships among thinking, reading, writing, and creating texts and images and introduces you to ways of becoming a critical thinker and reader and a thoughtful writer.

istockphoto.com/track5

Although the process of becoming a critical thinker involves solitary activities like reading, writing, and reflecting, it is a process that is also very social in nature. Our minds develop in unique ways by exchanging ideas with others: discussing, debating, questioning. When was the last time you experienced a mental "lightbulb" go off when working with others?

The Thinking-Writing Model:
Rhetoric, Situation, and Process

I write to understand as much as to be understood.

—ELIE WIESEL

Critical Thinking
Focus: Thinking
   through writing

Writing Focus:
   The writing
   process

Reading Theme:
   Writing as
   self-expression

Writing Activity:
   Reflecting on
   past critical
   thinking

Thinking and Writing in College

The writer E. M. Forster once remarked, "How do I know what I think until I see what I say?" What did he mean by this? That you can't write better than you think! In many ways college is a whole new world. Not only are you expected to do more work in your courses, but you also are expected to work at a higher level: to *write more analytically*, to *think more conceptually*, and to *read more critically* than ever before. As a college writer, a citizen, or a member of a profession, you are expected to write with depth, insight, and analytical understanding. In order to achieve this level of sophistication in writing, you need to develop comparably advanced thinking abilities.

Becoming an effective writer enables you to represent your experience with clarity and precision. As you may have learned from your communication experiences thus far, the very process of using language serves to generate ideas. As a vehicle for creating and communicating your ideas, writing can be thought of as a catalyst that stimulates your personal and intellectual development. Since the writing process also enlarges your understanding of the world, becoming an effective writer is at the heart of your education.

To improve your writing abilities, you need to write on a regular basis, integrating writing into your life as a vital and natural element. Therefore, this book offers you Thinking-Writing Activities. These can be done in various ways: out of class or in, individually or in pairs or groups, and in whatever format your instructor specifies. Your instructor might ask you to record your responses in a journal to be reviewed periodically or in a class website or online forum. Your writing may also be shared with classmates or used as a basis for discussion. The work you do for the Thinking-Writing Activities will help to prepare you for the Writing Projects that conclude each chapter. These will give you an opportunity to think deeply about important subjects, to express your own distinctive point of view in a thoughtful and organized fashion, and to analyze the ideas of others from a variety of sources. Collaborative Activities provide the opportunity to enrich your writing by working with other students.

Thinking-Writing Activity

RECALLING A LEARNING EXPERIENCE

Recall a memorable learning experience that you have had, either in school or outside. Describe that experience and explain why it has had a lasting impact on you. Discuss how the experience has contributed to your development as a thinker and writer.

Becoming a Critical Thinker and Thoughtful Writer

Who is a critical thinker, and how do you become one? Traditionally, when people refer to a critical thinker, they mean someone who has developed an understanding of today's complex world, a thoughtful perspective on ideas and issues, the capacity for insight and good judgment, and sophisticated reasoning and language abilities. Critical thinkers are able to

- Articulate their ideas clearly and persuasively in writing
- Understand and evaluate what they read
- Discuss ideas in an informed, productive fashion

By questioning and analyzing, by evaluating and making sense of information, you examine your own thinking and that of others. And by clearly expressing your ideas in writing, you enter a larger community of thinkers and writers who enrich and sharpen your own thoughts through their responses. These thinking and writing activities help you reach the best possible conclusions and decisions.

Qualities of a Thoughtful Writer

A thoughtful writer is a person who thinks critically while moving through the process of writing. This writer reflects deeply on the ideas to be expressed and thinks carefully about the language and organization needed to meet the goals of the writing situation. In short, a thoughtful writer is a critical thinker. No collection of writing tips and strategies will ever enable you to write thoughtfully if you're not thinking critically.

Throughout this text, we focus on four qualities that characterize critical thinkers and thoughtful writers, and we will tie these thinking-writing qualities into specific stages of the writing process.

- Curious
- Open-minded
- Knowledgeable
- Creative

Let's explore these qualities in greater depth.

Curious   Thoughtful writers explore situations with probing questions that penetrate beneath the surface of issues, instead of being satisfied with superficial explanations. (They *want* to learn, to discover . . .)

Open-minded   Thoughtful writers explore their subjects from many different perspectives, willing to listen carefully to every viewpoint and evaluate each perspective carefully and fairly. Rather than being locked in to one point of view or a single, limited framework, they strive to understand and communicate the complex dimensions of their themes. For example, if they are writing about a social issue, they strive to present different perspectives on the issue as they reason their way to an informed conclusion.

Knowledgeable   Thoughtful writers always work to support their opinions with facts, evidence, and reasons. They recognize that opinions have value only to the extent that they are *informed* opinions. On the other hand, if they lack knowledge of the subject, they acknowledge this and set out to research what they need to know.

Creative   Thoughtful writers strive to develop inventive approaches to subjects; their writing is fresh and imaginative, avoiding clichés and tired conventions. They seek to break out of established patterns of thinking and approach themes and ideas from innovative directions.

Thinking critically by carefully exploring your thinking process is one of the most satisfying aspects of being a mature, educated human being. Analogously, *writing thoughtfully* involves thinking critically as you move through the process of writing so that you can express your ideas effectively.

The Thinking-Writing Model

The paradox of acquiring any complex ability is that in the best of all possible worlds, you would learn all the component parts of the activity at the same time. For example, learning to drive a car requires you master a variety of component skills that operate simultaneously: watching the road ahead, steering, applying the appropriate pressure on the gas pedal, braking, keeping a proper distance from other vehicles, watching for traffic signs and traffic lights, keeping an eye open for pedestrians, and so on. Yet a book on driving, or a video, focuses on one skill at a time because that is how information is presented most easily. Somehow you have to make the leap from learning all of the skills separately in a linear, step-by-step fashion to using them all at the same time, in complex relationships with one another.

Learning the complex skills of thinking critically and writing thoughtfully poses a similar dilemma. Although it is essential to learn each of the component parts of these processes, what distinguishes critical thinkers and thoughtful writers is that they can use all of these individual skills simultaneously.

The visual Thinking-Writing Model (Figure 1.1) presents each of these processes in relationship to each other. As you work on the various chapters and activities in this book, you will become more familiar with the different dimensions of the thinking-writing process.

As you examine the model, the writing process typically begins with a question. What is the *Purpose* of this communication? What is the *Subject*? Who is the *Audience*? Who is the *Writer*, and what is the writer's perspective? Engaging these questions utilizes our core abilities to *Think Creatively* about ideas we want to communicate, *Think Critically* in order to organize and clarify these ideas, and *Write Thoughtfully* by using the appropriate vocabulary and language forms to communicate our ideas.

The writing process itself is dynamic and holistic. The key elements of the process are *Generating* ideas, *Defining* a focus, *Drafting, Organizing, Revising,* and *Proofreading.* For most writers, these activities rarely occur in a neat, orderly sequence: the process is much more organic and recursive. Effective writers also *Collaborate* with other people in order to help them produce the highest quality of writing, and their assistance can occur at any stage in the writing process.

At the very center of the model is *Communicating*, the process by which we share our thoughts, feelings, and experiences. Communication creates miraculous moments when our minds touch and engage other minds. The word *communicating* comes from the Latin word *communicare*, which means "to share, to impart, to make common." As members of a social species, we need to share thoughts and feelings with other human beings. As technologies allow speedier and speedier

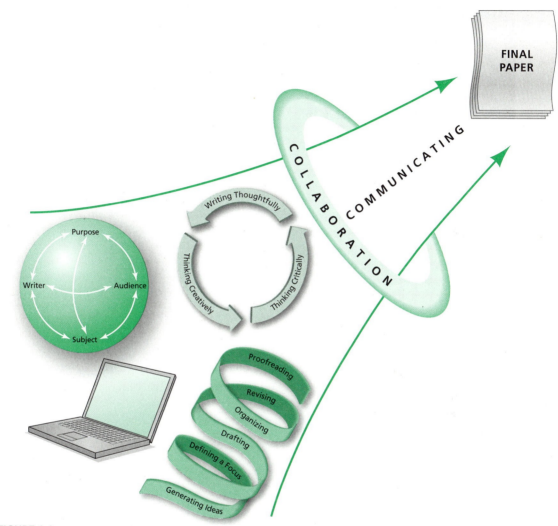

FIGURE 1.1
The Complete Thinking-Writing Model

communication throughout the world, critical thinking and thoughtful writing are evermore vital to the survival and progress of humanity.

This book is designed to offer you opportunities to build on the strengths you have and to grow as a critical thinker and thoughtful writer. The following Thinking-Writing Activity asks you to reflect on your own thinking-writing process as a starting point.

Thinking-Writing Activity

ANALYZING A WRITING EXPERIENCE

Describe in detail a writing experience that you found particularly satisfying or successful: for example, a paper you wrote for school, a market analysis you created for your company, or a letter in which you expressed important thoughts and feelings. After completing your description, answer the following questions in your journal or notebook.

- What was your goal or purpose in writing?
- What was the reaction of the people who read it—your audience?
- How did you think of the key ideas you included?
- How did you organize your ideas?
- Did you use other sources (such as readings) to provide support and context for your writing?
- In what ways did you revise your writing?
- How did you feel after completing your writing?

Your analysis will probably demonstrate that you already use many of the abilities that are integral to the Thinking-Writing Model. Carefully examine the Thinking-Writing Model in Figure 1.1. Before long, the model will become familiar, and you will be able to use it as a powerful guide to strengthen and clarify your thinking and writing. Let's explore the various dimensions of the Thinking-Writing Model and see how they work together to produce clear thinking and effective writing.

Rhetoric and the Writing Situation

Writing always occurs in a situation within which the act of writing takes place. Writers have reasons to write, someone to whom they wish to write, a subject about which they have something important to say, and a sense of self as a writer that they want to project. Although these ideas are of great importance today, they are not new. They come from the study of *rhetoric,* the principles developed in ancient times for speaking and writing effectively. Rhetoric is the art of inventing or discovering your ideas, arranging them in the most persuasive way, and then expressing them in suitable language in order to have the desired effect on their audiences. Today the word *rhetoric* has both a negative and a positive meaning: language that is insincere and not to be taken seriously—"mere rhetoric"—and the positive meaning with which this book is concerned, the study of the principles and rules for effective writing.

We begin our study of rhetoric with the components of the writing situation: purpose, audience, subject, and writer. In Figure 1.2, these four components appear in the first part of the model because they need to be considered when the writer begins to write, but they also need to be thought about at every stage of writing and communicating. To help you develop your rhetorical skills, these components are discussed individually at the beginning of each of the Writing Projects in subsequent chapters.

🖑 **ONLINE RESOURCES**
Classical Rhetoric
Visit your text website, accessed through **CengageBrain.com** to learn more about classical rhetoric.

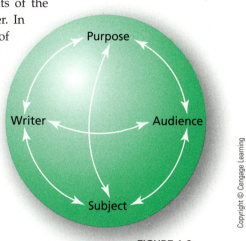

Copyright © Cengage Learning

FIGURE 1.2
The Writing Situation

Purpose

Every act of writing has a *purpose*. When you complete a paper for a college course, you hope to show your instructor that you have understood and can both apply and communicate concepts relevant to the class. In a business setting, your aim is to transmit information or requests in a memo or a report; in your civic life, you want to advocate for community interests through letters or petitions; in your private life, you write in your journal and email your friends so that you can later recall your activities and feelings. A crucial part of becoming a thoughtful writer is maintaining a clear sense of the specific audience and purpose for whatever subject you are writing on.

Audience

Thoughtful writers shape their work by consideration of their *audience*, the intended reader or readers. Although there are some instances when you write only for yourself (a diary entry, for example); you probably intend most of your writing to be read by someone else: the person receiving your letter, the coworkers reading your memo, the friend enjoying your blog, or the instructor grading your paper. The more you think about your audience, the more concerned you will be about using language and visuals to make yourself clear, and the better your writing will become. The real skill lies in writing so clearly and coherently that your audience receives exactly the same message that you intended to send.

Thoughtful writers are able to put themselves in their readers' place and to view their own writing through their readers' eyes. This perspective-taking helps them to craft their writing so that it will best communicate the ideas, arguments, experiences, and emotions they seek to convey. In other words, they think about

New Media & Thoughtful Writing

How to Write for the New Media

When we express ourselves in writing, our audience is not able to hear our vocal inflections or see our gestures and body language. The impression we make depends completely upon what we write. The same holds true for the use of email, which has changed the way many people communicate at work, in social settings, in the classroom, and at home. Consider the following questions:

- What are some of the differences between communicating via email, the spoken word, or another form of writing?
- Do you think an email is easier to misunderstand than other styles of writing? Why or why not? For example, have you ever
  - Received an email you thought was sarcastic, cruel, or too blunt?
  - Sent one that was misinterpreted?
  - Received "hoax" virus warnings?
  - Received chain letters promising unbelievable rewards?
  - Received jokes you didn't want?
- In your opinion, has the popularity of email changed the nature or frequency of these kinds of messages as compared to paper mail? If so, how has that happened? The central point is that in order to be an effective communicator in any medium, we have to be continually aware of our audience, asking ourselves the questions "How will my message be received or interpreted?" and "What 'voice' will be most successful in communicating my intended message?"

Writing is similar to speaking in this regard. Have you noticed that you speak differently to different groups of people in different situations? Depending upon whether and where you work, you may notice that your choice of words and even grammatical constructions vary from those you use when speaking with, for example, family members. For that matter, how you speak to children is probably different from how you speak to siblings or to parents and other elders. You have a different "speaking personality" in different situations.

What different email personalities do you have? What steps can you take to ensure that you come across as you intend when you use email? These are "language landmines" that you want to keep in mind as you compose and send your emails, texts, and tweets. Writing for new media effectively means developing a new set of writing strategies especially adapted to this new digital medium. In the following article by

Neal Jansons, "How to Write for the New Media," he identifies some of the writing strategies to work at developing.

How to Write for the New Media
by Neal Jansons

Here are some tricks and tips for developing a new media writing style.

1. Go Short

In school and literature, often we are taught that more is better. If you can slip in more detail, another source, or another idea, you should. Well, this is just plain wrong in the new media. Here we have to capture a reader who with the click of a mouse can be somewhere else. They are not a professor paid to read a paper or a book-reader sitting and relaxing in a nook. They are on a computer and working in a very "hot" (interactive) medium. **Keep your posts and articles between 400 and 700 words.** If you absolutely *must* go longer, consider splitting the post up into a series. DO NOT go for the "multi-pager." It does not work, nobody reads it and if you keep trying to write your *magnum opus* you will lose readers.

2. Avoid Big Blocks of Texts

Break your articles up into multiple paragraphs. What seems like over-formatting in a book or magazine can be perfect for a post because of the difference in how they are read. People's eyes react differently to text on a screen. **Use pictures, changes in font size, and lists to break your content up into meaningful chunks.** The goal is that at any point a person could finish up a section in just a few seconds and easily come back for the next chunk later.

3. Avoid the Passive Voice

In school we learn to speak in the passive voice to record facts. This makes things very "objective" and "neutral" sounding, but is not what people are looking for online. There are a billion other things they could be reading that can all be objective, but they will read *your* work because it is *yours*. **Make your writing drip with active verbs and your own personality.** Let your voice come through so strongly that the reader will hear you in their head.

(Continues)

@ NEW MEDIA & THOUGHTFUL WRITING (CONTINUED)

4. Lead the Reader

The formatting of online content is always a problem, but the best thing you can do is let your content guide the reader's eyes and mind. **Use lists, headings, and text styling to lead the reader's eyes to the important points.** This is what is sometimes called the "Command to Look" from a book by the same name.

5. Make Your Content "Hot"

This is the internet, web 2.0 thank you very much, and we want our content to be dynamic. We want links, video, and the ability to converse. **Pepper your articles with interactivity**, even to the point of asking questions for your readers to answer. If you refer to something, link it (but only the first time!), if you say there was a video, include it in the post.

6. K.I.S.S.

Keep it simple. No, really. Really simple. Avoid clarifying clauses, complicated thoughts, and involved sentences. This is not to say you can't write difficult ideas . . . just break them down. **Tell them what you are going to tell them, tell them, then tell them what you told them.** The reason for this is (again) about how people read on the internet. Since people are always multi-tasking, being able to come back to an article and read it in little chunks without losing the thread of the thought is absolutely necessary.

how much background information their audience will need, or won't need, to understand the intended message. Anticipating possible questions that their audience may have, they try to answer such questions at appropriate places. Understanding that the audience may have strong feelings about certain controversial topics, they consider those feelings as they write.

Subject

Writing has to be about someone or something—a *subject*. Sometimes the subject originates in your own experience, but often it comes from ideas and information provided by others. Much of college writing involves responding to ideas and concepts presented in textbooks, lectures, or research sources. Today,

Final Word

Following these simple steps you can increase your reader loyalty and the usefulness of your posts. People will be able to get what they need from your content easily and efficiently, which will make your posts and articles appealing and useful, which means people will come back to read more and pass on your work to other potential readers and clients. **Help your readers read and they will stay loyal, make them work too hard and they will just click something else.**

Source: From WriteNewMedia.com blog by Neal Jansons 1/23/10. Reprinted by permission of the author.

Thinking-Writing Activity

HOW WELL DO YOU COMMUNICATE?

How do you come across to your audience, and what can you do to improve the clarity of your message? One approach is to look through your sent email file and examine some of your older emails, asking yourself the questions "With the detachment of time, was this message written in a way that would best communicate my intended meaning, or could there have been possible misinterpretations?" and "How could I revise the message to make it less vague or ambiguous?" Once you have revised some of these older emails, think of some strategies to help make your future emails more successful in communicating the meaning you intend such as "I should make more use of examples to illustrate my point."

much of the research you will do for college begins on the Internet, so the ability to find and evaluate online sources is crucial. Your writing task is usually to demonstrate your understanding of the ideas presented and also to apply, analyze, synthesize, or evaluate the ideas being expressed. The quality of your writing depends on the quality of your thinking as you process ideas and present them in order to communicate your own informed perspective on the subject.

Writer

Of course, any writing situation calls for a *writer*, and the characteristics of the writer affect what is written and how it is produced. A writer's identity as a woman or a man or as a member of an ethnic or other social group often influences

Thinking Critically About Visuals

Perspective-Taking and Audience

Imagine this person is giving a talk about the importance of cooperation. How might the content, tone, intellectual level, and length of the talk be different if she were talking to a classroom full of first-graders or a roomful of Fortune 500 executives?

© 2010 Fuse/Jupiterimages Corporation

approaches and attitudes. The relationship of the writer to the language or dialect being used makes a difference; whether the writer is tired or energetic, happy or sad, and so forth, makes a difference, too.

The relationship of the writer to the intended audience also makes a difference. When writing email or blogs for friends, casual style and the admission of a lack of information on a subject are permissible. But college writers are expected to write with some authority as they join in a larger conversation of educated authors. If a piece of writing is about your own life and experiences, you automatically have that authority since no one knows your life better than you do. But many college assignments call for subjects related to class material, and you are still expected to write with authority. That is why the library and the Internet are so important to you; by gathering information you can become knowledgeable on almost any subject. One of the worst ways for a college writer to begin is, "I don't know much about this subject, but here goes."

FROM *My American Journey*

by Colin Powell

In the following excerpt from his best-selling autobiography *My American Journey*, former Secretary of State Colin Powell writes with authority about his life. Powell was born in New York City to immigrant parents from Jamaica. He attended public schools in the city, graduating from the City College of New York with a degree in geology. As a student at CCNY, he participated in ROTC, receiving a commission as an Army second lieutenant upon graduation. Powell served for thirty-five years, rising to the rank of four-star general and holding, from 1989 through 1993, the position of Chairman of the Joint Chiefs of Staff, the highest military position in the Department of Defense.

Powell's name has often been mentioned as a candidate for public office. He has been awarded two Presidential Medals of Freedom and the Congressional Gold Medal, among other military honors and decorations.

I have made clear that I was no great shakes as a scholar. I have joked over the years that the CCNY [City College of New York] faculty handed me a diploma, uttering a sigh of relief, and were happy to pass me along to the military. Yet, even this C-average student emerged from CCNY prepared to write, think, and communicate effectively and equipped to compete against students from colleges that I could never have dreamed of attending. If the Statue of Liberty opened the gateway to this country, public education opened the door to attainment here. Schools like my sister's Buffalo State Teachers College and CCNY have served as the Harvards and Princetons of the poor. And they served us well. I am, consequently, a champion of public secondary and higher education. I will speak out for them and support them for as long as I have the good sense to remember where I came from.

Shortly before the commissioning ceremony in Aronowitz Auditorium, Colonel Brookhart called me into his office in the drill hall. "Sit down, Mr. Powell," he said. I did, sitting at attention. "You've done well here (in ROTC). You'll do well in the Army. You're going to Fort Benning soon."

He warned me that I needed to be careful. Georgia was not New York. The South was another world. I had to learn to compromise, to accept a world I had not made and that was beyond my changing. He mentioned the black general Benjamin O. Davis, who had been with him at West Point, where Davis was shunned the whole four years by his classmates, including, I assumed, Brookhart. Davis had gotten himself into trouble in the South, Brookhart said, because he had tried to buck the system. The colonel was telling me, in effect, not to rock the boat, to be a "good Negro." . . .

The Army was becoming more democratic, but I was plunged back into the Old South every time I left the post. I could go into Woolworth's in Columbus, Georgia, and buy anything I wanted, as long as I did not try to eat there. I could go into a department store and they would take my money, as long as I did not try to use the men's room. I could walk along the street, as long as I did not look at a white woman. . . .

5   One night, exhausted and hungry, I locked up the house and headed back toward the post. As I approached a drive-in hamburger joint on Victory Drive, I thought, okay, I know they won't serve me inside, so I'll just park outside. I pulled in, and after a small eternity, a waitress came to my car window. "A hamburger, please," I said.

She looked at me uneasily. "Are you Puerto Rican?" she asked.

"No," I said.

"Are you an African student?" She seemed genuinely trying to be helpful.

"No," I answered. "I'm a Negro. I'm an American. And I'm an Army officer."

10   "Look, I'm from New Jersey," the waitress said, and "I don't understand any of this. But they won't let me serve you. Why don't you go behind the restaurant, and I'll pass you a hamburger out the back window."

Something snapped. "I'm not that hungry," I said, burning rubber as I backed out. As I drove away, I could see the faces of the owner and his customers in the restaurant windows enjoying this little exercise in humiliation. . . .

Racism was still relatively new to me, and I had to find a way to cope psychologically. I began by identifying my priorities. I wanted, above all, to succeed at my Army career. I did not intend to give way to self-destructive rage, no matter how provoked. If people in the South insisted on living by crazy rules, then I would play the hand dealt me for now. If I was to be confined to one end of the playing field, then I was going to be a star on that part of the field. Nothing that happened off-post, none of the indignities, none of the injustices, was going to inhibit my performance. I was not going to let myself become emotionally crippled because I could not play on the whole field. I did not feel inferior, and I was not going to let anybody make me believe I was. I was not going to allow someone else's feelings about me to become my feelings about myself. Racism was not just a black problem. It was America's problem. And until the country solved it, I was not going to let bigotry make me a victim instead of a full human being. I occasionally felt hurt; I felt anger; but most of all I felt challenged. I'll show you!

Questions for Reading Actively

1. What audience do you think Powell had in mind while writing? Identify a specific audience, either one person or a group of persons, to whom you would recommend this reading.

2. Describe the writer as specifically as you can. What is your attitude toward him, now that you have read this? Does this represent any change in your attitude toward Powell?

Questions for Thinking Critically

1. Describe an experience in which you were the victim of discrimination or prejudice. How did it make you feel? How did you deal with it?

2. Colin Powell was determined to achieve his goals, despite many obstacles. Describe in your own words the thinking approach he used to deal with the pervasive racism that he encountered.

3. Powell concludes his autobiography with an affirmation regarding the United States that seems particularly relevant in these perilous times: "We will come through because our founders bequeathed us a political system of genius, a system flexible enough for all ages and inspiring noble aspirations for all time. We will continue to flourish because our diverse American society has the strength, hardiness, and resilience of the hybrid plant we are."

    Explain whether you agree with Powell that America's ethnic diversity is a source of strength and resilience, and list the reasons why or why not.

Question for Writing Thoughtfully

1. What purpose or purposes do you think Powell had in mind while writing? How does he try to achieve his purpose(s)? List two specific examples from the reading to support your answer.

Writing Thoughtfully, Thinking Creatively, Thinking Critically

The next part of the Thinking-Writing Model, Figure 1.3, indicates the reciprocal relationships among writing thoughtfully, thinking creatively, and thinking critically. The ability to be creative is one of the four qualities that distinguish critical thinkers and thoughtful writers. When you first decide to write something, you need to come up with some initial ideas to write about. Your ability to *think creatively* makes producing such ideas possible. When you think creatively, you discover ideas—and connections among ideas—that are illuminating, useful, often exciting, sometimes original, and usually worth developing. We can define *thinking creatively* as discovering and developing ideas that are unusual and worthy of further elaboration.

Simultaneously (or *almost* simultaneously), these beginning ideas find form in language expressed in writing. Yet the process of writing thoughtfully elaborates and shapes the ideas that you are trying to express, especially if you are to bring your critical thinking abilities to bear on this evolving process. This extraordinarily complex process typically takes place in a very natural fashion as creative thinking and critical thinking work together to produce thoughtful writing, which in turn gives form to your ideas and communicates them to others.

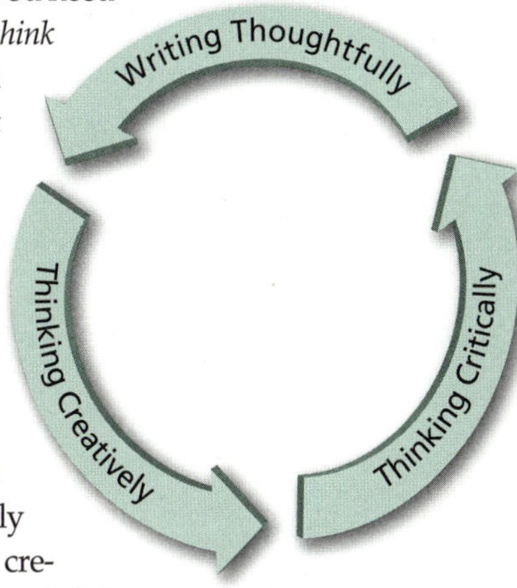

Writing Thoughtfully
Thinking Critically
Thinking Creatively
Copyright © Cengage Learning

FIGURE 1.3
Core Abilities

Effective writers not only use each of these processes but also are able to integrate them. For example, it is impossible to write thoughtfully without creating ideas that reflect your vision of the world or without using your critical thinking abilities to evaluate the accuracy and intelligibility of your writing. Unfortunately, these essential abilities are not always taught explicitly. Too often, writing is emphasized as a way of putting words together in conventional forms, not as a dynamic means of personal expression that liberates us to articulate our creative perspectives—tempered by critical evaluation.

The Writing Process

The Recursive Nature of the Writing Process

Despite the many different writing forms and contexts, the basic elements of the writing process remain constant:

- Generating ideas
- Defining a focus (main idea or *thesis*)
- Organizing ideas into various thinking patterns
- Drafting
- Revising, editing, and proofreading
- Collaborating, which can weave through all these activities

FIGURE 1.4
The Writing Process

These elements of the writing process occur within the writing situation as a result of creative and critical thinking, and they are depicted in the third part of the Thinking-Writing Model (Figure 1.4). For most writers, these activities rarely occur in a neat, orderly sequence. Instead, writers move in different ways, from generating ideas to drafting to more generating to organizing to revising to generating to editing—around and around—as they develop ideas and clarify them. And each element of the writing process depends upon the writer's awareness of subject, audience, and purpose.

You have probably discovered that the process of writing does not merely express your thinking; it also stimulates your thoughts, bringing to the surface new ideas and ways to explore them. So although you may begin a writing project by generating some ideas, you may find yourself returning to generate more ideas later on as you work to organize and draft your thoughts, developing new or refined concepts to write about. And as you gain more experience with collaboration, you may find yourself turning to others more frequently to benefit from their ideas and perspectives, which may send you back to generating, focusing, drafting, or organizing.

Generating Ideas

We have seen that most writing efforts begin with identifying something to write about—a subject. Since ideas are not created in isolation but are almost always related to a particular subject, you expand ideas by exploring that subject. Some writing projects have very specific requirements; others may be more open-ended. In most cases, however, you will be expected to come up with your own ideas. Even when you are responding to an assigned subject or a reading selection, you are typically expected to offer an original insight or viewpoint. As a thoughtful writer, you are expected to be open-minded, creative, and curious. At this stage of generating ideas, a number of strategies are useful, such as brainstorming, creating mind maps, freewriting, and asking key questions to stimulate your creative thinking. These strategies will be explored in depth in a later chapter.

Keeping a Journal or Blog

Keeping a journal or blog is rewarding in several ways. First, as you already know, the process of writing stimulates your mind and helps shape your thinking. Also, writing creates a record of your thoughts and feelings that you can return to and perhaps use as the starting place for a finished piece of writing. Journal entries should be freely written, with no concern for punctuation or polished prose. Nor should you evaluate your ideas. Just let them flow, write them in a notebook or a computer file, and make journal keeping a part of your daily life. A blog, or online journal, allows you to incorporate visuals and audio into your writing as well as join larger virtual communities and discussions.

Defining a Focus

After generating a number of possible ideas to write about, academic writers need to define a focus. Academic writing is *expected* to have a focus; classmates, instructors, and others interested in your subject expect more than a list of facts. Once selected, your main idea—known as a thesis or, for argumentative writing, a claim—will organize and direct your thinking. Your thesis or claim will also guide your exploration of the subject and suggest new ideas. Of course, a variety of main ideas can develop out of any particular situation, and your initial working thesis will probably need redefining as you draft your paper.

Sometimes you will need to do some drafting and organizing before you are ready to define your focus. And sometimes you will need to refocus your thesis as you do further drafting.

Organizing Ideas

Once you have a tentative thesis or claim, you may be ready to plan the organization of your paper. But at this point or even earlier, you may realize that you don't have enough information on your subject to fulfill your purpose. Remembering that a thoughtful writer is knowledgeable, you may need to generate more ideas or to consult other sources of information in order to write with authority. When you are ready to begin organizing, ask yourself, "What are my main points, and how should they be presented to my audience?" You can use a variety of thinking patterns as you organize your writing, such as reporting chronologically, comparing and contrasting, or dividing and classifying. Your choice of thinking pattern will depend on the subject you are exploring, your purpose, and your audience. We will examine these patterns in later chapters.

It usually helps to have a tentative organization to guide your drafting, but often your organization changes as you draft and revise. This is a natural and productive part of most people's writing processes.

Drafting

Drafting begins when you actually begin to write. *What* you write reflects your previous work from the initial stages of the writing process: generating ideas, defining a focus, and thinking about an organizational structure. Your writing expresses how far your thinking on the subject has progressed to that point. It is unlikely that your draft will emerge in finished form. In fact, your initial draft should undergo substantial revision until it finally represents your mind's best work. So don't get obsessed with trying to craft the perfect sentence, fashion the ideal metaphor, or secure the optimal word. You'll have time to do that later on. The most important goal in drafting is to get *started*. Get those vague and evolving ideas onto paper, where they can be examined, reflected upon, and refined.

Often you will find it useful to draft in sections, according to the plan you established. But be prepared to let the writing process take you to new places that you didn't anticipate. The process of writing is a catalyst for your thinking process, creating new ideas and leading in unexpected directions. Trusting your writing/thinking process leads to creative breakthroughs that will enrich your original plan.

Naturally, what you are drafting—a summary, an argument, a report—influences the way you express and organize your thinking. Much of your academic writing will be in the form of essays in which you are expected to take a position, analyze a concept, or interpret a subject. The structure normally used to organize ideas in an essay typically reflects the basic questions raised when you discuss ideas with others. As you draft, keep in mind the questions of a hypothetical audience (from Mina Shaughnessey's book *Errors and Expectations*):

What is your point? (stating the main idea)

I don't quite get your meaning. (explaining the main idea)

Prove it to me. (providing examples, evidence, and arguments to support the main idea)

So what? (drawing a conclusion)

Revising, Editing, and Proofreading

Because thinking and writing are recursive processes, you are continually revising your thinking and writing as you work on almost any paper. Whatever your drafting style, though, once you have expressed your thinking in language, you must be able to go back and "re-see" (the origin of the word *revise*) your drafts as clearly as possible.

Most writers have a hard time looking objectively at their own writing. They know what they mean; they sometimes like certain words, sentences, or clever ideas and don't want to change them. But thoughtful writers have acquired the ability to be critical readers of their own work and to accept the fact that they may need to make major changes in their drafts. Writers and researchers in many disciplines share their drafts with colleagues for feedback and additional perspective, a collaborative process called *peer review*. We will explore strategies for peer review in Chapter 3.

As they revise, they are aware of a second voice in their heads, their Reader/ Editor. This voice asks useful questions, not unlike those listed previously under Drafting:

Have you made your main point clear?

Have you proved your point to your audience by giving enough information and examples?

Could you reorganize any of your ideas to help your audience understand more easily?

Many writers wait until they are satisfied with the content and organization before they *edit* smaller components, such as paragraph division, topic sentences, sentence variety, connections, and transitions. Then they *proofread*, checking spelling and punctuation. And sometimes while they are editing or proofreading, they see content and organization problems that require more revision!

"Writing Is Not a McDonald's Hamburger"

by Natalie Goldberg

From *Writing Down the Bones*

Acclaimed as much for her intuitive, compassionate teaching of writing as she is for her own well-received prose, Natalie Goldberg's 1986 book *Writing Down the Bones* (from which "Writing Is Not a McDonald's Hamburger" is excerpted) has become a touchstone not only for aspiring writers but also for anyone wishing to live more

Source: From *Writing Down the Bones* by Natalie Goldberg. Copyright © 1986. Reprinted by arrangement with Shambhala Publications, Inc., Boston. www. Shambhala.com

creatively. Goldberg has continued to mine her personal life, her deeply engaged study of Zen Buddhism, and her painterly observations of the natural world (particularly the landscape around her home in Taos, New Mexico) in such books as *Wild Mind: Living the Writer's Life* (1990), *Long Quiet Highway: Waking Up in America* (1993), and *Thunder and Lightning: Cracking Open the Writer's Craft* (2000). Goldberg lives with her partner in Taos, New Mexico, and St. Paul, Minnesota.

Sometimes I have a student who is really good right from the beginning. I'm thinking of one in particular. The air was electric when he read, and he was often shaking. The writing process split him open; he was able to tell about being fourteen years old in a mental hospital, about walking the streets of Minneapolis tripping on LSD, about sitting next to the dead body of his brother in San Francisco. He said he had wanted to write for years. People told him he should be a writer, but anytime he sat down to write he couldn't connect the words on paper with the event or his feelings.

That is because he had an idea of what he wanted to say before he came to paper. Of course, you can sit down and have something you want to say. But then you must let its expression be born in you and on the paper. Don't hold too tight; allow it to come out how it needs to rather than trying to control it. Yes, those experiences, memories, feelings, are in us, but you can't carry them out on paper whole the way a cook brings out a pizza from the oven.

Let go of everything when you write, and try at a simple beginning with simple words to express what you have inside. It won't begin smoothly. Allow yourself to be awkward. You are stripping yourself. You are exposing your life, not how your ego would like to see you represented, but how you are as a human being. And it is because of this that I think writing is religious. It splits you open and softens your heart toward the homely world.

When I'm cranky now, miserable, dissatisfied, pessimistic, negative, generally rotten, I recognize it as a feeling. I know the feeling can change. I know it is energy that wants to find a place in the world and wants friends.

5   But yes, you can have topics you want to write about—"I want to write about my brother who died in San Francisco"—but come to it not with your mind and ideas, but with your whole body—your heart and gut and arms. Begin to write in the dumb, awkward way an animal cries out in pain, and there you will find your intelligence, your words, your voice.

People often say, "I was walking along [or driving, shopping, jogging] and I had this whole poem go through my mind, but when I sat down to write it, I couldn't get it to come out right." I never can either. Sitting to write is another activity. Let go of walking or jogging and the poem that was born then in your mind. This is another moment. Write another poem. Perhaps secretly hope something of what you thought a while ago might come out, but let it come out however it does. Don't force it.

The same student mentioned above was so excited about writing that he immediately tried to form a book. I told him, "Take it slow. Just let yourself write for a while. Learn what that is about." Writing is a whole lifetime and a lot of practice.

I understood his urgency. We want to think we are doing something useful, going someplace, achieving something—"I am writing a book."

Give yourself some space before you decide to write those big volumes. Learn to trust the force of your own voice. Naturally, it will evolve a direction and a need for one, but it will come from a different place than your need to be an achiever. Writing is not a McDonald's hamburger. The cooking is slow, and in the beginning you are not sure whether a roast or a banquet or a lamb chop will be the result.

Questions for Reading Actively

1. What purpose or purposes do you think Goldberg had in mind while writing? Specify any one thing in the reading that helps you to identify her purpose.

2. What audience do you think she had in mind while writing? What other audiences might benefit from reading this? What audiences might not benefit?

3. What is her subject? Be as specific as you can in describing it. What is her attitude toward her subject?

Questions for Thinking Critically

1. Goldberg, a Zen Buddhist, claims in paragraph 3 that she believes "writing is religious." How does she define and understand "religious," and what specific qualities of writing make it a "religious" activity or experience? Do you agree with her definition of "religious"? Compare your own definition of a "religious" activity or mindset with Goldberg's.

2. Athletes often describe their feeling at peak performance as being "in the flow." Goldberg describes something similar about the process of inspiration. Describe a time when you felt like you were "in the flow" of an activity (physical, artistic, or intellectual). How did you get "in the flow"? Is there a specific strategy or ritual that you use to help you get "in the flow"?

Question for Writing Thoughtfully

1. Goldberg uses an amusing metaphor to describe what writing is *not*. Do you agree with her metaphor? Create other metaphors that describe your feeling about writing (especially academic writing).

Collaborating

 When you work with other people in the writing process, you participate in collaboration. You can collaborate with others at every stage of the thinking and writing process. People can help one another generate ideas, identify a main idea to pursue, or suggest possible approaches and ways of organizing. Some entire pieces of writing, especially in business, are produced collaboratively by a team of writers. Since collaborating can occur in all writing process activities, the line representing collaboration circles around them in the model in Figure 1.1.

Writers often discover new perspectives when others review drafts of their writing. This is the moment when writers get a sense of how effective their efforts at communication are. No matter how clearly you try to keep your audience in mind as you write, you may not succeed at first. There is no substitute for having your audience (or people like your intended audience) let you know what you have and have not communicated clearly. With their suggestions, you can improve and refine your writing so that it will better convey what you intended. As a critical thinker and informed writer, you will learn to work with others in developing your thinking and writing, welcoming their advice when you are the sole author and contributing well when you are part of a writing team. Opportunities for collaborating are marked throughout the book with the icon to the previous page.

Of course, in writing collaboratively, you also have a responsibility to respond critically to the writing of others. *Critical* is related to *criticize*, which means "to question and evaluate." Unfortunately, the ability to criticize is often used destructively to tear down someone else's thinking. Criticism, however, should be *constructive*—analyzing for the purpose of developing better understanding. To develop your abilities to think critically and write thoughtfully, it is important to offer and receive constructive criticism.

Becoming a critical thinker and a thoughtful writer does not simply involve mastering certain life skills; it affects the entire way that you view the world and live your life. You already use critical thinking in many aspects of your life: how you make decisions, how you relate to others, and how you deal with controversial issues. These abilities can be improved with information, strategies, and practice, and you will continue to develop them as you move forward through college and your career.

Thinking-Writing Activity

EXPRESSING A DEEPER MEANING

This Thinking-Writing Activity gives you an opportunity to apply some of the ideas we have been exploring in this chapter. Think of a place—or, if you can, go and visit a place—that has special meaning for you, a place that led you to a realization about life. Write a description that effectively communicates *where* you are as well as expresses a deeper kind of meaning. What kind of meaning, exactly, is up to you, and depends on the feelings that the place evokes. Reach deep within yourself and discover an analogous feeling to articulate in your writing.

- Consider the audience for whom you are writing and the purpose you would like to accomplish.

- After writing your first draft, *rewrite* your paper to more fully express your feelings and ideas.

- Add details that communicate your meaning as specifically as possible.

- Craft your sentences so that they flow together and create a consistent "picture" of the place you are describing.

- Share your paper with your classmates. Ask them what feelings and ideas your description communicated to them.

- As a group, discuss which steps of the writing process for this assignment came easily and which required more effort.

CHAPTER 1   Summary

- Becoming a critical thinker and a thoughtful writer requires that you be curious, open-minded, knowledgeable, and creative.

- The components of any writing situation include the purpose, audience, subject, and writer.

- The writing process involves generating ideas, defining a focus, organizing ideas, drafting, revising, editing, and proofreading.

- Collaborating with others can be helpful at any stage of the writing process. The constructive criticism of others can help the writer gain different and valuable perspectives.

AP Photo/Alden Pellett

Writer Julia Alvarez and her husband raise organic coffee that they import to the United States. They put the proceeds into a small school and library in the mountain village of Los Marranitos where their farm is located in the Dominican Republic, which is aimed at helping children and adults learn to read. Of her own experience immigrating to the U.S., Alvarez says, "Not understanding the language, I had to pay close attention to each word—great training for a writer." What do you do when you come to an unfamiliar phrase, allusion, or word in a reading?

Reading:
Making Meaning

"Read not to contradict nor to believe, but to weigh and consider."

—FRANCIS BACON

Critical Thinking Focus:
Reflecting on reading and making meaning

Writing Focus:
Thinking about rhetorical choices and writing in response to reading

Reading Theme:
Using your response to reading as a subject for writing

Reading in College

Let's begin this chapter with a question: What does it mean to read? Not so long ago, to "read" meant to turn the pages of a book, a newspaper, or an owner's manual. Reading was a physical activity that required lamplight or daylight, and texts were physical objects that you carried around in a backpack or briefcase. When you went to the library, it was usually to borrow a book that you would read and then return two weeks later. When you woke up in the morning, you read a newspaper as you drank your coffee. And when you got home from classes, you stayed up late into the night with your textbooks and a dictionary.

The physical act of reading—of opening, turning, flipping back and forth, underlining, inserting a bookmark—seems at times to be almost quaint, like roller-skating instead of rollerblading, or using a dial-up modem instead of a high-speed digital connection. And yet reading—the deciphering of, and interacting with, ideas and language—is at the core of a liberal education. You read to be entertained, to be informed, to learn. Even though most of us might do most of our "reading" without ever getting near a book, the fundamental skills of deciphering and interacting are equally applicable to the screen and the page. And whatever, however, or wherever you plan to communicate in your professional life, those fundamental reading skills will make you a better writer in any medium.

Reading Actively

To read actively is to work at deciphering the many layers of a text. An active reader has a dictionary (online or print) at hand, along with annotating tools, plenty of time, and the will to jot down questions and comments either on the printed page (or printout), in a reading journal, or in a word processing document. When you read actively, you give your full concentration and attention to the text. (Passive reading, on the other hand, is usually marked by boredom and daydreaming. If you look up from the page or screen and can't remember what you were just "reading," you weren't really reading at all—you were just looking at words.)

Active reading is also productive reading. You have a sense, as you begin to read, of what you might expect to discover. Active—and critical—reading also imply *re*-reading; the following strategies will require you to work through a new text at least twice, becoming familiar with its structure as you delve into its content.

The following strategies for active reading will help to make any reading task—academic, professional, or even leisurely—more productive. They also apply equally to print texts and websites.

Review the Table of Contents or Chapter Outlines

The table of contents and chapter outlines of a book or website provide you with the general structure and organization of a text. By beginning with these elements, you can develop an overall understanding of the reading, the organization of its major ideas, and the way specific details fit into this organization. It's as if you are taking an aerial view of the territory you are going to explore, looking for key landmarks, examining the patterns of connecting roads, and developing a sense of the terrain.

Review the table of contents in this book, taking particular note of the topics that are covered and the way these topics are organized. Now look at where this chapter fits in relation to the overall design of the book. How do the topics of this chapter relate to the other topics in the book?

Thinking-Writing Activity

TAKING A READING INVENTORY

In your journal, respond to any or all of these questions. Your teacher may ask you to share and discuss your responses with other students.

1. Is there anyone in your life to whom you read—a child, an older person, a friend? (Or perhaps you read aloud as part of a religious service or a professional presentation.) In what contexts do you read aloud? How does reading aloud define or contribute to your relationship to your audience?

2. Who taught you to read? Do you remember learning to read? Have you helped anyone else learn to read?

3. What was the last thing you read out of sheer curiosity or pleasure? Were you surprised by your response to that text? Would you recommend it to a friend, or was this purely a "guilty" pleasure?

Read the Introductory Paragraphs and the Concluding Paragraphs or Summary

After reviewing the table of contents or chapter outline, review next the opening and closing paragraphs or summary. In academic textbooks, authors generally explain the major goals of the chapter in the introduction and then conclude by reviewing the key topics that have been explored. Reviewing these sections should help you fill in the mental map you are creating of the reading assignment and help you develop a plan for exploring the material.

Other kinds of writing—essays, journalism, blogs—often include a thesis statement in the opening paragraph and summarize the overall argument or problem in the concluding paragraph. Note the topic sentence of each paragraph, which will give you an overall sense of the text's structure and organization.

Review the opening and concluding sections of this chapter. What additional information have you gathered about the chapter?

Scan the Reading Assignment, Taking Particular Note of Section Headings, Illustrations, and Diagrams

The next step is to scout the territory by completing a rapid scan of what lies ahead. Move quickly through the material, focusing on the section headings, boxed or shaded areas, illustrations, diagrams, and other defining features. This should help you continue to fill in and elaborate your mental map, noting key points, concepts, definitions, and relationships.

Quickly scan this chapter, noting the features mentioned above. What new information have you gathered as a result of this scouting process?

Thinking-Writing Activity

PREVIEWING A READING ASSIGNMENT

Select a reading assignment from one of your courses, and before beginning to read, apply the previewing strategies that we have been considering:

- Examine the table of contents or chapter outline.
- Read the introductory paragraphs and the concluding paragraphs or summary.
- Scan the reading assignment, taking particular note of section headings, illustrations, and diagrams.

Then write a short paragraph, reporting specifically what each of the three strategies showed you about the assignment.

Annotating

Annotation is one of the most productive techniques that you will use in your college reading. It involves writing, or entering, your reactions to a text as you are reading, either with pen or pencil on paper or with your computer's graphic tools to annotate something that you have downloaded. When annotating, you are talking *with* the text, not allowing it to talk *at* you.

Your annotations will reflect your agreement and disagreement with what you read, your questions, what you see as important ideas, where you see relationships among parts of the texts, and where you see connections with additional ideas. Some methods are

- Underlining and numbering key points
- Circling key words and drawing lines to show relationships—for example, between a main idea and support for it
- Using question marks to indicate parts that you do not understand
- Commenting on the author's ideas or language or writing techniques
- Noting connections with your life or with other texts

Most word processing programs include annotation features such as highlighting, changing a font color, or inserting comments and questions. To annotate an online source, either save the online text in your word processing file or simply print out the page and highlight it on paper. (Many websites for periodicals, newspapers, and journals offer a "printer-friendly" option for articles, which allows you to print only the text, on continuous pages, without having to "click" through each separate page or print out banner advertisements.)

Summarizing

When you summarize a text, you use your own language to briefly and succinctly restate the author's main point. A summary follows the structure and organization of the original text, and might directly quote (using quotation marks) particularly interesting or apt words and phrases. When you summarize, you do not comment on or evaluate the text (that comes later); instead, writing the summary is a cognitive tool to ensure that you understand both the content and the structure of the text.

Summarizing is a strategy that is most effective at your second or third reading of a text, after you have annotated the text and looked up any unfamiliar terms or concepts.

Reading Critically

After reading actively in order to understand the content of a text, a thoughtful reader looks at it again, this time to read it critically. As a critical reader, you will analyze the text and evaluate its ideas and methods of presenting them. You will think of other subjects or issues to which the text might be connected.

Asking Questions

Asking questions will help you read critically. One set of useful questions is based on the components of writing that you learned in Chapter 1: purpose, audience, subject, writer, and context.

1. What is the *purpose* of the selection, and how is the author trying to achieve it?
2. Who is the intended *audience*, and what assumptions is the writer making about it?
3. What is the *subject* of the selection, and how would you evaluate its cogency and reliability?
4. Who is the *writer*, and what perspective does she bring to the writing selection?
5. What is the larger *context* in which this selection appears? Is the writer responding to a particular event or participating in an ongoing debate?

Some questions often used to generate writing also help with critical reading.

Questions of Interpretation   Questions of interpretation probe for relationships among ideas.

Is a *time sequence* given in this text? If so, what is its importance?

Is a *process of growth or development* explained in this text? If so, what is its importance?

What is *compared or contrasted* in this text? What are the purposes of any comparisons?

What is the *context* of the selection, and what contextual components might be significant? (For example, the time of its writing, characteristics of that time, the relationship to other works by the same author, whether or not it is a translation)

Are *causes* discussed in this text? If so, what is suggested about those causes and their effects?

Questions of Analysis   Questions of analysis look at parts of a text and the relationship of those parts to the whole, and at the reasoning being presented.

Is this text divided into identifiable *sections?* What are they? Are sections arranged logically?

What *evidence* or *examples* support the ideas presented in the text?

Does the text give *alternatives* to the ideas presented?

Questions of Evaluation   Questions of evaluation establish the truth, reliability, applicability—the value of the text. They usually address the effectiveness of the writing as well.

NEW MEDIA & THOUGHTFUL WRITING (& READING)

Amplifying with Audio

People who are blind or have vision impairments, or have dyslexia or other types of learning disabilities, may not be able to read or may have difficulty reading a printed page. To get the information they want, they might read in a Braille format, listen to audio recordings of someone reading, have someone read to them, or have a computer "read" to them with the aid of optical character recognition (OCR) software.

Even if you do not have vision problems or a learning disability, you may still benefit from hearing an audio version of something you have read. Some people learn better through certain types of stimuli. For example, many people consider themselves visual learners (they learn best by observing), while others consider themselves kinesthetic learners (they learn best by doing) or auditory learners (they learn best through listening). Some theorists would even argue that learning is optimized when it is multimodal, in other words, if you engage in more than one or all three types of learning.

Studying a reading in written form allows you to do things that an audio version does not—like observing spellings, paragraph length variety across the reading at a glance, and more. But, likewise, listening to an audio version of a reading provides experiences that the written version does not, particularly if the audio is provided by the author of the piece. For instance, when you listen to authors read their own work, you can more readily hear the tone, inflection, and pace they intended. This can be particularly helpful in studying certain types of literature and poetry.

What is the *significance* of the ideas in this text?

What is the apparent level of *truth* in this text? What criteria for truth does it meet?

What are the sources of information in this text? Are they *reliable*? Why?

Can the ideas in this text be *applied* to other situations?

What is *effective* about the writing in this text? Clarity?

The right tone? Appropriate—or imaginative—word choices? Organization?

Of course, you are not likely to ask all these questions about everything you read, and you will find other questions to ask as well.

You can find audio versions of popular fiction books at bookstores, on book websites, and in libraries in cassette and CD format. Some vendors may even offer the audio as an MP3 download. And, with the advent of text readers (e.g., the Kindle and Google's reader application), you can store and access a large number of books in one little lightweight, handheld device which can read to you.

Using audio recordings properly can positively augment your learning experience and should not be approached as a passive activity. A critical thinking and active learning perspective should be engaged regardless of which mode of learning stimuli you choose.

Thinking-Writing Activity

MULTIMODAL LEARNING

Visit your text website, accessed through **cengagebrain.com**, and read the poems offered there, first silently to yourself and then out loud. Then click on the link next to each poem to hear an audio recording of someone reading it. Describe what more you got out of the poem after reading it aloud and then after hearing someone else read it.

Next, click on the link to NPR.org and read the transcript of an interview. Then listen to the audio recording of it. Describe what more they got out of the interview when they got to hear the audio.

Using a Problem-Solving Approach

Successful readers often approach difficult reading passages with a problem-solving approach.

Step 1: *What is the problem?* What don't I understand about this passage? Are there terms or concepts that are unfamiliar? Are the logical connections between the concepts confusing? Do some things just not make sense?

Step 2: *What are the alternatives?* What are some possible meanings of the terms or concepts? What are some potential interpretations of the central meaning of this passage?

Thinking-Writing Activity

A PROBLEM-SOLVING APPROACH TO READING

Step 1: What parts (if any) of this passage do you find confusing?

Step 2: What are some possible definitions of the italicized words, and what are some potential interpretations of this passage?

Existentialism: (a) _____

                      (b) _____

Free: (a) _____

                      (b) _____

Overall Meaning: (a) _____

                      _____

Overall Meaning: (b) _____

                      _____

Step 3: What contextual clues can you use to help you define these concepts and determine the overall meaning? What knowledge of this subject do you have, and how can this knowledge help you understand this passage?

Step 4: Judging from your evaluation in Step 3, which of the possible definitions and interpretations do you think are most likely? Why?

Step 5: How do your conclusions compare with those of the other students in the class? Should you revise your definitions or interpretation?

Select a challenging passage from a course textbook and apply the preceding problem-solving approach.

A Problem-Solving Approach to Reading

Visit your text website, accessed through **CengageBrain.com**, to learn more about the problem-solving approach to reading.

Step 3: What is the evaluation of the possible alternatives? What are the "clues" in the passage, and what alternative meanings do they support? What reasons or evidence support these interpretations?

Step 4: What is the solution? Judging from my evaluation and what I know of this subject, which interpretation is most likely? Why?

Step 5: How well is the solution working? Does my interpretation still make sense as I continue my reading, or do I need to revise my conclusion?

Of course, expert readers go through this process very quickly, much faster than it takes to explain it. Although this approach may seem a little cumbersome at first, the more you use it, the more natural and efficient it will become. Let's begin by applying it to a sample passage. Carefully read the following passage from the French philosopher Jean-Paul Sartre's "Existentialism Is Humanism," and use the problem-solving approach to determine the correct meanings of the italicized concepts and the overall meaning of the passage.

> *Existentialism*, of which I am a representative, declares with greater consistency that if God does not exist there is at least one being whose existence comes before its essence, a being which exists before it can be defined by any conception of it. That being is man or, as Heidegger has it, the human reality. What do we mean by saying that *existence precedes essence*? We mean that man first of all exists, encounters himself, surges up in the world—and defines himself afterwards. If man as the existentialist sees himself as not definable, it is because to begin with he is nothing. He will not be anything until later, and then he will be what he makes of himself. Thus, *there is no human nature*, because there is no God to have a conception of it. Man simply is. Not that he is simply what he conceives himself to be, but he is what he wills, and as he conceives existence. *Man is nothing else but that which he makes of himself.* This is the first principle of existentialism. . . . If, however, it is true that existence is prior to essence, *man is responsible for what he is*. Thus, the first effect of existentialism is that it puts every man in possession of himself as he is, and places the entire responsibility for his existence squarely upon his own shoulders. . . . That is what I mean when I say that man is *condemned to be free*. Condemned, because he did not create himself, yet is nevertheless at liberty, and from the moment that he is thrown into this world he is responsible for everything he does. . . . In life, a man commits himself, draws his own portrait and there is nothing but that portrait.

Practicing Active and Critical Reading: One Student's Approach

Here is how one student, Joshua Bartlett, used previewing, problem solving, annotating, and summarizing with an essay that his philosophy professor assigned to show students how ideas from more than 2,500 years ago can apply to their lives today.

Previewing   Because this was an instructor's handout, Joshua's previewing started with a look at the title, the first two paragraphs, and the concluding paragraph. Because this is a short essay, Joshua moved quickly to scanning, reading through, and annotating. He was a bit confused when he read the first paragraph since the class had not yet begun studying Plato.

Problem Solving   Joshua realized that his major *problem* with this text was his lack of knowledge about Plato and Socrates. He decided that his *alternatives* were (1) to look them up in his philosophy class book or the encyclopedia or (2) to go on reading. He quickly *evaluated* the alternatives. Consulting his book or the encyclopedia would take some time, and he wanted to finish this assignment before he had to go to work. He knew that he would learn about Plato and Socrates next week in his class. His previewing had shown him that these problem paragraphs would be explained later in the essay. He *solved the problem* by deciding to go on reading. He felt that his solution *worked well* when he was able to summarize the essay.

Annotating   Joshua gave Tanner's essay a second and then a third reading, each time using a colored pen to draw his attention to specific points in the text. He underlined important points, placed question marks next to parts he did not understand, and commented on the writer's rhetorical strategies to better help him understand the writer's argument.

Summarizing   Joshua's philosophy professor asked the students to prepare a summary of the essay and be ready to share it with the class. She did this so that class discussion would be focused. Joshua took his annotations to class, too, so he was able to participate effectively. Here is his summary:

> "On Plato's Cave" claims that much of what we see, hear, and read may give us inaccurate images and projections of points of view and that we need to try to discover what is really solid, rather than believe what might not be. This essay begins by quoting Plato's description of human beings chained in a cave, seeing only reflections of people, animals, and material items. The essay connects this fantasy situation with our experiences with the media, and even with what parents and teachers tell us. The essay says that Plato tells of a person escaping from the cave and seeing the real world. It says that we, too, can climb out of darkness by understanding how received information and our resulting beliefs need to be examined so that we can have "substantiated knowledge."

On Plato's Cave

by Sonja Tanner

In the seventh book of Plato's dialogue *The Republic*, he offers an image of education in which humans are likened to prisoners in a cave. To understand this fully, we can attempt to render this image.

"Next, then," (Socrates) said, "make an image of our nature in its education and (want) of education, likening it to a condition of the following kind. See human beings as though they were in an underground cave-like dwelling with its entrance, a long one, open to the light across the whole width of the cave.

They are in it from childhood with their legs and necks in bonds so that they are fixed, seeing only in front of them, unable because of the bond to turn their heads all the way around. Their light is from a fire burning far above and behind them. Between the fire and

I guess we'll learn about Socrates next week—then I'll get this funny use of word.

spooky

the prisoners there is a road above, along which we see a wall, built like the partitions

puppet-handlers set in front of the <u>human beings</u> and over which they show the puppets."

    "I see," (Glaucon) said.

    "Then also see along this wall human beings carrying all sorts of artifacts, which

project above the wall, and statues of men and other animals wrought from stone, wood,

and every kind of material...." (514a1–515a2, Allan Bloom, trans.)

    We see persons at the bottom of a cave, <u>chained so as</u> to prevent them from leaving

the cave and from turning around to see what is behind them. Positioned in this way,

they can only watch the shadows projected onto the back wall of the cave, by the

passing of the artifacts in front of the fire. Behind the prisoners is a low wall which

obscures the persons carrying these artifacts. This projection is like those we create

around campfires, or in front of slide projectors, where a set of hands may look like a

barking dog or a flying bird. A similar distortion takes place in the cave. Further up the

cave is a fire and beyond that lies the cave's opening to the sunlight.

    Having sketched what is happening within the cave literally, we must now try

to <u>interpret what this image means figuratively.</u> When Glaucon remarks upon how

strange these prisoners are, Socrates tells him <u>that they are like us.</u> How are we like

these passive and helpless prisoners? <u>Do we ever receive information or entertainment</u>

<u>without thinking about where it actually comes from?</u> Although Plato was writing over

two thousand years before the invention of cathode ray tubes, the modern example

of television may show us what he meant. If the projected images are analogous to

those televised to us, then what might the <u>persons behind the wall represent? Acting</u>

<u>as filters of information, they might be seen as television networks, advertisers, or</u>

<u>the media in general.</u> They and their motivations for presenting information about the

world to us through their particular perceptual lenses are obscured from view like the

persons who pass behind the wall in the cave. As the chains prevent the prisoners from

turning to see what is causing the images they watch, we are sometimes prevented

by ignorance or uncritical thinking from recognizing the interests and persons served

by the way in which information is presented to us. When we are unaware as to how

perceptual lenses shape what it is we then believe, the information we receive and the

beliefs we build upon this information may be distorted, like the shadows projected

onto the wall. Many other persons shape the information we receive and the beliefs

[Margin annotations, handwritten:]

? the ones in the cave? no

who?

OK—clearer than bonds

—or with a flashlight

aha! where?

important point

now it's making sense

important point

This whole paragraph is important

may be the thesis

They sure do!

we hold. Authorities of all sorts fulfill this function—politicians, journalists, parents, teachers, writers and sometimes even ourselves.

Plato does not think us doomed to this unreflective state, however. Escape from the cave, though mysterious, is possible. Someone is apparently released from their bonds, turns around, and despite the confusion and pain from the dazzling light and arduous ascent, both of which they are unaccustomed to, is able to leave the cave. Just as when we leave a matinee movie and enter bright sunlight, we are at first dazzled and our eyes need a few moments to adjust to the light, the ascendant may experience disorientation or confusion upon first turning around. Turning from the shadows, this person discovers the objects causing these projections and the persons carrying them and, once outside the cave, the beings which these artifacts are made to resemble. The journey upwards is one of turning from images to their originals, ending ultimately in one's view of the sun itself, which, as the earth's source of heat and light, is a cause of all of the beings described in this allegory.

But how is escape from chains which bind at the neck and legs possible? Does someone release the prisoner and force them up into the light, and if so, who is this and why do they do it? Perhaps we are taking this image too literally in seeing this as a physical journey. Taking a cue from the aforementioned example in which the projections represent beliefs and information we take on uncritically, perhaps this journey is not physical but mental. The chains may signify ignorance and the uncritical taking over of second-hand opinions or beliefs and, as such, the chains themselves may even be self-imposed. Such an intellectual journey begins with a recognition that what we see and believe are only images, and by turning away from such appearances towards reality.

If the ascent is intellectual, rather than physical, a problem presents itself. Although Plato describes the release of a prisoner as though she or he were dragged up and out of the cave by the scruff of their neck, this type of force seems unlikely to guide an intellectual journey. Could one truly be forced or compelled to think independently? What else would motivate the journey? This is a particularly difficult question given the description of both ascent and return back into the cave as arduous, painful, and as subjecting one to derision and danger from the prisoners. What benefit could make good of undergoing such difficulties to leave the cave? We have been assuming here that the compulsion Plato describes as motivating the **ascent is a force external to the ascendant, but internal forces motivate us as well.** Why take the treacherous journey

[margin annotations: !! ; good comparison ; ! ; escape → journey ; another explanation ; repeats ; probably not ; hard to understand (read slow!)]

out of the cave? Perhaps simply because we <u>want</u> to. Our motivation upwards may be a desire for knowledge, as opposed to mere beliefs. If desire is the impetus for the <u>ascent,</u> this places <u>responsibility</u> for one's <u>education squarely on the shoulders of the individual.</u> We may have <u>assistance, encouragement</u> and <u>sometimes</u> even external forces compelling us upwards, but ultimately, our success depends <u>upon</u> our own <u>desire</u> for <u>knowledge and truth,</u> and our willingness to give up what we are accustomed to—the passive life and familiar comforts of cave-dwelling—for the rewards of rational and grounded knowledge.

the margin notes:

!

Aha—again!
This sounds
like my dad!

The cave makes
sense here

We are now able to locate ourselves on the (trajectory of enlightenment.) Looking at and discussing images are a first stage in education according to Plato and indeed that is precisely what we have done here thus far. The next step then seems to be turning away from the images we accept unreflectively and towards questions as to why we believe what we do, who or what are the sources of these beliefs, and how reliable are these sources, which can distinguish unfounded beliefs from substantiated knowledge. Maybe this ascent is undertaken by us on a regular basis, rather than simply once, in our lives.

important phrase

Here's the main
point

One of those
essays that leads
up to it—doesn't
state it at the
beginning the
way my English
teacher wants us
to do

Using Metacognitive Strategies

Metacognition is a process we have been working on throughout this book. While *cognition* refers to the process of thinking, *metacognition* refers to a form of thinking *about* the thinking process. For example, think about what you will be doing this evening, and as you are thinking about this, make a special effort to stand outside your thinking process and observe it while it is going on. This process of becoming an observer to your own thinking process—"reflecting" on your thinking—may feel strange, but it is well within your power if you concentrate. In the following space, describe some of the characteristics of the thinking process that you observed yourself engaging in. For instance, did you find you were talking to yourself? Did your thinking make use of still or moving visual images? Did you feel ideas were rushing through your mind like a river, or were your thoughts organized in an orderly fashion? Did you find one idea led to another idea, which led to another idea, through a series of associations?

Characteristics of My Thinking Process:

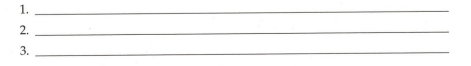

1. _____

2. _____

3. _____

Thinking-Writing Activity

YOUR REACTIONS

1. Write your reactions to the strategies for active and critical reading in this chapter. Which have you used before? How do they work for you? Which do you want to try now as you do your college reading?

2. How would you annotate "On Plato's Cave"?

3. Do you think that Joshua wrote an accurate summary of it? Would you summarize it differently?

If you can, share your reactions with classmates and notice agreements and disagreements.

By participating in this activity you were actually engaging in the process of *metacognition*, working to become aware of the process you use to think about something.

While the process of reading is a thinking (cognitive) activity, expert readers also engage in metacognition while they are reading. In other words, they are aware of their thinking process as they are reading, and they use this awareness to improve their thinking. This awareness can be expressed as a variety of questions:

Goals: What are my goals in reading this passage? How well am I meeting these goals?

Comprehension: How well do I understand what I am reading? What parts do I understand, and what parts am I confused about?

Anticipation: What events are going to take place following the ones I am reading about? How will the author develop and elaborate on these ideas?

Author's Purpose: What is the author's point of view, and why did she adopt this particular perspective? How has her point of view affected the information she selected and the manner in which she presented this information?

Evaluation: Is this information accurate? Do the ideas make sense? What evidence and reasons does the author provide to support her perspective?

As you work to answer these questions, you are likely to find that you are *rereading* key sections, and this rereading is an essential part of the process of reading effectively.

Thinking-Writing Activity

PRACTICING METACOGNITION

Although developing metacognitive reading abilities is a complex process that takes place over time, you can begin using these strategies immediately. Select a chapter from one of your textbooks. As you read, make a conscious effort to ask—and to answer—metacognitive questions noted above. Record your experience, identifying the questions that you found yourself asking, and how the process of asking—and trying to answer—these questions while you were reading affected your understanding of the material. The metacognitive questions are part of a reading worksheet located below that you can use for reference later.

READING WORKSHEET

Reading Assignment: _____

Reading Environment: _____

Reading Schedule: _____

Date Due: _____

Day   *Time Planned for Reading*

_____   _____

_____   _____

READING STRATEGIES

Problem Solving

Step 1: What is the problem in understanding the reading?

Step 2: What are the possible meanings and interpretations?

Step 3: What are the contextual clues, reasons, or evidence?

Step 4: What meaning or interpretation is most likely?

Step 5: How well is my conclusion working?

Metacognition

What are my *goals* in reading this passage, and how well am I meeting these goals?

What parts do I *understand,* and what parts are *confusing*?

How will the author *elaborate* and *develop* ideas I am reading about?

What is the author's *point of view,* and why did she adopt this particular perspective?

Do the ideas *make sense*? What *evidence* and *reasons* support the ideas presented?

Annotation

"Grounds for Fiction"

by Julia Alvarez

Poet, novelist, and teacher Julia Alvarez was born in New York City but raised in the Dominican Republic. Her novel *In the Time of the Butterflies* (1994) is based on the true story of the four Mirabal sisters who fought against the brutal Trujillo dictatorship, and her enormously popular *How the Garcia Girls Lost Their Accents* (1991) deftly explores the relationships among sisters. Both novels were critically acclaimed, nominated for and winning several important prizes. Her most recent novel, *Saving the World*, was published in 2006.

In recent years, Alvarez and her husband have started an organic coffee farm in the Dominican Republic; she recently brought a group of her American college students to the farm to work alongside local farmers and teach literacy classes in the community.

Every once in a while after a reading, someone in the audience will come up to me. *Have I got a story for you!* They will go on to tell me the story of an aunt or sister or next-door neighbor, some moment of mystery, some serendipitous occurrence, some truly incredible story. "You should write it down," I always tell them. They look at me as if they've just offered me their family crown jewels and I've refused them. "I'm no writer," they tell me. "You're the writer."

"Oh, you never know," I reply, so as to encourage them. What I should tell them is that writing ideas can't really be traded in an open market. If they could be, writers would be multimillionaires. Who knows what mystery (or madness) it is that drives us to our computers for two, three, four years, in pursuit of some sparkling possibility that looks like dull fact to everyone else's eyes. One way to define a writer is she who is able to make what obsesses her into everyone's obsession. I am thinking of Goethe, whose *Sorrows of Young Werther*, published in 1774, caused a spate of suicides in imitation of its young hero. Young Werther's blue frock coat and yellow waistcoat became the fad. We have all been the victims of someone's too-long slide show of their white-water rafting trip or their recounting of a convoluted, boring dream. But a Mark Twain can turn that slide show into the lively backdrop of a novel, or a Jorge Luis Borges can take the twist and turn of a dream and wring the meaning of the universe from it.

But aside from talent—and granted, that is a big aside, one that comes and goes and shifts and grows and diminishes, so it is also somewhat unpredictable—how can we tell when we've got it: that seed of experience, of memory, that voice of a character or fleeting image that might just be grounds for fiction? The answer is that we can never tell. And so another way to define a writer is someone who is willing to find out. As James Dickey once explained to an audience, "I work on the process of refining low-grade ore. I get maybe a couple of nuggets of gold out of fifty tons of dirt. It is tough for me. No, I am not inspired."

"Are you all here because you want to muck around in fifty tons of dirt?" I ask my workshop of young writers the first day. Not one hand goes up unless I've told them the Dickey story first.

5   In fact, my students want to know ahead of time if some idea they have will make a good story. "I mean, before I spend hours and hours on it," one young man explained. I told my students what Mallarmé told his friend the painter Degas, when Degas complained that he couldn't seem to write well although he was "full of ideas." Mallarmés's famous answer was, "My dear Degas, poems are not made out of ideas. Poems are made out of words." I told my student that if a young writer had come up to me and told me that he was going to write a story about a man who wakes up one morning and finds out that he has been turned into a cockroach, I would have told him to forget it. That story would never work. "And I would have stopped Kafka from writing his 'Metamorphosis,'" I concluded, smiling at my student, as if he might be a future Kafka.

"Well, it's just two pages," he grumbled. "And I have this other idea that might be better. About a street person who is getting Alzheimer's."

"Write both stories, and I'll read them and tell you what I think of them," I said. He looked alarmed. So I leveled with him. I told him that if he didn't want to spend hours and hours finding out if the kernel of an idea, the glimmer of an inspiration, the flash of a possibility would make a good story, he should give up the *idea* of wanting to be a writer.

As much as I can break down the process of writing stories, I would say that this is how it begins. I find a detail or image or character or incident or cluster of events. A certain luminosity surrounds them. I find myself attracted. I come forward. I pick it up, turn it around, begin to ask questions, and spend hours and weeks and months and years trying to answer them.

I keep a folder, a yellow folder with pockets. For a long time it had no label because I didn't know what to label it: WHATCHAMACALLITS, filed under *W,* or also under *W,* STORY-POEM-WANNABES. Finally, I called the folder CURIOSIDADES, in Spanish so I wouldn't have to commit myself to what I was going to do in English with these random little things. I tell my students this, too, that writing begins before you ever put pen to paper or your fingers down on the keyboard. It is a way of being alive in the world. Henry James's advice to the young writer was to be someone on whom nothing is lost. And so this is my folder of the little things that have not been lost on me; news clippings, headlines, inventory lists, bits of gossip that I've already sensed have an aura about them, the beginnings of a poem or a short story, the seed of a plot that might turn into a novel or a query that might needle an essay out of me.

10   Periodically, when I'm between writing projects and sometimes when I'm in the middle of one and needing a break, I go through my yellow folder. Sometimes I discard a clipping or note that no longer holds my attention. But most of my curiosidades have been in my folder for years, though some have migrated to new folders, the folders of stories and poems they have inspired or found a home in.

Here's one of these curiosidades that is now in a folder that holds drafts of a story that turned into a chapter of my novel *¡YO!* This chapter is in the point of view of Marie Beaudry, a landlady who, along with other narrators, gets to tell a story on Yolanda García, the writer. The little curiosity that inspired Marie's voice was a note I found in the trash of an apartment I moved into. It has nothing at all to do with what happens in my story.

> Re and Mal: Here's the two keys to your father's apt. Need I say more excepting that's such a rotten thing you pulled on him. My doing favors is over as of this morning. Good luck to you two hard-hearted hannahs. I got more feeling in my little finger than the two of you got in your whole body.
>
>   Jinny

I admit that when I read this note, I wanted to move out of that apartment. I felt the place was haunted by the ghost of the last tenant against whom some violation had been perpetrated by these two hard-hearted hannahs, Re and Mal. Over the years that handwritten note stayed in my yellow folder and eventually gave me the voice of my character Marie Beaudry.

Here's another scrap from deep inside one of the pockets. It's the title of an article in one of my husband's ophthalmological journals: "Treatment of Chronic Postfiltration Hypotony by Intrableb Injection of Autologous Blood." I think I saved that choice bit of medical babble because of the delight I took in the jabberwocky phenomenon of that title.

> 'Twas brillig and the slithy toves
> Did gyre and postfiltrate the wabe;
> All hypotonious was the blood,
> And autologous the intrableb.

I have not yet used it in a story or poem, but who knows, maybe someday you will look over the shoulder of one of my characters and see that he is reading this article or writing it. I can tell you that this delight in words and how we use and misuse them is a preoccupation of mine.

Maybe because I began my writing life as a poet, the naming of things has always interested me:

> Mother, unroll the bolts and name
> the fabrics from which our clothing came,
> dress the world in vocabulary:
> broadcloth, corduroy, denim, terry.

Actually, that poem, "Naming the Fabrics," besides being inspired, of course, by the names of fabrics, was also triggered by something I picked up while reading *The 1961 Better Homes and Garden Sewing Book,* page 45: "During a question and answer period at a sewing clinic, a woman in the audience asked this question: 'I can sew beautifully; my fitting is excellent; the finished dress looks as good as that of any professional—but how do I get up enough courage to cut the fabric?'" I typed out this passage and put it away. A few months later, this fear found its way from my yellow folder to my poem, "Naming the Fabrics":

> I pay a tailor to cut his suits
> from seersucker, duck, tweed, cheviot,
> those names make my cutting hand skittish—
> either they sound like sex or British.

Since I myself have no sewing skills to speak of, I didn't know about this fear that seamstresses experience before cutting fabric. Certainly, the year 1961, when this sewing book was published, brings other fears to mind: the Berlin Wall going up; invaders going down to the Bay of Pigs; Trujillo, our dictator of thirty-one years, being assassinated in the Dominican Republic. But this housewife in Indiana had her own metaphysical fears to work out on cloth. "How do I get up enough courage to cut the fabric?" Her preoccupation astonished me and touched me for all kinds of reasons I had to work out on paper.

15   You might wonder what a "serious writer" was doing reading *The 1961 Better Homes and Garden Sewing Book*. Wouldn't my time have been better spent perusing Milton or Emily Dickinson or even the *New York Review of Books* or *The Nation*? All I can say in my defense is that I believe in Henry James's advice: be someone on whom nothing is lost. Or what Deborah Kerr said in *Night of the Iguana*, "Nothing human disgusts me." I once heard a writer on *Fresh Air* tell Terry Gross that one of the most important things he had ever learned in his life was that you could learn a lot from people who were dumber than you. You can also learn a lot from publications that are below your literary standards: housekeeping books, cookbooks, manuals, cereal boxes, and the local newspapers of your small town.

These last are the best. Even if some of this "news" is really glorified gossip—so what? Most of our classics are glorified gossip. Think of the Wife of Bath's inventory of husbands or the debutante's hair-rape in "The Rape of the Lock." How about Madame Bovary's steamy affair? Is what happened to Abelard over his Héloïse or to Jason for pissing off Medea any less infamous than the John and Lorena Bobbit story of several years ago? The wonderful Canadian writer Alice Munro admits that she likes reading *People* magazine, and "not just at the checkout stand. I sometimes buy it." She goes on to say that gossip is "a central part of my life. I'm interested in small-town gossip. Gossip has that feeling in it, that one wants to know about life."

I've gotten wonderful stories from the *Addison Independent,* the *Valley Voice,* even the *Burlington Free Press* that would never be reported in the *Wall Street Journal* or the *New York Times:*

11-Year-Old Girls Take Car on Two-State Joyride

Two 11-year-old girls determined to see a newborn niece secretly borrowed their grandfather's car, piled clothes on the front seat so they could see over the steering wheel and drove more than 10 hours.

Neither one of them had ever driven a car before, said Michael Ray, Mercer County's juvenile case worker. The youngsters packed the Dodge Aries with soda, snacks, and an atlas for their trek from West Virginia to the central Kentucky town of Harrodsburg. "They were determined to see that baby," said caseworker Ray.

You could write a whole novel about that. In fact, in Mona Simpson's latest novel, *A Regular Guy,* eleven-year-old Jane di Natali is taught by her mother to drive their pickup with wood blocks strapped to the pedals so her short legs can reach them. Little Jane takes off on her own to see her estranged father hundreds of miles away. I wonder if Mona Simpson got her idea for Jane's odyssey from reading about these two eleven-year-olds.

Here's another article I've saved in my yellow folder:

Misdiagnosed Patient Freed After 2 Years

A Mexican migrant worker misdiagnosed and kept sedated in an Oregon mental hospital for two years because doctors couldn't understand his Indian dialect is going home.

Adolfo Gonzales, a frail 5-foot-4-inch grape picker who doesn't speak English or Spanish, had been trying to communicate in his native Indian dialect of Trique.

Gonzales, believed to be in his 20s, was born in a village in Oaxaca, Mexico. He was committed in June 1990 after being arrested for indecent exposure at a laundromat. Charges later were dropped.

I couldn't get this story out of my head. First, I was—and am—intensely interested in the whole Scheherazade issue of how important it is to be able to tell our stories to those who have power over us. Second, and more mundanely, I was intensely curious about those charges that were later dropped: indecent exposure at a laundromat. What was Adolfo Gonzales doing taking his clothes off in a laundromat? Why was he in town after a hard day of grape picking? I had to find answers to these questions, and so I started writing a poem. "It's a myth that writers write what they know," the writer Marcie Hershman has written. "We write what it is that we need to know."

The next payday you went to town
to buy your girl and to wash your one
set of working clothes.
In the laundromat, you took them off
to wring out the earth you wanted
to leave behind you.

from *"Two Years Too Late"*

20   Of course, you don't even have to go to your local paper. Just take a walk downtown, especially if you live in a small town, as I do. All I have to do is have a cup of coffee at Steve's Diner or at Jimmy's Weybridge Garage and listen to my neighbors talking. Flannery O'Connor claimed that most beginners' stories don't work because "they don't go very far inside a character, don't reveal very much of the character. And this problem is in large part due to the fact that these characters have no distinctive speech to reveal themselves with." Here are some examples of my fellow Vermonters talking their very distinctive and revealing speech.

He's so lazy he married a pregnant woman.
I'm so hungry I could eat the north end out of a southbound skunk.
The snow's butt-high to a tall cow.
More nervous than a long-tailed cat in a room full of rocking chairs.
I'm so sick that I'd have to get well to die.

Of course if, like Whitman, you do nothing but listen, you will also hear all kinds of bogus voices these days, speaking the new doublespeak. In our litigious, politically overcorrected, dizzily spin-doctored age, politicians and public figures have to use language so that it doesn't say anything that might upset anyone. Here's a list of nonterms and what they really stand for:

Sufferer of fictitious disorder syndrome: Liar
Suboptimal: Failed
Temporarily displaced inventory: Stolen
Negative gain in test scores: Lower test scores
Substantive negative outcome: Death

We're back to "Treatment of Chronic Postfiltration Hypotony by Intrableb Injection of Autologous Blood," what Ken Macrorie in his wonderful book about expository writing, *Telling Writing,* calls "Engfish"—homogenized, doctored-up, approximate language that can't be traced to a human being.

I tend to agree with what Dickinson once said about poetry, "There are no approximate words in a poem." Auden even went so far as to say that he could pick out a potential poet by a student's answer to the question, "Why do you want to write poetry?" If the student answered, "I have important things to say," then he was not a poet. If he answered, "I like hanging around words listening to what they say," then maybe he was going to be a poet.

I got enmeshed in one such string of words when I visited the United Nations to hear my mother give a speech on violation of human rights. At the door an aide handed me the list of voting member countries and the names caught my eye: Dem Kampuchea, Dem Yemen, Denmark, Djibouti, Dominica, Dominican Republic, Ecuador, Egypt....When I got home, I started writing a poem, ostensibly about hearing my mother give that speech, but really because I wanted to use the names of those countries:

I scan the room for reactions,
picking out those countries
guilty of her sad facts.
Kampuchea is absent,
absent, too, the South African delegate.
I cannot find the United States.
Nervous countries predominate,
Nicaragua and Haiti,
Iraq, Israel, Egypt.

from *"Between Dominica and Ecuador"*

But of course, it's not just words that intrigue writers, but the stories, the possibilities of human character that cluster around a bit of history, trivia, gossip.

For instance, Anne Macdonald's book, *Feminine Ingenuity,* inspired a character trait of the mother in *How the García Girls Lost Their Accents.* According to Macdonald, at the beginning of the twentieth century, 5,535 American women were granted patents for inventions, including a straw-weaving device, an open-eye needle for sewing hot-air balloons, and special planking designed to discourage barnacles from attaching themselves to warships. These intriguing facts gave me a side of the mother's character I would never have thought up on my own. Inspired by the gadgetry of her new country, Laura García sets out to make her mark: soap sprayed from the nozzle head of a shower when you turn the knob a certain way; instant coffee with creamer already mixed in; time-released water capsules for your potted plants when you were away; a key chain with a timer that would go off when your parking meter was about to expire. (And the ticking would help you find your keys easily if you mislaid them.)

Sometimes the inspiration is history. History . . . that subject I hated in school because it was so dry and all about dead people. I wish now my teachers had made me read novels to make the past spring alive in my imagination. For years, I wanted to write about the Mirabal sisters, but I admit I was put off by these grand historical abstractions. It wasn't until I began to accumulate several yellow folders' worth of vivid little details about them that these godlike women became accessible to me. One of my first entries came from my father, who had just returned from a trip to the Dominican Republic: "I met the man who sold the girls pocketbooks at El Gallo before they set off over the mountain. He told me he warned them not to go. He said he took them out back to the stockroom supposedly to show them inventory and explained they were going to be killed. But they did not believe him." I still get goosebumps reading my father's letter dated June 5, 1985. It went in my yellow folder. That pocketbook-buying scene is at the end of the novel I published nine years later.

25   So what are you to conclude from this tour of my yellow folder? That this essay is just an excuse to take you through my folder and share my little treasures with you? Well, one thing I don't want you to conclude is that this preliminary woolgathering is a substitute for the real research that starts once you have a poem or story going. In "Naming the Fabrics," for instance, though I was inspired by the plaintive question asked at a sewing clinic, I still had to go down to the fabric store and spend an afternoon with a very kind and patient saleslady who taught me all about gingham and calico, crepe and gauze. I spent days reading fabric books, and weeks working on the poem, and years going back to it, revising it, tinkering with it. For my story "The Tent," I had to call up the National Guard base near Champaign, Illinois, and get permission from the base commander to go observe his men setting up a tent. ("What exactly do you need this for?" he asked at least half a dozen times.) Sometimes I think the best reason for a writer to have a reputable job like being a professor at a university or a vice president of Hartford Insurance Company is so you can call up those base commanders or bother those salesladies in fabric stores as if you do have a real job. Otherwise, they might think you are crazy and lock you up like poor Adolfo Gonzales.

On the whole, I have found people to be kind and generous with their time, especially when you ask them to talk about something they know and care about. Many people have actually gone beyond kindness in helping me out. I remember calling up the local Catholic priest, bless his heart, who really deserves, I don't know, a plenary indulgence for tolerance in the face of surprise. Imagine getting an early-morning call (my writing day starts at 6:30, but I really don't do this kind of phone calling till about 7:30 since I do want my sources to be lucid). Anyhow, imagine an early-morning call at your rectory from a woman you don't know who asks you what is the name of that long rod priests have with a hole on one end to sprinkle people with holy water? I'd be lying if I tried to make drama out of the phone call and say there was a long pause. Nope. Father John spoke right up, "Ah yes, my aspergill."

One thing I should add—the bad news part of all this fun, but something writers do have to think about in this litigious age—what is grounds for fiction can also be, alas, grounds for suing. All three of my novels have been read by my publisher's lawyer for what might be libelous. Thank goodness Algonquin's lawyer is also a reader who refuses to vacuum all the value out of a book in order to play it safe. Still, I have had to take drinks out of characters' hands and make abused ladies disabused and make so many changes in hair coloring and hairstyle that I could start a literary beauty parlor.

But even if your fictional ground is cleared of litigious material, there might still be grounds for heartache. Your family and friends might feel wounded when they can detect— even if no one else can—the shape of the real behind the form of your fiction. And who would want to hurt those very people you write for, those very people who share with you the world you are struggling to understand in your fiction for their sake as well as your own?

I don't know how to get around this and I certainly haven't figured out what the parameters of my responsibility are to the real people in my life. One of my theories, which might sound defensive and self-serving, is that there is no such thing as straight-up fiction. There are just levels of distance from our own life experience, the thing that drives us to write in the first place. In spite of our caution and precaution, bits of our lives will get into what we write. I have a friend whose mother finds herself in all his novels, even historical novels set in nineteenth-century Russia or islands in the Caribbean where his mother has never been. A novelist writing about Napoleon might convey his greedy character by describing him spooning gruel into his mouth, only to realize that her image of how a greedy man eats comes from watching her fat Tío Jorge stuff his face with sweet habichuelas.

30   I think that if you start censoring yourself as a novelist—*this is out of bounds, that is sacrosanct*—you will never write anything. My advice is to write it out, and then decide, by whatever process seems fair to you—three-o'clock-in-the-morning insomniac angst sessions with your soul, or a phone call with your best friend, or a long talk with your sister—what you are going to do about it. More often than not, an upset reaction has more to do with people's wounded vanity or their own unresolved issues with *you* rather than what you've written. I'm not speaking now of meanness or revenge thinly masquerading as fiction, but of a writer's serious attempts to render justice to the world she lives in, which includes, whether she wants it to or not, the people she loves or has tried to love, the people who have been a part of the memories, details, life experiences that form the whole cloth of her reality—out of which, with fear and a trembling hand, she must perforce cut her fiction.

But truly, this is a worry to put out of your head while you are writing. You'll need your energy for the hard work ahead: tons and tons of good *ideas* to process in order to get those nuggets of pure prose. What Yeats once said in his poem "Dialogue of Self and Soul" could well be the writer's pledge of allegiance:

I am content to follow to its source,
every event in action or in thought.

And remember, no one is probably going to pay you a whole lot of money to do this. You also probably won't save anyone's life with anything you write. But so much does depend on seeing a world in a grain of sand and a heaven in a wildflower. Maybe we are here only to say: house, bridge, aspergill, gingham, calico, gauze. "But to say them," as Rilke said, "remember oh, to say them in a way that the things themselves never dreamed of existing so intensely."

But this is too much of an orchestral close for the lowly little ditty that starts with a newspaper clipping or the feel of a bolt of gingham or a cup of coffee at the

Weybridge Garage. The best advice I can give writers is something so dull and simple you'd never save it in your yellow folder. But go ahead and engrave it in your writer's heart. If you want to be a writer, anything in this world is grounds for fiction.

Questions for Reading Actively

1. In rereading the essay, highlight all the cultural allusions Alvarez makes—the writers she cites, the paintings she mentions, the literary characters who obsess her, even the tabloid news stories she finds entertaining. Using the Internet (and working with partners, if you like), look up any allusions that are unfamiliar, and annotate your text by writing explanations of those allusions in the margins. What is Alvarez's purpose for all these allusions? How do you, as a reader, respond to the breadth of her interests?

2. How does Alvarez demonstrate the four qualities of an active, thoughtful, and critical reader? In what ways is she curious, open-minded, knowledgeable, and creative in her reading and her use of what she reads?

3. After you have annotated the essay to clarify any unfamiliar allusions, respond to any or all of the previous metacognitive reading questions. Do any portions of the essay resist your questioning? Compare notes with your classmates—what is most difficult about Alvarez's essay, and why?

Questions for Thinking Critically

1. An *apologia* is a kind of argument, a defense that someone writes to explain and justify his or her actions, beliefs, or opinions. It's different from an *apology*, in which someone admits wrongdoing. In what ways does Alvarez present an apologia for herself as a writer? How, conversely, would she respond to a writer who might feel compelled to offer an apology for something he or she had written?

2. What does it mean to be *inspired*? (Look up the word; are you surprised by its etymology?) Where does Alvarez find inspiration? Look into the creative habits of another artist (in any medium) whose work you admire. From where does she draw her inspiration?

Question for Writing Thoughtfully

1. Get an empty folder. For one week, make an effort to put anything in that folder that catches your interest—an email from a friend, a photograph from the newspaper, the menu from a coffee shop, the stub from a movie ticket. At the end of the week, dump the contents of the folder on your desk. What story do these scraps tell you about yourself? about your life? Can you arrange them into any sort of "narrative," either creative or very close to true? You could also exchange folders with a classmate. What stories could you tell about your classmate based on what's in his folder?

Thinking Critically About Visuals

How Selective Should You Be?

What type of material do you think an aspiring writer should be reading? What does writer Julia Alvarez say about this? Do you agree with her? Why or why not?

© B. O'Kane/Alamy

Making Meaning

Words are not simple entities with one clear meaning that everyone agrees on. Instead, most words are complex, multidimensional carriers of meaning; their exact meaning often varies from person to person. These differences in meaning can lead to disagreements and confusion. To understand how words function, you have to examine the way that words serve as vehicles to express meaning.

Words arouse a variety of ideas, feelings, and experiences. Taken together, these responses express the total meaning of the words for each individual.

Linguists believe that this total meaning is actually composed of four different types of meaning:

- semantic meaning
- perceptual meaning
- syntactic meaning
- pragmatic meaning

Let us examine each of them in turn.

Semantic Meaning (Denotation)

The *semantic meaning* of a word expresses the relationship between a *linguistic event* (speaking or writing) and a *nonlinguistic event* (an object, idea, or feeling). For example, saying "chair" relates to an object you sit in, while saying "college education" relates to the experience of earning an academic degree through postsecondary study.

The semantic meaning of a word, also referred to as its *denotative meaning*, expresses the general properties of the word, and these properties determine how the word is used within its language system. How do you discover the general properties that determine word usage? Besides examining your own knowledge of the meaning and use of words, you can check dictionary definitions. They tend to focus on the general properties that determine word usage. For example, a dictionary definition of *chair* might be "a piece of furniture consisting of a seat, legs, and back, and often arms, designed to accommodate one person."

However, to understand a word's semantic meaning fully, you often need to go beyond defining its general properties to identifying examples that embody those properties. If you are sitting in a chair or can see one from where you are, examine its design. Does it embody all the properties identified in the definition? (Sometimes unusual examples embody most, but not all, the properties of a word's dictionary definition—for example, a beanbag chair lacks legs and arms.) If you are trying to understand the semantic meaning of a word, it is generally useful to see both the word's general properties and examples that illustrate them.

Perceptual Meaning (Connotation)

The total meaning of a word also includes its *perceptual meaning*, which expresses the relationship between a linguistic event and an individual's consciousness. For each of us, words elicit personal thoughts and feelings based on previous experiences and past associations. A person might relate saying "chair" to his favorite chair in his living room or the small chair that he built for his daughter. Perceptual meaning also includes an individual's positive and negative responses to the word. When you read or hear the word *book*, what positive or negative feelings does it arouse? What about *textbook*? *mystery book*? *comic book*? *cookbook*? In each case, the word probably elicits distinct feelings, and these contribute to the meaning each word has for you. For this reason, perceptual meaning is also sometimes called *connotative meaning*, the literal or basic meaning of a word plus all it suggests or connotes to you.

Syntactic Meaning

A third component of a word's total meaning is its *syntactic meaning*, which defines its relation to other words in a sentence. The syntactic meaning defines three relationships among words:

- *Content:* words that express the major message of the sentence
- *Description:* words that elaborate or modify the major message of the sentence
- *Connection:* words that join the major message of the sentence

For example, in the sentence "The two novice hikers crossed the ledge cautiously," *hikers* and *crossed* represent the content, or major message, of the sentence. *Two* and *novice* describe *hikers*, and *cautiously* elaborates on *crossed*.

At first, you may think that this sort of relationship among words involves nothing more than semantic meaning. The following sentence, however, clearly demonstrates the importance of syntactic meaning in language: "Invisible fog rumbles in on lizard legs." Although *fog* does not *rumble*, and it is not *invisible*, and the notion of moving on *lizard legs* seems incompatible with *rumbling*, the sentence does "make sense" at some level of meaning—namely, at the syntactic level. One reason it does is that there are three basic content words—*fog*, *rumbles*, and *legs*—and two descriptive words—*invisible* and *lizard*.

The third major syntactic relationship is connection. Connective words join ideas, thoughts, or feelings being expressed. For example, you could connect content meaning to either of the two sentences in the following ways:

The two novice hikers crossed the ledge cautiously *after* one of them slipped.

Invisible fog rumbles in on lizard legs, *but* acid rain doesn't.

When you add the content words *one slipped* and *rain doesn't*, you join the ideas, thoughts, and feelings they represent to the ideas, thoughts, or feelings expressed earlier (*hikers crossed* and *fog rumbles*) by using the connective words *after* and *but*.

The second reason that "Invisible fog rumbles in on lizard legs" makes sense at the syntactic level of meaning is that the words of that sentence obey the syntax, or order, of English. Most English speakers would have trouble making sense of "Invisible rumbles legs lizard on fog in"—or of "Barks big endlessly dog brown the," for that matter. Because of syntactic meaning, each word in the sentence derives part of its total meaning from the ways in which it is combined with the other words in that sentence.

Pragmatic Meaning

The fourth element that contributes to the total meaning of a word is its *pragmatic meaning*. The pragmatic meaning of a word involves the person who is writing and the situation in which the word is written. For example, the statement "That

Thinking-Writing Activity

SYNTACTIC MEANING

Look at the following sentences and explain the difference in meaning between the two in each pair.

1. a. The process of obtaining an *education at college* changes a person's future possibilities.

   b. The process of obtaining a *college education* changes a person's future possibilities.

2. a. She felt *happiness* for her long-lost brother.

   b. She felt the *happiness* of her long-lost brother.

3. a. The most important thing to me is *freedom from* the things that restrict my choices.

   b. The most important thing to me is *freedom* to make my choices without restrictions.

4. a. Michelangelo's painting of the Sistine Chapel ceiling represents his *creative* genius.

   b. The Sistine Chapel ceiling represents the *creative* genius of Michelangelo's greatest painting.

5. a. I *love* the person I have been involved with for the past year.

   b. I am *in love* with the person I have been involved with for the past year.

student likes to borrow books from the library" allows a number of pragmatic interpretations:

1. Was the writer outside looking at *that student* carrying books out of the library?

2. Did the writer have this information because he or she is a classmate of *that student* but did not actually see the student carrying books?

3. Was the writer in the library watching *that student* check the books out?

The correct interpretation or meaning of the sentence depends on what was actually taking place in the situation—in other words, its pragmatic meaning, which is also called its *situational meaning*.

The four types of meanings you just examined—semantic, perceptual, syntactic, and pragmatic—create the total meaning of a word. That is, all the dimensions of a word—all the relationships that connect linguistic events with nonlinguistic events, with your consciousness, with other linguistic events, and with situations in the world—make up the meaning you assign to the word. Later, we will build on the ideas of this section.

Thinking-Writing Activity

PRAGMATIC MEANING

For each of the following sentences, try describing a pragmatic context that identifies the person writing and the situation for which it is being written.

1. A *college education* is currently necessary for many careers that formerly required only high school preparation.

2. The utilitarian ethical system is based on the principle that the right course of action is that which brings the greatest *happiness* to the greatest number of people.

3. The laws of this country attempt to balance the *freedom* of the individual with the rights of society as a whole.

4. "You are all part of things, you are all part of *creation*, all kings, all poets," all musicians, you have only to open up, to discover what is already there. —Henry Miller

5. "If music be the food of *love*, play on."—Shakespeare

After completing the activity, compare your answers with those of your classmates. In what ways are the answers similar or different? Analyze the ways in which different pragmatic contexts (persons speaking and situations) affect the meanings of the italicized words.

CHAPTER 2   Summary

- To get the most out of what you are reading, you need to read actively and critically. Reading actively involves reviewing tables of contents or chapter outlines; reading the introductory paragraphs and concluding paragraphs or summary; scanning the reading assignment, taking particular note of section headings, illustrations, and diagrams; annotating; and summarizing.

- Reading critically entails asking questions of interpretation, analysis, and evaluation, and using a problem-solving approach.

- Metacognition (or thinking about your thinking) can aid active critical reading.

- To get the full meaning of what you read, you should consider the semantic, perceptual, and pragmatic meanings of the words and how they are being used together.

© William Radcliffe/Science Faction/Corbis

As the scientist who proposed the theory of evolution, Charles Darwin (1809–1882) relied on close and careful study of empirical evidence. Wrestling with his own religious faith in light of his scientific observations, Darwin recognized the enormous cultural and philosophical impact his work would have on his audience. Your own writing and thinking will have greater significance and meaning to you as you push the limits of your own understanding. Breakthroughs in thinking lead to vital, lively writing and insightful, informed beliefs. Do you know of any current research that is challenging people's beliefs?

Writing: Using Independent Thought and Informed Beliefs

"The mere process of writing is one of the most powerful tools we have for clarifying our own thinking."

—JAMES VAN ALLEN

From Insight to Writing to Informed Beliefs (and Back Again)

Thinking, writing, reading—these are the tools you use to understand your world, develop relationships with others, and make intelligent decisions in your quest to live a meaningful life. The underlying theme of this book is the way these potentially powerful tools are intrinsically related to one another. Every day you make choices in many areas of your life, choices that are guided by the beliefs you have developed. Successful choices are generally the product of enlightened beliefs that we have developed as a result of thinking critically, reading actively, and writing thoughtfully, as well as through lived experience. Whether the choices involve how best to write a research paper, enliven your social life, or pursue a challenging career, these fundamental abilities provide you with the means to construct beliefs that will guide your choices.

Using these four core qualities listed below as a framework, this chapter extends and deepens them by exploring other related qualities that characterize critical thinkers, active readers, and thoughtful writers, including the following:

- Thinking actively
- Thinking independently
- Viewing a situation from different perspectives
- Supporting diverse perspectives with evidence and reasons

The chapter then presents readings in which authors think critically by reflecting on experiences that have affected their beliefs. Concluding the chapter is a Writing Project that asks you to think critically and write thoughtfully about an experience that had an important impact on a belief that you held or hold. You should keep this Writing Project in mind as you read the chapter and work on Thinking-Writing Activities.

Critical Thinking Focus: Thinking about thinking

Writing Focus: Reflecting on experiences

Reading Theme: Experiences that have affected beliefs

Writing Project: Recalling the impact of experience on a belief

NEW MEDIA & THOUGHTFUL WRITING

Blogs

As we mentioned in Chapter 1, keeping a journal or blog is rewarding in a number of ways. An additional benefit of journaling in blog format is that you can get feedback on your writing through the comments section (provided you decide to make that section 'open' under your privacy settings). People who visit your blog may offer useful constructive criticism, alternative viewpoints on your topic, or additional sources for exploring your ideas further. Being open to feedback from every possible source inevitably will enrich your writing experience. Charles Darwin, whom we discussed at the opening of this chapter, wrote in his seminal work *The Origin of Species* (1859) "that something might perhaps be made out of this question [about the origin of species] by patiently accumulating and reflecting on all sorts of facts which could possibly have any bearing on it."

Another useful way you can use blogs to enhance your writing experience is to take advantage of a blog aggregator, such as Blogger.com, Bloglines.com, or Google Reader. You can add the RSS (or 'really simple syndication' feed) URLs for the blogs or news feeds you are interested in and the aggregator will keep track of all of them for you, showing you at a glance when a blog or news feed has a new posting and allowing you to read that posting on the aggregator's page. If you have a particular interest or research topic you want to learn more about, you can add blogs and news feeds on that topic that present differing viewpoints, and, in this way, you can stay well-informed on a subject you may want to write about.

Thinking-Writing Activity

BLOGGING

Go to a site like Blogger.com or Google.com/reader and use the site's aggregator options to start keeping track of blogs and newsfeeds on the topics you will be investigating for this class (and other classes too, if you like). Then create your own blog and share the address with your classmates. Blog about your ideas for writing topics and provide links to your potential research sources. Throughout the course, visit your classmates' blogs and leave constructive feedback via the comments section. Also remember to check back on your own posts to read the comments left there. You may find your classmates have provided very helpful suggestions.

Thinking Actively and Writing

When you think critically, you are *actively* using your intelligence, knowledge, and abilities to deal effectively with life's situations. Similarly, when you write thoughtfully, you act in the following ways:

- You *become involved* in the subject you are writing about, and because the writing process stimulates your thinking, you often discover ideas that you were unaware of until you started writing. Also, if you keep a journal or notebook and make writing part of your daily life, you find yourself more involved in and more reflective about your world.

- You *take initiative* as you develop confidence in your writer's voice, so you express your own perspectives instead of imitating the ideas of others.

- You *follow through* as you revise and edit in order to produce your best effort.

- You *take responsibility* for your work. That is, you begin assignments promptly and schedule enough time to complete them. Though your professors will guide you, and your classmates and writing center tutors will make suggestions about your drafts, you are in charge of your writing, and it is up to you to complete it honestly and well.

When you are thinking actively, you are not just waiting for something to happen. You are engaged in the process of achieving goals, making decisions, analyzing issues, and writing thoughtfully.

Influences on Your Thinking

As our minds grow and develop, we are exposed to influences that encourage us to think actively. We also, however, have many experiences that encourage us to think passively. For example, some analysts believe that when people, especially children, spend much of their time watching television or playing video games instead of reading and writing, they are being encouraged to think passively, thus inhibiting their intellectual growth.

You are influenced to think passively if an employer gives you detailed instructions for performing every task that permit no exception or deviation. On the other hand, when an employer gives you general areas of responsibility within which you are expected to make thoughtful and creative decisions, you are being stimulated to think actively and independently. Of course, certain people or activities can act as either active or passive influences, depending on specific situations and your individual responses. For example, consider employers. If you are performing a routine, repetitive task—such as a summer job in a peanut-butter cracker plant, hand-scooping 2,000 pounds of peanut butter a day—the very nature of the work encourages passive, uncritical thinking (although it might also lead to creative daydreaming!).

In college, you will find that your course work and teachers encourage you to think actively by expecting you to apply, analyze, synthesize, and evaluate the information you are acquiring. Professors may assign independent research projects, give essay exams, and require you to write papers in which you must bring your informed perspective to the course material.

Thinking Independently

Answer the following questions on the basis of what you believe to be true.

	Yes	No	Not Sure
1. Is the earth flat?			
2. Is the soul immortal?			
3. Should marijuana be legalized?			
4. Should music lyrics and videos be censored?			
5. Should we always follow "the Golden Rule" ("do unto others as you would have them do unto you")?			

Thinking-Writing Activity

ACTIVE AND PASSIVE INFLUENCES

Here is a list of some of the influences we all experience in our lives, along with space for adding others you are aware of. As you read through the list, place an *A* next to items that you believe influence you to think actively and a *P* next to items that make you more passive.

Activities	*People*
Reading	Family members
Writing	Friends
Watching television	Employers
Surfing the Internet	Advertisers
Drawing and painting	Teachers
Playing video games	Police officers

Playing sports   Religious leaders

Listening to music   Politicians

_____   _____

_____   _____

Identify one important influence in your life that stimulates you to think actively; then identify one that encourages you to think passively. Write explanations of how each has affected your thinking. Provide at least two specific examples for each influence.

Your responses to these questions reveal aspects of the way your mind works, beliefs you have developed that you express in your speaking and writing. How did you arrive at these conclusions? Your views on these and many other issues probably had their beginnings with your family, especially your parents or other adults who raised you. When you were little, you were very dependent on those adults, and you were influenced by the way they saw the world. As you grew up, you learned how to think, feel, and behave in various situations. Very likely your teachers included your brothers and sisters, friends, religious leaders, instructors, books, and the media. You absorbed most of what you learned passively, without even being aware of doing so. Many of your ideas about the issues raised in the five questions you just answered probably were shaped by experiences you had while growing up.

"I keep my core beliefs written on my palm for easy reference."

As a result of your ongoing experiences, however, your mind—and your thinking—have continued to mature. Instead of simply accepting the views of others, you have gradually developed the ability to examine your earlier thinking and to decide how much of it still makes sense to you and whether you should accept it. Now, when you think through important ideas, use this standard when making a decision: Are there good reasons or evidence that support this thinking? If there are, you can actively decide to adopt the ideas. If not, you can modify or reject them.

How do you know when you have examined and adopted beliefs yourself instead of simply borrowing them from others? One indication of having thought your beliefs through is being able to explain why you believe in them, giving the reasons that led you to your conclusions.

Still, not all reasons and evidence are equally strong or accurate. For example, in Europe before the fifteenth century, the common belief that the earth was flat was supported by the following reasons and evidence:

People of Authority: Many educational and religious authorities taught that the earth was flat.

Recorded References: The written opinions of scientific experts supported belief in a flat earth.

Observed Evidence: No person had ever circumnavigated the earth.

Personal Experience: From a normal vantage point, the earth *looks* flat.

Thinking-Writing Activity

EVALUATING BELIEFS

For each of the five beliefs you expressed at the beginning of this section, explain how you arrived at it and state the reasons and evidence that you believe support it.

1. *Example:* Is the earth flat?
   Belief: No, it is round.
   Reasons/Evidence:

   a. People of Authority: My parents and teachers taught me this.

   b. Recorded References: What references support your beliefs? I read about the earth in science textbooks and saw films and videos.

   c. Observed Evidence: I have seen a sequence of photographs taken from outer space that show the earth as a globe.

   d. Personal Experience: When I flew across the country, I could see the horizon line changing.

2. Is the soul immortal?

3. Should marijuana be legalized?

4. Should music lyrics and videos be censored?

5. Should we follow "the golden rule" in our relationships with others?

To evaluate the strengths and accuracy of the reasons and evidence you identified for holding your beliefs on the five issues, address questions such as the following:

People of Authority: Are the authorities knowledgeable in this area? Are they reliable? Have they ever given inaccurate information? Do other authorities disagree with them?

Recorded References: What references support your belief? What are the credentials of the authors? Do other authors disagree with their opinions? On what reasons and evidence do the authors base their opinions?

Observed Evidence: What is the source and foundation of the evidence? Can the evidence be interpreted differently? Does the evidence support the conclusion?

Personal Experience: What were the circumstances under which the experiences took place? Were distortions or mistakes in perception possible? Have other people had either similar or conflicting experiences? Are there other explanations for your experiences?

As a college writer, you are going to apply these questions to material you encounter while gathering information for essays, projects, or reports. The opposite of thinking for yourself is simply accepting the thinking of others without examining or questioning it. Learning to become an independent thinker is a complex, ongoing process.

Viewing a Situation from Different Perspectives

Critical thinkers listen to other views and new ideas and examine them carefully. No one person has *all* the answers! Your beliefs represent just one perspective on whatever problem you want to solve or situation you are trying to understand. In addition to your own particular viewpoint, there may be others, equally important, that you need to consider if you are to develop a more complete understanding of the problem or situation. Learning to think critically and write thoughtfully, in fact, requires this.

Audience and Perspective   Effective writing depends on always having a clear sense of your readers, the audience for whom you are writing. The ability to remain focused on that audience includes being able to see things from their point of view, to think empathetically within their frame of reference, and to understand their perspective. Perspective taking is essential to becoming a thoughtful writer.

To begin with, exploring topics from a variety of vantage points is often the best way to present a comprehensive analysis of the subject you are writing about. When you are tied to only one perspective, your writing tends to be one-sided and superficial. In order to produce your most accomplished writing, you need to be open to the informed comments and suggestions of others and flexible enough to use that feedback to refine your writing.

For most of the issues and problems you will explore and write about in college, one viewpoint is simply not adequate to provide a full and satisfactory understanding. To increase and deepen your knowledge, you must seek other perspectives. In academic and professional writing, you will be expected to seek actively (and *listen to*) other people's viewpoints. It is often very difficult to see things from points of view other than your own; if you are not careful, you can make the serious mistake of assuming that the way you see things is the way they really are.

In order to identify with perspectives other than your own, then, you also have to work to grasp the reasons for these alternate viewpoints. This approach, which stimulates you to evaluate your beliefs critically, is enhanced by writing. Writing about beliefs encourages people to explain their reasons for holding them and provides a vehicle for sharing their thinking with those who have contrasting points of view.

Thinking-Writing Activity

TWO SIDES OF A BELIEF

Describe in detail a belief about which you feel very strongly. Then explain the reasons or experiences that led you to this belief. Next, describe a point of view that differs from your belief. Identify some of the reasons someone would have that point of view.

Purpose and Perspective   Being open to new ideas and different viewpoints means being *flexible* enough to change or modify one's own ideas in the light of new information or better insight. People do have a tendency to cling to the beliefs they were brought up with and the conclusions they have arrived at. If you are going to continue to grow and develop as a thinker, however, you have to be willing to change or modify your beliefs when evidence suggests that you should.

In contrast to open and flexible thinking, *un*critical thinking tends to be one-sided and close-minded. People who think uncritically are convinced that they alone see things as they really are and that everyone who disagrees with them is wrong. It is very difficult for them to step outside their own viewpoints and look at issues from other people's perspectives. Words often used to describe this type of person include *dogmatic, subjective,* and *egocentric.*

Thinking Critically About Visuals

Understanding Different Sides of Complex Issues

As critical thinkers and thoughtful writers, we have an obligation to appreciate diverse perspectives on complex issues and develop informed opinions that are supported by compelling reasons. Have you ever taken part in or attended a protest or a demonstration regarding an issue that was important to you? Although it's essential to stand-up for what we believe, how can we also try to appreciate why people on different sides of the issue have conflicting perspectives?

Joe Raedle/Getty Images

Supporting Diverse Perspectives with Reasons and Evidence

When you are thinking critically, you can offer sound reasons for your views. As a thoughtful writer, you cannot simply take a position on an issue or make a claim; you have to back up your views, reinforce them with information that you feel supports your position. There is an important distinction between *what* you believe and *why* you believe it.

If you want to know all sides of an issue, you have to be able to give supporting reasons and evidence not just for your own views but also for the views of others.

Consider the issue of whether side air bags should be standard equipment for cars. As you try to make sense of this issue, you should attempt to identify not just the reasons for your view but also the reasons for other views. Following are reasons that support each view of this issue.

Issue

Cell phone use while driving should be prohibited.

Cell phone use while driving should be permitted.

Supporting reasons:

1. Studies show that using cell phones while driving increases accidents.

Supporting reasons:

1. Many people feel that cell phones are no more distracting than other common activities in cars.

Now see if you can identify additional supporting reasons for each of these views on cell phone use while driving.

For each of the following issues, identify reasons that support each side.

Issues

1. Multiple-choice and true/false exams should be given in college-level courses.

2. It is better to live in a society in which the government plays a major role in citizens' lives.

3. The best way to deal with crime is to impose long prison sentences.

4. When a couple divorces, the children should choose the parent with whom they wish to live.

1. Multiple-choice and true/false exams should not be given in college-level courses.

2. It is better to live in a society that minimizes the role of the government in citizens' lives.

3. Long prison sentences will not reduce crime.

4. When a couple divorces, the court should decide all custody issues regarding the children.

Thinking-Writing Activity

VIEWING DIFFERENT PERSPECTIVES

Seeing different perspectives is crucial to getting a more complete understanding of ideas expressed in passages you read. Read the two passages that follow. Then, for each passage, do these four things:

1. Identify the main idea of each passage.

2. List the reasons that support the main idea.

3. Develop another view of the main issue.

4. List the reasons that support the other view.

If we want auto safety but continue to believe in auto profits, sales, styling, and annual obsolescence, there will be no serious accomplishments. The moment we put safety ahead of these other values, something will happen. If we want better municipal hospitals but are unwilling to disturb the level of spending for defense, for highways, or for household appliances, hospital service will not improve. If we want peace but still believe that countries with differing ideologies are threats to one another, we will not get peace. What is confusing is that up to now, while we have wanted such things as conservation, auto safety, hospital care, and peace, we have tried wanting them without changing consciousness, that is, while continuing to accept those underlying values that stand in the way of what we want. The machine can be controlled at the "consumer" level only by people who change their whole value system, their whole worldview, their whole way of life. One cannot favor saving our wildlife and wear a fur coat.

* * * *

Most wicked deeds are done because the doer proposes some good to himself. The liar lies to gain some end; the swindler and thief want things which, if honestly got, might be good in themselves. Even the murderer may be removing an impediment to normal desires or gaining possession of something his victim keeps from him. None of these people usually does evil for evil's sake. They are selfish or unscrupulous, but their deeds are not gratuitously evil. The killer for sport has no such comprehensible motive. He prefers death to life, darkness to light. He gets nothing except the satisfaction of saying, "Something which wanted to live is dead. There is that much less vitality, consciousness, and, perhaps, joy in the universe. I am the Spirit that Denies." When a human wantonly destroys one of humankind's own works, we call him Vandal. When he wantonly destroys one of the works of God, we call him Sportsman.

Developing Informed Beliefs

The process of developing informed beliefs is ongoing and lifelong. It is also a process that is essential for you to achieve success and happiness since your beliefs constitute the "map" you use to guide your choices. If your belief map is accurate, your choices will reflect a clear understanding of the world. However, if your belief map is inaccurate or incomplete, you are in jeopardy of making ineffective or wrong-headed choices.

Developing informed beliefs involves the core qualities of a critical thinker and thoughtful writer to which we have been referring: *curious, open-minded, knowledgeable, creative*. The themes of this chapter complement these qualities:

- *Thinking actively* provides the impetus for asking questions, keeping an open mind, seeking knowledge, and being inventive.
- *Thinking independently* is achieved by being curious, going beyond familiar points of view, engaging in research to develop one's own informed opinions, and transcending conventional norms to achieve creative insights.
- *Viewing situations from different perspectives* is the essence of questioning narrow points of view in order to become truly open-minded. Perspective taking is

also the vehicle one uses to develop genuine knowledge and achieve creative insights.

- *Supporting diverse perspectives with reasons and evidence* is the outgrowth of questioning, open-minded explorations, and utilizing one's knowledge.

Thinking-Writing Activity

CREATING A BELIEF MAP

Just as maps help you to navigate your way through unfamiliar territory, belief mapping is a creative strategy for visualizing a path through new and challenging ideas. You can use belief mapping to help you better understand the origins of your own beliefs and positions as well as to plan ways to become a more active and independent thinker. In Chapter 4, we will explore how to use mapping and other visual strategies to help plan writing assignments.

To create a belief map, return to the topics in the Thinking-Writing Activity on page 60 and follow these guidelines:

- Select a topic (either an activity or a person) that has had a *passive* influence on your thinking. This is the starting point of your journey.

- Next, select a topic (again, an activity or a person) that has had an *active* influence on your thinking. This is the route you will travel.

- Finally, select a personal, academic, or career goal. This is your destination.

- Using any visual or artistic medium that appeals to you (such as a simple pencil sketch, a collage, or graphic-arts software), create a map that shows how the active influences on your thinking will help you navigate from your starting point to your goal. What kinds of obstacles might you expect along the way? How would you visually represent those obstacles? How would you describe them to someone on a similar journey?

Experiences That Affect Beliefs

In the following narratives, three writers reflect on learning experiences that caused them to evaluate and in some cases revise beliefs about themselves, the world in which they live, other people, and ways to live their lives.

As you read the selections, keep in mind one set of critical reading questions that we identified in Chapter 2.

- Who is the *writer*, and what perspective does he or she bring to the writing selection?

- What is the *subject* of the selection, and how would you evaluate its cogency and reliability?

- Who is the intended *audience,* and what assumptions is the writer making about it?
- What is the *purpose* of the selection, and how is the author trying to achieve it?

Following each selection are questions designed to stimulate and guide your critical thinking, active reading, and thoughtful writing.

FROM *An American Childhood*

by Annie Dillard (b. 1945)

Annie Dillard's engagement with nature and its reflection of the spiritual life informs her extensive creative and nonfiction writing. A poet, novelist, and essayist, Dillard won the Pulitzer Prize for her memoir *Pilgrim at Tinker Creek* (1974). Her close observations of the environment and her ongoing spiritual quests combine in her views on writing, as in this passage from "Write Till You Drop": "The sensation of writing a book is the sensation of spinning, blinded by love and daring. It is the sensation of a stunt pilot's turning barrel rolls, or an inchworm's blind rearing from a stem in search of a route. At its worst, it feels like alligator wrestling, at the level of the sentence." In the following memoir, she describes how her parents encouraged her early explorations of the natural world.

After I read *The Field Book of Ponds and Streams* several times, I longed for a microscope. Everybody needed a microscope. Detectives used microscopes, both for the FBI and at Scotland Yard. Although usually I had to save my tiny allowance for things I wanted, that year for Christmas my parents gave me a microscope kit.

In a dark basement corner, on a white enamel table, I set up the microscope kit. I supplied a chair, a lamp, a batch of jars, a candle, and a pile of library books. The microscope kit supplied a blunt black three-speed microscope, a booklet, a scalpel, a dropper, an ingenious device for cutting thin segments of fragile tissue, a pile of clean slides and cover slips, and a dandy array of corked test tubes.

One of the test tubes contained "hay infusion." Hay infusion was a wee brown chip of grass blade. You added water to it, and after a week it became a jungle in a drop, full of one-celled animals. This did not work for me. All I saw in the microscope after a week was a wet chip of dried grass, much enlarged.

Another test tube contained "diatomaceous earth." This was, I believed, an actual pinch of the white cliffs of Dover. On my palm it was an airy, friable chalk. The booklet said it was composed of the silicaceous bodies of diatoms—one-celled creatures that lived in, as it were, small glass jewelry boxes with fitted lids. Diatoms, I read, come in a variety of transparent geometrical shapes. Broken and dead and dug out of geological deposits, they made chalk, and a fine abrasive used in silver polish and toothpaste. What I saw in the microscope must have been the fine abrasive— grit enlarged. It was years before I saw a recognizable, whole diatom. The kit's diatomaceous earth was a bust.

5   All that winter I played with the microscope. I prepared slides from things at hand, as the books suggested. I looked at the transparent membrane inside an onion's skin and saw the cells. I looked at a section of cork and saw the cells, and at scrapings from the inside of my cheek, ditto. I looked at my blood and saw not much; I looked at my urine and saw long iridescent crystals, for the drop had dried.

All this was very well, but I wanted to see the wildlife I had read about. I wanted especially to see the famous amoeba, who had eluded me. He was supposed to live in the hay infusion, but I hadn't found him there. He lived outside in warm ponds and streams, too, but I lived in Pittsburgh, and it had been a cold winter.

Finally late that spring I saw an amoeba. The week before, I had gathered puddle water from Frick Park, it had been festering in a jar in the basement. This June night after dinner I figured I had waited long enough. In the basement at my microscope table I spread a scummy drop of Frick Park puddle water on a slide, peeked in, and lo, there was the famous amoeba. He was as blobby and grainy as his picture; I would have known him anywhere.

Before I had watched him at all, I ran upstairs. My parents were still at the table, drinking coffee. They, too, could see the famous amoeba. I told them, bursting, that he was all set up, that they should hurry before his water dried. It was the chance of a lifetime.

Father had stretched out his long legs and was tilting back in his chair. Mother sat with her knees crossed, in blue slacks, smoking a Chesterfield. The dessert dishes were still on the table. My sisters were nowhere in evidence. It was a warm evening; the big dining-room windows gave onto blooming rhododendrons.

10   Mother regarded me warmly. She gave me to understand that she was glad I had found what I had been looking for, but that she and Father were happy to sit with their coffee, and would not be coming down.

She did not say, but I understood at once, that they had their pursuits (coffee?) and I had mine. She did not say, but I began to understand then, that you do what you do out of your private passion for the thing itself.

I had essentially been handed my own life. In subsequent years my parents would praise my drawings and poems, and supply me with books, art supplies, and sports equipment, and listen to my troubles and enthusiasms, and supervise my hours, and discuss and inform, but they would not get involved with my detective work, nor hear about my reading, nor inquire about my homework or term papers or exams, nor visit the salamanders I caught, nor listen to me play the piano, nor attend my field hockey games, nor fuss over my insect collection with me, or my poetry collection or stamp collection or rock collection. My days and nights were my own to plan and fill.

When I left the dining room that evening and started down the dark basement stairs, I had a life, I sat with my wonderful amoeba, and there he was, rolling his grains more slowly now, extending an arc of his edge for a foot and drawing himself along by that foot, and absorbing it again and rolling on. I gave him some more pond water.

I had hit pay dirt. For all I knew, there were paramecia, too, in that pond water, or daphniae, or stentors, or any of the many other creatures I had read about and never seen: volvox, the spherical algal colony; euglena with its one red eye; the elusive glassy diatom; hydra, rotifers, water bears, worms. Anything was possible. The sky was the limit.

Questions for Reading Actively

1. Examine the structure of Dillard's essay. How much time passes over the course of the essay, and how can you tell? When does she "pause" in her narrative, and why?

2. In paragraph 11, Dillard asks a rhetorical question (a question that a writer does not answer, but leaves to the reader). Although it's just one word, what is the full meaning of that question? How would you, as a reader, answer it, based on what you know of Dillard's parents? based on your own parents, or your own experience as a parent?

Questions for Thinking Critically

1. When Annie Dillard rushed to share her discovery of the amoeba with her parents, they politely declined. What reaction had she expected, and what did this reveal about her beliefs regarding her relationship with her parents?

2. Her parents' lack of interest in this and other passions in her life led her to a conclusion: "I had essentially been handed my own life." Explain why you think she reached this conclusion.

3. Based on your own experience, do you believe that the best way to achieve "your own life" is through your parents' lack of involvement in your life?

4. The author states that "you do what you do out of your private passion for the thing itself." This "private passion" is a kind of curiosity, a key characteristic of a critical thinker. Describe a "private passion" of your own that you pursue not to please others but because of your personal curiosity and enthusiasm.

Question for Writing Thoughtfully

1. Compare the vocabulary of the final paragraph with the rest of the essay. Why do you think Dillard concludes her essay with this kind of language?

"Reversing Established Orders"

by Stephen Jay Gould (1941–2002)

From *Leonardo's Mountain of Clams and the Diet of Worms: Essays on Natural History*

Stephen Jay Gould started his academic career as a professor of geology at Harvard University but expanded his interests into evolutionary biology. He was curator of invertebrate paleontology at Harvard's Museum of Comparative Zoology and a writer with a gift for translating complex scientific theories into informed, but witty, prose that nonscientists can understand and enjoy. His essays appeared in magazines such as *Natural History* and *Discover* and were collected in the books *Ever Since Darwin, The Panda's Thumb, The Flamingo's Simile,* and *Leonardo's Mountain of Clams and the Diet of Worms*, in which the following essay appears. This essay illustrates the ongoing process by which natural scientists use inferences to discover factual information and to construct theories explaining that information.

We all know how the world works. A fisherman asks his boss in Shakespeare's *Pericles:* "Master, I marvel how the fishes live in the sea," and receives the evident response, "Why, as men do a-land; the great ones eat up the little ones." Consequently, when humorists invent topsy-turvy worlds, they reverse such established orders and then emphasize the rightness of their absurdity. Alice's Wonderland works on the principle of "sentence first—verdict afterwards." In Gilbert and Sullivan's town of Titipu, the tailor Ko-ko, condemned to death by decapitation, is elevated instead to the rank of Lord High Executioner because—it is so obvious; after all—a man "cannot cut off another's head until he's cut his own off." Pish-tush explains all this in a spirited song with a rousing chorus: "And I am right, and you are right, and all is right too- loora-lay."

Social and literary critics of the so-called postmodernist movement have emphasized, in a cogent and important argument often buried in the impenetrable jargon of their discourse, that conventional support for established orders usually relies upon claims for the naturalness of "dualisms" and "hierarchies." In creating dualisms, we divide a subject into two contrasting categories; in imposing hierarchy upon these dualisms, we judge one category as superior, the other as inferior. We all know the dualistic hierarchies of our social and political lives—from righteous versus infidel of centuries past to the millionaire CEOs who deserve tax cuts versus single mothers who should lose their food stamps in our astoundingly mean-spirited present. The postmodernists correctly argue that such dualisms and hierarchies represent our own constructions for political utility (often nefarious), rather than nature's factual and inevitable dictate. We may choose to parse the world in many other ways with radically different implications.

Our categorizations of nature also tend to favor dualistic hierarchies based upon domination. We often divide the world ecologically into predators and prey, or anatomically into complicated and dominant "higher" animals versus simpler and subservient "lower" forms. I do not deny the utility of such parsings in making predictions that usually work—big fish do generally eat little fish, and not vice versa. But the postmodernist critique should lead us to healthy skepticism, as we scrutinize the complex and socially embedded reasons behind the original formulations of our favored categories. Dualism with dominance may primarily record a human imposition upon nature, rather than a lecture directed to us by the birds and bees.

Natural historians tend to avoid tendentious preaching in this philosophical mode (though I often fall victim to such temptations in these essays). Our favored style of doubting is empirical: if I wish to question your proposed generality, I will search for a counterexample in flesh and blood. Such counterexamples exist in abundance, for they form a staple in a standard genre of writing in natural history—the "wonderment of oddity" or "strange ways of the beaver" tradition. (Sorry to be so disparaging—my own ignoble dualism, I suppose. The stories are terrific. I just often yearn for more intellectual generality and less florid writing.)

5   Much of our fascination with "strange cases" lies in their abrogation of accepted dualisms based on dominance—the "reversing established orders" of my title. As an obvious example, and paragon of this literature, carnivorous plants have always elicited primal intrigue—and the bigger and more taxonomically "advanced" the prey, the more we feel the weirdness. We yawn when a Venus's flytrap ensnares a mosquito, but shiver with substantial discomfort when a large pitcher plant devours a bird or rodent.

I keep a file marked "Reversals" to house such cases. I have long been on the lookout for optimal examples, where all three of the most prominent dualisms based on dominance suffer reversal: predator and prey, high and low, large and small—in other words, where a creature from a category usually ranked as small in body, primitive in design, and subject to predation eats another animal from a category generally viewed as bigger, anatomically superior, and rapacious. I now have four intriguing examples, more than enough for an essay. Since we postmodernists abjure hierarchical ranking, I will simply present my stories in the nonjudgmental chronological order of their publication (though postmodernism in this sense—and truly I am not a devotee of this movement—may be a cop-out and an excuse, for not devising a better logical structure for this essay!).

* * * *

1. FROGS AND FLIES. Frogs eat flies. If flies eat frogs, then we might as well be headed for bedlam or the apocalypse. My colleague Tom Eisner of Cornell University is revered throughout our profession as the past master of natural oddities with important and practical general messages. One day in August 1982, at a small pond in Arizona, Eisner and several colleagues noted thousands of spadefoot toads congregating on the muddy shore as they emerged to adulthood in near synchrony from their tadpole stage. Eisner and colleagues described their discovery in a technical publication:

> Spaced only centimeters apart in places, they were all of minimal adult size (body length, 1.5 to 2 cm [less than an inch]). Conspicuous among them were toads that were dead or dying, apparently having been seized by a predator in the mud and drawn partly into the substrate, until only their head, or head and trunk, projected above ground. We counted dozens of such semisubmerged toads.

They then dug deeper and to their great surprise, found the predator "a large grublike insect larva, subsequently identified as that of the horsefly *Tabanus punctifer.*" In other words, flies can eat toads! (Although astonishment may be lessened in noting that the tiny toads are much smaller than enormous fly larvae.) Unusually large insects and maximally small vertebrates have also been featured in the few other recorded cases of such reversals—frogs, small birds, even a mouse, consumed by praying mantids, for example.

The fly larvae force themselves into the mud, rear end first, until their front end, bearing the mouthparts, lies flush with the surface. The larvae then catch toads by hooking their pointed mandibles into the hind legs or belly, and then dragging the toad partway into the mud. The larvae—please remember that many tales in natural history are not pleasant by human standards—then suck the toad dry (and dead) by ingesting blood and body fluids only.

10   I loved the wry last sentence of the paper by Eisner and his colleagues—unusual in style for a technical article, but odd stories have always permitted some literary license:

> The case we report is a reversal of the usual toad-eats-fly paradigm, although . . . the paradigm may also prevail in its conventional form. Adult *Scaphiopus* [the spadefoot toad] might well on occasions have predatory access to the very *Tabanus* flies that as larvae preyed upon their conspecifics.

J. Greenberg, reporting for *Science News* (November 5, 1983), began his commentary with the emotional impact of such reversals:

> This is the Okeechobee Fla. Little League team thrashing the New York Yankees; this is Wally Cox beating out Burt Reynolds for the girl; this is Grenada invading the United States. "This is unlike anything I've ever seen," says Thomas Eisner.

* * * *

2. LOBSTERS AND SNAILS. Decapod crustaceans (lobsters, crabs, shrimp) eat snails, as all naturalists know. In fact, the classic case of an extended evolutionary "arms race," elegantly documented over many years by my colleague Geerat Vermeij, involves increased strength of crab claws correlated with ever more efficient protective devices (spines, ribs, thicker and wavier shells) in snails over geological time. Land crabs are the overwhelmingly predominant predator of my own favorite subject for research, the Caribbean land snail *Cerion*. If snails eat decapods, we might as well retire.

Amos Barkai and Christopher McQuaid studied rock lobsters and whelks (snails of middling size) in waters around two islands, Marcus and Malgas, located just four miles apart in the Saldanha Bay area of South Africa. On Malgas, as all God-fearing folk would only rightly suspect, rock lobsters eat mollusks, mostly mussels and several species of whelks. Barkai and McQuaid write in their 1988 account: "The rock lobsters usually attacked the whelks by chipping away the shell margin with their mouth parts."

The local lobstermen report that, twenty years ago, rock lobsters were equally common on both islands. But lobsters then disappeared from Marcus Island, for unclear reasons, perhaps linked to a period of low oxygen in surrounding waters during the 1970s. In the absence of lobsters as the usual top predator, extensive mussel beds have become established, and the population density of whelks has soared. Barkai and McQuaid asked themselves: "Why do rock lobsters not recolonize Marcus Island despite the high availability of food?"

15   In an attempt to answer their own question, they performed the obvious experiment—and made an astonishing discovery. The food has become the feeder—this time by overwhelming in number, not equaling in size (the whelks are much smaller than the lobsters). The conventional passive voice of scientific prose does not convey excitement well, but a good story easily transcends such a minor limitation. So, in Barkai and McQuaid's own words; and without any need for further commentary from me (I would only be tempted to make some arch and utterly inappropriate statement about slave revolts—Spartacus and all that):

One thousand rock lobsters from Malgas Island were tagged and transferred to Marcus Island . . . The result was immediate. The apparently healthy rock lobsters were quickly overwhelmed by large numbers of whelks. Several hundreds were observed being attacked immediately after release and a week later no live rock lobsters could be found at Marcus Island . . . The rock lobsters escaped temporarily by swimming, but each contact with the substratum resulted in several more whelks attaching themselves until weight of numbers prevented escape. On average each rock lobster was killed within fifteen minutes by more than three hundred *Burnupena* [whelks] that removed all the flesh in less than an hour.

Sic semper tyrannis.

* * * *

3. FISH AND DINOFLAGELLATES. Fish don't generally eat dinoflagellates; why should they even deign to notice such microscopic algae, floating in the plankton? But dinoflagellates certainly don't eat fish; the very notion, given the disparity in sizes, is ludicrous to the point of incomprehensibility.

Dinoflagellates do, however, *kill* fish, by indirect mechanisms long known and well studied for their immense practical significance. Under favorable conditions, dinoflagellate populations can soar to 60 million organisms per liter of water. These so-called blooms can discolor and poison the waters—"red tide" is the most familiar example—leading to massive deaths of fish and other marine organisms.

J. M. Burkholder and a group of her colleagues from North Carolina State University have studied toxic blooms associated with fish kills in estuaries of the southeastern United States. The largest event resulted in the death of nearly one million Atlantic menhaden in the estuary of the Pamlico River. The oddity of this case lies not in the killing of fish per se, a common consequence of dinoflagellate blooms. We have always regarded the deaths of fishes and other marine organisms during red tides as passive and "unintended" results of dinoflagellate toxins, or other consequences of massive algal populations during blooms. No one had supposed that dinoflagellates might actively kill fish as an evolved response for their own explicit advantage, including a potential nutritional benefit for the algal cells. And yet the dinoflagellates do seem to be killing and eating fishes in a manner suggesting active evolution for this most peculiar reversal.

The dinoflagellate lives in a dormant state, lying on the sea floor within a protective cyst. When live fish approach, the cyst breaks and releases a mobile cell that swims, grows, and secretes a powerful, water-soluble neurotoxin, killing the fish. So far, so what?—though the presence of fish does seem to induce activity by the dinoflagellate (breaking of the cyst), thus suggesting a direct link. Anatomical and behavioral evidence both suggest that dinoflagellates have actively evolved their strategy for feeding on fishes. The swimming cell, breaking out from the cyst, grows a projection, called a peduncle, from its lower surface. The cells seem to move actively toward dead or dying fishes. Flecks of tissue, sloughed off from the fish, then become attached to the peduncle and get digested. The authors describe this reversal at maximum disparity in size among my four cases:

The lethal agent is an excreted neurotoxin. [It] induces neurotoxic signs by
fish including sudden sporadic movement, disorientation, lethargy and apparent
suffocation followed by death. The alga has not been observed to attack fish directly.
It rapidly increases its swimming velocity to reach flecks of sloughed tissue from
dying fish, however, using its peduncle to attach to and digest the tissue debris.

* * * *

20   4. Sponges and arthropods. Among invertebrates, sponges rank as the lowest of the
low (the bottom rung of any evolutionary ladder), while arthropods stand highest
of the high (just a little lower than the angels, that is, just before vertebrates on a
linear list of rising complexity). Sponges have no discrete organs; they feed by filtering
out tiny items of food from water pumped through channels in their body. Arthropods
grow eyes, limbs, brains, and digestive systems; many live as active carnivores. Most
arthropods wouldn't take much notice of a lowly sponge, but we can scarcely imagine
how or why a sponge might subdue and ingest an arthropod.

However, in a 1995 article, crisply titled "Carnivorous Sponges," J. Vacelet and
N. Boury-Esnault of the Centre d'Oceanologie of Marseille have found a killer sponge
(about as bizarre as a fish-eating dinoflagellate—but both exist). Relatives of this
sponge, members of the genus *Asbestopluma*, have only been known from very deep
waters (including the all-time record for sponges at more than 25,000 feet), where
behavior and food preferences could not be observed. But Vacelet and Boury-Esnault
found a new species in a shallow-water Mediterranean cave (less than one hundred
feet), where scuba divers can watch directly.

The deep sea is a nutritional desert, and many organisms from such habitats develop
special adaptations for procuring large and rare items (while relatives from shallow
waters may pursue a plethora of smaller prey). *Asbestopluma* has lost both filtering
channels through the body and the specialized cells (called choanocytes) that pump the
water through. So how does this deep-water sponge feed?

The new species grows long filaments that extend out from the upper end of the body. A
blanket of tiny spicules, or small skeletal projections, covers the surface of the filaments. The
authors comment: "The spicule cover . . . gives the filaments a 'Velcro'-like adhesiveness"—
the key to this feeding reversal at maximal anatomical distance for invertebrates. The sponge
captures small crustaceans on the filaments—and they can't escape any more than a fuzz
ball can detach itself from the Velcro lining of your coat pocket. The authors continue:
"New, thin filaments grew over the prey, which was completely enveloped after one day and
digested within a few days." The sponge, in other words, has become a carnivore.

Four fascinating stories to give us pause about our preconceptions, particularly our
dualistic taxonomies based on the domination of one category over another. The little
guys sometimes turn tables and prevail—often enough, perhaps, to call the categories
themselves into question.

25   I see another message in these reversals—a consequence of the reassessment
that must always proceed when established orders crumble, or merely lose their claim
to invariance. In our struggle to understand the history of life, we must learn where
to place the boundary between contingent and unpredictable events that occur but

once and the more repeatable, lawlike phenomena that may pervade life's history as generalities. (In my own view of life, the domain of contingency looms vastly larger than all Western tradition, and most psychological hope, would allow. Fortuity pervades the origin of any particular species or lineage. *Homo sapiens* is a contingent twig, not a predictable result of ineluctably rising complexity during evolution. . . .)

The domain of lawlike generality includes broad phenomena not specific to the history of particular lineages. The ecological structure of communities should provide a promising searching ground, for some principles of structural organization must transcend the particular organisms that happen to occupy a given role at any moment. I imagine, for example, that all balanced ecosystems must sustain more biomass as prey than as predators—and I would accept such statements as predictable generalities, despite my affection for contingency. I would also have been willing to embrace the invariance of other rules for sensible repetition—that single-celled creatures don't kill and eat large multicellular organisms, for example. But these four cases of reversed order give me pause.

In a famous passage from the *Origin of Species*, Charles Darwin extolled the invariance of certain ecological patterns by using observed repetition in independent colonizations to argue against a range of contingently unpredictable outcomes:

> When we look at the plants and bushes clothing an entangled bank, we are tempted to attribute their proportional numbers and kinds to what we call chance. But how false a view is this! Every one has heard that when an American forest is cut down, a very different vegetation springs up; but it has been observed that the trees now growing on the ancient Indian mounds, in the Southern United States, display the same beautiful diversity and proportion of kinds as in the surrounding virgin forests. What a struggle between the several kinds of trees must here have gone on during long centuries, each annually scattering its seeds by the thousand; what war between insect and insect—between insects, snails, and other animals with birds and beasts of prey—all striving to increase, and all feeding on each other or on the trees or their seeds and seedlings, or on the other plants which first clothed the ground and thus checked the growth of the trees! Throw up a handful of feathers, and all must fall to the ground according to definite laws; but how simple is this problem compared to the action and reaction of the innumerable plants and animals which have determined, in the course of centuries, the proportional numbers and kinds of trees now growing on the old Indian ruins!

But the same patterns do not always recur from adjacent starting points colonized by the same set of species. Even the most apparently predictable patterns of supposedly established orders may fail. Remove the lobsters from waters around one South African island, and a new equilibrium may quickly emerge—one that actively excludes lobsters by converting their former prey into a ganging posse of predators!

Thus, I sense a challenge in these four cases, a message perhaps deeper than the raw peculiarity of their phenomenology—and the resulting attack upon our dualistic and hierarchical categories. We do not yet know the rules of composition for ecosystems. We do not even know if rules exist in the usual sense. I am tempted, therefore, to close with the famous words that D'Arcy Thompson wrote to signify our ignorance of the microscopic world (*Growth and Form*, 1942 edition). We are not quite so uninformed about the rules of composition for ecosystems, but what a stark challenge and what an inspiration to go forth: "We have come to the edge of a world of which we have no experience, and where all our preconceptions must be recast."

Questions for Reading Actively

1. In your own words, define the concept of *dualism with dominance* (paragraph 3). What is Gould's opinion of this concept and the ways in which it has been used to explain the natural world?

2. How is Gould's argument structured? What does Gould himself think about this method for structuring his argument?

Questions for Thinking Critically

1. How could you use what Gould calls "counterexamples" in biology (paragraph 4) to better develop your own perspectives and beliefs about a wide variety of issues?

2. In paragraph 15, Gould notes that "The conventional passive voice of scientific prose does not convey excitement well, but a good story easily transcends such a minor limitation." Compare Gould's sense of excitement and curiosity with Annie Dillard's recollection of her first sighting of an amoeba (p. 70). What qualities of critical thinking and thoughtful writing do these two authors share?

Questions for Writing Thoughtfully

1. How would you describe the audience Gould had in mind as he wrote this essay? Point out examples of Gould's language choices, allusions to scientific or cultural concepts, and other places in the essay where you think Gould is specifically appealing to this audience. Which parts of the essay do you find most accessible and appealing, and why? Which parts are most challenging for you?

2. What is the "message" that Gould sees in these reversals of seemingly established orders? In an essay, define that message in your own words and describe how it either challenges or upholds your own beliefs.

"The Case Against Chores"

by Jane Smiley (b. 1949)

Novelist and literature professor Jane Smiley has explored everything from the history of Greenland to thoroughbred horse racing in her fiction. A native of California, Smiley lived and taught for many years in Iowa. The influence of that state's proud rural culture is deeply felt in her novel *A Thousand Acres*, which won the Pulitzer Prize in 1991. Using the great Shakespearean tragedy *King Lear* as her inspiration, Smiley captured the vast sense of loss and despair felt by many Midwestern farm families during the rural economic crisis of the 1980s. Smiley's essays and book reviews have appeared in a range of periodicals. "The Case Against Chores" was originally published in *Harper's Magazine* in 1995.

I've lived in the upper Midwest for twenty-one years now, and I'm here to tell you that the pressure to put your children to work is unrelenting. So far I've squirmed out from under it, and my daughters have led a life of almost tropical idleness, much to their benefit. My son, however, may not be so lucky. His father was himself raised in Iowa and put to work at an early age, and you never know when, in spite of all my husband's best intentions, that early training might kick in.

Although "chores" are so sacred in my neck of the woods that almost no one ever discusses their purpose, I have over the years gleaned some of the reasons parents give for assigning them. I'm not impressed. Mostly the reasons have to do with developing good work habits or, in the absence of good work habits; at least habits of working. No such thing; as a free lunch any job worth doing is worth doing right, work before play, all of that. According to this reasoning, the world is full of jobs that no one wants to do. If we divide them up and get them over with, then we can go on to pastimes we like. If we do them "right," then we won't have to do them again. Lots of times, though, in a family, that *we* doesn't operate. The operative word is *you*. The practical result of almost every child-labor scheme that I've witnessed is the child doing the dirty work and the parent getting the fun: Mom cooks and Sis does the dishes; the parents plan and plant the garden, the kids weed it. To me, what this teaches the child is the lesson of alienated labor: not to love the work but to get it over with; not to feel pride in one's contribution but to feel resentment at the waste of one's time.

Another goal of chores: the child contributes to the work of maintaining the family. According to this rationale, the child comes to understand what it takes to have a family, and to feel that he or she is an important, even indispensable member of it. But come on. Would you really want to feel loved primarily because you're the one who gets the floors mopped? Wouldn't you rather feel that your family's love simply exists all around you, no matter what your contribution? And don't the parents love their children anyway, whether the children vacuum or not? Why lie about it just to get the housework done? Let's be frank about the other half of the equation too. In this day and age, it doesn't take much work at all to manage a household, at least in the middle class— maybe four hours a week to clean the house and another four to throw the laundry into the washing machine, move it to the dryer, and fold it. Is it really a good idea to set the sort of example my former neighbors used to set, of mopping the floor every two days, cleaning the toilets every week, vacuuming every day, dusting, dusting, dusting? Didn't they have anything better to do than serve their house?

Let me confess that I wasn't expected to lift a finger when I was growing up. Even when my mother had a full-time job, she cleaned up after me, as did my grandmother. Later there was a housekeeper. I would leave my room in a mess when I headed off for school and find it miraculously neat when I returned. Once in a while I vacuumed, just because I liked the pattern the Hoover made on the carpet. I did learn to run water in my cereal bowl before setting it in the sink.

5

Where I discovered work was at the stable, and, in fact, there is no housework like horsework. You've got to clean the horses' stalls, feed them, groom them, tack them up, wrap their legs, exercise them, turn them out, and catch them. You've got to clip them and shave them. You have to sweep the aisle, clean your tack and your boots, carry bales of hay and buckets of water. Minimal horsekeeping, rising just to the level of humaneness, requires many more hours than making a few beds, and horsework turned out to be a good preparation for the real work of adulthood, which is rearing children. It was a good preparation not only because it was similar in many ways but also because my desire to do it, and to do a good job of it, grew out of my love of and interest in my horse. I can't say that cleaning out her bucket when she manured in it was an actual joy, but I knew she wasn't going to do it herself. I saw the purpose of my labor, and I wasn't alienated from it.

Probably to the surprise of some of those who knew me as a child, I have turned out to be gainfully employed. I remember when I was in seventh grade, one of my teachers said to me, strongly disapproving, "The trouble with you is you do only what you want to do!" That continues to be the trouble with me, except that over the years I have wanted to do more and more.

My husband worked hard as a child, out-Iowa-ing the Iowans, if such a thing is possible. His dad had him mixing cement with a stick when he was five, pushing wheelbarrows not long after. It's a long sad tale on the order of two miles to school and both ways uphill. The result is, he's a great worker, much better than I am, but all the while he's doing it he wishes he weren't. He thinks of it as work; he's torn between doing a good job and longing not to be doing it at all. Later, when he's out on the golf course, where he really wants to be, he feels a little guilty, knowing there's work that should have been done before he gave in and took advantage of the beautiful day.

Good work is not the work we assign children but the work they want to do, whether it's reading in bed (where would I be today if my parents had rousted me out and put me to scrubbing floors?) or cleaning their rooms or practicing the flute or making roasted potatoes with rosemary and Parmesan for the family dinner. It's good for a teenager to suddenly decide that the bathtub is so disgusting she'd better clean it herself. I admit that for the parent, this can involve years of waiting. But if she doesn't want to wait, she can always spend her time dusting.

Questions for Reading Actively

1. What kinds of reasons and evidence does Smiley offer to support her argument? Do you consider these reasons and evidence to be authoritative? What does her choice of reasons and evidence reveal about Smiley's intended audience?

2. How does Smiley use rhetorical questions to appeal to her readers? What is your reaction to these questions?

Questions for Thinking Critically

1. How does the concept of *dualism with dominance* described by Stephen Jay Gould in "Reversing Established Orders" (p. 72) apply to Smiley's description of "chores" as part of a family dynamic?

2. In paragraph 5, Smiley makes a startling analogy. What is it? Do you agree? How might student writer Eli Sharp (p. 85) respond to that analogy?

3. In what ways do Jane Smiley's and Annie Dillard's (p. 69) childhoods resemble each other? What kinds of arguments do both writers make for the benefits of encouraging curiosity and independence in children? Do you agree or disagree?

Question for Writing Thoughtfully

1. What experience did Smiley have that changed her beliefs about chores? At what point in her essay does she describe this experience? Does the placement of that information have an impact on the reader? Try rewriting her essay with the information about that experience introduced at a different point. What is the effect?

Writing Project: An Experience That Influenced a Belief

The Thinking-Writing Activities and the readings and questions in this chapter have encouraged you to become an active thinker, to examine your beliefs, and to observe how some thoughtful people have reflected on their learning experiences. As you work on this project, reread what you wrote for the activities and think about the events discussed in the readings.

The Writing Situation

Begin by considering the elements discussed in the Writing Situation section of the Thinking-Writing Model.

Purpose   Your primary purpose in writing this essay is to make clear to your readers what your belief is, narrate your experience in an interesting way, and connect the two effectively. You are not trying to convince your readers that they should adopt your belief. You are showing them what your belief is and the impact of your experience. A second purpose is to stimulate your own increased understanding of your belief, your ability to evaluate that belief, and your larger understanding of other people's beliefs.

Write an essay telling of an experience that had an important influence on a belief that you held or hold. The belief might be about yourself, about another person involved in the experience, or about the issue that the experience illustrates. The experience may have helped form your belief, changed, or strengthened it.

You should explain your belief, of course, and describe the experience, reflecting on what happened as you tell of its effects. You may want to discuss the sources of the belief (see pages 62 and 63). Follow your instructor's directions for length, format, and so forth.

Audience   When you write about your own experiences, you are an important part of the audience. This form of writing, as you have seen in Annie Dillard's essay (p. 69), acts as a catalyst for self-discovery by encouraging you to reflect on your past experiences. As you write, your guiding ideas should include these questions:

- How effectively am I communicating the reality of this experience?
- How effectively have I analyzed the significance of this experience and the impact that it had?

You will also be writing for the other readers with whom you'll share this piece of writing. Consider these questions when thinking about your audience:

- How much information about my belief should I include to help my readers to understand it and know where it came from?
- How much would my readers be likely to know about the background of the experience I am writing about? What in that background is important for them to understand?
- What details of the experience should I include to make it real for my readers? What details can I leave out?

In other words, you need to put yourself in your readers' position and view your writing through their eyes.

Subject   When you write about your own experience or create an autobiographical narrative, you are using a common and effective means of communication. Real experiences provide living examples, not abstract or hypothetical ideas. Think of how often speakers, writers, and people you know tell about experiences in order to illustrate a point. This assignment demonstrates that interaction. The belief you are writing about is probably a somewhat abstract idea; your experience is real. In a later chapter you will consider narration again and be reminded that a story illuminates an idea, but does not really prove that the idea is true.

Most of us like to learn about what someone did and what he or she thinks it means, and most of us enjoy telling of our own experiences. As you think about your many beliefs and your many experiences, try to identify a belief that will interest an audience and an experience that you can represent in sharp detail.

Writer This Writing Project, like the others in Part One of this book, asks you to use your own experience as the basis of an essay. This makes you the authority on the subject, which should give you confidence. Your challenges are to shape your story and to connect it directly to your belief.

The Writing Process

One of this book's main goals is to help you discover your own writing process, to tap its strengths and to reduce its weaknesses. This project provides a good opportunity for you to reflect on your writing process.

Generating Ideas Think about a suitable experience to write about. Look for an experience that had a profound effect on your belief and that may have implications for other people's lives. Once you have found your topic, ask yourself questions and make notes about your responses. Questions you might ask include these:

- What happened? Outline the major events of the experience.
- How did you respond? What were your thoughts, reactions, feelings?
- What roles did other people play? Was the location important? Recall specific details about what people did and said, and about the setting, to make your retelling vivid for your audience.
- What was the result of the experience? How did it affect your belief?
- As you reflect on it, what was the experience's value for you? How has it influenced your life?

You may also refer to the questions for generating ideas in Chapter 4.

Defining a Focus In a few sentences, summarize the main point you wish to make in your essay, given your subject, audience, and purpose. Then evaluate your focus: Is it specific enough for you to convey it clearly in an essay? Is it interesting so that your audience will find it worth reading about? Is it thoughtful so that it serves the purpose of reflection?

At this point, consider whether or not the experience you have chosen is an appropriate subject for your purpose and audience. If not, you can begin again by looking for another experience to write about.

Organizing Ideas Think about how you can order the elements of your experience. Will you start at the beginning and describe them chronologically? Or will you start at a later point in time and use a flashback to the beginning of the experience?

Where will you include your observations and reflections about the experience: at the end or at various places throughout?

Drafting   As you translate your ideas, notes, and early versions into coherent writing, you will need to decide how to draft in ways that will help you revise your work effectively. Because the essay you are about to write will have three distinct components—your belief, your experience, and their connections—you may want to draft each component separately and then think about connecting them.

Drafting Hints

1. Spread out all the work you did while generating ideas and drafting a focus so that you can see it while you write the sections of your draft.

2. Draft briskly. You will revise and correct later.

3. If you stop or are interrupted while drafting, be sure to save what you have written.

4. When you return to drafting, reread what you saved to resume the flow of your ideas.

Revising   One of the best strategies for revision is to get an audience's reactions to your draft. Your classmates, or peers, can help you see where your draft is already successful and where it needs improvement. If your instructor allows class time for peer review, be sure to have a draft ready so that you can benefit from this activity.

 Revising Strategy: Peer Response Groups   This activity works best with groups of three or four.

1. The group selects a timekeeper, who allots ten minutes to each writer. Regardless of how many response process steps have been completed, after ten minutes the group goes on to the next writer's work.

2. One person begins by reading aloud his or her draft while group members listen.

3. The writer next reads his or her writing aloud a second time. *Do not skip this step*.

4. Group members listen and write notes or comments.

5. The writer then asks each group member this question and jots down their responses: "What questions do you have about my original belief and its sources?"

6. The writer next asks each member these questions and takes notes as each answers: "What questions do you have about the experience I described? What else do you need to know about it?"

7. The writer then asks each member these questions and records their responses: "Do you understand why my belief changed as a result of this experience and what my belief is now? What could I add to make my writing clearer?"

As soon as possible after peer review, you should revise your draft based on your peers' questions and comments. Then, if possible, put it aside for a day or two before continuing with revision. In an online classroom, you can post or email drafts of your paper and ask for written responses to the questions in Steps 5–7. Ask your instructor about additional ways to use technology for collaborative writing.

Reread your revised draft to yourself out loud, slowly. Then think about each of the following questions. As you consider ways to improve your draft based on your answers, stop and make changes to your draft before you move on to the next question.

1. How could you improve the first paragraph? How could you get your readers' attention and make them want to read on?

2. How could you improve the order of your draft? Could you rearrange some paragraphs?

3. How could you improve the flow of your draft? Where would transitions help your audience?

4. How could you improve your sentences? Pay particular attention to sentences that are difficult to read aloud. Your audience will have trouble following them! Could you shorten hard-to-read long sentences or write them as two sentences? Where could you use parallel structure to make your sentences more graceful?

Proofreading   After you prepare a final draft, check for use of standard grammar and punctuation. Proofread carefully for omitted words and punctuation marks. Run your spell-checker program, but be aware of its limitations. Proofread again to detect the kinds of errors the computer can't catch.

Your essay should now be completed to the very best of your ability, and, of course, you will need to submit a copy to your instructor by the due date. But also try to share it with other audiences. Would members of your family enjoy reading it? Would other people who were involved in the experience want to know how it affected you? Would someone with whom you currently have a relationship understand you better by reading it?

The following essay shows how a student responded to this assignment.

Student Writing

Eli Sharp's Writing Process

In response to an assignment asking him to agree or disagree with a belief expressed in one of the assigned readings, Eli Sharp, a student at City College of San Francisco, chose to disagree with Jane Smiley's belief expressed in "The Case Against Chores" (p. 78) that children should not be assigned chores. The assignment also required Sharp to consult other sources and cite them according to MLA style.

To begin generating ideas, Sharp started with his own immediate emotional reaction to Smiley's essay. "The hardest part was getting out of my reactive emotional response," he wrote in response to a query from his professor. "I was trying to be in an inquiring and open-minded state, rather than just defending my own belief."

The move from personal, subjective experience to a broader outlook was supported by Sharp's reading of other sources, an eclectic mix of authors and philosophers whose own insights into childhood helped Sharp to refine his own argument. "I knew that I wanted to convince my audience, my professor and classmates, of the soundness of my belief, so I had to work through my emotional reaction and more closely examine the bases for my own belief in the value of chores," he said. As he worked, Sharp kept track of the necessary source information and was careful to ensure that everything he quoted, paraphrased, or summarized was correctly cited both in the body of the essay and on the works-cited page that is required for MLA papers.

As you read Eli Sharp's essay, note how he often refers to specific points made in "The Case Against Chores." These references both support Eli's own argument as well as help his audience—even an audience that might not be familiar with Smiley's essay—understand the larger context.

An Argument for Chores

by Eli Sharp

In her essay "The Case Against Chores," Jane Smiley argues that children are both immediately and ultimately better off it they are not required by their parents, family, or other guardians to do household chores. She succinctly sums up the conventional rationales for assigning chores and dismisses them. In her own upbringing she "wasn't expected to lift a finger," and the closest she came to cleaning up after herself was "to run water in [her] cereal bowl before setting it in the sink." All the same, she developed work habits and skills tending a stable, as, she explains, she "wasn't alienated from [the work]" (73).

Smiley seems, first of all, to assume that the reader will share in her high opinion of herself as a well-known academic and a professional writer. True, she is esteemed by her peers and enjoys an elevated social status. But are these the only qualities that chore-doling Iowans want to engender in their children? I would argue that all too often those who make a living with their minds are viewed not with awe or respect by those who do so with their hands, but with some degree of suspicion, mistrust, and the sense that somehow such people are shirking "real work."

Be this as it may, I find Smiley's argument unconvincing on many grounds. I think she's guilty of faulty inductive reasoning, or "hasty generalization," in claiming that because she turned out so well, most other children will too. And again, when, having "[. . .] over the years gleaned some of the *reasons* parents give for assigning [chores,]" (italics mine), she assumes her work in this regard is done (72). If she's gleaned some of the reasons and remains unimpressed, the other ones couldn't possibly be any better. Even in her title Smiley seems a bit grandiose in her assessment of her own views. It's not just "A" case against chores; it's "The" case against chores.

Perhaps Smiley most compromises the validity of her argument in my eyes with her comment about learning to run some water in her cereal bowl before setting it in the sink. Is this a chore? I hardly consider a rudiment of self-accountability, such as cleaning up after herself, to be a chore. Maybe one of those reasons for assigning tasks that she didn't glean was that children should be weaned of the idea that they can expect to be served by others, including their parents. Or is this only true of certain segments of society, those who are to learn how to serve?

Whatever Smiley's views on wider issues may be, I see the case for assigning chores to children at some stage of their development and dependence on the family as being far more sound, reasonable, and convincing than that against. For one, not all children will opt for such benevolent pastimes as stable cleaning, in the absence of assigned chores. In his short but wonderfully lucid and honest essay on his own boyhood misbehavior, Andrew O'Hagan writes, "We all took and assigned roles in cruel little dramas of our own devising. Our talk would be full of new and interesting ways to worry or harass our parents . . . ." He goes on to describe a twelve-year-old neighbor girl who claimed to grind up light bulbs and put them in her father's porridge (43). While I don't suggest that assigning chores would have any influence whatsoever on such behavior, O'Hagan's point in mentioning this questionable claim is that the idea was lauded by him and his boyhood friends. Having some chores to do can keep children from having too much time on their hands to hang around with their peers and get into trouble. "Something happened when we all got together . . . ," O' Hagan writes, "We were competitive, deluded, and full of our own small powers. . . . As only dependents can be, we were full of our own independence" (40–41). Chores can help remind children of their dependence.

Smiley makes much of the insufficiency of this argument and stresses the idea that children should be loved, valued, and accepted for who they are, not what they do for the family. On the latter point, of course, I agree. However, it is the transition from dependence on the family to dependence on society, and the relative independence required, which interests me here. I suggest that some transitional stage, involving the introduction to the rules and mores of the society in which the family lives, is highly desirable. In a capitalist state society like ours, where semi-socialist institutions are required to play a subordinate role to "free enterprise," or unregulated competitive organizations, it greatly behooves a child to learn that her society does *not* value her for who she "is," but precisely for what she does, or what she's "worth" in terms of wealth, as the case may be. I don't contend that this situation owes to any specific historical cause, much less a particular political or social agenda, but that it is a normal extension of human nature, in absence of understanding and acknowledgement of a higher law. In this sense I follow Jean-Jacques Rousseau as he writes:

> Such was . . . the origin of society and law, . . . which irretrievably destroyed natural liberty, eternally fixed the law of property and inequality, converted clever usurpation into unalterable right, and, for the advantage of a few ambitious individuals, subjected all mankind to perpetual labour, slavery, and wretchedness. (79)

I believe the facts of daily life bear out this view despite the best efforts and intentions of the leaders and shapers of our society. President John F. Kennedy, in his inaugural address of January 20, 1969 (as examined by Robert Bellah in his essay on civil religion), spoke: "The same revolutionary beliefs for which our forebears fought are still at issue around the globe—the belief that the rights of man come not from the generosity of the state but from the hand of God." Nonetheless, the address concludes, "Here on earth God's work must truly be our own." Of this speech Bellah astutely observes that "It might be argued that the passages quoted reveal the essentially irrelevant role of religion in the very secular society that is America. . . . [Religion] gets only a sentimental nod . . . , before a discussion of the really serious business with which religion has nothing whatever to do" (41). The laws that govern our daily lives, in the modern world, are economic, not moral, and it is to a child's benefit to be prepared for this realization. Without entering into the question of the advisability of bringing children into such a world in the first place, I submit that the least parents can do is to *gradually* wean their child from the loving, nurturing environment of the family into the so-called "working world."

"She also taught me 'to speak the truth and shame the Devil!'" writes the poet and author Robert Graves of his mother. "Her favourite biblical exhortation went: 'My son, whatever thy hand findeth to do, do it with all thy might'" (32). This exhortation, central to many of the world's religions, sheds light on another possible advantage of chores. They give the child the opportunity to discover the simple pleasure of exertion itself.

Chores tend to be simple, manual labor. Growing up in northern Michigan, in a home built by my parents and their friends and heated entirely with wood-burning ovens, I have extensive experience with chores of this type. It really was an unusual amount of physical labor for boys (my brother and I) in the twentieth century. Felling, cutting, and splitting cordwood; shoveling masses of snow; gardening; composting; mowing; and occasionally harvesting maple sap, in addition to the usual household chores, were all on the list.

While Smiley says she took straight to stable work without the least outside obligation, there's no way I would have worked like I did without having my tasks clearly outlined for me. And, more to the point, I learned to enjoy physical labor, even in harsh conditions. The work was not oppressive, monotonous, dangerous, arbitrary, or, by a far cry, to someone else's reward and my detriment.

I was not a driven child, and I am not a driven adult. Having chores to do helped me better appreciate my leisure time. "Oh the happy, happy, never-to-be-recalled days of childhood!" writes the great novelist Lev Tolstoy. "How could one fail to love and cherish memories of such a time? Those memories refresh and elevate the soul and are a source of my best enjoyment" (52). So it is with me. The sheer physical, sensory enjoyment of the world is my abiding memory of childhood. My early childhood was virtually pure leisure, and chores were imposed on me only later in life, gradually. I often didn't want to do them beforehand, and made this very clear, but I also often enjoyed doing them once I started, and better enjoyed my meals and beverages and slept better afterward. There were more chores in winter than summer, and less daylight to do other things anyway. Still, I was never excessively tasked and spent more time playing than working, even in winter.

In view of all these advantages of assigning chores to children, all borne out in my own experience, I think the most significant is the lesson of self-accountability to be gleaned from these tasks. Children learn first-hand how much work goes into maintaining their own comfort and well-being. They may decide that such experience is unpleasant and distasteful and spend much of their adult lives seeking "better service," or expecting to be cleaned up after. But it is my opinion that they are far less likely to do so with the added experience of having been required, at some stage of their development, to take part in the daily work and maintenance of their own household.

Works Cited

Bellah, Robert N. "Civil Religion in America." *Daedalus* 134 (Fall 2005): 40–55. Print.

Graves, Robert. *Goodbye to All That*. New York: Doubleday, 1957. Print.

O'Hagan, Andrew. "Bad Bastardness." *Leopard 3, Frontiers*. Ed. Christopher MacLehose. London: Harvill, 1994. 38–44. Print.

Rousseau, Jean-Jacques. "On the Origin of Inequality." *Rousseau/Kant (13/14)*. Trans. G.D.H. Cole (1913). Chicago: Great Books Foundation, 1955. 22–109. Print.

Smiley, Jane. "The Case Against Chores." *Critical Thinking, Thoughtful Writing*. By John Chaffee. 4th ed. Boston: Houghton, 2008. 71–73. Print.

Tolstoy, L. N. *Childhood, Boyhood, Youth*. Baltimore: Penguin, 1972. Print.

Alternative Writing Projects

- An Author's Change in Belief

  Explain how one of the authors of the readings in Chapter 3 changed or strengthened one or more beliefs. Be sure to present in your own words the author's original belief, what circumstances changed or strengthened it, and what it was after these circumstances. Give the title and author's name, probably at the beginning of your essay, and put quotation marks around any of the author's words that you use.

- A Friend's or Relative's Belief

  Interview a friend or relative about one of that person's most important beliefs. Prepare your questions ahead of time and write down the answers carefully. Look ahead to later chapters for some guidelines to conducting an interview. Use what your friend or relative tells you as the basis for an essay about this belief, how it developed, and what it means in the life of the person who holds it.

- A Belief That You Have Observed

  Look around your community. Can you see evidence of some belief in action? For example, is there evidence that people believe in keeping up (or showing off) their homes or gardens or cars? Is there evidence of a belief in helping one's neighbors or in keeping to oneself? Is there evidence of belief in the importance of education, political action, sports? nice clothes? Use your observation as the basis for an explanation of the belief that you have noticed and your thinking about its significance.

CHAPTER 3 Summary

- Thinking actively as part of your writing process requires that you become involved, take initiative, follow through, and take responsibility.

- Part of thinking actively involves becoming aware of the influences on your thinking.

- By continually reexamining your long-held beliefs, holding them up to the scrutiny of reason and evidence, and comparing them to the different perspectives of others, you can ensure that your beliefs are your own and not just those passed down from other people.

- Developing informed beliefs involves being curious, open-minded, knowledgeable, and creative and is a lifelong process.

Courtesy of the National Institute of Health

Geneticist Barbara McClintock, whose work on genetics won a Nobel Prize in 1983, began her inquiry with a simple observation: what determined the colors of kernels of Indian corn? Astrophysicist Alan Lightman describes McClintock's love of puzzle solving as being key to the most creative work done by scientists, which underscores an important point—creativity is not a talent possessed only by the likes of poets, painters, and musicians. Rather, creativity is a natural human ability that should be a central part of everyone's life. What role does creativity play in the writing process?

Thinking: Becoming More Creative and Visually Aware

"You must expect the unexpected, because it cannot be found by search or trail."

—HERACLITUS

Creative Thinking, Critical Viewing, and Writing

Creative writing is often thought of as imaginative fiction, poetry, or drama, for which the author invents characters and situations. Creativity also plays an important role in *expository writing*, in which facts, ideas, and concepts are explored, developed, and argued.

You use creative thinking in selecting and narrowing your topic (if you are allowed to pick your own topic), in the way you generate and research ideas, in the way you organize ideas, and in the way you focus on your ideas with your thesis. You also use creative thinking to develop ideas with carefully chosen details and examples. Creative thinking helps you to develop analogies and metaphors to help your readers grasp your ideas. Finally, creative thinking allows you to write imaginative, inviting introductions that will make your readers eager to read further, and to write carefully crafted conclusions that tie in elegantly with your introductions. Of course, your critical thinking abilities are also involved in all these steps, helping you to decide which of your creative ideas to include and which to discard.

The challenge to be creative in your writing is a difficult one, but the possibilities for creativity are vast. Focusing on the following four areas for creativity in expository writing will help you further develop the creative thinking abilities you may already have. This chapter deals with the first two.

- Creativity in topic selection
- Creativity in generating ideas, researching, and drafting
- Creativity in using specific details and examples
- Creativity in writing introductions and conclusions

Critical Thinking Focus: The qualities of a creative thinker

Writing Focus: Generating original ideas

Reading Theme: The creative thinking process

Writing Project: Imagining your life lived more creatively

Creativity in Topic Selection

The topic of an essay is the subject you write about, one of the four components of the writing situation. Some topics are personal and ask you to draw on your own life experiences, others are impersonal and clearly require research, and still others are a blend of the personal and impersonal. Furthermore, some topics are fairly specific, such as, "Write about your favorite sports figure," or "Write about the effects of the war in Iraq." Others are more general: "Write about some aspect of political science." A first step is to think creatively about how to shape an assigned topic into one that interests you and that you can handle in the assigned length. A visual way to do this is to "narrow with arrows."

> My favorite sports figure → my favorite football player → my favorite quarterback → Eli Manning
>
> Effects of the war in Iraq → different types of effects → social effects → effects on national security → effects on airports and passengers
>
> Political science → elections → the 2008 presidential election → Obama's victory → why he won

Notice that at any point, the arrows could take you in a different direction.

> My favorite sports figure → my favorite baseball player → my favorite shortstop → Derek Jeter
>
> Effects of the war in Iraq → different types of effects → financial effects → effects on the price of oil → long-term effects on energy consumption
>
> Political science → elections → the 2008 presidential election → new campaign strategies → candidates' use of social media to advertise and communicate

Moving from Topic to Thesis

A topic is what you are going to write about, and a thesis is what you are going to say about it. Once you have narrowed your topic, try stating it as a question.

> Why is Eli Manning my favorite sports figure?
>
> What are the effects of the war in Iraq on energy consumption in the United States?
>
> How did Obama manage to win the presidential election?

If the answer to your question will require research, read as much as you can about the general topic area, looking for ways to modify your tentative topic question or even to change your question altogether. If you are working with a personal topic, begin making notes whether or not you have enough information to answer your question. You can broaden or narrow your topic question as you proceed.

> When you think that you have enough information, try answering your question in a complete sentence.

> Eli Manning's amazing athletic ability, great leadership skills, and generous contributions to our community make him my favorite sports figure.

> The war in Iraq has a rippling effect on America's economy: the rising price of oil contributes to inflation.

> Barrack Obama won the 2008 presidential election because he ran a strategic and modern campaign, he got the endorsement of well-respected leaders, and his intelligent and empassioned speeches inspired and motivated large segments of the population.

Treat the answer to your question as a tentative thesis, but expect to modify or even discard your original question. Becoming aware of the need to make these changes is something that most writers experience, so don't become discouraged when it occurs. Instead, congratulate yourself for being willing to put in the time and effort needed for the creative process as you shape your topic.

Creativity in Generating Ideas

Books about writing sometimes speak as though generating ideas, researching, and drafting are three entirely separate stages, and the writer finishes one stage before beginning the next. This may even be true in some cases, but often writers find themselves getting new ideas while researching or beginning to draft only to realize the need for more research or brainstorming.

Here are some strategies your open and curious mind can use to develop creative ideas in your writing. Your journal, blog, or notebook is a good place to practice these strategies.

Brainstorming   *Brainstorming* is an activity in which, working individually or with a group of people, you list all the ideas you can think of related to a given topic. The goal is to produce as many ideas as possible in a specific time period. While you are engaged in this idea-generating process, it is important to relax and let your mind run free.

These guidelines should help you:

- Set a timer and keep thinking until it goes off.
- Go for quantity. You want to generate as many ideas as you can.

- Write down *all* the ideas you generate.
- Build on ideas.
- Don't criticize or discard any ideas.

Imagine, for example, that you are assigned the following topic for a research paper:

There are many problems that students face on college campuses. Identify one such problem and then write a research paper that analyzes the causes of and possible solutions to the problem. Why does the problem occur, and what can be done to deal with it? Your paper should include relevant research findings as well as your own perspective on this problem.

Using the brainstorming strategy with a friend, you might come up with a list that includes the following student problems on your campus:

parking	classes too large
library closed too early	not enough access to computers
political tensions	plagiarism
binge drinking	use of drugs
registration too complicated	tests and papers coming in clumps
not enough social activities	some teachers just lecturing
increasing thefts	curriculum not well organized
financial aid cutbacks	

Mind Maps   *Mind maps* are visual presentations of the various ways ideas can be related to one another. For example, the Thinking-Writing Model is represented as a mind map in Figure 4.1. Mind maps are also a powerful approach for writing, helping you to generate ideas and to begin organizing them into various relationships. They are well suited to the writing process for a number of reasons. *First,* the organization grows naturally, reflecting the way your mind naturally makes associations and arranges information. *Second,* the organization can easily be revised to reflect new information and your developing understanding of how it should be organized. *Third,* you can express a range of relationships among the various ideas. *Fourth,* instead of being identified once and then forgotten, each idea remains an active part of the overall pattern, suggesting new possible relationships. *Fifth,* you do not have to decide initially on a beginning, subpoints, and so on; you can do this after your pattern is complete, so you save time and avoid frustration. For example, imagine that from your list of problems on campus you select "abuse of alcohol" as a paper topic. Your mind map might resemble Figure 4.1.

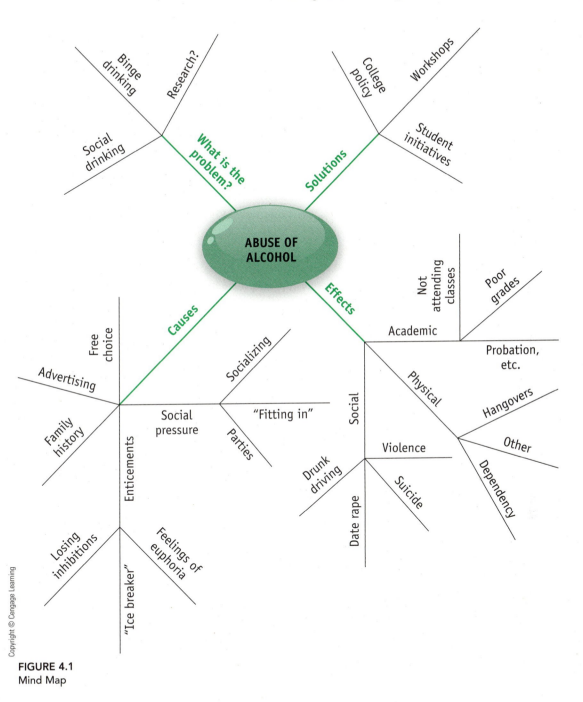

FIGURE 4.1
Mind Map

Thinking-Writing Activity

CREATE A MIND MAP

For this activity, you will experiment with a mind map. Your instructor will direct your choice of topic.

These guidelines should help you:

- Draw a circle in the middle of the page, and write your topic in the circle.
- Draw a few lines coming out from the circle, and label them with ideas about your topic.
- See which of your lines you could develop further. Then draw more lines from those, and label them with ideas and details about those aspects of your topic.
- Keep going until you have no more ideas about the topic, or until you see a section of your map developing into a cluster of ideas that you could write about.

Freewriting *Freewriting* is a sort of written brainstorming in which you write with a minimum of conscious reflection. But rather than simply list ideas, freewriters usually write in sentences. The goal is to let your ideas flow freely, without inhibition, giving your mind the opportunity to develop creative ideas in unique combinations.

These guidelines should help you:

- Set a timer and keep writing until it goes off.
- Write at a steady, comfortable pace for the entire time. If you get stuck, it is OK to write, "I am stuck. I can't think of any more ideas. I hope I get another idea," until a new idea comes to you. *Don't stop writing!*
- Don't criticize or make corrections.
- After the time limit is up, read carefully what you have written. Think about it for a few minutes. Then try the process again, starting with the most interesting ideas from your first try.

An example of freewriting about the problem of alcohol abuse might begin something like this:

Alcohol is a real problem on campus. Every party, that's all people do, is drink too much and then get silly. I think it's ok for people to drink some if they want to. They say it relaxes them and makes it easier to talk to strangers. But it's out of control, and that's a problem. There are a lot of students that drink all the time. They must be failing their classes, they sleep until noon, and they look lousy. There's got to be a better way to socialize and have fun with people besides getting bombed out of your mind....

Questioning   *Asking questions* that explore a topic provides another strategy for generating ideas, just as asking questions about a topic supports critical reading. In fact, the ability to ask appropriate and penetrating questions about visual and written texts is one of the most powerful thinking and communicating tools writers possess. Asking questions enables them to go beyond the obvious, to think, read, see, and write in ways that are in-depth, complex, and articulate. Questions come in many different forms and are used for many different purposes. For instance, questions can be classified in terms of the ways people organize and interpret information. The following are six such categories of questions:

1. Fact   4. Synthesis

2. Interpretation   5. Evaluation

3. Analysis   6. Application

Thoughtful writers ask appropriate questions from all of these categories. Listed next is a description of the six categories of questions, along with sample questions from each category.

1. **Questions of Fact.** Questions of fact seek to determine the basic information of a situation: who, what, when, where, how, why. These following seek information that is relatively straightforward and objective:

   Who, what, when, where, how, why?

   Describe _____.

2. **Questions of Interpretation.** Questions of interpretation seek to select and organize facts and ideas, discovering the relationships among them. Examples of such relationships include the following:

   Chronological relationships—relating things in time sequence

   Process relationships—relating aspects of growth, development, or change

   Comparison/contrast relationships—relating things in terms of their similar or different features

   Causal relationships—relating events in terms of the way some are responsible for causing others

   These questions can help you discover relationships:

   Can you retell _____ in your own words?

   What is the *main idea* of _____?

   What is the *time sequence* relating the following events: _____?

   What are the steps in the *process of growth* or *development* in _____?

How would you *compare* and *contrast* the features of _____ and _____?

What was/were the *cause(s)* of _____? What was/were the *effect(s)* of _____?

3. **Questions of Analysis.** Questions of analysis seek to separate an entire process or situation into its component parts and understand the relation of these parts to the whole. These questions or statements attempt to classify various elements, outline component structures, articulate various possibilities, and clarify the reasoning being presented:

What are the *parts* or *features* of _____?

Classify according to _____.

Outline/diagram/web _____.

What *evidence* can you present to support _____?

What are the *possible alternatives* for _____?

Explain the *reasons* you think _____.

4. **Questions of Synthesis.** The goal of questions of synthesis is to combine ideas to form a new whole or to arrive at a conclusion, making inferences about future events, creating solutions, and designing plans of action:

What would you *predict/infer* from _____?

What ideas can you *add to* _____?

How would you *create/design* a new _____?

What might happen if you *combined* _____ with _____?

What *solutions/decisions* would you suggest for _____?

5. **Questions of Evaluation.** The aim of evaluation questions is to help you make informed judgments and decisions by determining the relative value, truth, or reliability of things. The process of evaluation involves identifying your criteria or standards and then determining to what extent the things being evaluated meet those standards.

How would you evaluate _____ and what *standards* would you use?

Do you *agree* with _____? *Why or why not?*

How would you *decide* about _____?

What *criteria* would you use to *assess* _____?

6. **Questions of Application.** The purpose of application questions is to help you take the knowledge or concepts you have gained in one situation and apply them to other situations.

How is _____ *an example* of _____?

How would you *apply* this rule/principle to _____?

Additional Tips for Generating Ideas

- When brainstorming, write down every idea, no matter how unusable it may seem at the time.

- Phone your voice mail and leave yourself a message if an idea strikes you while you're away from home.

- Talk to other people about your topic. Knowledgeable people will add information; those unfamiliar with the topic will ask useful questions.

- Ask a librarian for research suggestions.

- Note conflicting information or opinions. They are the heart of academic discussion.

- Search at Yahoo! or Google for businesses or organizations that can provide information.

- Identify and interview experts on your topic. (Be sure to acknowledge them as sources.)

- Scan television schedules for related programs.

- Search online for sources of information.

- When drafting, don't necessarily begin with the introduction. Instead, begin with whatever section is easiest to write.

- Be willing to modify your thesis as you go along so that you don't lock yourself into a position too early.

- Avoid premature organization; draft sections on separate pages or as separate computer files. Then try arranging them in various orders.

- If you are interrupted while drafting, read what you have already written to get back into the flow.

Creative and Critical Thinking About Images

Many professional writers in a variety of contexts integrate images with their texts. From college and military recruitment brochures to advertisements to a company's annual reports, images work in both a subtle and an overt way to persuade us to do, believe, or buy something. As a creative thinker and thoughtful writer, you should begin to pay attention to the relationships between images and text in what you read. You should also think about the ways in which images can inspire, support, and reflect your own written work. (See Thinking Critically About Images on pages 1–1 to 1–8)

Images and the Writing Situation

Just as writers consider audience, subject, and purpose as they think through their writing and conduct their research, so too do creators of images (painters, cartoonists, graphic artists, photographers, and others). Whether they are recording events as they happen or reflecting imaginatively on their personal experiences, visual artists in all media are fundamentally aware that they are *communicating*—that, even without words, their images will tell a story, make an argument, show a process, or provide information.

Images and Your Audience   In your college career, you will often be asked to present information in a visual manner. Classes in the sciences and social sciences require you to present numerical data in the form of charts, graphs, and maps. In the visual arts and humanities, you may be asked to analyze a painting's message and style or to describe a film director's approach to setting a scene. Be sure to ask your instructors for each of your classes how to locate, correctly cite, and usefully include images in your own essays and research papers.

Images and Your Subject   Creative thinking teaches us that there are many different ways of experiencing and communicating information. When you use any of the idea-generation strategies discussed earlier in this chapter, try to incorporate visual as well as verbal descriptions and information. You could collect images from magazines, books, and online sources, printing them out or scanning them electronically to create a kind of visual "mind map." Or you could look online at sites such as the National Archives, *Flickr.com*, and Google Images, all of which allow you to search for images using key words related to your subject.

ONLINE RESOURCES
Finding Images Online
Visit your text website, accessed through **CengageBrain.com**, for more information on finding images online.

Images and Your Purpose   When you have gathered images that relate to your topic, you can use questions of fact, interpretation, analysis, synthesis, evaluation, and application (pages 99–100) to help you sort through the visuals and select those that best support your purpose in writing. For example, a witty or satirical editorial cartoon about federal response to Hurricane Katrina might be appropriate for an argument essay in which you analyze the political impact of that disaster, but for a paper about the storm's long-term environmental effects, you would be better served by a map showing the loss of land or a satellite photograph showing the extent of flood damage.

Reading Images Critically

As you search for images to use in your essays, reports, and arguments, remember that the content of an image—just like the content of a text—is composed of elements that work together to convey a message. Some of these elements are similar to those you consider when evaluating a piece of writing: setting, point of view, relationships between characters, an objective or subjective perspective. Other elements are specifically visual: the use of color, the manipulations of Photoshop or other image-moderating techniques, cropping (cutting), and the arrangement of images on a page or screen. And, of course, images are frequently accompanied by text that describes and contextualizes what you are seeing; this text, called a *caption,* should also be a part of your critical interpretation of visual evidence.

In Chapter 2, we explored four different types of meaning: semantic, perceptual, syntactic, and pragmatic. Each of these four kinds of meaning can also apply to your critical "reading"—or viewing—of visual content. Let's see how each type of meaning can be used to understand how just one compelling image can convey many different layers of meaning.

Semantic Meaning (Denotation)

As we learned in Chapter 2, the denotative or *semantic meaning* of a word expresses the relationship between the word itself and an idea or feeling. When you think about the relationship between images and ideas, beginning with the denotative (or literal) meaning can help you to understand its larger purpose and argument. Photographers and artists refer to the *composition* of an image—the arrangement of elements within the frame—and that is one way to think of a picture's denotative meaning. The photograph in the *Thinking Critically About Visuals* box, for example, shows an urban scene with a boy holding a bird. The caption supplied with the photograph, however, gives us a richer level of context. You already know that a denotative or semantic reading of a word is enriched by understanding both its general properties and specific examples. Were you asked to imagine, or draw, a picture of a boy holding a bird, your image might be very different—and probably much more bucolic. The caption, however, adds a level of specificity to the picture's semantic message. The picture might *literally* be about a boy with a bird, but its *connotative* message is far more powerful—and far less lovely.

Perceptual Meaning (Connotation)

Just as words can elicit personal and subjective feelings, so do images. You would respond quite differently to the picture if the boy, Feliciano, were smiling. Here, too, the relationship between an image and its caption is important to analyze. Remember that the images you see in the media are captured by one kind of journalist (a photographer, a cameraman) but later interpreted by reporters and editors in the newsroom. The interpretation that a journalist gives to a visual image can profoundly affect the way an audience interprets that image. Visually, the composition of *Thinking Critically About Visuals* photograph conveys a definite connotative or *perceptual meaning*: the boy is sad; the background is littered and abandoned; the overall sense is of urban blight. The words in the caption accompanying the photograph reinforce this meaning: *vacant lots, slumlords, dump, addicts.*

Learning to critically examine the relationships between the words and the images in a news report can help you dig deeper into an issue's impacts—and can also help you detect bias. This relationship between images and their larger contexts can be described as syntactic meaning.

Syntactic Meaning

A word's *syntactic meaning* (see page 53 in Chapter 2) depends on its relationships with other words—relationships of content, description, and connection. The content of a photograph or image is similar to its semantic meaning—What's this all about? But once you begin to connect that content to the way it is verbally described (by a caption, in this case) as well as visually composed (what is most important or dominant in the

Thinking Critically About Visuals

© Brenda Ann Kenneally/Corbis

Analyzing and Interpreting Visuals

August 6, 2001. Feliciano holds up a bird that mistakenly got into some oil paint that was dumped in one of the vacant lots in the neighborhood along Broadway in Brooklyn. Local slumlords pay addicts a few dollars to dump construction debris, and much of it ends up in the nearest lot. The bird died despite Feliciano's efforts to save it.

The caption above notes that the bird died "despite Feliciano's attempts to save it." What does that statement suggest about the relationship between the photographer and his subject? Why are the boy and the bird so close to the front of the image (and, therefore, close to *you* as a reader) instead of the slick of dumped paint?

ONLINE RESOURCES
Brenda Ann Kenneally
Visit your text website, accessed through **CengageBrain.com**, for additional information on photographer Brenda Ann Kenneally.

frame; what is the emotional impact of the image; what is the relationship between the photographer and the subject?), you begin to unravel the image's syntactic meaning. A third level of syntactic meaning has to do with the connection of these ideas and their ability to make sense—to convey a larger, more meaningful idea. The *Thinking Critically About Visuals* photograph and its caption work together to make a profound argument about urban pollution and its littlest victims. That that image and caption work so well together to make such a clear, direct argument contributes to our understanding of the fourth type of meaning: pragmatic, or situational.

Pragmatic Meaning

This final type of meaning has to do with the context or situation of the image—who created it, who or what is in it, and the ultimate purpose of and audience for the image. You'll find that many journalists and media outlets will attempt to give context and meaning to a large-scale catastrophe by focusing on the specific lives it impacts—as you'll see in several of the photos in the color section of this chapter. The photographer who took the picture on page 104, Brenda Ann Kenneally, is renowned for her work documenting troubled urban families; you can find many portfolios of her work online.

Thinking-Writing Activity

RECALLING A CREATIVE WRITING EXPERIENCE

1. Write about a time when you expressed yourself creatively in writing. It may have been in an important email, a memorable poem, or a paper for a school course. Respond to the following questions as you recall the writing experience.

   - What was the writing situation that required your creativity?
   - How did you go about finding a creative idea or approach?
   - Was it successful?
   - How do you feel as you recall this experience?

2. Share your experience with the class and listen carefully to the experiences of other students. On the basis of your own writing experience and those of your peers, make some inferences or general statements about creativity.

Living Creatively

We human beings have a nearly limitless capacity to be creative; our imaginations give us the power to conceive of new possibilities and to put these innovative ideas into action. Using creative resources in this way enriches our lives and brings a special meaning to our activities. Although we might not go to the extreme of saying that the uncreative life is not worth living, it is surely preferable to live a life enriched by the joys of creativity.

Many people think that being creative is beyond them, that creativity is a mysterious gift bestowed on only a chosen few. One reason for this misconception is that people often confuse being "creative" with being "artistic"—skilled at art music, poetry, imaginative writing, drama, or dance. Although artistic people are certainly creative, there are an infinite number of ways to be creative that are *not* artistic. Being creative is a state of mind and a way of life. As the writer Eric Gill expresses it: "The artist is not a different kind of person, but each one of us is a different kind of artist."

Are you creative? Yes! Think of all the activities that you enjoy: cooking, styling a wardrobe, raising children, playing sports, rapping, dancing, repairing an engine, blogging, designing a web page. Whenever you are investing your own personal ideas, applying your own personal stamp, you are being creative. To the extent that you are expressing your unique ideas developed through inspiration and experimentation, you are being creative. Similarly, if your moves on the dance floor or the basketball court express your distinctive personality, you are being creative, as you are when you stimulate the original thinking of your children or make your friends laugh with your own brand of humor. Living life creatively means bringing your perspective and creative talents to all the areas of your life.

Becoming More Creative: Understand and Trust the Process

Although the forces that discourage you from being creative are powerful, they can nevertheless be overcome with four productive strategies:

- Understand and trust the creative process.
- Eliminate the "Voice of Judgment."
- Make creativity a priority.
- Establish a creative environment.

Thinking-Writing Activity

REFLECTING ON PAST INHIBITIONS TO CREATIVITY

Reflect on your own creative development and describe some of the fears and pressures that inhibit your own creativity. For example, have you ever been penalized for trying a new idea that didn't work out? Have you ever suffered the wrath of the group for daring to be different and violating the group's unspoken rules? Do you feel that your life is so filled with responsibilities and demands that you don't have time to be creative?

Discovering your creative talents requires that you understand how the creative process operates and then have confidence in the results it produces. There are no fixed procedures or formulas for generating creative ideas because creative ideas by definition go beyond established ways of thinking to the unknown and the innovative. As the ancient Greek philosopher Heraclitus once said, "You must expect the unexpected, because it cannot be found by search or trail."

Although there is no fixed path to creative ideas, there are activities you can pursue that make the birth of creative ideas possible. In this respect, generating creative ideas is similar to gardening. You need to prepare the soil; plant the seeds; ensure proper watering, light, and food; and then be patient until the ideas begin to sprout. Following are some steps for cultivating your creative garden.

Absorb yourself in the task: Creative ideas don't occur in a vacuum. They emerge after a great deal of work, study, and practice. For example, if you want to come up with creative ideas in the kitchen, you need to learn more about the art of cooking. The more knowledgeable you are, the better prepared you will be to create innovative dishes. Similarly, if you are developing a creative perspective for a college research paper, you need to immerse yourself in the subject, becoming knowledgeable about the central concepts and issues. Absorbing yourself in the task "prepares the soil" for your creative ideas.

Allow time for ideas to incubate: After absorbing yourself in the task or problem, the next stage is to stop working on it. When your conscious mind stops actively working on the task, the unconscious dimension of your mind continues working—processing, organizing, and ultimately generating innovative ideas and solutions. This process is known as *incubation* because it mirrors the process in which baby chicks gradually evolve inside the egg until the moment when they break out through the shell. In the same way, your creative mind is at work while you are going about your business until the moment of *illumination,* when the incubating idea finally erupts to the surface of your conscious mind. People report that these illuminating moments—when their mental lightbulbs go on—often occur when they are engaged in activities completely unrelated to the task. For example, you may suddenly realize how to organize your research paper while you are working out at the gym.

Seize on the ideas when they emerge and follow them through: Generating creative ideas is of little use unless you recognize them when they appear and then act on them. Too often people don't pay much attention to these ideas when they occur, or they dismiss them as too impractical. Have confidence in your ideas, even if they seem a little strange. Many of the most valuable inventions in history began as improbable ideas ridiculed by the popular wisdom. For example, the idea of Velcro started with burrs covering the pants of the inventor as he walked through a field, and Post-It notes resulted from the accidental invention of an adhesive that was weaker than normal. In other words, thinking effectively means thinking creatively and thinking critically. After you use your *creative thinking* abilities to generate innovative ideas, you must employ your *critical thinking* abilities to evaluate and refine those ideas and design a practical plan for implementing them. For example,

@ THINKING CRITICALLY ABOUT NEW MEDIA

Creative Applications

The world is changing at warp speed, and many of these changes have to do with what is popularly termed the "new media," forms of information and communication technologies that were made possible by the creation of the Internet, wireless phones, and text communication devices. Virtually every aspect of our lives has been affected by the development and use of these technologies, including the way we think and write, communicate with one another, research and gather information, develop and sustain relationships, create our sense of self-identity, and construct "virtual" realities that have complex connections to the space-and-time world in which we go about the business of living. For example, it used to be that communicating with someone else involved speaking in person, writing a letter, or talking on a landline telephone. We can now speak by cell phone directly to most anyone on the planet from wherever we are whenever we want. What's more, we can use the technologies of email, instant messaging, text messaging, or twittering to stay socially connected to a large number of people on a continual basis. And through the development of social networking sites like Facebook, YouTube, and LinkedIn, people have been able to create "virtual communities." These virtual communities transcend geographical boundaries, and as the new media critic and writer Howard Rheingold explains, these globalised societies are self-defined networks, which resemble what we do in real life. "People in virtual communities use words on screens to exchange pleasantries and argue, engage in intellectual discourse, conduct commerce, make plans, brainstorm, gossip, feud, fall in love, create a little high art and a lot of idle talk."

However, accompanying this new universe of possibilities provided by new media are many risks and challenges that, more than ever, make it necessary to develop and apply our critical thinking abilities as we navigate our way through this digital universe. To this end, I have included a number of readings in this edition that address various aspects of new media, and, in addition, each chapter contains a section on "Thinking Critically About New Media." It's essential that we have the strategies and insight to make sure that these powerful new vehicles of communication are used to enhance our lives, not complicate and damage them.

One of the themes of this chapter has been creative thinking, and new media has offered an unprecedented opportunity to roam far and wide in our search for information that will enrich our creative endeavors. But new media also affords us the chance to gather many different perspectives on our projects, with others' ideas serving as catalysts to our creative imaginations. For example, the columnist David Pogue suggests that companies should use what he calls "crowdsourcing" to generate new ideas. To try this out, he asked his Twitter followers for their best tech-product enhancement ideas. He reports that "They responded wittily, passionately—and immediately (this is Twitter, after all)." Ideas that were tweeted back included:

- Cell phone batteries that recharge through kinetic motion as you walk around
- Technology that lets you use your hand as a TV remote control (the TV recognizes your gestures)
- A camera warning that responds to voice commands and also tells you if your thumb is in the way of the lens
- Laptop computers with built-in solar panels for charging batteries
- Music players that can be shifted to "Karaoke mode"

ONLINE RESOURCES
Finding Images Online
Visit your text website, accessed through **CengageBrain.com**, to find a link to the column with its complete list of creative ideas.

Thinking-Writing Activity

CREATIVE "CROWDSOURCING"

Following up on David Pogue's ingenious use of "crowdsourcing" to generate creative ideas, try some crowdsourcing of your own to generate innovative ideas to improve the quality of your life. Send several queries out to your network of friends asking them for their creative ideas, and then compile these into a master list that you share with everyone (be sure to give credit!). Here are some possible topics:

- Ideas for organizing the many activities in your life more efficiently
- Ideas for making studying more entertaining *and* effective
- Ideas for having a party with a totally unique theme

you should write down your creative idea about organizing your research paper and then begin drafting to see if it will work.

Eliminate the Voice of Judgment

The biggest threat to your creativity lies within yourself, the negative *Voice of Judgment (VOJ)*. This term was coined by Michael Ray and Rochelle Myers, the authors of *Creativity in Business,* a book based on a Stanford University course. The VOJ can undermine your confidence in every area of your life, including your creative activities. For example, when you are drafting a paper, the VOJ may whisper:

"This is a stupid idea, and no one will like it."

"Even if I could pull this idea off, it probably won't amount to much."

These statements, and countless others like them, have the ongoing effect of making you doubt yourself and the quality of your creative thinking. As you lose confidence, you become more timid, reluctant to follow through on ideas and present them to others. After a while your cumulative insecurity will discourage you from even generating ideas in the first place, and you will end up simply conforming to established ways of thinking and the expectations of others. In so doing, you surrender an important part of yourself, the vital and dynamic creative core of your personality.

How do you eliminate this unwelcome and destructive inner voice? There are a number of effective strategies. Remember, though, that the fight, although worth the effort, will not be easy.

Become aware of the VOJ: You have probably been listening to the negative messages of the VOJ for so long that you may not even consciously be aware of it. To conquer the VOJ, you first need to recognize it when it speaks.

Restate the judgment in a more accurate or constructive way: Sometimes there is an element of truth in our self-judgments, but we may have blown the reality out of proportion. For example, if you receive a low grade on a writing assignment, your VOJ may say, "You're a failure." But you need to assess the situation accurately: "I got a low grade on this paper—I wonder what went wrong and how I can improve my performance in the future."

Get tough with the VOJ: You can't be a wimp if you hope to overcome the VOJ. Instead, you have to be strong and determined, responding as soon as the VOJ appears: "I'm throwing you out and not letting you back in!" You may feel peculiar at first, but this will soon become an automatic response when those negative judgments appear.

Create positive voices and visualizations: The best way to destroy the VOJ for good is to replace it with positive encouragement. As soon as you have stomped on, say, the judgment "You're a jerk," replace it with "No, I'm an intelligent, valuable person with many positive qualities and talents." Similarly, make extensive use of positive visualization—"see" yourself performing well on assignments, being entertaining and insightful with other people, and succeeding gloriously in your courses and activities.

Use other people for independent confirmation: The negative judgments coming from the VOJ are usually irrational, but until they are dragged out into the light of day for examination, they can be very powerful. Sharing your VOJ with people you trust is an effective strategy because they can provide an objective perspective that will reveal the irrationality and destructiveness of negative judgments.

Establish a Creative Environment

An important part of eliminating the negative voice in your mind is to establish environments in which your creative resources can flourish. This means finding or developing physical environments conducive to creative expression as well as supportive social environments. Sometimes, working with other people can be stimulating and energizing to your creative juices; at other times, you may need a private place to work without distraction. You have to find the environment(s) best suited to your own creative process; then make a special effort to do your work there.

The people in your life who form your social environment play an even more influential role in encouraging or inhibiting your creative process. When you are surrounded by people who are positive and supportive, their presence will increase your confidence and encourage you to risk expressing your creative vision. They can stimulate your creativity by providing you with fresh ideas and new perspectives. By engaging in brainstorming, they can help you generate ideas and then later can help you figure out how to refine and implement the most valuable ones.

Make Creativity a Priority

Having diminished the negative Voice of Judgment in your mind, established a creative environment, and committed yourself to trusting your creative gifts, you are now in a position to live and write more creatively. But how do you actually do this? Start small. Identify some habitual patterns in your life and break out of them. Choose new experiences whenever possible—for example, order unfamiliar items from a menu, get to know people outside your circle of friends, or deliberately choose a new type of introduction for a paper—and strive to develop fresh perspectives on aspects of your life. Resist falling back into the ruts you were in previously; remember that living things are supposed to be continually growing, changing, and evolving, *not* acting in repetitive patterns like machines.

Where Do Ideas Come From?

Creativity is the process we use to discover and develop ideas that are unusual and worthy of further elaboration. But how do we get creative ideas? Where do they come from? The following readings from the worlds of science and business may give us some clues.

"Revenge of the Right Brain"

by Daniel H. Pink

When I was a kid growing up in a middle-class family, in the middle of America, in the middle of the 1970s, parents dished out a familiar plate of advice to their children: Get good grades, go to college, and pursue a profession that offers a decent standard of living and perhaps a dollop of prestige. If you were good at math and science, become a doctor. If you were better at English and history, become a lawyer. If blood grossed you out and your verbal skills needed work, become an accountant. Later, as computers appeared on desktops and CEOs on magazine covers, the youngsters who were *really* good at math and science chose high tech, while others flocked to business school, thinking that success was spelled MBA.

Tax attorneys. Radiologists. Financial analysts. Software engineers. Management guru Peter Drucker gave this cadre of professionals an enduring, if somewhat wonky, name: knowledge workers. These are, he wrote, "people who get paid for putting to work what one learns in school rather than for their physical strength or manual skill." What distinguished members of this group and enabled them to reap society's greatest rewards, was their "ability to acquire and to apply theoretical and analytic knowledge." And any of us could join their ranks. All we had to do was study hard and play by the rules of the meritocratic regime. That was the path to professional success and personal fulfillment.

But a funny thing happened while we were pressing our noses to the grindstone: The world changed. The future no longer belongs to people who can reason with computer-like logic, speed, and precision. It belongs to a different kind of person with a different kind of mind. Today—amid the uncertainties of an economy that has gone from boom to bust to blah—there's a metaphor that explains what's going on. And it's right inside our heads.

Scientists have long known that a neurological Mason-Dixon line cleaves our brains into two regions—the left and right hemispheres. But in the last 10 years, thanks in part to advances in functional magnetic resonance imaging, researchers have begun to identify more precisely how the two sides divide responsibilities. The left hemisphere handles sequence, literalness, and analysis. The right hemisphere, meanwhile, takes care of context, emotional expression, and synthesis. Of course, the human brain, with its 100 billion cells forging 1 quadrillion connections, is breathtakingly complex. The two hemispheres work in concert, and we enlist both sides for nearly everything we do. But the structure of our brains can help explain the contours of our times.

5   Until recently, the abilities that led to success in school, work, and business were characteristic of the left hemisphere. They were the sorts of linear, logical, analytical talents measured by SATs and deployed by CPAs. Today, those capabilities are still necessary. But they're no longer sufficient. In a world upended by outsourcing, deluged with data, and choked with choices, the abilities that matter most are now closer in spirit to the specialties of the right hemisphere—artistry, empathy, seeing the big picture, and pursuing the transcendent.

Source: From "Revenge of the Right Brain" by Daniel H. Pink, in WIRED magazine, Issue 13.02, February 2005. Adapted from *A Whole New Mind: Moving from the Information Age to the Conceptual Age*, copyright © Daniel H. Pink, to be published in March by Riverhead Books. Printed by permission of the publisher.

Beneath the nervous clatter of our half-completed decade stirs a slow but seismic shift. The Information Age we all prepared for is ending. Rising in its place is what I call the Conceptual Age, an era in which mastery of abilities that we've often overlooked and undervalued marks the fault line between who gets ahead and who falls behind.

To some of you, this shift—from an economy built on the logical, sequential abilities of the Information Age to an economy built on the inventive, empathic abilities of the Conceptual Age—sounds delightful. "You had me at hello!" I can hear the painters and nurses exulting. But to others, this sounds like a crock. "Prove it!" I hear the programmers and lawyers demanding.

OK. To convince you, I'll explain the reasons for this shift, using the mechanistic language of cause and effect.

The effect: the scales tilting in favor of right brain-style thinking. The causes: Asia, automation, and abundance.

Asia

10   Few issues today spark more controversy than outsourcing. Those squadrons of white-collar workers in India, the Philippines, and China are scaring the bejesus out of software jockeys across North America and Europe. According to Forrester Research, 1 in 9 jobs in the US information technology industry will move overseas by 2010. And it's not just tech work. Visit India's office parks and you'll see chartered accountants preparing American tax returns, lawyers researching American lawsuits, and radiologists reading CAT scans for US hospitals.

The reality behind the alarm is this: Outsourcing to Asia is overhyped in the short term, but underhyped in the long term. We're not all going to lose our jobs tomorrow. (The total number of jobs lost to offshoring so far represents less than 1 percent of the US labor force.) But as the cost of communicating with the other side of the globe falls essentially to zero, as India becomes (by 2010) the country with the most English speakers in the world, and as developing nations continue to mint millions of extremely capable knowledge workers, the professional lives of people in the West will change dramatically. If number crunching, chart reading, and code writing can be done for a lot less overseas and delivered to clients instantly via fiber-optic cable, that's where the work will go.

But these gusts of comparative advantage are blowing away only certain kinds of white-collar jobs—those that can be reduced to a set of rules, routines, and instructions. That's why narrow left-brain work such as basic computer coding, accounting, legal research, and financial analysis is migrating across the oceans. But that's also why plenty of opportunities remain for people and companies doing less routine work—programmers who can design entire systems, accountants who serve as life planners, and bankers expert less in the intricacies of Excel than in the art of the deal. Now that foreigners can do left-brain work cheaper, we in the US must do right-brain work better.

Automation

Last century, machines proved they could replace human muscle. This century, technologies are proving they can outperform human left brains—they can execute sequential, reductive, computational work better, faster, and more accurately than even those with the highest IQs. (Just ask chess grandmaster Garry Kasparov.) Consider jobs in financial services. Stockbrokers who merely execute transactions are history. Online trading services and market makers do such work far more efficiently. The brokers who survived have morphed from routine order-takers to less easily replicated advisers, who can understand a client's broader financial objectives and even the client's emotions and dreams.

Or take lawyers. Dozens of inexpensive information and advice services are reshaping law practice. At CompleteCase.com, you can get an uncontested divorce for $249, less than a 10th of the cost of a divorce lawyer. Meanwhile, the Web is cracking the information monopoly that has long been the source of many lawyers' high incomes and professional mystique. Go to USlegalforms.com and you can download—for the price of two movie tickets—fill-in-the-blank wills, contracts, and articles of incorporation that used to reside exclusively on lawyers' hard drives. Instead of hiring a lawyer for 10 hours to craft a contract, consumers can fill out the form themselves and hire a lawyer for one hour to look it over. Consequently, legal abilities that can't be digitized—convincing a jury or understanding the subtleties of a negotiation—become more valuable.

15   Even computer programmers may feel the pinch. "In the old days," legendary computer scientist Vernor Vinge has said, "anybody with even routine skills could get a job as a programmer. That isn't true anymore. The routine functions are increasingly being turned over to machines." The result: As the scut work gets offloaded, engineers will have to master different aptitudes, relying more on creativity than competence. Any job that can be reduced to a set of rules is at risk. If a $500-a-month accountant in India doesn't swipe your accounting job, TurboTax will. Now that computers can emulate left-hemisphere skills, we'll have to rely ever more on our right hemispheres.

Abundance

Our left brains have made us rich. Powered by armies of Drucker's knowledge workers, the information economy has produced a standard of living that would have been unfathomable in our grandparents' youth. Their lives were defined by scarcity. Ours are shaped by abundance. Want evidence? Spend five minutes at Best Buy. Or look in your garage. Owning a car used to be a grand American aspiration. Today, there are more automobiles in the US than there are licensed drivers—which means that, on average, everybody who can drive has a car of their own. And if your garage is also piled with excess consumer goods, you're not alone. Self-storage—a business devoted to housing our extra crap—is now a $17 billion annual industry in the US, nearly double Hollywood's yearly box office take.

But abundance has produced an ironic result. The Information Age has unleashed a prosperity that in turn places a premium on less rational sensibilities—beauty, spirituality, emotion. For companies and entrepreneurs, it's no longer enough to create a product, a service, or an experience that's reasonably priced and adequately functional. In an age of abundance, consumers demand something more. Check out your bathroom. If you're like a few million Americans, you've got a Michael Graves toilet brush or a Karim Rashid trash can that you bought at Target. Try explaining a designer garbage pail to the left side of your brain! Or consider illumination. Electric lighting was rare a century ago, but now it's commonplace. Yet in the US, candles are a $2 billion a year business—for reasons that stretch beyond the logical need for luminosity to a prosperous country's more inchoate desire for pleasure and transcendence.

Liberated by this prosperity but not fulfilled by it, more people are searching for meaning. From the mainstream embrace of such once-exotic practices as yoga and meditation to the rise of spirituality in the workplace to the influence of evangelism in pop culture and politics, the quest for meaning and purpose has become an integral part of everyday life. And that will only intensify as the first children of abundance, the baby boomers, realize that they have more of their lives behind them than ahead. In both business and personal life, now that our left-brain needs have largely been sated, our right-brain yearnings will demand to be fed.

As the forces of Asia, automation, and abundance strengthen and accelerate, the curtain is rising on a new era, the Conceptual Age. If the Industrial Age was built on people's backs, and the Information Age on people's left hemispheres, the Conceptual Age is being built on people's right hemispheres. We've progressed from a society of farmers to a society of factory workers to a society of knowledge workers. And now we're progressing yet again—to a society of creators and empathizers, pattern recognizers, and meaning makers.

20   But let me be clear: The future is not some Manichaean landscape in which individuals are either left-brained and extinct or right-brained and ecstatic—a land in which millionaire yoga instructors drive BMWs and programmers scrub counters at Chick-fil-A. Logical, linear, analytic thinking remains indispensable. But it's no longer enough.

To flourish in this age, we'll need to supplement our well-developed high tech abilities with aptitudes that are "high concept" and "high touch." High concept involves the ability to create artistic and emotional beauty, to detect patterns and opportunities, to craft a satisfying narrative, and to come up with inventions the world didn't know it was missing. High touch involves the capacity to empathize, to understand the subtleties of human interaction, to find joy in one's self and to elicit it in others, and to stretch beyond the quotidian in pursuit of purpose and meaning.

Developing these high concept, high touch abilities won't be easy for everyone. For some, the prospect seems unattainable. Fear not (or at least fear less). The sorts of abilities that now matter most are fundamentally human attributes. After all, back on the savannah, our caveperson ancestors weren't plugging numbers into spreadsheets or debugging code. But they were telling stories, demonstrating empathy, and designing innovations. These abilities have always been part of what it means to be human. It's just that after a few generations in the Information Age, many of our high concept, high touch muscles have atrophied. The challenge is to work them back into shape.

Want to get ahead today? Forget what your parents told you. Instead, do something foreigners can't do cheaper. Something computers can't do faster. And something that fills one of the nonmaterial, transcendent desires of an abundant age. In other words, go right, young man and woman, go right.

Question for Reading Actively

1. Identify and describe the social forces that the author believes are responsible for moving us from the Information Age to the Conceptual Age.

Question for Thinking Critically

1. Explain the differences between what the author characterizes as the Industrial Age, the Information Age, and the Conceptual Age. Why does he feel that being a "knowledge worker" will be no longer sufficient for achieving success in the new Conceptual Age?

Question for Writing Thoughtfully

1. According to the author, the thinking abilities associated with left-brain thinking are linear, logical, and analytic, while the thinking abilities associated with right-brain thinking involve artistry, empathy, inventiveness, and seeing the big picture. Using examples, explain how being able to think in both of these ways is advantageous for most careers.

"The 6 Myths of Creativity"

by Bill Breen

Bill Breen is the senior editor of *Fast Company,* a print and online magazine that has covered the business of new media and technology since the dot-com boom of the mid-1990s. A graduate of Colorado College (BA) and Trinity College, Dublin (MA), Breen studied literature in preparation for his career as a "word wrangler." Breen has written extensively on environmental issues as well as on business and technology.

Creativity

These days, there's hardly a mission statement that doesn't herald it, or a CEO who doesn't laud it. And yet despite all of the attention that business creativity has won over the past few years, maddeningly little is known about day-to-day innovation in the workplace. Where do breakthrough ideas come from? What kind of work environment allows them to flourish? What can leaders do to sustain the stimulants to creativity—and break through the barriers?

Teresa Amabile has been grappling with those questions for nearly thirty years. Amabile, who heads the Entrepreneurial Management Unit at Harvard Business School and is the only tenured professor at a top B-school to devote her entire research program to the study of creativity, is one of the country's foremost explorers of business innovation.

Eight years ago, Amabile took her research to a daring new level. Working with a team of PhDs, graduate students, and managers from various companies, she collected nearly 12,000 daily journal entries from 238 people working on creative projects in seven companies in the consumer products, high-tech, and chemical industries. She didn't tell the study participants that she was focusing on creativity. She simply asked them, in a daily email, about their work and their work environment as they experienced it that day. She then coded the emails for creativity by looking for moments when people struggled with a problem or came up with a new idea.

"The diary study was designed to look at creativity in the wild," she says. "We wanted to crawl inside people's heads and understand the features of their work environment as well as the experiences and thought processes that lead to creative breakthroughs."

5

Amabile and her team are still combing through the results. But this groundbreaking study is already overturning some long-held beliefs about innovation in the workplace. In an interview with *Fast Company,* she busted six cherished myths about creativity. (If you want to quash creativity in your organization, just continue to embrace them.) Here they are, in her own words.

1. Creativity Comes from Creative Types

When I give talks to managers, I often start by asking, Where in your organization do you most want creativity? Typically, they'll say R&D, marketing, and advertising. When I ask, Where do you *not* want creativity? Someone will inevitably answer, "Accounting." That always gets a laugh because of the negative connotations of creative accounting. But there's this common perception among managers that some people are creative, and most aren't. That's just not true. As a leader, you don't want to ghettoize creativity; you want everyone in your organization producing novel and useful ideas, including your financial people. Over the past couple of decades, there have been innovations in financial accounting that are extremely profound and entirely ethical, such as activity-based costing.

The fact is, almost all of the research in this field shows that anyone with normal intelligence is capable of doing some degree of creative work. Creativity depends on a number of things: experience, including knowledge and technical skills; talent; an ability to think in new ways; and the capacity to push through uncreative dry spells. Intrinsic motivation—people who are turned on by their work often work creatively—is especially critical. Over the past five years, organizations have paid more attention to creativity and innovation than at any other time in my career. But I believe most people aren't anywhere near to realizing their creative potential, in part because they're laboring in environments that impede intrinsic motivation. The anecdotal evidence suggests many companies still have a long way to go to remove the barriers to creativity.

2. Money Is a Creativity Motivator

The experimental research that has been done on creativity suggests that money isn't everything. In the diary study, we asked people, "To what extent were you motivated by rewards today?" Quite often they'd say that the question isn't relevant—that they don't think about pay on a day-to-day basis. And the handful of people who were spending a lot of time wondering about their bonuses were doing very little creative thinking.

Bonuses and pay-for-performance plans can even be problematic when people believe that every move they make is going to affect their compensation. In those situations, people tend to get risk averse. Of course, people need to feel that they're being compensated fairly. But our research shows that people put far more value on a work environment where creativity is supported, valued, and recognized. People want the opportunity to deeply engage in their work and make real progress. So it's critical for leaders to match people to projects not only on the basis of their experience but also in terms of where their interests lie. People are most creative when they care about their work and they're stretching their skills. If the challenge is far beyond their skill level, they tend to get frustrated; if it's far below their skill level, they tend to get bored. Leaders need to strike the right balance.

10

3. Time Pressure Fuels Creativity

In our diary study, people often thought they were most creative when they were working under severe deadline pressure. But the 12,000 aggregate days that we studied showed just the opposite: People were the least creative when they were fighting the clock. In fact, we found a kind of time-pressure hangover—when people were working under great pressure, their creativity went down not only on that day but the next two days as well. Time pressure stifles creativity because people can't deeply engage with the problem. Creativity requires an incubation period; people need time to soak in a problem and let the ideas bubble up.

In fact, it's not so much the deadline that's the problem; it's the distractions that rob people of the time to make that creative breakthrough. People can certainly be creative when they're under the gun, but only when they're able to focus on the work. They must be protected from distractions, and they must know that the work is important and that everyone is committed to it. In too many organizations, people don't understand the reason for the urgency, other than the fact that somebody somewhere needs it done today.

4. Fear Forces Breakthroughs

There's this widespread notion that fear and sadness somehow spur creativity. There's even some psychological literature suggesting that the incidence of depression is higher in creative writers and artists—the depressed geniuses who are incredibly original in their thinking. But we don't see it in the population that we studied.

We coded all 12,000 journal entries for the degree of fear, anxiety, sadness, anger, joy, and love that people were experiencing on a given day. And we found that creativity is positively associated with joy and love and negatively associated with anger, fear, and anxiety. The entries show that people are happiest when they come up with a creative idea, but they're more likely to have a breakthrough if they were happy the day before. There's a kind of virtuous cycle. When people are excited about their work, there's a better chance that they'll make a cognitive association that incubates overnight and shows up as a creative idea the next day. One day's happiness often predicts the next day's creativity.

5. Competition Beats Collaboration

There's a widespread belief, particularly in the finance and high-tech industries, that internal competition fosters innovation. In our surveys, we found that creativity takes a hit when people in a work group compete instead of collaborate. The most creative teams are those that have the confidence to share and debate ideas. But when people compete for recognition, they stop sharing information. And that's destructive because nobody in an organization has all of the information required to put all the pieces of the puzzle together.

15 ## 6. A Streamlined Organization Is a Creative Organization

Maybe it's only the public-relations departments that believe downsizing and restructuring actually foster creativity. Unfortunately, I've seen too many examples of this kind of spin. One of my favorites is a 1994 letter to shareholders from a major U.S. software company: "A downsizing such as this one is always difficult for employees, but out of tough times can come strength, creativity, and teamwork."

Of course, the opposite is true: Creativity suffers greatly during a downsizing. But it's even worse than many of us realized. We studied a 6,000-person division in a global electronics company during the entire course of a 25 percent downsizing, which took an incredibly agonizing 18 months. Every single one of the stimulants to creativity in the work environment went down significantly. Anticipation of the downsizing was even worse than the downsizing itself—people's fear of the unknown led them to basically disengage from the work. More troubling was the fact that even five months after the downsizing, creativity was still down significantly.

Unfortunately, downsizing will remain a fact of life, which means that leaders need to focus on the things that get hit. Communication and collaboration decline significantly. So too does people's sense of freedom and autonomy. Leaders will have to work hard and fast to stabilize the work environment so ideas can flourish.

Taken together, these operating principles for fostering creativity in the workplace might lead you to think that I'm advocating a soft management style. Not true. I'm pushing for a smart management style. My thirty years of research and these 12,000 journal entries suggest that when people are doing work that they love and they're allowed to deeply engage in it—and when the work itself is valued and recognized— then creativity will flourish. Even in tough times.

Questions for Reading Actively

1. In your own words, describe the "6 Myths of Creativity."

2. How did Teresa Amabile, the Harvard Business School professor who studies creativity in the workplace, design her research? What kinds of information was she looking for? What seems especially surprising or interesting about her approach to research?

3. Who is the audience for Bill Breen's article? How can you tell?

Question for Thinking Critically

1. Compare Daniel Pink's description of the kind of thinking that is necessary to be successful in today's business world ("Revenge of the Right Brain," p. 112) with the qualities that Amabile identifies as motivating creativity in business. How is the advice similar or different?

Questions for Writing Thoughtfully

1. Select one of the "6 Myths of Creativity" that has special application to your own studies, work, or life. How has this myth challenged or blocked your ability to be

creative? In an essay, describe the myth in your own words and devise a plan for overcoming this challenge or block and becoming more creative.

2. In your experience, which of the four strategies for becoming more creative (p. 106) is most important for innovation and success? In your response, refer to Daniel Pink's essay (p. 112) or Teresa Amabile's research.

Writing Project: Imagining Your Life Lived More Creatively

According to a French proverb, "Only he who does nothing makes a mistake." The chapter's Writing Project asks you to think creatively to imagine changes in your life. Doing this can, in fact, be very difficult. But it is important to do to avoid future regrets; often people most regret the things they did not do as they lived their lives.

Imagine how some part of your life could be more satisfying or exciting. You will need to focus on one or more specific areas of your life, such as an important relationship, your college work, or a job that would be ideal for you. Visualize how your future will be when you creatively transform this part of your life, and think about what you must do in the present to achieve this imagined goal. Create or locate images that inspire or evoke your goal as well as how you plan to achieve it. Follow your instructor's directions for length, format, and so on.

The Writing Situation

Begin by considering the key elements of the Thinking-Writing Model.

Purpose   Your purpose is to use the strategies for thinking, living, and writing this chapter presents to create a new vision of your own life. Doing this will require you to step back from your life, to become an observer of how you have lived, or are living, or might be living, and then to create a potentially different vision.

Your essay will begin with, and include, at least one actual image.

Audience   You have an interesting and varied audience. You are your own most important audience, for who else could be more interested in the subject? Beyond yourself, you may choose to show your writing to key people in your life, especially if any of them would be affected by the changes you propose. Their reactions to early drafts could be very helpful as you revise.

Your classmates may be part of your audience if your writing is going to be shared with them. All the readers mentioned so far will be interested in what you say, and especially in the changes you propose, so include enough background information about how your life was, or is, for them to understand the impact of those changes.

Subject   Thinking and writing about our own lives can be exciting yet challenging. Often we are so busy just living our lives that we don't take time to think about how they might be different. We begin to think that whatever *is* has to be.

A potential problem is that you may believe that there is little in your life that can be changed. You are not necessarily being asked to propose major changes. What you end up writing about could be a different life or simply a richer, more fully realized version of your life now.

Writer   As the expert on your own life, you write with authority on this project. If you are the creative type, you should welcome the chance to let your imagination go! If you consider yourself unimaginative, take this opportunity to develop your creative side, using any of the strategies discussed in this chapter.

The Writing Process

The following sections guide you through the stages of the writing process. Try to be particularly conscious of how creative thinking can help you discover and connect ideas.

Generating Ideas   Review your responses to the Thinking-Writing Activities in this chapter. You will probably see a number of ideas that pertain to this project. Then, to discover more ideas and a possible focus, follow these suggestions and jot down your responses.

- Think about two or three things you do that are particularly important to you. How might they become more satisfying if you became more creative in your approach?

- Envision your life five years from now. What activities do you hope to be involved in? How could they be shaped by creative thinking? What would your ideal job situation be?

- Recall an event from the past in which you experienced a creative breakthrough. What was your flash of insight? Can you apply that creative insight to your current situation or future life?

- Choose a situation and brainstorm or ask questions about it.

- For a week, keep a journal about how you experience your work and work environment each day. (See "The 6 Myths of Creativity," p. 116.) What situations seem to inspire your creativity? What situations stifle your creativity?

- Collect images that suggest "creativity" to you, even if you can't quite articulate *why* they seem creative.

- Ask yourself if you have enough ideas to begin drafting your paper. If not, you may want to try again by examining another aspect of your life.

Defining a Focus   After reviewing the material you created, consider which area of your life would be most exciting to focus on. Then write a few sentences about that change. For example:

> I think that I would like to be a more creative cook. Why? How? So that my housemates and I can have more enjoyable meals when it's my turn in the kitchen; so that I can really enjoy cooking. . . . Some ways that I can do this is to take a cooking course, check some really different cookbooks out of the library—like from other countries or other regions, or vegan, or barbecue. I should spend some time with my uncle who makes such good one-dish meals, find some tasty web sites, and watch some of those cooking shows instead of surfing away.

This writer has a focus: becoming a more creative cook. She can now decide how to draft the thesis—as a simple statement or a "blueprinted" sentence that lays out the organization of the paper.

> *Simple statement:* I want to change my life by becoming a more creative cook.
>
> *Blueprinted sentence:* I plan to become a more creative cook by taking a cooking course, checking some good cookbooks out of the library, spending more time with my uncle, finding some tasty websites, and watching some cooking shows.

If you do write a blueprinted sentence, consider whether you have listed the changes in an order that your audience can easily comprehend. Once you have established an order, use it to structure your essay.

Organizing Ideas   After you have decided on a focus, you can

- describe your current or past situation
- describe some changes you would like to make or wish you had made
- describe the improved situation
- select images that more specifically reflect your situation and/or your goal

Does this thinking suggest a method of organization? Is that organization effective, or is it too stodgy for a paper about creative thinking? How about narrating the events from a future perspective, after you have made some changes?

Map out an organizational plan that you think might work. Consult with your instructor if you are taking a creative approach to organization.

Drafting   As you translate your ideas into coherent writing, you need to draft in ways that will help you revise effectively. Because the essay you are about to write will have three distinct components—your present situation, the changes you would make, and how your life would be different—you may want to draft each component separately and then think about connecting them.

Thinking Critically About Visuals

Seeing and Believing

It is important that you, as a student, a citizen, and a consumer, apply your critical thinking abilities to what you *see* as well as to what you *read.* Learning to test the authority and credibility of visual as well as verbal sources of information will help you to develop creative, responsible, and purposeful ways to use images in your own writing. A good way to begin is to ask questions of fact, interpretation, analysis, synthesis, evaluation, and application as you consider the accuracy and purpose of a visual image that accompanies a printed text.

The images in this portfolio, and the questions and activities offered here and on this text's website, will help you to recognize how images in the media can sometimes present biased or incomplete information.

AP Photo/Charlie Riedel

A bird is mired in oil on the beach at East Grand Terre Island along the Louisiana coast on June 3, 2010, after an enormous oil spill in the Gulf of Mexico.

Thinking Critically About The Image

1. What emotions and/or thoughts does this photo inspire?
2. Contrast this image to the image of a bird that got into some oil paint in the "Reading Images Critically" section of Chapter 4. Compare the two images in terms of semantic, perceptual, syntactic, and pragmatic meaning.

Female body builders pose for a competition.

Thinking Critically About the Image

1. What is your reaction to the women in this photograph? Do you think that the concepts "masculinity and femininity" are outdated relics of earlier cultures? Or do you believe that these concepts reflect basic qualities of the human species that are still relevant today?

2. Some might interpret this level of body building as achieving the pinnacle of physical fitness, while others may interpret it as going to an unnecessary extreme. What message does this photo convey about fitness and health?

3. Write a short essay describing the ways a competition like this is similar or dissimilar to the Miss Universe pageant. In your essay, define and discuss the concepts of objectification and empowerment.

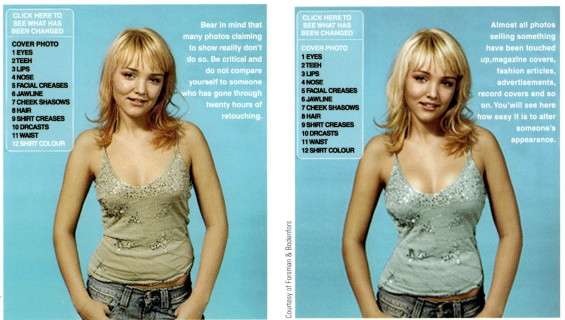

Left photo:

CLICK HERE TO SEE WHAT HAS BEEN CHANGED

COVER PHOTO
1 EYES
2 TEEH
3 LIPS
4 NOSE
5 FACIAL CREASES
6 JAWLINE
7 CHEEK SHASOWS
8 HAIR
9 SHIRT CREASES
10 DRCASTS
11 WAIST
12 SHIRT COLOUR

Bear in mind that many photos claiming to show reality don't do so. Be critical and do not compare yourself to someone who has gone through twenty hours of retouching.

Courtesy of Forsman & Bodenfors

Right photo:

CLICK HERE TO SEE WHAT HAS BEEN CHANGED

COVER PHOTO
1 EYES
2 TEEH
3 LIPS
4 NOSE
5 FACIAL CREASES
6 JAWLINE
7 CHEEK SHASOWS
8 HAIR
9 SHIRT CREASES
10 DRCASTS
11 WAIST
12 SHIRT COLOUR

Almost all photos selling something have been touched up, magazine covers, fashion articles, advertisements, record covers and so on. You'will see here how easy it is to alter someone's appearance.

Courtesy of Forsman & Bodenfors

These photos show the same model before her photo shoot and after the image has been "worked on" through air-brushing and photo-shopping.

Thinking Critically About the Image

1. As with the concepts of "masculinity" and "femininity," the concept of "beauty" varies widely depending on culture and time period. How do the two images above contrast in terms of visual impact?

2. What does the common practice of air-brushing and photo-shopping to manipulate images like this say about our values and concepts of "beauty" as a society?

(Visit http://demo.fb.se/e/girlpower/retouch to see an interactive version of this photo, which allows you to see each individual change more clearly.)

© REUTERS/Chris/Corbis

Iraqi boys play with toy guns in a Baghdad alley, May 31, 2003.

Thinking Critically About the Image

1. In time of war, children are typically the most tragic victims. This photo and the one on the opposite page illustrate the different effects war can have on children. What are the likely *long-term* impacts war will have on these children? How do you think war has affected the thinking and emotions of these Iraqi boys?

2. What do you think the intentions of the photographers were in each of these photos? What makes the photos so provocative? What approach did the photographers use in order to convey their meaning?

© Faleh Kheiber/Reuters/Corbis

In April 2006, the Iraqi Culture Ministry sponsored an eleven-day festival of children's theater in an effort to give children "a respite from the daily bloodshed and violence" of the ongoing war and insurgency. These girls study ballet in Baghdad.

Thinking Critically About the Image

1. By placing these images next to each other (or on facing pages), what kind of context might a photojournalist or propagandist suggest—either deliberately or accidentally?

2. Chapter 10 defines and discusses causal claims and causal fallacies. In an essay, examine how either or both of the photographs on these facing pages could be used to support or expose either a causal claim or a causal fallacy about the war in Iraq.

Homeless people sleep on a heating grate outside a Manhattan fur shop during the winter.

Thinking Critically About the Image

1. What are the ethical implications of photojournalism? Should photojournalists offer assistance—for example, buying food for or offering money to these homeless men—or does that compromise a journalist's objectivity?

2. What would be the thesis or claim of an opinion piece or argument that used this photograph as evidence? Compare possible claims with other students in your class. How many different ways can you find to "read" this photograph?

Damon Winter/The New York Times/Redux

Lionel Michaud finally finds his ten-month-old daughter Christian, or rather her body, on a pile of corpses after the January 2010 earthquake in Haiti. (This photo is mentioned in the reading "Making Sense of Haiti," by Amy Davidson in Chapter 9.)

Thinking Critically About The Image

1. This photo was made available to the public by *The New York Times*. Do you think it is effective in highlighting the devastation of the event for people who live far from the scene of the disaster? Or do you think it represents an invasion of the media into an individual's private moment?

2. The dead Haitian citizens in this photo are shown in a jumbled pile, some in positions that might be considered by some to be undignified. Is the photojournalist not showing respect for the dead by making this photo public? Does it matter that this scene was in a public place?

3. You have likely seen World War II pictures showing the dead victims of the Holocaust. (If not, you can easily look such photos up online.) Those pictures are in black-and-white, were taken in the 1940s, and depict the Jewish victims of a Nazi extermination; whereas, the photo on this page is in color, was taken in 2010, and depicts victims of a natural disaster. However, both types of photos show the dead of one distinct ethnic population who were killed, and they depict the dead in undignified positions. What other similarities or differences do you see (e.g., in perspective, lighting, focus)? How do these similarities and differences affect how you view the photos? What purpose do the photos serve?

A Palestinian soldier on patrol in Beirut, Lebanon, pets a kitten in this photo from 1982.

Thinking Critically About the Image

1. Photojournalists, just like print journalists, are keen observers of detail. Chapter 7 of this book discusses objective and subjective writing. In a paragraph, describe objectively what you see in this photograph. Then, write a subjective paragraph in which you interpret this image. Why is it important to form a critical understanding of how images are selected by journalists, politicians, and others in the media?

2. How does paradox work to make this photograph especially striking?

Drafting Hints

1. If you are drafting on a word processor, double or even triple space. Be sure to save your work every few minutes if your program does not do so automatically.

2. Consider drafting the three components of this essay as three separate files. You could name them "Present Situation," "Changes," and "New and Different Life." Then you can easily copy and paste them to see what organization would work best.

3. If you are drafting by hand, skip lines and write on only one side of the paper. That way you can easily rearrange them if you decide to reorganize.

Revising   One of the best revision strategies is to get an audience's reactions to your draft. Your classmates can help you see where your draft is already successful and where it needs improvement. If your instructor allows class time for peer review, have a draft ready.

Revising Strategy: Peer Response with Silent Writer   This activity, which works best with groups of three or four, introduces a different method for peer review than the one in Chapter 3. In this method, the writer is silent after reading the draft aloud twice and listens as peers respond. Follow all the steps of the directions carefully.

1. The group selects a timekeeper, who allots ten minutes to each writer. Regardless of how many steps in the response process have been completed, after ten minutes the group moves on to consider the next writer's work.

2. One person begins by reading his or her draft aloud while group members listen, giving the writer their full attention.

3. The writer then reads the draft aloud a second time. Group members listen again, this time taking notes.

4. Group members read their comments to the writer. Responses that are stated as "I" messages and are geared to helping the writer to revise work well:

   Weak response: "I like it. It sounds okay to me." (*no specific help given to writer*)

   Marginally useful: "I thought the description of your new neighborhood was entertaining." (*encouragement for the writer*)

   Useful: "Can you give me an example of the kind of task you would perform in your new job?" (*The writer learns what information the reader needs.*)

   Very useful: "I was confused when you said your aunt came into the room. I thought you said earlier that you were alone in the house." (*Again, the writers hear from someone who wasn't there when it happened, someone who needs more information.*)

5. The writer listens to questions and comments and may take notes but does *not* answer or respond aloud. The writer may ask questions after all group members have commented.

6. Continue the process until each group member has used ten minutes of response time.

As soon as possible after peer review, you should revise your draft based on your peers' questions and comments. Then, if possible, put it aside for a day or two before continuing.

Reread your revised draft out loud, slowly. Think about each of the following questions.

1. How could you improve your thesis?

2. How could you improve the order of your draft? Here you need to balance creativity against the needs of your readers. Is there a more creative way to arrange your essay without sacrificing the needs of your readers?

3. Could you provide transitions between sections of your essay to help your readers follow your ideas?

4. Is your use of language creative? Could you provide more specific adjectives and adverbs?

5. Have you given your essay an inventive title that will make your readers want to read it?

Editing and Proofreading   To prepare a final draft, edit for standard grammar and punctuation. Proofread carefully to detect omitted words and punctuation marks. Run your spell-checker program, but be aware of its limitations. Finally, ask someone you trust to proofread after you are finished.

The following essays show how two students responded to the idea of living their lives more creatively. Before writing, each of them used one of the methods on pages 106–107 for generating ideas.

Student Writing

Jessie Lange's Writing Process: Freewriting

I have to write a paper about a legend I didn't even understand. There are stairs going up a tower to a place that is a kind of nirvana, a place of happiness, but you can only reach the top if you don't believe in the legend itself. Hello? If you don't believe it, why would you spend your time climbing up? Ok, Ok, I needed to think. Usually getting outside helps me think better so I tried that up at our place in the country. I did have a great experience. I saw some deer in the mist at night. They were really hard to see and when I put up my lamp to get more light, instead of seeing them better, they almost disappeared in the light. So I turned out the light and I could see them better in the dark. I'm thinking that maybe this is like the legend. The opposite of what you would expect happens. Maybe the legend is about trying too hard. I'll try this angle and see what happens.

Discovering Creativity by Not Looking for It

by Jessie Lange

There have been numerous times when I have sat in front of a blank computer screen, a writing assignment in hand, feeling completely uninspired and uncreative. Without having even begun I think, "Now what?" There have been numerous times when I've just started filling up that screen with meaningless, dry words that really have no effect on me or anyone else. Yes, I'm getting the job done, but not the job I'd like—not my best work, not anywhere near it. One thing that I've found in my life is that in your most uncreative ruts sometimes you can't pull yourself out all on your own. You can't always, sitting in an idea-less vacuum, turn on the creativity. Sometimes you will save yourself time and produce a much more fulfilling piece of work if you take the time out to go *out* of the world of your blank screen. For me this has always meant literally getting outdoors, because somehow it always seems that I find *outside* what I've been looking for *inside*.

It was the first English assignment of my senior year of high school—an interpretation of a Buddhist legend—and I was struggling with its meaning. The legend is about a set of stairs leading to the top of the tower from where you can see the "whole horizon" and the "loveliest landscape"—a symbol of attaining nirvana. The paradox in the legend is that you can only reach the top if you do not believe in the legend itself. How would those who believe, then, ever reach the top? How can you even start the climb without making the conscious decision to do so?

Being in the country on weekends has many benefits, one of them being that I could go outside to clear my head. I lit my Williams Sonoma oil lamp and walked out into the night that offered the occasional drizzle and a strong breeze that ruffled the leaves of the tree I lay down under. I was there for an hour, feeling the drops on my face and the dampness settling into my body, before it happened. I rolled over and looked out into the field, because I sensed something the way that you can and will when you're listening with your entire body. Farther out, right before the lawn becomes high grass and eventually woods, were four white shapes moving across my line of vision. The same deer I casually glanced at during

Image copyright Stéphane Bidouze 2010. Used under license from Shutterstock.com

the day were like ghosts grazing out there at night. Just faint, light vaporous figures against the pitch black. That moment was like seeing the "whole horizon." Those animals, moving with such grace, were unaware of my presence. For all they knew, I was another tree silently overseeing their nightly ritual. Watching these beasts—because that's what they are, wonderfully wild animals—I was witnessing a scene that could have taken place in this same spot on this same night hundreds or thousands of years before. I reached for my lantern and turned up the flame, holding it in front of me for a better view. This light, however, obstructed my vision rather than illuminating it. It was only when I put the flame aside and cupped my hands around my eyes, creating a deeper darkness, that I could really see the deer.

And then I realized that perhaps that was why only those who do not believe the legend ever climb the stairs of the tower—because when you actively search for things, like holding the light, perhaps you prevent yourself from seeing them. Had I not put my writing aside and taken that walk, I would never have found this answer, the answer I was looking for. I wrote my English essay and I also learned something about creativity in my own life. Some of your most creative moments happen when you're not looking. In the journey up the steps of the tower toward creativity, sometimes it is not those who are keenly searching for a victory of sorts, but those who are instead turning down the light, that begin the climb.

Alternative Writing Projects

1. Write an essay explaining your original, creative solution to a physical problem, one involving a piece of equipment, the use of space, overcoming some barrier, and so on. Be sure to incorporate images that illustrate the problem, the solution, or both. Here are some examples:

   - Crowd control or better seating at concerts and sporting events
   - A device that makes some activity easier or more accessible for the disabled
   - New design or redesign of highways and roads in your area
   - An imaginative new tool or transportation device

2. Write an essay explaining your original, creative solution to a social problem, such as homelessness, tensions between racial groups, or drug use among young teenagers.

3. Write an essay explaining your original, creative plan for the perfect house, the perfect party, or the perfect vacation.

CHAPTER 4   Summary

- Creative ways to generate ideas include brainstorming, using mind maps, freewriting, and questioning.

- Six types of questions can help you generate ideas and narrow your topic: questions of fact, interpretation, analysis, synthesis, evaluation, and application.

- Images are a form of communication too and should be considered from a critical thinking perspective.

- In evaluating images, you should identify their audience, subject, and purpose to help determine their semantic, perceptual, syntactic, and pragmatic meanings.

- You can live a more creative life by eliminating "the voice of judgment," establishing a creative environment, and making creativity a priority.

© Bettmann/CORBIS

Frederick Douglass, who was born into but later escaped slavery, led a life defined by passionate questioning and risk taking. He had the profound revelation that slavery is as demeaning to slave owners as it is to slaves themselves. A society that tolerates such injustice, he realized, is never going to be truly capable of any form of justice. What would you consider to be the greatest injustice confronting the United States today?

Drafting: Making and Analyzing Decision

"The strongest principle of growth lies in human choice."

—GEORGE ELIOT

A decision is a kind of commitment. You make decisions, of varying degrees of importance and impact, every day of your life. How carefully you approach that decision, how thoughtfully you evaluate your choices, and how meaningfully you follow through on your commitment to what you have decided varies with the degree of that decision's importance. For example, a knowledgeable and open-minded evaluation of your current lifestyle might lead you to decide to make a few fundamental changes—you might get more exercise, resolve to drink less on the weekends, opt for salad instead of fries. Your decision to live more healthfully might be based on the advice of your doctor and the example set by an athletic friend, but until you *commit* yourself to that decision, you're never going to succeed at lowering your cholesterol or waking up refreshed on Monday morning.

When you decide on a topic for an essay, you are also making a commitment. In the previous chapter, we looked at the process of deciding on a topic—engaging your creativity, your curiosity, your open-mindedness and your knowledge in order to *decide* on the most engaging and appropriate topic for you to write about. In this chapter, we'll examine strategies for following through on that decision, applying those same four qualities to the decision making inherent in each stage of the drafting process.

In addition, this chapter includes essays by and about people forced to make extraordinary decisions under the most perilous circumstances. Their insight, creativity, strength, and thoughtfulness are truly inspiring.

Thinking Critically About Visuals

What's My Next Move?

Image copyright Tyler Olson, 2009. Used under license from Shutterstock.com

Our success in life—and sometimes our survival—depends on developing the ability to solve challenging problems in organized and creative ways. Can you think of other situations in which one decision could mean the difference between life and death for one or many people?

Decisions While Drafting

Most decisions made while drafting a piece of writing are not made in a "first this, then that" sequential order. As Chapter 1 points out, writing processes are usually recursive. Ideas are generated, drafts are made, more ideas come, revisions are necessary, more planning, maybe more drafting—back and forth until the writer says this is it. However, throughout this recursive process, writers must make decisions on subjects, audiences, purposes, and specific ideas and words.

Actually, there is a *first decision*. That is, of course, to take the step from generating ideas to drafting. Some people do this easily; others postpone it. You need to understand your own tendency here and be sure to have some strategies that get you going. Some of the strategies in Chapter 4 used to generate ideas are also useful for beginning to draft. For example,

- *Focused freewriting*. Writing freely on the selected topic can get a draft started, especially if the writer resolves to write and not stare at the screen or the blank page.
- *Listing ideas about the topic and then expressing the ideas in sentences.*
- *Deciding to write on the topic for a set amount of time,* maybe one-half hour.
- *Deciding to draft a specific section first,* usually the one you know most about.

Once you start drafting, you will face other decisions.

Decide What Your Purpose for Writing Is   Usually in college and at work, the purpose is clear. You want to complete the lab report or the English paper to fulfill the assignment as well as you can, or you want your proposal or your application to be accepted. However, if you are composing an email to go to your family list about reunion plans or a letter to the editor about a community problem, you might need to define your purpose. Do you want family members to help? Do you want the city council to act?

In your notebook or a separate file, write a sentence beginning "My purpose(s) for this (essay, email, memo) are…" and list them. Then write a sentence beginning "In order to fulfill my purpose, I should…" You are the audience for these sentences and those following the other decisions. These sentences will almost surely not be part of your draft. They will help you decide what to include.

Decide Who Your Audience Is and What Its Needs Are   As with purpose, the primary audience is often obvious in college and workplace writing—the instructor or the supervisor—but your classmates and fellow workers might be an audience, too. You often know what those audiences expect since assignments and office formats are usually explicit. If you are writing for family members or community groups, as you draft, you should think about what background information is necessary or superfluous, what tone is suitable, what level of vocabulary is appropriate, and what special needs that audience may have.

In your notebook or a separate file, write a sentence beginning "My audience is . . . Then write a sentence beginning, "My audience will expect . . .; my audience will need to know . . .; my audience will already know . . ."

Decide What Your Subject Is and Why It Is Interesting   As we have seen, your subject for writing can be drawn from your personal experience, or it can be a topic assigned by an instructor. If you are allowed to choose a subject, now is the time to exercise your creativity. Try the suggestions for creativity in topic selection and generating ideas presented in Chapter 3.

Decide Who You Are as a Writer   Finding your voice and taking a stand are key steps not only of the writing process but also of your intellectual development. To make a decision about what voice and tone to use in your paper, consider again your audience and purpose. Are you speaking as someone who is an expert on an issue, writing on a subject about which you have considerable personal experience? Alternatively, are you writing for an audience of experts whose conversation about a subject or issue you would like to join? As you read more widely in a variety of disciplines and attend lectures and seminars by experts in a range of fields, you will become more familiar with the different voices and vocabularies used to express ideas for specific audiences. As your knowledge increases, it will be time for you to experiment with different voices and approaches to convey that knowledge.

Decide on a Working Thesis   This is a time to be open-minded. After some drafting, you need to think again about the thesis you may have started with or think about formulating one if you have not yet done so. Reread the material in Chapter 4 about moving from a topic to a thesis statement. As you continue to draft, you will decide exactly how to state it and where to place it.

In your notebook or a separate file, write a sentence beginning "As I see it now, the thesis for this piece is . . ." Then write "Or perhaps it is better said as . . ."

Decide What Information to Use and What More You Need   Review your idea-generating activities. Look again at your tentative thesis. What information do you need to support it and to fulfill your purpose? Think about what you know; think about what you should know more about. Think about what your audience needs to know. The Critical Reading Questions of Interpretation, Analysis, and Evaluation in Chapter 2 can be helpful in this decision.

In your notebook or a separate file, write a sentence beginning "The ideas about . . . are important to my thesis." Then a sentence beginning "I need to know more about . . ." Then a sentence beginning "My audience needs to know . . ."

Decide When to Outline to Bring Order to Your Draft   Some writers make an outline or a plan before drafting; some writers outline after drafting; some writers do not outline but instead revise and redraft until they are satisfied with the organization of the piece.

A rough outline, which indicates the order of sections but is not carefully formatted, usually helps a draft get into shape. Sometimes, a draft benefits from being outlined more than once. Formal outlines, with logical patterns of letters, numbers, sentences, and phrases, can be done when a piece is close to being finished. See your handbook for formal outline specifications if you are asked to do one or if you want to be very sure about your paper's organization.

In your notebook or a separate file, outline the material in your draft, using an informal or a formal system as you find helpful.

Decide on an Introduction and a Conclusion   Although you will look carefully at these parts of your draft as you revise and refine, don't forget to work out possible beginnings and endings as you draft.

Explore as many different types of introductions and conclusions as you can if you are writing something for which there can be choices. (Some kinds of writing, such as lab reports, have expected formats that include types of beginnings and endings.)

Following are some types of beginnings:

- Background information or context
- A relevant anecdote
- A quotation or proverb that relates to the topic
- A striking statement (to be contradicted or supported)
- The problem to be addressed in the paper
- Questions connected to the content of the paper
- The who, what, where, when, how, and why of the paper's focus
- The claim, thesis, or main point
- Combinations of these types

Explore the many possibilities for endings, such as

- A summary of the paper's information
- A recommendation or call for action
- An apt quotation or proverb
- A telling anecdote
- The thesis or main point restated or stated at the end instead of the beginning
- A suggestion of the need for more discussion of the issue

A conclusion must provide a sense of closure to the piece; readers should recognize it as an ending (you should not have to write "The End"!).

Neither introductions nor conclusions should be apologetic ("I don't know much about this, but . . ."); nor should their tone differ from that of the body of the paper.

Decisions in Your Life

Throughout your life you will continue to make decisions and to deal with decisions others make that affect your life. Recalling a previous decision about your education, your relationships, your athletic activities, or any other part of your life will remind you of how important those choices are.

Thinking-Writing Activity

ANALYZING A PREVIOUS DECISION

Think back to an important decision you made that turned out well and describe the experience as specifically as possible by reconstructing the reasoning process you used to make your decision.

- How did you *define* the decision to be made?
- What *choices* did you consider?
- What were the various *pros and cons* of each possible choice?
- What specific plan of action did you use to implement your ideas?
- How did you review your decision to make any necessary adjustments?

Using a method to help you decide about important issues will help you make intelligent decisions and avoid poor choices.

An Organized Approach to Making Decisions

As you were reflecting on the successful decision you wrote about in the previous Thinking-Writing Activity, you probably noticed your mind working in a systematic way as you thought your way through the decision-making process. Of course, we often make important decisions with less thoughtful analysis by acting impulsively and are later forced to cope with the consequences. Our intuitions can be a useful guide to success when they are *informed intuitions*—based on lessons learned from past experience and thoughtful reflection. Naturally, there are no guarantees that careful analysis will lead to a successful result—there are often too many unknown elements and factors beyond our control. But we can certainly improve our success rate by becoming more knowledgeable about the decision-making process.

This approach consists of five steps. As you master these steps, you will be able to apply them in a natural and flexible way.

Step 1: Define the Decision and Its Goals Clearly (Audience)

This seems like an obvious step, but decision making frequently goes wrong at the starting point. For example, imagine that you are trying to decide on an academic major. In order to make an informed decision, you have to project yourself into the future, imagining the career that will be right for you. Your goals will likely include

- financial security
- personal fulfillment
- an opportunity to make use of your special talents
- employment opportunities and job security

Keeping these goals in mind as you consider various majors will give you the greatest success in discovering the field that best suits you. Your audience for this thinking exercise includes not just yourself but also anyone who can help you achieve those goals. The more specific your definition of the decision—and its goals—is, the clearer your analysis and the greater the likelihood of your success will be. Here's a strategy you can use to best define your decision:

> STRATEGY: Write a one-page analysis describing your decision-making situation that defines your goals as clearly and specifically as possible. Write for an audience beyond yourself. Your audience might be your parents, your partner, or your career counselor.

Step 2: Consider All Possible Choices (Subject)

Successful decision makers explore all possible choices, not simply the obvious ones. In fact, the less obvious choices often turn out to be the most effective ones. For instance, one student couldn't decide whether to major in accounting or business management. While discussing his situation with his friends, he revealed that his real interest was in website design. Although he was very talented, he considered this area only a hobby, not a possible career choice. His friends pointed out that designing websites could prove to be his best career opportunity, but he first needed to see it as a possibility.

> STRATEGY: List as many possible choices for your situation as you can—obvious and not obvious, practical and impractical. Ask other people for additional suggestions and keep an open mind—don't censor or prejudge any ideas. Evaluating many different possibilities will help you select a truly interesting and engaging subject.

Step 3: Gather All Relevant Information and Evaluate the Pros and Cons of Each Possible Choice (Purpose)

Each of the possible choices you identified will have certain advantages and disadvantages, so it is essential that you analyze these pros and cons in an organized fashion. This analysis will help you to define and focus your purpose. In the case of the student discussed in step 2, the career choice of accounting might on the one hand offer advantages like ready employment opportunities, the flexibility of working in many different situations and geographical locations, a moderate to high income, and job security. On the other hand, disadvantages might be that accounting does not reflect the student's deep and abiding interest, that he might become bored with it over time, and that the career might not result in the personal challenge and fulfillment that he needs.

> STRATEGY: Using a format similar to the following, analyze the pros and cons of each of your possible choices. The "pro" list will likely help you to visualize the true purpose motivating your choice.

In many cases, you may lack sufficient information to make an informed choice. Unfortunately, this has never prevented people from plunging ahead anyway, making a decision that is more a gamble than an informed choice. But it makes much more sense to seek out the information you need in order to determine which of your choices has the best chance of success. In the case of the student, he would need certain crucial information to determine which career would be best for him: What sort of academic preparation and experience is required for the various careers? What are the prospects for employment in these areas, and how well do the positions pay? What are the day-to-day activities in each career? How happy are the people in the various careers?

STRATEGY: For each possible choice that you have identified, create questions regarding information you need; then obtain that information. Your purpose here is to clarify the resources you need to achieve your goal.

Step 4: Select the Choice That Seems Best Suited to the Situation

The first three steps are designed to help you analyze your decision situation: to define clearly the decision in terms of your goals, to generate possible choices, and to evaluate the pros and cons of the choices you have identified. In the fourth step, you must synthesize what you have learned, weaving together all the various threads into a conclusion that you consider your best choice. In academic writing, synthesis often evolves from the drafting process as you discern new connections among different perspectives and resources. How do you do this? There is no one simple way to identify your best choice, but the following are two useful strategies for guiding your deliberations.

STRATEGY: Identify and prioritize the goal(s) of your decision situation and determine which of your choices best meets these goals.

This process will probably involve reviewing and perhaps refining your definition of the decision situation. For example, for the student we have been discussing, goals included choosing a career that would (a) provide financial security, (b) provide personal fulfillment, (c) make use of special talents, and (d) offer plentiful work opportunities along with job security.

Once identified, these goals can be ranked in order of priority, which will then suggest what the best choice would be. If the student ranks goals *a* and *d* at the top of the list, a choice of accounting or business administration may make sense. However, if the student ranks goals *b* and *c* at the top, pursuing a career in website design and illustration may be the best selection.

Project yourself into the future, imagining as realistically as you can the consequences of each possible choice. Write your thoughts down and discuss them with your friends or colleagues.

Step 5: Implement a Plan of Action and Monitor the Results, Making Necessary Adjustments

Once you have made your best choice, you need to develop and implement a plan of action. The more specific your plan, the greater the likelihood of its success. If, for instance, the student in the example in step 2 decides to pursue a career in website design, his plan should include reviewing the major that best meets his needs, discussing his situation with students and faculty in that department, planning what courses to take, and perhaps speaking with people working in the field. This step of the decision-making process is similar to the work of creating a research plan for writing (Chapter 14).

STRATEGY: Create a plan that details the steps you would take to implement your decision, along with a time line for taking these steps.

Naturally, your plan is merely a starting point. As you actually begin taking the steps in your plan, you may discover that you need to make changes and adjustments. You might find new information that suggests that your choice may be wrong. For example, as the student takes courses in HTML and design, he may realize that his interest in the field is not as serious as he once thought and that although he likes this area as a hobby, he does not want it to be his life's work. In this case, he should reconsider his other choices, perhaps adding some choices that he did not contemplate before.

STRATEGY: After implementing your choice, evaluate its success by identifying what is working and what is not; then make the necessary adjustments to improve the situation.

Summary for Making Decisions in Writing and in Life

1. Define the decision clearly.
2. Consider all possible choices.
3. Gather all relevant information and evaluate the pros and cons of each possible choice.
4. Select the choice that seems best suited to the situation.
5. Implement a plan of action and monitor the results, making necessary adjustments.

Analyzing Decisions

The following readings illustrate decisions of tremendous, life-altering import. Frederick Douglass describes how he and fellow slaves made the momentous decision to escape to the North in 1835. Philosopher Peter Singer explores our process of decision making with respect to the problem of world hunger: the decisions that we *do* make and the decisions that we *ought* to make from an ethical point of view.

FROM *Narrative of the Life of Frederick Douglass, an American Slave*

by Frederick Douglass

Frederick Bailey was born into slavery in 1818, his mother a field worker and his father rumored to be her white master. He spent his early childhood with his grandmother. When he was six years old, his grandmother brought him to the Lloyd Plantation, one of the oldest and largest plantations in Maryland. Frederick only saw his mother once more; she died when he was seven years old.

In 1825, Frederick was sent to live at the Baltimore home of Hugh and Sophia Auld. Sophia, a religious woman, began to teach Bailey (not yet known as Douglass) to read—until she was abruptly forbidden to continue the lessons by her husband, who believed that teaching a slave to read and write was too dangerous. Douglass quickly realized that literacy was a powerful tool for gaining his freedom.

In 1838, after laboring at various plantations and in a Baltimore shipyard, Douglass decided to flee north to New York City. Through the Underground Railroad, Douglass and his wife then moved further north to New Bedford, Massachusetts. To further protect himself from bounty hunters looking for runaway slaves, Frederick Bailey changed his name to Frederick Douglass. In 1845, he published the autobiographical *Narrative of the Life of Frederick Douglass, an American Slave,* which quickly became a bestseller.

During the Civil War, Douglass met several times with President Abraham Lincoln. After the Civil War, Douglass was perhaps the most important black advocate for equal rights and suffrage (the right to vote) in America. Douglass died in Washington, D.C., on February 20, 1895.

At the close of the year 1834, Mr. Freeland again hired me of my master, for the year 1835. But, by this time, I began to want to live ~ *upon free land* ~ as well as ~ *with freeland;* ~ and I was no longer content, therefore, to live with him or any other slaveholder. I began, with the commencement of the year, to prepare myself for a final struggle, which should decide my fate one way or the other. My tendency was upward. I was fast approaching manhood, and year after year had passed, and I was still a slave. These thoughts roused me—I must do something. I therefore resolved that 1835 should not pass without witnessing an attempt, on my part, to secure my liberty. But I was not willing to cherish this determination alone. My fellow-slaves were dear to me. I was anxious to have them participate with me in this, my life-giving determination. I therefore, though with great prudence, commenced early to ascertain their views and feelings in regard to their condition, and to imbue their minds with thoughts of freedom. I bent myself to devising ways and means for our escape, and meanwhile strove, on all fitting occasions, to impress them with the gross fraud and inhumanity of slavery. I went first to Henry, next to John, then to the others. I found, in them all, warm hearts and noble spirits. They were ready to hear, and ready to act when a feasible plan should be proposed. This was what I wanted. I talked to them of our want of manhood, if we submitted to our enslavement without at least one noble effort to be free. We met often, and consulted frequently, and told our hopes and fears, recounted the difficulties, real and imagined, which we should be called on to meet. At times we were almost disposed to give up, and try to content ourselves with our wretched lot; at others, we were firm and unbending in our determination to go. Whenever we suggested any plan, there was shrinking—the odds were fearful. Our path was beset with the greatest obstacles; and if we succeeded in gaining the end of it, our right to be free was yet questionable—we were yet liable to be returned to bondage. We could see no spot, this side of the ocean, where we could be free. We knew nothing about Canada. Our knowledge of the north did not extend farther than New York; and to go there, and be forever harassed with the frightful liability of being returned to slavery—with the certainty of being treated tenfold worse than before—the thought was truly a horrible one, and one which it was not easy to overcome. The case sometimes stood thus: At every gate through which we were to pass, we saw a watchman—at every ferry a guard—on every bridge a sentinel—and in every wood a patrol. We were hemmed in upon every side. Here were the difficulties, real or imagined—the good to be sought, and the evil to be shunned. On the one hand, there stood slavery, a stern reality, glaring frightfully upon us,—its robes already crimsoned with the blood of millions, and even now feasting itself greedily upon our own flesh. On the other hand, away back in the dim distance, under the flickering light of the north star, behind some craggy hill or snow-covered mountain, stood a doubtful freedom—half frozen—beckoning us to come and share its hospitality. This in itself was sometimes enough to stagger us; but when we permitted ourselves to survey the road, we were frequently appalled. Upon either side we saw grim death, assuming the most horrid shapes. Now it was starvation, causing us to eat our own flesh;—now we were contending with the waves, and were drowned;—now we were overtaken, and torn to pieces by the fangs of the terrible bloodhound. We were stung by scorpions, chased by wild beasts, bitten by snakes, and finally, after having nearly reached the desired spot,—after swimming rivers, encountering wild beasts, sleeping in the woods, suffering hunger and nakedness,—we were overtaken by our pursuers, and, in our resistance, we were shot dead upon the spot! I say, this picture sometimes appalled us, and made us

rather bear those ills we had,
Than fly to others, that we knew not of.

In coming to a fixed determination to run away, we did more than Patrick Henry, when he resolved upon liberty or death. With us it was a doubtful liberty at most, and almost certain death if we failed. For my part, I should prefer death to hopeless bondage.

Sandy, one of our number, gave up the notion, but still encouraged us. Our company then consisted of Henry Harris, John Harris, Henry Bailey, Charles Roberts, and myself. Henry Bailey was my uncle, and belonged to my master. Charles married my aunt: he belonged to my master's father-in-law, Mr. William Hamilton.

The plan we finally concluded upon was, to get a large canoe belonging to Mr. Hamilton, and upon the Saturday night previous to Easter holidays, paddle directly up the Chesapeake Bay. On our arrival at the head of the bay, a distance of seventy or eighty miles from where we lived, it was our purpose to turn our canoe adrift, and follow the guidance of the north star till we got beyond the limits of Maryland. Our reason for taking the water route was, that we were less liable to be suspected as runaways; we hoped to be regarded as fishermen; whereas, if we should take the land route, we should be subjected to interruptions of almost every kind. Any one having a white face, and being so disposed, could stop us, and subject us to examination.

5   The week before our intended start, I wrote several protections, one for each of us. As well as I can remember, they were in the following words, to wit:—

"This is to certify that I, the undersigned, have given the bearer, my servant, full liberty to go to Baltimore, and spend the Easter holidays. Written with mine own hand, & c., 1835."

WILLIAM HAMILTON,

"Near St. Michael's, in Talbot county, Maryland."

We were not going to Baltimore; but, in going up the bay, we went toward Baltimore, and these protections were only intended to protect us while on the bay.

As the time drew near for our departure, our anxiety became more and more intense. It was truly a matter of life and death with us. The strength of our determination was about to be fully tested. At this time, I was very active in explaining every difficulty, removing every doubt, dispelling every fear, and inspiring all with the firmness indispensable to success in our undertaking; assuring them that half was gained the instant we made the move; we had talked long enough; we were now ready to move; if not now, we never should be; and if we did not intend to move now, we had as well fold our arms, sit down, and acknowledge ourselves fit only to be slaves. This, none of us were prepared to acknowledge. Every man stood firm; and at our last meeting, we pledged ourselves afresh, in the most solemn manner, that, at the time appointed, we would certainly start in pursuit of freedom. This was in the middle of the week, at the end of which we were to be off. We went, as usual, to our several fields of labor, but with bosoms highly agitated with thoughts of our truly hazardous undertaking. We tried to conceal our feelings as much as possible; and I think we succeeded very well.

After a painful waiting, the Saturday morning, whose night was to witness our departure, came. I hailed it with joy, bring what of sadness it might. Friday night was a sleepless one for me. I probably felt more anxious than the rest, because I was, by common consent, at the head of the whole affair. The responsibility of success or failure lay heavily upon me. The glory of the one, and the confusion of the other, were alike mine. The first two hours of that morning were such as I never experienced before, and hope never to again. Early in the morning, we went, as usual, to the field. We were spreading manure; and all at once, while thus engaged, I was overwhelmed with an indescribable feeling, in the fulness of which I turned to Sandy, who was near by, and said, "We are betrayed!" "Well," said he, "that thought has this moment struck me." We said no more. I was never more certain of any thing.

The horn was blown as usual, and we went up from the field to the house for breakfast. I went for the form, more than for want of any thing to eat that morning. Just as I got to the house, in looking out at the lane gate, I saw four white men, with two colored men. The white men were on horseback, and the colored ones were walking behind, as if tied. I watched them a few moments till they got up to our lane gate. Here they halted, and tied the colored men to the gate-post. I was not yet certain as to what the matter was. In a few moments, in rode Mr. Hamilton, with a speed betokening great excitement. He came to the door, and inquired if Master William was in. He was told he was at the barn. Mr. Hamilton, without dismounting, rode up to the barn with extraordinary speed. In a few moments, he and Mr. Freeland returned to the house. By this time, the three constables rode up, and in great haste dismounted, tied their horses, and met Master William and Mr. Hamilton returning from the barn; and after talking awhile, they all walked up to the kitchen door. There was no one in the kitchen but myself and John. Henry and Sandy were up at the barn. Mr. Freeland put his head in at the door, and called me by name, saying, there were some gentlemen at the door who wished to see me. I stepped to the door, and inquired what they wanted. They at once seized me, and, without giving me any satisfaction, tied me—lashing my hands closely together. I insisted upon knowing what the matter was. They at length said, that they had learned I had been in a "scrape," and that I was to be examined before my master; and if their information proved false, I should not be hurt.

[Douglass and his companions were caught, jailed, and released to their owners.]

Questions for Reading Actively

1. Frederick Douglass and many other nineteenth-century abolitionist writers used biblical metaphors to describe the experience of slavery and the quest for freedom. (In the next chapter, on page 184, you'll see how Martin Luther King also uses biblical imagery to describe the moral imperative for civil rights.) How effective are the religious images and allusions that Douglass makes? (Some of these allusions are quite subtle; for example, why does he specify "thirty-nine lashes" of the whip that slaves who dared attend Sabbath school risked? or his use of the word *betrayed* in paragraph 8?) What does this language suggest about Douglass's audience?

2. In this excerpt Douglass describes at least one major decision that he makes. Describe, in your own words, one such decision. What steps did he take before making a commitment to that decision? Which factors were most important to him in making that decision?

Questions for Thinking Critically

1. Throughout his *Narrative,* Douglass emphasizes the power of literacy. What does literacy mean to Douglass, and why does he make an effort (even at great personal danger) to teach other slaves to become literate? Would Douglass and Malcolm X (page 164 in Chapter 6) share a common definition of *literacy*?

2. Douglass says of his "fellow-slaves": "We were linked and interlinked with each other. I loved them with a love stronger than anything I have experienced since." Given Douglass's audience for his autobiography, why does he feel it so necessary to describe the intensity of these feelings? (Remember, too, that at the time he wrote this autobiography, Douglass was married and a father.)

3. To inspire his close friends and fellow slaves at the Freeland home, Douglass "talked to them of our want of manhood, if we submitted to our enslavement without at least one noble effort to be free." What does he mean? What is a "noble effort to be free," and have you ever made such an effort? Are *you* truly "free" to make decisions about how you live your life?

Question for Writing Thoughtfully

1. In academic writing, students are often discouraged from using the first person in making an argument. How would the impact of Douglass's argument be affected if he had written in the third person? When is one person's experience enough for an argument to be completely authoritative and effective?

"The Solution to World Hunger"

by Peter Singer

The Australian philosopher Peter Singer, who teaches at Princeton University, is perhaps the world's most controversial ethicist. Many readers of his book *Animal Liberation* were moved to embrace vegetarianism, while others recoiled at Singer's attempt to place humans and animals on an even moral plane. Similarly, his argument that severely disabled infants should, in some cases, receive euthanasia has been praised as courageous by some—and denounced by others, including anti-abortion activists, who have protested Singer's Princeton appointment.

Singer's penchant for provocation extends to more mundane matters, like everyday charity. A recent article about Singer in *The New York Times* revealed that the philosopher gives one-fifth of his income to famine-relief agencies. "From when I first saw pictures in newspapers of people starving, from when people asked you to donate some of your pocket money for collections at school," he mused, "I always thought, 'Why that much—why not more?'"

Is it possible to quantify our charitable burden? In the following essay, Singer offers some unconventional thoughts about the ordinary American's obligations to the world's poor and suggests that even his own one-fifth standard may not be enough.

In the Brazilian film "Central Station," Dora is a retired schoolteacher who makes ends meet by sitting at the station writing letters for illiterate people. Suddenly she has an opportunity to pocket $1,000. All she has to do is persuade a homeless 9-year-old boy to follow her to an address she has been given. (She is told he will be adopted by wealthy foreigners.) She delivers the boy, gets the money, spends some of it on a television set and settles down to enjoy her new acquisition. Her neighbor spoils the fun, however, by telling her that the boy was too old to be adopted—he will be killed and his organs sold for transplantation. Perhaps Dora knew this all along, but after her neighbor's plain speaking, she spends a troubled night. In the morning Dora resolves to take the boy back.

Suppose Dora had told her neighbor that it is a tough world, other people have nice new TV's too, and if selling the kid is the only way she can get one, well, he was only a street kid. She would then have become, in the eyes of the audience, a monster. She redeems herself only by being prepared to bear considerable risks to save the boy.

At the end of the movie, in cinemas in the affluent nations of the world, people who would have been quick to condemn Dora if she had not rescued the boy go home

Source: "The Solution to World Hunger," by Peter Singer. Reprinted by permission of the author.

to places far more comfortable than her apartment. In fact, the average family in the United States spends almost one-third of its income on things that are no more necessary to them than Dora's new TV was to her. Going out to nice restaurants, buying new clothes because the old ones are no longer stylish, vacationing at beach resorts—so much of our income is spent on things not essential to the preservation of our lives and health. Donated to one of a number of charitable agencies, that money could mean the difference between life and death for children in need.

All of which raises a question: In the end, what is the ethical distinction between a Brazilian who sells a homeless child to organ peddlers and an American who already has a TV and upgrades to a better one—knowing that the money could be donated to an organization that would use it to save the lives of kids in need?

5   Of course, there are several differences between the two situations that could support different moral judgments about them. For one thing, to be able to consign a child to death when he is standing right in front of you takes a chilling kind of heartlessness; it is much easier to ignore an appeal for money to help children you will never meet. Yet for a utilitarian philosopher like myself—that is, one who judges whether acts are right or wrong by their consequences—if the upshot of the American's failure to donate the money is that one more kid dies on the streets of a Brazilian city, then it is, in some sense, just as bad as selling the kid to the organ peddlers. But one doesn't need to embrace my utilitarian ethic to see that, at the very least, there is a troubling incongruity in being so quick to condemn Dora for taking the child to the organ peddlers while, at the same time, not regarding the American consumer's behavior as raising a serious moral issue.

In his 1996 book, "Living High and Letting Die," the New York University philosopher Peter Unger presented an ingenious series of imaginary examples designed to probe our intuitions about whether it is wrong to live well without giving substantial amounts of money to help people who are hungry, malnourished or dying from easily treatable illnesses like diarrhea. Here's my paraphrase of one of these examples:

Bob is close to retirement. He has invested most of his savings in a very rare and valuable old car, a Bugatti, which he has not been able to insure. The Bugatti is his pride and joy. In addition to the pleasure he gets from driving and caring for his car, Bob knows that its rising market value means that he will always be able to sell it and live comfortably after retirement.

One day when Bob is out for a drive, he parks the Bugatti near the end of a railway siding and goes for a walk up the track. As he does so, he sees that a runaway train, with no one aboard, is running down the railway track. Looking farther down the track, he sees the small figure of a child very likely to be killed by the runaway train. He can't stop the train and the child is too far away to warn of the danger, but he can throw a switch that will divert the train down the siding where his Bugatti is parked. Then nobody will be killed—but the train will destroy his Bugatti. Thinking of his joy in owning the car and the financial security it represents, Bob decides not to throw the switch. The child is killed. For many years to come, Bob enjoys owning his Bugatti and the financial security it represents.

Bob's conduct, most of us will immediately respond, was gravely wrong. Unger agrees. But then he reminds us that we, too, have opportunities to save the lives of children. We can give to organizations like Unicef or Oxfam America. How much would we have to give one of these organizations to have a high probability of saving the life of a child threatened by easily preventable diseases? (I do not believe that children are more worth saving than adults, but since no one can argue that children have brought their poverty on themselves, focusing on them simplifies the issues.) Unger called up some experts and used the information they provided to offer some plausible estimates that include the cost of raising money, administrative expenses and the cost of delivering aid where it is most needed. By his calculation, $200 in donations would help a sickly 2-year-old transform into a healthy 6-year-old—offering safe passage through childhood's most dangerous years. To show how practical philosophical argument can be, Unger even tells his readers that they can easily donate funds by using their credit card and calling one of these toll-free numbers: (800) 367-5437 for Unicef; (800) 693-2687 for Oxfam America.

10   Now you, too, have the information you need to save a child's life. How should you judge yourself if you don't do it? Think again about Bob and his Bugatti. Unlike Dora, Bob did not have to look into the eyes of the child he was sacrificing for his own material comfort. The child was a complete stranger to him and too far away to relate to in an intimate, personal way. Unlike Dora, too, he did not mislead the child or initiate the chain of events imperiling him. In all these respects, Bob's situation resembles that of people able but unwilling to donate to overseas aid and differs from Dora's situation.

If you still think that it was very wrong of Bob not to throw the switch that would have diverted the train and saved the child's life, then it is hard to see how you could deny that it is also very wrong not to send money to one of the organizations listed above. Unless, that is, there is some morally important difference between the two situations that I have overlooked.

Is it the practical uncertainties about whether aid will really reach the people who need it? Nobody who knows the world of overseas aid can doubt that such uncertainties exist. But Unger's figure of $200 to save a child's life was reached after he had made conservative assumptions about the proportion of the money donated that will actually reach its target.

One genuine difference between Bob and those who can afford to donate to overseas aid organizations but don't is that only Bob can save the child on the tracks, whereas there are hundreds of millions of people who can give $200 to overseas aid organizations. The problem is that most of them aren't doing it. Does this mean that it is all right for you not to do it?

Suppose that there were more owners of priceless vintage cars—Carol, Dave, Emma, Fred and so on, down to Ziggy—all in exactly the same situation as Bob, with their own siding and their own switch, all sacrificing the child in order to preserve their own cherished car. Would that make it all right for Bob to do the same? To answer this question affirmatively is to endorse follow-the-crowd ethics—the kind of ethics that led many Germans to look away when the Nazi atrocities were being committed. We do not excuse them because others were behaving no better.

15   We seem to lack a sound basis for drawing a clear moral line between Bob's situation and that of any reader of this article with $200 to spare who does not donate it to an overseas aid agency. These readers seem to be acting at least as badly as Bob was acting when he chose to let the runaway train hurtle toward the unsuspecting child. In the light of this conclusion, I trust that many readers will reach for the phone and donate that $200. Perhaps you should do it before reading further.

Now that you have distinguished yourself morally from people who put their vintage cars ahead of a child's life, how about treating yourself and your partner to dinner at your favorite restaurant? But wait. The money you will spend at the restaurant could also help save the lives of children overseas! True, you weren't planning to blow $200 tonight, but if you were to give up dining out just for one month, you would easily save that amount. And what is one month's dining out, compared to a child's life? There's the rub. Since there are a lot of desperately needy children in the world, there will always be another child whose life you could save for another $200. Are you therefore obliged to keep giving until you have nothing left? At what point can you stop?

Hypothetical examples can easily become farcical. Consider Bob. How far past losing the Bugatti should he go? Imagine that Bob had got his foot stuck in the track of the siding, and if he diverted the train, then before it rammed the car it would also amputate his big toe. Should he still throw the switch? What if it would amputate his foot? His entire leg?

As absurd as the Bugatti scenario gets when pushed to extremes, the point it raises is a serious one: only when the sacrifices become very significant indeed would most people be prepared to say that Bob does nothing wrong when he decides not to throw the switch. Of course, most people could be wrong; we can't decide moral issues by taking opinion polls. But consider for yourself the level of sacrifice that you would demand of Bob, and then think about how much money you would have to give away in order to make a sacrifice that is roughly equal to that. It's almost certainly much, much more than $200. For most middle-class Americans, it could easily be more like $200,000.

Isn't it counterproductive to ask people to do so much? Don't we run the risk that many will shrug their shoulders and say that morality, so conceived, is fine for saints but not for them? I accept that we are unlikely to see, in the near or even medium-term future, a world in which it is normal for wealthy Americans to give the bulk of their wealth to strangers. When it comes to praising or blaming people for what they do, we tend to use a standard that is relative to some conception of normal behavior. Comfortably off Americans who give, say, 10 percent of their income to overseas aid organizations are so far ahead of most of their equally comfortable fellow citizens that I wouldn't go out of my way to chastise them for not doing more. Nevertheless, they should be doing much more, and they are in no position to criticize Bob for failing to make the much greater sacrifice of his Bugatti.

At this point various objections may crop up. Someone may say: "If every citizen living in the affluent nations contributed his or her share I wouldn't have to make such a drastic sacrifice, because long before such levels were reached, the resources would have been there to save the lives of all those children dying from lack of food or medical care. So why should I give more than my fair share?" Another, related, objection is that the Government ought to increase its overseas aid allocations, since that would spread the burden more equitably across all taxpayers.

Yet the question of how much we ought to give is a matter to be decided in the real world—and that, sadly, is a world in which we know that most people do not, and in the immediate future will not, give substantial amounts to overseas aid agencies. We know, too, that at least in the next year, the United States Government is not going to meet even the very modest United Nations-recommended target of 0.7 percent of gross national product; at the moment it lags far below that, at 0.09 percent, not even half of Japan's 0.22 percent or a tenth of Denmark's 0.97 percent. Thus, we know that the money we can give beyond that theoretical "fair share" is still going to save lives that would otherwise be lost. While the idea that no one need do more than his or her fair share is a powerful one, should it prevail if we know that others are not doing their fair share and that children will die preventable deaths unless we do more than our fair share? That would be taking fairness too far.

Thus, this ground for limiting how much we ought to give also fails. In the world as it is now, I can see no escape from the conclusion that each one of us with wealth surplus to his or her essential needs should be giving most of it to help people suffering from poverty so dire as to be life-threatening. That's right: I'm saying that you shouldn't buy that new car, take that cruise, redecorate the house or get that pricey new suit. After all, a $1,000 suit could save five children's lives.

So how does my philosophy break down in dollars and cents? An American household with an income of $50,000 spends around $30,000 annually on necessities, according to the Conference Board, a nonprofit economic research organization. Therefore, for a household bringing in $50,000 a year, donations to help the world's poor should be as close as possible to $20,000. The $30,000 required for necessities holds for higher incomes as well. So a household making $100,000 could cut a yearly check for $70,000. Again, the formula is simple: whatever money you're spending on luxuries, not necessities, should be given away.

Now, evolutionary psychologists tell us that human nature just isn't sufficiently altruistic to make it plausible that many people will sacrifice so much for strangers. On the facts of human nature, they might be right, but they would be wrong to draw a moral conclusion from those facts. If it is the case that we ought to do things that, predictably, most of us won't do, then let's face that fact head-on. Then, if we value the life of a child more than going to fancy restaurants, the next time we dine out we will know that we could have done something better with our money. If that makes living a morally decent life extremely arduous, well, then that is the way things are. If we don't do it, then we should at least know that we are failing to live a morally decent life—not because it is good to wallow in guilt but because knowing where we should be going is the first step toward heading in that direction.

25   When Bob first grasped the dilemma that faced him as he stood by that railway switch, he must have thought how extraordinarily unlucky he was to be placed in a situation in which he must choose between the life of an innocent child and the sacrifice of most of his savings. But he was not unlucky at all. We are all in that situation.

Questions for Reading Actively

1. In his essay, Singer outlines a moral argument for making charitable donations to save the lives of people living in poverty. How does he support his argument? Which of his examples are most powerful and why?

2. Singer says he does "not believe that children are more worth saving than adults, but since no one can argue that children have brought their poverty on themselves, focusing on them simplifies the issues." What does this statement imply about adults?

Questions for Thinking Critically

1. Singer uses a provocative example to dramatize our moral responsibility in reducing world hunger: a child imperiled on a railroad track. Do you agree with Singer's point that it is our moral obligation to save a child's life if we are able to without great sacrifice on our part? Why or why not?

2. Stated in even stronger terms, Singer believes that if we *don't* take the initiative to donate a significant portion of our income to help alleviate world hunger, then we are guilty of the moral equivalent of murder. Do you agree or disagree with this conclusion? Why or why not? If not, what counter arguments would you propose to Singer? How do you think he would respond?

3. If you put yourself in the situation that Singer describes, what would you be willing to sacrifice in order to save the life of a child with whom you had no personal connection? Whatever your level of sacrifice, would it be fair to say that this reflects the value you place on a human life?

4. Even if people are persuaded by the powerful logic of Singer's reasoning, why do you think they might be reluctant to take the next logical step of contributing much of their income to save the lives of starving children? Do you think their actions are justified?

Question for Thoughtful Writing

1. Think of another social dilemma. What is the average person's role in aiding or alleviating that problem? Write a couple of paragraphs about the average person's role in terms of the decisions that individual *does* or *does not* make.

Thinking-Writing Activity

PREPARING FOR DECISIONS

1. Make a list of whatever important decisions in your academic or personal life you have to make now or will have to make in the near future.

2. Select one decision and apply the five-step decision-making method that begins on page 133. As you think through your decision, be sure to identify all your possible choices and to follow your thoughts wherever they lead.

There are no guarantees in life. Our decisions may or may not turn out well. Still, following an organized method for making decisions can at least assure us of having explored and evaluated many possible choices and then having selected the one that seemed to best meet our needs. In other words, we will know that we made the best decision that we could have at the time.

NEW MEDIA & THOUGHTFUL WRITING

Issues with Communication

New media has created a rapidly expanding universe of possibilities, and with this expansion comes the need to expand one's critical thinking abilities to successfully navigate our way through unfamiliar terrain.

In this section we are going to briefly consider the way new media has affected our relationships with others. As is obvious, online communication has greatly expanded the frequency of our contact with others as well as the number of people with whom we are in touch. But with this ease of communication has come new challenges as well. For example, how many times have you regretted impulsively pressing the "send" button on a message written in the heat of the moment? For most of us, this is an all too frequent occurrence. As a rule of thumb, it's often a good idea to delay sending our composed message until we've had an opportunity to let things settle and review it with fresh vision. This also goes for important messages we send, professional or otherwise. We can almost always improve the content and clarity of our message by giving ourselves time to think about it for a while. It's helpful to recognize also that emailing and text-messaging can sometimes encourage a weakening of our inhibitions or internal censors, emboldening us to write things that we would probably not say in person. Again, making a practice of revisiting our message before sending it will doubtless save us from those next-day "How could I?" moments. And finally, we should always remind ourselves that email and text-messages are usually stripped down to the essentials, lacking the rich context that is provided when we are speaking to someone. Without our tone of voice, body language, or detailed articulation, the words and tone are often ambiguous, a situation that can easily lead to misunderstandings. Just because *we* know what we intend to say doesn't mean that the other person will interpret it in the same way. So when sending significant communications via new media the watchword is "Handle with care." Make the time and effort to say precisely what you intend in a way that leaves minimal chance that the recipient will take it any other way.

Analogously, social networking sites like Facebook and MySpace have opened up a Pandora's Box of trouble. These sites provide the unprecedented opportunity for individuals to create a "virtual self," building records of their social identities via descriptions, comments, photographs, and music. In addition to serving as powerful models of social communication, such public displays of private information play to the twin human impulses of showmanship and voyeurism. But problems arise when the "wrong" people visit our site and learn things about us we would never want them to know. For example, 30 percent of today's employers are using Facebook to check out potential employees prior to hiring! There are a number of ways to protect yourself from embarrassment, whether it's an employer, your parent, or your romantic partner. To begin with, you can think carefully about what you post on the site and also exercise care in who you invite to have access. Too often items are posted or people are invited without any consideration of future consequences and complications. Additionally, you can create lists of people in different categories— for example, professional, family, close friends, casual friends—and then regulate who gets to see what through the site's settings. It may seem like a bother, but in the long run you will likely be thankful you took the time to take these basic precautions.

Thinking-Writing Activity

FACEBOOK TROUBLESHOOTING

Sometimes it's easier to detect problems that others face than to view our own potential problems. With this in mind, work with a group of friends to identify potential trouble spots (inappropriate disclosures, incriminating photographs). Once you have compiled the areas of concern, devise strategies for erasing the problems and avoiding similar difficulties in the future. In this regard, you might develop a list of criteria or "ground-rules" to guide you in your posting, and also strategies for organizing your page to head-off problems before they occur.

Writing Project: Analyzing a Decision to Be Made

This chapter includes both readings and Thinking-Writing Activities that encourage you to reflect on drafting and decision making. Be sure to reread what you wrote for those activities; you may be able to use your responses to complete this project.

> Write an essay in which you analyze a decision you must make now or in the near future. Be sure to select a decision for which you already have considerable information or want to obtain more. Include all five steps of the decision-making method. After you have drafted your essay, revise it as best you can. Follow your instructor's directions for length, format, and so on.

The Writing Situation

Begin by considering the key elements in the Thinking-Writing Model on pages 6–8 in Chapter 1.

Purpose   Use this opportunity to work through an important real-life decision to obtain the best possible outcome. If others will be involved in or affected by this decision, your paper can show them your best thinking about it, making them more likely to agree with your decision. Also, in writing this paper, you can practice the creative and critical thinking involved in the five-step decision-making method. You can hone your revision skills both by carefully working through the revision questions on page 152 and by using ideas about revision from Chapter 6 as well as ideas from this chapter.

Audience   An essay about a decision implies at least two potential audiences. In describing a decision you made and the process of making that decision, you could be writing for people who are faced with similar circumstances or a closely related predicament. For example, perhaps you are considering moving to a new city or country with many unknowns and risks, as Frederick Douglass did. Through describing your commitment to a decision, even at its most difficult, you can inspire people who have made a similar decision.

Subject   Decisions can be challenging to think about and difficult to make. Sometimes we haven't enough information to make an intelligent choice; sometimes we *think* we know what the right decision is yet are reluctant to actually make it. Therefore, we often tend to put off decision making for as long as possible. Keep in mind that not making a decision is, in a way, making a decision to do nothing. For this assignment, try to identify a decision that will have significant consequences.

It may be what area to major in, whether to get a part-time job, whether to participate in a sport or other extracurricular activity, or whether to get a dog. The more
significant the decision, the more helpful this assignment will be to you.

Writer   You approach this Writing Project as the expert on the subject since you
are analyzing one of your own decisions. One challenge here is to distinguish between your own expertise about the decision-making situation and your audience's
needs for enough background and information. Another challenge is to focus on
the material provided earlier in this chapter because this assignment moves away
from recollecting experience and asks you to apply the decision-making process to
a decision you need to make soon.

For example, Peter Singer demonstrates his expertise as a philosopher of ethics
by using striking examples and compelling reasoning to draw us in to an analysis
of our own values and decisions.

The Writing Process

The following sections will guide you through the stages of generating, planning,
drafting, and revising as you work on an essay about making a decision.

Generating Ideas   Try to be particularly conscious of both the creative and the
critical thinking you do while making your decision and of the critical thinking and
decision making you do as you revise.

- Is there a decision you must make in the near future? If so, this is a good
  opportunity for you to accomplish two things at once: writing your paper and
  making your decision.

- Think about how much additional information you would need to evaluate
  possible choices for this decision. Do you have time to locate and absorb
  all of it?

- Describe the decision-making situation and your goals as clearly as you can.

- Brainstorm as many possible choices as you can. Ask others involved in the
  decision to help.

- Eliminate choices that you know are impractical or undesirable.

- Determine what information you must find for each choice. Locate that
  information.

- Write each choice on a separate sheet of paper. Then divide the paper into two
  columns: pros and cons. Write as much as you can in each column.

- For each, freewrite for five minutes on what would happen and how you
  would feel if you selected that choice.

- Freewrite for five minutes on how you would know if any given choice was
  the right one.

Defining a Focus   Write a tentative thesis statement that clarifies your decision-making situation. You might write something like "After thinking about the situation carefully, I realize that I have only two possible choices." Or you might "blueprint" your paper by naming the possible choices: "My choices for housing next year come down to these three: living with my aunt, sharing an apartment with my friend, or looking for a live-in job situation." You may even decide to announce your decision in your thesis statement: "After carefully weighing my options, I have decided to major in business administration." Or you may find a more creative way to state your thesis.

Organizing Ideas   The five-step method for making decisions fits well with essay structure. Your description of the decision-making situation might be the beginning of an introduction, to be completed by your thesis statement. You could include your goals in the introduction or state them in a separate paragraph. Each of the potential choices, explained in as much detail as possible along with the pros and cons of that choice, could serve as a body paragraph. Your decision of the best choice and your plan for monitoring it could be the essay's conclusion.

Drafting   Begin with the easiest part to draft. Your description of the decision-making situation could begin the introduction, but consider what, if any, additional information your audience might need in order to understand the situation. The introduction can end with your tentative thesis statement.

In your conclusion or thesis statement, name the choice you have selected. You may want to explain why if you think your reason may not be obvious to your audience. Remember to explain how you will monitor the results of your decision.

Revising   One of the best revision strategies is to get an audience's reactions to your draft. Here are some questions to ask your peers about this assignment:

- What questions do you have about my decision-making situation and my goals?
- What questions do you have about the alternative choices I described? What else do you need to know about them? Can you suggest any others?
- Do you understand why I am making this decision?
- What could I add to clarify why this choice is best for me?

Armed with the information from peer review, you are now ready to begin revising by using the revision method presented on page 169 in Chapter 6. If possible, use the following directions for revising with a word processor as you work through the revision process.

Revising Strategy: Using a Computer to Revise   Use the revision method by creating a series of files, one for each time you revise using your word processor. This system will give you a complete record of your work so that you can track how each draft changes.

- Call your first draft Decision 1 and print and save it.

- Later, create a new file called Decision 2 by copying and pasting Decision 1. Then make changes to the draft as a whole, being guided by your answers from the peer review and your answers to the Think Big questions on page 169. Print and save this draft.

- Now, consider the Think Medium questions to evaluate your individual paragraphs. Create a new file called Decision 3 by copying and pasting Decision 2. Then make whatever changes are suggested by your answers to the Think Medium questions on page 170. Print and save this draft.

- Next, consider the Think Small questions. Create a new file called Decision 4 by copying and pasting Decision 3. Then make whatever changes at the sentence level that are suggested by your answers to the Think Small questions on page 170. Print and save this draft.

- Finally, consider the Think "Picky" questions. Create a new file called Decision 5 by copying and pasting Decision 4. Then make whatever changes are suggested by your answers to the Think "Picky" questions on page 171. Run the spelling and grammar checking features of your word processing program, and use your judgment about which suggested changes to make. Print and save this draft. Decision 5 should present your very best work. It is now ready to be submitted to your instructor and any other audience you select.

You should also review "A Step-by-Step Method for Revising Any Assignment" in Chapter 6 on pages 169–171.

Editing and Proofreading   Your essay should now have been completed to the best of your ability, and, of course, you will need to submit it to your instructor by the due date. But also consider other possible audiences for this essay. Do you want to share your ideas with other people involved in your decision-making situation? Would members of your family or your close friends benefit by reading it? If your paper is about a decision that others must also make, such as selecting a major, perhaps your student newspaper would be interested in publishing it as a model of good decision making that others could emulate.

The following essays show how two students responded to this assignment.

Student Writing

Wendy Agudo's Writing Process

Wendy Agudo began to compose the following essay after a chance remark her philosophy professor made in class. Wendy had already completed the Thinking-Writing assignment on page 134, reflecting on her decision in junior high to overcome her learning disability and earn the high grades she would need to go to college and pursue a career in television journalism. The day after she completed that assignment, her philosophy professor told her class that the French philosopher Jean-Paul Sartre had said that we were "condemned to be free." Wendy began with a freewriting to sort out her feelings about how that quotation related to her own experience and then used the five steps to organized decision making (pages 134–137) to begin to plan her paper.

> Jean-Paul Sartre "we are condemned to be free"—it wasn't anyone's fault, the accident. I don't blame my parents. I don't blame anyone, and they don't blame each other. It just happened. Moving to America when I was really little was probably the best thing they could have done for me. Back in Ecuador it would have been really hard for me to get the help I needed. But still I wouldn't have had to learn a new language, and mami and papa wouldn't have had to work so hard and leave me alone for so much time when I really needed them. I'm angry with Lidia because she doesn't even know how easy she has it. Lidia has always had the family support and the money and the time to do whatever she wants, but all she wants to do is sit around talking on her celly to her boy. We're at work together and we're on deadline and I'm trying to get her to shut up and pay attention and she just rolls her eyes and says something in Albanian over the phone. She has no respect but I can't be jealous, that's not right either. Does she think about where she'll be in two years? in ten years?

1. <u>Define the decision.</u> I decided not to let my brain injury get in the way of my goals.

2. <u>Consider all possible choices.</u> I didn't have a choice. Either I succeed or I fail. It's up to me.

3. <u>Gather all relevant information and evaluate the pros and cons of each choice.</u>

   - I could have stayed in the remedial class in junior high. PRO—less work. CON—where would I be today?

   - I could ignore Lidia and let her screw up. PRO—not having to confront Lidia. CON—it's my job to confront her and make sure she's learning skills. If I don't help her, then I fail at some level.

   - I could let Lidia learn for herself. It worked for me. You need to take responsibility for your own life.

4. <u>Select the choice that seems best suited to the situation.</u> I can't boss Lidia around. She needs to find out for herself what the consequences of her lack of responsibility will be. Besides she won't listen to me. I can be a better example for everyone in the peer training program if I just get my own work done and set a high standard for myself.

5. <u>Implement a plan of action.</u> I owe it to my parents and to myself to succeed. I can't get jealous of Lidia or let her own decisions make my own work look bad.

Freedom

by Wendy Agudo

It's funny how some people always seem to have an excuse for everything, refusing to take responsibility for their actions. All of us have, at some point, shrugged our shoulders and made an excuse for behavior we should have regretted, or at least apologized for—being late to meet a friend, not having an assignment completed on time, not visiting an elderly relative. But making these excuses implies that we are not really in control of our own lives. When we make an excuse for our behavior, we are really saying that some other force—a train conductor, the weather, a computer, whatever—has more control over our lives than we do. To make excuses is to place limits on the extent of your personal freedom.

I see this kind of refusal to take responsibility all the time at my job. I work as a peer trainer for a small non-profit television station, teaching other young people (high school through age 25) how to use field and studio digital cameras, digital and analog video editing, and media literacy. I was fortunate enough to begin this work at the age of 18, and now at the age of 20 I consider myself very skilled and motivated. Because of my experience in a professional environment, I tend to have high expectations for my peers in this training program, who are my own age and often a little older. When they are late for a meeting, or careless with their work, or would rather go out and have fun than stay late and edit a story, I am very disappointed. I hear excuses like "I have no time because of school," or "my family this" and "my intelligence that." I could come up with many more compelling excuses myself, but yet I don't.

I believe that we all make choices in life, and that there is no reason for failure or self-pity. Many factors have contributed to my sense of responsibility, my stubbornness, and my loyalty to my family. But the most significant challenge I have faced—and that I could use as an excuse, but don't—has to do with my health.

I was born in Ecuador. When I was two years old, I accidentally fell from the second-story window of my parents' house. I landed on a pile of broken concrete and suffered brain damage, which the doctor said would be permanent. My parents could have allowed this to be a limit on my freedom, but they refused. I know I was too young to think this, but I do know that somewhere around this time I didn't allow myself to let this keep me down. As I grew I got better. It was my choice to continue and get past it.

Or maybe it was just luck.

My story doesn't have an accidentally happy ending. After I recovered from the fall there were still limitations. I was slow to walk and speak, and was dyslexic. Then, when I was four years old, my family immigrated to the United States. I was enrolled in an English-speaking public school. Between my difficulties in reading, walking, and speaking, I had to work three times as hard as anyone else just to keep up. I stuttered and had a lisp, so even when I did manage to speak English, other children teased me. Due to my dyslexia I had trouble focusing and concentrating, so I had trouble reading. Eventually I was afraid to read anything. I saw all of the other kids round me finishing with two books before I was able to get through even one. I was so discouraged that I wanted to give up.

This is another example of freedom of choice. I could have chosen to work harder, to study more, but I allowed outside circumstances—my disability—to make the choice for me. I gave up, but giving up was my own choice. It wasn't determined for me and it wasn't something I couldn't avoid. I chose to give up out of my own free will. And that choice had consequences. For many years I had very low grades and was passed from one "special" classroom to another.

At some point during junior high I realized that I wasn't going to get anywhere with such low grades. I worked harder and harder and eventually got better. I defeated the dyslexia, but it hasn't gone away. I still have dyslexia, but it doesn't control me. At least now it's something that doesn't hold me back. Eventually, I graduated from high school with honors, and I am now enrolled in college and earning "A" grades. Not bad for someone with a damaged brain!

This brings me back to the high expectations I have for other people in my peer training program. Due to the fact that I had to work so hard to develop myself, I also developed what I call high standards. I look at another peer trainer, whom I will call Lidia, as a comparison. Lidia is five months older than I am, and is also an immigrant. Her family came to the United States from Albania when she was four years old, just like me. Her parents are both doctors, and she was raised with many privileges. Although we both grew up in the same New York City neighborhood, our lives were very different. For my parents to get here from Ecuador, they had to make a dangerous and lonely journey across South America by car and on foot. We had no family in America to welcome us, and my parents had to work illegally in sweatshops for many years. But Lidia's parents joined a large family of uncles, aunts, and cousins, and her parents were able to begin practicing medicine again within a year or two of their arrival.

I have read that the environment you grow up in determines the kind of life you lead. I guess that, based on that evidence, I should have been a mother when I was still a teenager, and shouldn't have gone to college at all. But environment doesn't determine everything, and freedom to choose your own destiny isn't limited because of one or two aspects. Even in poverty, even in prison—even with a damaged brain!—you still have the freedom to choose to work hard and to make the best of your circumstances.

Lidia is always complaining at work. She takes fewer college classes than I do, and only works ten hours at the television station each week (I work 30 hours, sometimes more). Yet she is always late for meetings, loses track of equipment, and doesn't take her work assignments seriously. She assumes that everything will be easy for her, and doesn't realize that that complacency limits the choices she can make about her life. When things go wrong, she makes excuses—her car broke down, or she was out late the night before. She doesn't know how fortunate she is, and she'll never achieve as much as she could.

I believe that freedom is unlimited, and your life is determined by matters of choice. If you choose to give up, to accept less of yourself, then you will forever limit your choices and your freedom. But if you choose to continue, no matter what the obstacles, you will eventually achieve your goals. I may be disappointed in other people, but I have never been disappointed in myself. My family has sacrificed too much for me to come this far, and I will not let them down.

Student Writing

Cynthia Brown's Writing Process

Cynthia Brown's approach to this writing project exhibits those qualities of creativity, open-mindedness, knowledge, and curiosity that are the hallmarks of a critical thinker. Rather than writing about a specific decision, Cynthia reflected on a key factor—time—and how her relationship to time shaped all the major decisions she had made in her life. Cynthia drew on readings from her writing class and notes from her philosophy class to inform her essay.

When I moved to New York, I thought I was going to go insane. As much as I loved the city, I could not bear to live here. However, I came to New York to attend college and decided it would be best to allow myself time to make this decision based on rationale as opposed to emotion. I spent the next two years carefully analyzing and weighing my options. With the passage of time, I have come to the conclusion that I cannot live the kind of life I want to live as a student if I stay in New York. I decided to transfer, upon graduation from my current college, to a small liberal arts college in the middle of nowhere. I used time to help me explore my options instead of feeling trapped within its confines. This allowed me to move through the two years with ease and come to a truly authentic decision regarding my life.

Freedom and the Constraint of Time

by Cynthia Brown

Do I believe that I am free?

The 18th-century French philosopher Baron d'Holbach says that we are drowning in a river, desperately trying to keep our heads above water, sinking, rising, sinking again, until we die. The American writer William James argued that we are free to act, to drag ourselves out of that river of circumstance any time we choose and set our own course. I believe that whatever your personal belief about the nature of your freedom, we are all captured and held by the whims of Time. Time is universal, preceding both existence and essence.

Take, for example, measurement. Everything we know about the material world, everything we experience, is measured by time. Distance, stability, stamina, progress, relationships . . . the list is endless. We run, not a mile, but ten minutes. We travel, not by miles, but by hours. We wait, not with patience but in days. To an imaginary objective observer, an angel or an alien, humans would all seem to be motivated not by internal desires or the pursuit of knowledge, but by the hands of the clock. An alien wouldn't know that you decided to stop speaking with your boyfriend because you had fallen in love with someone else; the alien would notice that the clock on your bedroom wall said 3:37 pm, and could just as easily assume that the time determined your heart's action.

People wear wristwatches, follow the sun across the sky, track the phases of the moon. New technology helps us to process time faster so we don't waste a moment of it. We have cell phones and computers so we can work faster, multitask, move several concepts and relationships through time simultaneously. We are racing time, desperate to control it, bend it to our will. Yet time is a universal law, a rule we must abide by. We might think that we are free to make decisions about our own lives, but whatever we "choose" is ultimately changed, decayed, or unraveled by the passage of time.

When we look into the heavens, we see stars and wonder just how small we are. How long would it take me to travel to the next galaxy, the next universe? Ask a physicist and she will answer you in increments of time: light years. Our imaginations can travel as far into the universe as they may please in the shortest segment time has to give us. We feel we can take a shortcut and go where we please, sometimes inventing new universes where time does not exist. We feel, briefly, ecstatically, that we have beaten time—and then we wake up, or come down, and find ourselves in a place where we are alone and helpless, desperate to come back to the places and people we know.

Suppose we were to look back at our lives and what has shaped us. Wouldn't it be nice to go back and change everything, to disappear without knowledge of our present life and be given a chance to start all over again? Alan Lightman, a renowned physicist, explores this idea in his novel *Einstein's Dreams*. Many of his stories claim that time is an endless cycle, never giving in or relenting to our wishes. Our clocks repeat themselves in a circle. We fall in and out of love, looking back at time spent in our relationships as so much wasted time, hardly daring to allow ourselves to experience the emotion itself. We are simultaneously anticipating the future and regretting the past. We move forward, waiting for time to heal our wounds.

Although we created a calendar to help us move through and keep track of time, it is an endless cycle. Day into night. Hour into hour. The refugee boy from Sudan, lost on the dark North Dakota prairie, asks a friend: "Can you tell me, please, is it now night or day?" We ask Time to be responsible, ignoring our own role in our destiny. While we are thinking of everything that has gone wrong with our lives, Time is passing through us, creating us, owning us. We are creating ourselves in Time. Are we really making our decisions based on our experience and careful analysis, or are we allowing Time to take control and be our guide?

We slip in and out of awareness of time. We wake in the morning fresh from our dreams and instinctively look at the clock. Some mornings we rise and say, "Shit, I'm late for class. My professor is going to be so mad. He wears a watch." And here, we have a choice. Do we go late, or not go at all? Both of these decisions come with consequences. We weigh them as we brush our teeth and pull a sweater over our heads. Is the decision we make truly free, or are we simply responding to the urgency of the ticking clock?

It's possible to leave the technology of clocks and cell phones behind, but just like the Lost Boys of Sudan, we are still instinctively aware of the cycles of the sun. We cannot live without sunlight; we cannot imagine the universe without darkness. Our secrets are kept in the dark, and we reveal ourselves to each other by shining a light on our deepest truths. We are determined to live in light and shadow, and from an early age we are trained to respond to the shifts from day to night and back again.

One of the earliest lessons I remember from preschool was how to tell time (tell it what? I wonder now…). We learned how to read the hands on a clock, and what the numbers on a digital dial meant; we were taught to "be on time," and were punished if we were late. As schoolchildren, responding to bells, we were taught to be driven by forces beyond what we can truly see—only measure (and isn't it ironic that we are not allowed to pray in schools? But that's another argument entirely). Were we learning because we were curious, eating because we were hungry, jumping up from our desks because we couldn't wait to get home? Or were we just responding, like a bunch of trained rats, to the sound of the bell?

And so we wait. We wait for time to tell us what will be and where we will end up next. Whether or not the alarm clock will let us live another day. All of our teachings and still we wait, for something as old as the universe itself, a force that will long outlast any choices or commitments or decisions we make. Time moves forward, carrying us with it whether we ask it to or not. For surely if we exist outside of this concept of time, lock ourselves in a windowless room for what we suspect are minutes, days, or years, we are certain to be driven to madness.

So when I am asked, "Are you free?"

I answer, "Well, I don't wear a wristwatch. Do you?"

Alternative Writing Projects

1. Write an essay in which you analyze a decision that must be made soon by a community or group to which you belong. Describe the circumstances leading up to this decision, and follow through the five steps of the decision-making method discussed in this chapter. When you consider alternate choices and their pros and cons, be sure to include the perspectives of several members of your community who will be affected by this decision.

2. The theme of the wandering pilgrim, or the prodigal son, is found in literature across cultures and time periods. What does it mean to "come home" after a life-changing experience? Is it more difficult to decide to run away, or to decide to come home? Have you had a comparable experience? What led you away? Why did you decide to go home? How did the experience change you?

3. Have you ever talked someone out of what you knew was a bad decision? What were the circumstances of that decision? What was your relationship to the person making the decision? What was the most effective, or surprising, argument that you made to change that person's mind?

CHAPTER 5   Summary

- When you begin to prepare your draft, you should first establish what your purpose for writing is. To determine this, you should ask yourself the following questions:

  - Who is my audience and what are its needs?

  - What is my subject and why is it interesting?

  - Who am I as a writer?

  - What should my working thesis be?

  - What information should I use and what more do I need?

  - When should I start outlining?

  - What should my introduction and conclusion be?

- In making decisions about your life, you should take an informed and strategic approach. Using the following organized steps should prove helpful:

  - Step 1: Define the decision clearly.

  - Step 2: Consider all possible choices.

  - Step 3: Gather all relevant information and evaluate the pros and cons of each possible choice.

  - Step 4: Select the choice that seems best suited to the situation.

  - Step 5: Implement a plan of action and monitor the results, making necessary adjustments.

- After following your decision-making plan through to completion, it is good practice to look back and analyze your decisions. By identifying decisions that aided in your success or failure, you learn important lessons about which strategies may be worth repeating and which should be avoided in the future.

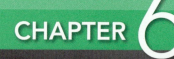
Courtesy of the University of Arizona, Bureau of Applied Research in Anthropology, School of Anthropology

Dr. Emory Sekaquaptewa, an anthropologist in the Bureau of Applied Research in Anthropology of the University of Arizona and chief judge of the Hopi tribe's Appellate Court, is working with a team of linguists and Hopi elders to rediscover and retell the sixteenth-century colonial history of his people. His creative, collaborative approach to history gives indigenous peoples not only a voice but also an active role in the recovery and perpetuation of their culture. What role have stories involving your family or your culture played in creating your own personal sense of history?

Revising: Using Language Thoughtfully

"Only where there is language is there world."

—ADRIENNE RICH

Critical Thinking Focus: Language and power

Writing Focus: Revising language to clarify thinking

Reading Theme: Using language ethically

Writing Project: The impact of language on our lives

Every time we use language and images, we send messages about our thinking and ourselves. When we speak or write, we are not simply making sounds or writing symbols; we are conveying ideas, sharing feelings, and describing experiences. At the same time, language itself shapes and influences thinking. When language use is careless—vague, general, indistinct, imprecise, foolish, inaccurate—it leads to the same sort of thinking. The reverse is also true: clear, precise language leads to clear, precise thinking, speaking, and writing.

The careless or imprecise use of language can be more consequential than a mediocre grade or a boring essay. When you write, you assume an audience; even if your audience is "only" your teacher, you still take on the responsibility of enlightening, entertaining, and truth telling. That assumption of an audience, so fundamental to rhetoric, implies that you are writing from an *ethical* perspective. The word *ethics* comes from the Greek term *ethos,* or "character." What you say, and how you say it, reveals to your audience what kind of person you are.

To write ethically also implies that you have a *responsibility* toward your reader, your subject, and yourself. To be responsible to your reader means that you write clearly, choosing the most appropriate language, constructing a logical argument that your reader can easily follow. To be responsible to your subject requires you to be as truthful as you can, given what you know. If you are writing an argument, it is your responsibility as an ethical writer to present opposing viewpoints fairly and accurately. Finally, you are responsible to your *ethos,* or how you appear in your writing. A carefully written, logically organized, interestingly illustrated essay reveals the presence of a thoughtful, interesting, curious mind.

This chapter explores the ethical implications of language—how it is used on both a personal and a social level to provoke, to haunt, to challenge, and to heal. Activities in this chapter discuss the *revision* part of the writing process, that careful reconsideration of your sources, organization, and word choice before you present your "final" paper to your audience.

Thinking-Writing Activity

LANGUAGE THAT OFFENDS

Has your attention been drawn to the ethical or responsible use of language on your campus or in your workplace? For example, does your campus have a speech code that defines hate speech or otherwise proscribed language? Are there words you are uncomfortable using or hearing in the classroom or the office? Are you uncomfortable with that language because it offends you or because you worry about offending someone?

Recognizing Effective Use of Language

One effective way to develop your ability to use language ethically and responsibly in communicating your thoughts, feelings, and experiences is to read widely. Highly regarded writers use word meanings accurately. They also often use many action verbs, concrete nouns, and vivid adjectives to communicate effectively. Another way to become a more sensitive and responsive writer is by seeking feedback from readers. In this section, you will be using all these strategies.

When thinking about how to use language effectively, we must consider not only our course assignments but also all the other forms of communication in which we participate and the different mediums in which we do so. The same rules do not apply for all types of writing. For instance, as Neal Jansons points out in the following article, writing successfully for new media requires a unique set of criteria.

Language, Thinking, and Learning

The following excerpt from *The Autobiography of Malcolm X* chronicles his discovery of the power of language while he was serving time in prison. Frustrated by not being able to communicate his ideas in writing, he committed himself to mastering the use of words by copying the dictionary. As you read, pay special attention to the way Malcolm X uses language to share his experiences with us. Do you find his personal quest inspiring? Why?

FROM *The Autobiography of Malcolm X*

by Malcolm X with Alex Haley

Born as Malcolm Little in Omaha, Nebraska, the son of an activist Baptist preacher and a mother busy with her eight children, Malcolm X saw racial injustice and violence from a very young age.

Malcolm dropped out of high school after a teacher's contemptuous discouragement of his ambitions to be a lawyer and became involved in criminal activities. After a conviction for burglary in Boston, he was sentenced to prison for ten years. (In the following excerpt from his autobiography, Malcolm X describes how he used this time for reflection and intellectual growth.) Paroled in 1952, Malcolm dropped the name *Little* (which he now referred to as his "slave name") and took up the name *X* to symbolize his lost African heritage.

In 1964, following a period of disappointment and disillusion with Elijah Muhammad, Malcolm X broke with the Nation of Islam, within which he had held a prominent position. Returning to the spiritual roots of his conversion to Islam, he made a hajj, or pilgrimage, to Mecca in Saudi Arabia. The sight of so many Muslims of so many different races and colors was deeply moving to Malcolm X, and upon his return to America he began working toward healing and reconciliation for all Americans of all races.

Unfortunately, the enemies he had made and the fears he had provoked did not leave Malcolm X much time to share this message; three assassins took him down as he spoke at the Audubon Ballroom in Harlem on February 15, 1965.

I became increasingly frustrated at not being able to express what I wanted to convey in letters that I wrote, especially those to Mr. Elijah Muhammad. In the street, I had been the most articulate hustler out there—I had commanded attention when I said something. But now, trying to write simple English, I not only wasn't articulate, I wasn't even functional. How would I sound writing in slang, the way I would *say* it, something such as, "Look, daddy, let me pull your coat about a cat, Elijah Muhammad—"

Many who today hear me somewhere in person, or on television, or those who read something I've said, will think I went to school far beyond the eighth grade. This impression is due entirely to my prison studies.

It had really begun back in the Charlestown Prison, when Bimbi first made me feel envy of his stock of knowledge. Bimbi had always taken charge of any conversation he was in, and I had tried to emulate him. But every book I picked up had few sentences which didn't contain anywhere from one to nearly all of the words that might as well have been in Chinese. When I just skipped those words, of course, I really ended up with little idea of what the book said. So I had come to the Norfolk Prison Colony still going through only book-reading motions. Pretty soon, I would have quit even these motions, unless I had received the motivation that I did.

I saw that the best thing I could do was get hold of a dictionary—to study, to learn some words. I was lucky enough to reason also that I should try to improve my penmanship. It was sad. I couldn't even write in a straight line. It was both ideas together that moved me to request a dictionary along with some tablets and pencils from the Norfolk Prison Colony school.

5

I spent two days just riffling uncertainly through the dictionary's pages. I'd never realized so many words existed! I didn't know *which* words I needed to learn. Finally, just to start some kind of action, I began copying.

In my slow, painstaking, ragged handwriting, I copied into my tablet everything printed on that first page, down to the punctuation marks.

I believe it took me a day. Then, aloud, I read back, to myself, everything I'd written on the tablet. Over and over, aloud, to myself, I read my own handwriting.

I woke up the next morning, thinking about those words—immensely proud to realize that not only had I written so much at one time, but I'd written words that I never knew were in the world. Moreover, with a little effort, I also could remember what many of these words meant. I reviewed the words whose meaning I didn't remember. Funny thing, from the dictionary's first page right now, that "aardvark" springs to my mind. The dictionary had a picture of it, a long-tailed, long-eared, burrowing African mammal, which lives off termites caught by sticking out its tongue as an anteater does for ants.

I was so fascinated that I went on—I copied the dictionary's next page. And the same experience came when I studied that. With every succeeding page, I also learned of people and places and events from history. Actually the dictionary is like a miniature encyclopedia. Finally the dictionary's A section had filled a whole tablet—and I went on into the B's. That was the way I started copying what eventually became the entire dictionary. It went a lot faster after so much practice helped me to pick up handwriting speed. Between what I wrote in my tablet, and writing letters, during the rest of my time in prison I would guess I wrote a million words.

10

I suppose it was inevitable that as my word-base broadened, I could for the first time pick up a book and read and now begin to understand what the book was saying. Anyone who has read a great deal can imagine the new world that opened. Let me tell you something: from then until I left the prison, in every free moment I had, if I was not reading in the library, I was reading on my bunk. You couldn't have gotten me out of books with a wedge. Between Mr. Muhammad's teachings, my correspondence, my visitors—usually Ella and Reginald—and my reading of books, months passed without my even thinking about being imprisoned. In fact, up to then, I never had been so truly free in my life.

The Norfolk Prison Colony's library was in the school building. A variety of classes was taught there by instructors who came from such places as Harvard and Boston universities. The weekly debates between inmate teams were also held in the school building. You would be astonished to know how worked up convict debaters and audiences would get over subjects like "Should Babies Be Fed Milk?"

Available on the prison library's shelves were books on just about every general subject. Much of the big private collection that Parkhurst had willed to the prison was still in crates and boxes in the back of the library—thousands of old books. Some of them looked ancient: covers faded, old-time parchment-looking binding. Parkhurst, I've mentioned, seemed to have been principally interested in history and religion. He had the money and the special interest to have a lot of books that you wouldn't have in general circulation. Any college library would have been lucky to get that collection.

As you can imagine, especially in a prison where there was heavy emphasis on rehabilitation, an inmate was smiled upon if he demonstrated an unusually intense interest in books. There was a sizable number of well-read inmates, especially the popular debaters. Some were said by many to be practically walking encyclopedias. They were almost celebrities. No university would ask any student to devour literature as I did when this new world opened to me, of being able to read and *understand.*

I read more in my room than in the library itself. An inmate who was known to read a lot could check out more than the permitted maximum number of books. I preferred reading in the total isolation of my own room.

15   When I had progressed to really serious reading, every night at about ten (P.M.) I would be outraged with the "lights out." It always seemed to catch me right in the middle of something engrossing.

Fortunately, right outside my door was a corridor light that cast a glow into my room. The glow was enough to read by, once my eyes adjusted to it. So when "lights out" came, I would sit on the floor where I could continue reading in that glow.

At one-hour intervals the night guards paced past every room. Each time I heard the approaching footsteps, I jumped into bed and feigned sleep. And as soon as the guard passed, I got back out of bed onto the floor area of that light-glow, where I would read for another fifty-eight minutes—until the guard approached again. That went on until three or four every morning. Three or four hours of sleep a night was enough for me. Often in the years in the streets I had slept less than that.

Questions for Reading Actively

1. For whom is Malcolm X writing, and what is his purpose? (In fact, if you read closely, you might detect more than one assumed audience, and many layers of purpose.) What language does he use and what images does he create to appeal to a specific audience?

2. Malcolm X uses contrast throughout this excerpt—especially the contrast between what his audience might *expect,* and what actually *occurs.* These contrasts are occasionally humorous, and often moving. Find three examples of these contrasts in this excerpt, and explain what makes them effective.

Questions for Thinking Critically

1. Malcolm X envied one of the other inmates, Bimbi, because his stock of knowledge enabled him to take charge of any conversation he was in. Explain why knowledge—and our ability to use it—leads to power in our dealings with others. Describe a situation from your own experience in which having expert knowledge about a subject enabled you, through writing, to influence the thinking of other people.

2. About pursuing his mastery of language and exploring books, Malcolm X states, "Up to then, I never had been so truly free in my life." Explain what you think he means by this statement. Then describe a time in your life when you felt "truly free."

Questions for Writing Thoughtfully

1. How does Malcolm X organize this excerpt from his autobiography? Why is this method of organization particularly effective? Create a simile to describe this organization strategy (for example, "it's like a light going on," or "it's like a tree putting out leaves after a long winter").

2. Malcolm X states that, although he was an articulate "street hustler," this ability was of little help in expressing his ideas in writing. Explain the differences between expressing your ideas orally and in writing, including the advantages and disadvantages of each form of language expression.

Making Decisions When Revising Drafts

Revision is the key to producing your best possible work. It is very rare for a first draft to represent the most effective writing of which a person is capable. Most accomplished writers expect their work to undergo a number of revisions based on their own reevaluation and on feedback from others. The difference between outstanding and mediocre writing often depends on revision.

Many of the concepts in the five-step decision-making approach discussed in Chapter 5 can be applied to revising your drafts.

- You *define the decision and your goals* by identifying what in a draft needs to be revised and what should be left as it is.

- You *consider possible choices* for improving a draft, especially with major components such as composing and placing the thesis statement, presenting evidence, and arranging material in sequences, sections, or paragraphs. You also often have various choices among words and sentence patterns when you work at the editing level of revision.

- You *gather relevant information* and *evaluate the pros and cons* of the different choices in order to select the one that best meets the needs of the writing situation. Sometimes you may want to write down the different possibilities; in other instances, you may just try them out in your mind.

- After *implementing* your choices by revising a draft, you *evaluate* your writing by *reading it again*, slowly and completely, to be sure that the whole piece is as good as you can make it.

 Collaborating with classmates or other trusted readers in all these decisions will usually be very helpful. Other readers can see your drafts more objectively and can help you "re-see" and revise them.

Specific Decisions to Make at Several Levels

The following suggestions should help you revise your drafts.

Read your entire draft slowly and carefully. You may find, as many writers do, that reading out loud helps you to identify parts that don't "sound" right. Also, ask someone whose judgment you trust to read the draft and help you to decide what improvement is needed. If your class allows peer review either in person or online, be prepared for this opportunity by having a draft ready.

The next step is to determine at what level you should begin to make changes. Revision means much more than correcting grammar, punctuation, and spelling. In fact, those corrections are often made separately, as editing and proofreading, to distinguish them from larger aspects of revision.

A helpful way to decide where to begin revising is to move through the following hierarchy of questions about your draft. If you find yourself answering any of the questions in a manner that suggests ways to improve your writing, stop and try to make the changes or additions to your draft before you move on to the next level. There is no point in worrying about punctuation if your draft lacks focus or good examples.

However, remember that revision, like all steps of the writing process, is recursive. You may detect content, organization, or wording problems while you are checking punctuation; you may fix a typo while you're rewording the thesis statement. The following hierarchy emphasizes the importance of looking first at major concerns, but you should be prepared to move around among the levels of revision as you make your decisions about a draft.

A Step-by-Step Method for Revising Any Assignment

The following method can be used both for revising your own papers and for reviewing your classmates' papers. It can be applied to any assignment. For easy reference as you move through the assignments in this book and those for other courses, an edited version of this method is reprinted on the inside back cover of this text. Refer to this method as you reach the Revising section of each Writing Project in the following chapters.

1. **Think big.** Look at the draft as a whole.
   - ❑ Does it fulfill the assignment's purpose in terms of topic and length?
   - ❑ Does it have a clear focus?
   - ❑ What parts of the draft, if any, do not relate to its focus?
   - ❑ How could the draft be reorganized to make it more logical for your audience?
   - ❑ What evidence could be added to help to accomplish your purpose?

❏ How could the flow between paragraphs be made smoother?

❏ Is your point of view about your subject consistent throughout?

❏ Develop alternatives based on the answers to these questions, decide which alternatives will improve your draft, and then make changes to your draft before proceeding to the next level of revision.

2. **Think medium.** Look at the draft paragraph by paragraph. First consider the *introduction*.

❏ How could you rewrite your lead to make your audience more interested in continuing to read? (See the suggestions for being creative with introductions in Chapter 5.)

❏ Can you make the tone of the introduction match the tone of the rest of the draft?

❏ How could you more effectively indicate your purpose for writing?

Then look at each of your *body paragraphs*.

❏ Does each support the thesis or claim?

❏ Does each present relevant, specific evidence about the subject not presented elsewhere?

❏ Which, if any, body paragraphs should be combined or eliminated?

❏ Have you chosen or created useful and interesting visuals?

❏ Which body paragraphs use topic sentences effectively? Which don't?

❏ Where could you use transitions to improve the flow within or between body paragraphs?

Now look at your *conclusion*. This is your last opportunity to accomplish your purpose with your intended audience.

❏ How could you make your conclusion more effective? (See the suggestions for being creative with conclusions in Chapter 5.)

❏ Does the tone of the conclusion match your overall tone?

Again, develop alternatives and make changes to your draft before proceeding to the next level.

3. **Think small.** Look at the draft sentence by sentence.

❏ Which sentences are difficult to understand? How could you reword them?

❏ Which, if any, sentences are so long that your audience could get lost in them?

❏ Where are there short, choppy sentences that can be combined?

❏ Which sentences seem vague? How could you clarify them?

❏ Which, if any, sentences have errors in standard English grammar or usage? How could you correct them?

Make necessary changes to your draft before proceeding to the next level.

4. **Think "picky."** Look at the draft as the fussiest critic might.

❏ Which words are not clear or not quite right for your meaning? What words could you use instead?

❏ Are any words spelled incorrectly? (Run the spell-checker program on your computer, but don't rely on it alone.)

❏ Are the pages numbered consecutively?

❏ Does the physical appearance of your draft meet the assignment's requirements for format?

❏ Is there anything else you can do to improve your draft?

Thinking-Writing Activity

USING THE REVISION METHOD

Apply each step of the revision method to an essay you have written for this course (your instructor will advise you about which one to select). Although this process may initially seem time-consuming and rather mechanical, you will soon begin to integrate these ideas in a more natural and flexible way. As you become more experienced as a writer, the revision method will eventually become an integral part of your writing process.

Beyond considering your own earlier experiences, you can deepen your understanding of revision by reading the following selection by an expert writer.

"The Maker's Eye: Revising Your Own Manuscripts"

by Donald M. Murray

Known as both a professional journalist and a brilliant teacher, Donald M. Murray won the Pulitzer Prize for his editorials in the *Boston Herald* in 1954. Since then, he has taught writing at the University of New Hampshire and Boston University and is now a columnist for *The Boston Globe*. He has acted as a writing coach for several national newspapers and written poetry for many journals. Now in retirement, he published his memoir, *My Twice-Lived Life,* in 2001.

Source: "The Maker's Eye: Revising Your Own Manuscripts." THE WRITER, 1973. Copyright 1973 by Donald M. Murray. Reprinted by permission of The Rosenberg Group on behalf of the author's estate.

Murray has also authored several books on the craft of writing and teaching writing, including *Learning by Teaching, Expecting the Unexpected,* and *Crafting a Life in Essay, Story, Poem*. His work has been highly influential in the way writing is taught. In this selection, he describes his own revision process, one that has served him well.

When students complete a first draft, they consider the job of writing done—and their teachers too often agree. When professional writers complete a first draft, they usually feel that they are at the start of the writing process. When a draft is completed, the job of writing can begin.

That difference in attitude is the difference between amateur and professional, inexperience and experience, journeyman and craftsman. Peter F. Drucker, the prolific business writer, calls his first draft "the zero draft"—after that he can start counting. Most writers share the feeling that the first draft, and all of those which follow, are opportunities to discover what they have to say and how best they can say it.

To produce a progression of drafts, each of which says more and says it more clearly, the writer has to develop a special kind of reading skill. In school we are taught to decode what appears on the page as finished writing. Writers, however, face a different category of possibility and responsibility when they read their own drafts. To them the words on the page are never finished. Each can be changed and rearranged, can set off a chain reaction of confusion or clarified meaning. This is a different kind of reading, which is possibly more difficult and certainly more exciting.

Writers must learn to be their own best enemy. They must accept the criticism of others and be suspicious of it; they must accept the praise of others and be even more suspicious of it. Writers cannot depend on others. They must detach themselves from their own pages so that they can apply both their caring and their craft to their own work.

5   Such detachment is not easy. Science fiction writer Ray Bradbury supposedly puts each manuscript away for a year to the day and then rereads it as a stranger. Not many writers have the discipline or the time to do this. We must read when our judgment may be at its worst, when we are close to the euphoric moment of creation.

Then the writer, counsels novelist Nancy Hale, "should be critical of everything that seems to him most delightful in his style. He should excise what he most admires, because he wouldn't thus admire it if he weren't . . . in a sense protecting it from criticism." John Ciardi, the poet, adds, "The last act of writing must be to become one's own reader. It is, I suppose, a schizophrenic process, to begin passionately and to end critically, to begin hot and to end cold; and, more important, to be passion-hot and critic-cold at the same time."

Most people think that the principal problem is that writers are too proud of what they have written. Actually, a greater problem for most professional writers is one shared by the majority of students. They are overly critical, think everything is dreadful, tear up page after page, never complete a draft, see the task as hopeless.

The writer must learn to read critically but constructively, to cut what is bad, to reveal what is good. Eleanor Estes, the children's book author, explains: "The writer must survey his work critically, coolly, as though he were a stranger to it. He must be willing to prune, expertly and hard-heartedly. At the end of each revision, a manuscript may look . . . worked over, torn apart, pinned together, added to, deleted from, words changed and words changed back. Yet the book must maintain its original freshness and spontaneity."

Most readers underestimate the amount of rewriting it usually takes to produce spontaneous reading. This is a great disadvantage to the student writer, who sees only a finished product and never watches the craftsman who takes the necessary steps back, studies the work carefully, returns to the task, steps back, returns, steps back, again and again. Anthony Burgess, one of the most prolific writers in the English-speaking world, admits, "I might revise a page twenty times." Roald Dahl, the popular children's writer, states, "By the time I'm nearing the end of a story, the first part will have been reread and altered and corrected at least 150 times. . . . Good writing is essentially rewriting. I am positive of this."

10   Rewriting isn't virtuous. It isn't something that ought to be done. It is simply something that most writers find they *have* to do to discover what they have to say and how to say it. It is a condition of the writer's life.

There are, however, a few writers who do little formal rewriting, primarily because they have the capacity and experience to create and review a large number of invisible drafts in their minds before they approach the page. And some writers slowly produce finished pages, performing all the tasks of revision simultaneously, page by page, rather than draft by draft. But it is still possible to see the sequence followed by most writers most of the time in rereading their own work.

Most writers scan their drafts first, reading as quickly as possible to catch the larger problems of subject and form, then move in closer and closer as they read and write, reread and rewrite.

The first thing writers look for in their drafts is *information*. They know that a good piece of writing is built from specific, accurate, and interesting information. The writer must have an abundance of information from which to construct a readable piece of writing.

Next, writers look for meaning in the information. The specifics must build a pattern of significance. Each piece of specific information must carry the reader toward meaning.

15   Writers reading their own drafts are aware of *audience*. They put themselves in the reader's situation and make sure that they deliver information which a reader wants to know or needs to know in a manner which is easily digested. Writers try to be sure that they anticipate and answer the questions a critical reader will ask when reading the piece of writing.

Writers make sure that the *form* is appropriate to the subject and the audience. Form, or genre, is the vehicle which carries meaning to the reader, but form cannot be selected until the writer has adequate information to discover its significance and an audience which needs or wants that meaning.

Once writers are sure the form is appropriate, they must then look at the *structure*, the order of what they have written. Good writing is built on a solid framework of logic, argument, narrative, or motivation which runs through the entire piece of writing and holds it together. This is the time when many writers find it most effective to outline as a way of visualizing the hidden spine by which the piece of writing is supported.

The element on which writers may spend a majority of their time is *development*. Each section of a piece of writing must be adequately developed. It must give readers enough information so that they are satisfied. How much information is enough? That's as difficult as asking how much garlic belongs in a salad. It must be done to taste, but most beginning writers underdevelop, underestimating the reader's hunger for information.

As writers solve development problems, they often have to consider questions of *dimension*. There must be a pleasing and effective proportion among all the parts of the piece of writing. There is a continual process of subtracting and adding to keep the piece of writing in balance.

20   Finally, writers have to listen to their own voices. *Voice* is the force which drives a piece of writing forward. It is an expression of the writer's authority and concern. It is what is between the words on the page, what glues the piece of writing together. A good piece of writing is always marked by a consistent, individual voice.

As writers read and reread, write and rewrite, they move closer and closer to the page until they are doing line-by-line editing. Writers read their own pages with infinite care. Each sentence, each line, each clause, each phrase, each word, each mark of punctuation, each section of white space between the type has to contribute to the clarification of meaning.

Slowly the writer moves from word to word, looking through language to see the subject. As a word is changed, cut, or added, as a construction is rearranged, all the words used before that moment and all those that follow that moment must be considered and reconsidered.

Writers often read aloud at this stage of the editing process, muttering or whispering to themselves, calling on the ear's experience with language. Does this sound right—or that? Writers edit, shifting back and forth from eye to page to ear to page. I find I must do this careful editing in short runs, no more than fifteen or twenty minutes at a stretch, or I become too kind with myself. I begin to see what I hope is on the page, not what actually is on the page.

This sounds tedious if you haven't done it, but actually it is fun. Making something right is immensely satisfying, for writers begin to learn what they are writing about by writing. Language leads them to meaning, and there is the joy of discovery, of understanding, of making meaning clear as the writer employs the technical skills of language.

25   Words have double meanings, even triple and quadruple meanings. Each word has its own potential for connotation and denotation. And when writers rub one word against the other, they are often rewarded with a sudden insight, an unexpected clarification.

The maker's eye moves back and forth from word to phrase to sentence to paragraph to sentence to phrase to word. The maker's eye sees the need for variety and balance, for a firmer structure, for a more appropriate form. It peers into the interior of the paragraph, looking for coherence, unity, and emphasis, which make meaning clear.

I learned something about this process when my first bifocals were prescribed. I had ordered a large section of the reading portion of the glass because of my work, but even so, I could not contain my eyes within this new limit of vision. And I still find myself taking off my glasses and bending my nose towards the page, for my eyes unconsciously flick back and forth across the page, back to another page, forward to still another, as I try to see each evolving line in relation to every other line.

When does this process end? Most writers agree with the great Russian writer Tolstoy, who said, "I scarcely ever reread my published writings, if by chance I come across a page, it always strikes me: all this must be rewritten; this is how I should have written it."

The maker's eye is never satisfied, for each word has the potential to ignite new meaning. This article has been twice written all the way through the writing process, and it was published four years ago. Now it is to be republished in a book. The editors make a few small suggestions, and then I read it with my maker's eye. Now it has been re-edited, re-vised, re-read, re-re-edited, for each piece of writing to the writer is full of potential and alternatives.

30   A piece of writing is never finished. It is delivered to a deadline, torn out of the typewriter on demand, sent off with a sense of accomplishment and shame and pride and frustration. If only there were a couple more days, time for just another run at it, perhaps then . . .

Questions for Reading Actively

1. Murray quotes several authors in his essay, identifying each with a short phrase. Does that additional information influence how you read that quote and "listen" to its speaker? In what way?

2. Reread that same essay aloud to yourself and see if your "ear's experience with language" suggests any additional changes.

Questions for Thinking Critically

1. Murray begins by contrasting the "student" and the "professional" writer. How do you, as a member of his audience, feel about your place in this comparison?

2. Compare the kind of writing that Murray is discussing to the writing that Malcolm X describes. How might Malcolm X interpret Murray's idea that "the words on the page are never finished"?

3. How does Murray establish his authority as a writer? Are you satisfied that he is someone whose advice you should follow? Why or why not?

Question for Writing Thoughtfully

1. Murray identifies elements for writers to examine when critically reading their drafts: information, audience, form, structure, development, dimension, and voice. Reread any essay you have written for this course, paying attention to each of these elements. How would you revise the essay further to better express your meaning?

Donald Murray discusses (paragraph 15) the importance of *audience* to writers and the revision process. It's evident from the last paragraph of his essay, however, that he is describing a revision process that is paper-based. Today's writers and professionals alike are far more likely to perform almost every step of the writing process on the computer. You are also probably very comfortable with going online, chatting with friends, looking up information, downloading music, and watching video *while* you are writing—and all at the same computer!

Just as you have access to an infinitely larger range of information and resources than scholars did even in the late twentieth century, your potential audience is likely to be not just local but also global. In the following article, journalist Mary Blume describes the impact of globalization on language. If you are to use language ethically and responsibly, you will need to learn to *listen*—to be attentive to the ways in which people from very different backgrounds and perspectives make efforts to communicate, to negotiate, and to share information.

"If You Can't Master English, Try Globish"

by Mary Blume

Essayist and reporter Mary Blume has lived in Paris since 1960 and covered the Paris beat for the *International Herald Tribune* for more than thirty years. Her books include *A French Affair: The Paris Beat 1965–1998* (1999) and *Cote d'Azur: Inventing the French Riviera* (1994). The *International Herald Tribune,* owned by the *New York Times,* is an English-language daily newspaper published internationally, with special focus on global affairs.

It happens all the time: during an airport delay the man to the left, a Korean perhaps, starts talking to the man opposite, who might be Colombian, and soon they are chatting away in what seems to be English. But the native English speaker sitting between them cannot understand a word.

They don't know it, but the Korean and the Colombian are speaking Globish, the latest addition to the 6,800 languages that are said to be spoken across the world. Not that its inventor, Jean-Paul Nerrière, considers it a proper language.

"It is not a language; it is a tool," he says. "A language is the vehicle of a culture. Globish doesn't want to be that at all. It is a means of communication."

Nerrière doesn't see Globish in the same light as utopian efforts such as Kosmos, Volapuk, Novial or staunch Esperanto. Nor should it be confused with barbaric Algol (for Algorithmic language). It is a sort of English lite: a means of simplifying the language and giving it rules so it can be understood by all.

5   "The language spoken worldwide, by 88 percent of mankind, is not exactly English," Nerrière says. "I don't think people who think this gives them an edge are right because it's not useful if they cannot be understood by English speakers." His primer, Parlez Globish, is an attempt to codify worldspeak and since its publication by Eyrolles in Paris last year, he says, his Web site www.jpn-globish.com has had almost 36,000 hits.

Source: "If You Can't Master English, Try Globish," by Mary Blume, *International Herald Tribune* Online, April 22, 2005. Copyright © 2006, I.H.T./iht.com. Reprinted by permission.

A retired IBM marketing executive, Nerrière speaks excellent English but switches to Globish if he is not getting through. "I look at their faces. Lack of understanding is very easy to decipher."

The main principles of Globish are a vocabulary of only 1,500 words in English (the OED lists 615,000), gestures and repetition. Grammar will be dealt with in the next volume, "Découvrez le Globish," due next month.

The Web site also includes song lyrics because Nerrière reckons this is an excellent way to learn words, even if they are not on the Globish 1,500. "Strangers in the Night" is one choice, but what is the student to do when Sinatra goes "scoobie-doobie-do"?

"Doesn't matter," Nerrière replies buoyantly. "I saw 'A Chorus Line' three or four times on Broadway and I know all the songs by heart. I never understood the line 'If Troy Donahue can be a movie star, you can be a movie star,' but I managed to reproduce it well enough in a way [that] it could be understood."

10 The point, he says, is to reach the threshold of understanding. But neither threshold nor understanding is on the 1,500-word list. "In Globish it would be the target, the goal, the objective. I use three words to reach the point where you would be understood everywhere."

The list goes from *able* to *zero*. *Niece* and *nephew*, for example, are not included, "but you can replace them with *the children of my brother*," Nerrière says. He feels he erred in putting in both *beauty* and *beautiful* and in including *much* and *many* but not *lot*.

"*Much* is for ideas; *many* is for things you can count. *A lot* works for both cases; the others require a little more understanding."

The seeds for Globish came about in the 1980s when Nerrière was working for IBM in Paris with colleagues of about forty nationalities. At a meeting where they were to be addressed by two Americans whose flight had been delayed, they started exchanging shoptalk in what Nerrière calls "une certaine forme d'anglais perverti." Then the Americans arrived and beyond their opening phrases, "Call me Jim," "Call me Bill," no one understood a word. And Jim and Bill, needless to say, did not understand perverted English.

One might say that, except for Jim and Bill of course, everyone was speaking Globish though they didn't know it. "They all, like me, spoke low-quality English, not really Globish. One might have a vocabulary of 2,000 words, another of 1,200 and not the same words. One of the things of interest in Globish is that with 1,500 words you can express everything. People all over the world will speak with the same limited vocabulary."

15 With many corporations imposing English as the lingua franca wherever their base, Nerrière sees a great future for Globish, which he has trademarked. Learning it by computer and practicing it by free-access telephone will make things even easier. And there is a new law in France that gives employees the right to twenty hours per year of instruction in a given subject.

"The idea is to increase their employability by teaching them skills unrelated to their present employment. For me, the odds of someone asking for a course in macramé are very small and the odds of asking for a course in Maltese are also small. Why not Globish? If it could be of use in this small grocery shop where I work, maybe it will help me in the big hotel where I hope to be."

There is another advantage, he argues. "At twenty hours a year you need twenty-four years to learn English with no result whatsoever since it would be spread too thin for the learner to remember what had been said two weeks earlier. With Globish you not only have free telephone access via the Internet, but you could get cheap lessons in places like India, where people speak good English and wages are low."

Nerrière reckons that with 182 hours plus learning "Strangers in the Night," the student should be able to communicate in Globish. It is not a pretty language—full of redundancies and lumpy constructions—but Nerrière repeats that it is nothing but a tool when proper English is not understood. "It is not the language of Hamlet, Faulkner or Virginia Woolf," he explains.

But the worst thing for the French about this international language is that it isn't French. Nerrière argues rather subtly that if people learned Globish, the French language would remain unsullied because franglais would die out.

20   "It would end this crazy French terror about English and francophonie. The French say you are killing the French language, and I say, no, we are saving it from being killed by English."

There is one possible hiccup in this scheme. The fluent Globish speaker will not be understood by native English speakers. No problem: Nerrière already is preparing a Globish version in English in addition to the Italian and Spanish editions, which will be out shortly. So he is not only protecting French from invasion, but he is getting Americans to become, so to speak, bilingual.

"Absolutely!" Nerrière says triumphantly. "This is the way to get Americans to learn another language."

Questions for Reading Actively

1. Given what you know about the *International Herald Tribune*, what can you assume about the audience for this article? Why would the subject of this article be interesting and relevant to that audience?

2. How does Jean-Paul Nerrière define *language*? How does he define *Globish*? What is the distinction between these two definitions, in Nerrière's view?

3. Do you think that Nerrière's plan to "get Americans to learn another language" could be successful? Consider your own experience learning (or not learning) another language in school as you form your response.

Question for Thinking Critically

1. What is the purpose of Globish? At the library, locate George Orwell's essay "Politics and the English Language" or his novel *1984*. How might Orwell interpret the purpose and necessity of Globish?

Questions for Writing Thoughtfully

1. The Writing Project in Chapter 8 (page 227) asks you to define a concept that is important to your life right now. Following the steps of this Writing Project, write an essay in which you define the concept of *language* within the context of your own academic, professional, or personal goals.

2. In paragraph 14, Nerrière suggests that Globish allows people to express all kinds of ideas while using a very limited vocabulary. What is the most recent new concept, term, or phrase that you have added to your vocabulary? In a brief narrative essay, describe how you first encountered this addition to your vocabulary and how knowing this term impacts some aspects of your life.

Using Language Ethically

Language reflects thinking, and thinking is shaped by language. Language not only provides multiple ways of expressing the same ideas, thoughts, and feelings but also helps to structure those thoughts. In turn, patterns of thinking breathe life into language.

The relationship between thinking and language is *interactive;* both processes are continually influencing each other in many ways. The interactive qualities of language also extend to its communicative purpose. We use language to persuade, to entertain, to inform, and to delight; yet we also know that language can be used to conceal the truth, to foment hatred, to create terror. As a critical thinker, it is your ethical responsibility to continually evaluate the quality and reliability of what you communicate to others through text, visuals, and speech. Malcolm X recognized, at a personal level, how powerful language can be; later in this chapter, Daniel Pipes explains how language, used for unethical purposes, can cause tremendous damage.

When language use is sloppy—vague, general, indistinct, imprecise, foolish, inaccurate, and so on—it leads to the same sort of thinking. And the reverse is also true. Clear and precise language leads to clear and precise thinking, as shown in Figure 6.1. The opposite of clear, effective language is language that fails to help the reader picture or understand what the writer means because it is vague or ambiguous.

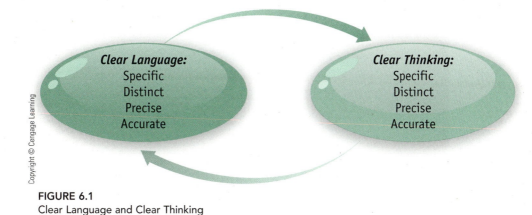

Copyright © Cengage Learning

FIGURE 6.1
Clear Language and Clear Thinking

Improving Vague Language

Although our ability to name and identify gives us the power to describe the world in a precise way, we often tend to describe it in words that are imprecise and general. Such nonspecific words are termed *vague* words. Consider the following sentences:

- I had a *nice* time yesterday.
- That is an *interesting* book.
- She is an *old* person.

In each of these cases, the italicized word does not provide a precise description of the thought, feeling, or experience that the writer or speaker is trying to communicate. Vagueness occurs whenever a word is used to represent an area of experience without clearly defining it. A *vague word* is one that lacks a clear and distinct meaning.

Although the vagueness of general measurement terms can lead to confusion, other forms of vagueness are more widespread and often more problematic. Terms such as *good* and *enjoyable,* for example, are imprecise and unclear. Vagueness of this sort permeates every level of human discourse, undermines clear thinking, and is extremely difficult to combat. To use language clearly and precisely, you must develop an understanding of the way language functions and commit yourself to breaking the entrenched habit of using vague expression.

Thinking-Writing Activity

VAGUE LANGUAGE

Most words of general measurement—short, tall, big, small, heavy, light, and so on—are vague. The exact meanings of these words depend on the specific situation in which they are used and on the particular perspective of the person using them. For example, give specific definitions for the following italicized words by filling in the blanks. Then compare your responses with those of your classmates. Can you account for the differences in meaning?

1. A *middle-aged* person is one who is _____ years old.
2. A *tall* person is one who is over _____ feet _____ inches tall.
3. It's *cold* when the temperature is _____ degrees.
4. A person is *wealthy* when he or she is worth _____ dollars.

Vagueness is always a matter of degree. In fact, you can think of your descriptive/informative use of language as falling somewhere on a scale between extreme generality and extreme specificity. The following statements move from the general to the specific.

General

| She is really smart.
| She does well in school.
| She gets straight A's.
↓ She earned an A1 in physics.

Specific

Although different situations require various degrees of specificity, you should work to become increasingly more precise in your use of language.

When you are revising your own work, try to recognize and improve vague language, remembering your obligation to your audience to be as clear as possible. Be on the lookout for vague words such as *nice, good, fine, interesting, well, special, bad, really, very, old, young, situation,* and so on. Resist the temptation to improve vague words by putting *very* or *really* in front of them. Instead, if you have written, "The dessert was good," ask yourself, "How or why was it good?" Then substitute your answer for the vague word: "The dessert was full of fresh, plump strawberries flavored with orange juice and bits of mint." Now your audience can enjoy it with you!

Using Figurative Language

Thus far in this section, we have been concerned with saying and writing exactly what we mean as precisely as possible. However, there is another way to use language to express thinking: to say something we do not literally mean. Of course, there are some writing situations for which figurative language is inappropriate. When in doubt, check with your instructor. But when we do use figurative language effectively, our readers or listeners understand that we are not speaking literally but rather that we are speaking figuratively, using a figure of speech. Here we will focus on two figures of speech that may already be familiar: *simile* and *metaphor*.

Both simile and metaphor are based on a special kind of comparative thinking called an analogy, which is a limited comparison of two essentially unlike things for the purpose of illuminating or enriching our understanding. Analogies differ from the more common comparisons that examine the similarities and differences of two items in the same general category, such as two items on a menu or two methods of learning a language. Similes and metaphors focus on unexpected likenesses between items from different categories. Thus, when we compare a baby's skin to velvet, we may be calling attention to the skin's color or softness, but we are not suggesting that it makes a nice jacket or can be dyed different colors.

Consider the following example:

Life's but a walking shadow, a poor player
That struts and frets his hour upon the stage,
And then is heard no more . . .
                              —Shakespeare, *Macbeth*

In this famous metaphor, Shakespeare is comparing two things that at first seem to have nothing in common: life and an actor. Yet a closer look reveals that even though they are dissimilar in many ways, they share some undeniable similarities.

It is simple to distinguish similes from metaphors. Similes are explicitly stated comparisons that include the words *as, like,* or *than.* For example, "To the goalie, Mia Hamm's shot appeared as a photon of light." On the other hand, metaphors are implicitly stated comparisons, usually using some part of the verb *to be,* and do not include the words *as, like,* or *than.* Thus, it would be a metaphor to say, "To the goalie, Mia Hamm's shot was a photon of light."

NEW MEDIA & THOUGHTFUL WRITING

New Media Metaphors for Our World

The advent of new media has given us a large number of new concepts that we can use as metaphors to better understand our world. For example, in the article in Chapter 10, "Playing God in the Garden," Michael Pollan describes how biotech companies describe the process of genetically engineering plants as giving the plants a new "software." And this is exactly how these companies want us to view the process of changing the DNA of the plant through genetic modification: simply inserting new "software" into the plant. But others argue that plants are not computers, they are alive, and changing them has implications for the environment—and for our health—that we don't fully understand. A better metaphor, they contend, is viewing the plant as an integral part of an "ecosystem."

Thinking-Writing Activity

Identify five concepts from new media: hardware, wired, twittering, tagging, etc.—and then explain how they are or might be used as metaphors to shape and understand our world.

When should you use figurative language in your writing? Extensive reading will help you develop a feel for opportunities, but here are four suggestions:

- **When you have trouble finding the right words.** Powerful or complex emotions can make you speechless or make you say things like "Words cannot express what I feel." For example, if you are trying to describe your feelings of love for someone, you might write, "As breathtaking as the first rose in spring, this is the first great love of my life," or "Like the fragile yet supple petals of the rose, my feelings are tender and sensitive."

- **When you want to express a profound thought in a strikingly original way.** For example, you want to express an idea about the meaning of life, which the simple word *life* does not convey. Shakespeare wrote, "(Life) is a tale/ Told by an idiot, full of sound and fury,/ Signifying nothing." Forrest Gump said, "Life is like a box of chocolates." You might write, "Life is a football game," or "Life is an earthquake."

- **When you want to add an extra dimension to a description.** The scientist Alan Lightman recalls that he "would save [his] math problems for last, right before bedtime, like bites of chocolate cake awaiting [him] after a long and dutiful meal of history and Latin." You might write, "The spilled flour settled all over the apartment like a soft snow."

- **When you want to amuse your audience.** The great pool hustler Minnesota Fats wrote, "A pool player in a tuxedo is like a hotdog with whipped cream on it." By putting together two things that don't go together, like hotdogs and whipped cream, Minnesota Fats made his audience smile. You might write, "My twin brothers get along like ice cream and sauerkraut."

Thinking-Writing Activity

CREATING SIMILES AND METAPHORS

1. Use your creative thinking skills to create a simile for a subject of your own choosing, noting at least two points of comparison.

2. Now use your creative thinking skills to create a metaphor (implied analogy) for a subject of your own choosing, noting at least two points of comparison.

3. Create a metaphor for life that represents your feelings and explain the points of similarity.

Figurative language that has become cliché is not effective. "He runs like a deer" and "I slept like a baby" were wonderful similes the first time they were used, but they have become old and tired: clichés. Use your creative thinking skills to write original, striking figures of speech.

Very skillful speakers and writers are able to weave similes and metaphors together into a striking tapestry. As you read the following selection by Martin Luther King Jr., notice how he uses figurative language effectively while being clear and precise about both the problem and the solution.

"I Have a Dream"

by Martin Luther King Jr.

The son of an influential Baptist minister, Martin Luther King Jr. began his involvement with the civil rights movement in 1955, when as a Baptist minister in Montgomery, Alabama, he led the Montgomery bus boycott after Rosa Parks, an African-American woman, heroically refused to give up her seat at the front of a public bus.

Greatly influenced by the nonviolent resistance of Mohandas K. Ghandi, King advocated an approach to protesting injustice that continues to resonate in progressive movements worldwide. Through education and outreach, marches, silent sit-ins at segregated lunch counters, and other acts of nonviolent resistance, King and his followers consistently met acts of barbarism with gestures of peace. He was awarded the Nobel Peace Prize in 1964.

And yet the violence he so peacefully—but forcefully—resisted eventually claimed him (as it did Ghandi). Dr. King was assassinated while standing on the balcony of the Lorraine Motel in Memphis, Tennessee, on April 4, 1968.

The speech that follows was delivered during the great March on Washington in 1963. That peaceful march and demonstration for human rights remains one of the most indelible images of twentieth-century American culture.

Five score years ago, a great American, in whose symbolic shadow we stand, signed the Emancipation Proclamation. This momentous decree came as a great beacon light of hope to millions of Negro slaves who had been seared in the flames of withering injustice. It came as a joyous daybreak to end the long night of captivity.

But one hundred years later, we must face the tragic fact that the Negro is still not free. One hundred years later, the life of the Negro is still sadly crippled by the manacles of segregation and the chains of discrimination. One hundred years later, the Negro lives on a lonely island of poverty in the midst of a vast ocean of material prosperity. One hundred years later, the Negro is still languishing in the corners of American society and finds himself an exile in his own land. So we have come here today to dramatize an appalling condition.

In a sense we have come to our nation's capital to cash a check. When the architects in our republic wrote the magnificent words of the Constitution and the Declaration of Independence, they were signing a promissory note to which every American was to fall heir. This note was a promise that all men would be guaranteed the unalienable rights of life, liberty, and the pursuit of happiness.

It is obvious today that America has defaulted on this promissory note insofar as her citizens of color are concerned. Instead of honoring this sacred obligation, America has given the Negro people a bad check; a check which has come back marked "insufficient funds." But we refuse to believe that the bank of justice is bankrupt. We refuse to believe that there are insufficient funds in the great vaults of opportunity of this nation. So we have come to cash this check—a check that will give us upon demand the riches of freedom and the security of justice. We have also come to this hallowed spot to remind America of the fierce urgency of *now*. This is no time to engage in the luxury of cooling off or to take the tranquilizing drugs of gradualism. *Now* is the time to make real the promises of Democracy. *Now* is the time to rise from the dark and desolate valley of segregation to the sunlit path of racial justice. *Now* is the time to open the doors of opportunity to all of God's children. *Now* is the time to lift our nation from the quicksands of racial injustice to the solid rock of brotherhood.

5   It would be fatal for the nation to overlook the urgency of the moment and to underestimate the determination of the Negro. This sweltering summer of the Negro's legitimate discontent will not pass until there is an invigorating autumn of freedom and equality. 1963 is not an end, but a beginning. Those who hope that the Negro needed to blow off steam and will now be content will have a rude awakening if the nation returns to business as usual. There will be neither rest nor tranquility in America until the Negro is granted his citizenship rights. The whirlwinds of revolt will continue to shake the foundations of our nation until the bright day of justice emerges.

But there is something that I must say to my people who stand on the warm threshold which leads into the palace of justice. In the process of gaining our rightful place we must not be guilty of wrongful deeds. Let us not seek to satisfy our thirst for freedom by drinking from the cup of bitterness and hatred. We must forever conduct our struggle on the high plane of dignity and discipline. We must not allow our creative protest to degenerate into physical violence. Again and again we must rise to the majestic heights of meeting physical force with soul force. The marvelous new militancy which has engulfed the Negro community must not lead us to a distrust of all white people, for many of our white brothers, as evidenced by their presence here today, have come to realize that their destiny is tied up with our destiny and their freedom is inextricably bound to our freedom. We cannot walk alone.

And as we walk, we must make the pledge that we shall march ahead. We cannot turn back. There are those who are asking the devotees of civil rights, "When will you be satisfied?" We can never be satisfied as long as the Negro is the victim of the unspeakable horrors of police brutality. We can never be satisfied as long as our bodies, heavy with the fatigue of travel, cannot gain lodging in the motels of the highways and the hotels of the cities. We cannot be satisfied as long as the Negro's basic mobility is from a smaller ghetto to a larger one. We can never be satisfied as long as a Negro in Mississippi cannot vote and a Negro in New York believes he has nothing for which to vote. No, no, we are not satisfied, and we will not be satisfied until justice rolls down like waters and righteousness like a mighty stream.

I am not unmindful that some of you have come here out of great trials and tribulations. Some of you have come fresh from narrow jail cells. Some of you have come from areas where your quest for freedom left you battered by the storms of persecution and staggered by the winds of police brutality. You have been the veterans of creative suffering. Continue to work with the faith that unearned suffering is redemptive.

Go back to Mississippi, go back to Alabama, go back to South Carolina, go back to Georgia, go back to Louisiana, go back to the slums and ghettos of our northern cities, knowing that somehow this situation can and will be changed. Let us not wallow in the valley of despair.

10 I say to you today, my friends, that in spite of the difficulties and frustrations of the moment I still have a dream. It is a dream deeply rooted in the American dream.

I have a dream that one day this nation will rise up and live out the true meaning of its creed: "We hold these truths to be self-evident; that all men are created equal."

I have a dream that one day on the red hills of Georgia the sons of former slaves and the sons of former slaveowners will be able to sit down together at the table of brotherhood.

I have a dream that one day even the state of Mississippi, a desert state sweltering with the heat of injustice and oppression, will be transformed into an oasis of freedom and justice.

I have a dream that my four little children will one day live in a nation where they will not be judged by the color of their skin but by the content of their character.

15 I have a dream today.

I have a dream that one day the state of Alabama, whose governor's lips are presently dripping with the words of interposition and nullification, will be transformed into a situation where little black boys and black girls will be able to join hands with little white boys and white girls and walk together as sisters and brothers.

I have a dream today.

I have a dream that one day every valley shall be exalted, every hill and mountain shall be made low, the rough places will be made plain, and the crooked places will be made straight, and the glory of the Lord shall be revealed, and all flesh shall see it together.

This is our hope. This is the faith with which I return to the South. With this faith we will be able to hew out of the mountain of despair a stone of hope. With this faith we will be able to transform the jangling discords of our nation into a beautiful symphony of brotherhood. With this faith we will be able to work together, to pray together, to struggle together, to go to jail together, to stand up for freedom together, knowing that we will be free one day.

20 This will be the day when all of God's children will be able to sing with new meaning:

My country, 'tis of thee, Sweet land of liberty, Of thee I sing: Land where my fathers died, Land of the pilgrims' pride, From every mountain-side Let freedom ring.

And if America is to be a great nation, this must become true. So let freedom ring from the prodigious hilltops of New Hampshire. Let freedom ring from the mighty mountains of New York. Let freedom ring from the heightening Alleghenies of Pennsylvania!

Let freedom ring from the snowcapped Rockies of Colorado!
Let freedom ring from the curvaceous peaks of California!

25   But not only that; let freedom ring from Stone Mountain of Georgia!
Let freedom ring from Lookout Mountain of Tennessee!
Let freedom ring from every hill and molehill of Mississippi. From every
    mountainside, let freedom ring.

When we let freedom ring, when we let it ring from every village and every hamlet, from every state and every city, we will be able to speed up that day when all of God's children, black men and white men, Jews and Gentiles, Protestants and Catholics, will be able to join hands and sing in the words of the old Negro spiritual, "Free at last! free at last! thank God almighty, we are free at last!"

Questions for Reading Actively

1. Of the rich metaphors King uses, which two or three do you find most effective or striking? Why?

2. This text is at once a speech and a sermon. Locate a recording of King's delivery of this great sermon, and listen to his delivery. How does King's voice, his emphasis on particular phrases, his call-and-response engagement with his audience, change the way you silently "read" the printed text?

3. The cadences and the figurative language of "I Have a Dream" are profoundly influenced by King's lifelong immersion in the African-American Baptist church. Are those rhythms and biblical allusions familiar to you? Do you need to understand those allusions in order to fully appreciate the ethical and moral implications of his call to action?

Questions for Thinking Critically

1. Do you have faith in individual people, or in society as a whole, to address and correct a specific injustice? Describe an injustice that you have witnessed, and evaluate how either individuals or a community has responded to that injustice.

2. King dreams of a nation where people are judged by the "content of their character"—their *ethic*. What is the content of your own character? How do you measure up to your own ethical ideals?

Question for Writing Thoughtfully

1. King exhorts the marchers to "continue to work with the faith that unearned suffering is redemptive." In the same year as the March on Washington, Malcolm X delivered a speech in Detroit in which he noted that "there is nothing in our book, the Koran, that teaches us to suffer peacefully. Our religion teaches us to be intelligent. Be peaceful, be courteous, obey the law, respect everyone; but if someone puts his hands on you, send him to the cemetery." Can these two views be reconciled? How do you think injustice should best be fought? Describe your point of view in a short essay.

Using Language to Influence

Because of the intimate relationship between language and thinking, people naturally use language to influence the thinking of others. One of the reasons Dr. King's speech was so influential was that he invoked the cadences and the vocabulary of the Bible. President Bill Clinton used the same strategy when he promised Americans "a new covenant" between the government and the people.

Thinking Critically About Visuals

Reading the Unwritten

Are citizens entitled to universal health care? In this mural, *The History of Medicine in Mexico, and the People Demanding Health,* which was created for a wall in the Hospital de la Raza in Mexico City, Mexico, the artist Diego Rivera dramatizes the struggle of the poor for access to a health care system that favors the rich. Murals like this have a rich history as a visual language to express important ideas. Who might be the audience for this mural, and what message did the artist want to communicate? Can you describe other murals that you have seen and what you thought their audiences and messages were intended to be?

Schalkwijk / Art Resource, NY ©ARS, NY
Drs. Neftali Rodrigues and Anotnio Diaz Lombardo

Thinking-Writing Activity

THINKING CRITICALLY ABOUT EUPHEMISMS

Select an important social problem such as drug use, crime, poverty, juvenile delinquency, support for wars in other countries, racism, or unethical or illegal behavior in government. List several euphemisms commonly used to describe the problem; then explain how these euphemisms can lead to dangerous misperceptions and serious consequences.

Later, George W. Bush became president after promoting an agenda of "compassionate conservatism." Conversely, the term *weapons of mass destruction* was so terrifying that many people believe it was one of the reasons that Congress voted to support the war in Iraq.

Manufacturers and advertising professionals choose language just as carefully to influence buying decisions. Americans are told that the Energizer bunny "keeps going and going." We are invited to "Join the Pepsi generation" and challenged to stop eating chips: "I bet you can't eat just one." And we are told over and over, "It's Miller time."

Whatever your political positions or buying habits, there are people who make a profession of using language to influence others' thinking. They are interested in influencing—and sometimes in controlling—your thoughts, feelings, and behavior. To avoid being unconsciously manipulated by these efforts, you need to be aware of how language functions. This knowledge will help you to distinguish actual arguments, information, and reasons from techniques of persuasion that others use to get you to accept their views without thinking critically. Three types of language often used to promote the uncritical acceptance of views are euphemistic language, clichés, and emotive language.

Euphemistic Language

The term *euphemism* is derived from a Greek word meaning "to speak with good words." Using a euphemism involves substituting a pleasanter, less objectionable expression for a blunt or more direct one. For example, an entire collection of euphemisms exists to disguise the unpleasantness of death: *passed away, went to her reward, departed this life,* and *blew out the candle.*

Why do people use euphemisms? Probably to help smooth out the "rough edges" of life, to make the unbearable bearable and the offensive inoffensive. Sometimes people use them to make their occupations sound more dignified (a garbage collector, for instance, might be called a "sanitation engineer"). Sometimes euphemisms can be humorous, as are the following "New Euphemisms for Bad Stuff at School."

Course failure	Unrequested course reregistration
Incomplete course grade	An unrequited educational encounter
Suspension	Mandatory discontinued attendance
Absence	A non-school learning experience

Euphemisms can become dangerous, though, when they are used to evade or to create misperceptions of serious issues. An alcoholic may describe herself as a "social drinker," thus denying her problem and need for help. A politician may indicate that one of his statements was "somewhat at variance with the truth"—meaning that he lied. Another example would be to describe rotting slums as "substandard housing," making deplorable conditions appear reasonable and the need for action less urgent. In the following brief essay, foreign, policy analyst Daniel Pipes argues against the use of euphemistic language to describe acts of terrorism.

"Beslan Atrocity: They're Terrorists—Not Activists"

by Daniel Pipes

Policy analyst Daniel Pipes is frequently consulted by media, industry, universities, and governments worldwide for his expert opinions and analysis of ongoing developments in the Middle East. He is the director of the Middle East Forum, a think tank that provides analysis about radical Islam to business, academic, and government entities. He was director of the Foreign Policy Research Institute from 1986 to 1993, and has been a board member of the United States Institute of Peace. The following article was written after Islamic terrorists took over a school in Beslan, Russia, in 2004, a siege that led to the deaths of four hundred people. Most of the dead were children, their teachers, and their parents, who had been celebrating the first day of the school year.

"I know it when I see it" was the famous response by a U.S. Supreme Court justice to the vexed problem of defining pornography. Terrorism may be no less difficult to define, but the wanton killing of schoolchildren, of mourners at a funeral, or workers at their desks in skyscrapers surely fits the know-it-when-I-see-it definition.

The press, however, generally shies away from the word *terrorist,* preferring euphemisms. Take the assault that led to the deaths of some four hundred people, many of them children, in Beslan, Russia, on September 3. Journalists have delved deep into their thesauruses, finding at least twenty euphemisms for terrorists:

Source: From "Beslan Atrocity: They're Terrorists—Not Activists," by Daniel Pipes, *New York Sun,* September 7, 2004. Reprinted with permission of Daniel Pipes.

Assailants—National Public Radio

Attackers—the Economist

   Bombers—the *Guardian*

Captors—the Associated Press

Commandos—Agence France-Presse

   refers to the terrorists both as

   "members du commando" and

   "commando"

Criminals—the *Times* (London)

Extremists—United Press International

Fighters—the *Washington Post*

Group—*The Australian*

Guerrillas—in a *New York Post* editorial

Gunmen—Reuters

Hostage-takers—the *Los Angeles Times*

Insurgents—in a *New York Times*

   headline

Kidnappers—the *Observer* (London)

Militants—the *Chicago Tribune*

Perpetrators—the *New York Times*

Radicals—the BBC

Rebels—in a *Sydney Morning Herald*

   headline

Separatists—the *Christian Science*

   Monitor

And my favorite:

Activists—the *Pakistan Times*

The origins of this unwillingness to name terrorists seems to lie in the Arab-Israeli conflict, prompted by an odd combination of sympathy in the press for the Palestinian Arabs and intimidation by them. The sympathy is well known; the intimidation less so. Reuters' Nidal al-Mughrabi made the latter explicit in advice for fellow reporters in Gaza to avoid trouble on the web site www.newssafety.com, where one tip reads: "Never use the word *terrorist* or *terrorism* in describing Palestinian gunmen and militants; people consider them heroes of the conflict."

The reluctance to call terrorists by their rightful name can reach absurd lengths of inaccuracy and apologetics. For example, National Public Radio's *Morning Edition* announced on April 1, 2004, that "Israeli troops have arrested twelve men they say were wanted militants." But CAMERA, the Committee for Accuracy in Middle East Reporting in America, pointed out the inaccuracy and NPR issued an on-air correction on April 26: "Israeli military officials were quoted as saying they had arrested twelve men who were 'wanted militants.' But the actual phrase used by the Israeli military was 'wanted terrorists.'"

5   (At least NPR corrected itself. When the *Los Angeles Times* made the same error, writing that "Israel staged a series of raids in the West Bank that the army described as hunts for wanted Palestinian militants," its editors refused CAMERA's request for a correction on the grounds that its change in terminology did not occur in a direct quotation.)

Metro, a Dutch paper, ran a picture on May 3, 2004, of two gloved hands belonging to a person taking fingerprints off a dead terrorist. The caption read: "An Israeli police officer takes fingerprints of a dead Palestinian. He is one of the victims (*slachtoffers*) who fell in the Gaza strip yesterday." One of the victims!

Euphemistic usage then spread from the Arab-Israeli conflict to other theaters. As terrorism picked up in Saudi Arabia such press outlets as *The Times (London)* and the Associated Press began routinely using *militants* in reference to Saudi terrorists. Reuters uses it with reference to Kashmir and Algeria.

Thus has *militants* become the press's default term for terrorists.

These self-imposed language limitations sometimes cause journalists to tie themselves into knots. In reporting the murder of one of its own cameramen, the

BBC, which normally avoids the word *terrorist,* found itself using that term. In another instance, the search engine on the BBC web site includes the word *terrorist* but the page linked to [it] has had that word expurgated.

10   Politically correct news organizations undermine their credibility with such subterfuges. How can one trust what one reads, hears, or sees when the self-evident fact of terrorism is being semi-denied?

Worse, the multiple euphemisms for *terrorist* obstruct a clear understanding of the violent threats confronting the civilized world. It is bad enough that only one of five articles discussing the Beslan atrocity mentions its Islamist origins; worse is the miasma of words that insulates the public from the evil of terrorism.

Questions for Reading Actively

1. How are the terms listed by Daniel Pipes euphemistic? That is, why are these terms (in Pipes's opinion) less accurate, or less objectionable, than the term *terrorist*?

2. What does the word *wanton* (paragraph 1) mean, and what are the connotations of its use by Pipes to describe the actions of terrorists?

3. To what does Pipes attribute the use of euphemisms to describe terrorist actions?

4. What other euphemisms can you identify that are used to describe current events?

Questions for Thinking Critically

1. Go online to find more information about the attacks on the Beslan school. Which of the terms listed by Pipes did you find in the articles and analysis you consulted? Which term, based on your interpretations of the events, seems most accurate?

2. Working with a small group, look up each of the terms listed by Pipes in a good dictionary and in a thesaurus. In what ways are the derivations and usages of these terms similar, and in what ways are they different? Which words are considered to be synonyms for each other? Create a spectrum (see page 195) ranging from "most objectionable" to "least objectionable" and place each term at a point on that spectrum that reflects your research.

Question for Writing Thoughtfully

1. The conservative Fox News network uses the term *homicide bombers,* as opposed to the more commonly used *suicide bombers,* to describe people who blow themselves up when they set off bombs meant to kill others as well. What is the difference between these two terms? Which terms, in your opinion, is more accurate? In an extended definition essay (see page 276 in Chapter 8), explain your thinking.

Thinking-Writing Activity

CLICHÉ AND PROVERB

Different societies and different time periods give rise to different clichés.

1. Write down two or three phrases that you consider to be clichés. Try to recall where you have read or heard them. Share this writing with classmates to see if they know these phrases and if they think that they are clichés.

2. Proverbs and famous quotations are also often repeated, but they function differently from clichés because they tend to encourage thinking.

3. Write down a proverb or a famous quotation that you know, and write a few sentences about how it stimulates your thinking.

4. Select a cliché and write a few sentences about how it does not help you think clearly about an issue to which it could apply.

Clichés

Clichés function in a similar way to *euphemisms* in that they tend to dilute meaning and avoid the complexities of an issue. A cliché is an overused phrase, usually employing figurative language, and so often repeated that the phrase becomes an automatic pattern. For example, if someone says "Sly as a . . .," what word comes next? Or "Sharp as a . . ."? On page 183, in the discussion of figurative language, the point was made that clichés usually start off as fresh wordings. People like the way the phrase sounds and repeat it over and over, year after year. After a while, the phrase loses its freshness and also its clear reference to what is being discussed.

What does it really mean to be "drunk as a skunk"? First of all, skunks do not imbibe alcohol. But, more important, this cliché is not helpful to a discussion of intoxication. The issue may be a drinker's health or safety—or the safety of those around that person. What does it really mean to say that someone is "sly as a fox"? The issue may be manipulative behavior that can cause serious problems, not just wily strategies.

In addition, the use of clichés indicates lazy thinking. Imagine how clever it must have seemed the first time someone said in a meeting that the group should "think outside the box." Yet a person who uses that phrase now is not being clever, just repeating a tired phrase, and will probably be considered inarticulate. Clichés may not create serious problems in casual conversation, but they do cloud meaning and should not be used in your academic writing.

Thinking-Writing Activity

EVALUATING EMOTIVE LANGUAGE

Identify examples of emotive language in the following passages and explain how the writer is using that language to influence people's thoughts and feelings.

> We need another and a wiser and perhaps a more mystical concept of animals. Remote from universal nature, and living by complicated artifice, man in civilization surveys the creature through the glass of his knowledge and sees thereby a feather magnified and the whole image in distortion. We patronize them for their incompleteness, for their tragic fate of having taken form so far below ourselves. And therein we err, and greatly err. For the animal shall not be measured by man. In a world older and more complete than ours they move finished and complete, gifted with senses that you have lost or never attained, living by voices you shall never hear.
>
> —Henry Beston, *The Outermost House*

> Every criminal, every gambler, every thug, every libertine, every girl ruiner, every home wrecker, every wife beater, every dope peddler, every moonshiner, every crooked politician, every pagan Papist priest, every shyster lawyer, every white slaver, every brothel madam, every Rome-controlled newspaper, every black spider—is fighting the Klan. Think it over. Which side are you on?
>
> —From a Ku Klux Klan circular

Emotive Language

What is your immediate reaction to each of the following words?

tyrant	*peaceful*	*disgusting*	*God*	*filthy*
mouthwatering	*bloodthirsty*	*freedom*	*jihad*	

Most of these words probably arouse strong feelings in you. In fact, this ability to evoke feelings accounts for the extraordinary power of language.

Certain words (like those just listed) are used to stand for the emotive areas of your experience. These emotive words symbolize the whole range of human feelings from powerful emotions ("I detest you!") to the subtlest of feelings.

Emotive language often plays a double role: it not only symbolizes and expresses our feelings but also arouses or *evokes* feelings in others. When you tell someone, "You're my best friend," you usually are not simply expressing your feelings for the person; you also hope to inspire that person to have similar feelings for you. Even when communicating factual information, we make use of the emotive influence of language to interest other people in what we are saying.

ONLINE RESOURCES
Classical Rhetoric
Visit the student website for *Critical Thinking, Thoughtful Writing* at **cengagebrain.com** to learn more about classical rhetoric.

For example, visit your English CourseMate, accessed through CengageBrain.com and compare the *New York Times* account of the events of 9/11 with the *People's Daily* account. Which account do you find more emotive? Which seems more objective? Which do you find more engaging? Why?

Although an emotive word may be an accurate description of feelings, it is not the same as a factual statement because it is true only for the speaker—not for others. For instance, even though you may feel that a movie is "tasteless" and "repulsive," someone else may find it "exciting" and "hilarious." By describing your feelings about the movie, you are giving your personal evaluation, which often may differ from the personal evaluations of others (it is not unusual to see conflicting reviews of the same movie). A factual statement, on the other hand, is a statement with which rational people will agree, providing that suitable evidence to verify it is available (for example, the fact that mass transit uses less energy than automobiles). When emotive words are used in larger groups (such as sentences, paragraphs, compositions, poems, plays, or novels), they become even more powerful. Martin Luther King Jr., speech "I Have a Dream" (p. 184) is a dramatic example of the force of effective emotive language.

One way to think about the meaning and power of emotive words is to see them on a scale or continuum, from mild to strong. For example:

overweight   fat   obese

The thinker Bertrand Russell used this continuum to illustrate how we perceive the same trait in various people:

- I am *firm.*
- You are *stubborn.*
- He/she is *pigheaded.*

We usually tend to perceive ourselves favorably ("I am firm"). I am speaking to you face to face, so I view you only somewhat less favorably ("You are stubborn"). But since a third person is not present, I can use stronger emotive language ("He/she is pigheaded"). Try this technique with two other emotive words:

1. I am . . .   You are . . .   He/she is . . .
2. I am . . .   You are . . .   He/she is . . .

Emotive words usually signal that a personal opinion or evaluation, rather than a fact, is being stated. Speakers occasionally do identify their opinions as opinions, using phrases like "In my opinion" or "I feel that." Often, however, speakers do not identify their opinions as such because they want you to treat their judgments as facts. In these cases, the combination of the informative use and the emotive use of language can be misleading and even dangerous.

A final point to consider about emotive language is that it can be used in a reverse way, as we have seen in the section on euphemism. George Orwell gives examples of this in his classic essay "Politics and the English Language." He points out that such usages deliberately drain the emotion from terms in order to lessen the shock of the information being conveyed. "Defenseless villages are bombarded from the air, the inhabitants driven out into the country-side, the cattle machine-gunned, the huts set on fire with incendiary bullets: this is called *pacification*."

Writing Project: The Impact of Language on Our Lives

This chapter explores the essential role of language in developing sophisticated thinking abilities. The goal of clear, effective thinking and communication is accomplished through the joint efforts of thought and language. Learning to use the appropriate language style, which depends on the social context in which you are operating, requires both critical judgment and flexible expertise with various language forms. Critically evaluating the pervasive attempts of advertisers and others to bypass your critical faculties and influence your thinking involves insight into the way language and thought create and express meaning. We will be examining these relationships between language and thought further in upcoming chapters.

The following Writing Project provides an opportunity for you to apply what you have learned in this chapter to your own writing.

> Write a paper in which you discuss some specific aspect of your experience with language. Analyze some way or ways in which words have affected you. You could write about a favorite poem or song lyric, about how the language of a religious ceremony or political statement influenced you, or about advertisements that made you desire or reject a product. You might tell of the impact of statements made by your parents, grandparents, teachers, or friends. You could recount one event or several situations, positive or negative effects. Whenever possible, connect your experience to concepts explained in this chapter. Follow your instructor's directions for topic limitations, length, format, and so on.

The guidelines you need to consider are those involved in writing any paper that connects your personal experience with a complex issue.

1. Present your experience vividly and use specific details.
2. Clearly state your point or thesis about the effect(s) the experience had on you. Think about the best place in your paper to do this.

3. Be explicit about the connections you see between your experience and the concepts about language that they illustrate. You may want to quote from the chapter. If you do, cite material as directed by your instructor.

4. Consider using some of the language techniques explored in this chapter (such as figurative language).

The Writing Situation

Begin by considering the key elements in the Thinking-Writing Model on pages 6–7 in Chapter 1.

Purpose   One purpose you have here is to connect abstract ideas about language with real-life experiences so that you and your readers can understand the concepts better. As with any writing project, another major purpose is to make your points clear and convincing to your audience.

Audience   As always, consider who could benefit from reading your paper. Perhaps your ideas would appeal to a larger audience, in which case you could submit your writing for publication, possibly in the "My Turn" column in *Newsweek*, the opinion pages of your campus newspaper, or some other publication or website.

Subject   Because language is such a large subject, one involving fairly simple as well as very complex ideas, writing about a real-life experience can clarify—and test—the ideas you choose to write about.

Writer   Because this project draws on your own experience, you are in a position of authority. However, the project asks you to focus on an aspect of your experience that you might not have thought about before, and it requires an analytical approach rather than a narrative one, even though you may decide to tell of an event. Therefore, you will need a sort of double consciousness as a writer: you first want to recall your experience as directly as you can, but then you will have to distance yourself as you analyze the effect of language on the experience.

The Writing Process

The following sections will guide you through the stages of generating, planning, drafting, and revising as you work on this writing assignment.

Generating Ideas

1. Think of times when something you heard, read, or even said had an impact on you. Did someone use harsh language that upset you or comforting language that soothed you? Did you say something funny, helpful, embarrassing, or astute? Has a particular phrase ever made you want to do or try something? Why?

2. Do you find any common denominator among several experiences, or does one experience stand out and ask to be told as a single story?

3. Have your significant language experiences involved spoken words more often than written ones?

4. Have any of your experiences involved more than one language or more than one dialect or level of usage?

Defining a Focus   What do you want your audience to understand about the way the experience has affected you? If you are going to recount several experiences, is it important to make that clear in your thesis? Draft a thesis statement that makes a point about your experience(s).

Share your tentative thesis with classmates. Do they consider your idea worthwhile? Next, list things you might say to develop your thesis. How do your peers respond?

Organizing Ideas   The organization of this paper will depend on whether you are discussing one or more experiences. However you approach it, you will need to consider what arrangement will best help your audience understand the effects of your experience. If you are using specific concepts from the chapter, you will have to think about how and where to present them so that their relevance is clear. Using a mind map or a web may help you organize your ideas. Here is one possible format:

First experience	*Second experience*	*Why the two experiences are related*
Circumstances	Circumstances	_____
What was said	What was said	_____
How it affected you	How it affected you	_____

Drafting   Start with the part that will be easiest to write. Look at your freewriting, your possible thesis statement, and your list or map of ideas. Now, work those early-stage writings into a coherent draft. Remember that shaping ideas is your biggest concern at this stage. Trust yourself to speak about your own experiences and to explain what they mean to you.

After you have drafted enough material, give attention to paragraphs. Where does your material cluster into divisions? Which paragraphs need topic sentences? Where in the paragraphs should topic sentences be placed?

Draft an opening paragraph and a conclusion. What connections exist between them? Will they create an effective beginning and a good ending for your essay?

Revising   Begin your revision by referring to "A Step-by-Step Method for Revising Any Assignment," on page 169. Each author included in this chapter offers guidelines and inspiration for revising and clarifying your writing. What would Donald Murray draw your attention to? Are your word choices as specific, insightful, and sharp-eyed as Malcolm X's engagement with a dictionary would provide?

The following essay shows how one student responded to this assignment. While revising, she applied concepts about language she had learned in this chapter. Her essay is followed by a poem by Roberto Obregon.

Student Writing

Jessie Lange's Writing Process

Student Jessie Lange decided to write about an experience she had with her younger brother. She took the advice given, to start with the part that would be easiest to write. She began to describe her experience, which would become the third paragraph of her essay below, this way:

> After my first four months of college, I returned home for the winter break. After all this, I returned home to be more affected by one word uttered by my younger brother than I had been by my classes.

Then Jessie thought about the precise language used in the readings in this chapter, and she realized that her readers would not know what "all this" meant and her readers also would not know how much younger her brother was. So she revised in this way:

> After my first four months of college, I returned home for the winter break. After four months of reading inspirational writers, attending the lectures of powerful speakers, learning about language itself in my linguistics course, speaking French, and having discussions with intelligent professors who are at the top of their field, I returned home to be more affected by one word uttered by my twelve-year-old brother than I had been by any of the speaking and listening I'd engaged in first semester.

Jessie continued this process as she drafted and revised, and finally produced this essay.

The Power of Language

by Jessie Lange

Language is indeed one of the most powerful things we possess. It is how we communicate our ideas, how we put our abstract feelings for others into words, and it is what we use to describe and evaluate our human experience. Being a "good speaker" in public is something we value highly as we do effective communication in our personal lives. One of the most incredible things about language is the power that just a phrase or even a single word can have. In fact, just a few words often have more of an impact than long speeches and rambling sentences. How does it happen that a small combination of letters can have such a tremendous effect on us?

In the play *Kiss of the Spider Woman* by Manuel Puig, one of the characters, Molina, comments on the power of language. Molina, a gentle soul and an expert storyteller, is desperately in love with the man with whom he is sharing a prison cell. "How does it happen that sometimes someone says something and wins someone else over forever?" he wonders. If only he knew, he could win the love of his cell-mate, Valentin. What Molina is acknowledging is that it doesn't take an infinite number of words to say something powerful. It can be a phrase or even a single word that has the most profound impact on others. In this case, it is the "one thing" uttered that causes another to fall in love with you. In the everyday, there are particular words and phrases that stay with us, that we roll over in our minds, repeating them to ourselves again and again. There are certain words that have such an impact that they stay with us eternally longer than the time it took to utter them. I recently had a personal experience with the effects of this.

After my first four months of college, I returned home for the winter break. After four months of reading inspirational writers, attending the lectures of powerful speakers, learning about language itself in my linguistics course, speaking French, and having discussions with intelligent professors who are at the top of their field, I returned home to be more affected by one word uttered by my twelve-year-old brother than I had been by any of the speaking or listening I'd engaged in first semester. My brother and I have always been extremely close. We do not have the "sibling rivalry" I so often hear about from others. And so being apart had been a struggle. The fact that we had been apart so long and the impending separation just a few weeks away were probably much of the reason his words had such an effect on me. We were saying goodnight one night and my brother who, in many ways, is a miniature me, was holding my hand. I'd just finished assuring him that he was the "bomb" and he was smiling at me. Somewhere out of his slim twelve-year-old frame a thought emerged in the form of speech: "I wish I could take you with me," he said. "Where?" I asked, thoroughly confused. His smile broadened. "Everywhere," he said matter-of-factly. Such a simple word but, to me, so profoundly meaningful, causing a complete overflow of emotion. I had visions of never letting go of his hand. Of bringing him to college with me, of going to school with him, of bringing him all through my life and never missing a day or a second of his getting older. Just one word: *Everywhere.*

If I've learned anything about language, it's that the cliché "quality, not quantity" definitely applies. It took one utterance from my brother to almost bring me to tears. With one word, I could imagine myself holding his fingers in mine wherever I went, wherever we went.

Alternative Writing Projects

1. Write an essay about the most current uses of doublespeak. Be sure to have a focus, a main point that your examples support.

2. Write an essay about how names define or don't define who we are.

CHAPTER 6   Summary

- One effective way to develop your ability to recognize and use language effectively and ethically is to read widely.
- When making decisions when revising drafts, it is good practice to follow these steps:
  - Define your goals.
  - Consider possible choices.
  - Gather relevant information and evaluate the pros and cons.
  - Implement your choice by drafting, and evaluate it by rereading what you wrote.
- When writing for new media, keep the following advice in mind:
  - Go short.
  - Avoid big blocks of text.
  - Avoid passive voice.
  - Lead the reader.
  - Make your content "hot."
  - K.I.S.S. (keep it simple . . .)
- Remember the following tips for revising your own writing or reviewing the writing of a peer:
  - Think big—look at the draft as a whole.
  - Think medium—look at the draft paragraph by paragraph.

- Think small—look at the draft sentence by sentence.
- Think "picky"—look at the draft as the fussiest critic might.
- You have a responsibility as a writer to use language ethically. One way to ensure your writing is ethical is to clear up any ambiguities or vagueness.
- Consider using figurative language, like similes and metaphors, when you:
  - Have trouble finding the right words
  - Want to express a profound thought in a strikingly original way
  - Want to add an extra dimension to a description
  - Want to amuse your audience
- Euphemisms and clichés should be used carefully and sparingly to avoid diluting serious issues and making your ideas sound boring and unoriginal.
- Emotive words usually signal that a personal opinion or evaluation is being presented. These words convey strong power to capture your audience's attention, but they should not be used as substitute for presenting facts.

PART 2

Thinking and Writing to Shape Our World

All of us actively shape, as well as discover, the world of our experience in which we live. Our world does not exist as a finished product waiting for us to perceive it, think about it, and describe it with words and pictures. Instead, we are active participants in composing our world, organizing, and interpreting sensations into a coherent whole. Many times, our shaping of this world will reflect basic thinking patterns that we rely on constantly whenever we think, act, speak, or write.

Part Two explores four basic ways of relating and organizing: relationships in space and time, relationships of comparison, relationships of cause, and relationships of classification and definition. The Writing Projects at the end of each chapter ask you to integrate ideas from other sources into your essays as you explore these relationships and the thinking/organizing patterns that develop from them.

Thos Robinson/Stringer/Getty Images

Dr. Oliver Sacks, a neurologist who explores and writes about neurology, was born in 1933 to two London physicians. As a 2002 article in *Wired* magazine puts it, Sacks's greatest revolution has to do with the way in which medical cases are described. Traditionally, in case descriptions the doctor is the "hero," diagnosing and struggling to cure a disease. For Sacks, however, his great interest is in how people with incurable neurological conditions themselves struggle to adapt to a suddenly challenging world—a difference of perspective. Dr. Sacks' work has inspired numerous playwrights, poets, composers, and artists, and he was awarded the Lewis Thomas Prize, which "recognizes the scientist as poet," in 2002 by Rockefeller University. What roles do perception and perspective play in writing?

Writing to Describe and Narrate: Exploring Perceptions

". . . a thing is not seen because it is visible, but conversely, visible because it is seen . . ."

—PLATO

The way we make sense of the world is through thinking, but our first experiences of the world come to us through our senses: sight, hearing, smell, touch, and taste. These senses are our bridges to the world, making us aware of what occurs outside us. The process of becoming aware of the world through our senses is known as *perceiving*.

This chapter and Chapter 11 will explore the way the perceiving process operates and how it relates to the ability to think, read, and write effectively. In particular, these chapters examine the way each of us shapes personal experience by actively selecting from, organizing, and interpreting the information provided by our senses. In a way, we each view the world through a pair of individual "contact lenses" that reflect our past experiences and our unique personalities. As critical thinkers, we want to become aware of the nature of our own lenses in order to offset any bias or distortion they may be causing. We also want to become aware of the lenses of others so that we can better understand why they view things the way that they do.

Developing insight into the nature of people's lenses—our own and others'—is essential to becoming an effective writer. When we write, it's helpful to understand our own point of view, to be aware of our own biases. That doesn't mean that we should strive to be completely "objective." In fact, such absolute objectivity is not possible because we can never completely remove our personal lenses. However, understanding our lenses helps us achieve our goals as writers. For example, if we want to present our ideas objectively, then we can work to compensate for our inherent bias. On the other hand, if our intention is to persuade others, we may choose to enhance and strengthen our point of view.

Analogously, we need to understand our audience's lenses if we are to communicate our thoughts and feelings effectively through our writing. This involves appreciating their point of view and understanding their biases. We can then use this knowledge to craft our writing, shape our language, and utilize the appropriate terminology and logic.

Critical Thinking Focus:
Understanding perceptions

Writing Focus:
Detail and order in chronologies

Reading Theme:
Narratives and process descriptions

Writing Project:
Narrative showing the effect of a perception

Once again, we can see the essential union of writing and thinking, communicating and knowing. This chapter will provide you with a foundation for understanding how you develop your beliefs and knowledge about the world and how you can communicate your ideas through clear, expressive, and compelling writing. Let's begin by exploring our main source of information—the perceiving process. Some of the most basic patterns of thinking and of presenting ideas draw directly on perceptions. This chapter will focus on three such patterns: description, process, and narrative.

Thinking Critically About Perceptions

Becoming Aware of Your Own Perceptions

At almost every waking moment of life, our senses are being bombarded by a tremendous number of stimuli: images to see, noises to hear, odors to smell, textures to feel, and flavors to taste. Experiencing all such sensations at once could create what the nineteenth-century American philosopher William James called "a bloomin' buzzin' confusion." Yet to us, the world usually seems much more orderly and understandable. Why is this so?

In the first place, our sense equipment can receive sensations only within certain limited ranges. For example, there are many sounds and smells that animals can detect but we cannot; animals' sense organs have broader ranges in these areas than ours do. A second reason we can handle sensory bombardment is that from the stimulation available, we select only a small amount on which to focus our attention. To demonstrate this, complete the following Thinking-Writing Activity.

This simple exercise demonstrates that for every sensation on which you focus, there are countless others that you are simply ignoring. If you were aware of everything that was happening at every moment, you would be completely overwhelmed. By selecting particular sensations, you are able to make sense of your world in a relatively orderly way. That is, you are *perceiving*, a process by which you actively select, organize, and interpret what is experienced by the senses.

Copyright © Cengage Learning

FIGURE 7.1
Recognizing a Pattern

It is tempting to think that our senses simply record what is happening out in the world, as if we were human camcorders. We are not, however, passive receivers of information, containers into which sense experience is poured. Instead, we are active participants who are always trying to understand the sensations we are encountering. As we perceive the world, our experiences are the result of combining the sensations we receive with our understanding of these sensations. For instance, examine the collection of markings in Figure 7.1.

What do you see? If all you see is a collection of black spots, try turning the illustration sideways; you will probably perceive a familiar animal.

From this example you can grasp how, when you perceive the world, you are doing more than simply recording what your senses experience; instead, you are actively making sense of these sensations. The collection of black spots suddenly became the figure of an animal because your mind was able to actively organize the spots into a pattern you recognized. Or think about times when you looked up at white, billowy clouds and saw different figures and designs. The figures you were perceiving were not actually in the clouds but were the result of your giving meaningful form to shapes you were experiencing.

The same is true for virtually everything we experience. Our perceptions of the world result from combining information provided by our senses with the way we actively make sense of this information. And since making sense of information is what we are doing when we are thinking, perceiving the world involves using our minds in an active way. Of course, we are usually not aware that we are using our minds to interpret sensations we are experiencing. We simply see the animal or the figures in the clouds as if they were really there.

Thinking-Writing Activity

WHAT DO YOU SENSE RIGHT NOW?

Respond to the following questions in writing, using a spontaneous, free-flowing style. Record your sensations as you experience them rather than first taking time to reflect and deliberate.

1. What can you *see?* (for example, the shape of the letters on the page, the design of the clothing on your arm)

2. What can you *hear?* (for example, the hum of the air circulator, the rustling of a page)

3. What can you *feel?* (for example, the pressure of the clothes against your skin, the texture of the page on your fingers)

4. What can you *smell?* (for example, the perfume someone is wearing, the odor of stale cigarette smoke)

5. What can you *taste?* (for example, the aftertastes of your last meal)

Compare your responses with those of your classmates. Did they perceive sensations different from the ones you perceived? If so, how do you explain these differences?

Actively Selecting, Organizing, and Interpreting Sensations   When we actively perceive the sensations we are experiencing, we are usually engaged in three distinct activities:

- *Selecting* certain sensations to pay attention to
- *Organizing* these sensations into a design or pattern
- *Interpreting* what this design or pattern means

In the case of Figure 7.1, you were able to perceive an animal because you selected certain markings to concentrate on, organized these markings into a pattern, and interpreted this pattern as representing a dog.

Of course, when we perceive, the three operations of selecting, organizing, and interpreting are usually performed quickly, automatically, and often simultaneously. Also, because they are so rapid and automatic, we are not normally aware of performing these operations.

Take a few moments to explore more examples that illustrate how you actively select, organize, and interpret your perceptions of the world. Carefully examine Figure 7.2. Do you see both the young woman and the old woman? If you do, try switching back and forth between the two images. As you do so, notice how for each image, you are doing the following things:

- *Selecting* certain lines, shapes, and shadings on which to focus your attention
- *Organizing* these lines, shapes, and shadings into different patterns
- *Interpreting* these patterns as representing things you can recognize—a hat, a nose, a chin

So far, we have been exploring how the mind actively participates in the ways we perceive the world. By combining the sensations we are receiving with the way our minds select, organize, and interpret these sensations, we perceive a world that is stable and familiar. Thus, each of us develops a perspective on the world, one that usually makes sense to us.

The process of perceiving takes place on various levels. At the most basic level, *perceiving* refers to the selection, organization, and interpretation of sensations: for example, being able to perceive various objects such as a basketball. However, we also perceive larger patterns of meaning at more complex levels, as in watching the action of a group of people engaged in a basketball game. Although these are different situations, both engage us in the process of perceiving.

Noting Differences in People's Perceptions

As we have noted, we are not usually aware of our active participation in perceiving the world. We normally assume that what we are perceiving is what is actually taking place.

FIGURE 7.2
Young Woman/Old Woman

Only when we find that our perception of an event differs from others' perceptions of it are we forced to examine the manner in which we are selecting, organizing, and interpreting the event. Many artists and photographers believe that what an individual viewer sees in a picture mirrors something within the viewer himself.

In most cases, people in a group will have a variety of perceptions about what is taking place in the photograph below. Some will see the couple as engaged in a serious disagreement. Others may see them thoughtfully discussing a serious issue related to the baby on the bed. In each case, the perception depends on how the viewer is actively using his or her mind to organize and interpret what is taking place.

Thinking Critically About Visuals

Thinking-Writing Activity

COMPARING YOUR PERCEPTIONS WITH OTHERS

Carefully examine this photograph of a man and a woman sitting on a bed with a baby in the background and then explore your reactions. What do you think is happening in this picture? Explain by answering the following questions.

1. Describe as specifically as possible what you perceive as taking place in the picture.

2. Describe what you think will take place next.

3. Identify which details of the picture inform your perceptions.

4. Compare your perceptions with those of your classmates. List several perceptions that differ from yours.

© 2010 Radius Images/Jupiterimages Corporation.

@ THINKING CRITICALLY ABOUT NEW MEDIA

Distinguishing Perception from Reality

Sure, the Internet is full of information, but much of this information is based on perceptions that are incomplete, biased, and outright false. How do we tell the difference between beliefs that are relatively accurate, objective, and factual from those that aren't? The short answer is that we need to come armed with our full array of critical thinking abilities combined with a healthy dose of skepticism. Consider these examples:

Phony Journalism   "One could say my life itself has been one long soundtrack. Music was my life, music brought me to life, and music is how I will be remembered long after I leave this life. When I die there will be a final waltz playing in my head that only I can hear." When Dublin University student Shane Fitzgerald posted this poetic but phony quote on the Wikipedia obituary for the French composer Maurice Jarre, he said he was testing how our globalized, increasingly Internet-dependent media was upholding accuracy and accountability in an age of instant news. His report card: Wikipedia passed; Journalism flunked. Although Wikipedia administrators quickly detected and removed the bogus quote, it wasn't quick enough to prevent journalists from around the world cutting and pasting it to dozens of blogs and newspaper websites. And the offending quote continued its viral spread until, after a full month went by, Fitzgerald blew the whistle on his editorial fraud. His analysis? "I am 100 percent convinced that if I hadn't come forward, that quote would have gone down in history as something Maurice Jarre said, instead of something I made up. It would have become another example where, once anything is printed enough times in the media without challenge, it becomes fact."

Phony Degrees   Want a college degree—or even a Ph.D.—in engineering, medicine, philosophy, or virtually any subject you choose, without having to attend all of those classes and pay all of that tuition? No problem! Your options range from having to take a limited number of online courses to simply coming up with the right cash payment, and an official looking diploma will be on its way before you can say *summa cum laude*! Phony degrees are nothing new: black markets in fake diplomas are known to have existed as far back as fourteenth-century Europe. But today's new media has raised the scam to a high art, with modern diploma mills providing detailed transcripts, verification services, and even fake accrediting agencies to legitimize fake schools. The only problem with using a phony degree to pad your resume? In addition to being uneducated and unqualified, of course, there's the likelihood of getting caught and watching your career disappear like invisible ink on a fraudulent diploma.

Counterfeit Websites   Counterfeit websites are sites disguising themselves as legitimate sites for the purpose of disseminating misinformation. For example, *www .martinlutherking.org* disseminates hateful information about one of the greatest African-American leaders of our era while pretending to be, on the surface, an "official" Martin Luther King Jr. site. While the home page depicts a photograph of King and his family and links titled "Historical Writings," "The Death of a Dream," and "Recommended Books," subsequent pages include defamatory allegations and links to white power organizations and literature.

Thinking-Writing Activity

DETECTING AND ANALYZING FAULTY PERCEPTIONS ON THE WEB

1. Here's an opportunity to put your critical thinking skills to use as a detective. Surf the web and identify at least one example of each of the misleading or bogus sites or advertisements listed below, and then critically evaluate them in terms of their accuracy, authenticity, reliability, and objectivity.

   - Phony journalism
   - Phony degrees
   - Counterfeit websites

2. Next, explore one or more "hoax-busting" websites and write your own personal guide to identifying and debunking false and misleading perceptions presented on the web.

Writing Thoughtfully About Perceptions

Although the verb *describe* can be used to mean the giving of any detailed account, it more precisely indicates the reporting of sensory impressions: what you see, hear, feel, smell, or taste—your perceptions. Look back at the questions on page 207 to note how your five senses responded; also, reflect on what you have been reading about selecting, organizing, and interpreting sensations. This material should help you understand the two types of descriptions that you will be writing about in the Thinking-Writing Activity on page 217, descriptions that you might also write in other college courses or in work situations.

Writing Objectively and Subjectively

Descriptions can be broadly divided into two categories: *objective,* involving as little judgment as possible, or *subjective,* involving whatever personal judgment is appropriate to a writer's purpose.

Objective descriptions are often expected in scientific, medical, engineering, and law enforcement writing. The purpose of an objective description is to help the audience sense an object or situation as it is. Later, judgments and implications can be drawn from objective descriptions, but the cleanest possible rendering is needed as a starting point. Of course, the selection and presentation of *any* ideas or information involve conscious and unconscious judgments. However, when objectivity is the purpose, you should try to perceive with as little bias as you can and to describe in language that is as neutral as possible.

In other writing situations, descriptions are intended to be more subjective. Then the explicit purpose is to shape the audience's opinion of the object under scrutiny. Subjective descriptions occur in literary texts of all kinds: stories, poems, personal essays, and biographies; in argumentative pieces; and in personal writing such as letters to friends and journal entries. Think of how a novelist describes characters or settings; think of how an attorney might reword the police report's objective description of a victim in order to influence a jury; think of how you would describe your new special person to a close friend! You may want to use the first person (*I*) when writing a subjective description to help your audience realize that this description is how you see it. When writing a subjective description, you will be selecting details purposefully and using language that creates the effect that you want your audience to experience.

Objective Language	Subjective Language
A German shepherd	A vicious, snarling dog
A lake at night	A shimmering mirror of moonlight
Drove at 85 mph	Recklessly tore down the road
A six-foot five-inch man	A towering man
Quit my job	Told them to take their job and shove it
Filed for divorce	Got revenge on the lowlife
Won the election	Stole victory from the real winner

Contrasting Objective and Subjective Writing

The reading that follows has, as its subject, the abilities of animals to perceive and "feel." However, the reading is both "objective" and "subjective," as the author—who is autistic—writes about her own processes of thinking and feeling.

"Animal Feelings"

by Temple Grandin

From *Animals in Translation: Using the Mysteries of Autism to Decode Animal Behavior*

Dr. Temple Grandin, a professor of animal science at Colorado State University, is renowned for her work on developing humane facilities for both the care and the slaughter of livestock. As a person with autism, she has written extensively on the ways in which people with autism perceive the world and the similarities between her own perceptions and those of animals. Her work was first brought to wide attention by neurologist and author Oliver Sacks in his book *An Anthropologist on Mars,* the title of which is Grandin's phrase for describing how she feels around "neurotypical" people. Grandin's books include *Thinking in Pictures: And Other Reports from My Life with Autism* (1996) and *Animals in Translation: Using the Mysteries of Autism to Decode Animal Behavior* (2005), from which the following selection is excerpted.

Animals Aren't Ambivalent

Mammals and birds have the same feelings people do. Researchers are just now discovering that lizards and snakes probably share most of these emotions with us, too. Just to give a couple of examples: the skink lizard in Australia is monogamous, and rattlesnake mamas here in the United States protect their young from predators the same way a mammal would. The fact that some snake mothers take care of their babies came as a big surprise, since researchers have always believed snakes weren't social at all and that mothers abandoned their babies after birth. We still don't know much about the social lives of snakes, but at least now we know that they *have* a social life.

   We know animals and humans share the same core feelings partly because we know quite a bit how our core emotions are created by the brain, and there's no question animals share that biology with us. Their emotional biology is so close to ours that most of the research on the neurology of emotions—or *affective neuroscience*—is done with animals. When it comes to the basics of life, like getting eaten by a tiger or protecting the young, animals feel the same way we do.

   The main difference between animal emotions and human emotions is that animals don't have *mixed emotions* the way normal people do. Animals aren't ambivalent; they don't have *love-hate* relationships with each other or with people. That's one of the reasons humans love animals so much; animals are loyal. If an animal loves you he loves you no matter what. He doesn't care what you look like or how much money you make.

Source: From "Animal Feelings," in *Animals in Translation: Using the Mysteries of Autism to Decode Animal Behavior*, Temple Grandin and Catherine Johnson, 2005, pp. 88–93. Reprinted with permission of the Authors.

This is another connection between autism and animals: autistic people have mostly simple emotions, too. That's why normal people describe us as *innocent*. An autistic person's feelings are direct and open, just like animal feelings. We don't hide our feelings, and we aren't ambivalent. I can't even imagine what it would be like to have feelings of love and hate for the same person.

5   Some people will probably think this is an insulting thing to say about autistic people, but one thing I appreciate about being autistic is that I don't have to deal with all the emotional craziness my students do. I had one fantastic student who flunked out of school because she broke up with her boyfriend. There's so much psychodrama in normal people's lives. Animals never have psychodrama.

Children don't, either. Emotionally, children are more like animals and autistic people, because children's frontal lobes are still growing and don't mature until sometime in early adulthood. I mentioned earlier that the frontal lobes are one big association cortex, tying everything together, including emotions like love and hate that would probably be better off staying separate. That's another reason why a dog can be like a person's child: children's emotions are straightforward and loyal like a dog. A seven-year-old boy or girl will race through the house to greet Dad when he comes from work the same way a dog will. I think animals, children, and autistic people have simpler emotions because their brains have less ability to make connections, so their emotions stay more separate and compartmentalized.

Of course, no one knows why an autistic *grown-up* has trouble making connections, since our frontal lobes are normal-sized. All we know right now is that researchers find "decreased connectivity among cortical regions and between the cortex and subcortex." The way I visualize it is that a normal brain is like a big corporate office building with telephones, faxes, e-mail, messengers, people walking around and talking—a big corporation has zillions of ways for messages to get from one place to another. The autistic brain is like the same big corporate office building where the only way for anyone to talk to anyone else is by fax. There's no telephone, no e-mail, no messengers, and no people walking around talking to each other. Just faxes. So a lot less stuff is getting through as a consequence, and everything starts to break down. Some messages get through okay; other messages get distorted when the fax misprints or the paper jams; other messages don't get through at all.

The point is that even though autistic people have a normal-sized neocortex including normal-sized frontal lobes, our brains *function* as if our frontal lobes were either much smaller or not fully developed. Our brains function more like a child's brain or an animal's brain, but for different reasons.

When the different parts of the brain are relatively separate from each other and don't communicate well, you end up with simple, clear emotions due to compartmentalization. A child can be furious at his mom or dad one second, then completely forget about it the next, because being mad and being happy are separate states. A child hops from one to the other depending on the situation.

10   You see the exact same thing with animals. Strong emotions in animals are usually like a sudden thunderstorm. They blow in and then blow back out. Two dogs who live together in the same house can be snarling one second, then go back to being best friends the next. Normal people need a lot more time to get over an angry emotion, and even when a normal adult does get over a bad emotion, he's made a lasting

connection between the angry emotion and the person or situation that made him angry. When a normal person gets furiously angry with a person he loves, his brain hooks up *anger* and *love* and remembers it. Thanks to his highly developed frontal lobes, which connect everything up with everything else, his brain learns to have mixed emotions about that person or situation.

Another big difference between animals and people is that animals probably don't have the complex emotions people do, like shame, guilt, embarrassment, greed, or wanting bad things to happen to people who are more successful than you. There are different schools of thought about simple and complex emotions, but the definition I use is brain-based. Simple emotions are the primary emotions such as fear and rage that come from the reptilian and the mammalian brains. Complex emotions, or secondary emotions, also come from the reptilian and the mammalian brains, but they light up the neocortex as well. The secondary emotions build on the primary emotions and involve more thought and interpretation. For instance, shame, guilt, and embarrassment probably all come out of the same primary emotion of *separation distress,* which I'll talk about shortly. Your culture and upbringing teach you when to feel shame versus when to feel embarrassment or guilt, but all three start out in the brain as the pain of being isolated.

I don't want to give the impression that animals *never* have more than one feeling at the same time. Later on I'll talk about the fact that cows often feel curious and afraid at the same time. (Jaak Panksepp, author of *Affective Neuroscience*, classifies curiosity as a core emotion.) Biologically it's possible for more than one basic emotional system to be activated in an animal's brain at the same time, so technically an animal is capable of experiencing a mixed emotion.

But in real life one emotion usually ends up completely replacing the other, and some of the core emotions probably do "turn off" others. For instance, brain research shows that play and rage are incompatible emotions, which anyone who has ever watched two dogs play fighting can tell you. Once in a while a play fight will turn into a real fight, and when that happens the two dogs don't show the slightest sign (friendly tail wags, toothy smiles) that they're experiencing happy play feelings along with angry fight feelings. Once a play fight has turned real, *all* of the dog's body language and vocal communication is angry.

No Freud for Dogs

Another huge difference between animals and people: I don't think animals have the defense mechanisms Sigmund Freud described in humans. Projection, displacement, repression, denial—I don't think we see these things in animals. Defense mechanisms defend against anxiety, and all defense mechanisms depend on repression in some way. Using repression, you push whatever it is you're afraid of down into your unconscious mind and focus your conscious mind on a stand-in. Or, in the case of the higher, more mature defense mechanisms, like humor, altruism, or intellectualization, you use humor, empathy, and thought to push away the "real" emotion, which is fear.

The reason I believe animals don't have Freudian defense mechanisms is that animals and autistic people don't seem to have repression. Or, if they do, they have it only to a weak degree. I don't think I have any of Freud's defense mechanisms, and I'm always amazed when normal people do. One of the things that blows my mind about normal human beings is denial. When I see a packing plant getting into a bad situation, I'll say, "That's not going to work," and everyone will immediately think I'm being really negative. But I'm not. It would be obvious to anyone outside the situation that what they're doing isn't going to work, but people inside the bad situation can't see it because their defense mechanisms protect them from seeing it until they're ready. That's denial, and I can't understand it at all. I can't even imagine what it's like.

15   That's because I don't have an unconscious. Normal people can push bad things out of their conscious minds into their unconscious minds, but I can't. Normal people can't always *keep* the bad stuff locked up, of course, but at least they have more freedom from it than I do. That's why I can't watch any violent movies with rape or torture scenes. The pictures stay in my conscious mind. Once they're there, I can't get rid of them. The only way I can block a bad image is by thinking about something else, but the bad image still pops back up in my mind, like a pop-up ad on the Internet. The way I think about it is that a normal brain has a built-in pop-up zapper, but my brain doesn't. To get rid of the pop-up image I have to consciously click on another screen.

I don't know *why* my brain doesn't have an unconscious, but I think it's connected to the fact that pictures are my "native language," not words. Lots of studies show that the language parts of your brain block your memory for images. Language doesn't *erase* your image memories; the images are still there, inside your head. But language keeps the images from becoming conscious. Psychologists call this *verbal overshadowing,* and I'll talk about it more in my chapter on animal thinking. For the time being, let's just say that while I don't know why I don't seem to have an unconscious, I think my problems with language have a lot to do with it. Language isn't a natural ability for me, so maybe the language parts of my brain don't have the same power to overshadow the pictures.

I know it's a leap to go from saying that I don't have an unconscious to saying I don't have defense mechanisms, but based on my personal experience I think it's true. No one has ever tried to test animals for defense mechanisms, but animals act as if they don't have them, either. You never see an animal act as if a dangerous situation is safe. You might see a dog act like he's not afraid when he is, but that's not the same thing. The dog knows there's danger and is using a standard dog strategy to avoid provoking the threatening dog any further.

A friend of mine has two dogs, one a gentle female collie and the other a macho golden retriever. (You might not have thought a golden retriever could be macho, but this one is.) When my friend walks the collie *alone* past the two ferocious-acting German shepherds down the street, the collie looks straight ahead and acts as if she's deaf and blind. She does this because staring is a provocation. She's averting her eyes to avoid challenging them.

The reason we can say the collie is only pretending not to be afraid of the other dogs when she's alone, instead of not feeling fear because she'd repressed it, is that she stops orienting to motion. All animals orient to movement. It's automatic. Since no dog can be oblivious to two German shepherds who are charging straight toward her, the collie has to consciously override her most basic orienting response. She has to *actively* ignore the other dogs.

Questions for Reading Actively

1. Note which paragraphs of the excerpt from "Animal Feelings" are subjective and which paragraphs are objective. How does the subject of each paragraph influence whether or not the author, Temple Grandin, chooses the subjective or objective voice?

2. Grandin uses comparison and contrast effectively in this reading. What are the subjects and concepts that she compares and contrasts? What kind of evidence does she use to illustrate these comparisons?

3. What is the difference between "simple" and "complex" emotions?

Question for Thinking Critically

1. Go online for more information about Temple Grandin and about autism. How do Grandin's history and writing challenge your perceptions of people with autism?

Questions for Writing Thoughtfully

1. Temple Grandin objectively considers and analyzes her own processes of perception in order to better understand the lives of animals. In a descriptive essay, analyze the ways in which you perceive a certain emotion or "feeling." What circumstances cause you to feel that emotion? Has your response to those circumstances changed as you have matured? Describe one or two key influences on how you perceive a specific circumstance and tell how you have learned an emotional response.

2. In an objective essay, describe the behavior of an animal or a group of animals (wild or domestic) with which you are familiar. Before you begin, look up the term *personification*. In your essay, be particularly aware of moments when you personify the behavior that you are objectively observing and describing. How do audience and circumstance influence whether or not a writer might use personification to describe behavior? What does personification suggest about the limits of human perceptions?

Thinking-Writing Activity

CREATING OBJECTIVE AND SUBJECTIVE DESCRIPTIONS

Write two separate paragraphs in which you describe the same person or object in two different ways. Make one paragraph as objective as possible; make the other primarily subjective in order to create a particular impression for your readers. Each paragraph should have about six to eight sentences.

Which of these paragraphs will have a strong topic sentence? Why? Which may not have a topic sentence or may have one that makes no claim? Why?

Chronological Relationships

Chronological forms of writing organize events or ideas in a time sequence. The focus in chronological writing is on using description to illustrate growth, development, or change—from a person's life story to the steps in creating a favorite dish. The *chronological pattern* organizes a topic into a series of events in the time sequence in which they occurred. Many chronologies are narratives or stories. The process mode of thinking organizes an activity into a series of steps necessary for reaching a certain end. Here the focus is on describing aspects of growth, development, or change, as you might do when explaining how to prepare a favorite dish or perform a new dance.

Narratives

Perhaps the oldest and most universal form of chronological expression is the *narrative*, a story about real or fictional experiences. Many people who study communication believe that narrative is the starting point for other patterns of presentation because we often process our perceptions in storylike ways.

Every human culture has used narratives to pass on values and traditions from one generation to the next, as exemplified by such enduring works as the *Odyssey*, the Bible, and the Koran. One of America's great storytellers, Mark Twain, once said that a good story has to accomplish something and arrive somewhere. In other words, if a story is to be effective in engaging the interest of the audience, it has to have a purpose. The purpose may be to provide more information on a subject, to illustrate an idea, to lead the audience to a particular way of thinking, or to entertain. An effective narrative does not merely record the complex, random, and often unrelated events of life. Instead, it has focus, an ordered structure, and a meaningful point of view.

Writing About Processes

A second type of time-ordered thinking pattern is the *process relationship*, which describes events or experiences in terms of their development. From birth, we are involved with processes in every facet of life. They can be classified in various ways: *natural* (such as growing physically), *mechanical* (such as assembling a bicycle), *physical* (such as learning a sport), *mental* (such as developing a way of thinking), and *creative* (such as writing a poem).

Writing about a process involves two basic tasks. The first is to divide the process being analyzed into parts or stages. The second is to explain the movement of the process through these parts or stages from beginning to end. The stages identified should be separate and distinct and should involve no repetition or significant omissions.

Processes are explained for two purposes. One is to give instructions on how to do something, such as build a wall or set up a computer. Instructions will often use the pronoun *you* and imperative or command verb forms. This is an excellent example of grammar, meaning, and purpose working together. The other purpose of process writing, is to describe a process but not necessarily teach someone to do it.

In your academic reading, you'll notice both kinds of process writing. For example, a biology textbook will explain the process of photosynthesis—something that your professor might expect you to understand, but certainly not to do yourself! (If you could, you'd be green.) On the other hand, when your biology professor gives you instructions for dissecting a frog, those instructions describe a process that you are expected to do.

Examples of Process Writing

Read the following two examples of process writing. What is the purpose of each? How can you tell? What are some words in each that indicate sequence?

> Jacketing was a sleight-of-hand I watched with wonder each time, and I have discovered that my father was admired among sheepmen up and down the valley for his skill at it: He was just pretty catty at that, the way he could get that ewe to take on a new lamb every time. Put simply, jacketing was a ruse played on a ewe whose lamb had died. A substitute lamb quickly would be singled out, most likely from a set of twins. Sizing up the tottering newcomer, Dad would skin the dead lamb, and into the tiny pelt carefully snip four leg holes and a head hole. Then the stand-in lamb would have the skin fitted onto it like a snug jacket on a poodle. The next step of disguise was to cut out the dead lamb's liver and smear it several times across the jacket of pelt. In its borrowed and bedaubed skin, the new baby lamb then was presented to the ewe. She would sniff the baby impostor endlessly, distrustful but pulled by the blood-smell of her own. When in a few days she made up her dim sheep's mind to accept the lamb, Dad snipped away the jacket and recited his victory: Mother him like hell now, don't ye? See what a hellava dandy lamb I got for ye, old sister? Who says I couldn't jacket day onto night if I wanted to, now-I-ask-ye?
>
> —Ivan Doig, *This House of Sky*

> If you are inexperienced in relaxation techniques, begin by sitting in a comfortable chair with your feet on the floor and your hands resting easily in your lap. Close your eyes and breathe evenly, deeply, and gently. As you exhale each breath let your body become more relaxed. Starting with one hand direct your attention to one part of your body at a time. Close your fist and tighten the muscles of your forearm. Feel the sensation of tension in your muscles. Relax your hand and let your forearm and hand become completely limp. Direct all your attention to the sensation of relaxation as you continue to let all tension leave your hand and arm. Continue this practice once or several times each day, relaxing your other hand and arm, your legs, back, abdomen, chest, neck, face, and scalp. When you have this mastered and can relax completely, turn

your thoughts to scenes of natural tranquility from your past. Stay with your inner self as long as you wish, whether thinking of nothing or visualizing only the loveliest of images. Often you will become completely unaware of your surroundings. When you open your eyes you will find yourself refreshed in mind and body.

—Laurence J. Peter, The Peter Prescription

Thinking-Writing Activity

WRITING PROCESS DESCRIPTIONS

Write two substantive paragraphs about two processes that you understand very well. In one, give instructions to a specific audience who would benefit from learning how to perform this activity. In the other, explain a process—but do not give instructions.

In the following essay, surgeon and writer Atul Gawande uses the description of a technical medical procedure to describe the ways in which young surgical residents become experienced, confident practitioners of their art.

"The Learning Curve"

by Atul Gawande

Atul Gawande received his MD from Harvard Medical School and an MPH from the Harvard School of Public Health. He is a doctor at a Boston hospital and a staff writer for *The New Yorker*, contributing essays on public health issues as well as specific cases and experiences from his own practice. A collection of these essays, *Complications: A Surgeon's Notes on an Imperfect Science*, was published in 2002.

The patient needed a central line. "Here's your chance," S., the chief resident, said. I had never done one before. "Get set up and then page me when you're ready to start."

It was my fourth week in surgical training. The pockets of my short white coat bulged with patient printouts, laminated cards with instructions for doing CPR and reading EKGs and using the dictation system, two surgical handbooks, a stethoscope, wound-dressing supplies, meal tickets, a penlight, scissors, and about a dollar in loose change. As I headed up the stairs to the patient's floor, I rattled.

This will be good, I tried to tell myself: my first real procedure. The patient—fiftyish, stout, taciturn—was recovering from abdominal surgery he'd had about a week earlier. His bowel function hadn't yet returned, and he was unable to eat. I explained to him that he needed intravenous nutrition and that this required a "special line" that would go into his chest. I said that I would put the line in him while he was in his bed, and that it would involve my numbing a spot on his chest with a local anesthetic, and then threading the line in. I did not say that the line was eight inches long and would go into his vena cava, the main blood vessel to his heart. Nor did I say how tricky the procedure could be. There were "slight risks" involved, I said, such as bleeding and lung collapse; in experienced hands, complications of this sort occur in fewer than one case in a hundred.

But, of course, mine were not experienced hands. And the disasters I knew about weighed on my mind: the woman who had died within minutes from massive bleeding when a resident lacerated her vena cava; the man whose chest had to be opened because a resident lost hold of a wire inside the line, which then floated down to the patient's heart; the man who had a cardiac arrest when the procedure put him into ventricular fibrillation. I said nothing of such things, naturally, when I asked the patient's permission to do his line. He said, "OK."

5   I had seen S. do two central lines; one was the day before, and I'd attended to every step. I watched how she set out her instruments and laid her patient down and put a rolled towel between his shoulder blades to make his chest arch out. I watched how she swabbed his chest with antiseptic, injected lidocaine, which is a local anesthetic, and then, in full sterile garb, punctured his chest near his clavicle with a fat three-inch needle on a syringe. The patient hadn't even flinched. She told me how to avoid hitting the lung ("Go in at a steep angle," she'd said. "Stay *right* under the clavicle"), and how to find the subclavian vein, a branch to the vena cava lying atop the lung near its apex ("Go in at a steep angle. Stay *right* under the clavicle"). She pushed the needle in almost all the way. She drew back on the syringe. And she was in. You knew because the syringe filled with maroon blood. ("If it's bright red, you've hit an artery," she said. "That's not good.") Once you have the tip of this needle poking in the vein, you somehow have to widen the hold in the vein wall, fit the catheter in, and snake it in the right direction—down to the heart, rather than up to the brain—all without tearing through vessels, lung, or anything else.

To do this, S. explained, you start by getting a guide wire in place. She pulled the syringe off, leaving the needle in. Blood flowed out. She picked up a two-foot-long twenty-gauge wire that looked like the steel D string of an electric guitar, and passed nearly its full length through the needle's bore, into the vein, and onward toward the vena cava. "Never force it in," she warned, "and never, ever let go of it." A string of rapid heartbeats fired off on the cardiac monitor, and she quickly pulled the wire back an inch. It had poked into the heart, causing momentary fibrillation. "Guess we're in the right place," she said to me quietly. Then to the patient: "You're doing great. Only a few minutes now." She pulled the needle out over the wire and replaced it with a bullet of thick, stiff plastic, which she pushed in tight to widen the vein opening. She then removed this dilator and threaded the central line—a spaghetti-thick, flexible yellow plastic tube—over the wire until it was all the way in. Now she could remove the wire. She flushed the line with a heparin solution and sutured it to the patient's chest. And that was it.

Today, it was my turn to try. First, I had to gather supplies—a central-line kit, gloves, gown, cap, mask, lidocaine—which took me forever. When I finally had the stuff together, I stopped for a minute outside the patient's door, trying to recall the steps. They remained frustratingly hazy. But I couldn't put it off any longer. I had a page-long list of other things to get done: Mrs. A needed to be discharged; Mr. B needed an abdominal ultrasound arranged; Mrs. C needed her skin staples removed. And every fifteen minutes or so I was getting paged with more tasks: Mr. X was nauseated and needed to be seen; Miss Y's family was here and needed "someone" to talk to them; Mr. Z needed a laxative. I took a deep breath, put on my best don't-worry-I-know-what-I'm-doing look, and went in.

I placed the supplies on a bedside table, untied the patient's gown, and laid him down flat on the mattress, with his chest bare and his arms at his sides. I flipped on a fluorescent overhead light and raised his bed to my height. I paged S. I put on my gown and gloves and, on a sterile tray, laid out the central line, the guide wire, and other materials from the kit. I drew up five cc's of lidocaine in a syringe, soaked two sponge sticks in the yellow-brown Betadine, and opened up the suture packaging.

S. arrived. "What's his platelet count?"

10   My stomach knotted. I hadn't checked. That was bad: too low and he could have a serious bleed from the procedure. She went to check a computer. The count was acceptable.

Chastened, I started swabbing his chest with the sponge sticks. "Got the shoulder roll underneath him?" S. asked. Well, no, I had forgotten that, too. The patient gave me a look. S., saying nothing, got a towel, rolled it up, and slipped it under his back for me. I finished applying the antiseptic and then draped him so that only his right upper chest was exposed. He squirmed a bit beneath the drapes. S. now inspected my tray. I girded myself.

"Where's the extra syringe for flushing the line when it's in?" Damn. She went out and got it.

I felt for my landmarks. *Here?* I asked with my eyes, not wanting to undermine the patient's confidence any further. She nodded. I numbed the spot with lidocaine. ("You'll feel a stick and a burn now, sir.") Next, I took the three-inch needle in hand and poked it through the skin. I advanced it slowly and uncertainly, a few millimeters at a time. This is a big goddamn needle, I kept thinking. I couldn't believe I was sticking it into someone's chest. I concentrated on maintaining a steep angle of entry, but kept spearing his clavicle instead of slipping beneath it.

"Ow!" he shouted.

15   "Sorry," I said. S. signaled with a kind of surfing hand gesture to go underneath the clavicle. This time, it went in. I drew back on the syringe. Nothing. She pointed deeper. I went in deeper. Nothing. I withdrew the needle, flushed out some bits of tissue clogging it, and tried again.

"Ow!"

Too steep again. I found my way underneath the clavicle once more. I drew the syringe back. Still nothing. He's too obese, I thought. S. slipped on gloves and a gown. "How about I have a look?" she said. I handed her the needle and stepped aside. She plunged the needle in, drew back on the syringe, and, just like that, she was in. "We'll be done shortly," she told the patient.

She let me continue with the next steps, which I bumbled through. I didn't realize how long and floppy the guide wire was until I pulled the coil out of its plastic sleeve, and, putting one end of it into the patient, I very nearly contaminated the other. I forgot about the dilating step until she reminded me. Then, when I put in the dilator, I didn't push quite hard enough, and it was really S. who pushed it all the way in. Finally, we got the line in, flushed it, and sutured it in place.

Outside the room, S. said that I could be less tentative the next time, but that I shouldn't worry too much about how things had gone. "You'll get it," she said. "It just takes practice." I wasn't so sure. The procedure remained wholly mysterious to me. And I could not get over the idea of jabbing a needle into someone's chest so deeply and so blindly. I awaited the X-ray afterward with trepidation. But it came back fine: I had not injured the lung and the line was in the right place.

My second try at placing a central IV line went no better than the first. The patient was in intensive care, mortally ill, on a ventilator, and needed the line so that powerful cardiac drugs could be delivered directly to her heart. She was also heavily sedated, and for this I was grateful. She'd be oblivious of my fumbling.

My preparation was better this time. I got the towel roll in place and the syringes of heparin on the tray. I checked her lab results, which were fine. I also made a point of draping more widely, so that if I flopped the guide wire around by mistake again, it wouldn't hit anything unsterile.

For all that, the procedure was a bust. I stabbed the needle in too shallow and then too deep. Frustration overcame tentativeness and I tried one angle after another. Nothing worked. Then, for one brief moment, I got a flash of blood in the syringe, indicating that I was in the vein. I anchored the needle with one hand and went to pull the syringe off with the other. But the syringe was jammed on too tightly so that when I pulled it free I dislodged the needle from the vein. The patient began bleeding into her chest wall. I held pressure the best I could for a solid five minutes, but still her chest turned black and blue around the site. The hematoma made it impossible to put a line through there anymore. I wanted to give up. But she needed a line and the resident supervising me—a second-year this time—was determined that I succeed. After an X-ray showed that I had not injured her lung, he had me try on the other side, with a whole new kit. I missed again, and he took over. It took him several minutes and two or three sticks to find the vein himself, and that made me feel better. Maybe she was an unusually tough case.

When I failed with a third patient a few days later, though, the doubts really set in. Again, it was stick, stick, stick, and nothing. I stepped aside. The resident watching me got it on the next try.

* * * *

Surgeons, as a group, adhere to a curious egalitarianism. They believe in practice, not talent. People often assume that you have to have great hands to become a surgeon, but it's not true. When I interviewed to get into surgery programs, no one made me sew or take a dexterity test or checked to see if my hands were steady. You do not even need all ten fingers to be accepted. To be sure, talent helps. Professors say that every two or three years they'll see someone truly gifted come through a program—someone who picks up complex manual skills unusually quickly, sees tissue planes before others do, anticipates trouble before it happens. Nonetheless, attending surgeons say that what's most important to them is finding people who are conscientious, industrious, and boneheaded enough to keep at practicing this one difficult thing day and night for years on end. As a former residency director put it to me, given a choice between a PhD who had cloned a gene and a sculptor, he'd pick the PhD every time. Sure, he said, he'd bet on the sculptor's being more physically talented; but he'd bet on the PhD's being less "flaky." And in the end that matters more. Skill, surgeons believe, can be taught; tenacity cannot. It's an odd approach to recruitment, but it continues all the way up the ranks, even in top surgery departments. They start with minions with no experience in surgery, spend years training them, and then take most of their faculty from these homegrown ranks.

25   And it works. There have now been many studies of elite performers—concert violinists, chess grand masters, professional ice skaters, mathematicians, and so forth—and the biggest difference researchers find between them and lesser performers is the amount of deliberate practice they've accumulated. Indeed, the most important talent may be the talent for practice itself. K. Anders Ericsson, a cognitive psychologist and an expert on performance, notes that the most important role that innate factors play may be in a person's *willingness* to engage in sustained training. He has found, for example, that top performers dislike practicing just as much as others do. (That's why, for example, athletes and musicians usually quit practicing when they retire.) But, more than others, they have the will to keep at it anyway.

* * * *

I wasn't sure I did. What good was it, I wondered, to keep doing central lines when I wasn't coming close to hitting them? If I had a clear idea of what I was doing wrong, then maybe I'd have something to focus on. But I didn't. Everyone, of course, had suggestions. Go in with the bevel of the needle up. No, go in with the bevel down. Put a bend in the middle of the needle. No, curve the needle. For a while, I tried to avoid doing another line. Soon enough, however, a new case arose.

The circumstances were miserable. It was late in the day, and I'd had to work through the previous night. The patient weighed more than three hundred pounds. He couldn't tolerate lying flat because the weight of his chest and abdomen made it hard for him to breathe. Yet he had a badly infected wound, needed intravenous antibiotics, and no one could find veins in his arms for a peripheral IV. I had little hope of succeeding. But a resident does what he is told, and I was told to try the line.

I went to his room. He looked scared and said he didn't think he'd last more than a minute on his back. But he said he understood the situation and was willing to make his best effort. He and I decided that he'd be left sitting propped up in bed until the last possible minute. We'd see how far we got after that.

I went through my preparations: checking his blood counts from the lab, putting out the kit, placing the towel roll, and so on. I swabbed and draped his chest while he was still sitting up. S., the chief resident, was watching me this time, and when everything was ready I had her tip him back, an oxygen mask on his face. His flesh rolled up his chest like a wave. I couldn't find his clavicle with my fingertips to line up the right point of entry. And already he was looking short of breath, his face red. I gave S. a "Do you want to take over?" look. Keep going, she signaled. I made a rough guess about where the right spot was, numbed it with lidocaine, and pushed the big needle in. For a second, I thought it wouldn't be long enough to reach through, but then I felt the tip slip underneath his clavicle. I pushed a little deeper and drew back on the syringe.

30   Unbelievably, it filled with blood. I was in. I concentrated on anchoring the needle firmly in place, not moving it a millimeter as I pulled the syringe off and threaded the guide wire in. The wire fed in smoothly. The patient was struggling hard for air now. We sat him up and let him catch his breath. And then, laying him down one more time, I got the entry dilated and slid the central line in. "Nice job" was all S. said, and then she left.

    I still have no idea what I did differently that day. But from then on my lines went in. That's the funny thing about practice. For days and days, you make out only the fragments of what to do. And then one day you've got the thing whole. Conscious learning becomes unconscious knowledge, and you cannot say precisely how.

* * * *

I have now put in more than a hundred central lines. I am by no means infallible. Certainly, I have had my fair share of complications. I punctured a patient's lung, for example—the right lung of a chief of surgery from another hospital, no less—and, given the odds, I'm sure such things will happen again. I still have the occasional case that should go easily but doesn't, no matter what I do. (We have a term for this. "How'd it go?" a colleague asks. "It was a total flog," I reply. I don't have to say anything more.)

    But other times everything unfolds effortlessly. You take the needle. You stick the chest. You feel the needle travel—a distinct glide through the fat, a slight catch in the dense muscle, then the subtle pop through the vein wall—and you're in. At such moments, it is more than easy; it is beautiful.

* * * *

It is 2 P.M. I am in the intensive-care unit. A nurse tells me Mr. G.'s central line has clotted off. Mr. G. has been in the hospital for more than a month now. He is in his late sixties, from South Boston, emaciated, exhausted, holding on by a thread—or a line, to be precise. He has several holes in his small bowel, and the bilious contents leak out onto his skin through two small reddened openings in the concavity of his abdomen. His only chance is to be fed by vein and wait for these fistulae to heal. He needs a new central line.

35   I could do it, I suppose. I am the experienced one now. But experience brings a new role: I am expected to teach the procedure instead. "See one, do one, teach one," the saying goes, and it is only half in jest.

    There is a junior resident on the service. She has done only one or two lines before. I tell her about Mr. G. I ask her if she is free to do a new line. She misinterprets this as a question. She says she still has patients to see and a case coming up later. Could

I do the line? I tell her no. She is unable to hide a grimace. She is burdened, as I was burdened, and perhaps frightened, as I was frightened.

She begins to focus when I make her talk through the steps—a kind of dry run, I figure. She hits nearly all the steps, but forgets about checking the labs and about Mr. G.'s nasty allergy to heparin, which is in the flush for the line. I make sure she registers this, then tell her to get set up and page me.

I am still adjusting to this role. It is painful enough taking responsibility for one's own failures. Being handmaiden to another's is something else entirely. It occurs to me that I could have broken open a kit and had her do an actual dry run. Then again, maybe I can't. The kits must cost a couple of hundred dollars each. I'll have to find out for next time.

Half an hour later, I get the page. The patient is draped. The resident is in her gown and gloves. She tells me that she has saline to flush the line with and that his labs are fine.

"Have you got the towel roll?" I ask.

She forgot the towel roll. I roll up a towel and slip it beneath Mr. G.'s back. I ask him if he's all right. He nods. After all he's been through, there is only resignation in his eyes.

The junior resident picks out a spot for the stick. The patient is hauntingly thin. I see every rib and fear that the resident will puncture his lung. She injects the numbing medication. Then she puts the big needle in, and the angle looks all wrong. I motion for her to reposition. This only makes her more uncertain. She pushes in deeper and I know she does not have it. She draws back on the syringe: no blood. She takes out the needle and tries again. And again the angle looks wrong. This time, Mr. G. feels the jab and jerks up in pain. I hold his arm. She gives him more numbing medication. It is all I can do not to take over. But she cannot learn without doing, I tell myself. I decide to let her have one more try.

Questions for Reading Actively

1. Why does Gawande conclude this essay as he does? How do you, as a reader, respond?

2. Obviously, Gawande is not writing for an audience who are about to perform the insertion of a large intravenous tube into the main blood vessel of the heart. Yet he gives a significant amount of detail as he describes the process of doing so. Each time he describes the insertion of such a tube, or "central line," his perceptions of the procedure change. What are the differences in Gawande's perceptions of each incident? What is Gawande's purpose for each description?

Questions for Thinking Critically

1. Gawande describes a kind of apprenticeship, a way in which knowledge and skills are passed along from one surgeon to another through example and practice. Is apprenticeship always the best way to learn, or teach, a particular skill or body of knowledge?

2. "Skill, surgeons believe, can be taught; tenacity cannot." Do you agree, or disagree? Describe a time in your life when being *tenacious* helped you to overcome an obstacle, to master a skill, or to solve a problem.

3. Why does Gawande describe the experience in paragraph 33 as "beautiful"? What, exactly, is "beautiful" about it? Have you experienced that same kind of "beauty" in accomplishing something difficult?

Question for Writing Thoughtfully

1. How does Gawande use chronology to organize his essay? Why is this a particularly effective organizational choice, given his subject and purpose?

Writing Project: A Narrative Showing the Effect of a Perception

The readings and Thinking-Writing activities in this chapter encourage you to become more aware of your perceptions, to use description to convey those perceptions, and to choose the appropriate organizing structure (chronology, narrative, and/or process) for writing about those perceptions.

Write a narrative essay describing the influence another person's perceptions had on your understanding of yourself, on a skill or body of knowledge you are learning, or on a significant decision you have made (or are in the process of making). When were you first made aware of this issue, conflict, idea, or skill? How did this other person (or persons) make their perceptions known to you? Were you initially in conflict with that other person, or have you always been in agreement? If there have been points of conflict in your relationship, did you learn and grow from them? How have your own perceptions grown and changed since knowing this other person (or persons)?

As part of your preparation for writing your essay, find a magazine or newspaper article dealing with the perception and quote from it at least once in your essay. Document the quoted material according to your instructor's directions. If an academic documentation format such as that of the Modern Language Association (MLA) or American Psychological Association (APA) is required, be sure that your entry conforms exactly to the models in a writing handbook.

The Writing Situation

Begin by considering the key elements in the Thinking-Writing Model on pages 6–7 in Chapter 1.

The following principles for writing narratives are not fixed rules; you may have good reasons for not following some of them. In general, though, they should help you to write an effective essay.

1. Identify the relevant issue fully so that the narrative has a meaningful context.

2. State your thesis well; place it effectively in your paper.

3. Use description to introduce your readers to the people involved and to let them visualize the place. Consider whether subjective or objective description, or a combination of the two, will best serve your purpose.

4. Tell the story as fully as seems appropriate for your intended audience, without either rambling excessively or leaving out important details or events.

5. Be sure to begin and end effectively. The conclusion is likely to be especially important in this essay since you may want to reiterate your main point there.

Purpose   You have a variety of purposes here. You have the opportunity to recall and relate a significant experience. You also can think about an issue that concerns you and learn more about it by finding the required article. In addition, you will be improving your ability to connect what you read with your own ideas, something you must do regularly as a college student. Most important, you can inform your classmates, your instructor, and your other readers about an issue that concerns you or skill that interests you and about the impact of another person's perception of that same issue.

Audience   As always, you are a member of your own audience and perhaps the person who will enjoy the narrative most since it is connected with your life. Your classmates will be a good audience, both to learn from your narrative and to share your experience. In addition, they are valuable as peer reviewers of your draft, reacting as intelligent readers who are also immersed in the assignment. Of course, anyone else who has had a similar experience would also benefit from reading your essay. Perhaps your campus newspaper would be interested. Finally, your instructor remains the audience who will judge how well you have planned, drafted, and revised. As a writing teacher, he or she cares about a clear focus, logical organization, specific details, and correctness. Keep these aspects in mind as you revise, edit, and proofread.

Subject   Although you and your readers are probably concerned about many perceptual issues, both you and they may need to be reminded of how an issue and a person's perceptions of it can affect someone else.

Writer   You are in a dual position here. You are, of course, the expert on your own story. This is both an advantage and a disadvantage: no one can argue with you about your story, but you still need to remember that your audience was not there. You must provide them with sufficient background and description to make them feel as if they did share your experience, but you don't want to overwhelm them with details. Therefore, you will need to be selective as you decide what to include and what to omit. Also, remember that you are not the expert on the article from which you plan to quote, so do think carefully about what it says and where to use it in your own work.

The Writing Process

The following sections will guide you through the stages of generating, planning, drafting, and revising as you work on a descriptive and illustrative narrative.

Generating Ideas

1. You may immediately recall a meaningful experience that you want to narrate. If not, think about past events that were worrisome, frightening, amusing, or exciting and then think again about the context of the event.

2. You may be deeply involved in dealing with others' perceptions of issues because of who you are, where you live, or which organizations you support. If so, you should have no problem identifying a concern you want to address. If not, look around, talk with friends and family members, read newspapers and magazines, and watch the news.

3. Think locally. Look at issues in your community or those connected with your college or job. Then try to recall any experiences in which another person's perceptions had an impact on you.

Defining a Focus   Draft a thesis statement that connects your experience with the perception you plan to write about. You may want to emphasize the directness of the connection, or you may need to show that what is not obvious is indeed related. Perhaps you may wish to emphasize a time element: "I didn't understand at the time, but now I see that . . ." or "I knew at that moment that . . ." You may want to focus on the impact this perception has had on your life.

Organizing Ideas   You could tell the story first and then connect it with the perceptual stereotype. Or you might make statements about the perception regularly throughout the narration as different events illustrate various aspects of the situation. In either case, your use of chronological order will help your audience follow the events of your story. Therefore, unless you see some serious reason not to do so, give background information first and then guide your audience through the time sequence of the events. You need to consider what arrangements will best help your audience see their connection to the issue. Be sure to select and place carefully the material quoted from your source and to incorporate it smoothly into your writing by introducing and commenting on it.

If you are using process writing in your essay, determine if the process itself can provide the organizational structure for the entire essay. Otherwise, be sure that each step of the process is clearly explained within each relevant paragraph.

Drafting   Begin with the easiest part to write, possibly the experience itself. Tell it fully; then plan to increase its effectiveness by including sharp details and a tight sequence of events at the revision stage. The paragraphs within the narrative may or may not have topic sentences. This is one of the differences between narration and exposition. Since your purpose is to connect the experience with others' perceptions, you may want to have topic sentences for the paragraphs that do that.

After you have drafted the narrative, draft the paragraphs that state the thesis and make the connection between the experience and the issue. Then establish and write any necessary transitions.

Revising, Editing, and Proofreading   Use the step-by-step method on pages 169–171 in Chapter 6 to revise your essay and prepare a final draft.

The following essay demonstrates how a student writer used a combination of description, process writing, and chronological ordering to illustrate how the perceptions of other people influenced his own decision.

Student Writing

Joshua Chaffee's Writing Process

Living so close to "Ground Zero," the site where the World Trade Center used to stand in New York City, Joshua Chaffee had an overwhelming number of perceptions, emotions, and experiences to sort through as he contemplated this essay. This experience was to define both his perceptions of his community and how he understood himself. Joshua knew he wanted to draw upon his experience as he approached this essay, but he also knew that he had to be careful with his organization and his descriptions. Often, when writing about something so overwhelming—and something experienced, even at a distance, by so many people—it becomes difficult to stay focused on your audience and your purpose. Joshua brought in the perceptions of other people to balance his own feelings. Here is an excerpt from Joshua's rough outline for this essay.

1. How did New Yorkers respond to 9/11?—keep it personal and specific; what did I personally witness? (Probably keep my emotions out of it—stick to what I perceived, not how I "felt"—that's too subjective and probably overwhelming. . . .)

2. Connect those perceptions to why I want to be a journalist. Can I talk to or find an article by another New York journalist who covered 9/11?—need to make a logical connection between 9/11 and why I want to be a journalist . . .

3. Incorporate as assignment for the "Feature Writing" course—how writing about New York (the La Frieda interview? the profile I did of Alan Kaufman and his pickle shop?) can give a voice to all New Yorkers, and connect that to my response to 9/11.

4. Conclusion?—maybe connect whatever I choose from "Feature Writing" to the behavior I witnessed on 9/11? A larger observation about why I love New York and want to stay here and do something for New Yorkers. . . .

We're All at Ground Zero

by Joshua Chaffee

From my bedroom window, I can see the six-story remainder of the World Trade Center's steel siding, forked in the ground, shooting up towards its former resting place in the New York City skyline. The site is lit through the entire night with an otherworldly glow, and men are working there, at "Ground Zero," when I go to sleep and when I wake up.

Outside my house, hundreds of people gather to cheer and offer their gratitude towards the workers. Each night I have joined them. At one point, a truck stops beside the crowd and a fireman inside exclaims, "We've just contacted two Port Authority Police Officers on the second floor and we're digging them out right now!" What follows is an eruption of yelling and cheering far greater than I have ever heard.

In an interview I did with former *New York Times* columnist turned novelist Anna Quindlen, she told me, "September 11th was a time that made me proud of the journalism profession. Journalists provided a huge public service to people because they created an instant sense of community. It was a time when I seriously considered writing columns again." After 9/11, Anna Quindlen re-affirmed her passion for journalism, while I discovered mine for the first time. It hit me on a Monday in late October of 2001.

About a month into the journalism course I was taking junior year, I found myself wedged in between Pat and Lisa La Frieda, scribbling madly onto a notepad because the air coolers in the meat locker were too loud for me to use my tape recorder. Outside the sun had yet to come up and, only weeks after September 11th, the air still smelled of ash. Inside, Pat La Frieda wore the same long, bloodstained white jacket and black knit cap characteristic of Italian-American butchers generations ago, when his grandparents owned La Frieda Meats. As he spoke to me, men hoisted sides of beef onto their shoulders while others sprayed the floor tiles with hoses to flush the blood into drains. The smell of cold, fresh meat permeated every corner of the long white room, a smell Pat relished as he slowly strolled past the lockers.

La Frieda Meats is located in Greenwich Village, one block east of the Hudson River and across the street from a controversial empty lot where an 18-story, luxury high-rise is planned to go up. The high-rise would be eight stories taller than any building near it, thus casting a long six-block shadow over the neighborhood. Pat had a lot to say on the topic. One question and he took off like a racehorse: "People have got to welcome advancement. You can't live in the past, saying how the Village used to be. Look, when my grandparents owned this meat packing business, they delivered the meat by horse drawn wagons every morning. Where would I be if I still used horses today!"

However, on the other side of me, his sister Lisa had a different point of view. Lisa is a large woman with heavy dark makeup. She jumped in, cutting off Pat, "Yeah, but you know what'll happen when they put in a luxury building? All the tenants will start screaming about my trucks coming in at four in the morning. And paying that much for an apartment, they probably got the right to complain." Sandwiched between Pat and Lisa, I tried to keep up with their words, which were barely audible above the meat coolers. I couldn't hold back a smile, though. Walking around a meat packing warehouse at six in the morning before school and talking to Pat and Lisa—I would rather be here than anywhere else, including my bed.

That Monday night I wrote about Pat and Lisa La Frieda, piecing their ideas into my article on the effects of the anticipated luxury high-rise. Hours later, I found myself still at my computer with a bowl of Chex Mix, writing and thinking about the interviews that morning. I understood what I had felt when I was standing in that frigid warehouse. I had realized my passion, and knew exactly what I wanted to be doing in the future. As a journalist, I have the opportunity to go out and have a half-hour conversation with some of the most interesting people—people I might otherwise never speak to. Then I come home and write about them; I give Pat and Lisa La Frieda a voice that they might never have used before—a voice that can be heard by hundreds of people.

The city is too big to know everyone's story. Most people don't know Alan Kaufman, the owner of the only remaining fresh pickle shop in the Lower East Side; or Joe Oliva, the 16-year security guard at Night Court, where every criminal arrested in Manhattan comes to be arraigned; or Chef José, the chef at a private Manhattan school, who was the head chef at United Airlines for most of his life. But, by opening up the worlds of everyone around us, journalists can unite a community.

This, I believe, is what Anna Quindlen meant by journalists creating "an instant sense of community," and this is what attracts me to the profession. Immediately after September 11, we all felt alone and frightened. But journalists showed us that everyone else was experiencing the same feelings, and that together we could help each other to understand and move on from what happened. When we are alone, our surroundings can seem overwhelming and unfriendly. But, through the telling of people's stories and the revealing of the true fabric of the city, New York can begin to feel as intimate as your family, and as small as a Village. All around the city people have come together. The city has united in a community of shared pain, devoted to its country and to each other. Everyone felt his or her hearts come down with those towers, but as we start to rebuild, we have each other for support.

Alternative Writing Projects

1. Ask someone with an interesting profession for permission to observe her or him at work. Keep careful notes, and if allowed, take audio and video recordings of that person at work. Write up an objective report of your findings. What were your perceptions of that kind of work before you began making your observations? How did your perceptions change? Next, draw up a list of questions for your subject based on your observations. Finally, write an objective profile of a day in the life of that particular kind of worker, using his or her own subjective comments as illustrations and evidence.

2. Create a podcast walking tour of a part of your campus or your community. Your audience will only be able to rely on your ability to verbally evoke particular sights, smells, and circumstances, so your descriptions must be especially rich and accurate. Then exchange podcasts with another student and offer each other constructive criticism on the quality of each other's language and the accuracy of each other's descriptions.

CHAPTER 7 Summary

- By actively selecting, organizing, and interpreting sensations, you can become better aware of your own perceptions. Then you will be better equipped to note the differences in the perceptions of others.

- To write thoughtfully, you need to know the difference between subjective perceptions, which include judgment, and objective perceptions, which include as little judgment as possible, and strive to be as objective in your writing as you can.

- Chronological writing focuses on illustrating growth, development, or change and can take the form of a narrative or process essay.

Jean-Christian Bourcart/Getty Images

Dr. Steven Pinker, a psychologist of language at Harvard University, has proposed that the human ability to not only *use* language but to think in terms of concepts and abstractions is wired into our very genes, and Pinker and other linguists such as Noam Chomsky have sought to prove that the human brain has evolved to recognize fundamental linguistic structures from a very early age. If there *is* a language gene, is there then also a music gene? What are the possible social and ethical impacts of these kinds of neurobiological research findings on what we as a society value about our humanity?

Writing to Classify and Define: Exploring Concepts

"Our life is what our thoughts make it."

—Marcus Aurelius

Internet, beauty, hip-hop culture, channel surfing, truth, bungee jumping, attitude, and *thinking* are only a few examples of concepts in a world filled with them. As you speak and write, you refer to concepts you have formed. Your academic study involves learning new concepts as well, and success in college and in your career requires understanding the conceptualizing process.

When you read textbooks or listen to lectures and take notes, you have to grasp key concepts and follow them as they are developed and supported. Many courses require you to apply the key concepts you have learned to new sets of circumstances. When you write essays, conduct research, or participate in group projects, you are expected to focus on certain concepts, develop and present a thesis (itself a concept), and support it with relevant evidence.

Your academic writing will often require the definition of terms or concepts. Chapter 6 discussed the fact that words are complex carriers of meaning—with meanings varying from person to person. This chapter will explore further implications of this complexity as it pertains to your writing.

The Writing Project in the chapter asks you to write a full definition of a concept that is important to your life. As you write this essay, you will see that definition usually involves using all the patterns of thinking that Chapter 7 discussed.

Definition is a very important thinking and writing pattern. When you write an essay that defines a concept, that concept is the subject of your essay. A clear idea of your audience will help you determine the kind of illustrations you will need to provide as well as the complexity of the language with which you describe those illustrations. Finally, the purpose of your essay (to demonstrate to your instructor that you have understood a concept, to introduce a complex concept to an audience unfamiliar with the subject, to explore how a concept has changed over time, and so on) will determine the rhetorical strategies you will use. The analytical activity of classification, which underlies defining, is essential to good thinking. Definition and classification rely on comparative relationships in order to establish categories by means of similarities and in order to distinguish among concepts within

Critical Thinking Focus: The conceptualizing process

Writing Focus: Defining and applying concepts

Reading Theme: Gender issues

Writing Project: Defining an important concept

categories by identifying differences. Definitions usually include descriptions and sometimes employ causal, chronological, or process analyses to make distinctions or to show the development of a concept. Understanding the thinking patterns that you have already worked with and being able to use them effectively can ease the difficult task of defining concepts.

To help you define significant concepts, this chapter will explain the conceptualizing process, present readings that involve definitions, and give you opportunities to define some terms that are significant in various aspects of your life.

What Are Concepts?

Concepts are general ideas that you use to organize your experience and, in so doing, bring order to your life. In the same way that words are the vocabulary of language, concepts are the vocabulary of thought. As organizers of your experience, concepts work in conjunction with language to identify, describe, distinguish, and relate all the various aspects of your world.

Developing expertise in the conceptualizing process improves your ability to form, apply, and relate concepts. This complex conceptualizing process is going on all the time in your mind, enabling you to think in a distinctly human way. When you form opinions or make judgments, you are applying and relating concepts.

How do you use concepts to organize and make sense of experience? Think back to the first day of the semester. For most students, this is a time to evaluate their courses by trying to determine which concepts apply.

- Will this course be interesting? useful? challenging?
- Is the instructor stimulating? demanding? understanding?
- Are the other students friendly? intelligent? conscientious?

Thinking-Writing Activity

CHANGING YOUR CONCEPTS

Identify an initial concept you had about an event in your life (a new job, attending college, getting married, and so on). After identifying your initial concept, describe the experiences that led you to change or modify the concept; then explain the new concept you formed to explain the situation. Your essay should include the following elements and use these rhetorical strategies:

- The initial concept (definition)
- New information provided by additional experiences (narration and description)
- The new concept formed to explain the situation (definition)

Each of these descriptive words or phrases represents a concept you are attempting to apply so that you can understand what is occurring at the moment and also anticipate what will occur. As the course progresses, you gather more information from experiences in class. This information may support your initial concepts, or it may conflict with them. If it supports them, you tend to maintain them ("Yes, I can see that this is going to be a difficult course"). When the information you receive conflicts with your initial concepts, you tend to find new concepts to explain the situation ("No, I can see that I was wrong—this course isn't going to be as difficult as I first thought"). A diagram of this process might look something like the one in Figure 8.1 below.

Throughout this thinking process you are making evaluations that establish classifications of kinds or types: What *kind* of course—difficult? easy? What *kind* of instructor? What *kind* of reading? What *kind* of student am I in relation to this course? And you are consciously or unconsciously using definitions that you have formulated: When I say "difficult course," I mean one that . . . When I say "demanding instructor," I mean one who . . . And so on.

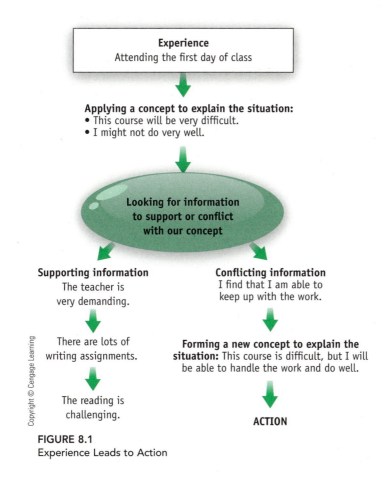

Copyright © Cengage Learning

FIGURE 8.1
Experience Leads to Action

The Importance of Concepts

Learning to understand and write about concepts will help you in every area of your life: academic, career, and personal. In college study, each academic discipline or subject uses many different concepts to organize experience, give explanations, and solve problems. Here is a sampling of college-level concepts: *entropy, subtext, Gemeinschaft, cell, metaphysics, relativity, parallel processing, prehistory, unconscious, aesthetic, minor key, interface, health, quantum mechanics, schizophrenia.* To make sense of how disciplines function, you need to understand what the concepts of that discipline mean, how to define them, how to apply them, and how they relate to other concepts.

Although each academic discipline has its own unique and specific concepts, some concepts change their definition according to the disciplinary "lens" used to interpret it. In the following passage from *Colour: Art & Science*, physiologist Trevor Lamb describes how the concept of *color* is understood by different academic disciplines.

> Although the idea of "colour" may seem a simple concept, it conjures up very different ideas for each of us. To the physicist, colour is determined by the wavelength of light. To the physiologist and psychologist, our perception of colour involves neural responses in the eye and the brain, and is subject to the limitations of our nervous system. To the naturalist, colour is not only a thing of beauty but also a determinant of survival in nature. To the social historian and linguist, our understanding and interpretation of colour are inextricably linked to our own culture. To the art historian, the development of colour in painting can be traced both in artistic and technological terms. And for the painter, colour provides a means of expressing feelings and the intangible, making possible the creation of a work of art. . . . In the field of colour, the arts and the sciences now travel in unison, and together they provide a rich and comprehensive understanding of the subject.

You will regularly present your understanding of definitions, of applications, and of relationships among concepts in your written work. You will also learn the methods of investigation, patterns of thought, and forms of reasoning that various disciplines use to form larger conceptual theories and methods. Successful completion of writing, research, and presentation assignments in your college courses will depend on your understanding of the key concepts that form the core of each discipline.

Regardless of their specific knowledge content, all careers require conceptual abilities, whether you are trying to apply a legal principle, develop a promotional theme, or devise a new computer program. Similarly, expertise in forming and applying concepts helps you to make sense of your personal life, understand others, and make informed decisions. The Greek philosopher Aristotle said that the intelligent person is a "master of concepts."

The Structure of Concepts

Concepts, in addition to being general ideas that you use to identify and organize your experience, are useful for distinguishing and connecting one thing to another. Concepts allow you to organize your world into patterns that make sense to you.

In their role of organizers of experience, concepts act to group aspects of your experience on the basis of their similarity. Consider the object that you usually write with: a notebook computer. The concept *notebook computer* represents an instrument that you use for writing. Now look around the classroom at other instruments people are using to write. You use the concept *notebook computer* to identify these as well, even though they may look quite different from yours. Thus, the concept *notebook computer* not only helps you to make distinctions in your experience by indicating how notebook computers differ from handhelds, cell phones, or desktops; it also helps you to determine which items are similar enough to all be called notebook computers. When you put items into a group with a single description—such as *notebook computers*—you are focusing on their similarities:

- They use internal hard drives.
- They are used for writing, research, communication, and entertainment.
- Each is portable.

Being able to see and name the similarities among certain things in your experience is the way you form concepts and is crucial for making sense of your world. If you were not able to do this, everything in the world would appear to be different, with its own individual name.

The Process of Classifying

The process by which you group things on the basis of their similarities is known as *classifying*. Classifying is a natural human activity that goes on all the time. In most cases, however, you are not conscious of classifying something in a particular sort of way; you do so automatically. The process of classifying is one of the main ways that you order, organize, and make sense of your world. Because no two things or experiences are exactly alike, your ability to classify things into various groups is what enables you to recognize things in your experience. When you perceive a notebook computer, you recognize it as a *kind* of object you have seen before. Even though you may not have seen this particular notebook computer, you recognize that it belongs to a category of things that is familiar.

The best way to understand the structure of concepts is to visualize them by means of a model. Examine Figure 8.2. The *sign* is the word or symbol used to name or designate the concept; for example, the word *triangle* is a sign. The *referents* represent all the various examples of the concept; the three-sided figure we are using as our model is an example of the concept *triangle*. The *properties* of the concept are the features that all things named by the word or sign share in common; all examples of the concept *triangle* share the characteristics of being a polygon and having three sides. These are the properties that we refer to when we define concepts; thus, "A triangle is a three-sided polygon."

Properties
(Qualities that all examples of the concept share in common)

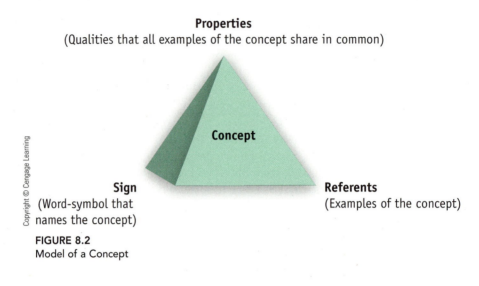

Concept

Sign
(Word-symbol that
names the concept)

Referents
(Examples of the concept)

FIGURE 8.2
Model of a Concept

Properties
Wheels, chassis, engine, seats for passengers

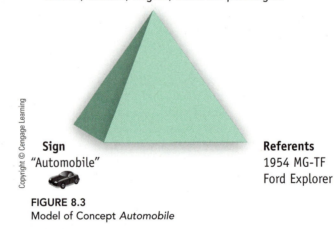

Sign
"Automobile"

Referents
1954 MG-TF
Ford Explorer

FIGURE 8.3
Model of Concept *Automobile*

Let's take another example. Suppose you wanted to explore the structure of the concept *automobile*. The sign that names the concept is the word *automobile* or the symbol ██. Referents of the concept include the 1954 MG-TF currently residing in the garage as well as the Ford Explorer parked in front of the house. The properties that all things named by the sign *automobile* include are wheels, a chassis, an engine, seats, and so on. Figure 8.3 shows a conceptual model of the concept *automobile*.

Thinking-Writing Activity

DIAGRAMMING CONCEPTS

Using the model we have developed, diagram the structure of three of the following concepts as well as those of two concepts of your own choice: *dance, success, student, religion, music, friend.*

Forming Concepts

You form—and apply—concepts to organize your experience, make sense of what is happening, and anticipate what may happen in the future. You form concepts by the interactive processes of *generalizing* (focusing on the common properties shared by a group of things) and *interpreting* (finding examples of the concept). The common properties form the necessary requirements that must be met in order for you to be able to apply the concept to your experience. If you examine the diagrams of concepts in the last section, you can see that the process of forming concepts involves moving back and forth between the referents (examples) of the concept and the properties (common features) shared by all examples of the concept. Let's further explore the way this interactive process of forming concepts operates.

Consider the following conversation between two people trying to form and clarify the concept *philosophy.*

A: What is your idea of what philosophy *means*?

B: Well, I think philosophy involves expressing important beliefs that you have—like discussing the meaning of life, assuming that there is a meaning.

A: Is explaining my belief about who's going to win the Super Bowl engaging in philosophy? After all, this is a belief that is very important to me—I've got a lot of money riding on the outcome!

B: I don't think so. A philosophical belief is usually a belief about something that is important to everyone—like what standards we should use to guide our moral choices.

A: What about the message that was in my fortune cookie last night: "Eat, drink, and be merry, for tomorrow we diet!"? This is certainly a belief that most people can relate to, especially during a holiday season! Is this philosophy?

B: I think that's what my grandmother used to call "foolosophy"! Philosophical beliefs are usually deeply felt views to which we have given a great deal of thought—not something plucked out of a cookie.

A: What about my belief in the golden rule "Do unto others as you would have them do unto you" because "What goes around comes around"? Doesn't that have the qualities that you mentioned?

B: Now you've got it!

As we review this dialogue, we can see that forming the concept *philosophy* works hand in hand with applying the concept to different examples. When two or more things work together in this way, we say that they *interact*. In this case, there are two parts of this interactive process.

We form concepts by generalizing, by focusing on the similar features among different things. In the previous dialogue, the things about which generalizations are being made are types of beliefs—beliefs about the meaning of life or about standards we use to guide our moral choices. By focusing on the similar features of these beliefs, the dialogue's two participants develop a list of properties philosophical beliefs share, including (1) beliefs dealing with important issues in life about which everyone is concerned and (2) beliefs reflecting deeply felt views—views to which people have given much thought. These common properties act as the requirements a viewpoint must meet to be considered a philosophical belief.

We apply concepts by interpreting, by looking for different examples of a concept and seeing if they meet the requirements of the concept we are developing. In the preceding dialogue, one participant attempts to apply the concept of *philosophy* to the following examples:

a belief about the outcome of the Super Bowl

a fortune cookie message: "Eat, drink, and be merry, for tomorrow we diet."

Each of these proposed examples suggests the development of new requirements for the concept to help clarify how the concept can be applied. Applying a concept to different possible examples thus becomes the way we develop and gradually sharpen our idea of it.

Even when a proposed example turns out not to be a valid one, the process of questioning often clarifies our understanding of that concept. For instance, although the proposed example of a belief about the outcome of the Super Bowl turned out not to be an example of the concept *philosophy*, examining it helped to clarify the concept and suggest other examples.

The process of developing concepts involves a constant back-and-forth movement between generalizing and interpreting. As the back-and-forth movement progresses, we gradually develop a list of specific requirements for an example of the concept; at the same time, we gain a clearer sense of how the concept is defined. We are also developing a collection of examples that embody the qualities of the concept and demonstrate situations in which the concept applies. This interactive process is illustrated in Figure 8.4.

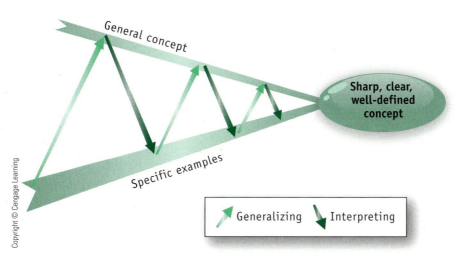

FIGURE 8.4
Movement from General Concept to Well-Defined Concept

Thinking-Writing Activity

FORMING A CONCEPT

Select a type of music with which you are familiar and write a dialogue similar to the one just examined. In the course of the dialogue, be sure to include the following:

1. Examples from which you are generalizing (such as specific bands)

2. General properties shared by various types of this music (e.g., "Jazz is a uniquely American form of music that uses complex rhythms and improvisation.")

3. Examples to which you are trying to apply the developing concept (such as the music of Marian McPartland, Miles Davis, or Thelonius Monk)

Forming concepts involves performing the operations of generalizing and interpreting together for two reasons:

1. You cannot form a concept unless you know how it might apply. If you have absolutely no idea what *jazz* or *philosophy* might exemplify, you cannot begin to form the concept, even in vague or general terms.

2. You cannot gather examples of the concept unless you know what they might be examples of. Until you begin to develop some idea of what the concepts *jazz* or *philosophy* might be (based on certain similarities among various things), you won't know where to look for examples of the concept (or how to evaluate them).

THINKING CRITICALLY ABOUT NEW MEDIA

Using New Media to Research a Concept

It's difficult to imagine, but it wasn't that long ago that if you wanted to research a subject, you had to physically go to the library and use the card catalog or periodical room to conduct your research. The creation of computers and the Internet has changed all of that, of course. Not only don't you have to go to a library, you don't even have to be sitting in front of a computer—through your cell phone or PDA you literally have the world at your fingertips.

In this new information universe, it's not simply our mobility that has been revolutionized, it's the *way* in which we're able to conduct research, roaming far and wide, with one link leading to another, and to another, and so on. It's very much the way in which our brain makes connections: spontaneously, dynamically, and at lightning speed.

Of course, as we've seen, with that boundless sea of information out there, it's essential that we keep our critical thinking abilities dialed up to the maximum so that we can distinguish the true from false, objective from subjective, and fact from fiction. It's been said that in this new media age "We're drowning in information but we're starved for knowledge." The reason for this is that "information" is *not* "knowledge." As we have seen in earlier chapters, information doesn't become knowledge until the human mind has *acted* upon it: analyzing, synthesizing, applying, evaluating, *thinking critically* about it.

Thinking-Writing Activity

MEDIA AS A CONCEPT

What is your concept of what media is? Go through the process of generalizing, interpreting, and then narrowing your ideas until you have specific examples and a sharp, clear, well-defined concept. Now compare your results with those of your classmates.

This interactive process is the way that you usually form all concepts, particularly the complicated ones. In college, much of your education is focused on carefully forming and exploring key concepts such as *democracy, dynamic equilibrium,* and *personality.*

Applying Concepts

Making sense of our experience means finding the right concept to explain what is going on. To determine whether the concept we have selected fits a situation, we have to determine whether the requirements that form the concept are being met.

To figure out which concept applies to the situation, we must do the following:

1. Be aware of the properties that form the boundaries of the concept.

2. Determine whether the experience meets those requirements, for only if it does can we apply the concept to it.

If we have the requirements of the concept clearly in mind, we can proceed to figure out which of these requirements are met by the experience. This is how we apply concepts, which is one of the most important ways we have for figuring out what is taking place in our experience.

Determining the Requirements of a Concept

In determining the requirements of a concept, we ask ourselves: *Would something still be an example of this concept if that thing did not meet this requirement?* If the answer to this question is *no*—that something would not be an example of this concept if it did not meet this requirement—we can say the requirement is a necessary part of the concept.

Consider the concept *dog*. Which of the following descriptions are requirements that must be met by an example of this concept?

1. Is an animal

2. Normally has four legs and a tail

3. Bites the mail carrier

It is clear that descriptions 1 and 2 are requirements that must be met to apply the concept *dog* because if we apply our test question—"Would something be an example of this concept if that thing did not meet this requirement?"—we can say that the thing would not be an example of the concept *dog* if it did not fit the first two descriptions: if it was not an animal and did not normally have four legs and a tail.

This does not seem to be the case, however, with description 3. If we ask ourselves the same test question, we can see that the thing might still be an example of the concept *dog* even if it did not bite the mail carrier. Even though some dogs do in fact bite mail carriers, this is not a requirement for being a dog.

Of course, there may be other things that meet these requirements but are not dogs. For example, a cat is an animal (description 1) that normally has four legs and a tail (description 2). What this means is that the requirements of a concept tell us only what attributes something must have to be an example of the concept. As a result, we often have to identify additional requirements that will define the concept more sharply. These requirements determine when the concept can be applied and indicate those things that qualify as examples of it. When we are able

Thinking Critically About Visuals

Fashion Statements as Concepts

There has always been a relationship between popular music and fashion, but this connection became even more prominent with the advent of music videos and MTV. For many performers today, fashion and dance choreography are an integral part of the overall music performance. For example, "Lady Gaga" (born Stefani Joanne Angelina Germanotta) uses elaborate costumes to frame her songs and has stated that "fashion is an inspiration for the song writing and her performances." We can contrast her "glam rock" (also exemplified by musicians like David Bowie, Freddy Mercury, Michael Jackson, and Madonna) with the fashion statements of other forms of music.

For example, in the mid-1970s, a grimmer countercultural youth movement was forming in New York City's underground music clubs and the streets of London.

Source: AP Photo/Peter Kramer

Punk, with its anarchic politics and shock-value fashion and music, had a bleak view of the potential for social change. However, just like the "glam rock" of Lady Gaga, and others, punk's fashion statements soon became part of the mainstream. What are some of the fashion statements of the forms of music with which you are familiar?

Playwright David Mamet has written: "The pursuit of Fashion is the attempt of the middle class to co-opt tragedy. In adopting the clothing, speech, and personal habits of those in straitened, dangerous, or pitiful circumstances, the middle class seeks to have what it feels to be the exigent and nonequivocal experiences had by those it emulates." In your own words, what is Mamet's argument about fashion? Can fashion choices that are meant to be political or social statements ever be frivolous, irresponsible, or counterproductive?

to identify all the requirements of the concept, we say these requirements are both necessary and sufficient for applying the concept.

Analyzing Complex Concepts

Although dealing with concepts like *dog* and *cat* may seem simple, matters become somewhat confusing when you start analyzing the more complex concepts you will encounter in your academic study. For example, consider the concepts of *masculinity* and *femininity*, two of the more emotionally charged and politically contentious concepts in our culture. There are many different perspectives on what these concepts mean, what they should mean, or whether we should be using them at all. See if you can identify properties and examples of these two concepts by completing the following Thinking-Writing Activity.

Thinking-Writing Activity

EXPLORING THE CONCEPTS OF MASCULINE AND FEMININE

Identify what you consider the essential properties (specific requirements that must be met to apply the concept) for each of these concepts as well as examples of people or behavior that illustrates these properties. For example, you might identify physical risk taking as a property of the concept *masculinity* and identify Russell Crowe as a person who illustrates this quality. Or you might identify intuition as a property of the concept *femininity*, illustrating this with the behavior "knowing without the conscious use of rational processes."

General Properties   *Specific Examples*

FEMININITY

1. _____   1. _____

2. _____   2. _____

3. _____   3. _____

MASCULINITY

1. _____   1. _____

2. _____   2. _____

3. _____   3. _____

Compare your list with those of your classmates. What similarities and differences do you notice? What factors might account for these similarities and differences? Look back at your responses after you have read the following selections.

A Casebook on Gender and Sexuality

It would seem to be the easiest characteristic to define, the most basic classification into which we can sort human beings: Are you a man or a woman? Is your behavior feminine or masculine? And yet the dazzling variety of human responses, preferences, fears, and favors blurs these apparently simple distinctions into a never-ending source of pleasure and conflict. Not surprisingly, the similarities and differences between men and women have inspired poets and storytellers as well as provoked the interests of social scientists and essayists. In the following casebook, writers across genres and perspectives attempt to define and classify the concepts of gender and sexuality.

"Choosing Clothes, but Not Husbands"

by Joseph Berger

Journalist Joseph Berger immigrated to New York City from Russia as a small boy just after the Second World War. He began his professional career as an English teacher at a Bronx, New York, public school and joined the staff of the *New York Post* as a reporter in 1971. He has covered religion, education, and science for the *Post* and *New York Newsday* and since 1985 for the *New York Times*, where "Choosing Clothes, but Not Husbands" first appeared in November 2004. In his 2001 memoir, *Displaced Persons: Growing Up American after the Holocaust*, Berger eloquently explored the tensions of a family caught between historical events, lost cultures, and missed opportunities. His insight and experience are evident in this article about female Afghan immigrants in New York City who are balancing tradition and possibility in their own lives.

By all appearances, Ashrat Khwajazadah and Naheed Mawjzada are thoroughly modern American women.

Long-haired and dark-eyed, they spurn the headscarves and modest outfits customarily worn by Afghan women, preferring hip-hugging slacks. Both of them are in their early twenties and both of them have taken a route still somewhat controversial among Afghans in Flushing, Queens—going to college to pursue professions. Ms. Khwajazadah studied speech pathology at Queens College and Ms. Mawjzada majors in political science at Adelphi University. Both also defy the ideal of a reticent Afghan womanhood, with Ms. Mawjzada speaking up forcefully when men talk politics at the dinner table.

But there are incongruities. Both of them, by design, have never dated. Like most young women in their Afghan enclave in Flushing, they are waiting for their parents to pick their spouses.

"It's been drilled into your head since you were a little girl: 'Don't talk with guys, don't ruin your reputation, everyone will gossip about you,'" said Ms. Khwajazadah, a high-spirited woman who came here as a two-year-old with her refugee parents. Nevertheless, she added, "I'm happy with my decision."

5 "I'm very close with my family and that helps me because they want to do what's best for me," she said.

In testing how far they can go in forsaking tradition, these women illustrate the delicate balance younger Afghans, particularly women, have had to strike as they grow up in a comparatively freewheeling society with parents—often uneducated and unable to speak English—who have held tight to their Afghan conventions.

To be sure, the Afghans' transition is an old immigrant story—one that could be told about the Irish, Italians and Jews of the nineteenth century or the newer groups that have seasoned New York City's stew. Those newcomers too looked on with anger or resignation as their children gradually (and their grandchildren more cavalierly) adopted the prevailing culture.

But the Afghan version has its own endemic twists, community advocates say. Older Afghans, particularly women, often have had no schooling whatsoever. Even today, some families insist that girls, whose non-Afghan friends roam freely, return home immediately after school. It is not uncommon for girls to be engaged as young as thirteen and be married by sixteen.

The Afghan story in New York has garnered more than the usual curiosity because Afghanistan has drawn so much attention on the world stage, first in the military response to September 11 and now as the fragile government of President Hamid Karzai tries to establish democracy, including expansion of women's rights.

10 There are 5,446 Afghans in New York City and over 9,100 in the metropolitan area, according to the 2000 census. A large proportion came here with grants of asylum after treacherous odysseys to escape either the Soviet occupation of 1979 or Taliban rule that began in 1996.

Manizha Naderi, the twenty-eight-year-old director of Women for Afghan Women, which offers counseling and instructional programs, remembers how at four years old she crossed the desert into Pakistan on a single motorcycle that also carried her parents, her two-year-old brother, nine-month-old sister and the driver.

The two largest enclaves of Afghans are in Flushing—north of Queens College and in the largely Chinese and Korean area north of Northern Boulevard. Flushing has four Afghan mosques, a half-dozen kabob houses and the Kouchi Market, which besides native spices and breads carries Afghan mandolins (rababs) and billiards-like board games (karams).

New Yorkers commonly encounter Afghan men in the fried chicken restaurants they own and in the ubiquitous sidewalk coffee carts of Midtown. But women are more out of sight. A quarter of Afghan women have never been to school and only half have completed high school, according to a study by Andrew A. Beveridge, a sociology professor at Queens College, and Kaisa Hagen, a student there. Only one quarter work outside the home, compared with 60 percent for other New York women.

Ms. Naderi said that "Afghanistan has a very patriarchal culture and women don't have rights," and those views migrate here.

15 "Men have corrupted views of Islam and actually believe women are second-class citizens and are there to take care of them," she said. "They don't let them go to school or to work."

Afghans from the capital, Kabul, are less bound by tradition than those from the villages, and those who fled the Soviets are more conservative than those who fled the Taliban. Some Afghan Muslims who have been here for decades are so acculturated they put up Christmas trees, but in general Afghans here are trying to sustain crucial remnants of their culture.

For more than a few families even the notion of educating their daughters beyond high school is regarded as daring, Ms. Naderi said. But more leaders are encouraging it. Mohammed Sherzad, the imam of Masjid Hazrat-I-Abubakr Sadiq, on Union Street in north Flushing (there is a similarly named mosque nearby from which Imam Sherzad was ousted) looks favorably upon women who postpone having children until they finish college.

"A good woman is one who is educated, both for her children and her society," he said.

Dr. Tahira Homayun, a gynecologist whose husband is an economic adviser to President Karzai, said some Afghan girls have more successful school careers than their brothers because struggling families often press boys to work.

20   Ms. Naderi said that as a result of the community's lingering patriarchal structures, violence toward wives is much more common than the community admits.

"There's a saying that the food your husband feeds you doesn't come for free," she said. "And men actually think they have a right under the Koran to beat their wives."

But no characteristic seems more ironclad than the convention of having parents arrange their children's marriages.

"Afghan people can't meet each other prior to getting engaged," said a sixty-five-year-old mother of six who was taking English classes given by Women for Afghan Women. She asked that her name not be used because seeing her name in print made her uncomfortable. "It's an embarrassment for the family."

Much of that stigma derives from the treasured principle of family honor. If a daughter chooses to find her own spouse, her father's stature will be diminished, the family name tainted by gossip, and her sisters may find it harder to marry.

25   "The girl is a trophy piece," said Ms. Mawjzada, the daughter of a coffee vendor who in addition to studying at Adelphi works in customer service at Geico insurance. "If the girl has a good reputation, the family has a good reputation."

Parents are more willing to close their eyes to a teenage Don Juan, and marriage customs for a man are also more lenient. Bashir Rahim, a twenty-nine-year-old computer technician, says if he meets a girl that interests him at a family gathering, he might ask her for her address, then send his parents to her home to start a conversation about marriage.

Girls learn by trial and error how far they can stretch tradition, but defying the code outright exacts a steep price. Ms. Naderi was married at sixteen to a man she chose on her own. Her mother and grandmother did not speak to her for ten years.

"My mother still tells me she can't look at people because they know her daughter married in this way," she said.

Masuda Sultan, a twenty-six-year-old Flushing woman who is doing graduate work in public administration at the Kennedy School of Government at Harvard, was not even sixteen when her father, the owner of a fried chicken restaurant in Harlem, contrived with an acquaintance to have her married to a doctor twice her age. She got to see her future husband three times before the wedding.

30 "I actually thought it could work," she recalled. "When your actions are limited and you're from a certain world and you're young and you respect your family, you go along with their wishes even if you have extreme doubts."

Key issues like how far she could go in school were left murky. But when it became clear after the wedding that Ms. Sultan wanted to put off having children until she finished college, the tensions became irreconcilable. Ms. Sultan lapsed into what she called a deep depression, and after three years she and her husband agreed to divorce, a rare and humiliating event in the Afghan community and one that often attaches blame to the woman. Ms. Sultan, who moved back with her parents into the same room she had shared with her sister, recalled that female friends found it so difficult to believe that she could leave her husband for the reasons she did that they asked if he beat or betrayed her.

"The core issue was really a different philosophy of what it means to be Afghan and what it means to be American," she said. "Ultimately I was being treated as a child and my role was set and I was told what I could and couldn't do."

Questions for Reading Actively

1. How does the author, Joseph Berger, use comparison and contrast to suggest conflict? What concepts does he compare and contrast?

2. Why would the subject of this article be of interest to readers of the *New York Times*? What other kinds of readers or audiences does this subject appeal to, and why?

Questions for Thinking Critically

1. How do the young Afghan women portrayed in this article negotiate the different concepts of femininity and women's social roles held by their traditional families and their new American communities?

2. How are certain concepts—such as *reputation, gossip,* and *honor*—used by the writer of this article and by the people he interviews? How does each concept and the impact of the word used to express it change according to its cultural context? (See Chapter 6 for more on the impact of language choices.)

3. What kinds of decision-making strategies do the young Afghan immigrants in this article use in order to appease their families while also fulfilling their own ambitions? Review Decisions in Your Life (in Chapter 5) and describe how applying these decision-making steps did, or could have, assisted these women in their decisions.

Question for Writing Thoughtfully

1. What kinds of evidence, illustration, and authority does the author cite in order to give substance to his thesis? This article was written in 2004. Do some research and create a list of new pieces of evidence, illustration, and authority that the author could use to update his article.

"Women and Femininity in the U.S. Popular Culture"

by Susan Grayson

From *New Dictionary of the History of Ideas*

Before the women's movement and deconstruction, the term *femininity* was understood as the opposite of the more obvious *masculinity*. Femininity represented those traits, characteristics, behaviors, or thought patterns not associated with a given society's expectations of men. Until the cultural upheaval of the late 1960s in the United States and elsewhere, the sweetly patient "angel of the house" persisted as the womanly ideal. Women learned to be feminine "in the image that suited the masculine desires" (quoted in Costa, p. 222), an image that included deference, respect, and obedience to males. In compensation, the woman held the passive power of the dispossessed. Submissive, soft-voiced, empathic, and maternal, the feminine woman would be willing to subordinate her own needs in order to better please others.

Femininity as a principle or "exquisite esthetic," as Susan Brownmiller puts it in *Femininity* (1984), "pleases men because it makes them appear more masculine by contrast . . . conferring an extra portion of unearned gender distinction on men, an unchallenged space in which to breathe freely and feel stronger, wiser, more competent, is femininity's special gift" (p. 16). This gift, however, costs the giver. Girls and young women learn they must adhere to standards of comportment, physical presentation, and appearance according to the demands and currency of their respective cultures and classes or face disapproval, even social failure, ostracism, rejection.

In a postbinary world, however, definitions of femininity as well as masculinity have blurred. Definitions of femininity are no longer standardized and are therefore seemingly open, writes Maggie Mulqueen in *On Our Own Terms*. They arise "*only* from the culture, not from theory. . . . In reality, though, the cultural prescriptions about femininity (and masculinity) are very narrow and influential" (p. 13). These influential prescriptions consist of social expectations and the pressure to conform, particularly in adolescence. A girl's sexual awakening and turbulent maturation eventually steer her toward pleasing boys and winning admiration, envy, and acceptance from her peers.

Beauty and Class

In addition, the reigning elements of femininity and their effect on women resonate according to one's class and race, criteria that can locate a woman along the continuum of behavior and attractiveness. Class is a fluid or changeable category; race is generally not, though beauty treatments can "standardize" ethnic features like hair color and texture (see below) or influence acceptable limits of body size.

Related to class are the awareness of and access to proper nutrition as well as the availability of leisure time for exercise, factors associated with the maintenance of lean body mass. The proportion of lean mass to body fat contributes to the impression of overall girth and therefore health. Few men, young or old, strive to be gaunt, and fewer men than women are dissatisfied with their bodies even if they are somewhat overweight. Instead, they value size especially if the bulk is muscle rather than fat. Men's "perceptions serve to keep them satisfied with their bodies, whereas women's serve to keep them dissatisfied," writes Sarah Grogan (pp. 144–145). American women of any age, however, find thinness the only tolerable size, despite evidence that men prefer somewhat rounder female bodies than women think they do.

Preferred body size and proportion reflect class-related tastes or expectations. Researchers have suggested that different social classes have distinct ideas of attractiveness, and magazines gear to these readers. The fleshiness of magazine models varies according to the social class of the targeted audience, be it male or female. Magazines for upwardly mobile homemakers have trim but not skinny models. Family-oriented magazines present more modest images typical of pleasant-looking housewives. So-called pulp magazines feature curvier bodies: "the lower the social class ranking of the magazine the bigger the chest and hip measurements of the models," observes Nora Scott Kinzer (p. 165). Magazine models are rarely if ever overweight; in fact, compared with their counterparts from the 1950s, they generally weigh less and have smaller measurements.

Viewing and Being Seen

Because she frequently feels on display, a woman monitors her physical appearance in mirrors, in store windows, and in the eyes and expressions of people who see her. Self-criticism originates not only in the woman herself but also from the internalized voice of male culture and the parents who teach her how to dress and present herself. John Berger's *Ways of Seeing* (1972) articulates the concepts of viewer and viewed by noting that the observer is generally male and the object observed, female. Though intended as an assessment of the subject in Western European painting, Berger's remarks apply equally to contemporary representations of women in the media: "Women watch themselves being looked at. . . . The surveyor of woman in herself is male: the surveyed female" (p. 47).

Women internalize femininity's burden of self-monitoring along with this same male gaze as they compare themselves, usually unfavorably, with the ideal face and body that they imagine the male conjures up in his mind's eye. In her article "The Persistence of Vision," Donna Haraway rejects the power that the male gaze assumes as it "mythically inscribes all the marked [e.g., female] bodies, that makes the unmarked category claim the power to see and not be seen, to represent while escaping representation. This gaze signifies the unmarked positions of Man and White" (quoted in Conboy, Medina, and Stanbury, p. 282). White males, the cliché goes, see a generic human being when they view themselves in the mirror; everyone else sees the markings of gender, race, or both.

Femininity, Attractiveness, and Science

Scientifically measurable differences in male and female prenatal hormone levels and in brain development, among other areas, have rekindled questions of the origins of, tendencies toward, and social reinforcements of masculinity and femininity as well as gender identity. Because the data lend themselves to different conclusions as to whether or not physical attractiveness has a scientific basis beyond its aesthetic component, studies from social theorists could lead to one set of interpretations; studies by sociobiologists and evolutionary psychologists to quite another.

Genetic survival, or maximizing the number of genes passed on in successive generations, is consistent with the latter's viewpoint regarding physical attractiveness. Sociobiologists and evolutionary psychologists would associate good looks with reproductive fitness and health. Traits like waist-to-hip ratio (WHR) and signs of overall health (luster of hair, vigor) attract attention from the opposite sex presumably because they indicate reproductive vigor. This paradigm, though, does not explain popular culture's preference for thin women rather than voluptuous or even overweight bodies with the optimal WHR; nor the preference for larger breasts, despite the irrelevance of breast size to milk production.

Moreover, while a wide pelvis should indicate a desirable mate for childbearing capacity, such was not the case in the last quarter of the twentieth century. Since the exaggerated thinness of the English model Twiggy, the ideal female figure of international supermodels resembles more the body of a twelve-year-old boy with long, slim limbs and small hips—androgynous rather than womanly. This preferred body type, however, seems unconnected to carrying and suckling an infant. The trend for a flat torso and stomach has replaced the breast as the focus of the female body. So prevalent are breast implants that one no longer can assume that a generous bra size is natural. A flat, well-muscled abdomen, on the other hand, indicates controlled food intake and a fitness routine. One anthropologist terms it "a modern-day virginity symbol" that suggests "a woman who has never borne children and thus has all of her years of fertility in front of her" (quoted in Bellafante, p. 9).

The American author Kim Chernin has discussed the relationship of female slimness to the power of the mother over infant sons, a power which a more robust-sized woman would recall unconsciously in men and which would threaten them. In fact, potential mothers are expected to be physically smaller and more delicate than men—thinner and less well-muscled than their protectors—but at the same time tall enough and long enough of bone to indicate good childhood nutrition and thus reproductive vitality. Today, particularly in puritanical America, slimness suggests self-control and mastery of sensuality in a society when fattening food is readily available and sex as much a sport as an erotic or intimate experience. Yet historically, a well-padded body was considered ideal as it indicated health and prosperity in centuries when starvation and illness were a constant threat.

Sociobiologists and evolutionary psychologists would identify reproduction as the main source of aggression and display in males and females. Despite social variations in these areas, reproductive rivalry, assertive courtship behaviors, and conflicts seem universal among males as they compete for potential mates. Feminine behavior appears to confer a further advantage in public by not threatening strangers. Women displaying such qualities as compliance, warmth, receptivity, and responsiveness can disarm interpersonal tension. The Norwegian social scientist Tore Bjerke notes that "the woman who looks and acts the most feminine (stereotypically speaking) is least likely to provoke an aggressive response after intruding on others" (Van der Dennen, p. 118).

Social constructionists could argue, however, that these trends become exaggerated by class, race, status, and any given society's standards of a pleasing physical appearance—what one could label an attractiveness quotient. This quotient differs for males and females according to their biological imperatives: for men, the need to inseminate as much as possible; for women, the need to choose the male who promises the greatest stability and capacity to provide materially for offspring.

Bionic Beauty and Distorted Views of the Self

In a culture saturated with idealized and retouched photos of models, comparisons of "ideal" and ordinary bodies seem inescapable, whether by others or by oneself. The American sociologist Leon Festinger's Social Comparison Theory of self-evaluation based on external models "would predict that people might use images projected by the media as standards for comparison" (Grogan, p. 100). Constant bombardment with an unattainable ideal of "models' bodies (slim and carefully arranged in the most flattering poses) would be expected to lead to unfavorable evaluation of the body of the perceiver" (Grogan, pp. 100–101). Some women do indeed report greater dissatisfaction with their own appearance than before exposure, others "no change," and some even report increased satisfaction. Grogan cites another study that correlates exposure and more negative body image to pre-test attitudes about the body. Clearly, studies of women exposed to media images have yielded mixed results.

In any case, such comparisons increase a young woman's sense that her appearance is substandard and urgently in need of repair. Forgotten is the reality that hair and makeup artists spend hours preparing models for these photos. Even then, the images can be airbrushed and pasted together. One actress (Julia Roberts) found magazine photos of herself to be a composite of different shots. Another (Kate Winslet) was displeased to find that her thighs had been slimmed in a picture air-brushed without her permission.

In their real lives, not even models or media stars resemble their carefully staged professional photos. How, then, can any woman without such resources escape disappointment with her appearance? Media images are partly to blame for the wounding and deflation so many feel in our narcissistic culture. Psychologists "argue that a failure to match the ideal leads to self-criticism, guilt and lowered self-worth"; this effect is stronger for women than for men because of more frequent exposure to photographs and the "cultural pressures on women to conform to an idealized body shape are more powerful and more widespread than those on men," says Grogan (p. 100). . . .

The American feminist Naomi Wolf addresses the conflict between social and biological requirements for attractiveness in *The Beauty Myth*. The Professional Beauty Qualification, or PBQ as she terms it, reflects the demands of a capitalist economy and the exploitation of sex and fantasy as incentives to consume and as criteria for hiring in the job market. The connection between publicity and success, status, sex appeal, and the admiration of others has long directed print and other forms of media.

Real-life achievements, based on talent, discipline, frustration, and hard work as much as on luck, seem disconnected from these images. Competency does not always help to secure or keep employment, according to widely publicized lawsuits of wrongful job termination for reasons other than weak performance. Some women have been fired because they were neither pretty enough nor slim enough to sell products in department stores, to read the news as television anchors, to work as flight attendants, or even to sing in the opera—an art form traditionally dependent on talent rather than appearance. The internationally respected soprano Deborah Voigt was dropped from a scheduled production of Richard Strauss's *Ariadne auf Naxos* because her weight strained both the costume and her credibility in the role. "Tenorissimo" Luciano Pavarotti, in contrast, was not fired for his enormous body. Rather, he chose to retire because he no longer could move on stage.

Of particular concern is the early-twenty-first century phenomenon of "makeover" programs (*What Not to Wear, How Do I Look, Date Patrol, Style Court,* and *Extreme Makeover*). The last is the most serious challenge to women's (and men's) health and well-being, fostering the fantasy that with enough money and cosmetic surgery or other procedures, anyone can have Hollywood-style glamour and, in fact, should. The program features multiple surgical procedures over a period of many hours and with good results. No information emerges about how the potential candidate's health history, suitability for extreme surgery, or physical condition are evaluated before selection is made. Minimal attention is spent on pain or complications of recovery. Television programs on stomach stapling (gastric bypass surgery) provide more information on the potential dangers of this last-chance solution to morbid obesity. Indeed, either way the patient is at serious risk. The problems with silicone breast implants are better publicized, but still women of all ages continue to desire large breasts that change the proportions of their bodies. Younger and younger adolescents ask for cosmetic surgery, a phenomenon that should not surprise a society with ever-growing numbers of young women suffering from eating disorders and body dysmorphic disorder.

"How healthy is the Surgical Age?" asks Wolf (p. 229), citing deaths caused by smoking, fasting, and other extreme methods of weight control and cosmetic surgery known as "body sculpting." She correctly aligns such practices with an intense stress that, she suggests, can contribute to mental instability. "Narcissists feel that what happens to their bodies does not happen to them" (p. 230). In other words, paying attention to various body parts or facial features contributes to a fragmented and fragmenting view of the self, a distorted sense of the body as abnormal or diseased. "The Surgical Age's definition of female 'health' is not healthy" (p. 231). . . .

A woman who chooses to submit to multiple plastic surgeries over a period of years in order to achieve a "Barbie-doll" look for her face and body may be determined to enjoy the attention, success, and glamorous social life she thinks beauty will bring. There may be a relationship between good looks and social success, in that attractiveness increases self-confidence, an appealing trait that draws people's attention. Self-confidence can be learned, however, and does not result from physical appearance alone. . . .

Beyond Questions of Science

The body, writes the American feminist Susan Bordo, is a "culturally mediated form" (in Conboy, Medina, and Stanbury, p. 103), in that its appearance reflects the discourse of its society and the state of women's power or lack thereof in that society. Beyond aesthetics, the ideal appearance and female body exist in relation to the bondage of dependency, racism, and social roles. The body, in other words, is territory conquered by masculine spectatorship, the site of a struggle over ownership of resources.

Women's beauty rituals comprise part of this cultural mediation. Rituals are the repeated acts of grooming beyond basic hygiene that serve to embellish according to the tastes and standards she has internalized from her peer group, magazines, and other media. Rituals can be as innocent as preteen makeup parties, as painful as piercing or tattoos, and as life-threatening as eating disorders for weight control. Some girls choose rituals to feel good about what is asked of them; some to bind the anxiety they feel as they dodge threats to their still-formulating sense of self; and some to overcome perceived shortcomings of which they are constantly reminded by advertising.

Successful advertising seeks to address a consumer's pleasure-seeking tendencies before the reality principal dampens her impulse to buy. Along with products, companies sell fantasies of pleasure, excitement, or well-being that will arise from the act of buying and using advertised items. Scenes of arousal need not include a partner. Pampering oneself with soothing lotions satisfies the need for attention without the risks involved in a relationship. Contemporary television and print commercials feature women experiencing what looks like self-stimulation and sexual arousal from shampoo and soap use in the shower.

In addition to bath and skin treatments, creamy foods like yogurts are advertised as sensual indulgences enjoyed by oneself. But for women, eating is already overdetermined. Intentionally or not, advertising can contribute to "emotionally induced compensatory eating," says Suzanne Z. Grunert (quoted in Costa, p. 68), and thus heighten the dilemma between the immediate comfort of eating and the potential for weight gain. Perhaps in compensation, shades of lipstick, eye shadow, and nail polish often are named after food. Instead of ingesting chocolate or cinnamon, one can wear them.

Ads for beauty and grooming aids fuel self-consciousness and vulnerability by making women aware of flaws they did not know they had. They stimulate an often-panicky desire to improve and, not surprisingly, create markets for products that promise to remedy imperfections from acne to wrinkles. Magazine articles, infomercials, and niche-marketed television programs bombard young women with images and messages they ignore at their own peril. Well-socialized girls change their hairstyles and adopt fashion trends in part to conform to the standards of their peer groups—actions that indicate how well they understand and respond to peer influences as seen in their shopping patterns. Product boycotts or grassroots truth-in-advertising campaigns fight to expose the "marketization" of cultural expression, but cannot fully counteract the impact of advertising and mass marketing and their by-product, peer pressure.

The cult of beauty in women represents an attempt to counteract an externally imposed sense of inadequacy. Feelings of failure arise from "a context where body image is subjective and socially determined. . . . A person's body image is not determined by the actual shape and size of that body, but by that person's subjective evaluation of what it means to have that kind of body within their particular culture," writes Grogan (p. 166). For women of any race, class, or gender identification, femininity becomes an investment of resources and discipline in order to gain fleeting attention "and some admiration but little real respect and rarely any social power" (Bartky, p. 73). Late-twentieth-century studies cited in Grogan (pp. 180–192) suggest that positive body image is linked to self-esteem and a sense of personal control over one's environment, both of which are problematic for women in a capitalist patriarchy. As long as societies teach women to evaluate themselves principally in terms of their femininity and attractiveness, self-assurance will belong more often to those who successfully conform to the cultural ideal. If instead girls and young women learn to appreciate their bodies as healthy, well-functioning instruments that enable them to lead productive lives, they will be closer to changing the conditions that relegate them to objectification.

Bibliography

Bartky, Sandra Lee. *Femininity and Domination: Studies in the Phenomenology of Oppression.* New York: Routledge, 1990.

Bellafante, Ginia. "At Gender's Last Frontier." *New York Times,* June 8, 2003, section 9, p. 9.

Bordo, Susan. *The Male Body: A New Look at Men in Public and in Private.* New York: Farrar, Straus and Giroux, 1999.

Brownmiller, Susan. *Femininity.* New York: Linden Press/Simon and Schuster, 1984.

Chernin, Kim. *The Obsession: Reflections on the Tyranny of Slenderness.* New York: Harper and Row, 1981.

Conboy, Katie, Nadia Medina, and Sarah Stanbury, eds. *Writing on the Body: Female Embodiment and Feminist Theory.* New York: Columbia University Press, 1997.

Costa, Janeen Arnold, ed. *Gender Issues and Consumer Behavior.* Thousand Oaks, Calif.: Sage, 1994.

Creed, Barbara. "Lesbian Bodies: Tribades, Tomboys, and Tarts." In *Feminist Theory and the Body,* edited by Janet Price and Margrit Shildrick. New York: Routledge, 1999.

Frost, Liz. *Young Women and the Body: A Feminist Sociology.* Houndsmills, U.K.: Palgrave, 2001.

Gilman, Sander. *Difference and Pathology: Stereotypes of Sexuality, Race, and Madness.* Ithaca, N.Y.: Cornell University Press, 1985.

Grogan, Sarah. *Body Image: Understanding Body Dissatisfaction in Men, Women, and Children.* London: Routledge, 1999.

Halprin, Sara. *Look at My Ugly Face: Myths and Musings on Beauty and Other Perilous Obsessions with Women's Appearance.* New York: Viking, 1995.

Kinzer, Nora Scott. *Put Down and Ripped Off: The American Woman and the Beauty Cult.* New York: Crowell, 1977.

Lakoff, Robin Tolmach, and Raquel Scherr. *Face Value: The Politics of Beauty.* Boston: Routledge and Kegan Paul, 1984.

Lippa, Richard. *Gender, Nature, and Nurture.* Mahwah, N.J.: Erlbaum, 2002.

Malson, Helen. *The Thin Woman: Feminism, Post-structuralism, and the Social Psychology of Anorexia Nervosa.* New York: Routledge, 1998.

Moore, Booth. "Beyond Her Years." *Los Angeles Times,* April 30, 2003, pp. E1, E9.

Mulqueen, Maggie. *On Our Own Terms: Redefining Competence and Femininity.* Albany: State University of New York Press, 1992.

Price, Janet, and Margrit Shildrick, eds. *Feminist Theory and the Body*. Edinburgh,
    U.K.: Edinburgh University Press, 1999.

Van der Dennen, J. M. G., ed. *The Nature of the Sexes: The Sociobiology of Sex Differences
    and the "Battle of the Sexes."* Groningen, The Netherlands: Origin Press, 1992.

West, Kasey. "Nappy Hair: A Marker of Identity and Difference." Available at
    http://www.beautyworlds.com/beautynappyhair.htm.

Zerbe, Kathryn. *The Body Betrayed: Women, Eating Disorders, and Treatment.*
    Washington, D.C.: American Psychiatric Press, 1993.

Susan Grayson

Source: From "Women and Femininity in the U.S. Popular Culture" by Susan Grayson. *From
New Dictionary of the History of Ideas.* COPYRIGHT 2005 The Gale Group, Inc. This material
is published under license from the publisher through the Gale Group, Farmington Hills,
Michigan. All inquiries regarding rights should be directed to the Gale Group. For permission to reuse this article, contact Copyright Clearance Center.

Question for Reading Actively

1. According to Susan Grayson, what are the properties of the concept *femininity*?
   What are some examples of this concept? How has the concept of *femininity*
   been created?

Question for Thinking Critically

1. In what ways can the concept of *femininity* that has developed in our culture
   be dangerous for women?

Question for Writing Thoughtfully

1. In an essay, explain whether you agree with the conceptual properties identified by Grayson. What properties of the concept *femininity* do you think
   should be included that were not addressed? Give at least one example of
   each property you identify.

"The Second Coming of the Alpha Male: A Prescription for Righteous Masculinity at the Millennium"

by Michael Segell

The Happy Warrior

In the past few years, curbing male aggression (and encouraging it in females) has
become a kind of clarion call among feminists and new-age men. In nearly all studies,
males demonstrate far more confrontational behavior and rough-and-tumble play than

Source: "The second coming of the alpha male: a prescription for righteous masculinity at
the millennium" by Michael Segell. From Esquire Magazine, 126 (4), October 1996. ©1996
Hearst Communications, Inc. All Rights Reserved. Reprinted by permission.

females and are responsible for almost all violent crime. But, as experts are quick to point out, violence is an aberrational by-product of aggression. What makes the difference is whether a rowdy boy is encouraged to channel his aggressiveness into productive challenges or is left to lose his way in life.

The firm hand of paternal guidance shows up repeatedly in analyses of accomplished tyros. A study of more than a hundred jet-fighter pilots revealed that most were firstborns who had unusually close relationships with their fathers; the fliers exuded enormous self-confidence, showed a great desire for challenge and success, and had little use for introspection. As Jerome Kagan, a developmental psychologist at Harvard, has repeatedly demonstrated in forty years of research on children, aggressiveness in a young child is highly correlated with what he calls assertive competence as an adult.

A few years ago, the merits of male assertiveness were given a boost by feminist psychologists who tried to prove the value of a concept called psychological androgyny. In tests measuring feminine and masculine characteristics, men and women who scored high in both—who were at once aggressive and nurturing, sensitive and rigid, dominant and submissive—were shown to have superior psychological health. To antimasculinists, this was proof that the ideal man had a highly developed feminine side. Later, though, the "androgyny is best" theory collapsed when more sophisticated analyses of data on "masculine" and "feminine" traits showed that the former accounted for all of the benefits. Aggression and dominance, not sensitivity and submissiveness, were responsible for superior self-esteem in both men and women.

One of the few long-term studies of men also confirms the dynamic link between self-assertion and a prosperous, virtuous life. Since 1937, researchers from the Grant Study of Adult Development have tracked the psychological and physical health of several classes of Harvard graduates. Among this elite group, which includes society surgeons and U.S. senators, college presidents and partners at Wall Street law firms, George Vaillant, a psychiatrist who has directed the study for the past thirty years, identified a special group of "best outcomes"—men who enjoyed not only material success but stable relationships and mental tranquility. He found that their urgent need to take charge was directly linked to their concern for and involvement with the commonweal: The best, as a group, gave six times as much money to charity as the worst yet exhibited six times as many displays of aggressive behavior as their less exalted classmates. As they grew older, they became more active in competitive sports than they'd been in college, whereas the less successful participants avoided competition altogether.

Boys take the rap for roughness, but girls may actually be meaner—perpetrators of a different, and sometimes more destructive, aggression. According to psychologist Robert Cairns, girls, at around age ten, develop a powerful, sophisticated technique that, although not physically assertive, uses alienation and rumormongering to vanquish a rival. This style of indirect aggression can emotionally devastate the victim, who often has no idea why, or even by whom, she's being attacked. Organizing social intrigues as a way of ganging up on a peer not only prolongs conflict but kindles larger group discord. As girls enter adulthood, they become even more skilled at using gossip, aspersions, and social ostracism to assault their adversaries. Margaret Mead once remarked that women should stay off the battlefield because they'd be too brutal. Unable to handle direct confrontation, they'd end up blowing everyone away when more modest strategies might do the job.

Boys, by contrast, tend to stick with a problem-solving style they've known since their first toy was snatched from them: confrontation. Unlike hidden female aggression, this up-front approach resolves conflict quickly and lets everyone in a group know what an individual's limits are. In a study of nineteen international crises that were ended by a surprise attack Peter Suedfeld, a Canadian psychologist, found that in the early stages of conflict, government ministers and heads of state—men—focused on gathering information, negotiating, seeking compromise, and diplomatically outwitting their opponents, but as tensions mounted, they gradually reduced the complexity of their thinking until a military strike became their only recourse.

Despite headlines about wife beating and war criminals, most men—even soldiers—are not naturally violent. In On Killing, military psychologist Dave Grossman argues persuasively that far from being bloodthirsty aggressors, most soldiers are loath to kill even a demonized enemy. Citing studies of previous wars, Grossman, a U.S. Army lieutenant colonel, concludes that as many as 85 percent of ordinary soldiers have done their best not to kill, firing their weapons over the enemy's head, busying themselves with supplies, and running away. "At the decisive moment," he says, "each man became, in his heart, a conscientious objector." After the battle of Gettysburg, for instance, about 80 percent of the more than twenty-five thousand muskets recovered from the battlefield were loaded. Since most of a soldier's time was spent loading his weapon and only a few seconds were needed to aim and fire, "the obvious conclusion is that most soldiers were not trying to kill the enemy."

Grossman's analyses raise profound questions about the nature of male violence in general and of the war hero in particular. In wars fought for virtuous causes, is it more honorable to kill or to shoot over an enemy's head? "I don't have the answer to that," he says. "The vast majority of soldiers who have chosen not to kill reflect something redeeming and reassuring about the nature of men. But I'm also proud to know there are soldiers who have a yearning for righteous combat, the willingness and courage to rise up during times of desperate need to fight the good fight."

The Ascendant Woman

For all but the most recent blip of history, men's brawn and women's lack of control of their reproductive destinies guaranteed that the dullest clod had status superior to his wife's. Even Ralph Kramden, a minor alpha male, got to be king of his castle. Those days are over, and the rapid adjustments men have been expected to make in this radical cultural experiment are producing chilling effects on relationships.

The root of jokes and vicious attacks on powerful women, from Eleanor Roosevelt to Hillary Clinton, from mothers-in-law to female bosses, lies deep within the male psyche. As psychologist Kagan says, "Psychological potency and the ability to dominate and to hide their weakness are the most urgent preoccupations of men." When a man does form a partnership with a woman who thinks of him as an equal rather than a superior, he often feels threatened. In the worst cases, this male insecurity results in physical violence; less impulsive men may respond with bullying, verbal abuse, or infidelity.

As evolutionary psychologist David Buss sees it, a modern husband in a dual-career marriage is vulnerable to "mate-value discrepancy." The very qualities that attracted him to his wife—her brains, professional status, sexual sophistication—put pressure on him to measure up to her standards, if not exceed them. According to the ancient mating paradigms outlined in Buss's book *The Evolution of Desire*, when a man feels that his wife is more desirable on the mating market than he is, he undermines and demeans her—from bitching about her cooking to complaining about her imaginary cellulite.

This strategy, documented in dozens of studies Buss has done around the world, is deployed to lower his mate's self-esteem and her perception of her attractiveness (still the most important determinant in a man's mate choice, she knows) and to decrease the likelihood that she'll defect from the relationship. The tactic, however loathsome, is a preemptive strike against a demonstrable threat to the modern marriage: When women are more successful than their husbands, they're twice as likely to ditch them if they're unhappy. To make matters worse, Buss says, the gender revolution has in fact magnified women's traditional mate preferences. They want men who can contribute at least as much to the family coffers as they themselves do, and powerful women place even more emphasis on selecting a man with superior earning power. For the New Man, the Ascendant Woman has raised the bar.

In a simpler one-paycheck era, men needed only compare themselves with women, who had subordinated their own sense of accomplishment to their husbands', to feel successful in their struggle to act good and manly. Even twenty years ago, newly minted alpha males who achieved status in the customary fashion—by beating out other males—still chose glamorous but unthreatening trophy wives as affirmations of their prestige. But in the gender-strained 1990s, some men are getting their signals crossed: Their ascendant mate triggers the kind of competition normally directed toward other men, and she becomes classified in some primitive sense as being like another male.

How do men satisfy their need to demonstrate assertiveness and confidence in a relationship with an equally powerful mate? The key, for both men and women, is to acknowledge the separate-but-equal attractions and skills of each gender. And here, the women's movement offers men an effective model. In the early years, feminists first affirmed what men had criticized in women—their expressiveness and empathy—and then emulated men's self-assertiveness to gain a foothold in the working world. Similarly, men need to celebrate anew the positive value of male qualities that have been repeatedly bashed—their natural aggressiveness, urge to dominate, and love of risk—then augment their social armament with a skill more common to women: sensitivity to their own and others' emotions. To attract and keep an assertive female—the thinking man's trophy wife—the aspiring alpha male needs to acquire a new power: psychological potency. This new manly attribute is critical at this transitional moment in the culture's gender experiment. According to Drew Westen, a psychologist at Harvard, men born before the 1980s harbor contradictory models of what a relationship should be. Consciously, we want a woman who is our equal—someone we can talk to man to man. But we also have a deep unconscious need to have our potency mirrored and bolstered by our wives in the same way our mothers did for our fathers. Women, too have a built-in conflict between wanting a powerful and heroic man who wears the pants in the family, the way Dad did, and being angered by and envious of such power. On one level, they want to affirm their mate's potency, but on another they may find it demeaning to do so. "It's not surprising," says Westen, "that a couple's interlocking motives can be at cross-purposes, not only within themselves but with each other."

How do we acquire the psychic chops to handle this conflict? "It's like asking, How do you grow up?" a psychiatrist told me. He was implying, of course, that, as in a Zen koan, the answer is contained in the question. A sense of control—over one's surroundings, destiny, and inner needs and desires—is essential to psychological autonomy. To be able to admit that you want the soft Mommy when you're getting too much of the Tiger Lady requires strength and courage, even if most men wouldn't think of it that way.

Men may be able to contribute the most to resolving this dilemma. During times of stress, we often attribute malevolent motives to our partner's behavior—explanations that have more to do with our own unexpressed fears and failures than with what's really going on. By acknowledging what troubles us, we can achieve supremacy over unconscious processes. In turn, we can short-circuit the primitive defenses that cause us to redirect stress, sadness, or a nagging sense of inadequacy into nasty assaults on our mates.

Understanding how utterly differently men and women respond to emotion and conflict is crucial here. Men are frequently oblivious to their internal states—an advantage while searching for air-crash victims in 120 feet of water but a serious impediment to intimacy. Women often initiate emotional confrontation as a way of communicating, while men, interpreting these entreaties as personal attacks, either shift into hyperarousal—fight mode—or flee. When an argument escalates, many men experience "flooding," an inundation of emotions from which they can retreat only by stonewalling. But implicit in this withdrawal is a sense of superiority—echoing the denigrating tactics deployed by men who sense mate-value discrepancy—and antipathy toward their mate's deepest feelings. "When men aren't expressive, they're passive-aggressive," says Robert Thy. "They're not angry, but everyone else is."

Short of physical violence, stonewalling leads to discord—and divorce—more surely than any other single male behavior. Again, men are in the best position to disrupt this pattern. The simple insight that's needed: Their mate's anger is not an expression of malice but of a desire to stay connected. By acknowledging and empathizing with her feelings, rather than trying to analyze and "fix" them, a man can break the insidious cycle that can lead to estrangement. A little self-reflection, not years of psychotherapy, is what's required.

Men also need to recognize that as feminism has co-opted their primary-breadwinner status, it has also loosened their bondage to economic necessity. No longer are men obliged to define themselves by their net worth alone. Unlike the gray-flannel-suited men of the 1950s, they are now free to perform a task central to masculinity's universal construct: caring for, rearing, and taking responsibility for their children and community. For men seeking new challenges to prove their adequacy, there is perhaps no greater one than reversing the decline of the role of the father in the family. Nor do single men need to be defined only by their pay stubs: There are plenty of fatherless children who could use a dose of male power in their lives.

Men can also show off their inherent talents by sharing them with their wives: Teach them the merits of doing rather than feeling, putting a filter on emotions in the workplace, and developing a problem-solving approach to conflicts—capabilities that have long served men so well. And men can still teach women how to act upon desire for the sake of simple, playful pleasure. Despite all the sundering of traditional conjugal bonds, each sex still has something that the other desperately wants.

A wise old friend, a retired psychiatrist, told me recently, "When men feel adequate, you never hear them talk about masculinity. It's when they feel less than capable that you hear a lot of talk about this thing called manhood." Like Achilles, the Greek embodiment of manliness, men who gather regularly to deconstruct masculinity could more profitably turn their energies away from self-absorption toward practical problem solving. They might then tease apart the riddle of their relationship to the New Woman—expanding their understanding of themselves, deepening their respect for her, and sharing in her glory the way women have traditionally shared in their husbands'. For men, the challenges of the modern relationship have never been more daunting. But the rewards for those willing to compete according to the new rules have never been more gratifying: the prosperity of a two-income family, the richness of an erotic life with a sexually assertive mate, the opportunity for greater intimacy and involvement with one's children. Perhaps the most significant finding of the Grant Study's Harvard grads was that the most accomplished men typically enjoyed long and satisfying relationships with their spouses; great success had not been won at the expense of poor marriages and neglected children. Embracing challenge, seeking out risk and channeling their natural aggression into business, sports, and community affairs, they proved lucky at work and in love.

The aspiring alpha male at the millennium would be wise to emulate them.

Questions for Reading Actively

1. According to Michael Segell, what are the properties of the concept *masculinity?* What are some examples of this concept?

2. What properties of the concept *masculinity* do you think should be included that were not addressed? For each property you identify, give at least one example.

Question for Thinking Critically

1. Segell believes that our culture should endeavor to transcend the traditional concepts of *masculinity* and *femininity* to form a new and more productive relationship between the genders while still retaining the positive differences between men and women. What are the revised concepts of *masculinity* and *femininity* that he is proposing, including his concept of *psychological potency?* Explain whether you agree or disagree with this proposal.

Question for Writing Thoughtfully

1. Some people feel that the concepts *masculinity* and *femininity* were formed by earlier cultures, are outdated in our current culture, and should be revised. Other people believe that these concepts reflect basic qualities of the human species, just like the sexual differences in other species, and should not be excessively tampered with. In an essay, explain where you stand on this issue, and describe the reasons that support your position.

"My Papa's Waltz"

by Theodore Roethke

From *The Collected Poems of Theodore Roethke*

The theme of fathers lost and found, fatherhood as conflicted and yearned for, permeates the work of Theodore Roethke. His German father, grandfather, and uncles owned and operated greenhouses in Saginaw, Michigan; the image of the greenhouse as a fragile shelter, a transparent place of life even in the most brutal of climates, gives a poignant force to several poems in his second volume of verse, *The Lost Son and Other Poems* (1948). The death of Roethke's father from cancer in 1923 shaped his adolescence and may have contributed to the severe bouts of depression that periodically shook him for the rest of his life. In an autobiographical essay, Roethke observed that "I believe that the spiritual man must go back in order to go forward"; this regression into the personal as well as poetic past in order to develop his own voice and persona shaped his poetic project.

Roethke held several university teaching appointments and was widely published during his life. He was awarded the Guggenheim Fellowship (1950), *Poetry* magazine's Levinson Prize (1951), and major grants from the Ford Foundation and the National Institute of Arts and Letters in 1952. His posthumously published and final book, *The Far Field* (1964), received the National Book Award.

The whiskey on your breath
Could make a small boy dizzy;
But I hung on like death:
Such waltzing was not easy.

We romped until the pans
Slid from the kitchen shelf;
My mother's countenance
Could not unfrown itself.

The hand that held my wrist
Was battered on one knuckle;
At every step you missed
My right ear scraped a buckle.

You beat time on my head
With a palm caked hard by dirt,
Then waltzed me off to bed
Still clinging to your shirt.

Questions for Reading Actively

1. Although poets often use figurative language in richly imaginative ways, there is just one simile in this poem. Where is that simile, and what does it reveal about the relationship between the father and the son?

2. Reading the poem out loud (to yourself, or to each other in the classroom), what do you notice about its rhyming and its rhythm? Do these patterns remind you of other kinds of poems, rhymes, or songs? In what way?

3. Is the narrator of the poem a small boy, or an adult writing from the perspective of a small boy? How can you tell?

Questions for Thinking Critically

1. Fatherhood, and the loss of or search for a father figure, is an overarching theme of Roethke's work. Based on this poem, how would you define Roethke's concept of fatherhood (not the specific father described here)?

2. In what ways do the father and the mother in this poem evoke the "masculine" and "feminine" qualities?

Question for Writing Thoughtfully

1. Think about your relationship with a parent, guardian, or other significant adult figure in your life and create a list of similes that express that relationship.

"Men and Their Hidden Feelings"

by Richard Cohen

Richard Cohen has been a columnist for the *Washington Post* since 1976. Born in New York City, he graduated from New York University and began his career as a journalist in New York. He joined *The Washington Post* in 1968 after attending the Columbia University Graduate School of Journalism, and after doing, as he puts it, "some postgraduate work" at Fort Dix, New Jersey, and Fort Leonard Wood, Missouri. At the *Post* he covered all sorts of stories—night police, city hall, education, state government, and national politics. His reporting has carried him into perilous situations in the Middle East and Africa, and Ground Zero immediately after the September 11 attacks. Cohen's graceful writing and engagement with topics of intimate interest as well as global import have earned him a devoted readership.

My friends have no friends. They are men. They think they have friends, and if you ask them whether they have friends they will say yes, but they don't really. They think, for instance, that I'm their friend, but I'm not. It's OK. They're not my friends either.

Source: From Richard Cohen, *"Men and Their Hidden Feelings" Washington Post* Writers Group, 1983. Copyright © 1983, The Washington Post Writers Group. Reprinted with permission.

The reason for that is that we are all men—and men, I have come to believe, cannot or will not have real friends. They have something else—companions, buddies, pals, chums, someone to drink with and someone to wench with and someone to lunch with, but no one when it comes to saying how they feel—especially how they hurt.

Women know this. They talk about it among themselves. I heard one woman describe men as the true Third World people—still not yet emerged. To women, this inability of men to say what they feel is a source of amazement and then anguish and then, finally, betrayal. Women will tell you all the time that they don't know the men they live with. They talk of long silences and drifting off and of keeping feelings hidden and never letting on that they are troubled or bothered or whatever.

If it's any comfort to women, they should know that it's nothing personal. Men treat other men the same way.

5   For instance, I know men who have suffered brutal professional setbacks and never mentioned it to their friends. I know of a guy who never told his best friend that his own son had a rare childhood disease. And I know others who never have sex with their wives, but talk to their friends as though they're living in the Playboy Mansion, either pretending otherwise or saying nothing.

This is something men learn early. It is something I learned from my father, who taught me, the way fathers teach sons, to keep my emotions to myself. I watched him and learned from him. One day we went to the baseball game, cheered and ate and drank, and the next day he was taken to the hospital with yet another ulcer attack. He had several of them. My mother said he worried a lot, but I saw none of this.

Legend has it that men talk a lot about sex. They don't. They talk about it only in the sense that it is treated like sports. They joke about it and rate women from 1 to 10. But they almost never talk about it in a way that matters—the quality of it. They almost never talk in real terms, in terms other than a cartoon, in terms that apply to them and the woman or women with whom they have a relationship.

Women do talk that way. Women talk about fulfillment, and they admit—maybe complain is the better word—to nonexistent sex lives. No man would admit to having virtually no sex life, yet there are plenty who do.

When I was a kid, I believed that it was men who had real friendships and women who did not. This seemed to be the universal belief, and boys would talk about this. We wondered about girls, about what made them so catty that they could not have friendships, and we really thought we were lucky to be men and have real friends.

10   We thought our friendships would last forever; we talked about them in some sort of Three Musketeer fashion—all for one and one for all. If one of us needed help, all of us would come running. We are still good friends, some of us, anyway, and I still feel that I will fight for them, but I don't think I could confide in them. No—not that.

Sometimes I think that men are walking relics—outmoded and outdated, programmed for some other age. We have all the essential qualities for survival in the wild and for success in battle, but we run like hell from talking about our feelings. We are, as the poet said in a different context, truly a thing of wonder.

Some women say that they have always had this ability to confide in one another— to talk freely. Others say that this is something relatively new—yet another benefit of the women's movement. I don't know. All I know is that they have it, and most men don't, and even the men who do—the ones who can talk about how they feel—talk to women. Have we been raised to think of feelings and sentiment as feminine? Can a man talk intimately with another man and not wonder about his masculinity? I don't know. I do know it sometimes makes the other men feel uncomfortable.

I know this is a subject that concerns me, and yet I find myself bottling it all up—keeping it all in. I've been on automatic pilot for years now.

It would be nice to break out of it. It would be nice to join the rest of the human race, connect with others in a way that makes sense, in a way that's meaningful—in a way that's more than a dirty joke and a slap on the back. I wonder whether it can be done.

15   If it can, it will happen because women will insist on it, because they themselves have shown the way, come out of the closet as women, talked about it, organized, defined an agenda, set their goals and admitted that as women—just as women—they have problems in common. So do men. It's time to talk about them.

Questions for Reading Actively

1. According to Cohen, what are the properties of men's relationships? Why does he think that these properties do not fit a definition of *friendship*?

2. What fundamental distinction does Cohen make between men and women? That is, how does he *classify* men and women? Do you agree with his classification? Why, or why not?

3. Examine the kind of evidence that Cohen offers in paragraph 5 to support his thesis. Would his argument be stronger if he had talked about, or named, *specific* men? What are the risks of generalizing about human behavior?

Questions for Thinking Critically

1. How do you think those men who might have considered themselves to be Cohen's "friends" felt after reading this column (which appeared in the *Washington Post*)? What are the risks that journalists—or any writers, really—take when they use material from their personal lives in their work?

2. Richard Cohen makes broad generalizations about categories of people. What are the inherent risks of making an argument based on very broad classifications or categories (such as "all men" or "all women")? How does Cohen successfully—or unsuccessfully—address those risks?

Question for Writing Thoughtfully

1. What are these "feelings" that Cohen describes? Is he arguing that men don't *have* feelings, or just that men don't *discuss* feelings? In an essay, explain whether or not you think it's as important to discuss feelings as to have them. Be sure to consider to what extent your response is based on your upbringing, current peer group, profession, or other such factors.

"Girl"

by Jamaica Kincaid

From *At the Bottom of the River*

Born on the Caribbean island of Antigua and named Elaine Potter Richardson by her parents, Jamaica Kincaid left home for America at the age of sixteen to work as an au pair in the wealthy New York City suburbs of Westchester. She moved to New York City to study photography and then spent a year at Franconia College in New Hampshire. In 1973, facing her family's disapproval over her published writing, she changed her first name to Jamaica, to evoke her Caribbean heritage, and her last name to Kincaid, simply because she liked the sound of it. Her articles in such magazines as *Ingenue* led, eventually, to a staff writing position at *The New Yorker,* where she wrote on a wide range of subjects (including gardening, her great passion). Her first novel, *A Small Place* (1988), delves into the painful legacy of colonization in the Caribbean, a theme that recurs throughout her fiction. She has also explored the impact of colonialism's legacy at the more intimate level of family, in such novels as *Lucy* (1990), *The Autobiography of My Mother* (1996), and *My Brother* (1997).

Wash the white clothes on Monday and put them on the stone heap; wash the color clothes on Tuesday and put them on the clothesline to dry; don't walk barehead in the hot sun; cook pumpkin fritters in very hot sweet oil; soak your little cloths right after you take them off; when buying cotton to make yourself a nice blouse, be sure that it doesn't have gum on it, because that way it won't hold up well after a wash; soak salt fish overnight before you cook it; is it true that you sing benna in Sunday school?; always eat your food in such a way that it won't turn someone else's stomach; on Sundays try to walk like a lady and not like the slut you are so bent on becoming; don't sing benna in Sunday school; you mustn't speak to wharf-rat boys, not even to give directions; don't eat fruits on the street—flies will follow you; *but I don't sing benna on Sundays at all and never in Sunday school;* this is how to sew on a button; this is how to make a buttonhole for the button you have just sewed on; this is how to hem a dress when you see the hem coming down and so to prevent yourself from looking like the slut I know you are so bent on becoming; this is how you iron your father's khaki shirt so that it doesn't have a crease; this is how you iron your father's khaki pants so they don't have a crease; this is how you grow okra—far from the house, because okra tree harbors red ants; when you are growing dasheen, make sure it gets plenty of water or else it makes your throat itch when you are eating it; this is how you sweep a corner; this is how you sweep a whole house; this is how you sweep a yard; this is how you smile to someone you don't like too much; this is how you smile to someone you don't like at all; this is how you smile to someone you like completely; this is how you set a table for tea; this is how you set a table for dinner; this is how you set a table for dinner with an important guest; this is how you set a table for lunch; this is how you set a table for breakfast; this is how to behave in the presence of men who don't know you very well, and this way they won't recognize immediately the slut I have warned you against becoming; be sure to wash every day, even if it is with your own spit; don't squat down to play marbles—you are not a boy, you know; don't pick people's flowers—you might catch something; don't throw stones at blackbirds, because it might not be a blackbird at all; this is how to make a bread pudding; this is how to make doukona; this is how to make pepper pot; this is how to make a good medicine for a cold; this is how to make a good medicine to throw away a child before it even becomes a child; this is how to catch a fish; this is how to throw back a fish you don't like, and that way something bad won't fall on you; this is how to bully a man; this is how a man bullies you; this is how to love a man, and if this doesn't work there are other ways, and if they don't work don't feel too bad about giving up; this is how to spit up in the air if you feel like it, and this is how to move quick so that it doesn't fall on you; this is how to make ends meet; always squeeze bread to make sure it's fresh; *but what if the baker won't let me feel the bread?;* you mean to say that after all you are really going to be the kind of woman who the baker won't let near the bread?

Questions for Reading Actively

1. Who is speaking in this monologue, and who is being spoken to? How can you tell?

2. What are the properties of correct behavior for a "girl," according to this speaker, and what are the consequences of defying that behavior?

3. There's a phrase that's repeated three times in this monologue. What is that sentence? Why is it repeated, and how does it foreshadow the very last lines of this monologue?

Questions for Thinking Critically

1. When you were growing up, who told you how to behave? Did anyone ever tell you (either explicitly, or by implication) that there were correct ways to behave like a "lady" or a "gentleman"? Were these household rules, or just friendly guidelines? Is there anything that the speaker of this monologue says that reminds you of something you were told when you were a child?

2. What kind of future does the speaker of this monologue foresee for the listener? Is there anything surprising in the advice given?

3. Did you find anything comic in this monologue? If so, what made you laugh, and why?

Question for Writing Thoughtfully

1. Write an essay similar to Kincaid's offering advice to your current child or grandchild, future child, niece or nephew, or some other young child.

Using Concepts to Classify

When you apply a concept to an object, idea, or experience, you are in effect classifying it by placing it in a group of things that are defined by the properties or requirements of the concept. The same things can often be classified in many different ways. For example, if someone handed you a tomato and asked, "Which category does this tomato belong in, fruit or vegetable?" how would you respond? The fact is that a tomato can be classified as both a fruit and a vegetable because its botanical definition does not seem consistent with its uses as a food.

Let's consider another example. Imagine that you are walking on undeveloped land with some other people when you come across an area of soggy ground with long grass and rotting trees. One person in your group surveys the parcel and announces, "That's a smelly marsh. All it does is breed mosquitoes. It ought to be covered with landfill and built on so that we can use it productively." Another member of your group disagrees with the classification "smelly marsh," stating, "This is a wetland of great ecological value. There are many plants and animals that need this area and other areas like it to survive. Wetland areas also help to prevent

THE TREE, as seen by...

the planner...   the parks department...   the publisher...

400 LUXURY HOMES TO BE ERECTED ON THIS SITE

the highways department...   the developer...   the landscape architect.

the rivers from flooding, by absorbing excess water during heavy rains." Which person is right? Should the wet area be classified as a "smelly marsh" or as a "valuable wetland"? Actually, the wet area can be classified both ways. The classification that you select depends on your needs and your interests.

These examples illustrate how the way you classify reflects and influences the way you see the world, the way you think about the world, and the way you behave in the world. You classify many of the things in your experience differently than others do because of your individual needs, interests, and values. For instance, smoking marijuana might be classified by some as "use of a dangerous drug" and by others as a "harmless good time." Some view SUVs as "gas guzzlers"; others see the same cars as "safer, more comfortable vehicles." Some people categorize body piercing as "perverse abuse" while others think of it as "creative self-expression." The way you classify aspects of your experience reflects the kind of individual you are and the way you think and feel about the world.

Classifying People and Their Actions

You also place people in various categories. The specific categories you select depend on who you are and how you see the world. Similarly, each of us is placed in a variety of classifications by other people. Here, for instance, are some of the categories in which certain people have placed this book's author:

Classification	*People Who Classify Him*
First-born son	His parents
Taxpayer	Internal Revenue Service
Tickler	His children
Bagel with cream cheese	Restaurant where he picks up his breakfast

Not only do you continually classify things and people and place them in various groups on the basis of common properties you choose to focus on; you also classify ideas, feelings, actions, and experiences.

Thinking-Writing Activity

CLASSIFICATION AND YOUR SELF

List some of the different ways that you can be classified and identify the people who would classify you that way.

_____   _____

_____   _____

_____   _____

Writing and Classifying

The intellectual act of classifying is an essential part of writing in three ways.

First, writings themselves are classified into many different forms. You know this already, of course. Novels, poems, essays, news stories, blogs, emails, lab reports—the list is almost endless. And each of these forms of writing has subclassifications: science fiction, political blogs, romance novels, and so forth. Different classifications of writing, or *genres*, have different purposes and styles. You are aware of this as a reader. As a college writer, you must become more aware of using styles and formats appropriate to the kind of writing that you are doing for your classes.

Thinking-Writing Activity

CLASSIFICATION AND ETHICS

Each of these following classifications represents a separate legal concept, one with its own properties and referents (examples). Of course, even when you clearly understand what the concept means, the complexity of the circumstances often makes it difficult to determine which concept applies.

Classification	Circumstance	Example
1. Manslaughter	Killing someone accidentally	Driving while intoxicated
2. Self-defense	_____	_____
3. Premeditated murder	_____	_____
4. Mercy killing	_____	_____
5. Diminished capacity	_____	_____

Court cases raise complex and disturbing issues. During a trial, trying first to identify the appropriate concept of the crime and then to determine which of the related concepts—*guilty* or *not guilty*—also applies is a challenging process. This is also true of many of life's other complex situations: you must work hard at identifying appropriate concepts to apply to the circumstances you are trying to make sense of, then be prepared to change or modify these concepts on the basis of new information or better insights. Explain, for instance, why the killing of another person might be classified in different ways, depending on the circumstances.

Second, almost any piece of writing is organized by classifying material into sections, chapters, or paragraphs in which the content is sorted and arranged in logical ways. Usually, writers put similar material together so that readers can think about related items that have been assembled for their easy comprehension. You—and other writers—do this when you revise drafts to create good paragraphs that each focus on one idea. You do this when you are sorting your research notes into topics (or categories) in order to organize a paper, report, or presentation.

Third, much writing concentrates on presenting *kinds, categories, types,* or *classifications* of concepts. Readings in this chapter discuss different classifications of masculinity and femininity. This book itself is divided into different categories of approaches to thinking and writing.

Thinking-Writing Activity

IDENTIFYING CLASSIFICATIONS

1. Think of any reading selection in this book that you recall as being well-organized. Turn to it and see how the writer classified or sorted the material into logical arrangements. Note the classifications of information. Perhaps topic sentences of paragraphs will show you what the writer has done.

2. Share your observations with classmates. See if they agree.

3. How did analyzing this piece of writing provide ideas about organizing your own work?

Defining Concepts

When you define a concept, you usually identify the necessary properties or requirements that determine when the concept can be applied. In fact, the word *definition* is derived from a Latin word meaning "boundary." A definition provides the boundaries of whatever territory in your experience can be described by the concept.

Definitions also use examples of the concept being defined. Consider the following:

Oxymoron   A rhetorical figure in which incongruous or contradictory terms are combined as in *a deafening silence* and *a mournful optimist.*

                                      —*The American Heritage Dictionary of the English Language*

An edible   Good to eat and wholesome to digest, as a worm to a toad, a toad to a snake, a snake to a pig, a pig to a man, and a man to a worm.

—Ambrose Bierce

Facts, theories   Facts and theories are different things, not rungs in a hierarchy of increasing certainty. Facts are the world's data. Theories are structures of ideas that explain and interpret facts. Facts do not go away when scientists debate rival theories to explain them. Einstein's theory of gravitation replaced Newton's, but apples did not suspend themselves in mid-air pending the outcome.

—Stephen Jay Gould

Contrast these definitions with the one illustrated in the following passage from Charles Dickens's *Hard Times:*

> "Bitzer," said Thomas Gradgrind. "Your definition of a horse." "Quadruped. Graminivorous. Forty teeth, namely twenty-four grinders, four eye teeth, and twelve incisive. Sheds coat in the spring; in marshy countries sheds hoofs, too. Hoofs hard, but requiring to be shod with iron. Age known by marks in mouth." That (and much more) Bitzer. "Now girl number twenty," said Mr. Gradgrind, "you know what a horse is."

Although Bitzer has certainly done an admirable job of listing some of the necessary properties or requirements of the concept *horse*, it is unlikely that "girl number twenty" has any better idea of what a horse is than she had before since Bitzer's definition relies exclusively on a technical listing of the properties characterizing the concept *horse* without giving any examples that might illustrate the concept more completely. Definitions like this which rely exclusively on a technical description of the concept's properties are not very helpful unless you already know what the concept means. A more concrete way of communicating the concept *horse* would be to point out various animals that qualify as horses and other animals that do not. You could also explain why they do not. (For example, "That can't be a horse because it has two humps and its legs are far too long.")

Even though examples do not take the place of a clearly understood definition, they are often very useful in clarifying, supplementing, and expanding such a definition. If someone asked you, "What is a horse?" and you replied by giving examples of different kinds of horses (thoroughbred racing horses, plow horses for farming, quarter horses for cowhands, circus horses), you certainly would be communicating a good portion of the meaning of *horse*. Giving examples of a concept complements and clarifies the necessary requirements for the correct use of that concept.

Giving an effective definition of a concept requires

- Identifying the general qualities of the concept, which determine when it can be correctly applied
- Classifying it, which means identifying its category, type, or "family"
- Using appropriate examples that embody its general qualities
- Differentiating it from other items in its classification

The process of providing definitions of concepts is basically the same process that you use to develop concepts.

Writing Thoughtfully to Define Concepts

Writing a full definition, often called an *extended definition*, is among the most important and most difficult of writing activities. Defining terms is a necessary part of college-level writing and speaking. For productive discussions about complex issues, all involved must agree on the meanings of significant terms, so clear definitions are often required. Difficulties arise because significant terms related to complex issues are usually abstract concepts, with possibilities of different definitions for different people. For example, the common political terms *conservative* and *liberal* often have varied meanings, even to people who identify themselves as one or the other.

No one has much trouble agreeing on definitions of physical objects. A table, a tree, a television set—not many arguments arise about what these objects are. But like *liberal* and *conservative*, concepts such as *religion, love, democracy, femininity,* and *masculinity* can be defined in different ways. If people discussing ideas like these do not establish definitions, their discussions will not be productive. Worse, these discussions sometimes lead to disagreements, arguments, and even wars. The readings and Thinking-Writing Activities in this chapter have been selected and planned to demonstrate the importance of definitions.

Notice how with both simple objects and complex concepts, defining is somewhat easier as long as a single word is being examined. As soon as modifying and classifying ideas are added, defining becomes more challenging and more significant to critical thinking. A *beautiful* table, a *good* tree to plant in a *small* yard, the *best* computer to buy for *your family room*—now these objects call for fuller definitions. The *kind* of democracy that can work in a country with a *history of despotism*, the *kind* of love that a *parent* might have for an *adult child*—these are the types of concepts that people must define in order to present arguments, to make decisions, to solve problems. These are the kinds of terms that you might want to define in the Writing Project in this chapter because they are the kinds that involve judgments; they are important to our lives because they influence our actions.

Clear, satisfying definitions can be as extended as book chapters, articles, or entire books; however, a definition often will be developed in a paragraph or two as a vital part of a paper or report. In the Writing Project for this chapter, you will write an essay that defines; you will see the need for using a variety of thinking/organizing patterns as you develop it. The guidelines for writing definitions are not fixed rules; there may be times when you would have good reasons for varying or adapting some of them. Try to use them, though, unless you have good reason not to.

Writing Project: Defining an Important Concept

This chapter has included readings, questions, and Thinking-Writing Activities that encourage you to define concepts that affect your life. Be sure to reread what you wrote for the activities; you may be able to use some of that material in completing this project.

> Write an essay in which you define a concept that is important to your life now or to your future life. Include explanations of why this concept is significant for you and why it needs defining or redefining. You may want to think of a concept that is expressed in a phrase rather than in a single word. Include material from two sources in addition to any dictionaries that you consult. Integrate your sources into your essay and document them as your instructor advises. After you have drafted your essay, revise it to the best of your ability. Follow your instructor's directions for topic limits, length, format, and so on.

Begin by considering the key elements in the Thinking-Writing Model in Chapter 1 on pages 6–7.

The Writing Situation

Purpose   You have several purposes here. You want to think about and formulate a definition that will be significant as you continue your college studies, decide on your profession, or enter a new phase in your personal life. Indeed, all of us need to be able to define the complex terms that are foundations for our thinking, our decisions, and our actions in life. In addition, you can improve your ability to present a full definition in order to clarify your own thinking and to increase your audience's understanding.

Audience   You have a multilevel audience. *You* are an important audience, for in facing the challenge of defining a complex concept, you can think more clearly about some aspect of your life. Your classmates can learn from your definition and also can be a valuable audience in peer reviews of a draft, reacting as intelligent readers who are not as knowledgeable as you about the concept that pertains to your life. In addition, you should think about and identify people outside your class who might enjoy or profit from reading your definition. If you are writing about a concept that impacts people in your community or on your campus, your paper can both share information and urge action.

Subject   All of us need to be able to define abstract, complex terms that are foundations for our thinking, our decisions, and our actions in life. College courses, family life, spiritual concerns, and romantic relationships all involve concepts that need to be well defined. Clear definitions help us understand what we mean when we speak and write, understand what others mean when they communicate with us, and—most important—avoid confusion and conflict. For this assignment, try to identify an important concept that is central to how you see yourself and your future. Concepts like *creative expression, enlightened free choice, authentic person, fulfillment, achieving potential, meaningful empathy, social responsibility, critical thinker*, and (of course) *thoughtful writer* are all examples with broad implications in a person's life.

Writer   This project provides you with the opportunity to participate in the "conversation of ideas" that is the lifeblood of thoughtful, reflective people in a society. By defining a complex concept, you are explaining how the concept you have selected has personal meaning for you. You are also suggesting to others— your audience—how they might think about your analysis of the concept. The definition you propose may help them understand something in their experience more clearly, or it may provide an added meaning they have not previously considered. The outside sources integrated into your analysis ensure that your definition is grounded in a common understanding that goes beyond your own experience.

The Writing Process

The following sections will guide you through the recursive stages of generating, planning, drafting, and revising as you work on an essay in which you define a significant concept. Try to be particularly conscious of both the critical thinking you do as you articulate your definition and the critical thinking and decision making you do as you revise.

Generating Ideas

- Refer back to the responses you wrote for the Thinking-Writing Activities for the readings on gender issues. These concepts are important in many people's lives, so perhaps you will write about one of them—or perhaps what you read and wrote will lead you to another concept to define.
- Think about the activities or concerns that are central to your life. Some of these are probably rather serious, as are the subjects discussed in this chapter,

but some parts are surely more lighthearted, like sports you play or watch, television comedies, thriller movies, or parties.

- Next, think of concepts inherent in some of your activities, such as a satisfying relationship or what it means to be a good athlete, college student, or practitioner of your religion.

- Now, list the properties of two or three concepts that you have identified. Include specific examples. How should each example be classified?

- Think about why any of these concepts need to be defined or redefined. Do people agree on the meaning? Have you formulated a meaning that is more precise and accurate?

- Share your lists and thinking with classmates and, if you can, with people involved in the area in which the concept is important.

- Use as many thinking patterns as you can to discover ideas about your concept. What is it different from? similar to? analogous to? Describe it; think about what causes it; think about what effects it has.

- Look up the concept's key words in a good college-level dictionary and also in the *Oxford English Dictionary*. Ask your instructor or one of your college librarians to explain the *OED* to you. See if you can use any of your concept's word history in your definition.

- Freewrite for at least five minutes about why the concept is important to your life, why it needs to be defined, and what information needs to be in your definition.

Defining a Focus

- Look at your freewriting and lists to see what main idea you are moving toward in your definition. Write this idea in any way that you can.

- Now draft a thesis statement that gives the key ideas in your definition. Recently a student defining *freedom of religion* had this as her thesis sentence: "To me, freedom of religion means more than simply being able to practice our religions as we believe that we should; it also means that we must understand and respect other people's religions." Another student, working on a definition of today's *superwoman*, wrote, "The main properties of a superwoman are being capable, tenacious, and independent."

- Be sure that your thesis statement emphasizes the meaning of the concept that you are defining.

Organizing Ideas   Essays emphasizing definition are not easy to organize because there are so many approaches to a clear definition of a complex concept. Because the thesis—the essence of the definition—needs to be placed in a context and explained in a number of ways, the question of where to state the thesis is especially crucial. This is the kind of essay in which it might come at the end. When you state the thesis at the end, you need to lead up to it or preview it throughout the essay. However, you will want to think of stating the thesis provisionally near the beginning and referring to it elsewhere in the paper as you establish your definition.

Identify the approaches that you have used in your generative writing and early drafts. Where have you used contrast, comparison, analogy, narration, and so on? The material developed by each of these approaches is likely to form a paragraph. The definitions that you have found in your dictionary and in the *Oxford English Dictionary* will need a paragraph or two to connect them with the definition that you are developing. As always, give careful thought to paragraphing. Try your drafted paragraphs in different orders to discover which will best help your readers understand your definition. Because it is important that your readers understand the need for a definition, explaining that need is an effective way to begin. Explaining the significance of this concept in your life might be part of the beginning or conclusion.

Guidelines for Writing Definitions of Concepts

1. Establish the need for a definition. Why is it needed? Do people disagree on the meaning of the concept? Are there multiple meanings? Are earlier definitions no longer satisfactory? Is this a new concept or new terminology?

2. Choose carefully the word or words in which you state the concept. Definitions provide precision, so you need to be sure that you have presented the concept in the words that are most indicative.

3. Incorporate two kinds of dictionary definitions: the short one that gives meaning, as in a regular college dictionary, and a longer one giving the history of the word's usage, which can be found in the *Oxford English Dictionary*. Word origins and past meanings can often illuminate the meaning that you want to present.

4. Be sure that you identify the category into which the concept fits.

5. Show comparative thinking. Point out similar concepts, but then make clear how your concept is distinct. Think of analogies that can illuminate the meaning of the concept.

6. Provide specific examples to show what the concept means. Illustrative anecdotes are often effective.

7. Include the meaning of the concept in the thesis statement. Give careful thought to where you state the thesis.

8. Throughout your definition, emphasize that you are establishing the meaning you believe the concept has within the context that you have identified.

9. Address the foregoing principles in separate paragraphs or sections of the definition. Provide each paragraph with a clear topic sentence whenever appropriate.

10. Document any sources that you use. Introduce source material into your definition, explain and comment on it, and cite it correctly.

Drafting   Be sure to identify source material as you include it in your draft. See the appendix for further guidelines on citing source material.

Begin with the easiest paragraph to draft. Explaining the concept's significance in your life is likely to be easy since you are writing about your thoughts and feelings; showing the need for a definition should not be difficult because you are writing about one of your convictions. As you draft, be sure that each paragraph contains real-life examples that pertain to the meaning of the concept—unless for some good reason a specific paragraph does not need examples.

After you draft your paragraphs, make every effort to write topic sentences that focus on how the material in each paragraph helps to establish the meaning of your concept.

As you draft the conclusion, be sure that it provides a satisfying ending with some reference to the thesis and emphasis on the meaning of the concept.

Revising, Editing, and Proofreading   Use the step-by-step method on pages 169–171 in Chapter 6 to revise and polish your essay.

The following two essays use definition and classification to define concepts. The first essay explores the meaning of the term *freedom*; the second investigates the concept of *masculinity*.

Student Writing

Nawang Doma Sherpa's Writing Process

An immigrant from the Himalayan nation of Nepal, student Nawang Doma Sherpa's perspective on *freedom* is informed both by the extraordinary choices and challenges she has made in her life as well as by her strong Buddhist faith. In her essay, she examines the concept of *freedom* through the lenses of both her immigrant experience and her faith, describing how achieving a sense of *freedom* has allowed her to define herself and her life. To generate ideas for her essay, she returned to her journal notes on the Thinking-Writing activity "Defining a Concept."

> General qualities of religion: I know what I believe, but everyone has their own very private reasons for what they believe in—it seems like everyone in my class has a different religion, but their faith—why they believe, or how they believe is the same. I think we're all looking for reasons for our lives. Why are we here?

Classification? What kind of human activity is it?: It's a mysterious activity. There has always been religion just as there have always been dreams. In Nepal our religion, Buddhism, determined so much—from how our days were structured to how we treated our parents and our neighbors. Here it seems like everyone has a different religion, or no religion at all. American society sometimes seems very religious—there's lots of talk about God and religion in politics for example—but it's not like the kind of everyday practice and discipline that I grew up with.

What is my definition of religion?: For me Buddhism is what I practice as well as what I believe. I live my life as a Buddhist, and it helps me to make rational choices about my life. Being free and contributing to make this world a better and more peaceful place is the only aim of Buddhism.

Freedom for Enlightenment

by Nawang Doma Sherpa

Human freedom is dependent upon two qualities: our relationships with others, and our need to believe in a higher purpose for our lives. All the different roles that each of us play in this world—child, student, peer, parent, and countless other relations—are intricate and interwoven with each other. In addition to the roles we each play, the mysterious phenomenon of religion both brings people together (as families and as entire societies) and drives them apart. In my own life, I have struggled with determining my freedom both in relationship to my family's traditions and expectations, and to my Buddhist faith.

I define myself on the basis of my achievements and flaws. In other words, I am who I am because of what I have done in my past—not because of the high goals and beautiful dreams I have set for my future. Both my own experience and the teachings of Buddhism have shown me that the future is both unpredictable and unknowable, but the past and present are reality and fact. The philosopher Jean-Paul Sartre noted that "man is nothing else but what he makes of himself," and I have come to share this view. We are free to determine our own fates, but we are not always fully aware of the responsibilities that come with this freedom. For me, religion and family duties helped me to acknowledge both my freedom and my responsibilities. However, it has not always been easy to accept these things.

I was born in Nepal into a middle class Sherpa family. They allowed me to pursue an education by attending a private girl's school for nine years and then a co-education school for another two years. After I graduated, I decided on my own to come to the United States. I moved to New York City, applied to college, and I now work to support myself and pay my tuition. This was a very unusual decision for a young girl from a traditional Nepalese family to make. Even though I am grown up, I still miss the love and care of my parents, especially the comfort of my mother's embrace and our home. My parents wanted me to stay in Nepal after I graduated, because it is traditional for girls of my social class to get married after they complete high school. But I made the decision to leave, to travel halfway around the world and live on very little money, entirely of my own free will. But if you ask me if I plan to spend the rest of my life away from Nepal, my family, and my home, I would not be able to answer you. I can only say that I will continue to make decisions based on my experience and my faith.

I practiced Buddhism, like most people in Nepal, and I feel free as a Buddhist. I could change my religion if I wanted to, because Buddhism encourages people to determine their own best choices for themselves rather than adhere strictly to one "perfect" or "correct" God. For me, Buddhism is rational. Ancestors have passed along the teaching of Buddha from generation to generation, and the core of that teaching is that we can free ourselves by understanding our inner self. The "eight-fold path" that all Buddhists follow determines how we relate to our selves and to each other: right speech, understanding, good deeds, determination, effort, awareness, thinking, and living. By understanding and accepting responsibility for our actions and beliefs, we achieve freedom. This makes us more responsible for who we are because by following this eight-fold path we will never hurt others and we will never fail in creating our image. Being free and contributing to make this world a better and more peaceful place is the only aim of Buddhism.

Freedom is possible, but with it comes responsibility. Freedom allows us to be conscious and aware, to explore and create new options and make choices that define us in the future. To deny your freedom is to deny responsibility for the choices that you make. I exercised free choice, and at the same time achieved freedom from my society's conservative expectations, by choosing to pursue a college education in America rather than getting married and staying in Nepal. But I have to accept the responsibility for this decision: my family misses me terribly, and I sometimes find it very difficult to balance work and school and to support myself financially. I am fortunate to have both the support of my family and the strength of my religion as I move forward into my future.

Student Writing

Jorden Carlsen's Writing Process

In response to an assignment asking him to develop an extended definition of an abstract concept related to the course readings, Jorden Carlsen, a student at City College of San Francisco, chose to explore the concept of *masculinity*.

Actually, I was stuck at first on choosing a topic. But masculinity is an interesting concept to me because its meaning is kind of vague; people aren't sure exactly what it means. So I thought it was open enough that I could come up with my own conclusions about it. What I wanted to do was to get the audience, my classmates and teacher, to agree that masculinity can be a positive ideal, and I didn't want to lose them along the way. I didn't want to make my essay too complex or outlandish.

To get started, I sat down and began writing ideas about masculinity on a piece of paper, just a list. From that, I could decide which direction to take. Then I began to do research. I used Google to find newspaper and magazine articles. I read about ten articles, and then I went back to my list to see which ideas I could support. Then I highlighted the parts of the articles I wanted to use to support these ideas.

I got rid of some of the ideas on my list and added some new ones. While I was doing this, I was able to write some sentences that I thought sounded good. These later became either topic sentences or supports in the body paragraphs of my essay.

Doing the research helped me get going. I could see that I could combine some of the ideas on my list to go together to form paragraphs. From there, I did an outline.

Deciding what ideas to use at the beginning was the hardest part. I began with what had attracted me to the topic, that the concept isn't exactly clear.

In the body, I decided to deal with some negative ideas about masculinity first and then move on to more positive ones and my own personal ideas. As I wrote, I actually convinced myself even more that my thesis was correct, that the concept of masculinity can be a positive tool for men. So my conclusion came right out of that. I was sold on the idea.

Masculinity Makes a Good Man

by Jorden Carlsen

Nowadays it is difficult to pin down exactly what characteristics make someone a "real" man, and when most of us say a "real man," we mean a masculine man. We know that such a man should be physically strong and not run away at the sight of a spider, but what else has come to mean a man is masculine? To some being masculine means that a man is never able to show any sign or weakness, and to others it means that all a man need do is be a good provider. I think there is more to it than that. I think that masculinity should be an ideal for men to live up to. It shouldn't limit a man's emotion or make him afraid to be seen as weak. Instead, the ideal of masculinity should be something that can encourage men to live up to their full potential in life. It should be something that makes men want to be good providers, stay in good physical shape, and be generally reliable. Masculinity can and should be used as a tool to help men make the most of themselves.

For some people the idea of *masculinity* has become self-defeating. For them it has become synonymous with experiencing uncomfortable social pressures, denying their emotions, having unsavory world-views, or having a fear of showing any kind of weakness. Sara B. Kimmel explains one view of this present situation in her article "Measuring Masculine Body Ideal Distress: Development of a Measure." This article is mainly concerned with many men's dissatisfaction with their bodies and the stress this dissatisfaction causes them. Kimmel notes that "boys and men are comparing themselves to increasingly unattainable masculine body images and are thus increasingly likely to evaluate their body image negatively." For these men, wanting to have a body that they see as masculine has made them unhappy with the body they have. As bad as it may sound, I think slight dissatisfaction can be a good thing for people who are out of shape in that it can encourage them to exercise or eat right, but like many things, can go too far and do more harm than good by, for example, leading to steroid use or eating disorders.

Kimmel also mentions an instrument called "The Conformity to Masculinity Norms Inventory," which has been used to assess conformity to masculine norms in the dominant culture in U.S. society. I found something among the topics included in their survey disturbing. Two of the factors that were included in the "Masculinity Norms" were "Power over Women" and "Disdain for Homosexuals." Why is it [that] people see these things as masculine? I certainly cannot tell you. I believe that a man should respect people, not control or show disdain for them. Doing so can only display a man's insecurities and other shortcomings that take away from the depth of character that makes a real man.

Another drawback to masculinity is that some believe that a real man should not show his emotion, or even worse, not have any. Is this another example of something taken too far? I think it is possible that this belief could have its origins in men's need to do what needs to be done. It has served men best in the past to be able to put their emotions aside and deal with the task at hand, but when there is no task that needs to be done, men don't need to hide their emotions. Yet in his essay titled "Complexion," Richard Rodriguez wrote, "More important than any of this was the fact that a man never verbally revealed his emotions" (516). Through his writing Rodriguez is able to show his range of emotion, which displays his personal strength to face adversity and shows that being emotional can be a part of being a "real" man.

Having a weakness doesn't make a man less masculine; it makes him human. But for some reason it has become construed that for a man to be masculine, he cannot have any weakness. This had led to many kinds of negative consequences for men the world over. I believe this a direct link to male violence. Many men now think that if anyone in any way, no matter how small, threatens to expose a weakness on their part, this person must be violently attacked in order to demonstrate that they are not weak. This has led to all kinds of despicable behavior from verbal attacks to gang warfare. These men don't see the irony that this behavior is covering up the bigger weakness of their own insecurity. Being vulnerable doesn't make men less masculine; it is how they handle the situation and themselves that makes them who they are.

What I believe to be basic to the view of what a man is supposed to be is his ability to provide. The pinnacle of manhood is his role of the hunter-gatherer. When a man can feed and clothe himself and his family, he is on the forefront of manliness. One of the main ideas in an article titled "Man-of-Action Heroes: The Pursuit of Heroic Masculinity in Everyday Consumption," written by Douglas B. Holt, professor of Marketing at the University of Oxford, and Craig J. Thompson, professor of Marketing at the University of Wisconsin, is that one of the main ideals of masculinity in America is that of a man who is a provider, what they call in the article "Breadwinner Masculinity" (427). These are the men who throughout history have been there for their families, clans, or villages, and have been able to keep everyone alive by bringing home the bacon. It may not always be glorious, but putting dinner on the table is often much more important to a culture's well-being than fighting on the battlefield. This is why men who work hard are seen as masculine. Advances in technology are taking working men farther and farther from hunting game and gathering crops, but that doesn't make them any less masculine. A man who spends eight hours a day doing quality control at the computer factory is putting dinner on the table just as much as an iron worker, and they both deserve the title of *masculine breadwinner*.

Take a moment to picture in your mind a masculine man. Chances have it that the man you saw wasn't extremely overweight or had arms that wouldn't stretch a rubber band put around his biceps. When most of us think of a masculine man, we tend to think of one who has an amount of physical prowess. This is mostly likely because strong men are more likely to be better protectors and better suited for the kind of physical labor that in the past kept our predecessors fed. This ideal can be good to encourage a man to stay healthy and in good shape. I know this from personal experience. When my running shoes have a fine layer of dust and I no longer recognize any of the people who work behind the counter at the gym, I know that I'm not living up to part of my potential. A man doesn't have to be an Olympic bodybuilder to have a masculine body. I see it more as a matter of physical ability. I don't do aerobic exercise because I think I'm fat. What gets my running shoes on is my personal drive to have physical stamina in case of the event I may need it, or want it. The physical side of masculinity is something that all men can tap into as encouragement to keep their body physically able, no matter their body type.

Much of what people perceive about masculinity is strength, but I think most people miss the most important strength of all: strength of character. This comes in many forms, from that of reliability to that of integrity. It's what I think about when I think about how a good man should behave. Real men do not take candy from children. They are the defenders of what is right and the ones who are willing to face risk for others. This is where the depth of masculinity lies. A man who is not a provider or [possessor] of any physical prowess will suddenly take on an air of masculinity when he stands up for what is right. Rodriguez wrote in his essay,

"To be formal is to be steady. A man of responsibility, a good provider. Someone formal is also constant. A person to be relied upon in adversity" (515). This is from the part of the essay where he is describing one of the three F's, the concept of what it is to be a man. Living up to the masculine ideal of character isn't always the easiest form of masculinity, but it is the most fulfilling.

Masculinity can be a good ideal for a man to live up to. It also can be taken too far or interpreted in a bad way that takes away from a man's character or leads him to unhealthy behavior, but if viewed correctly, and in the right context, it can be a guide for all men to help them live up to their potential. It can give them drive in life to do things that they may not have otherwise seen or had the motivation to do. *Masculinity* is just a concept, but it is one that has the power to lead a man to be more than he is, and that makes it powerful.

Works Cited

Holt, Douglas B., and Craig J. Thompson. "Man-of-Action Heroes: The Pursuit of Heroic Masculinity in Everyday Consumption." *Journal of Consumer Research* 31.2 (2004): 425–439. Print.

Kimmel, Sara B. "Measuring Masculine Body Ideal Distress: Development of a Measure." *International Journal of Men's Health* (Spring 2004): n. pag. Web. 18 Apr. 2005.

Rodriguez, Richard. "Complexion." *Great Writing*. Ed. Harvey S. Weiner and Nora Eisenberg. 3rd ed. San Francisco: McGraw, 2002: 513–516. Print.

Alternative Writing Projects

Compare and contrast how a distinctive concept (such as *masculinity* or *femininity*) is understood by two different cultures or social groups. Joseph Berger's essay (page 248 in Chapter 8) is an example of such an essay. You may draw upon your personal experience as part of your evidence to support your definition of a concept, and you might consider interviewing someone from a different culture or social group to compare the person's firsthand experiences with your own.

CHAPTER 8   Summary

- Concepts are general ideas that you use to organize your experience and, in so doing, bring order to your life. They also distinguish and connect one thing to another.

- The process by which you group things on the basis of their similarities is known as classifying.

- You form concepts by the interactive processes of generalizing and interpreting.

- To determine whether the concept you have selected fits a situation, you have to determine whether the requirements that form the concept are being met. There are many different perspectives on what some complex concepts mean, what they should mean, or whether they should be used at all.

- When you apply a concept to objects, ideas, experiences, actions, or people you are in effect classifying them by placing them in a group of things that are defined by the properties or requirements of the concept. The same things or individuals can often be classified in many different ways.

- When you define a concept, you usually identify the necessary properties or requirements that determine when the concept can be applied.

- For productive writing or discussions about complex issues, clear definitions are needed. Difficulties arise because significant terms related to complex issues are usually abstract concepts, which different people may define in various ways.

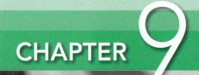
© vario images GmbH & Co.KG/Alamy

As you have probably been cautioned by your teachers and your friends, the Internet is an extraordinary source of an infinite array of perspectives and perceptions, but a significant percentage of that information ranges from the slightly biased to the completely wrong. The various projects of Wikimedia, a group of collaborative online resources founded by Internet entrepreneur Jimmy Wales, demonstrate how the collective input of responsible critical thinkers can create sources of information that are accurate, fair, and presented from a global array of perspectives and experiences. Why is that important?

To read more about Wikimedia, see the "New Media & Thoughtful Writing" box on p. 292.

Writing to Compare and Evaluate: Exploring Perspectives and Relationships

"Nothing that God ever made is the same thing to more than one person."

—Zora Neale Hurston

Critical Thinking Focus: Critically evaluating perceptions and perspectives

Writing Focus: Using comparative thinking

Reading Theme: Differing perspectives from history

Writing Project: Comparing perspectives on an issue or an event

Chapter 7 introduced the concept of *perceptions* and showed how writers use their perceptions when they describe, narrate, and explain processes. As critical thinkers, active readers, and thoughtful writers, however, we need to go beyond simply recognizing that people have different perceptions. We have to think carefully about perceptions. In addition, we need to see how *perceptions*—messages from the senses—are connected to *perspectives*—points of view that develop from and also influence perceptions.

This chapter emphasizes critical evaluation and comparison of perceptions and perspectives. It will help you think about the differing points of view that people bring to what they say and write. Perspectives often conflict with one another, so you then must try to determine which one makes the most sense. You need to be able to analyze the differences and similarities that you find.

Because so many life situations and college assignments involve comparing and contrasting perspectives in an organized way, this chapter presents strategies for using comparative analysis in thinking and writing. The Writing Project asks you to analyze different perspectives on one event or issue.

Perceptions and Perspectives

Perspectives, or points of view, are what people express when they speak and write and also the vantage points from which they perceive events or issues. So a complex interaction exists between perceptions and perspectives. People's perspectives are formed by beliefs, interests, needs, age, gender, nationality, ethnicity, health, education—the multiple factors of life. These factors of perspective influence perceptions; at the same time, perceptions continuously influence perspectives.

To understand how various people can be exposed to the same stimuli or events and yet have different perceptions, it helps to imagine that each of us views the

@ THINKING CRITICALLY ABOUT NEW MEDIA

Wikimedia

In your research, you may find various Wikimedia resources to be a useful starting point for your work. Wikipedia, a collaborative encyclopedia that was the first Wikimedia project, is written and edited entirely by volunteer contributors. There are now Wikipedia sites in more than sixty languages, and entries have been written in more than one hundred languages. In an interview, Wales pointed out that this diversity of perspective—bringing in marginalized cultures, voices, and languages to share their expertise with the world—is one of the greatest strengths of Wikimedia projects. "The Wikipedia for a lot of people harkens back to what we all thought the Internet was for in the first place," he observes. "When most people first started the Internet, they thought, oh, this is fantastic, people can communicate from all over the world and build knowledge and share information." Entirely nonprofit and volunteer-driven, Wikipedia is the ultimate expression of open-mindedness. Through a series of open-source, open-access chat rooms and other paths of communication, each Wikipedia entry is communally checked for accuracy, fairness, and the quality of its citations and illustrations. Until Wikipedia, print encyclopedias—for all their pretenses of objectivity—could only present one unified voice, one point of view, that was nearly impossible to amend or update once in print. With Wikipedia, both access to and control of information passes to a global community who use the technology to collaborate, learn, and grow.

Wiki resources grow organically through collaboration and community. The various projects of Wikimedia itself are built by tens of millions of mostly anonymous users in collaboration with one another, sharing and checking their created knowledge together. Users compare specific entries with their own knowledge, perspectives, and perceptions, and amend or add to each entry based on their own experience and information. As a fully volunteer project, Wikipedia depends on the ability and

world through personal "contact lenses," an analogy from the previous chapter. (You might think of the factors that go into forming perspectives as the prescription for the lenses!)

We aren't usually aware that we are wearing these lenses. Instead, without our realizing it, our lenses act as filters that select and shape what we perceive.

To understand how people perceive the world, we have to understand their individual lenses, which influence how they actively select, organize, and interpret

integrity of each contributor. For example, Wikipedia contributors have created "active improvement teams" that have implemented policies to check all entries for bias, to screen for spam, and to set and adhere to encyclopedia standards.

The software that structures all Wikimedia projects can be easily and freely adapted by anyone who wishes to create a communally edited website. You may, at some point in your academic career, be asked to create or participate in a wiki as a classroom project. The Wikimedia organization itself has branched out from Wikipedia to create wiki learning centers, online textbooks, dictionaries, a collection of quotations (in more than thirty languages), an archive of public-domain books and other texts, and even Wikispecies, a taxonomy database created by and for scientists but (as with all wikis) available to all.

Thinking-Writing Activity

USING WIKIMEDIA TO COLLABORATE AND COMMUNICATE

Earlier in this chapter, we explored different perspectives on the 2010 earthquake in Haiti. Gather into a group with two or three of your classmates and think of another disaster (e.g., the oil leak in the Gulf of Mexico, the flood in Pakistan, the eruption of the Eyjafjallajökull volcano). Decide amongst yourselves who will research which aspects of the disaster and then do your research separately. Use a free wiki host site (e.g., *https://www.google.com/sites*) as a place to compile your data, collaborate with your group members, and create your own web page about the disaster. The site should allow you to include whatever kind of media you would like (e.g., photos, video, audio, diagrams, and links), so use it to your advantage to highlight the different perspectives available regarding your subject. When the site is done, share it with the rest of your class and ask for their feedback.

the events in their experience. A diagram of the process might look like Figure 9.1. A more comic demonstration of the different "lenses" we all wear provides the punchline of the *Dilbert* cartoon on the next page.

Effective critical thinkers are aware of the lenses that they—and others—are wearing. People unaware of the nature of their own lenses can often mistake their own perceptions for objective truth, not having examined either the facts or others' perceptions of a given issue.

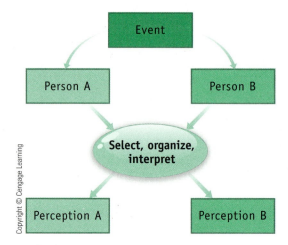

FIGURE 9.1
Differing Perceptions of an Event

Thinking-Writing Activity

DIFFERING PERSPECTIVES

Examine the following pairs of statements. In each pair, two people are being exposed to the same basic stimulus or event, yet the perception of one differs greatly from that of the other. Explain how the various perceptions might have developed.

1. a. That chili was much too spicy to eat.

   Explanation: _____

   b. That chili needed more hot peppers and chili powder to spice it up a little.

   Explanation: _____

2. a. People who wear lots of makeup and jewelry are very sophisticated.

   Explanation: _____

b. People who wear lots of makeup and jewelry are ostentatious and overdressed.

Explanation: _____

3. a. The music young people enjoy listening to is a highly creative cultural expression.

Explanation: _____

b. The music young people enjoy listening to is obnoxious noise.

Explanation: _____

4. a. I really enjoy how stimulating and intellectually challenging this English class is.

Explanation: _____

b. This English class is too much work. All the teacher wants to do is make us think, think, think. It makes my head hurt.

Explanation: _____

In the cartoon "The Investigation," each witness is giving what he or she (or it!) believes is an accurate description of the man in the center, and all are unaware that their descriptions are being influenced by who they are and the way that they perceive things.

Selecting Perceptions: Why Do We Notice the Things We Notice?

We tend to select perceptions about subjects that have been called to our attention. For instance, at the age of three, one author's child suddenly became aware of beards. On entering a subway car, she would ask in a penetrating voice, "Any beards here?" and proceed to count them out loud. In so doing, she naturally focused her parents' attention—as well as that of other passengers—on beards.

Another aspect of our perceiving lenses is our tendency to notice what we need, desire, or otherwise find interesting. When we go shopping, we focus on whatever items we are looking for. Walking down the street, we tend to notice certain kinds of people or events while completely ignoring others. Even while watching a movie or reading a book, we tend to concentrate on and remember the elements most meaningful to us. Another person can perform *exactly* the same actions—shop at the same store, walk down the same street, read the same book, or go to the same movie—and yet notice and remember entirely different things.

THE INVESTIGATION

Although we tend to focus on what is familiar, normally we are not aware of doing so. In fact, we often take for granted what is familiar to us—the taste of chili or eggs, the street that we live on, our family or friends—and normally don't think about how we perceive it. When something happens that makes the familiar seem strange and unfamiliar, though, we do become aware of our perceptions and start to evaluate them.

To sum up, we actively select our perceptions on the basis of

- What has been called to our attention
- What our needs or interests are
- What our moods or feelings are
- What seems familiar or unfamiliar
- What our backgrounds are

The way in which we select perceptions is a paramount factor in shaping the lenses through which we view the world, and it influences our writing to a great extent. Our writing is based on the points we choose to make, the details we select to include. Even when different people are writing about the same subject, the results are often very different because their lenses and their perspectives lead them to make different selections.

Organizing Perceptions

Not only do you actively select certain perceptions, you also actively organize them into meaningful relationships and patterns. Carefully examine Figure 7.2 in Chapter 7 on page 208. Do you see both the young woman and the old woman? If you do, try switching your perspective back and forth between the two images. As you do so, notice how for each image, you are doing the following things:

- *Selecting* certain lines, shapes, and shadings on which to focus your attention
- *Organizing* these lines, shapes, and shadings into different patterns
- *Interpreting* these patterns as representing things you can recognize—a hat, a nose, a chin

We naturally try to order and organize what we are experiencing into patterns and relationships that make sense to us. When we succeed in doing so, the completed whole means more than the sum of the individual parts. We are continually organizing the world in this way during virtually every waking moment. We do not live in a world of isolated sounds, patches of color, random odors, and individual textures. Instead, we live in a world of objects and people, language and music—a world in which all these individual stimuli are woven together. We are able to perceive this world of complex experiences because we can organize the individual stimuli we are receiving into relationships that have meaning for us.

This organizing process is integral to the writing process. When you write an essay, compose a letter, or create a story, you are actively organizing the ideas you selected to include various relationships. Instead of simply stringing together words, you are developing a coherent structure through which to communicate thoughts and feelings.

Interpreting Perceptions

Besides selecting and organizing perceptions, we also actively interpret what we perceive: we are figuring out what something means. One of the elements that influences interpretations is the *context*, or overall situation, within which the perception is occurring. For example, imagine that you see a man running down the street. Your interpretation of his action will depend on the specific context. For example, is there a bus waiting at the corner? Is a police officer running behind him? Is the man wearing a jogging suit?

We are continually trying to interpret what we perceive, whether it is a design, someone else's behavior, or a social situation. As in the example of someone running down the street, many perceptions can be interpreted in more than one way. When a situation has more than one possible interpretation, it is ambiguous. The more ambiguous a situation is, the greater its possible meanings or interpretations.

Casebook: Perception and Reality in Reporting the Earthquake in Haiti

On January 12, 2010, a catastrophic earthquake rocked the island of Haiti. Centered near the capital and most densely populated city of Port-au-Prince, the earthquake leveled thousands of buildings, including the Presidential Palace, burying several hundred thousand people alive and wreaking devastating havoc on the small, impoverished island. As with the hurricane Katrina that devastated New Orleans and the Mississippi coast in 2005, the world's perception of this event was framed, shaped, and communicated through the media's reporting, and the perceptions we form become our beliefs regarding the reality of what is occurring and our response to it. In his blog post on January 13, 2010, psychology and neuroscience writer Jonah Lehrer explores some of the paradoxes of this process.

"Haiti"

by Jonah Lehrer

"The news out of Haiti this morning is hellish; the Earth slips and thousands die. The early reports have the same feel as the 2004 Indian Ocean tsunami, in that every bulletin brings more awful news. I already find myself dreading tomorrow's newspaper, which will outline the full scope of the tragedy. Here is more information on where to donate. I'd like to take a moment and discuss a cruel paradox of such events, which is that the sheer scale of the suffering seems to inhibit our empathy. There are no stories yet, just anecdotal shards and heartbreaking photographs. And so all we get is ledes citing the horrifying statistics and shocking numbers of dead. But these numbers quickly get incomprehensible—we can't imagine a thousand corpses—and so the emotional event becomes an abstraction, which fails to trigger the proper moral reaction . . . the problem with statistics is that they don't activate our moral emotions. The depressing numbers leave us cold: our mind can't comprehend suffering on such a massive scale. This is why we are riveted when one child falls down a well, but turn a blind eye to the millions of people who die every year for lack of clean water. Or why we donate thousands of dollars to help a single African war orphan featured on the cover of a magazine, but ignore widespread genocides in Rwanda or Darfur. As Mother Theresa put it, 'If I look at the mass I will never act. If I look at the one, I will.'"

As you read the following accounts reflect on the interpretations that they are presenting and the perceptions that you are forming (and have formed) as a result of them. Then consider and respond to the questions that follow the articles.

Source: Jonah Lehrer, "Haiti" from *The Frontal Cortex,* January 13, 2010.

"Making Sense of Haiti"

by Amy Davidson

What does an earthquake look like? How can we envision what happened in Haiti— its destruction, its scale? There was the photograph, in the *Times* this morning, of Lionel Michaud, who had finally found his ten-month-old daughter Christian, or

Source: From Amy Davidson, "Making Sense of Haiti." From *The New Yorker,* Close Read. January 15, 2010. Copyright © 2010 The New Yorker. Reprinted by permission.

rather her body, on a pile of corpses, like a doll one of the other dead had lost hold of. Her mother, Michaud's wife, had also died, and he is sitting beside the jumble of bodies with his hand to his head as though he has no idea where to take things from here. And who would? Then there is the picture of a little boy named Reggie Claude, pulled from the rubble by Belgian and Spanish relief workers, who, beaming, hand him to his mother, who is rushing toward him. That is a true story, too. Both photographs capture part of what the earthquake has done. Maybe next to each other they show the way an earthquake is wanton and random—though that random part is not quite, especially in terms of the aftermath, as we know that poverty makes things worse.

What conveys the tragedy more? The bodies we see everywhere—bodies that people in Haiti still have to walk by and over, as the police have just begun, like watchmen in a plague city, to drive around asking residents to bring out their dead? Seven thousand people were buried in a mass grave yesterday. Or the pictures of the missing that a number of sites have collected—pictures taken before this happened, studio portraits and scenes from family gatherings? There are more photographs—the Boston *Globe's* Big Picture has a wrenching collection—conveying more dramas, all of which, despite their variety and glimpses of heroism, have the same moral: that something terrible has happened in Haiti.

Does it help to see it if you move back for a minute? The *Washington Post* has a GeoEye Satellite image of the quake area, which combines extreme distance—outer space—with queasy proximity. What do you see when you pan across blocks of pancaked houses? From directly overhead, you can't really tell how tall any of them were, or if what looks like a quilt of rags is an open-air morgue or an encampment. (The United Nations Development Program also has aerial pictures on its YouTube channel.) There are maps with colors marking the areas of greater and lesser destruction. And most abstract, and for that maybe most frightening, a roll of graph paper with the seismic readings from Tuesday. The *Times* has a map with pictures and little icons, including one for the penitentiary from which prisoners escaped in the chaos. Then there are lists with other information: where to contribute to help. Ten million dollars has been raised by text messaging—"Yele" to 501501, for a fund organized by Wyclef Jean, or "Haiti" to 90999, which sends ten dollars to the Red Cross.

Haiti isn't distant from America, really, or in any way an abstraction. Anyone, anywhere, facing what the Haitians face should touch us. But it's also true that Americans and their family members have been directly affected by the quake. It's no surprise, given the size of Florida's Haitian community, that the Miami *Herald's* coverage of the disaster has been outstanding; its main earthquake page also provides some real context. (Among other things, there are Patrick Farrell's Pulitzer-prize winning photographs of Haiti's children in the aftermath of last year's storms.) The *Times* also has updates on its Lede blog. And we've collected *The New Yorker's* coverage.

5   What is the range of an earthquake? An Estonian security guard was pulled from the rubble (dozens of his United Nations colleagues were not). The A.P. has a list

of foreign countries that lost people, and though, of course, at times like this we don't think of humanity in terms of borders, one still wonders how it came to be that a Peruvian and a Dane and fifteen Brazilians were all swallowed up by the Haitian quake. And one is grateful for the Belgian and Spanish rescuers, as well as those from other countries. Our contingent includes members of the 82nd Airborne. Cracks in the earth are not aligned with borders. Simon Winchester noted in the *Times* today that "the Enriquillo-Plantain Garden fault, the tectonic culprit behind Tuesday's earthquake, shares many similarities with the San Andreas." It's a strangely shifting world, in many senses.

Maybe, in the coming days, we'll get to a stage where pictures say less as numbers say more: the real number of the dead (now estimated at fifty thousand; "you can't dig fifty thousand graves," a rescuer told the Miami *Herald*), the tons of aid delivered. But not yet. We are still, though just barely, in the window of time in which family members and friends who can't find each other can have a little bit of hope. There are reports of civil disorder, and chaos at the airport, and nothing where it ought to be. There is no coherent story yet, and maybe there never will be. We still need pictures from Haiti.

Question for Reading Actively

1. In the first paragraph, two different photos are mentioned that are not shown. How does Davidson get you to "see" the images without showing the actual photos? What thoughts or emotions do her descriptions of the photos elicit?

Question for Thinking Critically

1. Davidson poses the question "How *do* we get our minds around a disaster on such an incomprehensible scale? Is it individual photographs and personal stories of rescue and death? Is it descriptions and statistics that detail the scope of the catastrophe? Is it video footage showing collapsed buildings, corpses stacked on the roads, and people desperate for food and medical attention? Is it photographs from the air that present a panorama of destruction? Or is it a roll of graph paper with the seismic readings of the earthquake? Or is it all of the above?" What do you think?

Question for Writing Thoughtfully

1. Davidson starts four of her paragraphs with a question or questions. What effect did this have? Did it prime your curiosity? Shape your initial thoughts on the paragraph's topic? Prejudice your perspective before you read more information? If so, how? If not, why not? How could you change the questions to change their effect?

Thinking Critically About Visuals

The Aftermath of the Earthquake in Haiti

What is the human price of devastation? A man builds coffins in front of his destroyed house in Port-au-Prince, Haiti in March 2010. The 7.0-magnitude earthquake that hit Haiti two months earlier in January left more than a million people living in makeshift camps. Building enough coffins before the thousands of dead bodies decayed was a tragic and hopeless endeavor. Did the scale of this tragic event heighten or inhibit your empathy for the victims? What images, statistics, or stories affected you most? Why do you think that is?

AP Photo/Esteban Felix

"Suffering"

by George Packer *"The New Yorker"*

The night after the earthquake, Haitians who had lost their homes, or who feared that their houses might collapse, slept outdoors, in the streets and parks of Port-au-Prince. In Place Saint-Pierre, across the street from the Kinam Hotel, in the suburb of Pétionville, hundreds of people lay under the sky, and many of them sang hymns: "God, you are the one who gave me life. Why are we suffering?" In Jacmel, a coastal town south of the capital, where the destruction was also great, a woman who had already seen the body of one of her children removed from a building learned that her second child was dead, too, and wailed, "God! I can't take this anymore!" A man named Lionel Gaedi went to the Port-au-Prince morgue

Source: "Suffering" by George Packer. From *The New Yorker* January 25, 2010. Copyright © 2010 The New Yorker. Reprinted by permission.

in search of his brother, Josef, but was unable to find his body among the piles of corpses that had been left there. "I don't see him—it's a catastrophe," Gaedi said. "God gives, God takes." Chris Rolling, an American missionary and aid worker, tried to extricate a girl named Jacqueline from a collapsed school using nothing more than a hammer. He urged her to be calm and pray, and as night fell he promised that he would return with help. When he came back the next morning, Jacqueline was dead. "The bodies stopped bothering me after a while, but I think what I will always carry with me is the conversation I had with Jacqueline before I left her," Rolling wrote afterward on his blog. "How could I leave someone who was dying, trapped in a building! . . . She seemed so brave when I left! I told her I was going to get help, but I didn't tell her I would be gone until morning. I think this is going to trouble me for a long time." Dozens of readers wrote to comfort Rolling with the view that his story was evidence of divine wisdom and mercy.

The earthquake seemed to follow a malignant design. It struck the metropolitan area where almost a third of Haiti's nine million people live. It flattened the headquarters of the United Nations mission, which would have taken the lead in coordinating relief, and killed dozens of U.N. employees, including, reportedly, the mission chief, Hédi Annabi. In a country without a building code, it wiped out whole neighborhoods of shoddy concrete structures, took down hospitals, wrecked the port, put the airport's control tower out of action, damaged key institutions from the Presidential Palace to the National Cathedral, killed the archbishop and senior politicians, cut off power and phone service, and blocked passage through the streets. There was almost no heavy equipment in the capital that could be used to move debris off trapped survivors, or even to dig mass graves. "Everything is going wrong," Guy LaRoche, a hospital manager, said.

Haitian history is a chronicle of suffering so Job-like that it inevitably inspires arguments with God, and about God. Slavery, revolt, oppression, color caste, despoliation, American occupation alternating with American neglect, extreme poverty, political violence, coups, gangs, hurricanes, floods—and now an earthquake that exploits all the weaknesses created by this legacy to kill tens of thousands of people. "If God exists, he's really got it in for Haiti," Pooja Bhatia, a journalist who lives in Haiti, wrote in the *Times*. "Haitians think so, too. Zed, a housekeeper in my apartment complex, said God was angry at sinners around the world, but especially in Haiti. Zed said the quake had fortified her faith, and that she understood it as divine retribution."

This was also Pat Robertson's view. The conservative televangelist appeared on "The 700 Club" and blamed Haitians for a pact they supposedly signed with the Devil two hundred years ago ("true story"), advising people in one of the most intensely religious countries on earth to turn to God. (Similarly, he had laid the blame for the September 11th attacks and Hurricane Katrina on Americans' wickedness.) In Robertsonian theodicy—the justification of the ways of God in the face of evil—there's no such thing as undeserved suffering: people struck by disaster always had it coming.

5   At the White House, President Obama, too, was thinking about divine motivation, and he asked the same question implied in the hymn sung by Haitian survivors under the night sky: "After suffering so much for so long, to face this new horror must cause some to look up and ask, Have we somehow been forsaken?" But Obama's answer was the opposite of Zed's and Robertson's: rather than claiming to know the mind of God, he vowed that America would not forsake Haiti, because its tragedy reminds us of "our common humanity."

Choosing the humanistic approach to other people's misery brings certain obligations. The first is humanitarian: the generous response of ordinary Americans, along with the quick dispatch of troops and supplies by the U.S. government, met this responsibility, though it couldn't answer the overwhelming needs of people in Haiti. But beyond rescue and relief lies the harder task of figuring out what the United States and other countries can and ought to do for Haiti over the long term, and what Haiti is capable of doing for itself. Before the earthquake, Hédi Annabi declared that the U.N. had stabilized Haiti to the point where its future was beginning to look a little less bleak. Bill Clinton, the U.N. special envoy to Haiti, has sounded even more optimistic about investment and growth, and after the earthquake he pointed to Haiti's new national economic plan as a sound basis for rebuilding.

Yet Haitian political culture has a long history of insularity, corruption, and violence, which partly explains why Port-au-Prince lies in ruins. If, after an earthquake that devastated rich and poor neighborhoods alike, Haiti's political and business elites resurrect the old way of fratricidal self-seeking, they will find nothing but debris for spoils. Disasters on this scale reveal something about the character of the societies in which they occur. The aftermath of the 2008 cyclone in Burma not only betrayed the callous indifference of the ruling junta but demonstrated the vibrancy of civil society there. Haiti's earthquake shows that, whatever the communal spirit of its people at the moment of crisis, the government was not functioning, unable even to bury the dead, much less rescue the living. This vacuum, which had been temporarily filled by the U.N., now poses the threat of chaos.

But if Haiti is to change, the involvement of outside countries must also change. Rather than administering aid almost entirely through the slow drip of private organizations, international agencies and foreign powers should put their money and their effort into the more ambitious project of building a functional Haitian state. It would be the work of years, and billions of dollars. If this isn't a burden that nations want to take on, so be it. But to patch up a dying country and call it a rescue would leave Haiti forsaken indeed, and not by God.

Questions for Reading Actively

1. Packer explores the way people try to find some sense or meaning in a natural disaster like this, some way to help them cope with the human loss and suffering. What are some of the explanations people offer to make sense of an event like this?

2. Why does Packer believe that the world has a moral obligation to help Haiti rebuild itself?

Question for Thinking Critically

1. Packer says, "If, after an earthquake that devastated rich and poor neighborhoods alike, Haiti's political and business elites resurrect the old way of fratricidal self-seeking, they will find nothing but debris for spoils." What does he mean by this?

Question for Writing Thoughtfully

1. Packer explores the ways religious, political, and socioeconomic perspectives can be used to understand the earthquake in Haiti. Write three paragraphs using these same perspectives to interpret the meaning of another event that has happened recently.

"Aftershock"

by Bryan Walsh, Jay Newton-Small, and Tim Padgett

Michaud Jonas returned to the ruins of the Palm Apparel factory to see if he could find his little sister's body—and, possibly, a job. Hundreds of workers were buried under the rubble of this T-shirt-manufacturing plant in the Port-au-Prince suburb of Carrefour, and Jonas' sister, 22, was one of them. The scent of decay around the neighborhood was overpowering. Yet though he mourned his loss—his brother and mother also died, when the family's home collapsed—he looked ahead. "Here was the worst place hit, so maybe it'll be the first place to recover," he said. "I need to find a job so I can help what's left of my family. They are depending on me."

For all the uncertainty and chaos in the early days following the quake, it was clear the world wanted to help. From the high-level work of former President Bill Clinton, the U.N. special envoy to Haiti, to the millions of dollars donated through text-messaging, there was no shortage of generosity in response to the devastation. Americans alone gave more than $190 million in the first week after the quake, on track with the response to the 2004 tsunami and Hurricane Katrina. While the U.S. military prepared a large mobilization of troops and support staff, NGOs with a long history of responding to natural disasters moved into Haiti as fast as they could. "We will be here today, tomorrow and for the time ahead," Secretary of State Hillary Clinton said on Jan. 16.

But that willingness to help collided at first with what was a logistical nightmare. Port-au-Prince's seaport was rendered unusable, its airport was barely functional, and roads were snarled by debris and the homeless. The temblor not only struck a country mired in poverty; it erupted just 15 miles (about 24 km) from that nation's capital. The result was a bureaucratic decapitation, meaning aid and personnel initially had to be shipped in, either through the neighboring Dominican Republic or secondary airports in Haiti. (The Asian tsunami, by contrast, didn't touch the capitals of affected countries.) Even after the Port-au-Prince airport was partly repaired and under the control of the U.S., landing slots were tight; some NGOs claimed that humanitarian flights were turned away for lack of space (though the U.S. insists that was only temporary). And for the locals, there was no Plan B. "With Katrina, if you could walk to the edge of a disaster area, you could get in a car, drive 40 miles, find a store and buy what you needed," says Caryl Stern, president and CEO of the U.S. fund for UNICEF. "Here, there is no car. There is no highway. There is no 40 miles away."

In the first week, workers handed out just 250,000 daily food rations to hundreds of thousands clamoring for them. But it's difficult to see how aid could have been

Source: "Aftershock" by Bryan Walsh, Jay Newton-Small and Tim Padgett. From Time.com blog, Swampland, January 20, 2010. © 2010 Time Inc. All rights reserved. Reprinted by permission.

distributed through a ruined Haiti much faster. Indeed, by one measure, things went better than expected: despite a security vacuum that U.S. soldiers now have to fill, fears of widespread violence seemed mostly unfounded, though there were local exceptions. As the shock of the quake receded, Haitians did what people have done throughout the world after natural disasters: they improvised, helping one another while they hoped for aid. Haitians "look more poised to come together and roll up our sleeves," says Jocelyn McCalla, a Haitian-American development consultant.

5   But that spirit won't be enough to keep Haiti going in the weeks and months ahead. For medium-term recovery, international aid will have to keep supplies flowing. Water will be the first priority. People can go hungry longer than they can go thirsty, and contaminated water can lead to outbreaks of diseases like cholera. Desalination will be one option—the aircraft carrier U.S.S. *Carl Vinson*, holding off the coast of Haiti, can donate 200,000 gal. (about 757,000 L) of fresh water a day. Steady food aid will be necessary for some time, though there are hopes that the earthquake left Haiti's agricultural sector mostly unscathed. The assistance efforts have to be visible, to assure Haitians they haven't been forgotten and to forestall rage on the ground.

There is also a pressing need for doctors and nurses who can handle traumatic injuries and provide disease care. There were more than 200,000 Haitians with HIV or AIDS before the quake. For them and people with other chronic conditions who need consistent drug treatment, interruption can mean death. Haiti's ruined public-health infrastructure will have to be rebuilt, and that will mean more than just replacing collapsed hospitals. Local talent will be needed—especially vital will be nurses and support staff. Without such a sustained effort, the "long-term ramifications could lead to more deaths than the event itself," says Tom Kirsch, the co-director of the Center for Refugee and Disaster Response at Johns Hopkins University.

Further ahead, a recovering Haiti must change the way it builds. The shoddiness of construction in Port-au-Prince made the death toll dramatically higher than it would have been had the quake struck in a sturdier place; the 1989 quake in the San Francisco Bay Area was of almost the same magnitude as Haiti's but killed only 63 people. A concrete block in Haiti might weigh an eighth of what its U.S. counterpart would, as unscrupulous contractors take kickbacks and building codes go unenforced. It wasn't only slums that tumbled, after all; grand buildings like the presidential palace and the headquarters of the U.N. mission collapsed too. Other developing countries in quake zones, like Colombia, build far more securely. "Earthquakes don't kill people," says Columbia University's Mutter. "Bad buildings kill people. And buildings are bad because people are poor."

That's exactly why recovery will never be complete unless Haiti can break out of the economic basement. The country has a per capita GDP of $1,300—six times less than that of the Dominican Republic, with which it shares the island of Hispaniola. While the Dominican Republic has enjoyed relative political stability, Haiti's history of corruption and turmoil has helped keep the country poor. Before the quake, Haiti had begun to do better, and in the initial phase of recovery, there will be jobs in reconstruction. Consistent aid policies that include microloans for small businesses and more-liberal tariffs that would nurture a low-cost export sector could help Haiti grow sustainably. A richer Haiti would be a safer Haiti. "Part of recovery has to mean charting a new role for Haiti in the global economy," says Ben Wisner, a research fellow at Oberlin College and a disaster expert.

What does the world owe Haiti? Beyond the moral imperative to help save the country, there is a practical incentive. Natural disasters—earthquakes, storms, floods—are unavoidable acts of God. But it's possible to build societies, from New Orleans to Port-au-Prince, that can weather them. Doing so would save lives and the tens of billions of dollars that are spent every time a fragile community gets wiped out. "The world can't afford more of these disasters," says Roger Bilham, a seismologist at the University of Colorado. "It's worth investing in these problems now, while we can." Haiti's buried were victims of poverty and neglect, not just the quake. But we owe it to the survivors—to people like Michaud Jonas—to help build a Haiti that will never again be so vulnerable.

Question for Reading Actively

1. Is the authors' perspective in this article reflective or forward looking? Point to examples to support your answer. According to the authors, what are Haiti's short-term and long-term recovery needs?

Question for Thinking Critically

1. In the last paragraph, the authors mention the terms "moral imperative" and "practical incentive." How would you define each of these terms? What is the difference between them? Do the authors suggest one or the other is a more compelling reason to do something? What do you think?

Question for Writing Thoughtfully

1. The authors mention several people by name in this article. Write the names down in a list and next to each name describe that person's perspective and how it supports the article (e.g., an authority who supplies expertise or reputable data).

Thinking-Writing Activity

FIVE ACCOUNTS OF THE ASSASSINATION OF MALCOLM X, 1965

Let's examine a situation in which a number of different people had differing perceptions about an event they were describing. Chapter 6 of this book contains a passage by Malcolm X (pages 164–167) written when he was just beginning his life's work. A few years later, this work came to a tragic end with his assassination at a meeting in Harlem. As you read through the various accounts, pay particular attention to the perceptions each presents. After reading the accounts, analyze some of the differences in these perceptions by writing answers to the questions that follow.

1. What details of the events has each writer selected to focus on?

2. How has each writer organized the selected details? Remember that most newspapers give what they consider the most important information first.

3. How does each writer depict Malcolm X, his followers, the gunmen, and the significance of the assassination?

The New York Times (February 22, 1965)

Malcolm X, the 39-year-old leader of a militant Black Nationalist movement, was shot to death yesterday afternoon at a rally of his followers in a ballroom in Washington Heights. The bearded Negro extremist had said only a few words of greeting when a fusillade rang out. The bullets knocked him over backwards.

A 22-year-old Negro, Thomas Hagan, was charged with the killing. The police rescued him from the ballroom crowd after he had been shot and beaten.

Pandemonium broke out among the 400 Negroes in the Audubon Ballroom at 160th Street and Broadway. As men, women and children ducked under tables and flattened themselves on the floor, more shots were fired. The police said seven bullets struck Malcolm. Three other Negroes were shot. Witnesses reported that as many as 30 shots had been fired. About two hours later the police said the shooting had apparently been a result of a feud between followers of Malcolm and members of the extremist group he broke with last year, the Black Muslims. . . .

Source: From *The New York Times*, February 22, 1965. Copyright © 1965 by The New York Times Co. Reprinted with permission.

Life (March 5, 1965)

His life oozing out through a half dozen or more gunshot wounds in his chest, Malcolm X, once the shrillest voice of black supremacy, lay dying on the stage of a Manhattan auditorium. Moments before, he had stepped up to the lectern and 400 of the faithful had settled down expectantly to hear the sort of speech for which he was famous—flaying the hated white man. Then a scuffle broke out in the hall and Malcolm's bodyguards bolted from his side to break it up—only to discover that they had been faked out. At least two men with pistols rose from the audience and pumped bullets into the speaker, while a third cut loose at close range with both barrels of a sawed-off shotgun. In the confusion the pistol man got away. The shotgunner lunged through the crowd and out the door, but not before the guards came to their wits and shot him in the leg. Outside he was swiftly overtaken by other supporters of Malcolm and very likely would have been stomped to death if the police hadn't saved him. Most shocking of all to the residents of Harlem was the fact that Malcolm had been killed not by "whitey" but by members of his own race.

Source: "The Violent End of the Man Called Malcolm." From the March 5, 1965 LIFE Magazine. Copyright © 1965 The Picture Collection Inc. Reprinted with permission. All rights reserved.

The New York Post (February 22, 1965)

They came early to the Audubon Ballroom, perhaps drawn by the expectation that Malcolm X would name the men who firebombed his home last Sunday. . . . I sat at the left in the 12th row and, as we waited, the man next to me spoke of Malcolm and his followers: "Malcolm is our only hope. You can depend on him to tell it like it is and to give Whitey hell."

Source: Copyright © 1965. Reprinted by permission of the New York Post.

There was a prolonged ovation as Malcolm walked to the rostrum. Malcolm looked up and said "A salaam aleikum (Peace be unto you)" and the audience replied "We aleikum salaam (And unto you, peace)."

Bespectacled and dapper in a dark suit, sandy hair glinting in the light, Malcolm said: "Brothers and sisters . . ." He was interrupted by two men in the center of the ballroom, who rose and, arguing with each other, moved forward. Then there was a scuffle at the back of the room. I heard Malcolm X say his last words: "Now, brothers, break it up," he said softly. "Be cool, be calm."

Then all hell broke loose. There was a muffled sound of shots and Malcolm, blood on his face and chest, fell limply back over the chairs behind him. The two men who had approached him ran to the exit on my side of the room, shooting wildly behind them as they ran. I heard people screaming, "Don't let them kill him." "Kill those bastards." At an exit I saw some of Malcolm's men beating with all their strength on two men. I saw a half dozen of Malcolm's followers bending over his inert body on the stage. Their clothes stained with their leader's blood.

Four policemen took the stretcher and carried Malcolm through the crowd and some of the women came out of their shock and one said: "I hope he doesn't die, but I don't think he's going to make it."

Associated Press (February 22, 1965)

A week after being bombed out of his Queens home, Black Nationalist leader Malcolm X was shot to death shortly after 3 (P.M.) yesterday at a Washington Heights rally of 400 of his devoted followers. Early today, police brass ordered a homicide charge placed against a 22-year-old man they rescued from a savage beating by Malcolm X supporters after the shooting. The suspect, Thomas Hagan, had been shot in the left leg by one of Malcolm's bodyguards as, police said, Hagan and another assassin fled when pandemonium erupted. Two other men were wounded in the wild burst of firing from at least three weapons. The firearms were a .38, a .45 automatic and a sawed-off shotgun. Hagan allegedly shot Malcolm X with the shotgun, a double-barrelled sawed-off weapon on which the stock also had been shortened, possibly to facilitate concealment. Cops charged Reuben Frances, of 871 E. 179th St., Bronx, with felonious assault in the shooting of Hagan, and with Sullivan Law violation—possession of the .45. Police recovered the shotgun and the .45.

Source: Paragraph on the assassination of Malcolm X, Associated Press, February 22, 1965. Reprinted by permission of the Associated Press.

The Amsterdam News (February 27, 1965)

"We interrupt this program to bring you a special newscast . . .," the announcer said as the Sunday afternoon movie on the TV set was halted temporarily. "Malcolm X was shot four times while addressing a crowd at the Audubon Ballroom on

Source: Excerpt from the *Amsterdam News*, February 27, 1965/Reprinted by permission of the New York Amsterdam News.

166th Street." "Oh no!" That was my first reaction to the shocking event that followed one week after the slender, articulate leader of the Afro-American Unity was routed from his East Elmhurst home by a bomb explosion. Minutes later we alighted from a cab at the corner of Broadway and 166th St. just a short 15 blocks from where I live on Broadway. About 200 men and women, neatly dressed, were milling around, some with expressions of awe and disbelief. Others were in small clusters talking loudly and with deep emotion in their voices. Mostly they were screaming for vengeance. One woman, small, dressed in a light gray coat and her eyes flaming with indignation, argued with a cop at the St. Nicholas corner of the block. "This is not the end of it. What they were going to do to the Statue of Liberty will be small in comparison. We black people are tired of being shoved around." Standing across the street near the memorial park one of Malcolm's close associates commented: "It's a shame." Later he added that "if it's war they want, they'll get it." He would not say whether Elijah Muhammed's followers had anything to do with the assassination. About 3:30 P.M. Malcolm X's wife, Betty, was escorted by three men and a woman from the Columbia Presbyterian Hospital. Tears streamed down her face. She was screaming, "They killed him!" Malcolm X had no last words. . . . The bombing and burning of the No. 7 Mosque early Tuesday morning was the first blow by those who are seeking revenge for the cold-blooded murder of a man who at 39 might have grown to the stature of respectable leadership.

Changes in Perceptions and Perspectives

Just as journalists, scientists, and disaster officials change their perspectives after gaining increased knowledge, your ways of viewing the world will develop and change through the experiences you have, the knowledge you acquire, and your reflections on your experiences and knowledge. As you think critically about perceptions, you will learn more about how you make sense of the world. This understanding may strengthen your perceptions, or it may change them.

Obtaining More Accurate Perceptions: Adjusting the Lenses

So far, we have emphasized the great extent to which, by selecting, organizing, and interpreting, we directly affect our perceptions. We have suggested that each of us views the world through his or her own unique lenses, that no two of us perceive the world in exactly the same way. In addition, the sources on which we rely for the most up-to-date and ostensibly most accurate, objective information are themselves compromised by different and conflicting perceptions and perspectives as they try to negotiate enormous amounts of changing information.

Because we actively participate in selecting, organizing, and interpreting the sensations we experience, our perceptions are often incomplete, inaccurate, or subjective. To complicate the situation further, our own limitations in perceiving are not the only factors that can cause us problems. Other people often purposefully create perceptions and misperceptions. An advertiser who wants to sell a product may try to create the impression that our lives will be changed if we use it. Or a person who wants to discredit someone else may spread untrue rumors about her.

Develop Awareness

The only way to correct the mistakes, distortions, and incompleteness of our perceptions is to become aware of the ordinarily unconscious process by which we perceive and make sense of the world. By doing so, we will be able to think critically about what is going on and to correct our mistakes and distortions. In other words, we can use our critical thinking abilities to create a clearer and more informed idea of what is taking place. We cannot rely on the validity of our perceptions alone. If we remain unaware of how our process of perceiving operates and of our active role in it, we will be unable to control it. We will be convinced that the way we see the world is the way the world is, even when our perceptions are mistaken, distorted, or incomplete.

Besides asking questions, we have to become aware of the personal perspectives that we bring to our perceptions. Each of us brings to every situation a whole collection of expectations, interests, fears, and hopes that can influence what we are perceiving.

Consider the following situations:

- You and your family have been advised to evacuate in the path of a forthcoming hurricane, but you remember from the experiences of people in New Orleans and Houston that to flee could leave your property vulnerable to looting or could result in a very long, hot, uncomfortable road trip that might not in the end have been necessary. How do you balance the recommendations of current authority with recent past experience?

- Your teacher asks you to evaluate the performance of a colleague who is giving a report to the group. You don't like this other student because he acts as if he's superior to everyone else in the group. How do you evaluate his report?

- You are asked to estimate the size of an audience attending an event that your organization has sponsored. How many people are there?

In each of these cases, your perceptions might be influenced by whatever hopes, fears, or prejudices you brought to the situation, causing your observations to be distorted or inaccurate. Although you usually cannot eliminate the personal feelings that influence your perceptions, you can become aware of these feelings and try to control them.

Get Input from Others

The first step in critically examining your perceptions is to be willing to ask questions about them. As long as you believe that the way you see things is the only way to see them, you will not be able to recognize when your perceptions are distorted or inaccurate.

For instance, if you believe that your interpretation of the photo in the Thinking-Writing Activity on page 209 is the only correct one, you will probably not consider other interpretations. But if you are willing to entertain other possible interpretations, you will open the way to more fully developing your perception of what is taking place.

As noted in Chapter 7, critical thinkers strive to see things from different perspectives. One of the best ways to do so is by communicating with others. This means exchanging and critically examining ideas in an open and organized way. Engaging in dialogue is one of the main ways to check your perceptions—by asking others what their perceptions are and comparing and contrasting them with yours.

This is exactly what you did when you discussed the various possible interpretations of the Thinking Critically About Visuals photo in Chapter 7. By comparing your perceptions with those of your classmates, you developed a more complete sense of how differently events can be viewed as well as an appreciation of the reasons supporting the different perspectives.

Find Evidence

Also, you should try to discover independent proof or evidence regarding your perceptions. You can evaluate the accuracy of your perceptions when evidence is available in the form of records, photographs, videotapes, or the results of experiments. What independent forms of evidence could verify your perceptions about the couple in the Thinking Critically About Visuals box in Chapter 7?

Keep an Open Mind

Thinking critically about perceptions means trying to avoid developing impulsive or superficial ones that you are unwilling to change. As explained in Chapter 3, a critical thinker is *thoughtful* in approaching the world and open to modifying his or her views in light of new information or better insights. Consider the following perceptions:

- Women are very emotional.
- Politicians are corrupt.
- All Muslims are potential terrorists.
- People who are good athletes are usually poor students.
- The government doesn't care about poor people.

These types of general perceptions are known as *stereotypes* because they express a belief about an entire group of people without recognizing the individual differences among members of the group.

For instance, it is probably accurate to say that there are some politicians who are corrupt, but this is not the same as saying that all, or even most, politicians are corrupt. Stereotypes affect our perceptions of the world because they encourage us to form inaccurate and superficial ideas about a whole group of people ("Teenagers are reckless drivers"). When we meet someone who falls into this group, we automatically perceive that person as possessing a stereotyped quality ("This person is a teenager, so he is a reckless driver"). Even if we find that the person does not fit our stereotyped perception ("This teenager is not a reckless driver"), this sort of superficial and thoughtless labeling does not encourage us to change our perceptions of the group as a whole. Instead, it encourages us to overlook the conflicting information in favor of our stereotyped perceptions ("All teenagers are reckless drivers—except this one"). In contrast, when we are perceiving in a thoughtful fashion, we try to see what a person is like as an individual instead of trying to fit him or her into a preexisting category.

Sometimes stereotypes are so built into a culture that it is difficult for a person to be aware of them until they are brought to his or her attention. The perspective, or view of the world, that the culture presents may not even acknowledge the possibility of other perspectives, so it can be very difficult for an individual to become aware of them and then to "switch lenses" to try to see a situation from those viewpoints.

True critical thinkers can and do switch lenses, and in their writing they help others to do so as well. The following two readings present varying perspectives on Native Americans. One was written by a famous eighteenth-century American; the other was written in the early twentieth century by a member of the Sioux nation. As you read these accounts, think about what factors probably contributed to the writers' perspectives.

"Remarks Concerning the Savages of North America"

by Benjamin Franklin

Perhaps no other figure so captures the American imagination—or the America as once imagined—as Benjamin Franklin. Born into a family of Boston soapmakers, Franklin became a printer's apprentice to his brother, James, at the age of twelve. As brothers tend to do, Benjamin and James quarreled repeatedly; in 1723, Benjamin ran away to Philadelphia. After several difficult years of hard work, Franklin was established enough in his own printing business to marry Deborah Read in 1730. He began publishing and contributing to a newspaper, the *Pennsylvania Gazette,* and in 1733 he started publishing Poor Richard's Almanack.

Franklin used his prominent position as a businessman and journalist to undertake civic initiatives that are still cornerstones of American communities. Franklin helped to establish the first free lending library, the first public hospital, and the first organized firefighting company in America. Politically, Franklin was elected to the Second Continental Congress in 1775 and helped to draft the Declaration of Independence. In 1776, Franklin was appointed the ambassador to the Court of Louis XVI for the American colonies. Franklin died at the age of eighty-four, back home in Philadelphia. His funeral was attended by 20,000 people.

In the following essay, excerpted from a longer work published in 1784, Franklin uses the term *savages* ironically. His admiration and respect for Native Americans is rooted in the diplomatic relationships he established with the Iroquois Nation in the 1760s. When, in 1763, a vigilante army of white settlers massacred a settlement of Conestoga Iroquois—including women and children—Franklin responded by mustering an army of Quakers and other citizens, including Governor Penn himself. The action probably saved more than one hundred Conestoga lives.

Savages we call them, because their Manners differ from ours, which we think the Perfection of Civility; they think the same of theirs.

Perhaps, if we could examine the Manners of different Nations with Impartiality, we should find no People so rude, as to be without any Rules of Politeness; nor any so polite, as not to have some Remains of Rudeness.

The Indian Men, when young, are Hunters and Warriors; when old, Counsellors; for all their Government is by Counsel of the Sages; there is no Force, there are no Prisons, no Officers to compel Obedience, or inflict Punishment. Hence they generally study Oratory, the best Speaker having the most Influence. The Indian Women till the Ground, dress the Food, nurse and bring up the Children, and preserve and hand down to Posterity the Memory of public Transactions. These Employments of Men and Women are accounted natural and honourable. Having few artificial Wants, they have abundance of Leisure for Improvement by Conversation. Our laborious Manner of Life, compared with theirs, they esteem slavish and base; and the Learning, on which we value ourselves, they regard as frivolous and useless. An Instance of this occurred at the Treaty of Lancaster, in Pennsylvania, *anno* 1744, between the Government of Virginia and the Six Nations. After the principal Business was settled, the Commissioners from Virginia acquainted the Indians by a Speech, that there was at Williamsburg a College, with a Fund for Educating Indian youth; and that, if the Six Nations would send down half a dozen of their young Lads to that College, the Government would take care that they should be well provided for, and instructed in all the Learning of the White People. It is one of the Indian Rules of Politeness not to answer a public Proposition the same day that it is made; they think it would be treating it as a light matter, and that they show it Respect by taking time to consider it, as of a Matter important. They therefore deferr'd their Answer till the Day following; when their Speaker began, by expressing their deep Sense of the kindness of the Virginia Government, in making them that Offer; "for we know," says he, "that you highly esteem the kind of Learning taught in those Colleges, and that the Maintenance of our young Men, while with you, would be very expensive to you. We are convinc'd, therefore, that you mean to do us Good by your Proposal; and we thank you heartily. But you, who are wise, must know that different Nations have different Conceptions of things; and you will therefore not take it amiss, if our Ideas of this kind of Education happen not to be the same with yours. We have had some Experience of it; Several of our young People were formerly brought up at the Colleges of the Northern Provinces; they were instructed in all your Sciences; but, when they came back to us, they were bad Runners, ignorant of every means of living in the Woods, unable to bear either Cold or Hunger, knew neither how to build a Cabin, take a Deer, or kill an Enemy, spoke our Language imperfectly, were therefore neither fit for Hunters, Warriors, nor Counsellors; they were totally good for nothing. We are however not the less oblig'd by your kind Offer, tho' we decline accepting it; and, to show our grateful Sense of it, if the Gentlemen of Virginia will send us a Dozen of their Sons, we will take great Care of their Education, instruct them in all we know, and make *Men* of them."

Having frequent Occasions to hold public Councils, they have acquired great Order and Decency in conducting them. The old Men sit in the foremost Ranks, the Warriors in the next, and the Women and Children in the hindmost. The Business of the Women is to take exact Notice of what passes, imprint it in their Memories (for they have no Writing), and communicate it to their Children. They are the Records of the Council, and they preserve Traditions of the Stipulations in Treaties 100 Years back; which, when we compare with our Writings, we always find exact. He that would speak, rises. The rest observe a profound Silence. When he has finish'd and sits down, they leave him 5 to 6 Minutes to recollect, that, if he has omitted anything he intended to say, or has anything to add, he may rise again and deliver it. To interrupt another, even in common Conversation, is reckon'd highly indecent. How different this is from the conduct of a polite British House of Commons, where scarce a day passes without some Confusion, that makes the Speaker hoarse in calling *to Order;* and how different from the Mode of Conversation in many polite Companies of Europe, where, if you do not deliver your Sentence with great Rapidity, you are cut off in the middle of it by the Impatient Loquacity of those you converse with, and never suffer'd to finish it!

5   The Politeness of these Savages in Conversation is indeed carried to Excess, since it does not permit them to contradict or deny the Truth of what is asserted in their Presence. By this means they indeed avoid Disputes; but then it becomes difficult to know their Minds, or what Impression you make upon them. The Missionaries who have attempted to convert them to Christianity, all complain of this as one of the great Difficulties of their Mission. The Indians hear with Patience the Truths of the Gospel explain'd to them, and give their usual Tokens of Assent and Approbation; you would think they were convinc'd. No such matter. It is mere Civility.

A Swedish Minister, having assembled the chiefs of the Susquehanah Indians, made a Sermon to them, acquainting them with the principal historical Facts on which our Religion is founded; such as the Fall of our first Parents by eating an Apple, the coming of Christ to repair the Mischief, his Miracles and Suffering, &c. When he had finished, an Indian Orator stood up to thank him. "What you have told us," says he, "is all very good. It is indeed bad to eat Apples. It is better to make them all into Cyder. We are much oblig'd by your kindness in coming so far, to tell us these Things which you have heard from your Mothers. In return, I will tell you some of those we had heard from ours. In the Beginning, our Fathers had only the Flesh of Animals to subsist on; and if their Hunting was unsuccessful, they were starving. Two of our young Hunters, having kill'd a Deer, made a Fire in the Woods to broil some Part of it. When they were about to satisfy their Hunger, they beheld a beautiful young Woman descend from the Clouds, and seat herself on that Hill, which you see yonder among the blue Mountains. They said to each other, it is a Spirit that has smelt our broiling Venison, and wishes to eat of it; let us offer some to her. They presented her with the Tongue; she was pleas'd with the Taste of it, and said, 'Your kindness shall be rewarded; come to this Place after thirteen Moons, and you shall find something that will be of great Benefit in nourishing you and your Children to the latest Generations.' They did so, and, to their Surprise, found Plants they had never seen before; but which, from that ancient time, have been constantly cultivated among us, to our great Advantage. Where her right Hand had touched the Ground, they found Maize; where her left hand had touch'd it, they found Kidney-Beans; and where her Backside had sat on it, they found Tobacco." The good Missionary, disgusted with this idle Tale, said, "What I delivered to you were sacred Truths; but what you tell me is mere Fable, Fiction, and Falshood." The Indian, offended, reply'd, "My brother, it seems your Friends have not done you Justice in your Education; they have not well instructed you in the Rules of common Civility. You saw that we, who understand and practise those Rules, believ'd all your stories; why do you refuse to believe ours?"

When any of them come into our Towns, our People are apt to crowd round them, gaze upon them, and incommode them, where they desire to be private; this they esteem great Rudeness, and the Effect of the Want of Instruction in the Rules of Civility and good Manners. "We have," say they, "as much Curiosity as you, and when you come into our Towns, we wish for Opportunities of looking at you; but for this purpose we hide ourselves behind Bushes, where you are to pass, and never intrude ourselves into your Company."

Their Manner of entering one another's village has likewise its Rules. It is reckon'd uncivil in travelling Strangers to enter a Village abruptly, without giving Notice of their Approach. Therefore, as soon as they arrive within hearing, they stop and hollow, remaining there till invited to enter. Two old Men usually come out to them, and lead them in. There is in every Village a vacant Dwelling, called *the Strangers' House*. Here they are plac'd, while the old Men go round from Hut to Hut, acquainting the Inhabitants, that Strangers are arriv'd, who are probably hungry and weary; and every one sends them what he can spare of Victuals, and Skins to repose on. When the Strangers are refresh'd, Pipes and Tobacco are brought; and then, but not before, Conversation begins, with Enquiries who they are, whither bound, what News, &c.; and it usually ends with offers of Service, if the Strangers have occasion of Guides, or any Necessaries for continuing their Journey; and nothing is exacted for the Entertainment.

The same Hospitality, esteem'd among them as a principal Virtue, is practis'd by private Persons; of which Conrad Weiser, our Interpreter, gave me the following Instance. He had been naturaliz'd among the Six Nations, and spoke well the Mohock Language. In going thro' the Indian Country, to carry a Message from our Governor to the Council at Onondaga, he call'd at the Habitation of Canassatego, an old Acquaintance, who embrac'd him, spread Furs for him to sit on, plac'd before him some boil'd Beans and Venison, and mix'd some Rum and Water for his Drink. When he was well refresh'd, and had lit his Pipe, Canassatego began to converse with him; ask'd how he had far'd the many Years since they had seen each other; whence he then came; what occasion'd the Journey, &c. Conrad answered all his Questions; and when the Discourse began to flag, the Indian, to continue it, said, "Conrad, you have lived long among the white People, and know something of their Customs; I have been sometimes at Albany, and have observed, that once in Seven Days they shut up their Shops, and assemble all in the great House; tell me what it is for? What do they do there?" "They meet there," says Conrad, "to hear and learn *good Things*." "I do not doubt," says the Indian, "that they tell you so; they have told me the same; but I doubt the Truth of what they say, and I will tell you my Reasons. I went lately to Albany to sell my Skins and buy Blankets, Knives, Powder, Rum, &c. You know I us'd generally to deal with Hans Hanson; but I was a little inclin'd this time to try some other Merchant. However, I call'd first upon Hans, and asked him what he would give for Beaver. He said he could not give any more than four Shillings a Pound; 'but,' says he, 'I cannot talk on Business now; this is the Day when we meet together to learn *Good Things*, and I am going to the Meeting.' So I thought to myself, 'Since we cannot do any Business to-day, I may as well go to the meeting too,' and I went with him. There stood up a Man in Black, and began to talk to the People very angrily. I did not understand what he said; but, perceiving that he look'd much at me and at Hanson, I imagin'd he was angry at seeing me there; so I went out, sat down near the House, struck Fire, and lit my Pipe, waiting till the Meeting should break up. I thought too, that the Man had mention'd something of Beaver, and I suspected it might be the Subject of their Meeting. So, when they came out, I accosted my Merchant. 'Well, Hans,' says I, 'I hope you have agreed to give more than four Shillings a Pound.' 'No,' says he, 'I cannot give so much; I cannot give more than three shillings and sixpence.' I then spoke to several other Dealers, but they all sung the same song,—Three and sixpence,—Three and sixpence. This made it clear to me, that my Suspicion was right; and, that whatever they pretended of meeting to learn *good Things*, the real purpose was to consult how to cheat Indians in the Price of Beaver. Consider but little, Conrad, and you must be of my Opinion. If they met so often to learn *good Things*, they would certainly have learnt some before this time. But they are still ignorant. You know our Practice. If a white Man, in travelling thro' our Country, enters one of our Cabins, we all treat him as I treat you; we dry him if he is wet, we warm him if he is cold, we give him Meat and Drink, that he may allay his Thirst and Hunger; and we spread soft Furs for him to rest and sleep on; we demand nothing in return. But, if I go into a white Man's House at Albany, and ask for Victuals and Drink, they say, 'Where is your Money?' and if I have none, they say, 'Get out, you Indian Dog.' You see they have not yet learned those little *Good Things*, that we need no Meetings to be instructed in, because our Mothers taught them to us when we were Children; and therefore it is impossible their Meetings should be, as they say, for any such purpose, or have any such Effect; they are only to contrive *the Cheating of Indians in the Price of Beaver*."

Questions for Reading Actively

1. What is Franklin's definition of *savage*? This term has long since ceased to be appropriate when used to refer to indigenous peoples; do you think that Franklin, writing two hundred years ago, was also aware of how

inappropriate this term could be? Explain your answer with reference to Franklin's own examples and argument.

2. What two ideals is Franklin comparing in this essay?

3. Franklin was widely known for his wit, of which there is a sly example in paragraph 6. Identify the joke. Why does Franklin include it? Is he simply being sarcastic, or is he making a much larger and subtle comparison of perspectives?

Questions for Thinking Critically

1. What does Franklin mean when he says, "Perhaps, if we could examine the Manners of different Nations with Impartiality, we should find no People so rude, as to be without any Rules of Politeness; nor any so polite, as not to have some Remains of Rudeness"?

2. What does the Iroquois speaker mean when he says, "If the Gentlemen of Virginia will send us a Dozen of their Sons, we will take great Care of their Education, instruct them in all we know, and make *Men* of them"?

3. In paragraph 9, Franklin recounts the experience of the Iroquois elder Canassatego when he went to a "great House" to "hear and learn *good Things*." Why does Franklin use Canassatego's exact language, rather than explaining or translating his perspective for his English-speaking colonial audience? What is the tremendous irony that Canassatego's perspective gives to the concept of *"good Things"*?

Question for Writing Thoughtfully

1. How does Franklin use comparison to structure this essay?

FROM *The School Days of an Indian Girl*

by Zitkala-Sa (Gertrude Simmons Bonnin)

A member of the Yankton Sioux nation, Zitkala-Sa was born on the Pine Ridge Reservation in South Dakota and raised in a traditional tipi on the Missouri River. At the end of the nineteenth and beginning of the twentieth centuries, many surviving Native American nations were forced from their traditional lands onto "reservations," lands managed by the American government. Children on these reservations were forced to sacrifice their native languages, cultures, and traditions, often sent away from their families to religious or secular boarding schools. In the following autobiographical essay, Zitkala-Sa recounts her time spent at a Quaker boarding school for Native American children in Wabash, Indiana. The experience left her feeling divided between identities and cultures, a division that galvanized her into pursuing further education and devoting her life to justice for Native Americans. She graduated from Earlham College with plans to become a teacher, and her musical talents brought her to the Boston Conservatory. In 1900, she went to Paris with the Carlisle Indian Industrial School (CIIS) as violin soloist for the Paris Exposition. But the loss and destruction of her own culture haunted her, and led to her first book, the 1901 collection *Old Indian Legends*.

Zitkala-Sa became increasingly active politically, along with her husband, Ray Bonnin of the Sioux nation. She worked to increase voter participation by Native Americans, and in 1930, she formed the National Council of American Indians, where she served as president until her death in 1938.

The Cutting of My Long Hair

The first day in the land of apples was a bitter-cold one; for the snow still covered the ground, and the trees were bare. A large bell rang for breakfast, its loud metallic voice crashing through the belfry overhead and into our sensitive ears. The annoying clatter of shoes on bare floors gave us no peace. The constant clash of harsh noises, with an undercurrent of many voices murmuring an unknown tongue, made a bedlam within which I was securely tied. And though my spirit tore itself in struggling for its lost freedom, all was useless.

A paleface woman, with white hair, came up after us. We were placed in a line of girls who were marching into the dining room. These were Indian girls, in stiff shoes and closely clinging dresses. The small girls wore sleeved aprons and shingled hair. As I walked noiselessly in my soft moccasins, I felt like sinking to the floor, for my blanket had been stripped from my shoulders. I looked hard at the Indian girls, who seemed not to care that they were even more immodestly dressed than I, in their tightly fitting clothes. While we marched in, the boys entered at an opposite door. I watched for the three young braves who came in our party. I spied them in the rear ranks, looking as uncomfortable as I felt.

A small bell was tapped, and each of the pupils drew a chair from under the table. Supposing this act meant they were to be seated, I pulled out mine and at once slipped into it from one side. But when I turned my head, I saw that I was the only one seated, and all the rest at our table remained standing. Just as I began to rise, looking shyly around to see how chairs were to be used, a second bell was sounded. All were seated at last, and I had to crawl back into my chair again. I heard a man's voice at one end of the hall, and I looked around to see him. But all the others hung their heads over their plates. As I glanced at the long chain of tables, I caught the eyes of a paleface woman upon me. Immediately I dropped my eyes, wondering why I was so keenly watched by the strange woman. The man ceased his mutterings, and then a third bell was tapped. Every one picked up his knife and fork and began eating. I began crying instead, for by this time I was afraid to venture anything more.

But this eating by formula was not the hardest trial in that first day. Late in the morning, my friend Judewin gave me a terrible warning. Judewin knew a few words of English, and she had overheard the paleface woman talk about cutting our long, heavy hair. Our mothers had taught us that only unskilled warriors who were captured had their hair shingled by the enemy. Among our people, short hair was worn by mourners, and shingled hair by cowards!

5   We discussed our fate some moments, and when Judewin said, "We have to submit, because they are strong," I rebelled.

"No, I will not submit! I will struggle first!" I answered.

I watched my chance, and when no one noticed I disappeared. I crept up the stairs as quietly as I could in my squeaking shoes,—my moccasins had been exchanged for shoes. Along the hall I passed, without knowing whither I was going. Turning aside to an open door, I found a large room with three white beds in it. The windows were covered with dark green curtains, which made the room very dim. Thankful that no one was there, I directed my steps toward the corner farthest from the door. On my hands and knees I crawled under the bed, and cuddled myself in the dark corner.

From my hiding place I peered out, shuddering with fear whenever I heard footsteps near by. Though in the hall loud voices were calling my name, and I knew that even Judewin was searching for me, I did not open my mouth to answer. Then the steps were quickened and the voices became excited. The sounds came nearer and nearer. Women and girls entered the room. I held my breath, and watched them open closet doors and peep behind large trunks. Some one threw up the curtains, and the room was filled with sudden light. What caused them to stoop and look under the bed I do not know. I remember being dragged out, though I resisted by kicking and scratching wildly. In spite of myself, I was carried downstairs and tied fast in a chair.

I cried aloud, shaking my head all the while until I felt the cold blades of the scissors against my neck, and heard them gnaw off one of my thick braids. Then I lost my spirit. Since the day I was taken from my mother I had suffered extreme indignities. People had stared at me. I had been tossed about in the air like a wooden puppet. And now my long hair was shingled like a coward's! In my anguish I moaned for my mother, but no one came to comfort me. Not a soul reasoned quietly with me, as my own mother used to do; for now I was only one of many little animals driven by a herder.

The Snow Episode

10   A short time after our arrival we three Dakotas were playing in the snowdrifts. We were all still deaf to the English language, excepting Judewin, who always heard such puzzling things. One morning we learned through her ears that we were forbidden to fall lengthwise in the snow, as we had been doing, to see our own impressions. However, before many hours we had forgotten the order, and were having great sport in the snow, when a shrill voice called us. Looking up, we saw an imperative hand beckoning us into the house. We shook the snow off ourselves, and started toward the woman as slowly as we dared.

Judewin said: "Now the paleface is angry with us. She is going to punish us for falling into the snow. If she looks straight into your eyes and talks loudly, you must wait until she stops. Then, after a tiny pause, say, 'No.'" The rest of the way we practiced upon the little word "no."

As it happened, Thowin was summoned to judgment first. The door shut behind her with a click.

Judewin and I stood silently listening at the keyhole. The paleface woman talked in very severe tones. Her words fell from her lips like crackling embers, and her inflection ran up like the small end of a switch. I understood her voice better than the things she was saying. I was certain we had made her very impatient with us. Judewin heard enough of the words to realize all too late that she had taught us the wrong reply.

"Oh, poor Thowin!" she gasped, as she put both hands over her ears.

15   Just then I heard Thowin's tremulous answer, "No."

With an angry exclamation, the woman gave her a hard spanking. Then she stopped to say something. Judewin said it was this: "Are you going to obey my word the next time?"

Thowin answered again with the only word at her command, "No."

This time the woman meant her blows to smart, for the poor frightened girl shrieked at the top of her voice. In the midst of the whipping the blows ceased abruptly, and the woman asked another question: "Are you going to fall in the snow again?"

Thowin gave her bad password another trial. We heard her say feebly, "No! No!"

20   With this the woman hid away her half-worn slipper, and led the child out, stroking her black shorn head. Perhaps it occurred to her that brute force is not the solution for such a problem. She did nothing to Judewin nor to me. She only returned to us our unhappy comrade, and left us alone in the room.

During the first two or three seasons misunderstandings as ridiculous as this one of the snow episode frequently took place, bringing unjustifiable frights and punishments into our little lives.

Within a year I was able to express myself somewhat in broken English. As soon as I comprehended a part of what was said and done, a mischievous spirit of revenge possessed me. One day I was called in from my play for some misconduct. I had disregarded a rule which seemed to me very needlessly binding. I was sent into the kitchen to mash the turnips for dinner. It was noon, and steaming dishes were hastily carried into the dining room. I hated turnips, and their odor which came from the brown jar was offensive to me. With fire in my heart, I took the wooden tool that the paleface woman held out to me. I stood upon a step, and, grasping the handle with both hands, I bent in hot rage over the turnips. I worked my vengeance upon them. All were so busily occupied that no one noticed me. I saw that the turnips were in a pulp, and that further beating could not improve them; but the order was, "Mash these turnips," and mash them I would! I renewed my energy; and as I sent the masher into the bottom of the jar, I felt a satisfying sensation that the weight of my body had gone into it.

Just here a paleface woman came up to my table. As she looked into the jar she shoved my hands roughly aside. I stood fearless and angry. She placed her red hands upon the rim of the jar. Then she gave one lift and a stride away from the table. But lo! the pulpy contents fell through the crumbled bottom to the floor! She spared me no scolding phrases that I had earned. I did not heed them. I felt triumphant in my revenge, though deep within me I was a wee bit sorry to have broken the jar.

As I sat eating my dinner, and saw that no turnips were served, I whooped in my heart for having once asserted the rebellion within me.

* * * *

Four Strange Summers

25   After my first three years of school, I roamed again in the Western country through four strange summers.

During this time I seemed to hang in the heart of chaos, beyond the touch or voice of human aid. My brother, being almost ten years my senior, did not quite understand my feelings. My mother had never gone inside of a schoolhouse, and so she was not capable of comforting her daughter who could read and write. Even nature seemed to have no place for me. I was neither a wee girl nor a tall one; neither a wild Indian nor a tame one. This deplorable situation was the effect of my brief course in the East, and the unsatisfactory "teenth" in a girl's years.

It was under these trying conditions that, one bright afternoon, as I sat restless and unhappy in my brother's cabin, I caught the sound of the spirited step of my brother's pony on the road which passed by our dwelling. Soon I heard the wheels of a light buckboard, and Dawee's familiar "Ho!" to his pony. He alighted upon the bare ground in front of our house. Tying his pony to one of the projecting corner logs of the low-roofed cottage, he stepped upon the wooden doorstep.

I met him there with a hurried greeting, and as I passed by, he looked a quiet "What?" into my eyes.

When he began talking with my mother, I slipped the rope from the pony's bridle. Seizing the reins and bracing my feet against the dashboard, I wheeled around in an instant. The pony was ever ready to try his speed. Looking backward, I saw Dawee waving his hand to me. I turned with the curve in the road and disappeared. I followed the winding road which crawled upward between the bases of little hillocks. Deep water-worn ditches ran parallel on either side. A strong wind blew against my cheeks and fluttered my sleeves. The pony reached the top of the highest hill, and began an even race on the level lands. There was nothing moving within that great circular horizon of the Dakota prairies save the tall grasses, over which the wind blew and rolled off in long, shadowy waves.

30   Within this vast wigwam of blue and green I rode reckless and insignificant. It satisfied my small consciousness to see the white foam fly from the pony's mouth.

Suddenly, out of the earth a coyote came forth at a swinging trot that was taking the cunning thief toward the hills and the village beyond. Upon the moment's impulse, I gave him a long chase and a wholesome fright. As I turned away to go back to the village, the wolf sank down upon his haunches for rest, for it was a hot summer day; and as I drove slowly homeward, I saw his sharp nose still pointed at me, until I vanished below the margin of the hilltops.

In a little while I came in sight of my mother's house. Dawee stood in the yard, laughing at an old warrior who was pointing his forefinger, and again waving his whole hand, toward the hills. With his blanket drawn over one shoulder, he talked and motioned excitedly. Dawee turned the old man by the shoulder and pointed me out to him.

"Oh han!" (Oh yes) the warrior muttered, and went his way. He had climbed to the top of his favorite barren hill to survey the surrounding prairies, when he spied my chase after the coyote. His keen eyes recognized the pony and driver. At once uneasy for my safety, he had come running to my mother's cabin to give her warning. I did not appreciate his kindly interest, for there was an unrest gnawing at my heart.

As soon as he went away, I asked Dawee about something else.

35   "No, my baby sister, I cannot take you with me to the party to-night," he replied. Though I was not far from fifteen, and I felt that before long I should enjoy all the privileges of my tall cousin, Dawee persisted in calling me his baby sister.

That moonlight night, I cried in my mother's presence when I heard the jolly young people pass by our cottage. They were no more young braves in blankets and eagle plumes, nor Indian maids with prettily painted cheeks. They had gone three years to school in the East, and had become civilized. The young men wore the white man's coat and trousers, with bright neckties. The girls wore tight muslin dresses, with ribbons at neck and waist. At these gatherings they talked English. I could speak English almost as well as my brother, but I was not properly dressed to be taken along. I had no hat, no ribbons, and no close-fitting gown. Since my return from school I had thrown away my shoes, and wore again the soft moccasins.

While Dawee was busily preparing to go I controlled my tears. But when I heard him bounding away on his pony, I buried my face in my arms and cried hot tears.

My mother was troubled by my unhappiness. Coming to my side, she offered me the only printed matter we had in our home. It was an Indian Bible, given her some years ago by a missionary. She tried to console me. "Here, my child, are the white man's papers. Read a little from them," she said most piously.

I took it from her hand, for her sake; but my enraged spirit felt more like burning the book, which afforded me no help, and was a perfect delusion to my mother. I did not read it, but laid it unopened on the floor, where I sat on my feet. The dim yellow light of the braided muslin burning in a small vessel of oil flickered and sizzled in the awful silent storm which followed my rejection of the Bible.

40   Now my wrath against the fates consumed my tears before they reached my eyes. I sat stony, with a bowed head. My mother threw a shawl over her head and shoulders, and stepped out into the night.

After an uncertain solitude, I was suddenly aroused by a loud cry piercing the night. It was my mother's voice wailing among the barren hills which held the bones of buried warriors. She called aloud for her brothers' spirits to support her in her helpless misery. My fingers grew icy cold, as I realized that my unrestrained tears had betrayed my suffering to her, and she was grieving for me.

Before she returned, though I knew she was on her way, for she had ceased her weeping, I extinguished the light, and leaned my head on the window sill.

Many schemes of running away from my surroundings hovered about in my mind. A few more moons of such a turmoil drove me away to the Eastern school. I rode on the white man's iron steed, thinking it would bring me back to my mother in a few winters, when I should be grown tall, and there would be congenial friends awaiting me.

Incurring My Mother's Displeasure

In the second journey to the East I had not come without some precautions. I had a secret interview with one of our best medicine men, and when I left his wigwam I carried securely in my sleeve a tiny bunch of magic roots. This possession assured me of friends wherever I should go. So absolutely did I believe in its charms that I wore it through all the school routine for more than a year. Then, before I lost my faith in the dead roots, I lost the little buckskin bag containing all my good luck.

45   At the close of this second term of three years I was the proud owner of my first diploma. The following autumn I ventured upon a college career against my mother's will.

I had written for her approval, but in her reply I found no encouragement. She called my notice to her neighbors' children, who had completed their education in three years. They had returned to their homes, and were then talking English with the frontier settlers. Her few words hinted that I had better give up my slow attempt to learn the white man's ways, and be content to roam over the prairies and find my living upon wild roots. I silenced her by deliberate disobedience.

Thus, homeless and heavy-hearted, I began anew my life among strangers.

As I hid myself in my little room in the college dormitory, away from the scornful and yet curious eyes of the students, I pined for sympathy. Often I wept in secret, wishing I had gone West, to be nourished by my mother's love, instead of remaining among a cold race whose hearts were frozen hard with prejudice.

During the fall and winter seasons I scarcely had a real friend, though by that time several of my classmates were courteous to me at a safe distance.

50   My mother had not yet forgiven my rudeness to her, and I had no moment for letter-writing. By daylight and lamplight, I spun with reeds and thistles, until my hands were tired from their weaving, the magic design which promised me the white man's respect.

At length, in the spring term, I entered an oratorical contest among the various classes. As the day of competition approached, it did not seem possible that the event was so near at hand, but it came. In the chapel the classes assembled together, with their invited guests. The high platform was carpeted, and gayly festooned with college colors. A bright white light illumined the room, and outlined clearly the great polished beams that arched the domed ceiling. The assembled crowds filled the air with pulsating murmurs. When the hour for speaking arrived all were hushed. But on the wall the old clock which pointed out the trying moment ticked calmly on.

One after another I saw and heard the orators. Still, I could not realize that they longed for the favorable decision of the judges as much as I did. Each contestant received a loud burst of applause, and some were cheered heartily. Too soon my turn came, and I paused a moment behind the curtains for a deep breath. After my concluding words, I heard the same applause that the others had called out.

Upon my retreating steps, I was astounded to receive from my fellow students a large bouquet of roses tied with flowing ribbons. With the lovely flowers I fled from the stage. This friendly token was a rebuke to me for the hard feelings I had borne them.

Later, the decision of the judges awarded me the first place. Then there was a mad uproar in the hall, where my classmates sang and shouted my name at the top of their lungs; and the disappointed students howled and brayed in fearfully dissonant tin trumpets. In this excitement, happy students rushed forward to offer their congratulations. And I could not conceal a smile when they wished to escort me in a procession to the students' parlor, where all were going to calm themselves. Thanking them for the kind spirit which prompted them to make such a proposition, I walked alone with the night to my own little room.

55   A few weeks afterward, I appeared as the college representative in another contest. This time the competition was among orators from different colleges in our state. It was held at the state capital, in one of the largest opera houses.

Here again was a strong prejudice against my people. In the evening, as the great audience filled the house, the student bodies began warring among themselves. Fortunately, I was spared witnessing any of the noisy wrangling before the contest began. The slurs against the Indian that stained the lips of our opponents were already burning like a dry fever within my breast.

But after the orations were delivered a deeper burn awaited me. There, before that vast ocean of eyes, some college rowdies threw out a large white flag, with a drawing of a most forlorn Indian girl on it. Under this they had printed in bold black letters words that ridiculed the college which was represented by a "squaw." Such worse than barbarian rudeness embittered me. While we waited for the verdict of the judges, I gleamed fiercely upon the throngs of palefaces. My teeth were hard set, as I saw the white flag still floating insolently in the air.

Then anxiously we watched the man carry toward the stage the envelope containing the final decision.

There were two prizes given, that night, and one of them was mine!

60   The evil spirit laughed within me when the white flag dropped out of sight, and the hands which furled it hung limp in defeat.

Leaving the crowd as quickly as possible, I was soon in my room. The rest of the night I sat in an armchair and gazed into the crackling fire. I laughed no more in triumph when thus alone. The little taste of victory did not satisfy a hunger in my heart. In my mind I saw my mother far away on the Western plains, and she was holding a charge against me.

Questions for Reading Actively

1. Zitkala-Sa uses a strikingly apt metaphor in paragraph 9. What is that metaphor? How many different layers of meaning does it have here?

2. In what ways do the Bible or representations of Christianity figure in this narrative?

3. What is the "evil spirit" that Zitkala-Sa refers to in paragraph 60?

Questions for Thinking Critically

1. Compare Zitkala-Sa's experience with the missionary school to the conversation between an Iroquois elder and a group of Virginia politicians who offered to educate six young Iroquois men at a Williamsburg, Virginia, college (the college, William and Mary, is today one of the oldest continuing institutions of higher learning in America). In what ways does Zitkala-Sa's experience reflect the observations of the Iroquois elders, both in terms of the perils of assimilation as well as the rifts created between family members?

2. Zitkala-Sa recounts her experiences through the perspective of a child. What are the advantages to this perspective in telling her story? What are the disadvantages?

Question for Writing Thoughtfully

1. Did your education—and think broadly here of "education," not just of "school"—involve the taming or controlling of some part of your spirit or personality? Write a short essay about what you gave up and why and what that loss taught you, if anything.

Writing Thoughtfully About Perspectives

Comparison and Contrast

Whenever we place two or more perspectives, or two or more other things, together and examine them for similarities and differences, we are engaging in the powerful thinking pattern called *comparison and contrast*. To be precise, when we *compare*, we are focusing on likenesses or areas of agreement; when we *contrast*, we are focusing on differences or areas of disagreement. Generally, the items examined are from the same category. We will discuss writing about items from the same category in the next section, Thinking in Comparisons. Sometimes, in order to make a point or to explain something, we may compare items from different categories. We will discuss these unusual comparisons in the Analogy section (pages 330–332).

Thinking in Comparisons

We use comparison and contrast informally in our daily lives when we make decisions such as what food to buy or which TV programs to watch. When we use comparison and contrast in a formal way by following certain established principles, we are using it to think critically to arrive at a significant conclusion. That is, we use it not only to list areas of similarity or difference but also to help achieve a clearer understanding or new insight. When we use comparison and contrast to examine different perspectives, we do so in order to understand each perspective, to see if one is superior to another, to see if we ourselves have yet another perspective, and so on.

The principles for using comparison and contrast to think critically are straightforward.

1. *Compare or contrast two or more things that have something essential in common (that is, items from the same category).* Thus, it makes sense to compare two accounts of the same event or two essays on the use of Standard English.

2. *Establish important bases or points for comparison and contrast.* In everyday situations, it is fairly easy to determine which points are important. In

deciding between two cars, the important points may be price, model, and safety features; exterior color or exact trunk capacity may be lesser concerns. But when you are working with written texts, finding points for comparison and contrast and deciding which of them are important require careful thought. When comparing or contrasting two accounts of the same event, important points might include the actual presence of the writers at the event or the writers' reliance on the accounts of others, the language the writers use to describe the participants or actions, and which details the writers have included or omitted. The writer's gender or the length of an account might or might not be significant.

3. *Develop or locate relevant, specific evidence for each point.* Opinions valued by critical thinkers are those supported by evidence. In everyday situations, evidence usually means facts: the prices of two different cars, the presence or absence of air bags, and so on. With written texts, the evidence comes from the texts themselves, in the form of either accurate paraphrases or direct quotations.

4. *Determine the significance of the comparison and contrast: What can be learned from it?* What should be done as a result? In everyday situations, this significance is often a determination: one car is superior to another and is therefore the one to purchase. When you are working with written texts, the significance may be that the texts disagree on important points; therefore, you may decide that one is more persuasive than the other.

"A Natural Disaster, and a Human Tragedy"

by Ted Steinberg

Ted Steinberg is a professor of history and law at Case Western University, with a particular interest in the history of American environmental law and policy. His book *Acts of God: The Unnatural History of Natural Disaster in America* (Oxford, 2000) was a nominee for a Pulitzer Prize. He has also written about the legal implications of American environmental policy for the *New York Times* and the *Los Angeles Times*, among numerous other newspapers and magazines. "A Natural Disaster, and a Human Tragedy" was published in the September 23, 2005, edition of *The Chronicle of Higher Education*, a leading newspaper and journal about academic life.

Is Hurricane Katrina "our tsunami," as the mayor of Biloxi, Miss., A. J. Holloway, has said? Does it make sense to compare today's disaster to a catastrophe that killed upward of 200,000 impoverished people, injured roughly half a million, displaced millions more,

Source: From "A Natural Disaster, and a Human Tragedy," by Ted Steinberg, *The Chronicle of Higher Education*, September 23, 2005, http://chronicle.com/free/v52/i05/05b01101.htm. Reprinted with permission of the author.

and was felt across a huge geographic span that included Sumatra, Thailand, India, Sri Lanka, and eastern Africa?

In searching for meaning in the current calamity, we can learn something about the root causes of such disasters by pinpointing the proper historical analogy.

Although it is no doubt an overstatement to compare Katrina to the 2004 tsunami, the two have some things in common. Both demonstrated the vulnerability of the poor in the face of natural calamity: Consider Katrina's victims who suffered through the aftermath at the Superdome and convention center. That was a man-made disaster that clearly could have been averted if the federal government, specifically the Federal Emergency Management Agency, had quickly marshaled the political will and resources to evacuate those without access to cars, instead of promoting on its Web site a faith-based charity that was clearly no match for the problem.

Likewise, both disasters demonstrated the tragic consequences of reckless coastal development. In Asia, industrial fish farms, tourist resorts, and refineries combined over the last generation to destroy huge stretches of coastal mangrove forest. The forest helps stabilize the land, and offers a form of natural protection that can soften the blow of a tsunami. Bangladesh experienced many fewer deaths in the disaster because of the conservation of its coastal mangroves than did Indonesia, where two-thirds of the forest has been destroyed.

5   In New Orleans, meanwhile, the dredging of channels to accommodate petrochemical companies has compromised huge amounts of marshland. Such changes, combined with the erosion of the area's barrier islands, and the Bush administration's policy of opening up more wetlands to development, weakened the natural frontline defense against a hurricane storm surge and left the city more vulnerable to death and destruction.

Both disasters also show the problems with neoliberal imperatives, based in a theory of political economy that idealizes the free market and chips away at the public sector at home, while worshiping at the altar of free trade and investment abroad. Foreign capital, whether in the form of tourism or the cash-cropping of fish, played a role in opening the coast around the Indian Ocean to the destructive force of the tsunami. In the aftermath of the disaster, the World Bank is leading the effort to expand the reach of those very same enterprises at the expense of the poor. The poor suffered the most in the calamity, and they are now experiencing the brutalizing effects of what the activist journalist Naomi Klein has rightly termed "disaster capitalism," as foreign corporations seek to profit from the reconstruction while the residents of the fishing villages that formerly occupied the area are being forced to relocate. In June 2005 Oxfam found that because the flow of aid has tended to go to business people and landowners, many of the poor have been made even poorer by the disaster.

What form the postdisaster rebuilding of the Gulf region will take remains to be seen. But this much is clear: Those poor people who had to suffer through the stench, the heat, and the overflowing toilets were victims of a way of thinking that goes back 25 years. Neoliberalism is a philosophy that has been shared by Republicans and Democrats alike (which is, by the way, why I'm not entirely convinced by those who argue that this kind of mistreatment would not have happened under a Kerry administration), and it was the root cause behind the failed evacuation. It is an ethos that deludes its adherents into thinking that "a thousand points of light" are better at solving America's problems than the federal government. It is a worldview that would rather put its faith in volunteer efforts than pony up the money and resources to safely evacuate the roughly 120,000 people in New Orleans who, we knew in advance, had no access to cars.

When it comes to hurricane evacuation, American officials ought to take a page out of Fidel Castro's handbook. The American news media never miss an opportunity to poke fun at the Communists. I would not want to defend all of Castro's policies, but whatever their faults, the Communists in Cuba have figured out how to use government resources to organize an efficient civil-defense system for protecting their people—staging exercises to practice evacuation, providing shelters in advance with medical personnel, and even bringing in trucks before a storm so people can save their material possessions. It hardly needs mentioning that being alive is one of the prerequisites for enjoying the freedom that Americans value so much.

So there is a great deal that the tsunami and the present hurricane have in common. But a much better historical comparison exists closer to home, one that highlights the irresponsible decision making and denial on the part of government officials that, combined with profit-driven land development, largely explains why the poor pay with their lives in such disasters. I have in mind the 1928 hurricane that took the lives of at least 1,836 people in Florida, the vast majority of them poor migrant workers who drowned as the waters of Lake Okeechobee rose up over a dike and pounded them to death.

10   That disaster is comparable to what is happening in the wake of Hurricane Katrina not just because the victims in both cases are overwhelmingly poor and African American. They compare because, in both cases, there were clear signs, in advance, that they were disasters waiting to happen—literally unnatural disasters.

In the case of the 1928 Florida hurricane, the warning was telegraphed several years in advance. Earlier in the century state authorities had overseen a massive drainage project that reclaimed land around the shores of Lake Okeechobee and turned it into valuable agricultural enterprises. Yet living around the lake had its price. In 1922 heavy rains caused the water to rise more than four feet and flooded Clewiston and Moore Haven, towns along the lake's southern shore that housed the black laborers who worked the rich agricultural land nearby.

In 1924 storms again raised the lake level, causing more flooding. Then, in the summer of 1926, heavy rains raised the level of the lake yet again, leading a journalist named Howard Sharp to beg state officials to take steps to lower the water: "The lake is truly at a level so high as to make a perilous situation in the event of a storm," he wrote in the *Tampa Tribune*.

The Everglades Drainage District, headed by some of the highest officials in the state, including Gov. John W. Martin and Attorney General J. B. Johnson, took no action to lower the water. By September 1 the level of Lake Okeechobee exceeded 18 feet. The levees around the lake were built to only 21 feet, and anyone even remotely familiar with the area knew that a stiff wind could cause the lake to rise as much as three feet. The mathematics of fatality and destruction were painfully obvious. Yet the drainage commissioners, beholden to wealthy agricultural and commercial interests—who wanted the lake water high to help with irrigating crops and navigation—refused to act.

Nobody listened, and on September 18, 1926, a Category 4 storm ripped across Florida and caused the waters of Lake Okeechobee to wash over a dike and kill at least 150 people (though 300 seems more likely) in Moore Haven, which had an entire population of only 1,200 at the time.

15   After the disaster, the attorney general explained: "The storm caused the loss and damage. . . . It is not humanly possible to guard against the unknown and against the forces of nature when loosed." Interpreting the event as a "natural" disaster masked the calamity's man-made causes and scarcely moved anyone to action to help ward off a future catastrophe, which, it turned out, was just around the corner.

On September 16, 1928, a powerful storm, with a barometric low of 27.43 inches—even lower than that recorded in 1926—swept ashore near Palm Beach. After the notorious 1900 Galveston hurricane (which left at least 8,000 dead), it was the deadliest storm in twentieth-century American history. Most of those who died were black migrant workers, virtually all of whom drowned in the towns along the southern shore of Lake Okeechobee, as the howling winds sent a wall of water crashing over the dikes in a grim repetition of what had happened two years before.

Sightseers, brimming with morbid curiosity, filed into the region to see the mounds of swollen, rotting corpses firsthand. According to one report, "the visitor would stare for moments entranced, then invariably turn aside to vomit." Bodies were still being found more than a month after the disaster, when searching ceased for lack of funds.

Again, Sharp seemed remarkably prescient, writing a week before the storm that those who advocated a high water level in Lake Okeechobee were taking "a terrible responsibility on themselves." And again, a member of the Everglades drainage commission—this time Ernest Amos, the state comptroller—called the disaster an "act of God," in what is surely one of history's more irresponsible outbursts of denial.

After Hurricane Katrina swept through New Orleans, President Bush, sounding much like state officials in Florida in the 1920s, said: "I don't think anybody anticipated the breach of the levees." Seeing the calamity as primarily the work of unforeseen and unpredictable forces, however, amounts to a form of moral hand-washing.

20   In fact, multiple warnings had gone out. FEMA has known about the potential for large loss of life in New Orleans, probably for a generation. Ten years ago *Weatherwise* magazine called New Orleans "the Death Valley of the Gulf Coast" because the city is surrounded by water and not particularly well served by major roadways. In 2000, in talking about the general decline in death rates from natural disasters in the twentieth century, I called attention in my book *Acts of God* to New Orleans and wrote: "Think twice before assuming that high death tolls are a thing of the past." Mark Fischetti, a contributing editor to *Scientific American*, made the same prediction in an excellent report in the magazine in 2001. The journalists John McQuaid and Mark Schleifstein reported extensively in 2002 on the potential for calamity in the *Times-Picayune*. And as recently as May 2005, Max Mayfield, the director of the National Hurricane Center, was quoted as saying, "I can't emphasize enough how concerned I am with southeast Louisiana because of its unique characteristics, its complex levee system."

Is the current disaster the American tsunami? No, it's the Hurricane Katrina calamity. But the same blind faith in the free market and private enterprise, coupled with the brutal downsizing of the public sector, and a very explicit pattern of denial in the face of impending natural calamity, help explain why America's most vulnerable saw their lives washed out to sea.

Questions for Reading Actively

1. Identify Ted Steinberg's thesis. How soon in his essay does he name those things that he will compare and contrast? What is the connection between those identifications and his thesis statement?

2. Does Steinberg use a block organization or a point-by-point organization for his essay?

3. Circle the words, phrases, and sentences Steinberg uses that signal relationships among those things he is comparing and contrasting.

Questions for Thinking Critically

1. From paragraph 6 on, Steinberg's argument becomes explicitly economic. How does he define *neoliberal imperatives,* and to what does he contrast such an economic system? Have other resources that you have consulted about the impact of hurricanes Katrina and Rita discussed the economic backgrounds?

2. In this chapter we have examined the need to develop and appreciate multiple perspectives as critical thinkers. How many fields of expertise—different academic and/or professional perspectives—does Steinberg draw upon to write his essay? In your own life as a worker, a student, and a citizen, how can you work to become better informed without necessarily becoming an "expert" yourself?

Question for Writing Thoughtfully

1. In the second paragraph of his essay, Steinberg argues for the need to find a "proper historical analogy" for understanding both the aftermath of Katrina and the devastation caused by the Asian tsunami of 2004. In your own words, describe this analogy. (The next section of this chapter will explore analogy more fully as a strategy for critical thinking.)

Analogy

We noted earlier that comparative relationships involve examining the similarities and differences of two items in the same general category, such as two perspectives, two items on a menu, or two methods of birth control. There is another kind of comparison, however, one that does not focus on things in the same category. Such comparisons are known as *analogies,* and their goal is to clarify or illuminate a concept from one category by saying that in some ways, it resembles a concept from a very different category.

The purpose of an analogy is not the same as the purpose of the comparison we have been discussing. We noted that the goal of comparing similar things is often to make a choice and that the process of comparing can provide us with information on which we can base an intelligent decision. The main goal of analogies, however, is not to choose or decide; it is to illuminate our understanding. Identifying similarities between very different things can often stimulate us to see these things in a new light or from a different perspective.

We often create and use analogies to put a point across. Used appropriately, an analogy can help to illustrate what we are trying to communicate. This device is particularly useful when we have difficulty finding the right words to represent our experiences. Similes and metaphors, two figures of speech based on analogy that help us to "say things for which we have not words," are discussed on pages 181–184 in Chapter 6.

In addition to communicating experiences that resist simple characterization, analogies are useful when a writer is explaining a complicated concept. For instance, we might compare the eye to a camera lens or compare the body's immune system to the National Guard (corpuscles are called to active duty and rush to the scene of danger when undesirable elements threaten the well-being of the organism).

Analogies are often used to describe shape or size. They help our readers to visualize size if we describe an object as "about the size of a dollar bill" or a piece of property as "roughly the size of two football fields."

Analogies enliven discourse by evoking images that illuminate the points of comparison. Consider the following analogies and explain the points of comparison.

"Laws are like cobwebs, which may catch small flies, but let wasps and hornets break through."—Jonathan Swift

"Like as the waves make towards the pebbled shore, so do our minutes hasten to their end."—William Shakespeare

"Some books are to be tasted, others to be swallowed, and some few to be chewed and digested."—Francis Bacon

"He has all the qualities of a dog, except its devotion."—Gore Vidal

In addition to *simple analogies* like the preceding ones that are designed to make one or two penetrating points, *extended analogies* have a more ambitious purpose. They attempt to illuminate a more complex subject by identifying a number of points of comparison. For example, we might seek to explain the theory of causal determinism by drawing an analogy between the universe and a watch or by analogizing the chemical interaction of molecules to a choreographed dance.

A word of caution about using analogies is in order here. Since they are based on items from different categories and have only limited points of similarity, be very careful when writing or reading arguments based on analogies. The failed

U.S. military policy in Vietnam was partially based on the "domino theory," which held that since the countries in Southeast Asia had common borders, if one country became Communist, the other countries would also "fall" to Communism, just as a row of dominoes would all fall if one were knocked down. However, the countries were separate entities, places with people, history, cultures, and policies of their own. They were not small game pieces like dominoes, so the theory proved false. Analogies do have value for describing and explaining, but by their very nature, they have limited value in an argument.

Writing Project: Comparing Perspectives on an Issue or Event

This chapter has included both readings and Thinking-Writing Activities that encourage you to reflect on the nature of perception and on comparing and contrasting different perspectives. Be sure to reread what you wrote for those activities; you may be able to use the material when completing this project.

Write an essay comparing and contrasting two or more written texts that present different perspectives on the same event or issue. Your primary purpose is to present some significant insights about the perspectives and the texts. Follow your instructor's directions for choosing texts and for the paper's length and format.

Begin by considering the key elements in the Thinking-Writing Model in Chapter 1 on pages 6–7.

The Writing Situation

Purpose   Along with presenting significant insights about the texts and their subject, you will better understand how to use the thinking patterns of comparison and contrast. Also, you will think more about the implications of different perspectives presented in various accounts. And, since comparative papers invite logical organization, your planning abilities should improve. Finally, you will be sharing your insights about the texts with your audience.

Audience   One audience for this paper would be anyone interested in the subject discussed in your choice of texts. This audience might be outside of your college since most events or issues that are written about have community, national, or international significance. If you can, identify such an audience and see if you can share your paper with them by publishing it in a newspaper or newsletter or by otherwise distributing it. If the texts pertain to history, sociology, psychology, or some other academic subject, perhaps people studying those subjects would want to read your essay.

You should consider whether or not your audience has read the texts that you are analyzing. If they have, you will not need to include much summary of content or explanation of context. If your readers have not read the texts, you will have to include a brief summary and perhaps an explanation of why the texts were written.

To communicate with your audience, you will need to include enough evidence from the texts to demonstrate your points. You should not merely *tell* your audience that a likeness or difference exists; you must *show* them the evidence so they can see it for themselves.

Subject   If your instructor specifies which texts you should compare and contrast, consider why he or she may have chosen them. A question to ask yourself is what those texts have in common. If your instructor has left the choice to you, remember that you must use texts that have something essential in common. It helps a great deal to pick texts that genuinely interest you, either because of their subject matter or because of their style. Or you may decide to select an issue or event that interests you and use your research skills to locate texts about the topic. In that case, it may be necessary to provide paraphrases or summaries of the texts for your audience.

Writer   This project asks you to bring your critical reading and thinking skills to other writers' works and to analyze their perspectives. Your position of authority and your comfort level may depend on how much you know about the subject. However, neither your personal opinions nor your experiences are the focus of this project. You must be as objective as possible as you write and as thoughtful as possible as you establish the significance of your analysis.

The Writing Process

The following sections will guide you through the stages of generating, planning, drafting, and revising as you work on your essay. Try to be particularly conscious of applying the principles discussed in this chapter and of the critical thinking you do when you revise.

Generating Ideas   Once you have decided which texts you will use, reread each of them several times. Likenesses and differences may not be immediately apparent, nor may any significance strike you at the start. Doing some preliminary writing may help.

- Make a list of the ideas in each text.
- Make a list of what you notice about each text. Are you struck by the opening, the choice of words, the author's bias or objectivity, the presence or absence of specific details, or any other elements or characteristics?
- After you have made these lists, begin to look for bases or points of likeness or difference. Doing this requires abstract thinking on your part, but patience will yield results.

- Collaboration can be productive. Talk with others about the texts.
- Read the student papers at the end of this chapter. They may help you to see what needs to be done.
- Carefully read any other models your instructor provides.
- Try freewriting for five minutes on what the texts have in common, then for five minutes on how they differ.
- Once you have established some bases for comparison or contrast, go back to the texts themselves and look for passages you could quote to illustrate your points.
- If you own the publication(s) in which the texts appear, use a highlighting pen to mark areas you may wish to quote. If you don't own them, copy the quotations or make photocopies to highlight.
- Now begin to think about significance. What are you beginning to observe about the texts? What are you beginning to feel about them?
- Try freewriting for five minutes on any or all of these questions:

    Does one text do a better job than the other? If so, in what way or ways?

    Do you agree with either or both texts? If not, what *is* your perspective?

    Have the texts caused you to reevaluate or change your own ideas or perspectives?

    Do the texts have different styles or vocabularies?

Defining a Focus   Write a thesis statement that will clearly inform your audience that you are going to explore similarities, differences, or both. You might decide to write something like "After studying both of these accounts carefully, I saw two distinct differences." Or you might decide to name the areas of likeness or difference: "The authors are similar in their recognition of the need for more education and their determination in pursuing that education." You may even decide to announce the personal significance of your comparisons in your thesis statement: "Seeing the biased way in which one of the texts presented this event made me wary of accepting any printed reports at face value."

Organizing Ideas   This assignment fits well with what you have already learned about essay structure but requires you to move a few steps beyond what you have accomplished previously. Your description of the issue or event and of the texts that describe it can give you an introduction that will end with your thesis statement. The actual discussion of likenesses and/or differences will take place in the body paragraphs, and the significance of your analysis can be introduced or expanded upon in the conclusion. The major decision you will have to make is whether to use block or point-by-point organization or some combination of the two.

Guidelines for Using Comparisons in Writing

When you are ready to present the results of your critical thinking in writing for others to read and consider, you need to present your thinking in such a way that readers will be able to follow it and, hopefully, agree with your conclusion. Therefore, for writing, you should also follow these principles:

1. *Early and accurately, introduce the things to be compared and contrasted.* When you work with written texts, this means identifying what the texts are (personal essays, poems, newspaper accounts, excerpts from books, and so on) and naming the titles and authors, probably in the introductory paragraph.

2. *Develop a thesis that states that you will examine likenesses and differences.* Because you will be discussing two or more things and introducing points about each, the audience will be confronting a difficult reading task. A clear statement of what is to come can offer them a framework to follow.

3. *Organize the comparison or contrast in the way that will be easiest for the audience to follow.* There are three ways to organize a comparison and contrast: block, point-by-point, or a careful combination of the two.

   - *Block* means that after the introduction, you first present all the material about the first subject; then, you present all the material about the second.

   - *Point-by-point* means that for each key point or basis of comparison, you first give information about one of the things being compared and contrasted, then give information about the other. In this way, you can move back and forth between the two things being compared and contrasted. The selection by Benjamin Franklin on pages 312–317 uses point-by-point organization.

   - You can also use a *combination* of these two patterns when there are some items of similarity or difference that you can present in blocks, followed by points that you may want to address separately. Topic sentences and transitions are very important in a combination method!

4. *Bring up the same bases or points of comparison or contrast for each subject, and in the same order.* An incomplete comparison results when, for instance, the language used in one text is addressed but the language used in another is not discussed. If an important detail appears in one text but not in the other, it is reasonable to simply tell the audience this: "No mention is made of a doctor in this account."

5. *Assist the audience by using words, phrases, or sentences that show relationships and shifts.* Logical connections that exist in your mind may not necessarily be apparent to your audience, but you can point them out by using appropriate expressions.

Comparison words and phrases	*Contrast words and phrases*
Same	Different, differ from, difference
Similar, similarly	In contrast
Like, alike	Unlike
Reminds me of	On the other hand
Resembles	Conversely
Shows connections with	Contrast
Both	Is separate from

6. *State the significance of your comparison and contrast at the place in the essay where it will be most effective.* Sometimes writers use the significance as the opening lead, sometimes they incorporate it into the thesis statement, and sometimes they save it for the conclusion. In deciding where to place it, ask yourself where it will have the greatest impact on your audience.

Drafting   Begin with the easiest paragraph to draft. If you are using point-by-point, remember to begin each body paragraph with a topic sentence indicating that this point will be discussed for both (or all) texts: for example, "Both accounts agree on the cause of the contamination." Then provide the audience with as much information as is needed to help them see what you mean. Use the quotations you highlighted to support your points and let the audience see that the texts really do say very similar—or very different—things. You will, of course, have to decide on the most logical order for the body paragraphs: which point to present first, which second, and so on.

Generally, readers have an easier time following point-by-point organization, but some writing situations call for block. Fortunately, word processors make it easy to move material around, so try it both ways to see which will be easier for your audience.

In your conclusion, name or expand upon the significance of your analysis, but be careful not to make too broad a statement. Consideration of two or three texts does not prove, for instance, that all texts are racist or sexist, but discovering racism or sexism in some texts should encourage you and your readers to be aware that these perspectives may be present in others.

Revising, Editing, and Proofreading   Use the Step-by-Step method in Chapter 6 on pages 169–171 to revise and polish your essay.

Student Writing

Jennifer Wade's Writing Process

Student Jennifer Wade felt an immediate and powerful personal connection to this chapter's readings by Benjamin Franklin and Zitkala-Sa. Sorting out her personal perspective and comparing it to the "official" or "objective" accounts she had obtained from family and archival history was a particular challenge for Jennifer and led to a very compelling essay in which she explores the ambivalence she feels as she tries to reconcile her European and her Cherokee ancestry. Many forms of academic and professional writing do not (by convention or by common agreement) allow for the use of the personal voice. In Jennifer's case, however, as with the readings by Matt Welch and Brian Thevenot, a personal perspective lends her essay a particular authority.

Where Did All of the Cherokees Go?

by Jennifer Wade

Almost twenty-five years ago on Tuesday, December 2, 1980, around one o'clock in the morning, my mother gave birth to me in an Indian hospital. Shortly after my birth I received an identification card from the United States Department of the Interior Affairs Tahlequah Agency. My identification card states that 5/64 of the red blood flowing through my veins is Cherokee Indian blood. I have oftentimes wondered why the government issues identification cards to the chosen few who are a part of something that has become almost nonexistent. What happened in order for the American government to go to great extremes to acknowledge such small traces of a certain descent? My identification card tells me who I am, yet I do not feel like a Cherokee Indian. Nor do I look like one.

According to the web site of the U.S. Department of the Interior, which includes the Bureau of Indian Affairs, the Cherokee nation adopted a new Constitution in 1975 that "establishes a Cherokee Register for the inclusion of any Cherokee for membership purposes in the Cherokee Nation." It was through this agreement that I was enrolled as a member of the Nation at my birth. My father gave me the Cherokee blood and shortly thereafter left me with my mother. She resented my father and everything about him, including my Cherokee heritage. I grew up being a part of something exclusive, and yet I never experienced the culture. As generations pass, the Cherokee Indians will become extinct. After twenty-five years I decided it was time for me to meet my ancestors. I wanted to know where I came from and what had happened to them.

As my research began, I found that I shared many of the beliefs and values my ancestors did. According to Professor Theda Perdue, the Cherokees believed Earth was created by something powerful. They believed the rock sky where everyone lived became overcrowded, and so a water beetle created an island and sent the Cherokee down to inhabit the new land (The Cherokee 13). It is as though God sent his people back to live as a mortal again. The Cherokees too had their own Adam and Eve, but they called them Kana'ti and Selu. From this man and woman came all others (13). Although the Cherokees speak an alien language and look like weather-beaten scavengers, their beliefs are similar to others'. Through this discovery, I have found that all ethnicities have a universal code of conduct.

Unfortunately, there are those who choose to ignore the universal code of conduct when interacting with other ethnicities. Frank W. Porter III, director of the Chelsea House foundation for American Indian Studies, makes this point clear: "The Europeans believed they had 'discovered' a New World," but their religious bigotry, cultural bias, and materialistic world-view kept them from appreciating and understanding the people who lived in it (7). These narcissistic views all but destroyed a strong nation of people. All that remain are a few American citizens with meaningless identification cards reminding us of what we once were, or could have been.

Comedian Chris Rock points out, in his stand-up routine *Bigger, Blacker, and Better*, "You ain't never gonna find a family of American Indians chillin' out in Red Lobster." You will not because they do not exist anymore. Somewhere in Oklahoma you may find people with long, straight, jet black hair and dark brown eyes who probably have an identification card, but they, like me, are only a glimpse of what the Cherokee Indians once were.

In a sense the Cherokee Indians caused their own demise. Had they had the mentality of their counterparts, the outcome may have been different. The Cherokees were generous and willing to compromise with the Europeans who were invading their homeland. Perdue explains that the Cherokees were "incredibly adaptable" (39). If they had chosen to live like the Europeans, could they have survived and lived peacefully together? In the book *Voices From the Trail of Tears*, Vicki Rozema reports of an article written in 1828 by Elias Boudinot in which a chief from a Cherokee tribe explains how generous the Cherokees had been as he sits in the house of General

Knox looking out his window at what once was free land where his people hunted and lived: "They [the white people] asked only to let them tie it [a great canoe] to a tree—we consented. They then said some of their people were sick, and they asked [to] put them under the shade of the trees," (4) and so the Cherokees consented. They kept consenting until everything they had was gone. Soon they were fighting to the death for the clothes on their back. Never before had the Cherokees encountered such an enemy. It was not enough for the Europeans to be satisfied with food and shelter; they wanted everything.

I am left with feeling guilt because I think like the European does. One is not enough; I want two. As the Cherokee nation died, so too did its teachings; *do unto others as they would do unto you* is a philosophy I was taught at an early age. The Cherokees understood this philosophy and applied it accordingly. The Europeans applied this philosophy as they saw fit. In most cases they had to receive in order to give. This is the "you scratch my back and I will scratch yours" mentality.

But despite my ambivalence, many others of Cherokee heritage are taking the initiative to keep our culture's heritage and traditions alive. Museums across the Carolinas (where the Cherokee nation originated) and Oklahoma (where I was born) commemorate both the livelihoods of the Cherokee peoples and the tragedies of the Trail of Tears. An effort to create a written language to preserve the rich Cherokee oral traditions of storytelling, genealogy, and folk wisdom is being perpetuated by the Internet.

It can be peculiar how the nature of human interaction can work. I am a descendant of European and Cherokee heritage because of events beyond any one person's control. Hundreds of years ago a big boat bumped into a peaceful nation of tribal people who were too generous in their offers. Today it is known as the United States of America. We are one of the strongest and largest nations in the world because of ruthless generals who wanted it all. Our history teaches us that George Washington and Benjamin Franklin liberated us from an unruly king and brought us a new world full of opportunity and prosperity. Although all of these statements are true, they do not tell us what it cost the world. From the very moment the first Europeans set foot on what they thought was India, the world lost a great nation of philosophical people. We are left with identification cards that remind us of the remnants of Cherokee blood pumping through the hearts of a select few.

a	e	i	o	u	v [ə̃]
Ꭰ a	Ꭱ e	Ꭲ i	Ꭳ o	Ꭴ u	Ꭵ v
Ꭶ ga Ꭷ ka	Ꭸ ge	Ꭹ gi	Ꭺ go	Ꭻ gu	Ꭼ gv
Ꭽ ha	Ꭾ he	Ꭿ hi	Ꮀ ho	Ꮁ hu	Ꮂ hv
Ꮃ la	Ꮄ le	Ꮅ li	Ꮆ lo	Ꮇ lu	Ꮈ lv
Ꮉ ma	Ꮊ me	Ꮋ mi	Ꮌ mo	Ꮍ mu	
Ꮎ na Ꮏ hna Ꮐ nah	Ꮑ ne	Ꮒ ni	Ꮓ no	Ꮔ nu	Ꮕ nv
Ꮖ qua	Ꮗ que	Ꮘ qui	Ꮙ quo	Ꮚ quu	Ꮛ quv
Ꮝ s Ꮜ sa	Ꮞ se	Ꮟ si	Ꮠ so	Ꮡ su	Ꮢ sv
Ꮣ da Ꮤ ta	Ꮥ de Ꮦ te	Ꮧ di Ꮨ ti	Ꮩ do	Ꮪ du	Ꮫ dv
Ꮬ dla Ꮭ tla	Ꮮ tle	Ꮯ tli	Ꮰ tlo	Ꮱ tlu	Ꮲ tlv
Ꮳ tsa	Ꮴ tse	Ꮵ tsi	Ꮶ tso	Ꮷ tsu	Ꮸ tsv
Ꮹ wa	Ꮺ we	Ꮻ wi	Ꮼ wo	Ꮽ wu	Ꮾ wv
Ꮿ ya	Ᏸ ye	Ᏹ yi	Ᏺ yo	Ᏻ yu	Ᏼ yv

Courtesy of Cengage Learning

FIGURE 9.2
Cherokee Syllabary

Works Cited

Leone, Bruno, and Brenda Stalcup, eds. *Native American Rights*. San Diego: Green Haven, 1998. Print.

Mooney, Thomas. *Exploring Your Cherokee Ancestry*. Park Hill: Cherokee National Historic Society, 1990. Print.

Perdue, Theda. *The Cherokees*. New York: Chelsea, 1989. Print.

Rozena, Vicki. *Voices From the Trail of Tears*. Winston: Blair, 2003. Print.

United States. Dept. of the Interior. *Indian Ancestry—Cherokee Indian Ancestry*. 10 Oct. 2003. Web. 3 Nov. 2005.

"Cherokee syllabary." *Wikipedia*. Wikipedia Foundation, n.d. Web. 30 October 2005.

Alternative Writing Project: Comparing Two Reviews

Find a recent review of a movie that you have seen or of a restaurant at which you have eaten. Compare the review with your experience. Do you agree with the reviewer? Identify specific examples of points you agree with and explain why. Do you disagree with the reviewer? Identify specific examples of these, too. Write an essay presenting your analysis of the review as it relates to your experience with the movie or at the restaurant.

CHAPTER 9   Summary

- Perceptions are messages from the senses, whereas perspective points of view that develop from and also influence perceptions.

- We actively select our perspectives based on what has been called to our attention, what our needs or interests are, what our moods and feelings are, what seems familiar or unfamiliar, and what our backgrounds are.

- We naturally try to order and organize our perceptions into patterns and relationships that make sense to us; this is important for writing.

- Context, or the overall situation, plays a big role in how we interpret our perceptions.

- Your ways of viewing the world will develop and change through the experiences you have, the knowledge you acquire, and your reflections on your experiences and knowledge.

- To obtain more accurate perceptions, you should develop your awareness, get input from others, find evidence, and keep an open mind.

- You can use comparison and contrast to think critically and to organize your writing.

Mike Segar/Reuters

With his commitment to the environment as well as his profound understandings of economics and commerce, environmental lawyer Robert F. Kennedy (son of the slain senator Robert Kennedy and nephew of John F. Kennedy) has forged an alliance between industry and environmentalists that, working together, has resulted in an organization called Riverkeepers and a Hudson River ecosystem that might be more thriving now than at any point in the previous 150 years. Kennedy recognizes that carefully supported arguments and persuasive negotiations between environmental activists, fishermen and sporting groups, local governments, and industry result in solutions that are broadly supported and easier to implement. What are the causes and effects at play in conservation of a river's environment?

Writing to Speculate:
Exploring Cause and Effect

"The present contains nothing more than the past, and what is found in the effect was already in the cause."

—HENRI BERGSON

Previous chapters have examined thinking and writing patterns that help us make sense of the world. As we explore our world, we humans tend to ask why things are as they are: Why do some marriages endure for years and others end in divorce? Why does a coastal area of the country have relatively calm summers for several years, then experience a record-breaking hurricane? Why do certain political ideas take hold during particular periods of history?

When we contemplate such questions, we are asking about (1) *causes*, factors that contribute to events and bring them about, and (2) *effects*, events that result directly or indirectly from causes or from other events. Much thinking about causes and effects occurs in an impromptu way. For example, about a divorce, we might guess, "I think the marriage failed because of financial problems." Though that might in fact be one reason, other factors are probably also involved. Determining causes is complicated because

- An event may have more than one cause
- An event may have various types of causes
- Determining causes with certainty is often impossible

When we think about causal relationships in an organized way, ever conscious of the difficulty and uncertainty of the task, we are using a critical thinking process called *causal analysis*.

The Writing Project in this chapter asks you to find information about some causes of a recent event and then to write a paper in which you present this information. The chapter should help you to write effectively about causal relationships.

Kinds of Causal Relationships

Causal patterns of thinking involve relating events in terms of the influence or effect they have on one another. The following statements are all examples of causal statements.

- Since I was the last to leave, I turned off the lights.
- Taking plenty of vitamin C really cured that terrible cold I had.
- I accidentally toasted my hand along with the marshmallows by getting too near the campfire.

In these statements, the words *since, turned off, cured,* and *getting too near* all point to the fact that something has caused something else to take place.

Words That Indicate Cause and Effect

Cause	*Effect*
because	because of
reason(s), for this reason (these reasons)	as a result, result, resulted in
affect, effect (verb)	consequently, consequence
bring about	therefore
a factor in	since
cure, infect	thus
lead, lead to	accordingly
produce (verb)	happens whenever
encourage, encouragement	follows from, follows that
discourage	ensues
influence	
solve	

What additional cause and effect words can you think of?

You are probably realizing that you make causal statements all the time and that you are constantly thinking in terms of causal relationships. In fact, the goal of much of your thinking is to figure out why something happened or how something came about. One advantage of causal analysis is that it enables you to make reasonable predictions because you are able to clarify the causal relationships involved and make predictions based on your understanding.

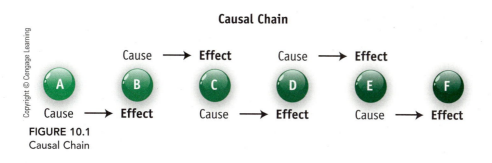

FIGURE 10.1
Causal Chain

The purpose of much of your academic writing will be causal analysis, either to demonstrate that you fully understand the factors contributing to a specific situation or result (for example, why a certain genetic mutation leads to Type I diabetes in humans) or the effects of particular behaviors (for example, why a combination of poor eating habits and lack of exercise can bring on Type II diabetes in susceptible adolescents and adults). Your audience may at first be your professor, but it's clear that this kind of thinking and the writing it produces will be useful in the workplace and the community as well. Thinking carefully and skeptically about causes and effects is excellent training for your further research, and it will help you to solve complex problems and make well-informed decisions.

Although you may think of causes and effects in isolation—A caused B—in reality, causes and effects rarely appear by themselves. There is not just one cause of a resulting effect; there is a whole string of causes, as illustrated by the structures in Figure 10.1. These interrelated causes form more complex patterns, including three that we will examine next: *causal chains, contributory causes,* and *interactive causes.*

Causal Chains

Consider the following scenario:

Your paper on the topic "life span and poverty" is due on Monday morning. You have reserved the whole weekend to work on it and are just getting started when the phone rings. A favorite childhood friend is in town and wants to stay with you for the weekend. You say *yes*. By Sunday night, you've had a great weekend but have made little progress on your paper. You brew a pot of coffee and get started. At 3:00 A.M. you are too exhausted to continue. Deciding to get a few hours' sleep, you set the alarm clock for 6:00 A.M., giving yourself plenty of time to finish up. When you wake up, it's nine o'clock; the alarm failed to go off. Your class starts in forty minutes. You have no chance of getting the paper done on time. On your way to class, you mentally review the causes of this disaster. No longer concerned about life after death, you are very worried about your own longevity after this class!

- What causes in this situation are responsible for your paper's being late?
- What do you think is the single most important cause?
- What do you think your instructor will identify as the most important cause? Why?

A *causal chain*, as illustrated by the preceding example, is a situation in which one thing leads to another, which then leads to another, and so on over a period of time. In writing about causal chains, your narrative would use chronological ordering (see page 195 in Chapter 7). There is not just one cause of the resulting effect. Which event or circumstance in the chain is the "tipping point," the most important contributing factor to the effect? Your answer will depend on your perspective on the situation. You might see the cause of the unfinished paper as a defective alarm clock. Your instructor, though, might see the cause of the problem as overall lack of planning.

Thinking-Writing Activity

CREATING A CAUSAL CHAIN

1. Create a scenario in which you make a series of decisions that culminates in a significant conclusion. For example, your decision to take a course outside of your major might lead to a conversation with the professor, which leads you to explore a career option that you had not previously considered, and so on. The scenario might be based on an actual experience in your life or one created through your imagination.

2. Review the scenario you have just created. Explain how the "real" cause of the final effect could vary, depending on your perspective on the situation.

Contributory Causes

In addition to operating in causal chains over a period of time, causes can also work simultaneously to produce an effect. This results in a situation in which a number of different *contributory causes* bring something about. Instead of working in isolation, each cause contributes to bringing about the final effect. When this situation occurs, each cause serves to support and reinforce the action of the other causes, a condition illustrated in Figure 10.2.

Consider the following situation:

It is the end of the term, and you have been working incredibly hard at school—writing papers, preparing for exams, finishing up course projects. You haven't been getting enough sleep, and you haven't been eating regular, well-balanced meals. To make matters worse, you have been under intense pressure in your personal life, having serious arguments with the person you have been dating,

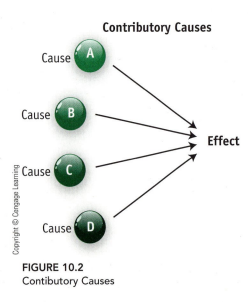

Contributory Causes

Cause A

Cause B

Cause C

Cause D

Effect

Copyright © Cengage Learning

FIGURE 10.2
Contibutory Causes

and this situation is constantly on your mind. It is the middle of the flu season, and many people you know have been sick with various respiratory infections. Walking home one evening, you get soaked by an unexpected downpour. By the time you get home, you are shivering. You soon find yourself in bed with a thermometer in your mouth—you are sick!

What was the "cause" of your illness? In this situation, you can see that evidently, a combination of factors led to your physical breakdown: low resistance, getting wet and chilled, being exposed to various germs and viruses, physical exhaustion, lack of proper eating, and so on. Taken by itself, no one factor might have been enough to cause your illness. Together, they all contributed to the final outcome. The readings on longevity later in this chapter demonstrate the complexity of interrelated causes.

Thinking-Writing Activity

CREATING A CAUSAL CHAIN

Creating a Contributory-Cause Scenario

Create a similar scenario, detailing the contributory causes that led to your asking someone for a date, choosing a major, losing or winning a game, or another effect.

Interactive Causes

Causes rarely operate in isolation but instead often influence (and are influenced by) other factors. Imagine that you are scheduled to give a PowerPoint presentation to a large group of people. As your moment at the podium approaches, you become anxious, which results in a dry mouth and throat, making your voice sound more like a croak. The prospect of sounding like a bullfrog increases your anxiety, which in turn dries your mouth and constricts your throat further, reducing your croak to something much worse—silence.

Different factors can relate to each other through reciprocal influences that flow back and forth from one to the other. Understanding this type of *interactive causal relationship* helps you to organize and make sense of your experiences. For instance, to comprehend social relationships (families, teams, groups of friends), you consider the complex ways in which each individual influences—and is influenced by—all the other members of the group. Student Daniel Eggers explored the complex interactive causal relationships that continue to affect poverty in the African-American community decades after Dr. Martin Luther King Jr.'s "I Have a Dream" speech (page 184 in Chapter 6). Understanding biological systems and other systems is similar to understanding social systems. To comprehend and explain how an organ such as the heart, liver, or brain functions, you have to describe its complex, interactive relationships with all the other parts of the biological system. Figure 10.3 illustrates these dynamic causal relationships.

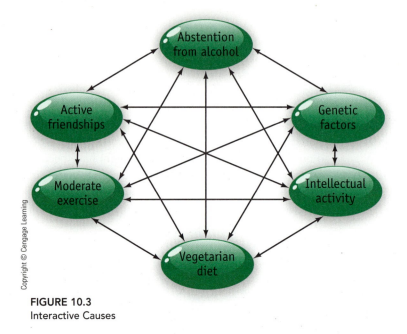

Copyright © Cengage Learning

FIGURE 10.3
Interactive Causes

Thinking-Writing Activity

IDENTIFYING CAUSAL PATTERNS

Read the following passages that illustrate causal patterns of thinking. For each passage, identify the kind of causal relationship (chain, contributory, or interactive). Draw a chart or figure that illustrates this relationship, and explain how the causes are related to one another.

1. Nothing posed a more serious threat to the bald eagle's survival than a modern chemical compound called DDT. Around 1940, a retired Canadian banker named Charles L. Broley began keeping track of eagles nesting in Florida. Each breeding season, he climbed into more than 50 nests, counted the eaglets and put metal bands on their legs. In the late 1940s, a sudden drop-off in the number of young produced led him to conclude that 80 percent of his birds were sterile. Broley blamed DDT. Scientists later discovered that DDE, a breakdown product of DDT, causes not sterility, but a fatal thinning of eggshell among birds of prey. Applied on cropland all over the United States, the pesticide was running off into waterways where it concentrated in fish. The bald eagles ate the fish and the DDT impaired their ability to reproduce. They were not alone, of course. Ospreys and pelicans suffered similar setbacks.—Jim Doherty, "The Bald Eagle and DDT"

2. It is popularly accepted that Hitler was the major cause of World War II, but the ultimate causes go much deeper than one personality. First, there were long-standing German grievances against reparations levied on the nation following its defeat in World War I. Second, there were severe economic strains that caused resentment among the German people. Third, there were French and English reluctance to work out a sound disarmament policy and American noninvolvement in the matter. Finally, there was the European fear that communism was a much greater danger than National Socialism. These factors contributed to the outbreak of World War II.—Gilbert Muller, *The American College Handbook*

3. You crunch and chew your way through vast quantities of snacks and confectioneries and relieve your thirst with multicolored, flavored soft drinks, with and without calories, for two basic reasons. The first is simple; the food tastes good, and you enjoy the sensation of eating it. Second, you associate these foods, often without being aware of it, with the highly pleasurable experiences depicted in the advertisements used to promote their sale. Current television advertisements demonstrate this point: people turn from grumpiness to euphoria after crunching a corn chip. Others water ski into the sunset with their loved ones while drinking a popular soft drink. People entertain on the patio with friends, cook over campfires without mosquitoes, or go to carnivals with granddad munching away at the latest candy or snack food. The people portrayed in these scenarios are all healthy, vigorous, and good looking; one wonders how popular the food they convince you to eat would be if they would crunch or drink away while complaining about low back pain or clogged sinuses.—Judith Wurtman, *Eating Your Way Through Life*

Ways of Testing Causes

Necessary Condition and Sufficient Condition

In addition to the three patterns of causality we have just examined, we need to consider necessary and sufficient conditions. A *necessary condition* is a factor that is required to bring about a certain result: for example, an intact light bulb is required for a lamp's illumination. However, by itself, an intact light bulb is not sufficient to provide illumination: you also need electricity, which is another necessary condition.

Thinking Critically About Visuals

Are You What You Eat?

As Michael Pollen explains in his article, "Playing God in the Garden" on p. 357, much of the food that we are ingesting has been treated with pesticides and genetically modified in ways that are unknown to us. This photo depicts farmers spraying a crop with powerful pesticides.

Abid Katib/Getty Images

Should we be concerned about the history of the food we are eating, the ways in which it has been treated and genetically altered before it arrives on our table? Notice how the farmers spraying pesticide are dressed in this photo. What kind of a causal relationship if any is implied by this or other elements of this photo?

A *sufficient condition* is a factor that of itself is always sufficient for bringing about a certain result. For example, a pinch on the arm is a sufficient cause for discomfort. Of course, even with a sufficient condition, there may be an additional necessary condition, or several necessary conditions, for a result to occur. Having healthy nerves in the arm and being conscious are two necessary conditions for someone's feeling a sensation when pinched on the arm.

Immediate Cause and Remote Cause

Yet another way to think critically about causes is to classify them by how close in time the cause is to its result. Something that happens just before an event that it causes is called an *immediate cause*. A factor that also helped to bring about this same event but that occurred further back in time is called a *remote cause*. For example, a last-minute touchdown could be the immediate cause of a football championship, but wise trades made for key players before the season began might be remote causes.

Identifying Causal Fallacies

Because causality plays such a dominant role in the way we make sense of the world, it is not surprising that people make many mistakes and many errors in judgment in trying to determine causal relationships. These mistakes and errors can lead to unsound arguments, or *fallacies*. The following are some of the most common fallacies associated with causality.

- Questionable cause
- Misidentification of the cause
- *Post hoc ergo propter hoc*
- Slippery slope

Questionable Cause

The fallacy of *questionable cause* occurs when someone presents a causal relationship for which no real evidence exists. Superstitious beliefs such as "If you break a mirror, you will have seven years of bad luck" usually fall into this category. Some people feel that astrology, a system of beliefs tying one's personality and fortunes in life to the position of the planets at the moment of birth, also falls into this category.

Consider the following passage from the *Confessions* of philosopher St. Augustine (C.E. 354–386). Does it seem to support the causal assertions of astrology or deny them? Why?

> Firminus had heard from his father that when his mother had been pregnant with him, a slave belonging to a friend of his father's was also about to bear. It happened that since the two women had their babies at the same instant, the men were forced to cast exactly the same horoscope for each newborn child down to the last detail, one for his son, the other for the little slave. Yet Firminus, born

THINKING CRITICALLY ABOUT NEW MEDIA

Causation vs. Correlation in the News

In any research methods class, you will hear the phrase "correlation does not equal causation" quite often. The Merriam-Webster dictionary defines *correlation* as "a relation existing between phenomena or things or between mathematical or statistical variables which tend to vary, be associated, or occur together in a way not expected on the basis of chance alone." For example, if researchers found that children with low self-esteem tended to have fewer friends, they couldn't say that low self-esteem impairs the children's ability to make friends because it might be just as likely that having few friends makes them have those feelings of low self-esteem—or there may even be a third factor that is affecting the first two factors. In other words, there may be a relationship, or correlation, between self-esteem and the ability to make friends, but you cannot say one *causes* the other if you cannot rule out all other possibilities. For this reason, researchers are very careful about how they present research results in the journal articles they write.

Some of the research being done in scientific circles can have a great impact on and applications for the general public, but the journal articles in which the research is presented are not typically written in a style that is very accessible to an average reader. They are often laden with field-specific jargon and go into great detail about statistics and methods. Someone not familiar with that field or statistic and methods would have a difficult time wading through it and grasping the significance of the findings. For that reason, the way the general public typically learns about new research that might be applicable to their lives is through media outlets, like news programs on television, the radio, and, increasingly more so, on the Internet.

The danger in relying on, for instance, an online news site or blog for your research information is that it would seem that many of the journalists who are interpreting the

to wealth in his parents' house, had one of the more illustrious careers in life whereas the slave had no alleviation of his life's burden.

Other examples of this fallacy include beliefs such as

- Lottery numbers that occur in dreams are more likely to be winners than random choices.
- Spending money is the best way to solve most problems.
- Movies that have the highest box-office numbers are of the best quality and most deserving of awards.

research data may not be any better at it than the average person. Whether it is because journalists do not have formal research methods training, because the journalist or news outlet is motivated to generate a provocative news story to increase their site traffic despite the facts, or because of some other unknown reason, too often journalists make the error of reporting correlation as causation. Other times, they may not outwardly state a cause-and-effect relationship, but they may imply it. This kind of misinformation can be not only unfortunate but also potentially harmful. As the George Mason University Statistical Assessment Service notes on its website, "there has been a lot of publicity over the purported relationship between autism and vaccinations, for example. As vaccination rates went up across the United States, so did autism. However, this correlation (which has led many to conclude that vaccination causes autism) has been widely dismissed by public health experts. The rise in autism rates is likely to do with increased awareness and diagnosis, or one of many other possible factors that have changed over the past 50 years" (http://stats.org/faq_vs.htm). When news sites report the vaccination may be a likely cause of autism, it may spur parents who read that to keep their children from being vaccinated, which most public health experts would not recommend. Therefore, when reading about research via an online news media site, it is very important you try to verify causation claims before sharing or acting on the information.

Thinking-Writing Activity

JUSTIFYING CLAIMS

Visit your text website, accessed through **cengagebrain.com**, and click on the links to online news articles reporting scientific research. Determine whether or not the claims of causation are justified and explain why.

Misidentification of the Cause

In causal situations we are not always certain about what is causing what—in other words, about what is the cause and what is the effect. For example, in the following pairs of items, which is the cause, and which is the effect? Why?

- Headaches and tension
- Failure in school and personal problems
- Shyness and lack of confidence
- Substance abuse and emotional difficulties

Sometimes a third factor is responsible for two effects that we are examining. Headaches and tension may both be the result of a third element—such as some new medication a person is taking. When we fail to recognize the third element, we commit the fallacy of *ignoring a common cause*. There also exists the fallacy of *assuming a common cause*—such as assuming that a person's sore toe and earache both stem from the same cause.

Post Hoc Ergo Propter Hoc

The translation of the Latin phrase *post hoc ergo propter hoc* is "After that, therefore because of that." It refers to situations in which, because two things occur closely together in time, we assume that one has caused the other. Suppose your team wins the game each time you wear your favorite shirt; you just may be tempted to conclude that the one event (wearing your favorite shirt) has some influence on the other event (winning the game). As a result, you may continue to wear this shirt "for good luck." It is easy to see how this sort of mistaken thinking can lead to all sorts of superstitious beliefs. Consider the following causal conclusion arrived at by Mark Twain's fictional character Huckleberry Finn in the following passage. How would you analyze his conclusion?

> I've always reckoned that looking at the new moon over your left shoulder is one of the carelessest and foolishest things a body can do. Old Hank Bunker done it once, and bragged about it; and in less than two years he got drunk and fell off a shot tower and spread himself out so that he was just a kind of layer. . . . But anyway, it all came of looking at the moon that way, like a fool.

Can you identify any of your own superstitious beliefs or practices that may have resulted from *post hoc* thinking?

Slippery Slope

The causal fallacy of *slippery slope* is illustrated in the following advice:

> Don't miss that first deadline, because if you do, it won't be long before you're missing all your deadlines. This will spread to the rest of your life, as you will be late for every appointment. This terminal procrastination will ruin your career, and friends and relatives will abandon you. You will end up a lonely failure who is unable to ever do anything on time.

Slippery slope thinking asserts that one undesirable action will inevitably lead to a worse action, which will necessarily lead to still a worse one, all the way down the "slippery slope" to some terrible disaster at the bottom. Although this progression may indeed occur, there certainly is no causal guarantee that it will. Create slippery slope scenarios for one of the following warnings:

- If you get behind on one credit card payment . . .
- If you fail that first test . . .
- If you eat that first potato chip . . .

Summary: Causal Fallacies

Questionable Cause:

Presenting a causal relationship for which no real evidence exists

Misidentification of Cause:

Uncertainty about what is the cause and what is the effect: ignoring a common cause, assuming a false common cause

Post Hoc Ego Propter Hoc:

Assuming a causal relationship between situations occurring closely together in time

Slippery Slope:

Asserting that one undesirable action will lead to a worse action, which will lead to still a worse one—down, down the slippery slope

Thinking-Writing Activity

DIAGNOSING CAUSAL FALLACIES

Review the four causal fallacies just described; then identify and explain the errors of reasoning illustrated in the following examples.

1. The person who won the lottery says she dreamed the winning numbers. I'm going to start writing down the numbers that I dream about.

2. Yesterday I forgot to take my vitamins, and I immediately got sick. That mistake won't occur again!

3. I'm warning you: if you miss a class, it won't be long before you flunk out of school and ruin your future.

4. I always take the first seat in the bus. Today I took another seat, and the bus broke down.

5. I think the reason I'm not doing well in school is that I simply don't have enough time to study, and my classes aren't interesting, either.

Detecting Causal Claims

Sometimes people use causal reasoning because they want us to see cause-and-effect relationships that they believe exist. When they do this, we say they are making *causal claims*. Consider the following examples.

1. Politicians assure us that a vote for them will result in better schools and lower taxes.
2. Advertisers tell us that using a detergent will leave our wash "cleaner than clean, whiter than white."
3. Doctors tell us that eating a balanced diet will result in a longer life.
4. Educators tell us that a college degree is worth an average of $830,000 additional income over an individual's lifetime.
5. Utility companies inform us that using nuclear energy will result in less pollution.

In each of these examples, certain causal claims are being made about how the world operates in an effort to persuade us to adopt a certain point of view. As critical thinkers, it is our responsibility to evaluate these various causal claims to determine whether they are valid or questionable.

Thinking-Writing Activity

EVALUATING CAUSAL CLAIMS

Explain how you might go about evaluating the causal claims previously listed.

- *Example:* Electing politicians and claims about getting better schools and lower taxes.
- *Evaluation:* Speak to teachers and principals about school needs. Understand what a politician in a specific office can and cannot do about education. Learn about budgets for school systems. Remember your own school experiences and think about why they were good or bad. Learn about taxes and schools in your area.

Exploring Cause and Effect: Modern Agriculture and Social Impact

The impact of human civilization on the environment has taken on increasing urgency as global warming, the razing of rain forests, the search for sustainable fuel sources, and our dependence on factory-farmed or genetically modified food are discussed and debated in the media. All these factors affect the most basic aspects of our lives, from the quality of our air to the safety of our next meal. In the following article, "Playing God in the Garden," Michael Pollen traces the genetically engineered history of the "New Leaf Superior" potatoes that he is planting in his garden, exploring a variety of disturbing questions as he does so. As you read this article, watch for the author's development of different kinds of causal connections, and evaluate the clarity and effectiveness of his arguments.

"Playing God in the Garden"

by Michael Pollan

Planting

Today I planted something new in my vegetable garden—something very new, as a matter of fact. It's a potato called the New Leaf Superior, which has been genetically engineered—by Monsanto, the chemical giant recently turned "life sciences" giant—to produce its own insecticide. This it can do in every cell of every leaf, stem, flower, root and (here's the creepy part) spud. The scourge of potatoes has always been the Colorado potato beetle, a handsome and voracious insect that can pick a plant clean of its leaves virtually overnight. Any Colorado potato beetle that takes so much as a nibble of my New Leafs will supposedly keel over and die, its digestive tract pulped, in effect, by the bacterial toxin manufactured in the leaves of these otherwise ordinary Superiors. (Superiors are the thin-skinned white spuds sold fresh in the supermarket.) You're probably wondering if I plan to eat these potatoes, or serve them to my family. That's still up in the air; it's only the first week of May, and harvest is a few months off.

Certainly my New Leafs are aptly named. They're part of a new class of crop plants that is rapidly changing the American food chain. This year, the fourth year that genetically altered seed has been on the market, some 45 million acres of American farmland have been planted with biotech crops, most of it corn, soybeans, cotton and potatoes that have been engineered to either produce their own pesticides or withstand herbicides. Though Americans have already begun to eat genetically engineered potatoes, corn and soybeans, industry research confirms what my own informal surveys suggest: hardly any of us knows it. The reason is not hard to find. The biotech industry, with the concurrence of the Food and Drug Administration, has decided we don't need to know it, so biotech foods carry no identifying labels. In a dazzling feat of positioning, the industry has succeeded in depicting these plants simultaneously as the linchpins of a biological revolution—part of a "new agricultural paradigm" that will make farming more sustainable, feed the world and improve health and nutrition—and, oddly enough, as the same old stuff, at least so far as those of us at the eating end of the food chain should be concerned.

This convenient version of reality has been roundly rejected by both consumers and farmers across the Atlantic. Last summer, biotech food emerged as the most explosive environmental issue in Europe. Protesters have destroyed dozens of field trials of the very same "frankenplants" (as they are sometimes called) that we Americans are already serving for dinner, and throughout Europe the public has demanded that biotech food be labeled in the market.

By growing my own transgenic crop—and talking with scientists and farmers involved with biotech—I hoped to discover which of us was crazy. Are the Europeans overreacting, or is it possible that we've been underreacting to genetically engineered food?

5   After digging two shallow trenches in my garden and lining them with compost, I untied the purple mesh bag of seed potatoes that Monsanto had sent and opened up the Grower Guide tied around its neck. (Potatoes, you may recall from kindergarten experiments, are grown not from seed but from the eyes of other potatoes.) The guide put me in mind not so much of planting potatoes as booting up a new software release. By "opening and using this product," the card stated, I was now "licensed" to grow these potatoes, but only for a single generation; the crop I would water and tend and harvest was mine, yet also not mine. That is, the potatoes I will harvest come August are mine to eat or sell, but their genes remain the intellectual property of Monsanto, protected under numerous United States patents, including Nos. 5,196,525, 5,164,316, 5,322,938 and 5,352,605. Were I to save even one of them to plant next year— something I've routinely done with potatoes in the past—I would be breaking Federal law. The small print in the Grower Guide also brought the news that my potato plants were themselves a pesticide, registered with the Environmental Protection Agency.

If proof were needed that the intricate industrial food chain that begins with seeds and ends on our dinner plates is in the throes of profound change, the small print that accompanied my New Leaf will do. That food chain has been unrivaled for its productivity—on average, a single American farmer today grows enough food each year to feed 100 people. But this accomplishment has come at a price. The modern industrial farmer cannot achieve such yields without enormous amounts of chemical fertilizer, pesticide, machinery and fuel, a set of capital-intensive inputs, as they're called, that saddle the farmer with debt, threaten his health, erode his soil and destroy its fertility, pollute the ground water and compromise the safety of the food we eat.

We've heard all this before, of course, but usually from environmentalists and organic farmers; what is new is to hear the same critique from conventional farmers, government officials and even many agribusiness corporations, all of whom now acknowledge that our food chain stands in need of reform. Sounding more like Wendell Berry than the agribusiness giant it is, Monsanto declared in its most recent annual report that "current agricultural technology is not sustainable."

What is supposed to rescue the American food chain is biotechnology—the replacement of expensive and toxic chemical inputs with expensive but apparently benign genetic information: crops that, like my New Leafs, can protect themselves from insects and disease without being sprayed with pesticides. With the advent of biotechnology, agriculture is entering the information age, and more than any other company, Monsanto is positioning itself to become its Microsoft, supplying the proprietary "operating systems"—the metaphor is theirs—to run this new generation of plants.

There is, of course, a second food chain in America: organic agriculture. And while it is still only a fraction of the size of the conventional food chain, it has been growing in leaps and bounds—in large part because of concerns over the safety of conventional agriculture. Organic farmers have been among biotechnology's fiercest critics, regarding crops like my New Leafs as inimical to their principles and, potentially, a threat to their survival. That's because Bt, the bacterial toxin produced in my New Leafs (and in many other biotech plants) happens to be the same insecticide organic growers have relied on for decades. Instead of being flattered by the imitation, however, organic farmers are up in arms: the widespread use of Bt in biotech crops is likely to lead to insect resistance, thus robbing organic growers of one of their most critical tools; that is, Monsanto's version of sustainable agriculture may threaten precisely those farmers who pioneered sustainable farming.

Sprouting

10 After several days of drenching rain, the sun appeared on May 15, and so did my New Leafs. A dozen deep-green shoots pushed up out of the soil and commenced to grow—faster and more robustly than any of the other potatoes in my garden. Apart from their vigor, though, my New Leafs looked perfectly normal. And yet as I watched them multiply their lustrous dark-green leaves those first few days, eagerly awaiting the arrival of the first doomed beetle, I couldn't help thinking of them as existentially different from the rest of my plants.

My New Leafs are different. Although Monsanto likes to depict biotechnology as just another in an ancient line of human modifications of nature going back to fermentation, in fact genetic engineering overthrows the old rules governing the relationship of nature and culture in a plant. For the first time, breeders can bring qualities from anywhere in nature into the genome of a plant—from flounders (frost tolerance), from viruses (disease resistance) and, in the case of my potatoes, from Bacillus thuringiensis, the soil bacterium that produces the organic insecticide known as Bt. The introduction into a plant of genes transported not only across species but whole phyla means that the wall of that plant's essential identity—its irreducible wildness, you might say—has been breached.

But what is perhaps most astonishing about the New Leafs coming up in my garden is the human intelligence that the inclusion of the Bt gene represents. In the past, that intelligence resided outside the plant, in the mind of the organic farmers who deployed Bt (in the form of a spray) to manipulate the ecological relationship of certain insects and a certain bacterium as a way to foil those insects. The irony about the New Leafs is that the cultural information they encode happens to be knowledge that resides in the heads of the very sort of people—that is, organic growers—who most distrust high technology.

One way to look at biotechnology is that it allows a larger portion of human intelligence to be incorporated into the plant itself. In this sense, my New Leafs are just plain smarter than the rest of my potatoes. The others will depend on my knowledge and experience when the Colorado potato beetles strike; the New Leafs, knowing what I know about bugs and Bt, will take care of themselves. So while my biotech plants might seem like alien beings, that's not quite right. They're more like us than like other plants because there's more of us in them.

Growing

To find out how my potatoes got that way, I traveled to suburban St. Louis in early June. My New Leafs are clones of clones of plants that were first engineered seven years ago in Monsanto's $150 million research facility, a long, low-slung brick building on the banks of the Missouri that would look like any other corporate complex were it not for the 26 greenhouses that crown its roof like shimmering crenellations of glass.

15   Dave Stark, a molecular biologist and co-director of Naturemark, Monsanto's potato subsidiary, escorted me through the clean rooms where potatoes are genetically engineered. Technicians sat at lab benches before petri dishes in which fingernail-size sections of potato stem had been placed in a nutrient mixture. To this the technicians added a solution of agrobacterium, a disease bacterium whose modus operandi is to break into a plant cell's nucleus and insert some of its own DNA. Essentially, scientists smuggle the Bt gene into the agrobacterium's payload, and then the bacterium splices it into the potato's DNA. The technicians also add a "marker" gene, a kind of universal product code that allows Monsanto to identify its plants after they leave the lab.

A few days later, once the slips of potato stem have put down roots, they're moved to the potato greenhouse up on the roof. Here, Glenda DeBrecht, a horticulturist, invited me to don latex gloves and help her transplant pinky-size plantlets from their petri dish to small pots. The whole operation is performed thousands of times, largely because there is so much uncertainty about the outcome. There's no way of telling where in the genome the new DNA will land, and if it winds up in the wrong place, the new gene won't be expressed (or it will be poorly expressed) or the plant may be a freak. I was struck by how the technology could at once be astoundingly sophisticated and yet also a shot in the genetic dark.

When I got home from St. Louis, I phoned Richard Lewontin, the Harvard geneticist, to ask him what he thought of the software metaphor. "From an intellectual-property standpoint, it's exactly right," he said. "But it's a bad one in terms of biology. It implies you feed a program into a machine and get predictable results. But the genome is very noisy. If my computer made as many mistakes as an organism does"—in interpreting its DNA, he meant—"I'd throw it out."

I asked him for a better metaphor. "An ecosystem," he offered. "You can always intervene and change something in it, but there's no way of knowing what all the downstream effects will be or how it might affect the environment. We have such a miserably poor understanding of how the organism develops from its DNA that I would be surprised if we don't get one rude shock after another."

Flowering

My own crop was thriving when I got home from St. Louis; the New Leafs were as big as bushes, crowned with slender flower stalks. Potato flowers are actually quite pretty, at least by vegetable standards—five-petaled pink stars with yellow centers that give off a faint rose perfume. One sultry afternoon I watched the bumblebees making their lazy rounds of my potato blossoms, thoughtlessly powdering their thighs with yellow pollen grains before lumbering off to appointments with other blossoms, other species.

20   Uncertainty is the theme that unifies much of the criticism leveled against biotech agriculture by scientists and environmentalists. By planting millions of acres of genetically altered plants, we have introduced something novel into the environment and the food chain, the consequences of which are not—and at this point, cannot be—completely understood. One of the uncertainties has to do with those grains of pollen bumblebees are carting off from my potatoes. That pollen contains Bt genes that may wind up in some other, related plant, possibly conferring a new evolutionary advantage on that species. "Gene flow," the scientific term for this phenomenon, occurs only between closely related species, and since the potato evolved in South America, the chances are slim that my Bt potato genes will escape into the wilds of Connecticut.

Yet what happens if and when Peruvian farmers plant Bt potatoes? Or when I plant a biotech crop that does have local relatives? A study reported in Nature last month found that plant traits introduced by genetic engineering were more likely to escape into the wild than the same traits introduced conventionally.

Andrew Kimbrell, director of the Center for Technology Assessment in Washington, told me he believes such escapes are inevitable. "Biological pollution will be the environmental nightmare of the 21st century," he said when I reached him by phone. "This is not like chemical pollution—an oil spill—that eventually disperses. Biological pollution is an entirely different model, more like a disease. Is Monsanto going to be held legally responsible when one of its transgenes creates a superweed or resistant insect?"

Kimbrell maintains that because our pollution laws were written before the advent of biotechnology, the new industry is being regulated under an ill-fitting regime designed for the chemical age. Congress has so far passed no environmental law dealing specifically with biotech. Monsanto, for its part, claims that it has thoroughly examined all the potential environmental and health risks of its biotech plants, and points out that three regulatory agencies—the U.S.D.A., the E.P.A. and the F.D.A.—have signed off on its products. Speaking of the New Leaf, Dave Stark told me, "This is the most intensively studied potato in history."

Significant uncertainties remain, however. Take the case of insect resistance to Bt, a potential form of "biological pollution" that could end the effectiveness of one of the safest insecticides we have—and cripple the organic farmers who depend on it. The theory, which is now accepted by most entomologists, is that Bt crops will add so much of the toxin to the environment that insects will develop resistance to it. Until now, resistance hasn't been a worry because the Bt sprays break down quickly in sunlight and organic farmers use them only sparingly. Resistance is essentially a form of co-evolution that seems to occur only when a given pest population is threatened with extinction; under that pressure, natural selection favors whatever chance mutations will allow the species to change and survive.

25   Working with the E.P.A., Monsanto has developed a "resistance-management plan" to postpone that eventuality. Under the plan, farmers who plant Bt crops must leave a certain portion of their land in non-Bt crops to create "refuges" for the targeted insects. The goal is to prevent the first Bt-resistant Colorado potato beetle from mating with a second resistant bug, unleashing a new race of superbeetles. The theory is that when a Bt-resistant bug does show up, it can be induced to mate with a susceptible bug from the refuge, thus diluting the new gene for resistance.

But a lot has to go right for Mr. Wrong to meet Miss Right. No one is sure how big the refuges need to be, where they should be situated or whether the farmers will cooperate (creating havens for a detested pest is counter-intuitive, after all), not to mention the bugs. In the case of potatoes, the E.P.A. has made the plan voluntary and lets the companies themselves implement it; there are no E.P.A. enforcement mechanisms. Which is why most of the organic farmers I spoke to dismissed the regulatory scheme as window dressing.

Monsanto executives offer two basic responses to criticism of their Bt crops. The first is that their voluntary resistance-management plans will work, though the company's definition of success will come as small consolation to an organic farmer: Monsanto scientists told me that if all goes well, resistance can be postponed for 30 years. (Some scientists believe it will come in three to five years.) The second response is more troubling. In St. Louis, I met with Jerry Hjelle, Monsanto's vice president for regulatory affairs. Hjelle told me that resistance should not unduly concern us since "there are a thousand other Bt's out there"—other insecticidal proteins. "We can handle this problem with new products," he said. "The critics don't know what we have in the pipeline."

And then Hjelle uttered two words that I thought had been expunged from the corporate vocabulary a long time ago: "Trust us."

"Trust" is a key to the success of biotechnology in the marketplace, and while I was in St. Louis, I asked Hjelle and several of his colleagues why they thought the Europeans were resisting biotech food.

30   Monsanto executives are quick to point out that mad cow disease has made Europeans extremely sensitive about the safety of their food chain and has undermined confidence in their regulators. "They don't have a trusted agency like the F.D.A. looking after the safety of their food supply," said Phil Angell, Monsanto's director of corporate communications. Over the summer, Angell was dispatched repeatedly to Europe to put out the P.R. fires; some at Monsanto worry these could spread to the United States.

I checked with the F.D.A. to find out exactly what had been done to insure the safety of this potato. I was mystified by the fact that the Bt toxin was not being treated as a "food additive" subject to labeling, even though the new protein is expressed in the potato itself. The label on a bag of biotech potatoes in the supermarket will tell a consumer all about the nutrients they contain, even the trace amounts of copper. Yet it is silent not only about the fact that those potatoes are the product of genetic engineering but also about their containing an insecticide.

At the F.D.A., I was referred to James Maryanski, who oversees biotech food at the agency. I began by asking him why the F.D.A. didn't consider Bt a food additive. Under F.D.A. law, any novel substance added to a food must—unless it is "generally regarded as safe" ("GRAS," in F.D.A. parlance)—be thoroughly tested and if it changes the product in any way, must be labeled.

"That's easy," Maryanski said. "Bt is a pesticide, so it's exempt" from F.D.A. regulation. That is, even though a Bt potato is plainly a food, for the purposes of Federal regulation it is not a food but a pesticide and therefore falls under the jurisdiction of the E.P.A.

Yet even in the case of those biotech crops over which the F.D.A. does have jurisdiction, I learned that F.D.A. regulation of biotech food has been largely voluntary since 1992, when Vice President Dan Quayle issued regulatory guidelines for the industry as part of the Bush Administration's campaign for "regulatory relief." Under the guidelines, new proteins engineered into foods are regarded as additives (unless they're pesticides), but as Maryanski explained, "the determination whether a new protein is GRAS can be made by the company." Companies with a new biotech food decide for themselves whether they need to consult with the F.D.A. by following a series of "decision trees" that pose yes or no questions like this one: "Does . . . the introduced protein raise any safety concern?"

35   Since my Bt potatoes were being regulated as a pesticide by the E.P.A. rather than as a food by the F.D.A., I wondered if the safety standards are the same. "Not exactly," Maryanski explained. The F.D.A. requires "a reasonable certainty of no harm" in a food additive, a standard most pesticides could not meet. After all, "pesticides are toxic to something," Maryanski pointed out, so the E.P.A. instead establishes human "tolerances" for each chemical and then subjects it to a risk-benefit analysis.

When I called the E.P.A. and asked if the agency had tested my Bt potatoes for safety as a human food, the answer was. . .not exactly. It seems the E.P.A. works from the assumption that if the original potato is safe and the Bt protein added to it is safe, then the whole New Leaf package is presumed to be safe. Some geneticists believe this reasoning is flawed, contending that the process of genetic engineering itself may cause subtle, as yet unrecognized changes in a food.

The original Superior potato is safe, obviously enough, so that left the Bt toxin, which was fed to mice, and they "did fine, had no side effects," I was told. I always feel better knowing that my food has been poison-tested by mice, though in this case there was a small catch: the mice weren't actually eating the potatoes, not even an extract from the potatoes, but rather straight Bt produced in a bacterial culture.

So are my New Leafs safe to eat? Probably, assuming that a New Leaf is nothing more than the sum of a safe potato and a safe pesticide, and further assuming that the E.P.A.'s idea of a safe pesticide is tantamount to a safe food. Yet I still had a question. Let us assume that my potatoes are a pesticide—a very safe pesticide. Every pesticide in my garden shed—including the Bt sprays—carries a lengthy warning label. The label on my bottle of Bt says, among other things, that I should avoid inhaling the spray or getting it in an open wound. So if my New Leaf potatoes contain an E.P.A.-registered pesticide, why don't they carry some such label?

Maryanski had the answer. At least for the purposes of labeling, my New Leafs have morphed yet again, back into a food: the Food, Drug and Cosmetic Act gives the F.D.A. sole jurisdiction over the labeling of plant foods, and the F.D.A. has ruled that biotech foods need be labeled only if they contain known allergens or have otherwise been "materially" changed.

But isn't turning a potato into a pesticide a material change?

40   It doesn't matter. The Food, Drug and Cosmetic Act specifically bars the F.D.A. from including any information about pesticides on its food labels.

I thought about Maryanski's candid and wondrous explanations the next time I met Phil Angell, who again cited the critical role of the F.D.A. in assuring Americans that biotech food is safe. But this time he went even further. "Monsanto should not have to vouchsafe the safety of biotech food," he said. "Our interest is in selling as much of it as possible. Assuring its safety is the F.D.A.'s job."

Meeting the Beetles

My Colorado potato beetle vigil came to an end the first week of July, shortly before I went to Idaho to visit potato growers. I spied a single mature beetle sitting on a New Leaf leaf; when I reached to pick it up, the beetle fell drunkenly to the ground. It had been sickened by the plant and would soon be dead. My New Leafs were working.

From where a typical American potato grower stands, the New Leaf looks very much like a godsend. That's because where the typical potato grower stands is in the middle of a bright green field that has been doused with so much pesticide that the leaves of his plants wear a dull white chemical bloom that troubles him as much as it does the rest of us. Out there, at least, the calculation is not complex: a product that promises to eliminate the need for even a single spraying of pesticide is, very simply, an economic and environmental boon.

No one can make a better case for a biotech crop than a potato farmer, which is why Monsanto was eager to introduce me to several large growers. Like many farmers today, the ones I met feel trapped by the chemical inputs required to extract the high yields they must achieve in order to pay for the chemical inputs they need. The economics are daunting: a potato farmer in south-central Idaho will spend roughly $1,965 an acre (mainly on chemicals, electricity, water and seed) to grow a crop that, in a good year, will earn him maybe $1,980. That's how much a french-fry processor will pay for the 20 tons of potatoes a single Idaho acre can yield. (The real money in agriculture—90 percent of the value added to the food we eat—is in selling inputs to farmers and then processing their crops.)

45   Danny Forsyth laid out the dismal economics of potato farming for me one sweltering morning at the coffee shop in downtown Jerome, Idaho. Forsyth, 60, is a slight blue-eyed man with a small gray ponytail; he farms 3,000 acres of potatoes, corn and wheat, and he spoke about agricultural chemicals like a man desperate to kick a bad habit. "None of us would use them if we had any choice," he said glumly.

Idaho farmers like Forsyth farm in vast circles defined by the rotation of a pivot irrigation system, typically 135 acres to a circle; I'd seen them from 30,000 feet flying in, a grid of verdant green coins pressed into a desert of scrubby brown. Pesticides and fertilizers are simply added to the irrigation system, which on Forsyth's farm draws most of its water from the nearby Snake River. Along with their water, Forsyth's potatoes may receive 10 applications of chemical fertilizer during the growing season. Just before the rows close—when the leaves of one row of plants meet those of the next—he begins spraying Bravo, a fungicide, to control late blight, one of the biggest threats to the potato crop. (Late blight, which caused the Irish potato famine, is an airborne fungus that turns stored potatoes into rotting mush.) Blight is such a serious problem that the E.P.A. currently allows farmers to spray powerful fungicides that haven't passed the usual approval process. Forsyth's potatoes will receive eight applications of fungicide.

Twice each summer, Forsyth hires a crop duster to spray for aphids. Aphids are harmless in themselves, but they transmit the leafroll virus, which in Russet Burbank potatoes causes net necrosis, a brown spotting that will cause a processor to reject a whole crop. It happened to Forsyth last year. "I lost 80,000 bags"—they're a hundred pounds each—"to net necrosis," he said. "Instead of getting $4.95 a bag, I had to take $2 a bag from the dehydrator, and I was lucky to get that." Net necrosis is a purely cosmetic defect; yet because big buyers like McDonald's believe (with good reason) that we don't like to see brown spots in our fries, farmers like Danny Forsyth must spray their fields with some of the most toxic chemicals in use, including an organophosphate called Monitor.

"Monitor is a deadly chemical," Forsyth said. "I won't go into a field for four or five days after it's been sprayed—even to fix a broken pivot." That is, he would sooner lose a whole circle to drought than expose himself or an employee to Monitor, which has been found to cause neurological damage.

It's not hard to see why a farmer like Forsyth, struggling against tight margins and heartsick over chemicals, would leap at a New Leaf—or, in his case, a New Leaf Plus, which is protected from leafroll virus as well as beetles. "The New Leaf means I can skip a couple of sprayings, including the Monitor," he said. "I save money, and I sleep better. It also happens to be a nice-looking spud." The New Leafs don't come cheaply, however. They cost between $20 and $30 extra per acre in "technology fees" to Monsanto.

50   Forsyth and I discussed organic agriculture, about which he had the usual things to say ("That's all fine on a small scale, but they don't have to feed the world"), as well as a few things I'd never heard from a conventional farmer: "I like to eat organic food, and in fact I raise a lot of it at the house. The vegetables we buy at the market we just wash and wash and wash. I'm not sure I should be saying this, but I always plant a small area of potatoes without any chemicals. By the end of the season, my field potatoes are fine to eat, but any potatoes I pulled today are probably still full of systemics. I don't eat them."

Forsyth's words came back to me a few hours later, during lunch at the home of another potato farmer. Steve Young is a progressive and prosperous potato farmer—he calls himself an agribusinessman. In addition to his 10,000 acres—the picture window in his family room gazes out on 85 circles, all computer-controlled—Young owns a share in a successful fertilizer distributorship. His wife prepared a lavish feast for us, and after Dave, their 18-year-old, said grace, adding a special prayer for me (the Youngs are devout Mormons), she passed around a big bowl of homemade potato salad. As I helped myself, my Monsanto escort asked what was in the salad, flashing me a smile that suggested she might already know. "It's a combination of New Leafs and some of our regular Russets," our hostess said proudly. "Dug this very morning."

After talking to farmers like Steve Young and Danny Forsyth, and walking fields made virtually sterile by a drenching season-long rain of chemicals, you could understand how Monsanto's New Leaf potato does indeed look like an environmental boon. Set against current practices, growing New Leafs represents a more sustainable way of potato farming. This advance must be weighed, of course, against everything we don't yet know about New Leafs—and a few things we do: like the problem of Bt resistance I had heard so much about back East. While I was in Idaho and Washington State, I asked potato farmers to show me their refuges. This proved to be a joke.

"I guess that's a refuge over there," one Washington farmer told me, pointing to a cornfield.

Monsanto's grower contract never mentions the word "refuge" and only requires that farmers plant no more than 80 percent of their fields in New Leaf. Basically, any field not planted in New Leaf is considered a refuge, even if that field has been sprayed to kill every bug in it. Farmers call such acreage a clean field; calling it a refuge is a stretch at best.

55   It probably shouldn't come as a big surprise that conventional farmers would have trouble embracing the notion of an insect refuge. To insist on real and substantial refuges is to ask them to start thinking of their fields in an entirely new way, less as a factory than as an ecosystem. In the factory, Bt is another in a long line of "silver bullets" that work for a while and then get replaced; in the ecosystem, all bugs are not necessarily bad, and the relationships between various species can be manipulated to achieve desired ends—like the long-term sustainability of Bt.

This is, of course, precisely the approach organic farmers have always taken to their fields, and after my lunch with the Youngs that afternoon, I paid a brief visit to an organic potato grower. Mike Heath is a rugged, laconic man in his mid-50's; like most of the organic farmers I've met, he looks as though he spends a lot more time out of doors than a conventional farmer, and he probably does: chemicals are, among other things, labor-saving devices. While we drove around his 500 acres in a battered old pickup, I asked him about biotechnology. He voiced many reservations—it was synthetic, there were too many unknowns—but his main objection to planting a biotech potato was simply that "it's not what my customers want."

That point was driven home last December when the Department of Agriculture proposed a new "organic standards" rule that, among other things, would have allowed biotech crops to carry an organic label. After receiving a flood of outraged cards and letters, the agency backed off. (As did Monsanto, which asked the U.S.D.A. to shelve the issue for three years.) Heath suggested that biotech may actually help organic farmers by driving worried consumers to the organic label.

I asked Heath about the New Leaf. He had no doubt resistance would come—"the bugs are always going to be smarter than we are"—and said it was unjust that Monsanto was profiting from the ruin of Bt, something he regarded as a "public good."

None of this particularly surprised me; what did was that Heath himself resorted to Bt sprays only once or twice in the last 10 years. I had assumed that organic farmers used Bt or other approved pesticides in much the same way conventional farmers use theirs, but as Heath showed me around his farm, I began to understand that organic farming was a lot more complicated than substituting good inputs for bad. Instead of buying many inputs at all, Heath relied on long and complex crop rotations to prevent a buildup of crop-specific pests—he has found, for example, that planting wheat after spuds "confuses" the potato beetles.

60   He also plants strips of flowering crops on the margins of his potato fields—peas or alfalfa, usually—to attract the beneficial insects that eat beetle larvae and aphids. If there aren't enough beneficials to do the job, he'll introduce ladybugs. Heath also grows eight varieties of potatoes, on the theory that biodiversity in a field, as in the wild, is the best defense against any imbalances in the system. A bad year with one variety will probably be offset by a good year with the others.

"I can eat any potato in this field right now," he said, digging Yukon Golds for me to take home. "Most farmers can't eat their spuds out of the field. But you don't want to start talking about safe food in Idaho."

Heath's were the antithesis of "clean" fields, and, frankly, their weedy margins and overall patchiness made them much less pretty to look at. Yet it was the very complexity of these fields—the sheer diversity of species, both in space and time—that made them productive year after year without many inputs. The system provided for most of its needs.

All told, Heath's annual inputs consisted of natural fertilizers (compost and fish powder), ladybugs and a copper spray (for blight)—a few hundred dollars an acre. Of course, before you can compare Heath's operation with a conventional farm, you've got to add in the extra labor (lots of smaller crops means more work; organic fields must also be cultivated for weeds) and time—the typical organic rotation calls for potatoes every fifth year, in contrast to every third on a conventional farm. I asked Heath about his yields. To my astonishment, he was digging between 300 and 400 bags per acre— just as many as Danny Forsyth and only slightly fewer than Steve Young. Heath was also getting almost twice the price for his spuds: $8 a bag from an organic processor who was shipping frozen french fries to Japan.

On the drive back to Boise, I thought about why Heath's farm remained the exception, both in Idaho and elsewhere. Here was a genuinely new paradigm that seemed to work. But while it's true that organic agriculture is gaining ground (I met a big grower in Washington who had just added several organic circles), few of the mainstream farmers I met considered organic a "realistic" alternative. For one thing, it's expensive to convert: organic certifiers require a field to go without chemicals for three years before it can be called organic. For another, the U.S.D.A., which sets the course of American agriculture, has long been hostile to organic methods.

65   But I suspect the real reasons run deeper, and have more to do with the fact that in a dozen ways a farm like Heath's simply doesn't conform to the requirements of a corporate food chain. Heath's type of agriculture doesn't leave much room for the Monsantos of this world: organic farmers buy remarkably little—some seed, a few tons of compost, maybe a few gallons of ladybugs. That's because the organic farmer's focus is on a process, rather than on products. Nor is that process readily systematized, reduced to, say, a prescribed regime of sprayings like the one Forsyth outlined for me— regimes that are often designed by companies selling chemicals.

Most of the intelligence and local knowledge needed to run Mike Heath's farm resides in the head of Mike Heath. Growing potatoes conventionally requires intelligence, too, but a large portion of it resides in laboratories in distant places like St. Louis, where it is employed in developing sophisticated chemical inputs. That sort of centralization of agriculture is unlikely to be reversed, if only because there's so much money in it; besides, it's much easier for the farmer to buy prepackaged solutions from big companies. "Whose Head Is the Farmer Using? Whose Head Is Using the Farmer?" goes the title of a Wendell Berry essay.

Organic farmers like Heath have also rejected what is perhaps the cornerstone of industrial agriculture: the economies of scale that only a monoculture can achieve. Monoculture—growing vast fields of the same crop year after year—is probably the

single most powerful simplification of modern agriculture. But monoculture is poorly
fitted to the way nature seems to work. Very simply, a field of identical plants will
be exquisitely vulnerable to insects, weeds and disease. Monoculture is at the root of
virtually every problem that bedevils the modern farmer, and that virtually every input
has been designed to solve.

To put the matter baldly, a farmer like Heath is working very hard to adjust his
fields and his crops to the nature of nature, while farmers like Forsyth are working
equally hard to adjust nature in their fields to the requirement of monoculture and,
beyond that, to the needs of the industrial food chain. I remember asking Heath what
he did about net necrosis, the bane of Forsyth's existence. "That's only really a problem
with Russet Burbanks," he said. "So I plant other kinds." Forsyth can't do that. He's part
of a food chain—at the far end of which stands a long, perfectly golden McDonald's
fry—that demands he grow Russet Burbanks and little else.

This is where biotechnology comes in, to the rescue of Forsyth's Russet Burbanks
and, if Monsanto is right, to the whole food chain of which they form a part.
Monoculture is in trouble—the pesticides that make it possible are rapidly being lost,
either to resistance or to heightened concerns about their danger. Biotechnology is
the new silver bullet that will save monoculture. But a new silver bullet is not a new
paradigm—rather, it's something that will allow the old paradigm to survive. That
paradigm will always construe the problem in Forsyth's fields as a Colorado potato beetle
problem, rather than as a problem of potato monoculture.

70   Like the silver bullets that preceded them—the modern hybrids, the pesticides and the
chemical fertilizers—the new biotech crops will probably, as advertised, increase yields.
But equally important, they will also speed the process by which agriculture is being
concentrated in a shrinking number of corporate hands. If that process has advanced more
slowly in farming than in other sectors of the economy, it is only because nature herself—
her complexity, diversity and sheer intractability in the face of our best efforts at control—
has acted as a check on it. But biotechnology promises to remedy this "problem," too.

Consider, for example, the seed, perhaps the ultimate "means of production" in
any agriculture. It is only in the last few decades that farmers have begun buying their
seed from big companies, and even today many farmers still save some seed every fall
to replant in the spring. Brown-bagging, as it is called, allows farmers to select strains
particularly well adapted to their needs; since these seeds are often traded, the practice
advances the state of the genetic art—indeed, has given us most of our crop plants.
Seeds by their very nature don't lend themselves to commodification: they produce more
of themselves ad infinitum (with the exception of certain modern hybrids), and for that
reason the genetics of most major crop plants have traditionally been regarded as a
common heritage. In the case of the potato, the genetics of most important varieties—
the Burbanks, the Superiors, the Atlantics—have always been in the public domain.
Before Monsanto released the New Leaf, there had never been a multinational seed
corporation in the potato-seed business—there was no money in it.

Biotechnology changes all that. By adding a new gene or two to a Russet Burbank or
Superior, Monsanto can now patent the improved variety. Legally, it has been possible to
patent a plant for many years, but biologically, these patents have been almost impossible
to enforce. Biotechnology partly solves that problem. A Monsanto agent can perform

a simple test in my garden and prove that my plants are the company's intellectual property. The contract farmers sign with Monsanto allows company representatives to perform such tests in their fields at will. According to Progressive Farmer, a trade journal, Monsanto is using informants and hiring Pinkertons to enforce its patent rights; it has already brought legal action against hundreds of farmers for patent infringement.

Soon the company may not have to go to the trouble. It is expected to acquire the patent to a powerful new biotechnology called the Terminator, which will, in effect, allow the company to enforce its patents biologically. Developed by the U.S.D.A. in partnership with Delta and Pine Land, a seed company in the process of being purchased by Monsanto, the Terminator is a complex of genes that, theoretically, can be spliced into any crop plant, where it will cause every seed produced by that plant to be sterile. Once the Terminator becomes the industry standard, control over the genetics of crop plants will complete its move from the farmer's field to the seed company—to which the farmer will have no choice but to return year after year. The Terminator will allow companies like Monsanto to privatize one of the last great commons in nature—the genetics of the crop plants that civilization has developed over the past 10,000 years.

75 At lunch on his farm in Idaho, I had asked Steve Young what he thought about all this, especially about the contract Monsanto made him sign. I wondered how the American farmer, the putative heir to a long tradition of agrarian independence, was adjusting to the idea of field men snooping around his farm, and patented seed he couldn't replant. Young said he had made his peace with corporate agriculture, and with biotechnology in particular: "It's here to stay. It's necessary if we're going to feed the world, and it's going to take us forward."

Then I asked him if he saw any downside to biotechnology, and he paused for what seemed a very long time. What he then said silenced the table. "There is a cost," he said. "It gives corporate America one more noose around my neck."

Harvest

A few weeks after I returned home from Idaho, I dug my New Leafs, harvesting a gorgeous-looking pile of white spuds, including some real lunkers. The plants had performed brilliantly, though so had all my other potatoes. The beetle problem never got serious, probably because the diversity of species in my (otherwise organic) garden had attracted enough beneficial insects to keep the beetles in check. By the time I harvested my crop, the question of eating the New Leafs was moot. Whatever I thought about the soundness of the process that had declared these potatoes safe didn't matter. Not just because I'd already had a few bites of New Leaf potato salad at the Youngs but also because Monsanto and the F.D.A. and the E.P.A. had long ago taken the decision of whether or not to eat a biotech potato out of my—out of all of our—hands. Chances are, I've eaten New Leafs already, at McDonald's or in a bag of Frito-Lay chips, though without a label there can be no way of knowing for sure.

So if I've probably eaten New Leafs already, why was it that I kept putting off eating mine? Maybe because it was August, and there were so many more-interesting fresh potatoes around—fingerlings with dense, luscious flesh, Yukon Golds that tasted as though they had been pre-buttered—that the idea of cooking with a bland commercial variety like the Superior seemed beside the point.

There was this, too: I had called Margaret Mellon at the Union of Concerned Scientists to ask her advice. Mellon is a molecular biologist and lawyer and a leading critic of biotech agriculture. She couldn't offer any hard scientific evidence that my New Leafs were unsafe, though she emphasized how little we know about the effects of Bt in the human diet. "That research simply hasn't been done," she said.

80   I pressed. Is there any reason I shouldn't eat these spuds?

"Let me turn that around. Why would you want to?"

It was a good question. So for a while I kept my New Leafs in a bag on the porch. Then I took the bag with me on vacation, thinking maybe I'd sample them there, but the bag came home untouched.

The bag sat on my porch till the other day, when I was invited to an end-of-summer potluck supper at the town beach. Perfect. I signed up to make a potato salad. I brought the bag into the kitchen and set a pot of water on the stove. But before it boiled I was stricken by this thought: I'd have to tell people at the picnic what they were eating. I'm sure (well, almost sure) the potatoes are safe, but if the idea of eating biotech food without knowing it bothered me, how could I possibly ask my neighbors to? So I'd tell them about the New Leafs—and then, no doubt, lug home a big bowl of untouched potato salad. For surely there would be other potato salads at the potluck and who, given the choice, was ever going to opt for the bowl with the biotech spuds?

So there they sit, a bag of biotech spuds on my porch. I'm sure they're absolutely fine. I pass the bag every day, thinking I really should try one, but I'm beginning to think that what I like best about these particular biotech potatoes—what makes them different—is that I have this choice. And until I know more, I choose not.

Questions for Reading Actively

1. What does it mean to say that a plant has been genetically "modified" or "engineered"? What are the New Leaf Superior potatoes able to do as a result of being genetically modified?

2. Of all the causes suggested in this article, which could be classified as contributory causes? Which are interactive causes? Can you identify any causal fallacies in the beliefs and observations of the people quoted and described in the article?

Questions for Thinking Critically

1. What are the potential risks to the environment of growing genetically engineered food? What are the potential risks to people in eating food that has been genetically modified?

2. Genetically modified food is designed to reduce the pesticides that farmers must use to protect their crops. What dangers does this heavy use of pesticides pose for the public?

3. How is organic farming able to avoid the heavy use of pesticides? Why isn't organic farming a larger share of the market?

Questions for Writing Thoughtfully

1. With reference to Figures 10.1, 10.2, and 10.3, create a diagram that illustrates the various causes that contribute to extreme longevity in the United States and elsewhere in the world. (This is a kind of summary—try this note-taking strategy to help you work through and understand a complex reading.)

2. Rank in order what your produce preferences would be (if you knew what you were eating by clear labeling!) and explain your reasoning.

   - Plants grown using traditional farming methods with repeated applications of pesticides
   - Genetically-modified plants
   - Organically grown plants

Writing Thoughtfully About Causal Relationships

Clearly, because of the complexity of determining cause and effect, writing a causal analysis requires special care. Causal analyses range all the way from rigorous scientific studies that can establish causes with some degree of certainty to theorizing about events in our personal lives. The causal analysis assignments you will encounter in college are likely to be of two types: those for which you conduct some kind of study to determine causality and then report your results, and those for which you research what others have said about the causes of an event and report their findings.

For the first type, you are likely to be given a format, such as for a lab report or an experimental design. It will be important for you to follow directions as you plan and conduct your study, and important for you to observe the conventions of the discipline in which you are writing as you prepare your report. Models are extremely helpful, so study them carefully if your professor provides them. If not, ask a librarian for guidance.

The second type, in which you report what others have said about the causes of an event, can be structured as an essay. Daniel Eggers's thoughtful analysis on page 375 is an example of such an essay. If you consult other sources of information, you must properly cite and document those sources (see Appendix).

Writing Project: Exploring Some Causes of a Recent Event

This chapter has included both readings and Thinking-Writing Activities that encourage you to think about causal relationships in your own life and in the environment. Be sure to reread what you wrote for those activities; you may be able to use some of the material when completing this project.

Write an essay in which you report and discuss some of the causes of a specific local or national event that occurred within the last three years. You might want to choose an event that had an environmental impact, or, depending on your interests or your instructor's assignment, you might want to write about something else that has affected the lives of many people (such as recent Supreme Court decisions or a current international crisis). Include material from two to four sources, being certain to cite and document those sources accurately.

After you have drafted your essay, revise it to the best of your ability. Follow your instructor's directions for topic choices, length, format, documentation style, and so on.

Begin by considering the key elements in the Thinking-Writing Model in Chapter 1 on pages 6–7.

The Writing Situation

Purpose   You have a variety of purposes here. You can satisfy your own curiosity about why an event occurred and explain the causes to others. You can improve your ability to think critically about causal relationships. You can hone your revision skills by working through the revision questions that follow.

Audience   You have a range of readers within your audience. *You* are an important audience, for in researching and analyzing causes, you can become a better thinker and possibly a more concerned citizen. Your classmates can be a valuable audience for review of a draft, reacting as intelligent readers who are not as knowledgeable as you about the causes of this event. Others interested in the event may find your essay enlightening. Finally, your instructor remains the audience who will judge how well you have planned, drafted, and revised. As a writing teacher, he or she cares about a clear focus, logical organization, specific details and examples, accurate documentation of sources, and correctness. Your classmates and your instructor will be interested in how you have applied this chapter's ideas.

Subject   You should reflect on the event or issue in terms of its causes and effects on the community. For example, if you decide to write about an event such as Hurricane Katrina that had a disproportionate effect on the poor, consider that all of us need to be concerned about both positive and negative environmental changes. Not only our future, but our children's and their children's futures depend on our careful stewardship of the earth. At the same time, there are competing economic and political pressures that can act against a strict conservationist view. By researching and analyzing a specific event, we can add to our own knowledge and that of our audience, thereby preparing all for responsible future action.

Writer   You will be using sources for this essay, but your paper should be written in your own voice and include your own observations and experiences. You will report and document the published writers' words and ideas and comment upon them as you think appropriate. If you find disagreement among your sources, don't discard any of them: the lack of agreement gives you a variety of views to report and consider.

The Writing Process

The following sections will guide you through the stages of generating, planning, drafting, and revising as you work on your essay. Try to be particularly conscious of both the critical thinking you find in your sources and the critical thinking you do as you examine them.

Generating Ideas

- Within your instructor's parameters for the assignment, begin by finding an event that interests you. If one comes to mind immediately, you can begin to research it. If not, begin by brainstorming a list of all the local and national events you can remember from the last few years.

- After you have selected an event, use your college library and the Internet. Consult Chapter 14 and your handbook about locating sources. Search for full texts of articles from reputable publications. Check titles for words like *causes, factors, results in, reasons,* or *underlie.*

- Locate or print the sources that you identify and read them, using the strategies for active and critical reading discussed in Chapter 2. First, check to see that they do indeed discuss the causes of the event, not just the event itself. Then see what causes they identify and how they label them (contributory, interactive, and so on). If they do not label them, try to do that yourself. Also, look for language that indicates the source's level of certainty about these causes ("has been definitely identified as a cause," or "may be partially responsible").

- Highlight sections of the source that you will include (if you own the source or have photocopied it). If you are required to do so, make note cards based on the marked sections.

- Think about how much information you have. Do you need more? If so, continue researching, reading, and marking until you have enough to answer the question "Why did this event take place?"

Defining a Focus   Write a thesis statement that will make clear to your audience that you are going to analyze *why* the event occurred or why the issue is critical. Here are two possible ways to frame this type of thesis.

The first is simply to report what your sources say and whether or not they are in agreement.

A second type of thesis requires you to take a position on the causal relationships involved. For example, you could write, "Having consulted four sources dealing with the causes of this event, I agree with three of them but reject a theory proposed in the fourth."

Organizing Ideas   If you made note cards, read through them two or three times. Then spread them all out on a table or desk so that you can see them all at once. Begin to group them into stacks: one to describe the event and one for each cause mentioned. Ideally, doing this will help you to integrate material from your different sources into various parts of your essay. You may decide not to use a few note cards; this often happens and indicates that you have done a good job of finding sufficient information. If you discover that you don't have enough information, you can do more research.

If you didn't make note cards, spread your marked sources out and try to plan how you will use information from each.

Review the principles for writing an essay of causal analysis on page 374 of this chapter. In addition, you will need to determine the order of your body paragraphs. For a causal chain, you will probably want chronological order. For contributory causes, you may want to use climactic (least to most important) order. For interactive causes, you may want to try different orders until you discover which will make the interaction of the causes easiest for your audience to understand.

Principles for Analyzing Causes

1. Be cautious. Causal relationships are difficult to prove. You may have to use wording such as *possible cause* or *may have affected*.

2. Name and describe the event or issue and people's reactions to it in your introduction.

3. In your thesis statement, indicate that you will be analyzing the causes of this event or issue or that you will be reporting what others have said about its causes.

4. Discuss each cause in a separate section (at least one body paragraph for each cause).

5. Amplify how or why each cause brought about the event or makes the issue important or controversial. Simply naming the cause is not enough.

6. Whenever possible, focus on immediate rather than remote causes. See page 349 to review these terms.

7. Use the labels in this chapter (contributory, causal chain, interactive, sufficient, and so on) to identify causal relationships if they are suitable for the style of your paper.

8. Represent accurately any sources that you use and document them honestly and correctly.

9. Avoid logical fallacies such as *post hoc ergo propter hoc*. See pages 351–355 to review these fallacies.

10. In your conclusion, name the causes and discuss the level of certainty for each of them. You may, of course, wish to do more than this in your conclusion.

Drafting   Draft one section from each stack of note cards. A highly specific description of the event could become the introduction. Quotations from eyewitnesses or participants in the event can help to interest your audience. The introduction can conclude with the tentative thesis statement you have written.

Begin each body paragraph with a topic sentence that names the possible or verifiable cause being discussed. Then provide the audience with as much information as necessary to help them understand how that cause actually could or did bring about the event.

Be sure to note the author, URL, and title and page of any information from any source you use. Do not trust yourself to add documentation as you revise your paper. It's easy to lose track and therefore to plagiarize accidentally.

In your conclusion, you can summarize the causes and discuss the level of certainty, or uncertainty, about them. If you found considerable disagreement among your sources, you can comment on that. If research is still ongoing about the causes, you can say so. You can, of course, do more than this in your conclusion, depending on your content.

On a separate page, draft a Works Cited list, using the format specified by your instructor.

Revising, Editing, and Proofreading   Use the step-by-step method in Chapter 6 on pages 169–171 to revise and polish your essay.

The following essay shows how two students responded to this assignment.

Student Writing

Daniel Eggers's Writing Process

In response to an assignment asking him to update and add to an argument put forth in one of the assigned readings, Daniel Eggers, a student at City College of San Francisco, chose to consider whether or not the dream proposed by Dr. Martin

Luther King Jr. had been achieved. When his research showed that it had not, he began to look for causes.

One of the most important decisions that I made in writing this essay was how to plan my approach. Since the validity of my arguments would be gauged through the supporting data, the majority of my effort went into locating appropriate sources, on which the framework of my essay would then be established. That is why I chose to produce a malleable thesis to begin with—so that I could later reshape it to allow the supporting sources to fit together nicely.

Although the majority of my effort went into locating sources, I still needed to produce a thesis and establish a framework to tie all of the sources together by creating supporting arguments for my thesis. My research suggested that there were many possible causes for racial inequality that were interrelated. Since the economy plays such an important role in American society, the first cause, to which all of the arguments could relate, was the involvement of African Americans in the economy. In the first paragraph I listed the origins of poverty for so many African Americans. These include the loss of low-skilled jobs, leading to deeper levels of poverty, which increases the development of ghettos and thus further isolates the African-American population. The causal chain could have gone in many different directions, but it was the material in my supporting sources that helped me to see the progression of causes.

Luckily, some of the sources I chose discussed recent events, such as the 2000 Presidential election and Hurricane Katrina, so writing comments about these sources came somewhat naturally. This is where I think the greatest advantage in writing this essay lay, with engaging a subject that ignited my curiosity, fascination, and interest.

Was It Only a Dream?

by Daniel Eggers

In the fall of 1963, on the one-hundredth anniversary of the Emancipation Proclamation, Martin Luther King Jr. stood before nearly two-hundred and fifty-thousand people in Washington, D.C., to present his famous speech, "I Have a Dream." This speech was a momentous event for the civil rights movement, and even today we are still able to hear King's voice saying the words: "I have a dream that one day this nation will rise up and live out the true meaning of its creed: 'We hold these truths to be self-evident; that all men are created equal'" (531). Through King's speech we are able to partake in his vision of a future where racial inequalities no longer exist. Many people, despite the giant steps taken by the civil rights movement, feel that racial equality will never be achieved. I, myself, having researched the events of the civil rights movement, as well as recent events concerning race, feel that, though one day we may see King's dream come true, we still have a long way to go before racial equality will become a reality.

Now, over forty years after King's speech, many African Americans are still an underprivileged group, especially because of their position in the economy. Michael Hughes and Carolyn J. Kroehler reported in *Sociology: the Core* that in 2001, "for every dollar in wealth owned by a white household, the average African American household owns [only] sixteen cents" (183–184). This considerable economic inequality places limitations on the lifestyles of many African Americans by barring their access to decent housing, good education, adequate healthcare, and nutritious foods. Though the problem of African American poverty is clearly shown through statistics, the origins of the problem are not easily defined. Hughes and Kroehler state that due to the vanishing number of low-skilled jobs in the last decade, "poor urban African Americans find themselves relegated to all-black neighborhoods where they are socially isolated from mainstream American life" (233). These all-black neighborhoods, or what some would refer to as ghettos, are symbols of economic inequality in America. King refers to these all-black neighborhoods in his speech as a source of discontent for the devotees of civil rights: "We will not be satisfied as long as the Negro's basic mobility is from a smaller ghetto to a larger one" (530).

Most who can recognize African American poverty as a sizable fracture in our society can reasonably argue that it must be granted the attention it deserves in order to be repaired. However, the problem of African American poverty seldom receives attention in mainstream America. The media largely ignores gradually developing social and economic problems and places the spotlight on immediate high-profile events. Such was the case with Hurricane Katrina, whose aftermath, given ample media coverage by all the major networks, revealed some desperate levels of African American poverty, as well as incompetence and neglect of city, state, and federal governments to provide relief to the victims. An article in the *Wall Street Journal* by Shelby Steele discusses the aftermath of Hurricane Katrina with its connection to racial issues. Steele states, in light of Katrina's aftermath, "Here was a poverty with an element of surrender in it that seemed to confirm the worst charges against [African Americans]: that [they] are inferior, that nothing really helps [them], that the modern world is beyond [their] reach" (20). The extensive media coverage given to Katrina, though horrifying and depressing, gave the American people an unforgettable example of extreme African American poverty stemming from the injustice of racial inequality.

Because the scales of economic distribution tilt disproportionately away from African Americans, the country has not obtained racial equality, but what steps can be taken to correct this inequity? Providing access to a good education seems to be one viable solution, and today there are numerous community colleges and vocational schools at which a person can acquire the necessary skills to earn a decent living. However, poverty looms like a cloud over many African Americans' prospects for acquiring an education. This is especially true because of the steady rise in the costs of tuition, housing, and transportation.

In addition to financial obstacles, some African American students are now facing a reversal of affirmative action when being considered for admission to higher education. One case occurred in Florida in 1999 with Governor Jeb Bush's abolishment of affirmative action in university admissions. K. Chandler reported in the *Westside Gazette* that due to this revocation of racial background being considered in the state universities' admissions process, the number of African American incoming freshmen to Florida universities dropped from a high of 17.6 percent in 1999 to 15.8 percent in 2004. A similar case is given by James T. Patterson in his book, *Brown v. Board of Education*, in which a 1996 Court of Appeals ruling required the University of Texas Law School to stop enforcing its affirmative action guidelines for admission. This decision resulted in African American enrollment there dropping from thirty-one to four in the following year (2006). Numbers like these illustrate the importance of affirmative action laws in maintaining equal opportunities in education for African Americans, and their reversal is a huge step backwards in the battle for racial equality.

There are many more holes in the system to explore when analyzing the racial inequalities within America. Consider the disenfranchisement of some African American voters during the 2000 presidential election in Florida. Bob Drogin reported in a *Los Angeles Times* article that in Gadsden County, a poor rural county of Florida predominantly occupied by African Americans, "one in eight voters' [. . .] ballots were rejected as invalid." This article contrasts the wealthier and predominantly white county of Leon, where only two in one thousand ballots were rejected, which causes questions to arise about the fairness of the voting process. Clearly these discrepancies resulted from issues concerning class and racial inequality. Drogan reported that Leon County could afford to purchase more effective ballot processing machines for each of its districts, which would notify a voter if a ballot was not filled out correctly, while in Gadsden County, because of the lack of funds to purchase ballot processing machines, the ballots had to be taken to a main election office to be processed.

These technicalities are significant because, had the 179,855 ballots—noted by Drogan—that went uncounted in Florida been processed, we could possibly have seen a different outcome in the election, especially since George W. Bush defeated Al Gore by a mere 537 votes. The disenfranchisement of some African Americans during this election is also significant because it shows just how far away they are from gaining the equal voting rights to which they are entitled under the Fifteenth Amendment.

What history shows is that as long as a minority group is fighting to gain equal rights, there will be a group who will do what it can to halt its progress. Such was the circumstance involving the *Brown v. Board of Education* case of 1954. James T. Patterson noted that in response to the ruling, which outlawed segregation in public schools, white supremacist groups mobilized to resist desegregation. For example, Bryant Bowles, who founded the National Association for the Advancement of White People, organized protests and ordered white students to boycott a high school in Delaware. It was not only through boycotts and protests that Bowles tried to slow the civil rights movement, but also through threats of violence toward people who supported that school's desegregation (74–75).

Today the methods of supremacists are less direct and more covert, using economic, political, and psychological oppression to maintain racial inequality. The previously mentioned examples of Katrina and the disenfranchisement of African Americans in the Florida 2000 election would suffice as modern methods of oppression, but every now and then a supremacist will slip in an ounce of truth concerning his/her opinion about race. Bob Herbert wrote a column in the *New York Times* that discusses some cruel words said on the radio by the former secretary of education in the Reagan cabinet, Bill Bennett: "I do know that it's true that if you wanted to reduce crime, you could—if that were your sole purpose—you could abort every black baby in this country, and your crime rate would go down." Bennett went on to say, "That would be an impossible, ridiculous, and morally reprehensible thing to do, but your crime rate would go down." Bennett's statement makes clear that racism, so prevalent throughout American history, still exists today.

African Americans have a problematic disposition within our culture. It's sort of a double standard where they are expected to fit in and be functioning cogs within the machine of American society, yet they are not truly accepted and are often treated as outsiders. W. E. B. DuBois describes this condition best in *The Souls of Black Folk* by saying, "One ever feels his two-ness,—an American, a Negro; two souls, two thoughts, two unreconciled strivings; two warring ideals in one dark body, whose dogged strength alone keeps it from being torn asunder" (38). But despite this disposition, along with the obstacles of oppression that were placed here as soon as the first enslaved Africans were brought to these shores, change will always be a constant, so the possibility for a future of justice and racial equality for African Americans may one day come to pass. However, the nation is still quite a distance from achieving this goal, but as long as we can recognize how far the civil rights movement has come and become aware of what must be done to push the movement forward, then the dream that millions of Americans from all racial groups share with Martin Luther King Jr. will never remain only a dream.

Works Cited

Chandler, K. "Black Enrollment in Florida Colleges Plummets as Percentage of Hispanics Surges." *Western Gazette*. 18 Aug. 2005. Web. 14 November 2005.

Drogin, Bob. "2 Florida Counties Show Election Day's Inequities." *Los Angeles Times*. Los Angeles Time, 12 Mar. 2001. Web. 16 Nov. 2005.

Du Bois, W. E. B. *The Souls of Black Folk*. Massachusetts: Bedford, 1997. Print.

Herbert, Bob. "Impossible, Ridiculous, Repugnant." *New York Times*. 6 Oct. 2005. Web. 16 Nov. 2005.

Hughes, Michael, and Carolyn J. Kroehler. *Sociology: The Core*. 7th ed. New York: McGraw, 2005. Print.

King, Jr., Martin Luther. "I Have a Dream." *Great Writing: A Reader for Writers*. 3rd ed. Ed. Harvey S. Wiener. New York: McGraw, 2002. 529–32. Print.

Patterson, James T. *Brown v. Board of Education: A Civil Rights Milestone and Its Troubled Legacy*. New York: Oxford UP, 2001. Print.

Steele, Shelby. "Witness: Blacks, Whites, and the Politics of Shame in America." *Wall Street Journal*. 26 Oct. 2005. Web. 14 Nov. 2005.

Alternative Writing Project: Utopias and Dystopias

In their article "How to Live to Be 100" (p. 38) authors Richard Corliss and Michael D. Lemonick suggest many lifestyle changes that, along with favorable genes, might help the average person to live to be at least 100 years old. In an essay, suggest ways in which a society made up of people who lived well past the century mark would be either a utopia or a dystopia. (Be sure to look up both words; your essay should define the term in your own words and within the context of your own argument.) How joyful would a society be, for example, if everyone practiced the physical discipline and appetite control some scientists suggest? What would be the benefits and challenges to a society where the population continually increased because people were living longer? Your essay could be quite imaginative, but even the most compelling science-fiction or fantasy is based on some semblance of probability—so be sure to complement your suppositions with some research.

CHAPTER 10   Summary

- Three kinds of causal relationships are:
  - *Causal chains*, situations in which one thing leads to another, which leads to another, and so on over a period of time;
  - *Contributory causes*, in which more than one cause works simultaneously to produce an effect; and
  - *Interactive causes*, that relate to each other through reciprocal influences that flow back and forth from one to the other.
- You can test a cause by determining its
  - *Necessary conditions*, factors that are required to bring about a certain result;
  - *Sufficient conditions*, factors that of themselves are always sufficient to bring about a certain result;
  - *Immediate causes*, things that happen just before an event that they cause; and

- *Remote causes*, things that happen just before an event, but further back in time, that they cause.
- Types of causal fallacies include
  - *Questionable cause*, presenting a causal relationship for which no real evidence exists;
  - *Misidentification of the cause*, uncertainty about what is the cause and what is the effect: ignoring or assuming a common cause;
  - *Post hoc ergo propter hoc*, assuming that, because two things occur closely together in time, one has caused the other; and
  - *Slippery slope*, asserting that one undesirable action will inevitably lead to a worse action, which will necessarily lead to a still worse one, and so forth, culminating in disaster.

PART 3

Thinking and Writing to Explore Issues and Take Positions

As you have become more confident in your thinking and writing abilities, you may also have developed more respect for the thinking and writing of others. You have probably observed how academic work and even democracy itself depend on understanding sources of beliefs and various perspectives. You have been learning how to evaluate information and how to express your own perspectives clearly.

Part One of this book helped you focus on yourself as a thinker and a writer, and you wrote from your experiences and observations. Part Two asked you to explore important thinking patterns and to incorporate some ideas from others into your writing. Here in Part Three assignments will lead to the presentation of your ideas and those from sources in well-reasoned writing.

The Writing Projects at the end of each chapter in Part Three ask you to integrate material from several sources into your written work. As you do so, you will learn effective, responsible ways of introducing, commenting on, and documenting ideas from others. You will consider the principles that underlie research and citation, and you will use appropriate formats for academic writing.

© Christopher Felver/Corbis

A successful businessman, Millard Fuller and his wife decided to give away nearly everything they owned and to devote their lives to serving the poor. In the early 1970s, the Fullers and their family moved to Africa, where they developed a system to involve people and communities in low-income areas in the building of their own homes. Realizing that this system could assist poor people in America, the Fullers moved back to the United States in 1976 and founded Habitat for Humanity, which "successfully removed the stigma of charity by substituting it with a sense of partnership." If you have participated in a community service project, what did you learn from the experience?

Writing to Analyze:
Believing and Knowing

"A belief is not merely an idea the mind possesses, it is an idea that possesses the mind."

—Robert Bolton

Writers write about what they believe, and their purposes often include explaining their beliefs and persuading others to adopt them. Yet what exactly are beliefs, and how are they constructed? When should they be kept, when should they be modified, and when should they be discarded? What are the differences between believing and knowing, and how do writers handle these differences? How do writers present beliefs they hold with varying degrees of certainty?

In this information age, we are flooded with data, stories, and pictures from television, radio, newspapers, magazines, books, and computers. Thus, critical thinkers and thoughtful writers face a continuing challenge to evaluate information they receive and to redefine their beliefs accordingly.

Chapter 3 examined the sources of beliefs, especially those related to personal life. This chapter continues that discussion by further examining the structure of beliefs, by presenting guidelines for evaluating beliefs, and by drawing distinctions between believing and knowing and between knowledge and truth. This chapter presents some of the ways in which beliefs take shape and some of the ways in which they are presented. The concepts of *interpretation, evaluation, conclusion, prediction, report, inference,* and *judgment* will provide a vocabulary to help you think about your beliefs and those of others.

The Writing Project at the end of the chapter asks you to analyze some influences on your beliefs about a social or an academic issue.

Ways of Forming Beliefs

Throughout our lives, we form beliefs about the world around us to explain why things happen as they do, to predict how things will happen, and to govern the choices we make. For example, consider the following statements and answer "Yes," "No," or "Not sure" to each.

1. Human beings need to eat in order to stay alive.
2. Smoking marijuana is a harmful activity.
3. Every human life is valuable.
4. Developing your mind is as important as taking care of your body.
5. People should care about other people, not just about themselves.

Your responses to these statements reflect certain beliefs you have, beliefs not all people share.

What exactly are beliefs? *Beliefs* represent an interpretation, evaluation, conclusion, or prediction that a person believes to be true. You may not have considered these different representations of beliefs before, but, if you think about it, you might see that most of your beliefs fit into one of these categories. Sometimes it might be important as you consider a belief to see which type it is. For example, *interpretation* suggests that other explanations are possible, and *prediction* makes clear that an event has not yet happened. Such understandings help when thinking critically about your beliefs.

The statement "I believe that the U.S. Constitution's guarantee of 'the right of the people to keep and bear arms' does not prohibit all governmental regulation of firearms" represents an interpretation of the Second Amendment. To say, "I believe that watching daytime talk shows is unhealthy because they focus almost exclusively on the seamy side of human life" expresses an *evaluation* of daytime talk shows. The statement "I believe that one of the main reasons two out of three people in the world go to bed hungry each night is that industrially advanced nations have not done a satisfactory job of sharing their resources" expresses a *conclusion* about the problem of world hunger. To say, "I believe that if drastic environmental measures are not undertaken to slow the global warming trend, the polar icecaps will melt and the earth will be flooded" is to make a *prediction* about events that will occur in the future.

Besides expressing an interpretation, evaluation, conclusion, or prediction about the world, a belief also expresses an *endorsement* of its accuracy—an indication that the belief is held to be true by the writer or speaker. This endorsement is a necessary dimension of a belief. For example, the statement "Astrological predictions are meaningless because there is no persuasive evidence that the position of the planets has any effect on human affairs" expresses a belief even though it doesn't specifically include the words *I believe*.

In addition, it is necessary to recognize that beliefs are not static—at least not if we apply a critical approach. We continually form and re-form our beliefs throughout much of our lives. This process often follows the following sequence:

1. We *form* beliefs in order to explain what is taking place. (These initial beliefs are often based on our past experiences.)

2. We *test* these beliefs by acting on the basis of them.

3. We *revise* (or "re-form") these beliefs if our actions do not achieve our goals.

4. We *retest* these revised beliefs by again using them as a basis for action.

As we actively participate in this ongoing process of forming and re-forming beliefs, we are using our critical thinking abilities to identify and critically examine our beliefs by, in effect, asking the following questions:

- How effectively do these beliefs explain what is taking place?
- To what extent are the beliefs consistent with other beliefs about the world?
- How effectively do the beliefs help us to predict what will happen in the future?
- To what extent are these beliefs supported by sound reasons and compelling evidence derived from reliable sources?

This process of critical exploration enables us to develop more understanding of various situations and to exert more control over them.

Thinking-Writing Activity

IDENTIFYING BELIEFS

Describe beliefs you have that fall in each of these categories (interpretation, evaluation, conclusion, prediction) and then explain the reason(s) you have for endorsing the beliefs.

1. **Interpretation** (an explanation or analysis of the meaning or significance of something)
   My interpretation is that . . .
   Supporting reason(s):

2. **Evaluation** (a judgment of the value or quality of something, based on certain standards)
   My evaluation is that . . .
   Supporting reason(s):

3. **Conclusion** (a decision made or an opinion formed after consideration of the relevant facts or evidence)
   My conclusion is that . . .
   Supporting reason(s):

4. **Prediction** (a statement about what will happen in the future)
   My prediction is that . . .
   Supporting reason(s):

Beliefs Based on Personal Experience

The introductory discussion of beliefs in Chapter 3 identified four sources of beliefs: people of authority, recorded references, observed evidence, and personal experience. The last two involve direct experience. Yet how we interpret and understand direct experience—what conclusions we draw from what we perceive—depends to some extent on what we already believe. In offering evidence to support their beliefs, people generally choose those perceptions and experiences that fit with their previous beliefs; contradictory experiences may be ignored or downplayed.

In the following pair of readings, two writers offer differing beliefs about the situation of the homeless in the United States, based on their perceptions of direct experience. B.C. chooses to live as a homeless person in "Homeless in Prescott, Arizona" while Katrina evacuee Donna Fenton does all she can to try to escape from her homelessness, as related in Nicholas Confessore's article "For Katrina Evacuee, Getting Help Is a Full-Time Job."

Before you begin to read, write down two or three of your beliefs about homelessness and the homeless. After you have read both pieces, write a few sentences about how your beliefs were affected by your reading these articles. If possible, share your statements with your classmates.

"Homeless in Prescott, Arizona"

by B.C.

This narrative was one of thousands of stories submitted to National Public Radio's National Story Project. In 1999, novelist Paul Auster asked listeners to NPR's *Weekend All Things Considered* program to submit brief stories about some incident or anecdote "that revealed the mysterious and unknowable forces at work in our lives. . . . In other words, true stories that sounded like fiction." For more than a year, Auster read selected stories on the radio program. In 2001, he collected and published 179 of the stories in *I Thought My Father Was God: And Other True Tales from NPR's National Story Project.*

Last spring I made a major life change, and I wasn't suffering from a midlife crisis. At fifty-seven I'm way beyond that. I decided I could not wait eight more years to retire, and I could not be a legal secretary for eight more years. I quit my job; sold my house, furnishings, and car; gave my cat to my neighbor; and moved to Prescott, Arizona, a community of thirty thousand, nestled in the Bradshaw Mountains with a fine library, community college, and a beautiful town square. I invested the proceeds from selling everything and I now receive $315 a month in interest income. That is what I live off of.

I am anonymous. I am not on any government programs. I do not receive any kind of welfare, not even food stamps. I do not eat at the Salvation Army. I do not take handouts. I am not dependent on anyone.

Source: "Homeless in Prescott, Arizona" by B. C. from *I thought my father was God and other true tales from NPR's National Story*, by Paul Auster, Nelly Reifler.

My base is downtown Prescott, where everything I need is within a radius of a mile and a half—easy walking. To go farther afield, I take a bus that makes a circuit of the city each hour and costs three dollars for a day pass. I have a post-office box—cost, forty dollars a year. The library is connected to the Internet, and I have an e-mail address. My storage space costs twenty-seven dollars a month, and I have access to it twenty-four hours a day. I store my clothes, cosmetic and hygiene supplies, a few kitchen items, and paperwork there. I rent a secluded corner of a backyard a block from my storage area for twenty-five dollars a month. This is my bedroom, complete with arctic tent, sleeping bag, mattress, and lantern. I wear a sturdy pack with a water bottle, flashlight, and Walkman, toiletries and rain gear.

Yavapai College has an Olympic-size pool and a women's locker room. I take college classes and have access to these facilities; cost, thirty-five dollars a month. I go there every morning to perform my "toilet" and shower. I go to the Laundromat with a small load of clothes whenever I need to; cost, fifteen dollars a month. Looking presentable is the most important aspect of my new lifestyle. When I go to the library, no one can guess I'm homeless. The library is my living room. I sit in a comfortable chair and read. I listen to beautiful music through the stereo system. I communicate with my daughter via e-mail and type letters on the word processor. I stay dry when it's wet outside. Unfortunately, the library does not have a television, but I've found a student lounge at the college that does. Most of the time I can watch *The News Hour, Masterpiece Theater*, and *Mystery*. To further satisfy my cultural needs, I attend dress rehearsals at the local amateur theater company, free of charge.

5   Eating inexpensively and nutritiously is my biggest challenge. My budget allows me to spend two hundred dollars a month for food. I have a Coleman burner and an old-fashioned percolator. I go to my storage space every morning and make coffee, pour it into my thermos, load my backpack, go to the park, and find a sunny spot to enjoy my coffee and listen to *Morning Edition* on my Walkman. The park is my backyard. It's a beautiful place to hang out when the weather is clement. I can lie on the grass and read and nap. The mature trees provide welcome shade when it's warm.

My new lifestyle has been comfortable and enjoyable so far because the weather in Prescott during the spring, summer, and fall has been delightful, though it did snow Easter weekend. But I was prepared. I have a parka, boots, and gloves, all warm and waterproof.

Back to eating. The Jack in the Box has four items that cost one dollar—Breakfast Jack, Jumbo Jack, a chicken sandwich, and two beef tacos. After I enjoy my coffee in the park, I have a Breakfast Jack. There's a nutrition program at the adult center where I can eat a hearty lunch for two dollars. For dinner, back to the Jack in the Box. I buy fresh fruit and veggies at Albertson's. Once in a while I go to the Pizza Hut—all you can eat for $4.49. When I return to my storage space in the evening, I make popcorn on my Coleman burner. I only drink water and coffee; other beverages are too expensive.

I've discovered another way to have a different eating experience and to combine it with a cultural evening. There's an art gallery downtown, and the openings of the new shows are announced in the newspaper. Two weeks ago I put on my dress and panty hose, went to the opening, enjoyed eating the snacks, and admired the paintings.

I've let my hair grow long, and I tie it back in a ponytail like I did in grade school. I no longer color it. I like the gray. I do not shave my legs or underarms and do not polish my fingernails [or] wear mascara, foundation, blush, or lipstick. The natural look costs nothing.

10   I love going to college. This fall, I'm taking ceramics, chorale, and cultural anthropology—for enrichment, not for credit. I love reading all the books I want to but never had enough time for. I also have time to do absolutely nothing.

Of course there are negatives. I miss my friends from back home. Claudette, who works at the library, befriended me. She was a feature writer for the local newspaper and is adept at getting information from people. Eventually, I told her who I was and how I live. She never pressures me to live differently, and I know she's there for me if I need her.

I also miss Simon my cat. I keep hoping that a cat will come my way, particularly before winter sets in. It would be nice to sleep and snuggle with a furry body.

I hope I can survive the winter. I've been told that Prescott can have lots of snow and long stretches of freezing temperatures. I don't know what I'll do if I get sick. I'm generally an optimist, but I do worry. Pray for me.

"For Katrina Evacuee, Getting Help Is a Full-Time Job"

by Nicholas Confessore

The following article was published in the *New York Times* in March 2006, almost six months after Hurricane Katrina devastated the Gulf Coast. Before joining the Metropolitan Desk as a reporter at the *Times*, Nick Confessore was a senior correspondent for *American Prospect* and an editor of the *Washington Monthly*.

Donna Fenton no longer consults the scrap of paper in her pocketbook when she needs the phone number for the Red Cross, or New York City's welfare office, or the Federal Emergency Management Agency.

"I know them all by heart," said Ms. Fenton, 37, who left Biloxi, MS, after Hurricane Katrina destroyed her home there. "I call them every day. That's my job."

She starts in the morning, calling from the rooms she and her family share at a Ramada hotel near La Guardia Airport, or from the hotel's basement conference room. She knows what numbers will lead to someone helpful and the ones that will plunge her into a thicket of indifference or incomprehension. She keeps going for hours, sometimes until 3 o'clock the next morning.

The days and nights can blur together, a fog of dial tones, beige wallpaper and overly cheerful automated voices. "Everything they asked for, I sent in," she said. "I sent it in the second time, and then I sent it in a third time."

5   What she wants, she says, is enough money to move into a new apartment in New York so she can begin anew the life that Katrina ripped apart. "It wasn't like we had any luxuries," she said. "But we were scraping by."

About 20 families left homeless by Katrina still live at the Ramada, and, all things considered, Ms. Fenton is among the more fortunate evacuees. Because she went to high school in New York, the city is not wholly foreign to her. She has found a job that pays about as well as the one she held managing two restaurants in Biloxi. Her husband, Matt, has found part-time work at an auto body shop.

Ms. Fenton is polite, organized and determined.

But more than five months after arriving in Queens with a change of clothes and a tapped-out bank account, moving on has been much harder than she thought it would be. Many obstacles she has encountered are familiar to other Katrina evacuees living in New York as they sort out their next moves and deadlines approach, after which the federal government will no longer pay for hotel rooms.

Some obstacles are more rare.

10 Ms. Fenton, who has lupus, collapsed at a Manhattan welcome center last September after filling out paperwork from half a dozen agencies and charities. Doctors found that days of irregular sleep and roadside food had worsened her condition, producing an enlarged heart and an irregular heartbeat.

"In the South," she said, "we eat a lot of vegetables. That's impossible to do in a hotel or on the road." She spent four days in the hospital.

A Red Cross worker placed Ms. Fenton, her husband, and four of her five children—Akreem, 16; Ashley, 14; LaTanya, 10; and Danielle, 9—at the Ramada, and gave her a debit card with a $1,565 limit. The children were placed in public school, but debit-card money quickly dwindled. "That doesn't go far for six people," she said.

So Ms. Fenton began working the phones. A $2,358 check for rent assistance from FEMA arrived in October. But a second check, for what the agency calls "immediate needs," never materialized. She also got no response from the Small Business Administration to a loan application she filed almost as soon as she arrived in the city. The FEMA check was soon used up—on clothes, food, and transportation, and for her family, as well as for her oldest son, William, 21, and his fiancée, Amanda McGee, who also live at the hotel.

Twice, Ms. Fenton said, she found apartments, but was afraid to sign leases because she was not sure FEMA's promised rental assistance would arrive.

15 Filling paperwork was a constant headache. Faxes to and from agencies seemed to disappear regularly. "It was like Russian roulette," she said.

FEMA granted her an extension to stay at the hotel, she said, but then forgot to issue an authorization code for the second of the two rooms her family occupied. That meant more time pleading on the phone.

A FEMA spokeswoman, Nicole Andrews, acknowledged last week that the process could be "pretty tough for anyone who has been traumatized like these people have."

There were bright spots. A recreation center in Brooklyn offered free memberships to the Ramada evacuees. At Christmas, a nearby church gave $100 gift cards to the families.

But Ms. Fenton's health was a continuing problem. In October, a hotel maid found her unconscious in her room. More hospital stays followed, six in all, as she battled to control her lupus. Then, in February, her appendix burst, resulting in a two-week hospital stay.

20 Her son William was told by doctors that he had post-traumatic stress syndrome stemming from the hurricane. More recently, her daughter LaTanya disappeared from the hotel and was found wandering the streets nearby. "She was saying that she didn't want to go back to the hotel," Ms. Fenton said.

Two weeks ago, an unlicensed driver slammed into their car, destroying the family's main means of transportation. Her husband has borrowed cars from colleagues at work to take the younger children to school.

A new apartment, however, has remained elusive, and with it a normal life. With all the time she spends on the phone, she said, she cannot start the job waiting for her at a Brooklyn check-cashing business.

In January, a real estate agent helped line up a new apartment in Bushwick, Brooklyn. But without another rental assistance check, Ms. Fenton was afraid to move, despite the apartment building owner's encouragement.

"I know I can't live there for free," she said. "I don't want to get us there and then stick this lady with not being able to pay the rent." She recently learned that the second rent check had been lost in the mail, and a replacement could not be issued until it was found.

25   "From what I'm hearing, it's a long process," said Ms. Fenton, still hopeful of moving to the Bushwick apartment.

She pulled on her coat. She needed to go to Manhattan to pick out furniture for the possible new apartment from a Salvation Army warehouse. It was her second trip there: the first time, the table and chairs she had ordered arrived with the legs broken.

"That's the most agitating part," she said. "Everything is done over and over. All of this has been done before."

Questions for Reading Actively

1. Identify passages in "Homeless in Prescott, Arizona" and "For Katrina Evacuee, Getting Help Is a Full-Time Job" that express interpretations, evaluations, conclusions, and predictions.

2. Compare and contrast B.C.'s beliefs about negotiating homelessness with the beliefs of Donna Fenton. What does each woman believe about who is responsible for helping the homeless? What accounts for the difference in their perceptions?

Questions for Thinking Critically

1. Does the term *homeless* accurately describe the way B.C. has chosen to live? Which woman—Donna Fenton or B.C.—seems to most closely reflect stereotypes about homelessness in America?

2. How did your beliefs affect your response to each reading?

Questions for Writing Thoughtfully

1. What differences can you find between the *New York Times'* expository presentation and B.C.'s narrative approach? What do you see as the strengths of each approach? To what extent are the purposes of each text similar, even though their writing situations are very different?

2. Are any of your beliefs about homelessness based on direct experience? If so, whose experiences are closer to yours: B.C.'s or Donna Fenton's? Write a first-person narrative like "Homeless in Prescott, Arizona" that describes your experience for an audience otherwise unfamiliar with homelessness.

Beliefs Based on Indirect Experience

No matter how much we have experienced in our lives, the fact is, of course, that no one person's direct experiences are enough to establish an adequate set of accurate beliefs. We all depend on the experience of others to provide us with beliefs and also to serve as foundations for those beliefs. For example, does Antarctica exist? How do we know? Have we ever been there and seen it with our own eyes? Probably not; nevertheless, we believe in the existence of Antarctica and its ice and penguins. Of all the beliefs each of us has, few are actually based on our direct personal experience. Instead, other people have in some way or form communicated to us virtually all these beliefs and the evidence for them. As we reach beyond our personal experiences to form and revise our beliefs, we find that information is provided by two sources: people of authority and recorded references.

As we have seen in the essays discussing homelessness by B.C. and about Donna Fenton, the beliefs of others cannot be accepted without question. Each of us views the world through individual lenses that shape and influence the way we select and present information. Comparing different sources helps to make these lenses explicit and highlights the different interests and purposes involved. In fact, examining sources may lead us to recognize that there are a variety of competing viewpoints, some fairly similar, some quite contradictory. In critically reviewing the beliefs of others, it is essential for us to pursue the same goals of accuracy and completeness that we set when examining beliefs based on personal experience. As a result, we focus on the reasons or evidence that support the information others are presenting.

Thinking-Writing Activity

THE ORIGIN OF A BELIEF

Select one of the beliefs that you identified in the Thinking-Writing Activity at the beginning of this chapter. What indirect sources helped shape it: your family, friends, teachers, religious leaders, television, the Internet? What direct personal experiences or observations have had an impact on it? Note specifically how some of these influences shaped your belief.

Evaluating Sources and Information

When we depend on information that others provide, we need to ask key questions. The most crucial part of determining the reliability of a source's information is determining the reliability of the source itself.

How Reliable Is the Source?

We know that some sources—such as advertising—can be very unreliable whereas other sources, such as *Consumer Reports* magazine (which does not accept advertising), are generally considered reliable. Sometimes, however, the reliability of a source of nformation is not immediately clear. In those cases, we have to use a variety of standards or criteria to evaluate a source's reliability, whether the source is written or audible.

Special care should be taken when evaluating information from websites. See Checklist for Evaluating the Quality of Internet Resources in Chapter 14 on pages 547–548.

What Are the Source's Purposes and Interests?

Evaluating information means thinking critically about the perceiving lenses through which the source of the information views the situation. Is this source presenting an argument or giving information? Are you looking at a report, an inference, or a judgment (see pages 412–419)? In other words, what is the rhetorical purpose of the piece? How is the purpose reflected in the selection of details and in wording and tone?

You also need to think about the piece's audience. Who is the intended audience? Is it friendly, neutral, or hostile? Is it informed or new to the subject? Writers or speakers can focus on specific audiences without being dishonorable, but sometimes they can emphasize one point of view or tap emotions in manipulative ways. Can you detect any slanting, or does this source's material seem balanced?

How Knowledgeable or Experienced Is the Source?

When seeking information from indirect sources, we want to locate people of authority or recorded references that can offer a special understanding of a subject. When a car begins making strange noises, we search for someone who knows cars. When we want to learn more about a social issue such as homelessness, we turn to articles and books written by people who have studied the problem.

In seeking information from sources, it is important to distinguish between nonexpert sources and expert sources who have training, education, and experience in a particular area. Also, any expert source's credentials should be up-to-date. A book about careers in the computer industry published twenty years ago is not likely to be reliable.

Sports and entertainment figures often endorse products in television commercials, but their testimony is not very convincing if those products have nothing to do with sports or entertainment (and if these "experts" have been paid large sums of money and told exactly what to say). Finally, we should not accept expert opinion without question or critical examination, even if the experts meet all of our criteria.

Was the Source Able to Make Accurate Observations?

You may have heard of law-enforcement training courses where actors stage simulated crimes before an unsuspecting class. Students in the class are then quickly informed that the situation has been staged to test their powers of observation and asked to record what happened in as much detail as they can remember. Invariably many witnesses are quite mistaken about much of what they remember while others can recall many fine details exactly. The same is true in any kind of eyewitness account: some people have quite sharp memories while others may "remember" many imagined details. In addition, a person's vantage point as a witness may color the reliability of the testimony. The amount of light, obstructions to vision, and other matters can make his or her perceptions less than wholly reliable.

The reliability of an indirect source also depends on the personal viewpoints and beliefs the source brings to a situation. These feelings, expectations, and interests often influence what a witness perceives without his or her full awareness of the process. For example, a group that sponsored an antiwar rally at a political convention might claim a crowd of more than five thousand while politicians issue a report estimating rally attendance at about two thousand. We have seen that two different writers can draw very different conclusions about what it means to be homeless. What further questions could be asked, and how might additional sources be located to evaluate the reliability of such differing sources?

How Reputable Is the Source?

When evaluating the reliability of sources, it is useful to consider how accurate and reliable their information has been in the past. If someone has consistently given sound information over a period of time, we gradually develop confidence in the accuracy of that person's reports. Police officers and news media reporters must continually evaluate the reliability of information sources. Of course, this works the other way as well. When people consistently give inaccurate or incomplete information, others lose confidence in their reliability. Nevertheless, few people provide information that is either completely reliable or completely unreliable. You probably realize that your own reliability tends to vary, depending on the situation, the type of information you are providing, and the person to whom you are giving it. Thus, in trying to evaluate information offered by others, you have to explore the following factors before arriving at a provisional conclusion, which you may have to revise later in light of additional information.

How Valuable Is Information from This Source?

Of course, you also need to assess the credibility of the information itself by asking these questions: What are the main ideas being presented? What evidence is provided? Does the information seem accurate? Is it up-to-date? Does anything seem false? Does anything seem to have been left out?

Thinking-Writing Activity

EVALUATING A SOURCE OF A BELIEF

Select one of the beliefs that you discussed in the Thinking-Writing Activity on page 388 that is based on sources such as people of authority or recorded references. Now, based on the criteria just discussed, evaluate the reliability of one source of your belief.

@ THINKING CRITICALLY ABOUT NEW MEDIA

Internet Hoaxes, Scams, and Urban Legends

As we have seen in this chapter, *fallacies* are unsound arguments that are often persuasive and appear to be logical because they usually appeal to our emotions and prejudices, and because they often support conclusions that we want to believe are accurate. One expression of fallacious thinking in new media can be found in the existence of *Internet Hoaxes:* messages, offers, solicitations, advice, or threats that are often seductive in their appeal but false and sometimes dangerous. The hoaxes come in all shapes and sizes: "helping" someone from an African country transfer twenty million dollars; receiving birthday greetings from a secret admirer; verifying your credit card information with an alleged bank; passing along a message to ten friends with the hope of receiving special blessings or cash; helping to provide medical care for an ill or injured child; and many, many more. Often these hoaxes are harmless, resulting in nothing more than us wasting time and bandwidth by forwarding phony chain letters. Other times, however, we risk donating money to scam artists, divulging credit or bank information to financial predators, or introducing destructive viruses into our computer by opening attached files from Internet anarchists.

Most virus warnings are hoaxes and can be spotted by the following signs:

- They falsely claim to describe an extremely dangerous virus.
- They use pseudo-technical language to make impressive sounding claims.
- They falsely claim that the report was issued or confirmed by a well-known company.
- They ask you to forward it to all your friends and colleagues.

You should avoid passing on warnings of this kind, as the continued re-forwarding of these hoaxes wastes time and email bandwidth. Sometimes you may receive hoaxes with a file attached that may be infected with a virus. A good principle is to delete all hoaxes and *never* open an attached file from a source that you don't know personally.

There are a number of sites devoted to uncovering these Internet hoaxes, including:

www.snopes.com (Urban Legends Reference Pages)

www.hoaxbusters.org

urbanlegends.about.com

Hoaxbusters.com offers a guide to help detect whether an email is a hoax or the real deal. Included below are their "Top Five Signs That an E-mail Is a Hoax." After you read through their warning signs, review the emails included above and see if the guidelines help you identify them as hoaxes. Then conduct some independent research of your own by locating three possible internet hoaxes and then analyzing their authenticity by applying the "Top Five Signs."

Top Five Signs That an E-mail Is a Hoax

The next time that you receive an alarming e-mail calling you to action, look for one or more of these five telltale characteristics before even thinking about sending it along to anybody else.

Urgent   The e-mail will have a great sense of urgency! You'll usually see a lot of exclamation points and capitalization. The subject line will typically be something like:

URGENT!!!!!!

WARNING!!!!!!

IMPORTANT!!!!!!

VIRUS ALERT!!!!!!

THIS IS NOT A JOKE!!!!!!

Tell All Your Friends   There will always be a request that you share this "important information" by forwarding the message to everybody in your e-mail address book or to as many people as you possibly can. This is a surefire sign that the message is a hoax.

This Isn't a Hoax   The body of the e-mail may contain some form of corroboration, such as a pseudoquote from an executive of a major corporation or government official. The message may include a sincere-sounding premise, such as this, for example: *My neighbor, who works for Microsoft, just received this warning so I know it's true. He asked me to pass this along to as many people as I can.*

Sometimes the message will contain a link to Snopes to further confuse people. The references to Snopes are just red herrings, though, meant only to give a sense of

(Continues)

THINKING CRITICALLY ABOUT NEW MEDIA (CONTINUED)

legitimacy to the hoax. The author knows that lots of folks will believe it because they see it in print and won't bother to really check it for themselves. Anyone actually bothering to check the story with Snopes would, of course, discover that it was not true. Hoax writers count on folks being too lazy to verify those stories before they hit the forward button.

It's all a bunch of baloney. Don't believe it for a second.

Watch for e-mails containing a subtle form of self-corroboration. Statements such as "This is serious!" or "This is not a hoax!" can be deceiving. Just because somebody says it's not a hoax doesn't make it so.

Dire Consequences   The e-mail text will predict dire consequences if you don't act immediately. You are led to believe that a missing child will never be found unless the e-mail is forwarded immediately. It may infer that someone won't die happy unless they receive a bazillion business cards. Or it may state that a virus will destroy your hard drive and cause green fuzzy things to grow in your refrigerator.

History   Look for a lot of >>>> marks in the left margin. These marks indicate that people suckered by the hoax have forwarded the message countless times before it has reached you.

In her book, *Cyberliteracy*, Laura Gurak identified three things that are common to all hoax and urban legend e-mail chain letters. They are the **hook**, the **threat**, and the **request**. To hook you in, a hoax will play on your sympathy, your greed, or your fears. It will threaten you with bad luck, play on your guilt, or label you a fool for not participating. And, of course, it will request that you forward the e-mail to all of your friends and family.

The hook catches your interest to make you read the whole e-mail. The hook may be a sad story about a missing or sick child, or about the latest computer virus. Once you're hooked, the threat warns you about the terrible things that will happen if you don't keep the chain going. The threat may be that someone will die if you don't respond, or that your computer will suffer a melt-down from the latest virus. Last is the request. It will implore you to send the message to as many others as possible. It may even promise a small donation to a group with a legitimate-sounding name because they are able to track every forwarded e-mail (also a hoax).

Thinking-Writing Activity

IDENTIFYING INTERNET HOAXES

Use the guidelines that you have just read about to identify the telltale signs of a hoax in these examples:

BILL GATES GIVEAWAY

Dear Friends,

Please do not take this for a junk letter. Bill Gates is sharing his fortune. If you ignore this you will repent later. Microsoft and AOL are now the largest Internet companies and in an effort to make sure that Internet Explorer remains the most widely used program, Microsoft and AOL are running an e-mail beta test. When you forward this e-mail to friends, Microsoft can and will track it (if you are a Microsoft Windows user) for a two-week time period. For every person that you forward this e-mail to, Microsoft will pay you $245.00, for every person that you sent it to that forwards it on, Microsoft will pay you $243.00, and for every third person that receives it, you will be paid $241.00. Within two weeks, Microsoft will contact you for your address and then send you a check.

BONZAI KITTENS

To anyone with love and respect for life: In New York there is a Japanese who sells bonsai-kittens." Sounds like fun huh? NOT! These animals are squeezed into a bottle. Their urine and feces are removed through probes. They feed them with a kind of tube. They feed them chemicals to keep their bones soft and flexible so the kittens grow into the shape of the bottle. The animals will stay their as long as they live. They can't walk or move or wash themselves. Bonsai-kittens are becoming a fashion in New York and Asia. See this horror at: http://www.bonsaikitten.com Please sign this email in protest against these tortures. If you receive an email with over 500 names, please send a copy to: anacheca@hotmail.com. From there this protest will be sent to USA and Mexican animal protection organizations.

(Continues)

@ THINKING CRITICALLY ABOUT NEW MEDIA (CONTINUED)

MISSING CHILD PICTURE

I am asking you all, begging you to please forward this email onto anyone and everyone you know, PLEASE. My 9 year old girl, Penny Brown, is missing. She has been missing for now two weeks. It is still not too late. Please help us. If anyone anywhere knows anything, sees anything, please contact me at zicozicozico@hotmail.com. I am including a picture of her. All prayers are appreciated!! In only takes 2 seconds to forward this on, if it was your child, you would want all the help you could get. Please. Thank you for your kindness, hopefully you can help us.

VIRUS WARNING

Just to let you know a new virus was started in New York last night. This virus acts in the following manner: It sends itself automatically to all contacts on your list with the title "A Virtual Card for You." As soon as the supposed virtual card is opened, the computer freezes so that the user has to reboot. When the ctrl+alt+del keys or the reset button are pressed, the virus destroys Sector Zero, thus permanently destroying the hard disk. Yesterday in just a few hours this virus caused panic in New York, according to news broadcast by CNN www.cnn.com. This alert was received by an employee of Microsoft itself. So don't open any mails with subject "A Virtual Card for You." As soon as you get the mail, delete it. Please pass on this email to all your friends. Forward this to everyone in your address book. I would rather receive this 25 times than not at all.

Believing and Knowing

Developing beliefs that are as accurate as possible is important to us as critical thinkers because the more accurate our beliefs are, the better we are able to understand the world around us and to make predictions about the future. As the preceding discussion has suggested, however, the accuracy of the beliefs we form can vary tremendously.

We use the word *knowing* to distinguish beliefs supported by strong reasons or evidence (such as the belief that life exists on earth) from beliefs for which there is less support (such as the belief that life exists on other planets) or from beliefs disproved by reasons or evidence to the contrary. This saying expresses another way to understand the difference between believing and knowing:

"You can believe what is not so, but you cannot know what is not so."

Thinking-Writing Activity

WEIGHING YOUR BELIEFS AND KNOWLEDGE

Look again at the beliefs you have written about for previous activities. Could you say about any of them "I know this" rather than merely "I believe this"? Why? Write answers to these questions.

Knowledge and Truth

Authorities often disagree about the true nature of a given situation or the best course of action. It is common, for example, for doctors to disagree about a diagnosis, for economists to differ on the state of the economy, or for psychiatrists to disagree on whether a convicted felon is a menace to society or a victim of social forces.

What do we do when experts disagree? As critical thinkers, we must analyze and evaluate all the available information, develop our own well-reasoned beliefs, and recognize when we lack sufficient information to arrive at well-reasoned beliefs. We must realize, too, that such beliefs may evolve over time as we obtain more information or improve our insight.

Although there are compelling reasons to view knowledge and truth as evolving, some people resist doing so. Either they take refuge in a belief in the absolute, unchanging nature of knowledge and truth as presented by the appropriate authorities, or they conclude that there is no such thing as knowledge or truth and that trying to seek either is futile.

Understanding Relativism

In this latter view of the world, known as *relativism,* all beliefs are considered "relative" to the person or context in which they arise. For the relativist, all opinions are equal in validity to all others; no one is ever in a position to say with confidence that one view is right and another one wrong. Although a relativistic view is appropriate in some areas of experience—for example, in matters of taste such as fashion—in many other areas it is not. Knowledge, in the form of well-supported beliefs, does exist. Some beliefs are better than others, not because an authority has proclaimed them so but because they can be analyzed in terms of the criteria discussed earlier in this chapter.

Understanding Falsifiable Beliefs

Another important criterion for evaluating certain beliefs is that the beliefs be *falsifiable*. This means that it is possible to state conditions—tests—under which the beliefs could be disproved and that the beliefs then pass those tests. For example, if you believe that you can create ice cubes by placing water-filled trays in a freezer, you can conduct an experiment to determine whether your belief is accurate. If no ice cubes form after you put the trays in the freezer, your theory is disproved. If, however, you believe that your destiny is related to the positions of the planets and stars (as astrologers do), it is not clear how you can conduct an experiment to determine whether your belief is accurate. Since a belief that is not falsifiable can never be proved, such a belief is questionable.

The Media and Truth

We are all aware in a general way that the media can shape our beliefs by the information they provide and the interpretations they give to that information. We may not be aware, however, of some of the subtle ways in which this is done or of the profound influences that result. As you read the essays in this chapter, consider how your beliefs might be shaped by the sources that these writers discuss.

In the following article, "The Story Behind the Story," the journalist Mark Bowden uses the specific example of the nomination of Sonia Sotomayor to the Supreme Court to support his more general thesis that traditional journalism is collapsing and that, as a result, "the quest for information has been superseded by the quest for ammunition." He says the catalyst for the collapse of journalism is a combination of cable television which has created a twenty-four-hour news cycle, and the power of new media to help feed the increasing hunger for news reporting and news commentary. As a result, Bowden is convinced that "[w]ork formerly done by reporters and producers is now routinely performed by political operatives and amateur ideologues of one stripe or another, whose goal is not to educate the public but to *win*. This is a trend not likely to change."

"The Story Behind the Story"

by Mark Bowden

If you happened to be watching a television news channel on May 26, the day President Obama nominated U.S. Circuit Court Judge Sonia Sotomayor to the Supreme Court, you might have been struck, as I was, by what seemed like a nifty investigative report.

First came the happy announcement ceremony at the White House, with Sotomayor sweetly saluting her elderly mother, who as a single parent had raised the prospective justice and her brother in a Bronx housing project. Obama had chosen a woman whose life journey mirrored his own: an obscure, disadvantaged beginning followed by blazing academic excellence, an Ivy League law degree, and a swift rise to power. It was a moving TV moment, well-orchestrated and in perfect harmony with the central narrative of the new Obama presidency.

But then, just minutes later, journalism rose to perform its time-honored pie-throwing role. Having been placed by the president on a pedestal, Sotomayor was now a clear target. I happened to be watching Fox News. I was slated to appear that night on one of its programs, *Hannity*, to serve as a willing foil to the show's cheerfully pugnacious host, Sean Hannity, a man who can deliver a deeply held conservative conviction on any topic faster than the speed of thought. Since the host knew what the subject matter of that night's show would be and I did not, I'd thought it best to check in and see what Fox was preoccupied with that afternoon.

With Sotomayor, of course—and the network's producers seemed amazingly well prepared. They showed a clip from remarks she had made on an obscure panel at Duke University in 2005, and then, reaching back still farther, they showed snippets from a speech she had made at Berkeley Law School in 2001. Here was this purportedly moderate Latina judge, appointed to the federal bench by a Republican president and now tapped for the Supreme Court by a Democratic one, unmasked as a Race Woman with an agenda. In one clip she announced herself as someone who believed her identity as a "Latina woman" (a redundancy, but that's what she said) made her judgment superior to that of a "white male," and in the other she all but unmasked herself as a card-carrying member of the Left Wing Conspiracy to use America's courts not just to apply and interpret the law but, in her own words, to *make policy*, to perform an end run around the other two branches of government and impose liberal social policies by fiat on an unsuspecting American public.

5   In the Duke clip, she not only stated that appellate judges make policy, she did so in a disdainful mock disavowal before a chuckling audience of apparently like-minded conspirators. "I know this is on tape and I should never say that, because we don't make law, I know," she said before being interrupted by laughter. "Okay, I know.

I'm not promoting it, I'm not advocating it, I'm . . . you know," flipping her hands dismissively. More laughter.

Holy cow! I'm an old reporter, and I know legwork when I see it. Those crack journalists at Fox, better known for coloring and commenting endlessly on the news than for actually breaking it, had unearthed not one but two explosive gems, and had been primed to expose Sotomayor's darker purpose *within minutes of her nomination!* Leaving aside for the moment any question about the context of these seemingly damaging remarks—none was offered—I was impressed. In my newspaper years, I prepared my share of advance profiles of public figures, and I know the scut work that goes into sifting through a decades-long career. In the old days it meant digging through packets of yellowed clippings in the morgue, interviewing widely, searching for those moments of controversy or surprise that revealed something interesting about the subject. How many rulings, opinions, articles, legal arguments, panel discussions, and speeches had there been in the judge's long years of service? What bloodhound producer at Fox News had waded into this haystack to find these two choice needles?

Then I flipped to MSNBC, and lo! . . . they had the exact same two clips. I flipped to CNN . . . same clips. CBS . . . same clips. ABC . . . same clips. Parsing Sotomayor's 30 years of public legal work, somehow every TV network had come up with precisely the same moments! None bothered to say who had dug them up; none offered a smidgen of context. They all just accepted the apparent import of the clips, the substance of which was sure to trouble any fair-minded viewer. By the end of the day just about every American with a TV set had heard the "make policy" and "Latina woman" comments. By the end of the nightly news summaries, millions who had never heard of Sonia Sotomayor knew her not only as Obama's pick, but as a judge who felt superior by reason of her gender and ethnicity, and as a liberal activist determined to "make policy" from the federal bench. And wasn't it an extraordinary coincidence that all these great news organizations, functioning independently—because this, after all, is the advantage of having multiple news-gathering sources in a democracy—had come up with exactly the same material in advance?

They hadn't, of course. The reporting we saw on TV and on the Internet that day was the work not of journalists, but of political hit men. The snippets about Sotomayor had been circulating on conservative Web sites and shown on some TV channels for weeks. They were new only to the vast majority of us who have better things to do than vet the record of every person on Obama's list. But this is precisely what activists and bloggers on both sides of the political spectrum do, and what a conservative organization like the Judicial Confirmation Network exists to promote. The JCN had gathered an attack dossier on each of the prospective Supreme Court nominees, and had fed them all to the networks in advance.

This process—political activists supplying material for TV news broadcasts—is not new, of course. It has largely replaced the work of on-the-scene reporters during political campaigns, which have become, in a sense, perpetual. The once-quadrennial clashes between parties over the White House are now simply the way our national business is conducted. In our exhausting 24/7 news cycle, demand for timely information and analysis is greater than ever. With journalists being laid off in droves, savvy political operatives have stepped eagerly into the breach. What's most troubling is not that TV-news producers mistake their work for journalism, which is bad enough, but that young people drawn to journalism increasingly see no distinction between disinterested reporting and hit-jobbery. The very smart and capable young men who actually dug up and initially posted the Sotomayor clips both originally described themselves to me as part-time, or aspiring, journalists.

10　　The attack that political operatives fashioned from their work was neither unusual nor particularly effective. It succeeded in shaping the national debate over her nomination for weeks, but more serious assessments of her record would demolish the caricature soon enough, and besides, the Democrats have a large majority in the Senate; her nomination was approved by a vote of 68–31. The incident does, however, illustrate one consequence of the collapse of professional journalism. Work formerly done by reporters and producers is now routinely performed by political operatives and amateur ideologues of one stripe or another, whose goal is not to educate the public but to *win*. This is a trend not likely to change.

Morgen Richmond, the man who actually found the snippets used to attack Sotomayor, is a partner in a computer-consulting business in Orange County, California, a father of two, and a native of Canada, who defines himself, in part, as a political conservative. He spends some of his time most nights in a second-floor bedroom/office in his home, after his children and wife have gone to bed, cruising the Internet looking for ideas and information for his blogging. "It's more of a hobby than anything else," he says. His primary outlet is a Web site called VerumSerum.com, which was co-founded by his friend John Sexton. Sexton is a Christian conservative who was working at the time for an organization called Reasons to Believe, which strives, in part, to reconcile scientific discovery and theory with the apparent whoppers told in the Bible. Sexton is, like Richmond, a young father, living in Huntington Beach. He is working toward a master's degree at Biola University (formerly the Bible Institute of Los Angeles), and is a man of opinion. For both Sexton and Richmond, Verum Serum is a labor of love, a chance for them to flex their desire to report and comment, to add their two cents to the national debate. Both see themselves as somewhat unheralded conservative thinkers in a world captive to misguided liberalism and prey to an overwhelmingly leftist mainstream media, or MSM, composed of journalists who, like myself, write for print publications or work for big broadcast networks and are actually paid for their work.

Richmond started researching Sotomayor after ABC News Washington correspondent George Stephanopoulos named her as the likely pick back on March 13. The work involved was far less than I'd imagined, in part because the Internet is such an amazing research tool, but mostly because Richmond's goal was substantially easier to achieve than a journalist's. For a newspaper reporter, the goal in researching any profile is to arrive at a deeper understanding of the subject. My own motivation, when I did it, was to present not just a smart and original picture of the person, but a fair picture. In the quaint protocols of my ancient newsroom career, the editors I worked for would have accepted nothing less; if they felt a story needed more detail or balance, they'd brusquely hand it back and demand more effort. Richmond's purpose was fundamentally different. He figured, rightly, that anyone Obama picked who had not publicly burned an American flag would likely be confirmed, and that she would be cheered all the way down this lubricated chute by the Obama-loving MSM. To his credit, Richmond is not what we in the old days called a "thumbsucker," a lazy columnist who rarely stirs from behind his desk, who for material just reacts to the items that cross it. (This defines the vast majority of bloggers.) Richmond is actually determined to add something new to the debate. "The goal is to develop original stories that attract attention," he told me. "I was consciously looking for something that would resonate."

But not just anything resonant. Richmond's overarching purpose was to damage Sotomayor, or at least to raise questions about her that would trouble his readers, who are mostly other conservative bloggers.

Richmond began his reporting by looking at university Web sites. He had learned that many harbor little-seen recordings and transcripts of speeches made by public figures, since schools regularly sponsor lectures and panel discussions with prominent citizens, such as federal judges. Using Google, Richmond quickly found a list of such appearances by Sotomayor, and the first one he clicked on was the video of the 2005 panel discussion at Duke University Law School. About 40 minutes into it, Richmond says, he was only half listening, multitasking on his home computer, when laughter from the sound track caught his ear. He rolled back the video and heard Sotomayor utter the line about making policy, and then jokingly disavow the expression.

15   "What I found most offensive about it was the laughter," he says. "What was the joke? . . . Here was a sitting appellate judge in a room full of law students, treating the idea that she was making policy or law from the bench as laughable." He recognized it as a telling in-joke that his readers would not find funny.

Richmond posted the video snippet on YouTube on May 2, and then put it up with a short commentary on Verum Serum the following day, questioning whether Sotomayor deserved to be considered moderate or bipartisan, as she had been characterized. "I'm not so sure this is going to fly," he wrote, and then invited readers to view the video. He concluded with sarcasm: "So she's a judicial activist . . . I'm sure she is a moderate one though! Unbelievable. With a comment like this I only hope that conservatives have the last laugh if she gets the nomination."

A number of larger conservative Web sites picked up the video, and on May 4 it was aired on television for the first time, by Sean Hannity.

On Malkin's Web site, Richmond had come across a short, critical reference to a speech Sotomayor had given at Berkeley Law School, in which, according to Malkin, the prospective Supreme Court nominee said "she believes it is appropriate for a judge to consider their 'experiences as women and people of color' in their decision making, which she believes should 'affect our decisions.'"

Malkin told me that her "conservative source" for the tidbit was privileged. She used the item without checking out the actual speech, which is what Richmond set out to find. He had some trouble because Malkin had placed the speech in 2002 instead of 2001, but he found it—the Honorable Mario G. Olmos Law & Cultural Diversity

Memorial Lecture—in the Berkeley Law School's *La Raza Law Journal*, bought it, and on May 5 posted the first detailed account of it on his blog. He ran large excerpts from it, and highlighted in bold the now infamous lines: "I would hope that a wise Latina woman with the richness of her experiences would more often than not reach a better conclusion than a white male who hasn't lived that life."

20   Richmond then commented:

"To be fair, I do want to note that the statement she made . . . is outrageous enough that it may have in fact been a joke. Although since it's published "as-is" in a law journal I'm not sure she is entitled to the benefit of the doubt on this. The text certainly does not indicate that it was said in jest. I have only a lay-person's understanding of law and judicial history, but I suspect the judicial philosophy implied by these statements is probably pretty typical amongst liberal judges. Personally, I wish it seemed that she was actually really trying to meet the judicial ideal of impartiality, and her comments about making a difference are a concern as this does not seem to be an appropriate focus for a member of the judiciary. I look forward to hopefully seeing some additional dissection and analysis of these statements by others in the conservative legal community."

The crucial piece of Richmond's post, Sotomayor's "wise Latina woman" comment, was then picked up again by other sites, and was soon being packaged with the Duke video as Exhibits A and B in the case against Sonia Sotomayor. Richmond told me that he was shocked by the immediate, widespread attention given to his work, and a little startled by the levels of outrage it provoked. "I found her comments more annoying than outrageous, to be honest," he said.

In both instances, Richmond's political bias made him tone-deaf to the context and import of Sotomayor's remarks. Bear in mind that he was looking not simply to understand the judge, but to expose her supposed hidden agenda.

Take the Duke panel first: most of the video, for obvious reasons, held little interest for Richmond. Most of the talk concerned how to make your application for a highly competitive clerkship stand out. Late in the discussion, a student asked the panel to compare clerking at the district-court (or trial-court) level and clerking at the appellate level. Sotomayor replied that clerks serving trial judges are often asked to rapidly research legal questions that develop during a trial, and to assist the judge in applying the law to the facts of that particular case. The appellate courts, on the other hand, are in the business of making rulings that are "precedential," she said, in that rulings at the appellate level serve as examples, reasons, or justifications for future proceedings in lower courts. She went on to make the ostensibly controversial remark that students who planned careers in academia or public-interest law ought to seek a clerkship at the appellate level, because that's where "policy is made."

25   This is absolutely true, in the sense she intended: precedential decisions, by definition, make *judicial* policy. They provide the basic principles that guide future rulings. But both Sotomayor and her audience were acutely aware of how charged the word *policy* has become in matters concerning the judiciary—conservatives accuse liberal judges, not without truth, of trying to set *national* policy from the bench. The polite laughter that caught Richmond's ear was recognition by the law students that the judge had inadvertently stepped in a verbal cow pie. She immediately recognized

what she had done, expressed mock horror at being caught doing so on tape, and then pronounced a jocular and exaggerated mea culpa, like a scoring runner in a baseball game tiptoeing back out onto the diamond to touch a base that he might have missed. Sotomayor went on to explain in very precise terms how and why decisions at the appellate level have broader intellectual implications than those at the lower level. It is where, she said, "the law is percolating."

Seen in their proper context, these comments would probably not strike anyone as noteworthy. If anything, they showed how sensitive Sotomayor and everyone else in the room had become to fears of an "activist court."

A look at the full "Latina woman" speech at Berkeley reveals another crucial misinterpretation.

To his credit, Richmond posted as much of the speech as copyright law allows, attempting to present the most important sentence in context. But he still missed the point. Sotomayor's argument was not that she sought to use her position to further minority interests, or that her gender and background made her superior to a white male. Her central argument was that the sexual, racial, and ethnic makeup of the legal profession has in fact historically informed the application of law, despite the efforts of individual lawyers and judges to rise above their personal stories—as Sotomayor noted she labors to do. Her comment about a "wise Latina woman" making a better judgment than a "white male who hasn't lived that life" referred specifically to cases involving racial and sexual discrimination. "Whether born from experience or inherent physiological or cultural differences . . . our gender and national origins may and will make a difference in our judging," she said. This is not a remarkable insight, nor is it even arguable. She said that although white male judges have been admirably able on occasion to rise above cultural prejudices, the progress of racial minorities and women in the legal profession has directly coincided with greater judicial recognition of their rights. Once again, her point was not that this progress was the result of deliberate judicial activism, but that it was a natural consequence of fuller minority and female participation.

Richmond seems a bright and fair-minded fellow, but he makes no bones about his political convictions or the purpose of his research and blogging. He has some of the skills and instincts of a reporter but not the motivation or ethics. Any news organization that simply trusted and aired his editing of Sotomayor's remarks, as every one of them did, was abdicating its responsibility to do its own reporting. It was airing propaganda. There is nothing wrong with reporting propaganda, per se, so long as it is labeled as such. None of the TV reports I saw on May 26 cited VerumSerum.com as the source of the material, which disappointed but did not surprise Richmond and Sexton.

30   Several hours of Internet snooping by Richmond at his upstairs computer wound up shaping the public's perception of Sonia Sotomayor, at least for the first few weeks following her nomination. Conservative critics used the snippets to portray her as a racist and liberal activist, a picture even Richmond now admits is inaccurate. "She's really fairly moderate, compared to some of the other candidates on Obama's list," he says. "Given that conservatives are not going to like any Obama pick, she

really wasn't all that bad." He felt many of the Web sites and TV commentators who used his work inflated its significance well beyond his own intent. But he was not displeased.

For his part, Sexton says: "It is a beautiful thing to live in this country. It's overwhelming and fantastic, really, that an ordinary citizen, with just a little bit of work, can help shape the national debate. Once you get a taste of it, it's hard to resist."

I would describe their approach as post-journalistic. It sees democracy, by definition, as perpetual political battle. The blogger's role is to help his side. Distortions and inaccuracies, lapses of judgment, the absence of context, all of these things matter only a little, because they are committed by both sides, and tend to come out a wash. Nobody is actually right about anything, no matter how certain they pretend to be. The truth is something that emerges from the cauldron of debate. No, not the truth: *victory*, because winning is way more important than being right. Power is the highest achievement. There is nothing new about this. But we never used to mistake it for journalism. Today it is rapidly replacing journalism, leading us toward a world where all information is spun, and where all "news" is unapologetically propaganda.

Without journalism, the public good is viewed only through a partisan lens, and politics becomes blood sport.

Television loves this, because it is dramatic. Confrontation is all. And given the fragmentation of news on the Internet and on cable television, Americans increasingly choose to listen only to their own side of the argument, to bloggers and commentators who reinforce their convictions and paint the world only in acceptable, comfortable colors. Consumers of such "news" become all the more entrenched in their prejudices, and ever more hostile to those who disagree. The other side is no longer the honorable opposition, maybe partly right; but rather always wrong, stupid, criminal, even downright evil. In a post-journalistic society, there is no disinterested voice. There are only the winning side and the losing side.

35   There's more here than just an old journalist's lament over his dying profession, or over the social cost of losing great newspapers and great TV-news operations. And there's more than an argument for the ethical superiority of honest, disinterested reporting over advocacy. Even an eager and ambitious political blogger like Richmond, because he is drawn to the work primarily out of political conviction, not curiosity, is less likely to experience the pleasure of finding something new, or of arriving at a completely original, unexpected insight, one that surprises even himself. He is missing out on the great fun of speaking wholly for himself, without fear or favor. This is what gives reporters the power to stir up trouble wherever they go. They can shake preconceptions and poke holes in presumption. They can celebrate the unnoticed and puncture the hyped. They can, as the old saying goes, afflict the comfortable and comfort the afflicted. A reporter who thinks and speaks for himself, whose preeminent goal is providing deeper understanding, aspires even in political argument to persuade, which requires at the very least being seen as fair-minded and trustworthy by those—and this is the key—who are inclined to

disagree with him. The honest, disinterested voice of a true journalist carries an authority that no self-branded liberal or conservative can have. "For a country to have a great writer is like having another government," Alexander Solzhenitsyn wrote. Journalism, done right, is enormously powerful precisely because it does not seek power. It seeks truth. Those who forsake it to shill for a product or a candidate or a party or an ideology diminish their own power. They are missing the most joyful part of the job.

Question for Reading Actively

1. Bowden believes that traditional journalism is collapsing, with "political operatives and amateur ideologues" replacing journalists engaged in investigative reporting. What evidence does Bowden cite to support this claim?

Questions for Thinking Critically

1. In a part of the article that is not included in the preceding excerpt, Bowden observes "What gave newspapers their value was the mission and promise of journalism—the hope that someone was getting paid to wade into the daily tide of manure, sort through its deliberate lies and cunning half-truths, and tell a story straight." Instead of trained reporters who are cynical, suspicious, and expert critical thinkers, new media has made it possible for almost anyone with a laptop or smart phone to participate in the national dialogue, leading to the onslaught of biased and prejudiced points of view that are presented as "objective." Based on your experience, do you consider this to be a serious problem?

2. What are the two quotes from Sonia Sotomayor that were repeatedly cited as evidence of her lack of objectivity? Why does Bowden believe that the meaning of these quotes was dramatically misrepresented?

Questions for Writing Thoughtfully

1. According to Bowden, in the new world of news reporting, "Power is the highest achievement . . . Today it is rapidly replacing journalism, leading us toward a world where all information is spun, and where all 'news' is unapologetically propaganda." Examine a variety of news shows on television or online, select several examples that support this perspective and several examples that conflict with it, and write up your evaluation.

2. If Bowden is right, in "a post-journalistic society, there is no disinterested voice. There are only the winning side and the losing side." What suggestions would you make to ensure that news reporting and commentary avoids bias, prejudice, and inaccuracy? Think about what we do as critical thinkers in order to avoid these pitfalls in evaluating the value and truth of information, and write a short essay outlining your ideas.

Thinking Critically About Visuals

"Seeing" is Not Always "Believing"

Henry Louis Gates, Jr., teaches undergraduate and graduate courses as a Professor of English at Harvard University. On July 16, 2009, Gates returned home from a trip to China to find he was unable to open the door to his house in Cambridge, Massachusetts. When he enlisted the help of his driver to try to get into the house, a person passing by mistook what they saw as a possible break-in and called the police. When Officer Crowley arrived on the scene, he and Gates got into a confrontation which resulted in the officer arresting Gates and charging him with disorderly conduct. As Gates is African American and the arresting officer was Caucasian, this event ignited controversy nationwide and was covered by the media for quite some time. Some believed that Crowley reacted too harshly to Gates based on his race. Others thought Crowley was just doing his job.

Pete Souza/The White House/PSG/Newscom

This event even caught the attention of President Obama, who was only a few months into his term as President at the time. Obama invited Gates and Crowley to the White House to discuss race relations and law enforcement over beer. Some thought meeting over beer was a public relations stunt; others thought it was a genuine gesture designed to get both sides of the story from the primary sources. What do you think? What roles do believing, knowing, perception, and the influence of media play in this story?

Ways of Presenting Beliefs

When you write, you are presenting your beliefs. No matter what its form—letters, research papers, blog, business documents, even stories and poems—your written expression states what you believe. When you write, you present your beliefs in three ways: reports, inferences, and judgments. Your choice of words establishes which of the three you are using:

- *Report:* My bus was late today.
- *Inference:* My bus will probably be late tomorrow.
- *Judgment:* The bus system is unreliable.

Now try to identify which of the three is being used in these statements:

1. Each modern nuclear warhead has over one hundred times the explosive power of the bomb dropped on Hiroshima.
2. With all the billions of planets in the universe, the odds are that there are other forms of life in the cosmos.
3. In the long run, the energy needs of the world will best be met by solar energy technology rather than nuclear energy or fossil fuels.

As you examine these various statements, you can see that they provide readers with different types of information. For example, the first statement in each list reports aspects of the world that can be verified—that is, checked for accuracy. Appropriate investigation can determine whether the bus was actually late today and whether modern nuclear warheads really have the power attributed to them. When you describe the world in ways that can be verified through investigation, you are *reporting factual information.*

Looking at the second statement in each list, you can see that each provides a different sort of information than the first one does. These statements cannot be verified. There is no way to investigate and determine with certainty whether the bus will indeed be late tomorrow or whether there is life on other planets. Although these conclusions may be based on facts, they go beyond them. When you describe the world in ways based on factual information yet go beyond it to make statements about what is not currently known, you are *inferring* conclusions about the world.

Finally, as you examine the third statement in each list, it is apparent that these statements differ from both factual reports and inferences. In each the speaker is applying certain standards (criteria) to deem the bus service as unreliable and solar energy as more promising than nuclear energy or fossil fuels. You are *judging* when you describe the world in ways that evaluate it on the basis of certain criteria.

You continually use these ways of describing and organizing your world—reporting, inferring, and judging—to make sense of your experience. In most instances, you are not aware that you are actually performing these activities, nor are you usually aware of the differences among them. Yet these three activities work together to help you see the world as a complete picture.

Thinking-Writing Activity

IDENTIFYING REPORTS, INFERENCES, AND JUDGMENTS

1. Write three statements that you believe—one as a report, one as an inference, and one as a judgment.

2. Locate a short article from a newspaper, magazine, or online news service and identify the reports, inferences, and judgments it contains.

3. Share your statements and your findings with classmates.

Reporting Factual Information

Statements written as reports express the most accurate beliefs you have about the world. Factual beliefs have earned this distinction because they are verifiable, usually by using one or more of your senses. For example, consider the following factual statement: "That young woman is wearing a brown hat in the rain." This statement about an event in the world is considered factual because you can verify it immediately with sensual experience—what you can (in principle or in theory) see, hear, touch, taste, or smell. It is important to say *in principle* or *in theory* because often you do not use all of your senses to check out what you are experiencing. Look again at the factual statement: you would normally be satisfied to see this event without insisting on touching the hat or giving the person a physical examination. If necessary, however, you could perform these additional actions.

You use the same reasoning when you believe other people's factual statements that you are not in a position to check immediately. For instance:

- The Great Wall of China is more than fifteen hundred miles long.
- There are large mountains and craters on the moon.
- Your skin is covered with germs.

You consider these factual statements because even though you cannot verify them with your senses at the moment, you could in principle or in theory do so *if* you were flown to China, *if* you were rocketed to the moon, or *if* you were to examine your skin with a powerful microscope. The process of verifying factual statements involves identifying the sources of information on which they are based and evaluating the reliability of these sources.

You communicate factual information to others by means of reports. A *report* is a description of something that has been experienced, then communicated in as accurate and complete a way as possible. Through reports you share your sensory experiences with other people, and this sharing enables you to learn much more about the world than you would if you were confined to knowing only what you experience.

Because factual reports play such an important role in the exchange and accumulation of information about the world, it is important that they be as accurate and complete as possible. This brings us to a problem. We have already seen in previous chapters that our perceptions and observations often are not accurate or complete. This means that sometimes when we think we are making true factual reports, they actually are inaccurate or incomplete. For instance, consider our earlier factual statement: "That young woman is wearing a brown hat in the rain." Here are questions you could ask concerning the accuracy of the statement:

- Is the woman actually young, or does she merely look young?
- Is the person actually a woman, or a man disguised as a woman?
- Is that really a hat the woman is wearing, or is it something else (such as a helmet or a paper bag)?

Of course, there are methods you could use to answer these questions. Can you describe some of them?

Besides difficulties with observations, the "facts" that you see in the world actually depend on more *general beliefs* that you have about how the world operates. Consider this question: "Why did the man's body fall from the top of the building to the sidewalk?" Having had some general science courses, you might respond, "The body was simply obeying the law of gravity" and consider that a factual statement. But how did people account for this sort of event before Newton formulated the law of gravity? Some popular responses might have included the following:

- Things always fall down, not up.
- The spirit in the body wanted to join with the spirit of the earth.

In the past, when people made statements like these—such as "Humans can't fly"— they thought they were stating facts. Increased knowledge and understanding have since shown these "factual beliefs" to be inaccurate, so they have been replaced by "better" beliefs. These better beliefs explain the world in a way that is more

Thinking-Writing Activity

EVALUATING FACTUAL INFORMATION

1. Locate and carefully read, watch, or listen to a report that deals with a major social issue.
2. Identify the main idea and key points of the article.
3. Describe the factual statements used to support the main idea.
4. Evaluate the accuracy of the factual information.
5. Evaluate the reliability of the sources of the factual information.

accurate and predictable. Will many of the beliefs now considered to be factually accurate also be replaced by more precise and predictable beliefs? If history is any indication, this will most certainly happen. Newton's formulations have already been replaced by Einstein's, based on the latter's theory of relativity. Einstein's have been refined and modified as well and may someday also be replaced.

Inferring from Evidence or Premises

Imagine yourself in the following situations:

1. It is 2:00 A.M. and your roommate comes crashing into the room. He staggers to his bed and falls across it, dropping (and breaking) a nearly empty whiskey bottle. Startled, you gasp, "What's the matter?" With alcohol fumes blasting from his mouth, he mumbles: "I jus' wanna hadda widdel drink!" What do you conclude?

2. Your roommate has just learned that she passed a math exam for which she had done absolutely no studying. Humming the refrain "I did it my way," she comes dancing over to you with a huge grin on her face and says, "Let me buy you dinner to celebrate!" What do you conclude about how she is feeling?

3. It is midnight and the library is about to close. As you head for the door, you spy your roommate shuffling along in an awkward waddle. His coat bulges out in front as if he's pregnant. When you ask, "What's going on?" he gives you a glare and hisses, "Shhh!" Just before he reaches the door, a pile of books slides from under his coat and crashes to the floor. What do you conclude?

In these examples, it would be reasonable to make the following conclusions:

1. Your roommate is drunk.
2. Your roommate is happy.
3. Your roommate is stealing library books.

Although these conclusions are reasonable, they are not factual reports; they are inferences. You have not directly experienced your roommate's "drunkenness," "happiness," or "stealing." Instead, you have inferred it on the basis of your roommate's behavior and the circumstances. What clues in these situations might lead to these conclusions? One way of understanding the inferential nature of these views is to ask yourself the following questions:

1. Have you ever pretended to be drunk when you weren't? Could other people tell?

2. Have you ever pretended to be happy when you weren't? Could other people tell?

3. Have you ever been accused of stealing something when you were perfectly innocent? How did this happen?

From these examples you can see that whereas factual beliefs can in principle be verified by direct observation, *inferential beliefs* go beyond what can be directly observed. For instance, in the previous examples, your observation of some of your roommate's actions led you to infer things that you were not observing directly—"He's drunk," "She's happy," "He's stealing books."

Making such simple inferences is something you do all the time. It is so automatic that usually you are not even aware that you are going beyond your immediate observations or that you may be having trouble distinguishing between what you *observe* and what you *infer*. Making such inferences enables you to see the world as a complete picture, to fill in the blanks and to supplement the fragmentary sensations being presented to your senses. Presenting your inferences along with your beliefs in writing paints a complete picture for your readers.

Your writing may also include *predictions* of what will occur in the near future. Predictions and expectations are also inferences because you attempt to determine what is currently unknown from what is already known.

It is possible that your inferences may be wrong; in fact, they frequently are. You may infer that the woman sitting next to you is wearing two earrings and then discover that she has only one. You may expect the class to end at noon but find that the teacher lets you out early—or late. In the last section, we concluded that not even factual beliefs are ever absolutely certain. Comparatively speaking, inferential beliefs are much more uncertain than factual beliefs, so it is important to distinguish between the two.

The distinction between what is observed and what is inferred is given particular attention in courtroom settings, where defense lawyers usually want witnesses to describe only what they observed—not what they inferred as they observed. When a witness includes an inference such as "I saw him steal it," the lawyer may object that the statement represents a "conclusion of the witness" and move to have the observation struck from the record. For example, imagine that you are a defense attorney listening to the following testimony. At what points would you object by saying, "This is a conclusion of the witness"?

> I saw Harvey running down the street, right after he knocked the old lady down. He had her purse in his hand and was trying to escape as fast as he could. He was really scared. I wasn't surprised because Harvey has always taken advantage of others. It's not the first time that he's stolen, either; I can tell you that. Just last summer he robbed the poor box at St. Anthony's. He was bragging about it for weeks.

Finally, keep in mind that even though in *theory* facts and inferences can be distinguished, in *practice* it is almost impossible to communicate with others in speech or writing by sticking only to factual observations. A reasonable approach is to state your inference along with the observable evidence on which the inference is based (e.g., John seemed happy because . . . .). Our language has an entire collection of terms (*seems, appears, is likely,* and so on) that signal when we are making an inference and not expressing an observable fact. Thoughtful writers use these words carefully and deliberately.

Many of the predictions that you make are inferences based on your past experiences and information that you presently have. Even when there appear to be sound reasons supporting them, these inferences are often wrong due to incomplete information or unanticipated events. The fact that even people whom society considers "experts" regularly make inaccurate predictions should encourage you to exercise caution when presenting your beliefs as inferences. Here are some examples:

> "So many centuries after the Creation, it is unlikely that anyone could find hitherto unknown lands of any value."
>
> —The Advisory Committee to King Ferdinand and Queen Isabella of Spain, before Columbus's voyage in 1492

> "What will the soldiers and sailors, what will the common people say to 'George Washington, President of the United States'? They will despise him to all eternity."
>
> —John Adams, 1789

> "What use could the company make of an electrical toy?"
>
> —Western Union's rejection of the telephone in 1878

> "The actual building of roads devoted to motor cars is not for the near future in spite of many rumors to that effect."
>
> —a 1902 article in *Harper's Weekly*

> "You ain't goin' nowhere, son. You ought to go back to driving a truck."
>
> —Jim Denny, Grand Ole Opry manager, firing Elvis Presley after one performance, 1954

Thinking-Writing Activity

FACTUAL AND INFERENTIAL BELIEFS

Examine the following list of statements, noting which are *factual beliefs* (based on observations) and which are *inferential beliefs* (conclusions that go beyond observations). For each factual statement, describe how you might go about verifying the information. For each inferential statement, describe a factual observation on which the inference could be based. (*Note:* Some statements may contain both factual beliefs and inferential beliefs.)

- When my leg starts to ache, that means snow is on the way.
- The grass is wet—it must have rained last night.

- I think that it's pretty clear from the length of the skid marks that the accident was caused by that person's driving too fast.
- Fifty men lost their lives in the construction of the Queensboro Bridge.
- Nancy said she wasn't feeling well yesterday—I'll bet that she's out sick today.

Now consider the following situations. What inferences might you be inclined to make on the basis of what you are observing? How could you investigate the accuracy of an inference?

- A student in your class is consistently late for class.
- You see a friend driving a new car.
- An instructor asks the same student to stay after class several times.
- You don't receive any birthday cards.

So far, we have been exploring relatively simple inferences. Many of the inferences people make, however, are much more complicated. In fact, much of our knowledge of the world rests on our ability to make complicated inferences in a systematic and logical way. However, just because an inference is more complicated does not mean that it is more accurate; in fact, the opposite is often the case. One of the masters of inference is the legendary Sherlock Holmes. In the following passage, Holmes makes an astonishing number of inferences upon meeting Dr. Watson. Study Holmes's conclusions carefully. Are they reasonable? Can you explain how he reaches them?

"You appeared to be surprised when I told you, on our first meeting, that you had come from Afghanistan."

"You were told, no doubt."

"Nothing of the sort. I knew you came from Afghanistan. From long habit the train of thoughts ran so swiftly through my mind that I arrived at the conclusion without being conscious of intermediate steps. There were such steps, however. The train of reasoning ran, 'Here is a gentleman of a medical type, but with the air of a military man. Clearly an army doctor, then. He is just come from the tropics, for his face is dark, and that is not the natural tint of his skin, for his wrists are fair. He has undergone hardship and sickness, as his haggard face says clearly. His left arm has been injured. He holds it in a stiff and unnatural manner. Where in the tropics could an English army doctor have seen much hardship and got his arm wounded? Clearly in Afghanistan.' The whole train of thought did not occupy a second. I then remarked that you came from Afghanistan, and you were astonished."

—Sir Arthur Conan Doyle, *A Study in Scarlet*

Thinking-Writing Activity

ANALYZING AN INCORRECT INFERENCE

Describe an experience in which you made an incorrect inference. For example, it might have been a situation in which you mistakenly accused someone, an accident based on a miscalculation, a poor decision based on an inaccurate prediction, or some other event. Analyze that experience by answering the following questions.

1. What was (were) your mistaken inference(s)?
2. What was the factual evidence on which you based your inference(s)?
3. Looking back, what could you have done to avoid making the erroneous inference(s)?

The following essay illustrates the ongoing process by which natural scientists use inferences to discover factual information and to construct theories explaining the information.

"Evolution as Fact and Theory"

by Stephen Jay Gould

Stephen Jay Gould started his academic career as a professor of geology at Harvard University but expanded his interests into evolutionary biology. He was curator of invertebrate paleontology at Harvard's Museum of Comparative Zoology and a writer with a gift for translating complex scientific theories into informed, but witty, prose that nonscientists can understand and enjoy. His essays appeared in magazines such as *Natural History* and *Discover* and were collected in the books *Ever Since Darwin, The Panda's Thumb,* and *The Flamingo's Smile.* This essay illustrates the ongoing process by which natural scientists use inferences to discover factual information and to construct theories explaining that information.

Kirtley Mather, who died last year at age 89, was a pillar of both science and the Christian religion in America and one of my dearest friends. The difference of half a century in our ages evaporated before our common interests. The most curious thing we shared was a battle we each fought at the same age. For Kirtley had gone to Tennessee with Clarence Darrow to testify for evolution at the Scopes trial of 1925. When I think that we are enmeshed again in the same struggle for one of the best documented, most compelling and exciting concepts in all of science, I don't know whether to laugh or cry.

According to idealized principles of scientific discourse, the arousal of dormant issues should reflect fresh data that give renewed life to abandoned notions. Those

Source: "Evolution as Fact and Theory" by Stephen Jay Gould. *Discover Magazine,* 1981. Reprinted by permission of the author.

outside the current debate may therefore be excused for suspecting that creationists have come up with something new, or that evolutionists have generated some serious internal trouble. But nothing has changed; the creationists have not a single new fact or argument. Darrow and Bryan were at least more entertaining than we lesser antagonists today. The rise of creationism is politics, pure and simple; it represents one issue (and by no means the major concern) of the resurgent evangelical right. Arguments that seemed kooky just a decade ago have re-entered the mainstream.

Creationism Is Not Science

The basic attack of the creationists falls apart on two general counts before we even reach the supposed factual details of their complaints against evolution. First, they play upon a vernacular misunderstanding of the word "theory" to convey the false impression that we evolutionists are covering up the rotten core of our edifice. Second, they misuse a popular philosophy of science to argue that they are behaving scientifically in attacking evolution. Yet the same philosophy demonstrates that their own belief is not science, and that "scientific creationism" is therefore meaningless and self-contradictory, a superb example of what Orwell called "newspeak."

In the American vernacular, "theory" often means "imperfect fact"—part of a hierarchy of confidence running downhill from fact to theory to hypothesis to guess. Thus the power of the creationist argument: evolution is "only" a theory, and intense debate now rages about many aspects of the theory. If evolution is less than a fact, and scientists can't even make up their minds about the theory, then what confidence can we have in it? Indeed, President Reagan echoed this argument before an evangelical group in Dallas when he said (in what I devoutly hope was campaign rhetoric): "Well, it is a theory. It is a scientific theory only, and it has in recent years been challenged in the world of science—that is, not believed in the scientific community to be as infallible as it once was."

5   Well, evolution *is* a theory. It is also a fact. And facts and theories are different things, not rungs in a hierarchy of increasing certainty. Facts are the world's data. Theories are structures of ideas that explain and interpret facts. Facts do not go away when scientists debate rival theories to explain them. Einstein's theory of gravitation replaced Newton's, but apples did not suspend themselves in mid-air pending the outcome. And human beings evolved from apelike ancestors whether they did so by Darwin's proposed mechanism or by some other, yet to be discovered.

Moreover, "fact" does not mean "absolute certainty." The final proofs of logic and mathematics flow deductively from stated premises and achieve certainty only because they are *not* about the empirical world. Evolutionists make no claim for perpetual truth, though creationists often do (and then attack us for a style of argument that they themselves favor). In science, "fact" can only mean "confirmed to such a degree that it would be perverse to withhold provisional assent." I suppose that apples might start to rise tomorrow, but possibility does not merit equal time in physics classrooms.

Evolutionists have been clear about this distinction between fact and theory from the very beginning, if only because we have always acknowledged how far we are from completely understanding the mechanisms (theory) by which evolution (fact) occurred. Darwin continually emphasized the difference between his two great and separate accomplishments: establishing the fact of evolution, and proposing a theory—natural selection—to explain the mechanism of evolution. He wrote in *The Descent of Man:* "I had two distinct objects in view; firstly, to show that species had not been separately created, and secondly, that natural selection had been the chief agent of change. . . . Hence if I have erred in . . . having exaggerated its [natural selection] power . . . I have at least, as I hope, done good service in aiding to overthrow the dogma of separate creations."

Thus Darwin acknowledged the provisional nature of natural selection while affirming the fact of evolution. The fruitful theoretical debate that Darwin initiated has never ceased. From the 1940s through the 1960s, Darwin's own theory of natural selection did achieve a temporary hegemony that it never enjoyed in his lifetime. But renewed debate characterizes our decade, and while no biologist questions the importance of natural selection, many now doubt its ubiquity. In particular, many evolutionists argue that substantial amounts of genetic change may not be subject to natural selection and may spread through populations at random. Others are challenging Darwin's linking of natural selection with gradual, imperceptible change through all intermediary degrees; they are arguing that most evolutionary events may occur far more rapidly than Darwin envisioned.

Scientists regard debates on fundamental issues of theory as a sign of intellectual health and a source of excitement. Science is—and how else can I say it?—most fun when it plays with interesting ideas, examines their implications, and recognizes that old information may be explained in surprisingly new ways. Evolutionary theory is now enjoying this uncommon vigor. Yet amidst all this turmoil no biologist has been led to doubt the fact that evolution occurred; we are debating *how* it happened. We are all trying to explain the same thing: the tree of evolutionary descent linking all organisms by ties of genealogy. Creationists pervert and caricature this debate by conveniently neglecting the common conviction that underlies it, and by falsely suggesting that we now doubt the very phenomenon we are struggling to understand.

10   Using another invalid argument, creationists claim that "the dogma of separate creations," as Darwin characterized it a century ago, is a scientific theory meriting equal time with evolution in high school biology curricula. But a prevailing viewpoint among philosophers of science belies this creationist argument. Philosopher Karl Popper has argued for decades that the primary criterion of science is the falsifiability of its theories. We can never prove absolutely, but we can falsify. A set of ideas that cannot, in principle, be falsified is not science.

The entire creationist argument involves little more than a rhetorical attempt to falsify evolution by presenting supposed contradictions among its supporters. Their brand of creationism, they claim, is "scientific" because it follows the Popperian model in trying to demolish evolution. Yet Popper's argument must apply in both directions. One does not become a scientist by the simple act of trying to falsify another scientific system; one has to present an alternative system that also meets Popper's criterion—it too must be falsifiable in principle.

"Scientific creationism" is a self-contradictory, nonsense phrase precisely because it cannot be falsified. I can envision observations and experiments that would disprove any evolutionary theory I know, but I cannot imagine what potential data could lead creationists to abandon their beliefs. Unbeatable systems are dogma, not science. Lest I seem harsh or rhetorical, I quote creationism's leading intellectual, Duane Gish, Ph.D., from his recent (1978) book *Evolution? The Fossils Say No!* "By creation we mean the bringing into being by a supernatural Creator of the basic kinds of plants and animals by the process of sudden, or flat, creation. We do not know how the Creator created, what processes He used, *for He used processes which are not now operating anywhere in the natural universe* [Gish's italics]. This is why we refer to creation as special creation. We cannot discover by scientific investigations anything about the creative processes used by the Creator." Pray tell, Dr. Gish, in the light of your last sentence, what then is "scientific" creationism?

The Fact of Evolution

Our confidence that evolution occurred centers upon three general arguments. First, we have abundant, direct, observational evidence of evolution in action, from both the field and the laboratory. It ranges from countless experiments on change in nearly everything about fruit flies subjected to artificial selection in the laboratory to the famous British moths that turned black when industrial soot darkened the trees upon which they rest. (The moths gain protection from sharp-sighted bird predators by blending into the background.) Creationists do not deny these observations; how could they? Creationists have tightened their act. They now argue that God only created "basic kinds," and allowed for limited evolutionary meandering within them. Thus toy poodles and Great Danes come from the dog kind and moths can change color, but nature cannot convert a dog to a cat or a monkey to a man.

The second and third arguments for evolution—the case for major changes—do not involve direct observation of evolution in action. They rest upon inference, but are no less secure for that reason. Major evolutionary change requires too much time for direct observation on the scale of recorded human history. All historical sciences rest upon inference, and evolution is no different from geology, cosmology, or human history in this respect. In principle, we cannot observe processes that operated in the past. We must infer them from results that still survive: living and fossil organisms for evolution, documents and artifacts for human history, strata and topography for geology.

15   The second argument—that the imperfection of nature reveals evolution—strikes many people as ironic, for they feel that evolution should be most elegantly displayed in the nearly perfect adaptation expressed by some organisms—the camber of a gull's wing, or butterflies that cannot be seen in ground litter because they mimic leaves so precisely. But perfection could be imposed by a wise creator or evolved by natural selection. Perfection covers the tracks of past history. And past history—the evidence of descent—is our mark of evolution.

Evolution lies exposed in the *imperfections* that record a history of descent. Why should a rat run, a bat fly, or porpoise swim, and I type this essay with structures built of the same bones unless we all inherited them from a common ancestor? An engineer, starting from scratch, could design better limbs in each case. Why should all the large native mammals of Australia be marsupials, unless they descended from a common ancestor isolated on this island continent? Marsupials are not "better," or ideally suited for Australia; many have been wiped out by placental mammals imported by man from other continents. This principle of imperfection extends to all historical sciences. When we recognize the etymology of September, October, November, and December (seventh, eighth, ninth, and tenth, from the Latin), we know that two additional items (January and February) must have been added to an original calendar of ten months.

The third argument is more direct: transitions are often found in the fossil record. Preserved transitions are not common—and should not be, according to our understanding of evolution . . .—but they are not entirely wanting, as creationists often claim. The lower jaw of reptiles contains several bones, that of mammals only one. The nonmammalian jawbones are reduced, step by step, in mammalian ancestors until they become tiny nubbins located at the back of the jaw. The "hammer" and the "anvil" bones of the mammalian ear are descendants of these nubbins. How could such a transition be accomplished?, the creationists ask. Surely a bone is either entirely in the jaw or in the ear. Yet paleontologists have discovered two transitional lineages of therapsids (the so-called mammal-like reptiles) with a double jaw joint—one composed of the old quadrate and articular bones (soon to become the hammer and anvil), the other of the squamosal and dentary bones (as in modern mammals). For that matter, what better transitional form could we desire than the oldest human, *Australopithecus afarensis*, with its apelike palate, its human upright stance, and a cranial capacity larger than any ape's of the same body size but a full 1,000 cubic centimeters below ours? If God made each of the half dozen human species discovered in ancient rocks, why did he create an unbroken temporal sequence of progressively more modern features—increasing cranial capacity, reduced face and teeth, larger body size? Did he create a mimic evolution and test our faith thereby?

Conclusion

I am both angry at and amused by the creationists; but mostly I am deeply sad. Sad for many reasons. Sad because so many people who respond to creationist appeals are troubled for the right reason, but venting their anger at the wrong target. It is true that scientists have often been dogmatic and elitist. It is true that we have often allowed the white-coated, advertising image to represent us—"Scientists say that Brand X cures bunions ten times faster than . . ." We have not fought it adequately because we derive benefits from appearing as a new priesthood. It is also true that faceless bureaucratic state power intrudes more and more into our lives and removes choices that should belong to individuals and communities. I can understand that requiring that evolution be taught in the schools might be seen as one more insult on all these grounds. But the culprit is not, and cannot be, evolution or any other fact of the natural world. Identify and fight your legitimate enemies by all means, but we are not among them.

I am sad because the practical result of this brouhaha will not be expanded coverage to include creationism (that would also make me sad), but the reduction or excision of evolution from high school curricula. Evolution is one of the half dozen "great ideas" developed by science. It speaks to the profound issues of genealogy that fascinate all of us—the "roots" phenomenon writ large. Where did we come from? Where did life arise? How did it develop? How are organisms related? It forces us to think, ponder, and wonder. Shall we deprive millions of this knowledge and once again teach biology as a set of dull and unconnected facts, without the thread that weaves diverse material into a supple unity?

20   But most of all I am saddened by a trend I am just beginning to discern among my colleagues. I sense that some now wish to mute the healthy debate about theory that has brought new life to evolutionary biology. It provides grist for creationist mills, they say, even if only by distortion. Perhaps we should lie low and rally around the flag of strict Darwinism, at least for the moment—a kind of old-time religion on our part.

But we should borrow another metaphor and recognize that we too have to tread a straight and narrow path, surrounded by roads to perdition. For if we ever begin to suppress our search to understand nature, to quench our own intellectual excitement in a misguided effort to present a united front where it does not and should not exist, then we are truly lost.

Questions for Reading Actively

1. Gould defines *facts* as the "world's data" and refers to observing an apple fall from the tree as Isaac Newton is alleged to have done. Identify some of the facts Gould presents as evidence to support the theory of evolution.

2. Gould defines *theories* as "structures of ideas that explain and interpret facts," such as Newton's theory of gravitation, which was introduced to explain facts like falling apples. In addition to facts, Gould states, the theory of evolution is supported by reasonable inferences. Identify some inferences that he cites as evidence.

3. Gould begins this essay with allusions to the Scopes trial of 1925, Darrow, and Bryan. He seems to assume that his readers will know what he is talking about. If you know about this event, how does this reference set the scene for his 1981 essay? If you don't know about it, was your understanding reduced?

Questions for Thinking Critically

1. What does Gould say about creationism? Find specific statements. Is Gould presenting reports, inferences, or judgments about this concept?

2. Gould calls Kirtley Mather a "pillar of both science and the Christian religion in America." Do you know people who are both scientific and spiritual? What do those people say about these two approaches to the world?

Question for Thinking Critically

1. Think about how the qualities of a critical reader and thinker can be useful in discussing issues related to evolution and creationism and write a short essay describing your reasoning.

The comic strip below was probably intended to be funny, but it reflects what Gould says about theories as "structures of ideas that explain and interpret facts." Historical facts are interpreted differently at different times; theories about history change. School textbooks about United States history of fifty years ago usually focused on the Founding Fathers, pioneers moving westward, and military actions. Books published now usually include material on Native Americans, women, slaves, and daily life. You might want to discuss this change with your grandparents or older friends.

Judging by Applying Criteria

Identify and write a description of a friend, a course you have taken, or the college you attend. Be sure your descriptions are specific and include what you think about the friend, the course, and the college.

1. _____ is a friend I have. He/she is . . .

2. _____ is a course I have taken. It was . . .

3. _____ is the college I attend. It is . . .

Now review your writing. Does it include factual descriptions? Note any facts that can be verified. Your writing may also contain inferences based on factual information. Can you identify any? In addition, your writing may include judgments about the person, the course, and the school—descriptions that express your evaluation based on certain criteria. Facts and inferences help you figure out what is actually happening (or will happen); the purpose of judgments is to express your evaluation about what is happening (or will happen). For example:

- My new car has broken down three times in the first six months. (Factual report)

- My new car will probably continue to have difficulties. (Inference)

- My new car is a lemon. (Judgment)

When you label your new car a "lemon," you are making a judgment based on certain criteria. For instance, a lemon is usually a newly purchased item—often an automobile—with which you have repeated problems. For another example of judging, consider the following statements:

- Carla always does her work thoroughly and completes it on time. (Factual report)
- Carla will probably continue to do her work in this fashion. (Inference)
- Carla is a very responsible person. (Judgment)

By judging Carla to be responsible, you are evaluating her on the basis of the criteria or standards that you believe indicate a responsible person. One such criterion is completing assigned work on time. Can you identify additional criteria for judging someone as being responsible?

Review your previous description of a friend, a course, or your college. Can you identify any judgments in your description? For each judgment you have listed, identify the criteria on which you based the judgment.

Many of our disagreements with others focus on differences in judgments. To write thoughtfully, you need to approach such differences intelligently by following these guidelines:

- Make explicit the criteria or standards used as a basis for the judgment.
- Try to establish the reasons that justify these criteria.

For instance, if you write "Professor Andrews is an excellent teacher," you are basing your judgment on certain criteria of teaching excellence. Once these standards are made explicit, they can be discussed to see whether they make sense and what justifies them. Of course, your idea of what makes an excellent teacher may be different from someone else's, so you can test your conclusion by comparing your criteria with those of your classmates. When disagreements occur, use these two steps for resolution.

In short, not all judgments are equally good or equally poor. The credibility of a judgment depends on the criteria used to make the judgment and on the evidence or reasons that support these criteria. For example, there may be legitimate disagreements about judgments on the following points:

- Who was the greatest United States president?
- Which movie deserves the Oscar this year?
- Which is the best baseball team this year?

However, in these and countless other cases, the quality of judgments depends on presenting the criteria used for the competing judgments and then demonstrating that your candidate best meets the agreed-upon criteria by providing supporting evidence and reasons. With this approach, you can often engage in intelligent discussion and establish which judgments are best supported by the evidence.

Thinking-Writing Activity

ANALYZING JUDGMENTS

Review the following two passages, which illustrate various judgments. For each passage, do the following:

1. Identify the evaluative criteria on which the judgments are based.

2. Describe the reasons or evidence the author uses to support the criteria.

3. Explain whether you agree or disagree with the judgments and give your rationale.

One widely held misconception concerning pizza should be laid to rest. Although it may be characterized as fast food, pizza is not junk food. Especially when it is made with fresh ingredients, pizza fulfills our basic nutritional requirements. The crust provides carbohydrates; from the cheese and meat or fish comes protein; and the tomatoes, herbs, onions, and garlic supply vitamins and minerals.

—Louis Philip Salamone, "Pizza: Fast Food, Not Junk Food"

Let us return to the question of food. Responsible agronomists report that before the end of the year millions of people if unaided might starve to death. Half a billion deaths by starvation is not an uncommon estimate. Even though the United States has done more than any other nation to feed the hungry, our relative affluence makes us morally vulnerable in the eyes of other nations and in our own eyes. Garrett Hardin, who has argued for a "lifeboat" ethic of survival (if you take all the passengers aboard, everybody drowns), admits that the decision not to feed all the hungry requires of us "a very hard psychological adjustment." Indeed it would. It has been estimated that the 3.5 million tons of fertilizer spread on American golf courses and lawns could provide up to 30 million tons of food in overseas agricultural production. The nightmarish thought intrudes itself. If we as a nation allow people to starve while we could, through some sacrifice, make more food available to them, what hope can any person have for the future of international relations? If we cannot agree on this most basic of values—feed the hungry—what hopes for the future can we entertain?

—James R. Kelly, "The Limits of Reason"

Distinguishing Among Reports, Inferences, and Judgments

Although the activities of reporting, inferring, and judging tend to be woven together in your experiences and in your writing, it is important to be able to distinguish these activities. Each plays a different role in helping you make sense of the world for yourself and for your audience, and you should be careful not to confuse these roles. For instance, although writers may appear to be reporting factual information, they may actually be expressing personal evaluations, which are not factual. Consider the statement "Los Angeles is a smog-ridden city drowning in automobiles." Although seeming to be reporting factual information, the writer really is expressing his or her personal judgment. Of course, writers can identify their judgments with such phrases as "in my opinion," "my evaluation is," and so forth.

Sometimes, however, writers do not identify their judgments. In some cases they do not do so because the context within which they are writing (such as a newspaper editorial) makes it clear that the information is judgment rather than fact. In other cases, however, they want their judgments to be treated as factual information. Confusing the activities of reporting, inferring, and judging, whether accidental or deliberate, can be misleading and even dangerous.

Confusing factual information with judgments can be personally damaging as well. For example, there is a big difference between these two statements:

- I failed my exam today. (Factual report)
- I am a failure. (Judgment)

Stating the fact "I failed my exam today" describes your situation in a concrete way, enabling you to evaluate (judge) it as a problem you can hope to solve through reflection and hard work. If, however, the situation causes you to make the judgment "I am a failure," this sort of general evaluation will not encourage you to explore solutions to the problem or improve your situation.

Finally, another main reason for distinguishing among the activities of reporting, inferring, and judging concerns the accuracy of statements. We noted, for instance, that factual statements tend to be reasonably accurate because they are by nature verifiable whereas inferences are usually much less certain. As a result, it is crucial to be aware of whether you are presenting a belief as a report, an inference, or a judgment. If you write the superintendent of your apartment building a note saying, "My thermostat is broken," an inference on your part based on the fact that you feel uncomfortably hot, you will feel foolish if you later discover that you have a fever and that the thermostat is functioning well.

Presenting Beliefs in Your Writing

Understanding and evaluating beliefs pertains in three particular ways to your college papers as well as to the writing you will do in other settings. First, as you are better able to distinguish among reports, inferences, and judgments, you will be able to present different types of beliefs more accurately. Although you may not often use the term *report, inference,* or *judgment,* you will word your beliefs in precise ways that indicate the level of speculation behind your statements.

Second, a strong relationship exists between the thesis of a paper and your beliefs about the topic. The thesis, most of all, expresses what you believe is the main point of your paper. As you work to clarify your thesis statement, you also clarify your beliefs about the issue you are addressing. And when you state the thesis clearly in your paper, you are making your beliefs clear to your readers.

Third, as a college writer and quite possibly as a working professional, you will regularly use source material in your papers. The techniques for evaluating beliefs will help you evaluate sources of information. Then, as you present in your researched writing what others have said, you can comment on their beliefs as you integrate the material into your papers. (See Chapter 14 on research.)

Writing Project: Analyzing Influences on Your Beliefs About a Social or Academic Issue

This chapter has included both readings and Thinking-Writing Activities that encourage you to think about the sources of your beliefs. Be sure to reread what you wrote for the activities as you may be able to use some of your work in completing this project.

> Write an essay in which you consider some influences on the development of your beliefs about a social issue or an idea related to an academic field. As much as possible, apply the concepts discussed in this chapter.
>
> As a college student, you receive much of your information about social or academic issues from print and electronic sources. Therefore, you should analyze at least two media sources such as newspaper, magazine, or journal articles; material from a web site; a film or a DVD; a book or book chapter. In addition, think about what your teachers and other people have told you and, perhaps, about personal experiences.

Begin by considering the key elements of the Thinking-Writing Model in Chapter 1 on pages 6–7.

The Writing Situation

Purpose   Your primary purpose here is to further your own development as a capable college student. You will be exploring some of the ways in which you come to accept concepts. In addition, you will be sharing your insights with your audience, which always provides another purpose: to write an effective paper.

On a technical level, you are required to take different kinds of information and pull them together. Such *synthesis* is the central purpose of many kinds of academic and professional writing. Most research papers, case studies, field reports, project summaries, product proposals, and business plans use information that must be analyzed and synthesized.

You also have an intellectual purpose. You will look closely at your own ways of defining what you believe and what you consider true as well as what you do not believe and what you consider false.

Audience   As usual, your classmates are a good audience for this paper, both in draft and finished versions, since they are doing the same assignment and will want to see how you handle it. In addition, people interested in the social issue or academic field will naturally be potential readers. If you are taking a class pertaining to your subject, you could share your paper with those students. If you are writing about a social issue relevant to your community, you could share your work in a newsletter or on a website.

Of course, your instructor remains the audience who will judge how well you have articulated your beliefs, how you have selected the influences on your beliefs, how you have handled the sources, and how you have planned, drafted, revised, and edited your essay.

Subject   Examining the sources of beliefs and evaluating evidence are among the most challenging of activities. If you are just beginning to learn about the issue on which you are writing, you may not have enough background to be very inquisitive or judgmental. However, you should be aware of criteria that any thoughtful student can detect: specific support for a claim, whether information is current, appropriateness of examples and authorities, and responsible attribution. Also, you have some understanding of reports, inferences, predictions, and judgments to apply to your analysis.

Writer   For this Writing Project, you should be as open as possible to new ways of thinking about your beliefs. After such critical analysis, some writers find that their beliefs have been strengthened; others may realize that some of their beliefs were based on unreliable information and need to be reevaluated.

As with the Writing Projects in Part One, you are in a position of authority here when you are writing about your own reactions and realizations. At the same time, since you are writing about a social issue or an academic field instead of about your personal life, you are a writer who is dealing with other people's beliefs in addition to your own. After writing the paper, you may want to consider whether you are a more accepting or more skeptical person.

The Writing Process

The following sections will guide you through the stages of planning, drafting, and revising your essay analyzing the sources of your beliefs.

Generating Ideas

- Identify some ideas in the Thinking-Writing Activities that you may be able to use. Then write informally about them.
- Think about teachers, books, films, articles, the Internet, and other sources of information in your field that have provided you with information that you believe. Why have they had this effect?

- Think about any sources that you are reluctant to trust or believe. Why have they had this effect?
- What concepts in this field do you believe most firmly?
- Are there some that you question?
- Freewrite for five minutes about your ideas for this project.
- Look at the list of questions for exploring topics in Chapter 4. Which of them can help you generate ideas for this project?

Defining a Focus

- The Writing Project itself provides a wide-angle focus, but you must sharpen it in order to produce an understandable paper.
- Notice if your issue or idea has several components. For example, the issue of high-stakes testing in public schools raises questions about the kind of tests used, the effects on students' passing to the next grade, the effects on school funding or ratings, and the effects on curriculum. You may want to focus only on one aspect. Perhaps your beliefs about evolution in biology or parallel processing in computer science are really beliefs about several components of the general idea.
- Write down your belief to be sure that you can state it well. If you haven't decided on one belief, write several. Are they interpretations, evaluations, conclusions, or predictions in your statement? Do these terms help you find a focus?
- Consider your level of belief. Are you strongly convinced that your belief is plausible? Do you have questions about it? Why?
- Focus on differences. Does a popular press, television, or website account differ from what a book says or what a professor has taught you?
- Draft a thesis statement that gives direction to the essay.
- Create a map, web, or rough outline so that you can see how ideas might cluster or separate. See Chapter 4 for idea-generation strategies.

Organizing Ideas

If you created a map or rough outline while you were looking for a focus, review it and try to be more specific about how to arrange the ideas for your paper.

- Have you drafted a tentative thesis that states your belief, one that says something about the sources of the belief, or one that includes both? What kind would be most effective?
- If you have several sources for your belief, does each one deserve at least a paragraph?
- If your beliefs have changed, have you discussed this matter in an effective place?

- If you are contrasting two differing perspectives, have you structured the contrast logically?
- If you are presenting similar perspectives, have you structured the comparison logically?
- Have you planned a conclusion? Does it refer to the influences on your beliefs?
- Remember that you may modify your plan or outline as you draft.

Drafting

- Begin with the part easiest to draft. Is it writing about your instructors or dealing with your print or electronic sources?
- Perhaps you should then shift to a part that is hard to draft and at least make some notes or write questions.
- Draft a new outline or map, if necessary, as you rethink what you want to say. Look at the preliminary thesis statement that you drafted. Do you need to rework it now, or should you wait until you have drafted more?
- Shape the paragraphs that will make up the body of your essay. Draft clear topic sentences; think about where the topic sentence should be placed in each paragraph.
- Draft an opening paragraph and a concluding paragraph, understanding that you may want to revise them substantially later.

Revising, Editing, and Proofreading   Use the Step-by-Step method in Chapter 6 on pages 169–171 to revise your essay and prepare a final draft.

Student Writing

Jessie Lange's Writing Process

The following essay was written for a criminal justice course. Jessie's professor asked students to demonstrate how media treatments of a current criminal justice issue helped to shape the beliefs they hold about that issue. For students in a criminal justice course, who might someday be dealing with offenders or victims of a particular kind of crime, the ability to distinguish between personal beliefs and objective evidence (and to make a distinction between how they might personally feel about an issue and what the law says about that issue) is of critical importance. But Jessie realized that as a concerned citizen, it was also her responsibility to be informed about criminal justice issues that might impact her as a woman, a voter, and a future parent. Jessie used the Thinking-Writing Activity entitled Evaluating Factual Information on page 395 to discuss her two key sources.

Dealing with Sex Offenders

by Jessie Lange

In the past few years we have heard much about Megan's Law, which states that people should be made aware of charged sex offenders in their community. While I wholeheartedly believe that people, for the protection of themselves and their children, have the right to know, there is another twist on the issue I hadn't thought about until I heard a story recently on *60 Minutes*. The story involved Stephanie's Law—a new law in place in some states under which sex offenders are kept *after* they have served their time to go through a therapy program in an attempt to "cure" them. The question that this provoked in me was not whether the state should have the right to hold sexual criminals beyond their sentence, but whether they can be cured at all. If not, should they ever be released back into a world where they are likely to do more damage, destroy more lives?

A recent *New York Times* article described a rehabilitation program in Texas whereby prisoners are immersed in religion—taking classes, having discussions, and owning up to their "sins." Interestingly, while there are 79 men convicted of "robbery, drug possession, and murder" participating, those convicted of sexual crimes are not accepted into the program. This is partly because they are "looked down on by other prisoners" and partly because, according to criminologists, "sexual criminals are the most difficult to rehabilitate."

In fact, there is a question as to whether this rehabilitation is even possible. Sexual criminals in particular seem to be under the influence of urges which are out of their control. The *60 Minutes* report said that, while many may have good intentions in being treated through therapy and returning to society, it may be out of their hands. They may say they understand their wrongs, they may feel cured, but if they are released it seems impossible for even the offenders to know if they will be able to control their impulses. If there is such a question, do they deserve a chance at freedom when it means potentially committing another crime?

There is no question in my mind that, while many sex offenders do not repent for what they have done and have no real interest in being cured, there are also many for whom their crimes are almost out of their hands—as disgusting to them as to anyone else. The *New York Times* ran an article entitled "Sex Offender Agrees to Be Castrated." In Illinois, a convicted child sex offender is having himself castrated "in an effort to win a lighter sentence." The offender, in fact, "volunteered to be castrated even before he was convicted" previously of an attack on a young girl. It seems as though the man is making an attempt to control his urges but, according to the article, "experts disagree on whether castration helps" in controlling these urges.

Both the *New York Times* and *60 Minutes* have good reputations as reliable media sources. I read this paper and watch this show regularly. (I'm pleased that my parents introduced me to them.) I think that these reports are as reliable as the popular press can be. If I decide to do research on this subject and write a substantial paper, I will have to use criminal justice and sociology journals and try to interview one or two experts, as well.

I have not had any personal experience with sex offenders, but I have read and heard enough to know that their crimes destroy not only the lives of victims but also the lives of families and friends of the victims and that their crimes can so haunt victims that these fears are never resolved. In addition, victims of sexual crimes may grow up to inflict these crimes on others, continuing the cycle. In my opinion, the damage done by sex offenders and the risk of untreatable urges to commit these crimes, a risk illustrated by the high percentage of repeat offenders, is too great to justify their release. At least not until there is a proven "cure," a sure-fire way to *know* that they are treatable, have been treated, and will not continue to make victims of others.

Through the media, I have come to understand that many may be operating on urges not within their control, but this does not justify their release. At some point the blame has to fall on the individual. If they were to learn that their rehabilitation was an impossibility, I think that those who are truly disgusted by their crimes might even agree that they are too dangerous to be returned to a society where they have already done so much damage.

Works Cited

Niebuhr, Gustav. "Using Religion to Reform Criminals." *New York Times* 18 Jan. 1998, late ed.: A16. Print.

"Sex Offender Agrees to Be Castrated." *New York Times* 18 Jan. 1998: A6. Print.

60 Minutes. WCBS, New York. 24 June 1997. Television.

Alternative Writing Project: Evolving Beliefs in an Academic Field

Locate a college or high school science, history, or literature textbook from forty or fifty years ago. Compare several specific points made in the decades-old book with points made in one of your textbooks in the same field.

In order to establish a context for what you observe, ask your instructor or a librarian to guide you to sources that discuss changes in theories in the field that your material is about. For example, in history, you could examine material about multicultural or gender-based approaches; in literature, material about "the canon"; in science, material about a specific discovery in genetics or physics.

Write an essay presenting the differences and similarities that you have found and comment on what beliefs they seem to reflect. Follow your instructor's directions for topic limitation, length, format, and citation methods.

CHAPTER 11 Summary

- A *belief* expresses an interpretation, evaluation, conclusion, or prediction about the world, as well as an endorsement of its accuracy; is formed, tested, revised, and retested over time; and can be based on your own personal experience or indirect experience.

- When we evaluate the sources and information related to a belief, it is important to consider the following questions:
  - How reliable is the source?
  - What are the source's purposes and interests?
  - How knowledgeable or experienced is the source?
  - Was the source able to make accurate observations?
  - How reputable is the source?
  - How valuable is information from this source?

- *Knowing* is distinguished from belief by strong reasons and evidence, and truth is often disagreed upon amongst experts, so it is important that we all analyze, evaluate, and develop our own well-reasoned beliefs and acknowledge when we do not have enough information to do so.

- A relativistic view of the world sees all opinions as equal in validity to all others. There are serious problems with this view as some opinions are clearly more informed and accurate than others in many areas of life.

- A belief can be seen as falsifiable if it is possible to state conditions—tests—under which the belief could be disproved but the belief passes those tests.

- The media can shape our beliefs in subtle yet profound ways.

- You can present your beliefs by reporting factual information, inferring from evidence or premises, or judging by applying criteria.

STR/AFP/Getty Images/Newscom

Muhammad Yunus established the Grameen Bank, which provides "microcredit" loans to Bangladeshi women living in poverty who wish to start businesses, work for which he received the Nobel Peace Prize in 2006. Going against traditional economic theory, Yunus' small-sum loans make a remarkable impact in the lives of these women and their communities. Not only do the women typically pay back the loans quickly, the percentage of repaid loans is higher than that of most First-World countries. This challenging, innovative way of thinking about poverty is a profound example of how creative thinking can solve even the most intractable problems. How do Yunus' microcredit loans relate to the reading in Chapter 5 by Peter Singer?

Writing to Propose Solutions: Solving Problems

"Whatever creativity is, it is in part a solution to a problem."

—BRIAN ALDISS

Problem solving is one of the most powerful of human thinking patterns, and writing is the main system we use to analyze challenging problems and propose solutions. On a personal level, you have probably written an email about a problem in your life. You may have been trying to sustain a romantic relationship with someone while geographically separated, helping a friend resolve a personal crisis, or writing to family members to coordinate a holiday reunion. To address civic problems, you and your neighbors may have written letters to newspapers or petitioned your local government. Writing memos, reports, and proposals to solve problems is an integral part of most careers, from finance to filmmaking.

Although proposing solutions is a common form of writing, it is challenging. In order to compose an insightful solution, you need to do the following:

- *Define the problem clearly.* Your audience needs to understand that there *is* a problem and know exactly what it is.

- *Analyze the problem systematically.* Complex problems are often a confusing tangle of needs, ideas, frustrations, goals, and pieces of information. You need to disentangle the issues so that your audience can understand the core of the problem and what alternatives are possible.

- *Propose a well-reasoned solution.* After presenting a lucid analysis of the problem, along with feasible alternatives, you need to reach a conclusion that you support with thoughtful reasoning and solid evidence. As part of your proposed solution, you should explain why other alternative solutions are less desirable than yours. You should also address anticipated objections to your solution and explain how these difficulties can be overcome.

You will notice that the problem-solving method is similar to the decision-making method discussed in Chapter 5. However, this chapter presents the process in more detail; the focus is on problems instead of on decisions, and you will be considering social as well as personal issues. The chapter readings address societal problems. Finally, the Writing Project involves analyzing a social or personal problem that needs a solution.

Problems in Personal and Civic Life

Throughout your life, you will continually be solving problems. As a student, for example, you deal with a steady stream of academic assignments—quizzes, exams, research projects, essays, papers, and audiovisual presentations. In order to solve these academic problems effectively—how to do well on an exam, for example—you need to define the problem (what areas will the exam cover, and what will its format be?), identify and evaluate various alternatives (what are possible study approaches?), and then combine all these factors to reach a solution (what will your study plan and schedule be?). Relatively simple problems like preparing for an exam do not require a systematic or complex analysis. You can solve them with effort and concentration. However, the difficult and complicated problems in your personal life, such as choosing a college major or ending a relationship, may be a different story. Because these are such crucial situations, you will need to solve such problems in the best possible way by using all your creative and critical thinking skills.

The problems that exist in society also need the very best thinking of all citizens. The fear of terrorism is far too real, parents feel stressed about their children's safety, drugs and alcohol continue to destroy lives, and both racism and sexism create conflicts. These problems may seem overwhelming, and it is true that you cannot control them in the same way that you can control your own life situations. Still, by thinking creatively and critically about such issues, and by gathering information, you can at least develop your own views about contending with them. Then you will be in a position to act on such problems and to vote for candidates whose positions are similar to yours.

Basics of the Problem-Solving Method

Consider the following personal problem:

> My best friend is addicted to drugs, but he won't admit it. Jack always liked to drink, but I never thought too much about it. After all, a lot of people like to drink socially, get relaxed, and have a good time. But over the last few years, he's started using other drugs as well as alcohol, and it's ruining his life. He's stopped taking classes at college and will soon lose his job if he doesn't change. Last week I told him that I was really worried about him, but he told me that he has no drug problem and that in any case it really isn't any of my business. I don't know what to do. I've known Jack since we were in elementary school together, and he's a wonderful person. It's as if he's in the grip of some terrible force and I'm powerless to help him.

In working through this problem, the writer of this description could only think of one possible course of action to try. But if he or she chose instead to approach the problem as a critical thinker, the writer would have to think carefully and systematically through several possibilities in order to reach a solution.

In order to think effectively in situations like this, we usually ask ourselves a series of questions. These are the questions to ask in a five-step problem-solving method:

1. What is the *problem*?
2. What are the *alternatives*?
3. What are the *advantages* and/or *disadvantages* of each alternative?
4. What is the *solution*?
5. How well is the solution *working*?

Put yourself in the position of the student whose friend seems to be addicted to drugs and alcohol and apply the questions to that problem.

1. What Is the Problem?

There are a variety of ways to define the problem. For instance, you might define it simply as "Jack has a drug dependency." You might view the problem as "Jack has a drug dependency, but he won't admit it." You might even define the problem as "Jack has a drug dependency, but he won't admit it—and I want to help him solve this problem." Notice that each redefinition of the problem results in a more *specific* definition, which in turn helps you better understand the essence of the problem and your responsibility with respect to it.

2. What Are the Alternatives?

In dealing with this problem, you can consider a wide variety of possible actions before selecting the best ones. Identify some of the alternatives.

> (Example): Speak to my friend in a candid and forceful way to convince him that he has a serious drug dependency.

3. What Are the Advantages and Disadvantages of Each Alternative?

Evaluate the strengths and weaknesses of each alternative you have identified so that you can weigh your choices and determine the best course of action.

> (Example): Speak to my friend in a candid and forceful way to convince him that he has a serious problem.

> *Advantage:* He may respond to my direct emotional appeal, acknowledge that he has a problem, and seek help.

> *Disadvantage:* He may react angrily, further alienating me from him and making it more difficult for me to have any influence on him.

4. What Is the Solution?

After evaluating the various alternatives, select the one you think would be most effective for solving the problem and describe the sequence of steps you would take to act on that alternative.

5. How Well Is the Solution Working?

The final step in the process comes after you have begun to implement your choice of action. You review the solution and decide whether it is working well. If it is not, you must modify your solution or perhaps try an alternate solution you disregarded earlier. In this situation, trying to figure out the best way to help your friend recognize addiction and seek treatment leads to a series of decisions. This is what the critical thinking process is all about—trying to make sense of what is going on in the world and acting appropriately in response. When we solve problems effectively, our thinking process exhibits a coherent organization, following the general approach just outlined.

This problem-solving method lends itself to the organization of an essay or argument. For your writing to be truly effective in describing a problem and proposing a solution, you will need to consider additional rhetorical issues.

Audience   When writing about Jack's situation, the evidence you draw on and the voice in which you write will have to do with your immediate audience. If you are writing directly to Jack, you will want to be as candid, caring, and explicit as possible. You might want to describe, in a letter to Jack, a particularly difficult or embarrassing moment when his addiction interfered with your relationship. On the other hand, if you are writing to Jack's family to urge members to intervene, you will want to be less personal about Jack's effects on your own life and instead describe the effect of his behavior on his grades and his job performance.

Purpose   When describing a personal problem and exploring possible solutions, your purpose depends not only on your immediate audience but also on the outcome you desire. For example, if you were to write directly to Jack in this situation, your purpose might be either to urge him to seek help to preserve your relationship—or to inform him that you have reached the limits of your tolerance, and you are ending your friendship although you still wish him well. Your purpose will, obviously, influence your choice of language as well as the structure of your writing.

If we can understand the way the mind operates when we are thinking effectively, we can apply this understanding to improve our thinking in new, challenging situations. In the remainder of this chapter, we will explore a more sophisticated version of this problem-solving approach and apply it to a variety of complex, difficult problems.

Thinking-Writing Activity

ANALYZING A PROBLEM SOLVED PREVIOUSLY

1. Write a description of a problem in your personal life that you have recently solved.

2. Explain how you went about solving the problem. What were the steps, strategies, and approaches you used to understand the problem and to make an informed decision about a possible solution?

3. Analyze your thinking process by applying the five-step problem-solving method we have been exploring.

4. Share your problem with classmates and have them try to analyze and solve it. Then explain the solution you arrived at.

The Problem-Solving Method in Detail

Imagine yourself in the following situation. What would be your next move, and what are your reasons for deciding on it?

> You are about to begin your second year of college, following a very successful first year. Until now, you have financed your education through a combination of savings, financial aid, and a part-time job (sixteen hours a week) at a local store. However, you just received a letter from your college saying that your financial aid package has been reduced by half due to budgetary problems. The letter concludes, "We hope this aid reduction will not prove to be too great an inconvenience." From your perspective, the loss of aid isn't an inconvenience—it's a disaster! Your budget last year was already tight, and with your job, you barely had enough time to study, participate in a few college activities, and have a modest (but essential) social life. To make matters worse, your mother has been ill, reducing her income and creating financial problems at home. You're panicking—what in the world are you going to do?

As noted earlier, at first a difficult problem often seems like a confused tangle of information, feelings, alternatives, opinions, considerations, and risks. The problem just described is a complicated situation that does not seem to have a single simple solution. Without applying a systematic approach, your thoughts might wander through the tangle of issues in this manner:

> I want to stay in school, . . . but I'm not going to have enough money. . . . I could work more hours at my job, . . . but I might not have enough time to study and get top grades . . . and if all I'm doing is working and studying, what about my social life? . . . and what about Mom and the kids? They will need my help. . . . I could drop out of school for a while, . . . but if I don't stay in school, what kind of future do we have?

Very often, when faced with difficult problems like this one, you simply may not know where to begin to try to solve them. Every issue is connected to many others. Frustrated by not knowing where to take the first step, you may give up trying to understand the problem. Or you may behave in one of the following ways:

1. Act impulsively without thought or consideration ("I'll just quit school").

2. Follow someone else's advice without seriously evaluating the suggestion ("Tell me what I should do—I'm tired of thinking about this").

3. Do nothing as you wait for events to make the decision for you ("I'll just wait and see what happens").

None of these approaches is likely to succeed in the long run, and each can gradually reduce your confidence in dealing with complex problems. An alternative to these reactions is to *think critically* about the problem, analyzing it with an organized approach based on the following five-step method.

Even when we are using an organized method for working through difficult problems and arriving at thoughtful conclusions, our minds may not always work

---

Detailed Method for Solving Problems

Step 1: What is the problem?

    a. What do I know about the situation?

    b. What results am I seeking in this situation?

    c. How can I define the problem?

Step 2: What are the alternatives?

    a. What are the boundaries of the problem situation?

    b. What alternatives are possible within these boundaries?

Step 3: What are the advantages and disadvantages of each alternative?

    a. What are the advantages?

    b. What are the disadvantages?

    c. What additional information do I need in order to evaluate this alternative?

Step 4: What is the solution?

    a. Which alternative(s) will I pursue?

    b. What steps can I take to act on this/these alternative(s)?

Step 5: How well is the solution working?

    a. What is my evaluation?

    b. What adjustments are necessary?

in a logical, step-by-step fashion. Effective problem solvers typically pass through all the steps we will be examining, but not always in sequence.

Instead, the best problem solvers take a flexible approach to the process, one in which they utilize a repertoire of problem-solving strategies as needed. Sometimes, exploring the various alternatives helps them to go back and redefine the original problem. Similarly, seeking to implement the solution can often suggest a new alternative or alternatives that combine the best points of previous ones. This recursive approach is shown in Figure 12.1.

The key point is that although the problem-solving steps are presented in a logical sequence here, you need not follow them in a mechanical and unimaginative fashion. At the same time, in learning a problem-solving method like this, it is generally not wise to omit steps because each one deals with an important aspect of the problem. As you become more proficient in using the method, you will find that you can apply its concepts and strategies to problem solving in an increasingly flexible and natural fashion, just as learning the basics of an activity like driving a car gradually results in a more integrated performance of the skills involved.

Before You Begin: Accepting the Problem

To solve a problem, you must first be willing to *accept* the problem by acknowledging that it exists and committing yourself to trying to solve it. Sometimes you may have difficulty recognizing a problem unless it is pointed out to you. At other times, you may actively resist acknowledging a problem, even when it is pointed out to you. The person who confidently states, "I don't really have any problems," sometimes has very serious problems—but is simply unwilling to acknowledge them.

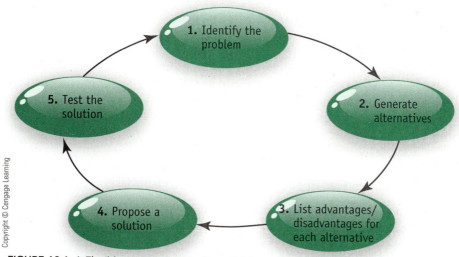

FIGURE 12.1 A Flexible Approach to Problem Solving

However, mere acknowledgment is not enough to solve a problem, and indeed it would make for a very brief and unsatisfying essay. Once you have identified a problem, you must commit yourself to solving it. Successful problem solvers are highly motivated and willing to persevere through the many challenges and frustrations of the problem-solving process. How do you find this motivation and commitment? There are not simple answers, but the following strategies may help:

- *List the benefits.* Making a detailed list of the benefits you will derive from successfully dealing with the problem is a good place to begin. Such a process helps you clarify why you might want to tackle the problem, motivates you to get started, and serves as a source of encouragement when you encounter difficulties or lose momentum.

- *Formalize your acceptance.* You can formalize your acceptance of a problem by "going on record," either by preparing a signed declaration or by signing a "contract" with someone else. This formal commitment can serve as an explicit statement of original intentions to which you can refer if your resolve weakens.

- *Accept responsibility for your life.* Former U.S. Attorney General Robert F. Kennedy, who was assassinated in 1968, once said, "Some people see things as they are, and ask, 'Why?' I see things as they could be, and ask, 'Why not?'" You have the potential to control the direction of your own life, but to do so, you must accept your freedom to choose and the responsibility that goes with it.

- *Create a "worst case" scenario.* Some problems persist because people are able to ignore their possible implications. When you create a worst-case scenario, you remind yourself, as graphically as possible, of the potentially disastrous consequences of your actions. For example, looking at vivid color photographs and research conclusions can remind a person that excessive smoking, drinking, or eating can lead to myriad health problems and social and psychological difficulties as well as death.

- *Identify the constraints.* If you are having trouble accepting a problem, it is usually because something is holding you back. For example, you might be concerned about the amount of time and effort involved, you might be reluctant to confront the underlying issues the problem represents, you might be worried about finding out unpleasant things about yourself or others, or you might be inhibited by other problems in your life, such as a tendency to procrastinate. Whatever the constraints, using this strategy involves identifying and describing all the factors that are preventing you from confronting the problem and then addressing them one at a time.

Step 1: What Is the Problem?

The problem-solving process begins by determining exactly what the central issues of the problem are. Otherwise, your chances of solving it are considerably reduced. You may even spend time trying to solve the wrong problem. For instance, consider the different formulations of the following problems. How might they lead a person in different directions when trying to solve it?

"School is boring" versus "I am bored in accounting class."
"I'm unlovable" versus "I was just turned down for a date."

In each of these cases, a very general conclusion (first formulation) has been replaced by a more specific characterization of the problem (second formulation).

General conclusions ("I'm a failure") do not suggest productive ways of resolving the difficulties. They are too absolute, too all-encompassing. On the other hand, more specific descriptions of the problem situation ("I just failed an exam") do permit you to attack problems with useful strategies. In short, the way you define a problem determines not only how you will go about solving it but also whether you feel that the problem can be solved at all. Correct identification of a problem is essential if you are going to be able to successfully analyze it and reach an appropriate conclusion. Incorrectly identifying the problem can lead to pursuing an unproductive, even destructive, course of action.

This process of identifying the problem and arriving at a specific characterization of it can help you to articulate a clear thesis (for an essay or research project) or claim (for an argument).

Consider the problem of the college student whose financial aid package was cut (pages 441–442) and analyze it using this problem-solving method. Ask:

1. What do I know about the situation?
2. What is my purpose for writing about the problem?
3. What results am I aiming for in this situation (what is my purpose)?
4. How can I define the problem?

Step 1A: What do I know about the situation?   Solving a problem begins with determining what you *know* to be the case and what you *think* may be the case. To explore the problem successfully, you need to have a clear idea of the details of your beginning circumstances. You can identify and organize what you know about the problem situation by posing key questions. By asking—and trying to answer—questions of fact, you are establishing a sound foundation for exploring your problem as well as developing an interesting, arguable thesis or claim. Imagine that you are the student described earlier who is facing a reduction in financial aid. Answer the following questions of fact—who? what? where? when? how? why?—about your problem.

- *Who* are the people involved in this situation?
  Who will benefit from my solving this problem?
  Who can help me solve this problem?
- *What* are the various parts or dimensions of the problem?
  What are my strengths and resources for solving this problem?

- *When* did the problem begin?
  When should the problem be resolved?

- *How* did the problem arise or develop?

- *Why* is solving this problem important to me?
  Why is this problem difficult to solve?

- Additional questions: _____

Step 1B: What results am I aiming for in this situation?   The second part of answering the question "What is the problem?" consists of identifying the specific results or objectives you are trying to achieve. Your purpose for writing about this problem is to solve it. If you are able to achieve your specific results or objectives, you will have satisfied your purpose for writing. Whereas the first part of step 1 oriented you in terms of the history of the problem and the current situation, this part encourages you to look to the future. To identify results, you need to ask yourself the question "What are the objectives that, once achieved, will solve this problem?" For instance, one of the results or objectives in the sample problem might be having enough money to pay for college. Describe additional results you might be trying to achieve in this situation.

1. Having enough money to pay for college.

2. _____

3. _____

4. _____

Step 1C: How can I define the problem?   After exploring what you know about the problem and the results you want to achieve, you need to conclude step 1 by defining the problem as clearly and specifically as possible. This is a crucial task in the problem-solving process because this definition will determine the direction of your analysis. Chapter 8 illustrates the thinking processes for successful definition.

Often, identifying the central issue of a problem is a complex process. For example, the statement "My problem is relating to other people" suggests a complicated situation with many interacting variables that resists simple definition. In fact, you may not even begin to develop a clear definition of the problem until you engage in the process of trying to solve it. Or you might begin by believing that your problem is, say, not having the ability to succeed but end by concluding that the problem is really a fear of success.

As you will see, the same insights also apply to social problems. For example, the problem of high school dropouts might initially be defined in terms of problems in the school system whereas later formulations might identify drug use or social pressure as the core of the problem.

Although there are no simple formulas for defining challenging problems, you can try several strategies to identify the central issue most effectively:

- *View the problem from different perspectives.* As you saw in Chapters 3, 7, and 8, perspective taking is a key ingredient of thinking critically; it can also help you to zero in on many problems. When you describe how various individuals might view a given problem—such as the high school dropout rate—the essential ingredients of the problems begin to emerge. In the student financial-aid problem, how would you describe the student's perspective? the college's perspective? the student's family's perspective?

- *Identify component problems.* Larger problems are often made up of component problems. To define a larger problem, it is often necessary to identify and describe the subproblems that comprise it. A student's poor school performance, for example, might result from a number of factors like ineffective study habits, inefficient time management, and preoccupation with a personal problem. Defining, and dealing effectively with, a larger problem means defining and dealing with the subproblems first. Can you identify two possible subproblems in the financial aid problem?

- *State the problem clearly and specifically.* A third defining strategy is to state the problem as clearly and specifically as possible as you examine your objectives for solving it. Stating this sort of precise description of the problem is an important step toward solving it. If you state the problem in very general terms, you won't have a clear idea of how best to proceed in dealing with it. However, if you can describe it in specific terms, your description will begin to suggest actions you can take to solve the problem. Examine the differences between the statements of the following problem:

General: "My problem is money."

More specific: "My problem is needing to budget my money so that I won't always run out of it near the end of the month."

Most specific: "My problem is my need to develop the habits and discipline to budget my money so that I won't always run out of it near the end of the month."

Review your analysis of the student's financial aid problem; then state the problem in writing as clearly and specifically as you can.

Step 2: What Are the Alternatives?

Once you have clearly and specifically identified a problem, your next move is to examine each possible action that might help you to solve it. Before you list the alternatives, however, it makes sense to explore the situation's boundaries to determine which actions are possible and which are not.

Step 2A: What are the boundaries of the problem situation?   Boundaries are limits that you simply cannot change. They are part of the problem, and they must be accepted and dealt with. At the same time, you must be careful not to identify as boundaries circumstances that *can* be changed. For instance, again imagining yourself as the student with the financial aid problem, you might assume that your problem must be solved in your current location, without realizing that transferring to a less expensive college could be one of your options. Identify additional boundaries that might be part of this sample situation and list some of the questions you should answer about these boundaries.

Step 2B: What alternatives are possible within these boundaries?   After you have established a general notion of the boundaries of the problem situation, you can proceed to identify the possible courses of action that can occur within them. Of course, identifying all the possible alternatives is not always easy; in fact, that may be part of your problem. Often we cannot see a way out of a problem because our thinking is set in certain ruts, fixed in certain perspectives. We may be blind to other approaches, either because we reject them without seriously considering them ("That will never work!") or because they simply do not occur to us. You can use several strategies to overcome these obstacles:

- *Discuss the problem with other people.* Discussing possible alternatives with others uses a number of the aspects of critical thinking we explored in Chapter 1. Other people can often suggest alternatives we haven't thought of since they are outside the situation and thus have a more objective perspective, and since they naturally view the world differently than we do because of their past experiences and their personalities. In addition, discussions are often creative experiences that generate ideas participants would not have come up with on their own.

- *Brainstorm ideas.* Group brainstorming builds on the strengths of working with other people to generate ideas and solve problems. In a typical brainstorming session, either in person or online, a group of people work together to propose as many ideas as possible in a specific time period. As ideas are produced, they are not judged or evaluated, as this tends to inhibit the free flow of ideas and discourage people from making suggestions. Evaluation is deferred until a later stage. People are encouraged to build on the ideas of others since the most creative ideas are often generated through the constructive interplay of various minds.

- *Change your location.* Your perspectives on a problem are often tied to the circumstances in which the problem exists. For example, a problem you may be having in school is connected with your daily experiences and your habitual reactions to them. Sometimes you need a fresh perspective, which you can gain by getting away from the problem situation so that you can view it more clearly in a different light. Perhaps spending a day or two out of town will help, or even taking a long walk in a different neighborhood.

Using these strategies, as well as your own reflections, identify as many alternatives to help solve the financial aid problem that you can think of.

1. Attend school part-time

2. _____

3. _____

4. _____

Step 3: What are the Advantages and Disadvantages of Each Alternative?

Once you have identified the alternatives, your next step is to evaluate them. Each possible course of action offers certain advantages in the sense that if you were to select that alternative, there would be some positive results. At the same time, each possible course of action probably also has disadvantages in the sense that if you were to select that alternative, you may incur a cost or risk some negative results. Determine how helpful each course of action would or would not be in solving the problem.

Step 3A: What are the advantages of each alternative?   The alternative we listed in step 2 for the sample problem ("Attend college part-time") might include the following advantages:

Alternative	Advantages
Attend college part-time	1. Doing this would remove some of the immediate time and money pressures I am experiencing while still allowing me to prepare for the future.
	2. I would have more time to focus on the courses that I would be taking and to work additional hours.

Identify the advantages of each of the alternatives that you listed in step 2. Be sure that your responses are thoughtful and specific. For example, how many additional hours could you work? How much additional income would doing that generate?

Step 3B: What are the disadvantages of each alternative?   The alternative we listed in step 2 for the sample problem might include the following disadvantages:

Alternative	Disadvantages
Attend college part-time	1. It would take me much longer to complete my schooling, thus delaying my progress toward my goals.
	2. I might lose motivation and drop out before completing school because the process would be taking so long.
	3. Being a part-time student might threaten my eligibility for financial aid.

Now identify the disadvantages of each of the alternatives that you listed for step 2. Make sure that your responses are thoughtful and specific. For example, how much longer would it take you to get your degree?

Step 3C: What additional information do I need to evaluate each alternative? The next part of step 3 consists of determining what you must know (information needed) to best evaluate and compare the alternatives. For each alternative there are questions that you must answer in order to establish which alternatives make sense and which do not. In addition, you need to figure out the most reliable sources for this information.

The information—and the sources of it—that must be located for the first alternative in the sample problem might include the following:

Information Needed

1. How long will it take me to complete my degree?

2. How long can I continue in school without losing interest and dropping out?

3. Will I threaten my eligibility for financial aid if I become a part-time student?

   Sources: Myself, other part-time students, school counselors, financial aid office

Identify the information needed and the sources of this information for each of the alternatives that you identified on pages 447–449. Be sure that your responses are thoughtful and specific.

Step 4: What is the Solution?

The purpose of steps 1 through 3 is to analyze your problem in a systematic and detailed fashion. After breaking down the problem in this way, your final step is to decide on a thoughtful course of action based on your increased understanding. Even though conducting this sort of analysis does not guarantee finding a specific solution to the problem, it should deepen your understanding of exactly what the problem is. And in locating and evaluating the alternatives, it should give you some very good ideas about the general direction in which you should move and the immediate steps you should take.

Step 4A: Which alternative(s) will I pursue?   There is no simple formula to tell you which alternatives to select. As you work through the different courses of action that are possible, you may find that you can immediately rule some out. In the sample problem, for example, you may know with certainty that you do not want to attend college part-time (alternative 1) because you will forfeit your remaining financial aid. However, it may not be as simple to select which of the other alternatives you wish to pursue. How do you decide?

The decisions we make usually depend on what we believe is most important to us. These beliefs are known as *values*. Our values are the starting points of our actions and strongly influence our decisions. For example, if we value staying alive (as most of us do), we will make many decisions each day that express this value—eating proper meals, not walking in front of moving traffic, and so on.

Our values help us set priorities in life—that is, decide what aspects of our lives are most important to us. We might decide that for the present, going to school is more important than having an active social life. In this case, going to school has higher priority than having an active social life. Unfortunately, our values are not always consistent with each other—we may have to choose either going to school or having an active social life. Both activities may be important to us; they are simply not compatible with each other. Very often the *conflicts* between our values constitute the problem. Let's examine some strategies for selecting alternatives that might help to solve the sample problem.

- *Evaluate and compare alternatives.* Although each alternative may have certain advantages and disadvantages, not all advantages are equally desirable or potentially effective. For example, giving up college entirely would certainly solve some aspects of the sample problem, but its obvious disadvantages would rule out this solution for most people. Thus, it makes sense to try to evaluate and rank the various alternatives on the basis of how effective they are likely to be and how they match up with your value system. A good place to begin is at the "Results" stage, step 1B. Examine each of your alternatives and evaluate how well it will contribute to achieving the results you are aiming for in the situation. You may want to rank the alternatives or develop your own rating system to assess their relative effectiveness.

  After evaluating the alternatives in terms of their anticipated *effectiveness*, the next step is to evaluate them in terms of their *desirability* relative to your needs, interests, and value system. Again, you can use either a ranking or a rating system to assess their relative desirability. After completing these two separate evaluations, you can select whatever alternatives seem most appropriate. Review the alternatives you identified in the sample problem; then rank or rate them according to their potential effectiveness and desirability.

- *Synthesize a new alternative.* After reviewing and evaluating the alternatives you have generated, you may develop a new alternative that combines the best qualities of several options while avoiding the disadvantages some of them would have if implemented exclusively. In the sample problem, you might combine attending college part-time during the academic year with attending school during summer session so that progress toward your degree wouldn't be impeded. Examine the alternatives you identified and develop a new option that combines the best elements of several of them.

- *Try out each alternative—in your imagination.* Focus on each alternative and try to imagine, as concretely as possible, what it would be like if you actually selected it. Visualize what impact your choice would have on your problem and what the implications would be for your life as a whole. By trying out the alternative in your imagination, you can sometimes avoid unpleasant results or unexpected consequences. As a variation of this strategy, you can sometimes test alternatives on a very limited basis in a practice situation. Suppose you are trying to overcome your fear of speaking out in groups. You can practice various speaking techniques with your friends or family until you find an approach that works for you.

Step 4B: What steps can I take to act on the alternative(s) chosen?   Once you have decided on an alternative to pursue, your next move is to plan what steps to take in acting on it. Planning the specific steps you will take is extremely important. Although thinking carefully about your problem is necessary, it is not enough if you hope to solve the problem. You have to take action. In the sample problem, for example, imagine that one of the alternatives you have selected is "find additional sources of income that will enable me to work part-time and attend school full-time." The specific steps you would take might include these:

- Contact the financial aid office to learn what other forms of monetary aid are available and how to apply for them.
- Contact some local banks to find out what sort of student loans they offer.
- Look for a higher-paying job to earn more money without working additional hours.
- Discuss your problem with students in similar circumstances in order to generate new ideas.

Identify the steps you would have to take to pursue the alternative(s) you identified on pages 447–449.

Plans, of course, do not implement themselves. Once you know what actions are needed, you have to make a commitment to taking the necessary steps. This is where many people stumble in the problem-solving process; they remain paralyzed by inertia or fear. Having a clear sense of purpose—and an audience who will be directly affected by your decisions—will help keep you motivated. To overcome such blocks and inhibitions, you sometimes need to reexamine your original acceptance of the problem, perhaps making use of some of the strategies you explored on pages 443–444. Once you get started, the rewards of actively attacking your problem are often enough incentive to keep you focused and motivated.

Step 5: How Well is the Solution Working?

As you work toward reaching a reasonable and informed conclusion, be wary of falling into the trap of thinking that there is only one "right" solution and that if you don't figure out what it is and implement it, all is lost. You should remind yourself that any analysis of problem situations, no matter how careful and systematic, is ultimately limited. You simply cannot anticipate or predict everything that will happen in the future. Consequently, every decision you make is provisional in the sense that your ongoing experience will inform you whether it is working out or needs to be modified.

Step 5A: What is my evaluation?   In many cases the relative effectiveness of your efforts will be apparent. In other cases you will find it helpful to pursue a more systematic evaluation along the lines suggested in the following strategies.

- *Compare the results with the goals.* The essence of evaluation is comparing the results of your efforts with your initial goals. For example, the goals of the sample problem are embodied in the results you specified on pages 447–449. Compare the anticipated results of the alternative(s) you selected. To what extent will your choice(s) meet these goals? Are any goals not likely to be met by your alternative(s)? If so, which ones? Could they be addressed by other alternatives? Asking these questions and others will help you to assess the success of your efforts and will provide a foundation for future decisions.

- *Get other perspectives.* As you have seen throughout the problem-solving process, getting the opinions of others is a productive strategy at virtually every stage, and this is certainly true of evaluation. It is not always easy to accept the evaluations of others, but keeping an open mind about outside opinions is a very valuable attitude to cultivate because it will stimulate and guide you to produce your best efforts.

    To receive specific, practical feedback, you need to ask specific, practical questions that will elicit such information. General questions ("What do you think of this?") typically receive overly general, unhelpful answers ("It sounds okay to me"). Be focused when soliciting feedback and remember that you do have the right to ask people for *constructive* comments—that is, to provide suggestions for improvement rather than just to tell you what they think is wrong. For example, you could say, "What do you know about me that you think will help me maintain my motivation to stay in school—even if it takes two years longer than I had planned?" Or you can ask, "Do you have any ideas about how I can cut my expenses by 10 percent each month?"

Step 5B: What adjustments are necessary?   As a result of your review, you may discover that the alternative you selected is not feasible or is not producing satisfactory results. Even when things initially appear to be working reasonably well, an active thinker continues to ask questions such as "What might I have overlooked?" and "How could I have done this differently?" Of course, asking—and trying to answer—questions like this is even more essential if solutions are hard to come by (as they usually are in real-world problems) and if you are to retain the flexibility and optimism you will need to tackle a new option.

"As soon as one problem is solved, another rears its ugly head."

Thinking-Writing Activity

ANALYZING A PROBLEM IN YOUR LIFE

This Thinking-Writing Activity provides you with the opportunity to apply the problem-solving method to an important *un*solved problem in your own life. First, select from your own life a problem that you are currently grappling with and have not been able to solve. Next, strengthen your acceptance of the problem by using several strategies described on pages 443–444. Finally, work your way through each of the problem-solving steps outlined on page 442. Write out responses to the questions in each step, and be sure to discuss your problem with other class members to generate fresh perspectives and unusual alternatives that might not have occurred to you. Your ultimate goal is to decide on a provisional solution to your problem and establish a plan of action that will help you move in the right direction.

Solving Social Problems

The problems we have analyzed up to this point are "personal" problems in the sense that they represent individual challenges we encounter as we live our lives. Problems are not only of a personal nature, however. We also face problems as

Thinking Critically About Visuals

"Necessity Is the Mother of Invention"

This photo is of a windmill designed and built by William Kamkwamba in 2003 in Masitala, a village in Malawi, Africa, for the purpose of generating power for his parents' home. At the time, Kamkwamba was just a teenager and he researched and taught himself how to build the windmill all on his own using local scrap materials that he could find. This vividly illustrates the point that creative problem-solving is both innovative and useful in a practical way, and that it often makes use of available materials—whatever they are—thus underscoring the wisdom of the statement "Necessity is the mother of invention." What other examples of creative innovation have you run into in the course of everyday life?

© Lucas Oleniuk/The Toronto Star/zReportage.com/ZUMApress.com

members of a community, the larger society, and the world. As with personal problems, we need to approach these kinds of problems in an organized and thoughtful way in order to explore the issues, develop a clear understanding, and decide on an informed plan of action.

Making sense of a complex, challenging situation is not a simple process. The famous newspaperman H. L. Mencken once said, "To every complex question there is a simple answer—and it's wrong!" In this chapter we have seen that complex problems do not have simple solutions, whether they are personal problems or larger social problems like racial prejudice or world hunger. We have also learned that by working through these complex problems thoughtfully and systematically, we can achieve a deeper understanding of their many interacting elements as well as develop and implement strategies for solving them.

A thoughtful problem solver employs all the critical thinking abilities we have examined in this book. And although we might agree with Mencken's evaluation of simple answers to complex questions, we would expand upon it: "To many complex questions there are complex answers—and these are well worth pursuing."

THINKING CRITICALLY ABOUT NEW MEDIA

Surfing Dangers and Addictions

Using the power and opportunities afforded by new media is intoxicating—but it is also potentially problematic. In the last chapter we explored the difficulties we can encounter when dealing with others on the Net. But you may encounter threats and challenges just by virtue of spending a lot of time online. These threats and challenges can be dealt with effectively if we take an informed, problem-solving approach, but we first have to be aware of what the dangers are.

To begin with, using the various aspects of new media can be addictive in the same way that watching television can be addictive. For example, have you ever found yourself "hypnotized" by the television, watching shows that you're not even that interested in? There are a variety of visual and psychological reasons why it's so difficult to stop watching television, many of which apply to the computer screen as well. Unlike real life, where we take in a tiny part of the visual panorama around us with the fovea (the sharp-focusing part of the eye), when we watch television we take in the entire frame of the image with our sharp foveal vision, making the experience more visually fascinating. Similarly, again in contrast to real life, the images on the screen are dynamic and almost always moving, creating an attention-grabbing bond that is difficult to tear ourselves away from. This continual eye-movement as we watch activity on screens also causes the eye to defocus slightly, a physiological activity that typically accompanies various fantasy, daydreaming, and drug-induced states. As Marie Winn in her seminal work *The Plug-In Drug*, observes: "This may very well be a reason for the trancelike nature of so many viewers' television experience, and may help to explain why the television image has so strong and hypnotic a fascination."

These same factors are at work whether we are watching a television screen or a computer screen. The difference is that new media is *interactive*: we can roam around the Net at will, follow an infinite succession of links and websites, and communicate with as many people as we wish to. It's no wonder that once we start our fingertips moving on the computer or communication device we're using, it's very difficult to get those fingers to stop. Although a certain amount of the time we spend engaged with new media is productive, much of it is not particularly useful, and it prevents us from engaging in other activities that *would* be more enriching and productive.

As with any addiction, seeking a solution involves recognizing that there *is* a problem and then using a problem-solving methodology like the one introduced in this chapter. Certainly a good place to begin is by strictly scheduling and limiting the time we spend "surfing" online or engaged in social exchanges. This is particularly true when it comes to email and text-messaging. And if we're engaged in a real-world activity, it's useful to discipline ourselves by checking for messages every hour or so rather than reading and responding to them as they come in. Research has shown that leaving and then returning to the activity in which you were engaged is a tremendous time-waster.

A more subtle threat to our well-being is described in the article on page 458 *Is Google Making Us Stupid?,* in which the author, Nicholas Carr, explores whether our immersion in new media is restructuring the way we think and process information, making it more difficult for us to concentrate on activities like reading for a lengthy period of time, spending time in quiet contemplation of important issues, or thinking in deep and complex ways. As Carr, a writer, explains: "Once I was a scuba diver in the sea of words. Now I zip along the surface like a guy on a Jet Ski."

Thinking-Writing Activity

READING PRINT VS. READING ONLINE

In anticipation of reading the following article, *Is Google Making Us Stupid?,* perform the following reading "experiment" to explore the differences between print and online reading. Select a news source that has both a print version and an online version such as *The New York Times, Washington Post, Chicago Tribune,* or *The Los Angeles Times.*

First read the online version, selecting and reading the articles of interest as you normally would. Then read the print version of the same publication but on a different date. What differences did you find between the two experiences? For example, did you find that

- you spent more time reading one of the versions?
- one version provided you with the more detailed and developed information?
- one version exposed you to a greater variety of topics and stories?
- one version more deeply engaged you in the process of reading and thinking?
- one version resulted in a greater recall of what you had read?

After responding to these questions, analyze and write about what factors accounted for the different experiences.

In the provocative article, "Is Google Making Us Stupid?," the writer Nicholas Carr wonders if the culture's pervasive use of the Web-based new media is restructuring the way that we think, making it more difficult for us to concentrate, contemplate, and read lengthy, complex books and articles. The author's concern is that using the Web encourages us to jump quickly from link to link, spending little time at any one particular place to think deeply and analytically about the ideas we are considering. Is this a problem about which we ought to be concerned?

Is Google Making Us Stupid?

by Nicholas Carr

"Dave, stop. Stop, will you? Stop, Dave. Will you stop, Dave?" So the supercomputer HAL pleads with the implacable astronaut Dave Bowman in a famous and weirdly poignant scene toward the end of Stanley Kubrick's *2001: A Space Odyssey*. Bowman, having nearly been sent to a deep-space death by the malfunctioning machine, is calmly, coldly disconnecting the memory circuits that control its artificial "brain." "Dave, my mind is going," HAL says, forlornly. "I can feel it. I can feel it."

I can feel it, too. Over the past few years I've had an uncomfortable sense that someone, or something, has been tinkering with my brain, remapping the neural circuitry, reprogramming the memory. My mind isn't going—so far as I can tell—but it's changing. I'm not thinking the way I used to think. I can feel it most strongly when I'm reading.

Immersing myself in a book or a lengthy article used to be easy. My mind would get caught up in the narrative or the turns of the argument, and I'd spend hours strolling through long stretches of prose. That's rarely the case anymore. Now my concentration often starts to drift after two or three pages. I get fidgety, lose the thread, begin looking for something else to do. I feel as if I'm always dragging my wayward brain back to the text. The deep reading that used to come naturally has become a struggle.

Source: "Is Google Making Us Stupid?" by Nicholas Carr. From *The Atlantic*, July/August 2008. Reprinted by permission of the author.

I think I know what's going on. For more than a decade now, I've been spending a lot of time online, searching and surfing and sometimes adding to the great databases of the Internet. The Web has been a godsend to me as a writer. Research that once required days in the stacks or periodical rooms of libraries can now be done in minutes. A few Google searches, some quick clicks on hyperlinks, and I've got the telltale fact or pithy quote I was after. Even when I'm not working, I'm as likely as not to be foraging in the Web's info-thickets' reading and writing e-mails, scanning headlines and blog posts, watching videos and listening to podcasts, or just tripping from link to link to link. (Unlike footnotes, to which they're sometimes likened, hyperlinks don't merely point to related works; they propel you toward them.)

For me, as for others, the Net is becoming a universal medium, the conduit for most of the information that flows through my eyes and ears and into my mind. The advantages of having immediate access to such an incredibly rich store of information are many, and they've been widely described and duly applauded. "The perfect recall of silicon memory," Wired's Clive Thompson has written, "can be an enormous boon to thinking." But that boon comes at a price. As the media theorist Marshall McLuhan pointed out in the 1960s, media are not just passive channels of information. They supply the stuff of thought, but they also shape the process of thought. And what the Net seems to be doing is chipping away my capacity for concentration and contemplation. My mind now expects to take in information the way the Net distributes it: in a swiftly moving stream of particles. Once I was a scuba diver in the sea of words. Now I zip along the surface like a guy on a Jet Ski.

5   I'm not the only one. When I mention my troubles with reading to friends and acquaintances—literary types, most of them—many say they're having similar experiences. The more they use the Web, the more they have to fight to stay focused on long pieces of writing. Some of the bloggers I follow have also begun mentioning the phenomenon. Scott Karp, who writes a blog about online media, recently confessed that he has stopped reading books altogether. "I was a lit major in college, and used to be [a] voracious book reader," he wrote. "What happened?" He speculates on the answer: "What if I do all my reading on the web not so much because the way I read has changed, i.e. I'm just seeking convenience, but because the way I THINK has changed?"

* * * *

Anecdotes alone don't prove much. And we still await the long-term neurological and psychological experiments that will provide a definitive picture of how Internet use affects cognition. But a recently published study of online research habits , conducted by scholars from University College London, suggests that we may well be in the midst of a sea change in the way we read and think. . . . They found that people using the sites exhibited "a form of skimming activity," hopping from one source to another and rarely returning to any source they'd already visited. They typically read no more than one or two pages of an article or book before they would "bounce" out to another site.

Sometimes they'd save a long article, but there's no evidence that they ever went back and actually read it. The authors of the study report:

> It is clear that users are not reading online in the traditional sense; indeed there are signs that new forms of "reading" are emerging as users "power browse" horizontally through titles, contents pages and abstracts going for quick wins. It almost seems that they go online to avoid reading in the traditional sense.

Thanks to the ubiquity of text on the Internet, not to mention the popularity of text-messaging on cell phones, we may well be reading more today than we did in the 1970s or 1980s, when television was our medium of choice. But it's a different kind of reading, and behind it lies a different kind of thinking—perhaps even a new sense of the self. "We are not only what we read," says Maryanne Wolf, a developmental psychologist at Tufts University and the author of *Proust and the Squid: The Story and Science of the Reading Brain*. "We are how we read." Wolf worries that the style of reading promoted by the Net, a style that puts "efficiency" and "immediacy" above all else, may be weakening our capacity for the kind of deep reading that emerged when an earlier technology, the printing press, made long and complex works of prose commonplace. When we read online, she says, we tend to become "mere decoders of information." Our ability to interpret text, to make the rich mental connections that form when we read deeply and without distraction, remains largely disengaged.

Reading, explains Wolf, is not an instinctive skill for human beings. It's not etched into our genes the way speech is. We have to teach our minds how to translate the symbolic characters we see into the language we understand. And the media or other technologies we use in learning and practicing the craft of reading play an important part in shaping the neural circuits inside our brains. Experiments demonstrate that readers of ideograms, such as the Chinese, develop a mental circuitry for reading that is very different from the circuitry found in those of us whose written language employs an alphabet. The variations extend across many regions of the brain, including those that govern such essential cognitive functions as memory and the interpretation of visual and auditory stimuli. We can expect as well that the circuits woven by our use of the Net will be different from those woven by our reading of books and other printed works.

Sometime in 1882, Friedrich Nietzsche bought a typewriter—a Malling-Hansen Writing Ball, to be precise. His vision was failing, and keeping his eyes focused on a page had become exhausting and painful, often bringing on crushing headaches. He had been forced to curtail his writing, and he feared that he would soon have to give it up. The typewriter rescued him, at least for a time. Once he had mastered touch-typing, he was able to write with his eyes closed, using only the tips of his fingers. Words could once again flow from his mind to the page.

10   But the machine had a subtle effect on his work. One of Nietzsche's friends, a composer, noticed a change in the style of his writing. His already terse prose had become even tighter, more telegraphic. "Perhaps you will through this instrument even take to a new idiom," the friend wrote in a letter, noting that, in his own work, his "'thoughts' in music and language often depend on the quality of pen and paper."

"You are right," Nietzsche replied, "our writing equipment takes part in the forming of our thoughts." Under the sway of the machine, writes the German media scholar Friedrich A. Kittler, Nietzsche's prose "changed from arguments to aphorisms, from thoughts to puns, from rhetoric to telegram style."

The human brain is almost infinitely malleable. People used to think that our mental meshwork, the dense connections formed among the 100 billion or so neurons inside our skulls, was largely fixed by the time we reached adulthood. But brain researchers have discovered that that's not the case. James Olds, a professor of neuroscience who directs the Krasnow Institute for Advanced Study at George Mason University, says that even the adult mind "is very plastic." Nerve cells routinely break old connections and form new ones. "The brain," according to Olds, "has the ability to reprogram itself on the fly, altering the way it functions."

As we use what the sociologist Daniel Bell has called our "intellectual technologies"—the tools that extend our mental rather than our physical capacities—we inevitably begin to take on the qualities of those technologies. The mechanical clock, which came into common use in the 14th century, provides a compelling example. In Technics and Civilization, the historian and cultural critic Lewis Mumford described how the clock "disassociated time from human events and helped create the belief in an independent world of mathematically measurable sequences." The "abstract framework of divided time" became "the point of reference for both action and thought."

The clock's methodical ticking helped bring into being the scientific mind and the scientific man. But it also took something away. As the late MIT computer scientist Joseph Weizenbaum observed in his 1976 book, *Computer Power and Human Reason: From Judgment to Calculation,* the conception of the world that emerged from the widespread use of timekeeping instruments "remains an impoverished version of the older one, for it rests on a rejection of those direct experiences that formed the basis for, and indeed constituted, the old reality." In deciding when to eat, to work, to sleep, to rise, we stopped listening to our senses and started obeying the clock.

15   The process of adapting to new intellectual technologies is reflected in the changing metaphors we use to explain ourselves to ourselves. When the mechanical clock arrived, people began thinking of their brains as operating "like clockwork." Today, in the age of software, we have come to think of them as operating "like computers." But the changes, neuroscience tells us, go much deeper than metaphor. Thanks to our brain's plasticity, the adaptation occurs also at a biological level.

The Internet promises to have particularly far-reaching effects on cognition. In a paper published in 1936, the British mathematician Alan Turing proved that a digital computer, which at the time existed only as a theoretical machine, could be programmed to perform the function of any other information-processing device. And that's what we're seeing today. The Internet, an immeasurably powerful computing system, is subsuming most of our other intellectual technologies. It's becoming our map and our clock, our printing press and our typewriter, our calculator and our telephone, and our radio and TV.

When the Net absorbs a medium, that medium is re-created in the Net's image. It injects the medium's content with hyperlinks, blinking ads, and other digital gewgaws, and it surrounds the content with the content of all the other media it has absorbed. A new e-mail message, for instance, may announce its arrival as we're glancing over the latest headlines at a newspaper's site. The result is to scatter our attention and diffuse our concentration.

The Net's influence doesn't end at the edges of a computer screen. . . . As people's minds become attuned to the crazy quilt of Internet media, traditional media have to adapt to the audience's expectations. Television programs add text crawls and pop-up ads, and magazines and newspapers shorten their articles, introduce capsule summaries, and crowd their pages with easy-to-browse info-snippets. When, in March of this year, *The New York Times* decided to devote the second and third pages of every edition to article abstracts , its design director, Tom Bodkin, explained that the "shortcuts" would give harried readers a quick "taste" of the day's news, sparing them the "less efficient" method of actually turning the pages and reading the articles. Old media have little choice but to play by the new-media rules.

Never has a communications system played so many roles in our lives—or exerted such broad influence over our thoughts—as the Internet does today. Yet, for all that's been written about the Net, there's been little consideration of how, exactly, it's reprogramming us. The Net's intellectual ethic remains obscure.

20   About the same time that Nietzsche started using his typewriter, an earnest young man named Frederick Winslow Taylor carried a stopwatch into the Midvale Steel plant in Philadelphia and began a historic series of experiments aimed at improving the efficiency of the plant's machinists. . . . once his system was applied to all acts of manual labor, Taylor assured his followers, it would bring about a restructuring not only of industry but of society, creating a utopia of perfect efficiency. "In the past the man has been first," he declared; "in the future the system must be first."

Taylor's system is still very much with us; it remains the ethic of industrial manufacturing. And now, thanks to the growing power that computer engineers and software coders wield over our intellectual lives, Taylor's ethic is beginning to govern the realm of the mind as well. The Internet is a machine designed for the efficient and automated collection, transmission, and manipulation of information, and its legions of programmers are intent on finding the "one best method"—the perfect algorithm—to carry out every mental movement of what we've come to describe as "knowledge work."

* * * *

Google has declared that its mission is "to organize the world's information and make it universally accessible and useful." It seeks to develop "the perfect search engine," which it defines as something that "understands exactly what you mean and gives you back exactly what you want." In Google's view, information is a kind of commodity, a utilitarian resource that can be mined and processed with industrial efficiency. The more pieces of information we can "access" and the faster we can extract their gist, the more productive we become as thinkers.

Where does it end? Sergey Brin and Larry Page, the gifted young men who founded Google while pursuing doctoral degrees in computer science at Stanford, speak frequently of their desire to turn their search engine into an artificial intelligence, a HAL-like machine that might be connected directly to our brains. "The ultimate search engine is something as smart as people—or smarter," Page said in a speech a few years back. "For us, working on search is a way to work on artificial intelligence." In a 2004 interview with *Newsweek*, Brin said, "Certainly if you had all the world's information directly attached to your brain, or an artificial brain that was smarter than your brain, you'd be better off." Last year, Page told a convention of scientists that Google is "really trying to build artificial intelligence and to do it on a large scale."

Such an ambition is a natural one, even an admirable one, for a pair of math whizzes with vast quantities of cash at their disposal and a small army of computer scientists in their employ. A fundamentally scientific enterprise, Google is motivated by a desire to use technology, in Eric Schmidt's words, "to solve problems that have never been solved before," and artificial intelligence is the hardest problem out there. Why wouldn't Brin and Page want to be the ones to crack it?

25   Still, their easy assumption that we'd all "be better off" if our brains were supplemented, or even replaced, by an artificial intelligence is unsettling. It suggests a belief that intelligence is the output of a mechanical process, a series of discrete steps that can be isolated, measured, and optimized. In Google's world, the world we enter when we go online, there's little place for the fuzziness of contemplation. Ambiguity is not an opening for insight but a bug to be fixed. The human brain is just an outdated computer that needs a faster processor and a bigger hard drive.

The idea that our minds should operate as high-speed data-processing machines is not only built into the workings of the Internet, it is the network's reigning business model as well. The faster we surf across the Web—the more links we click and pages we view—the more opportunities Google and other companies gain to collect information about us and to feed us advertisements. Most of the proprietors of the commercial Internet have a financial stake in collecting the crumbs of data we leave behind as we flit from link to link—the more crumbs, the better. The last thing these companies want is to encourage leisurely reading or slow, concentrated thought. It's in their economic interest to drive us to distraction.

Maybe I'm just a worrywart. Just as there's a tendency to glorify technological progress, there's a countertendency to expect the worst of every new tool or machine. In Plato's *Phaedrus*, Socrates bemoaned the development of writing. He feared that, as people came to rely on the written word as a substitute for the knowledge they used to carry inside their heads, they would, in the words of one of the dialogue's characters, "cease to exercise their memory and become forgetful." And because they would be able to "receive a quantity of information without proper instruction," they would "be thought very knowledgeable when they are for the most part quite ignorant." They would be "filled with the conceit of wisdom instead of real wisdom." Socrates wasn't wrong—the new technology did often have the effects he feared—but he was shortsighted. He couldn't foresee the many ways that writing and reading would serve to spread information, spur fresh ideas, and expand human knowledge (if not wisdom).

The arrival of Gutenberg's printing press, in the 15th century, set off another round of teeth gnashing. The Italian humanist Hieronimo Squarciafico worried that the easy availability of books would lead to intellectual laziness, making men "less studious" and weakening their minds. Others argued that cheaply printed books and broadsheets would undermine religious authority, demean the work of scholars and scribes, and spread sedition and debauchery. As New York University professor Clay Shirky notes, "Most of the arguments made against the printing press were correct, even prescient." But, again, the doomsayers were unable to imagine the myriad blessings that the printed word would deliver.

So, yes, you should be skeptical of my skepticism. Perhaps those who dismiss critics of the Internet as Luddites or nostalgists will be proved correct, and from our hyperactive, data-stoked minds will spring a golden age of intellectual discovery and universal wisdom. Then again, the Net isn't the alphabet, and although it may replace the printing press, it produces something altogether different. The kind of deep reading that a sequence of printed pages promotes is valuable not just for the knowledge we acquire from the author's words but for the intellectual vibrations those words set off within our own minds. In the quiet spaces opened up by the sustained, undistracted reading of a book, or by any other act of contemplation, for that matter, we make our own associations, draw our own inferences and analogies, foster our own ideas. Deep reading, as Maryanne Wolf argues, is indistinguishable from deep thinking.

30   If we lose those quiet spaces, or fill them up with "content," we will sacrifice something important not only in our selves but in our culture. In a recent essay, the playwright Richard Foreman eloquently described what's at stake:

> I come from a tradition of Western culture, in which the ideal (my ideal) was the complex, dense and "cathedral-like" structure of the highly educated and articulate personality—a man or woman who carried inside themselves a personally constructed and unique version of the entire heritage of the West. [But now] I see within us all (myself included) the replacement of complex inner density with a new kind of self—evolving under the pressure of information overload and the technology of the "instantly available."

As we are drained of our "inner repertory of dense cultural inheritance," Foreman concluded, we risk turning into "'pancake people'—spread wide and thin as we connect with that vast network of information accessed by the mere touch of a button."

I'm haunted by that scene in 2001. What makes it so poignant, and so weird, is the computer's emotional response to the disassembly of its mind: its despair as one circuit after another goes dark, its childlike pleading with the astronaut—"I can feel it. I can feel it. I'm afraid"—and its final reversion to what can only be called a state of innocence. HAL's outpouring of feeling contrasts with the emotionlessness that characterizes the human figures in the film, who go about their business with an almost robotic efficiency. Their thoughts and actions feel scripted, as if they're following the steps of an algorithm. In the world of 2001, people have become so machinelike that the most human character turns out to be a machine. That's the essence of Kubrick's dark prophecy: as we come to rely on computers to mediate our understanding of the world, it is our own intelligence that flattens into artificial intelligence.

Questions for Reading Actively

1. In your own words, state the *general* problem described by this article, and then list the specific *characterizations* of that problem. Is the prominence given to one of those characterizations in this article really the most important in the larger context of the general problem? Be prepared to show how the structure of this article demonstrates the relative importance of these specific characterizations.

2. Are there any voices missing from this article? If you were this writer's editor, whose voices and perspectives would you recommend including, and why?

Questions for Thinking Critically

1. Have you noticed in your own life that it's easier for you to move quickly around the Web than to spend concentrated time reading a book or lengthy article? Writing an extended essay or letter? Concentrating on an issue or problem for an extended period of time?

2. The author acknowledges that "the Net is becoming a universal medium, the conduit for most of the information that flows through my eyes and ears and into my mind" and that this puts him at risk for being a "mere decoder of information" rather than a deep thinker *about* information. Would you say that this is true for you as well? Why or why not?

Question for Writing Thoughtfully

1. Imagine that you are the president of your college and that you want students to use the full power of the Internet in their education but you also wish them to develop their abilities to think deeply, concentrate, and contemplate. Using the problem-solving method in this chapter, analyze this problem and write a short essay outlining some practical solutions for dealing with this challenge.

Taking a Problem-Solving Approach to Writing

Problem solving provides you with a framework that you can use in much of your writing. A problem-solving approach can assist you in generating ideas and organizing information for most subjects. For example, you can look at a writing assignment as a problem and use a modification of the five-step method, such as follows, as a way to work on it.

1. What exactly is the assignment? What is its purpose?

2. What are some alternative ways to complete it? Who is the obvious audience, and what other possible audiences should I consider?

3. What are the advantages and disadvantages of the alternatives? Am I prepared to change my subject or thesis if my initial approach doesn't work?

4. What is the best way for me to complete this assignment? How can I use conversations and peer review to gain additional perspectives?

5. After some drafting ask: How is my solution to the problem of the assignment working out?

Then, as you write any essay, you can use modifications of the problem-solving steps at any stage. Look at the thesis as a problem and ask the preceding questions about it. Look at any part of the paper and ask the questions. Actually, effective writers do this to some extent—perhaps less systematically—as they draft, plan, and revise. As you recall, Chapter 5 sets forth a similar pattern for approaching revision.

Research projects can also be seen and approached as problems. Just as you can apply a problem-solving approach to any writing assignment, so can you apply it to most research projects (see Chapter 14).

Writing Project: Proposing a Solution to a Problem

This chapter includes both readings and Thinking-Writing Activities that encourage you to familiarize yourself with the problem-solving model and the steps required for implementing it. Be sure to reread what you wrote for those activities, as you may be able to use some of that material when completing this project.

> Write an essay in which you apply the five-step problem-solving method to a local, national, or international problem or to a personal problem. If you are analyzing a social problem, you will have to do some research and locate several articles that provide background information about and discussion of the problem. If you are analyzing a personal problem, you will enrich your paper by consulting some sources that pertain to it. Be sure to document all sources honestly and correctly in the format required by your instructor.
>
> After you have drafted your essay, revise it to the best of your ability. Follow your instructor's directions about focus, length, scope, format, and so on.

Begin by considering the key elements in the Thinking-Writing Model in Chapter 1 on pages 6–8.

The Writing Situation

Purpose   You have a variety of purposes here. You can use this opportunity to learn about a major problem in order to arrive at the best possible solution—and thus become a better-informed citizen. You might be able to help solve the problem if you are involved in the situation. Also, you will be practicing the creative and critical thinking involved in the problem-solving model.

Audience   As usual, you will have several audiences for your paper. While working through the problem-solving model, you will be your own audience since in describing the problem and working through the alternative solutions, you will be determining the solution to the problem. As you begin to shape the answers to the model's questions into an essay, your audience will include readers other than yourself, so their needs should now occupy your attention.

Your classmates can be a valuable audience for peer review of a draft. They can react as intelligent readers who are not as knowledgeable as you are about the problem and its possible solutions but who can become interested as they read your description of it and your evaluation of the possible solutions. Finally, your instructor remains the audience who will judge how well you have analyzed the problem. As a writing teacher, he or she cares about a clear focus, logical organization, relevant details and examples, and accepted usage. Keep these factors in mind as you revise, edit, and proofread.

Subject   Problems are problems precisely because they are difficult to think about and to solve. Often this is true because we don't have enough accurate information to arrive at an intelligent solution. Working on this paper will encourage you to find good information and to think about viable alternative solutions. Since you will be deeply involved in the subject, select a problem that you care about, one that is challenging—but compelling—to write about.

Writer   This assignment provides you an opportunity to learn more about a problem that you care about but perhaps do not know enough about to propose a solid solution. You will use both online and print resources to increase your knowledge of the problem and give you the pleasure of having additional expertise about something significant. If your instructor asks or allows you to write about a personal problem, you might not have to do as much research, but you will have the opportunity to work out something that is of immediate concern. Equipped with the problem-solving model and the direction it provides, you should work as a confident writer as you complete this assignment.

The Writing Process

The following sections will guide you through the stages of generating, planning, drafting, and revising as you work on an essay about solving an important problem. Try to be particularly conscious of both the critical thinking you do while working through the problem-solving model and the critical thinking and decision making you do as you revise.

Generating Ideas   You may find yourself in one of three situations:

1. If your instructor's directions specify that you must write about a particular local, national, or international problem, you must begin there. You might start by working through the problem-solving model and answering each question on the basis of your current knowledge. Then you will be able to see what additional information you need to know and thus will be aware of what to look for as you research the problem.

2. If your instructor's directions allow you to choose any important local, national, or international problem, you might begin by brainstorming (alone or with a group) a list of each of these types of problems. Then you can select the one that seems most important, the one that interests you most, or the one about which you are most informed.

3. If your instructor's directions allow you to write about a personal problem, you might begin by brainstorming a list of problems you now face. It might help to make three columns: school problems, work problems, and personal problems. Then you can pick one, preferably one that you have to solve soon and for which you would need to gather information to write about.

Whichever situation describes yours, once you have worked through the problem-solving model, you will almost certainly spot gaps in your information. Think about how much additional information you will need in order to evaluate each of the alternative solutions. Then locate that information, asking a librarian for assistance if necessary.

Once you have filled in all the gaps and selected a solution—and a means to determine whether it is working—you are ready to turn your attention to presenting your information to your audience.

Defining a Focus   Write a thesis statement that will make clear to your audience that you are going to explore a problem-solving situation. You might decide to write something like "After thinking about the problem carefully, I realize that I have only two possible choices." Or you might decide to name the possible choices: "Newton's possible solutions to its budget problem include raising more revenue, cutting the budget, or some combination of the two." You may even decide to announce your chosen solution in your thesis statement: "After carefully weighing the alternatives, raising more revenue while continuing to cut the budget appears to be the best choice."

Organizing Ideas   The five-step method for solving problems fits well with essay structure. Your description of the problem together with its necessary history and other background information will give you a working introduction that can include your thesis statement. Each of the alternative solutions, explained in as much detail as possible, along with its advantages and disadvantages, will provide one section of the body (one or more paragraphs). Your determination of the best solution and how it could be monitored will provide a conclusion.

When you are asked to write a proposal, essay, or argument about solving a problem, as this chapter's Writing Project does, you can use the problem-solving method as a system of organization. The following principles for writing about problem solving may not apply to every instance, but they should help you convert answers to the questions in the problem-solving model into an effective essay.

1. Be aware of the needs of your audience. Your readers need specific details about background, history, special circumstances, and so forth, and they need to have this information presented in an order that they can understand. Begin your outline and draft by presenting this information in the clearest order you can devise. As you write and revise your essay, continually ask yourself, "Does my audience have all the information necessary to understand the point I am trying to make?"

2. Present all the information your audience needs in order to understand the problem before you begin to discuss alternative solutions.

3. Include a thesis statement indicating that you are going to discuss alternative solutions. If you are specifically writing an argument, be sure that your claim is debatable and that you give fair and equal consideration to opposing solutions.

4. Discuss each alternative solution by explaining what it would involve and by presenting its advantages and disadvantages. Provide enough specific information to allow your audience to see these advantages and disadvantages. Don't just say, "A program could be developed to help students see how to avoid date rape." Instead, begin a paragraph by saying: "Respected student leaders from honor societies and athletic teams could participate in a forum explaining how excessive drinking, certain drugs, and certain behaviors can lead to situations in which date rape might occur."

5. Present the alternative solutions in the order that will most help your audience comprehend them. In an argument, your rebuttal to each alternative should help your audience understand why you would select the one you did.

6. Conclude your essay by stating one solution, or some combination of solutions, and explain clearly why you chose it. If you have had time to implement the solution, describe whether or not it is working. If you have not yet implemented it, explain how you will determine whether or not it is working.

Drafting Begin with the easiest paragraph to draft. Keep your written answers to each part of the problem-solving model in front of you.

Remember to begin each section of the body with a topic sentence that names the alternative solution being considered. If you are discussing advantages or disadvantages in separate paragraphs, draft topic sentences that prepare your readers for that information—such as "Unfortunately, cutting the budget further will create serious disadvantages for many citizens." Then provide specific information.

You will, of course, have to determine the best order in which to arrange the section. Experiment until you find the one that seems most helpful to your audience.

Be sure to indicate the sources of your information. You do not have to use the correct citation format in a draft, but you do have to remind yourself exactly where you obtained the material so that you won't forget to cite it as you finish the paper.

In your conclusion, name the solution you have chosen. You may want to explain why you selected it if you think that will not be obvious to your audience. Remember to explain how you will evaluate the effectiveness of your solution.

Revising, Editing, and Proofreading Use the step-by-step method in Chapter 6 on pages 169–171 to revise your essay and prepare a final draft.

The following essay shows how a student responded to this assignment—by writing about a social problem and citing according to Modern Language Association (MLA) format.

Student Writing

Joshua Bartlett's Writing Process

As a college student, Joshua witnessed firsthand the impact of irresponsible attitudes toward alcohol among his peers. Even though he and his classmates were required to participate in various "alcohol awareness" education programs as part of freshman orientation at their campus, Joshua knew that the programs were not engaging, urgent, or serious enough to get the attention of young people like himself. Because Joshua was writing a formal argument, and because he was required to use sources to provide information, Joshua did not include anecdotes from his own personal experience. Had he been writing an opinion piece for his campus newspaper, he might well have described a campus party in which a fellow student was seriously hurt in an alcohol-related incident; he might even have described his own experiences with binge drinking. Although that evidence would certainly be compelling, it might not be adequately objective for an academic audience—and you can imagine how it might undermine his credibility with his professor! Instead, Joshua provides objective evidence from a range of sources to support his well-thought-out approach to the problem of alcohol abuse on college campuses.

To structure his draft, Joshua used the Detailed Method for Solving Problems (page 442).

Critical Thinking About Uncritical Drinking

by Joshua Bartlett

There is widespread agreement that excessive student drinking is a serious problem on many college campuses. However, there are different views on the causes of this problem and on the best solutions for it. In this paper I will present some perspectives on the problem of student drinking and conclude with suggestions on how to deal with this serious threat to student health and success.

Why do college students drink to excess? According to many experts, it is mainly due to the influence of the people around them. When most students enter college, they do not have a drinking problem. However, although few realize it, they are entering a culture in which alcohol is often the drug of choice, one that can easily destroy their lives. According to some estimates, 80 to 90 percent of the students on many campuses drink alcohol, and many of them are heavy drinkers (Engs 543). One study found that nearly 30 percent of university students consume more than 15 alcoholic drinks a week (Gerson A43). An additional study found that among those who drink at least once a week, 92 percent of the men and 82 percent of the women consume at least five drinks in a row, and half said they wanted to get drunk (Rosenberg 81).

The results of all this drinking are predictably deadly. Virtually all college administrators agree that alcohol is the most widely used drug among college students and that its abuse is directly related to emotional problems and violent behavior, ranging from date rape to death (Dodge, "Campus Crime" A331; Leatherman A33). For example, at one university, a 20-year-old woman became drunk at a fraternity party and fell to her death from the third floor ("Clemson" A3). At another university, two students were killed in a drunk-driving accident after drinking alcohol at an off-campus fraternity house; the families of both students have filed lawsuits against the fraternity (Dodge, "Beer Kegs Banned" A28). When students enter a college or university, they often become socialized into the alcohol-sodden culture of "higher education," at both formal and informal parties. The influence of peer pressure is enormous. Students often find it difficult to resist the pressures from their friends and fellow students to drink.

However, some observers of young people believe that, although peer pressure is certainly a factor in excessive college drinking, it is only one of a number of factors. They point out that the misuse of alcohol is a problem for all youth in our society, not just college students. For example, a recent study by the surgeon general's office shows that 1 in 3 teenagers consumes alcohol every week. This abuse leads to traffic deaths, academic difficulties, and acts of violence (Elson 64). Another study based on a large, nationally representative sample indicates that although college students are more likely to use alcohol, they tend to drink less per drinking day than nonstudents of the same age (Crowley 14); in other words, most college students who drink are more social drinkers than problem drinkers. One survey of undergraduate students found that college drinking is not as widespread as many people think (O'Hare 540). The conclusion from this data is that even though drinking certainly takes place on college campuses, it is no greater a problem than in the population at large.

Whatever the extent, the misuse of alcohol by college students is a serious situation with a number of probable causes. Certainly the influence of friends, whether in college or out, plays a role, as I've already discussed. But it is not the only factor. To begin with, there is evidence that family history is related to alcohol abuse.

For example, one survey of college students found more problem drinking among students whose parents or grandparents had been diagnosed with alcoholism (Perkins and Berkowitz 237–240). Another study found that college students who come from families with high degrees of conflict display a greater potential for alcoholism (Pardeck 342–343).

Another important factor to consider in the misuse of alcohol by young people is advertising. A recent article entitled "It Isn't Miller Time Yet, and This Bud's Not for You" underscores the influence advertisers exert on the behavior of youth (Siler 52). By portraying beer drinkers as healthy, fun-loving, attractive young people, they create role models that many youths imitate. In the same way that cigarette advertisers used to encourage smoking among our youth—without regard for the health hazards—so alcohol advertisers try to sell as much booze as they can to whoever will buy it—no matter what the consequences.

A final factor in the abuse of alcohol is the people themselves. Although young people are subject to a huge number of influences, in the final analysis, they are free to choose what they want to do. They don't have to drink, no matter what the social pressures. In fact, many students resist these pressures and choose not to drink excessively or at all. In short, some students choose to think critically, while others choose to drink uncritically.

In order to encourage good judgment by more students and to minimize the causes of excessive drinking, I think that the following strategies could help solve the college alcohol problem. Only the last one has any disadvantages to be considered.

1. Colleges should have orientation and educational programs aimed at preventing alcohol abuse, and colleges should give top priority to campaigns against underage and excessive drinking.

2. Advertising and promotion of alcoholic beverages on college campuses and in college publications should be banned. Liquor distributors should not sponsor campus events. In addition, alcoholic beverage companies should be petitioned not to target young people in their ads.

3. Depending on the campus culture, colleges should ban or restrict alcohol use on campus and include stiff penalties for students who violate the rules.

4. Students at residential colleges should be able to live in substance-free housing, offering them a voluntary haven from alcohol, other drugs, tobacco, and peer pressure.

5. Colleges should create attractive alcohol-free clubs or pubs.

6. Colleges should ban the use of beer kegs, a symbol of cheap and easy availability of alcohol.

7. Fraternities should eliminate all alcohol-based contests or hazing torments.

8. Where possible, the on-campus drinking age should be reduced to 18 so that students won't be forced to move parties off-campus. At off-campus parties, there is no college control, and as a result, students tend to drink greater quantities and more dangerous concoctions.

Of course, this suggestion has the disadvantages of being in conflict with laws in many states or counties and also of seeming to encourage drinking by connecting it even more extensively with social events. But it has the advantages of control and of eliminating the attraction of what's forbidden.

In conclusion, alcohol abuse on college campuses is an extremely serious problem that is threatening the health and college careers of many students. As challenging as this problem is, I believe that it can be solved if students, teachers, and college officials work together in harmony and with determination to implement the suggestions made in this paper.

Works Cited

"Clemson Issues Ban on Parties Using Alcohol." *Chronicle of Higher Education* 31 Jan. 1990: A3. Print.

Crowley, Joan E. "Educational Status and Drinking Patterns: How Representative Are College Students?" *Journal of Studies on Alcohol* 52.1 (1991): 10–16. Print.

Dodge, Susan. "Campus Crime Linked to Students' Use of Drugs and Alcohol." *Chronicle of Higher Education* 17 Jan. 1990: A331. Print.

——— "Use of Beer Kegs Banned by Some Colleges and National Fraternities." *Chronicle of Higher Education* 12 June 1991: A27–28. Print.

Elson, John. "Drink Until You Finally Drop." *Time* 16 Dec. 1991 : 64. Print.

Engs, Ruth C. "Family Background of Alcohol Abuse and Its Relationship to Alcohol Consumption Among College Students: An Unexpected Finding." *Journal of Studies on Alcohol* 51.6 (1990): 542–547. Print.

Gerson, Mark. "30 Pct. of Ontario's Students Called 'Heavy Drinkers.'" *Chronicle of Higher Education* 12 April 1989: A43. Print.

Leatherman, Courtney. "College Officials Are Split on Alcohol Policies; Some Seek to End Underage Drinking; Others Try to Encourage 'Responsible' Use." *Chronicle of Higher Education* 31 Jan. 1990: A33–35. Print.

O'Hare, Thomas M. "Drinking in College: Consumption Patterns, Problems, Sex Differences and Legal Drinking Age." *Journal of Studies on Alcohol* 51.6 (1990): 536–541. Print.

Pardeck, John T. "A Multiple Regression Analysis of Family Factors Affecting the Potential for Alcoholism in College Students." *Adolescence* 26.102 (1991): 341–347. Print.

Perkins, H. Wesley, and Alan D. Berkowitz. "Collegiate COAs and Alcohol Abuse: Problem Drinking in Relation to Assessment of Parent and Grandparent Alcoholism." *Journal of Counseling and Development* 69.3 (1991): 237–240. Print.

Rosenberg, Debra. "Bad Times at Hangover U." *Newsweek* 19 Nov. 1990: 81. Print.

Siler, Julie Flynn. "It Isn't Miller Time Yet, and This Bud's Not for You." *Business Week* 24 June 1991: 52. Print.

Alternative Writing Projects: Community Problems, Community Solutions

1. Prepare a concise PowerPoint presentation that addresses a specific campus or community problem and that proposes a specific solution. Your presentation should consist of no more than ten slides—about the time you would have to present your concerns at a public forum such as a student governance board or town council meeting. Plan to have two slides for each of the five steps of the Flexible Approach to Problem Solving in Figure 12.1. Your main purpose here is to be as concise as possible while issuing a call to action.

2. Apply the five-step problem-solving method to a local, national, or international problem that has already been successfully solved. You will be writing primarily in the past tense, and your purpose will be to describe *why* a particular solution worked so well. Your particular focus will be on step 5 of the process, Test the Solution, and your critical analysis will be focused on evaluation.

CHAPTER 12 Summary

We can become more effective *problem-solvers* by approaching complex problems in an organized way:

- Have I accepted the problem and committed myself to solving it?
- Step 1: What is the problem?
- Step 2: What are the alternatives?
- Step 3: What are the advantages and/or disadvantages of each alternative?
- Step 4: What is the solution?
- Step 5: How well is the solution working?

This approach to solving problems is effective not only for problems that you experience personally but also problems that you may face as citizens of a community, a society, and the world, and it also provides a framework that you can use in much of your writing.

As rigorously planned and carefully controlled as laboratory experiments, thought experiments are used by scientists and philosophers to explore possibilities that might not otherwise be ethically or physically tested. The Australian philosopher and ethicist Peter Singer, who teaches at Princeton University, uses thought experiments to explore such provocative social issues as animal rights, euthanasia, and the redistribution of wealth. His provocative, rigorous thinking challenges all of us to live ethically, in ways that do indeed shake the comfortable material foundations of our culture. What other topics in ethics might be well-suited to thought experiments?

Writing to Persuade:
Constructing Arguments

Principles of Argument

"I got into direct confrontation with everybody I love."

—LAURYN HILL

Critical Thinking Focus: Using reasons, evidence, and logic

Writing Focus: Convincing an audience

Reading Theme: Arguments about important issues

Writing Project: Arguing a position on a significant issue

People who study communication, argument, and rhetoric believe that much of what we say, write, and post online can be defined as *argument* because most statements seek listeners' or readers' agreement with the ideas being presented. Unless someone is just saying "Hmmmm" or "Hello" or is asking a question only to obtain information, the purpose of his or her statement usually is to make a point, to convince the audience of its validity, and often to bring about change or action. Essays, letters, stories, poems, movies, websites—and even paintings and clothes—can be considered arguments or have argumentative purposes.

This chapter is devoted to argument, even though most of your previous writing has had argumentative characteristics. Some writing is supposed to be predominantly argumentative, and you need to know how to create it and how to analyze it. Arguing effectively is essential to academic and professional success as well as to establishing your personal ethic. In addition, because both politicians and advertisers use argumentative techniques, you need to understand both valid and fallacious arguments in order to evaluate claims that people want you to accept.

This chapter will introduce concepts related to argument, provide readings and Thinking-Writing Activities to help you grasp them, and conclude with a Writing Project that asks you to write a logical, well-organized argument for a position that is important to you. The chapter will also explore ways to construct effective arguments and to evaluate arguments.

Thinking-Writing Activity

ANALYZING ARGUMENTATIVE WRITING

1. Select an essay or blog entry that you have written that you believe has an argumentative purpose. What is your thesis or claim? What specific evidence do you present? Who are your audiences? Does the paper advocate for any change or action? What is it?

2. Select a reading from a previous chapter that you consider argumentative. What is its claim? What evidence does it present? Who are its audiences? What change or action does it seek?

Classical Concepts of Argument

The concepts that guide logical argument are central to Western culture. Articulated by the philosophers and rhetoricians of ancient Greece and Rome, they have been studied and applied for more than two thousand years. Even though emotions, gut reactions, and intuition cannot be brushed aside—because they are so human— logical thinking and the resulting structured arguments are expected in business, government, and scholarship. Therefore, as a college composition student, you have both practical and historical reasons for giving attention to principles of argument or rhetoric.

The Greek philosopher Aristotle, in his famous work the *Rhetoric* and in other writings on logic, is the source of many concepts basic to our ideas of argument. But even Aristotle, more than three hundred years B.C.E., was responding to earlier works on rhetoric; and to this day, those who have followed him have modified and redefined his ideas and those of other classical rhetoricians. Those concepts include *ethos*, the character of the speaker or writer; *pathos*, the effect on the audience; and *logos*, the logic and substance of an argument. All three are powerful aspects of any argument. You should try to identify them in arguments that others address to you, and you should work hard to achieve effectiveness with each in arguments that you write.

Responsible writers try to present themselves as knowledgeable, reasonable, trustworthy, and sensitive to the tone appropriate to the situation—that is, to achieve their desired *ethos*. Critical thinkers are able to build clear and logical discussions, avoid fallacious reasoning, and handle opposing viewpoints courteously but firmly—that is, achieve their desired *logos*. A good combination of *logos* and *ethos* will engage audiences and elicit thoughtful responses—that is, achieve the desired *pathos*.

Some other centuries-old concepts are the techniques for generation or discovery of ideas, the arrangement of sections of an argument, the thinking methods of deduction and induction, techniques for refutation, and moral concerns about the use of rhetorical power for honorable ends.

Links to the Thinking-Writing Model The classical rhetoricians were concerned with oral communication; literacy for all, print, and electronics were yet to come. Speech is, of course, still essential to communication, both face to face and via electronic media. This book concentrates on writing, but the ancient concepts have never gone out of use, and they function well to promote effective writing. The topics in the Thinking-Writing Model (pages 6–8 in Chapter 1) that is the foundation of this book demonstrate contemporary applications of many classical principles.

Notice how subject, purpose, audience, and writer connect in multiple ways with the concepts of *logos*, *pathos*, and *ethos*. If *logos* means both content and the logic of its presentation, *logos* connects with the Thinking-Writing Model's topics of subject, defining a thesis, and organizing ideas as well as with thinking critically. *Pathos* connects, of course, with the Thinking-Writing Model's audience and purpose; *ethos*, with the writer and also with the editing and proofreading stages of revising since a well-finished paper gives a good impression of its writer.

The classical concepts of *discovery* and *arrangement* are clearly connected to the Thinking-Writing Model's notions of thinking creatively, generating ideas, organizing ideas, and drafting.

Responsible Rhetoric Today, the words *argument* and *rhetoric* are regularly used in conversation and in the media differently from the ways in which they are used in this chapter. Popularly, *argument* often means "a quarrel," and *rhetoric* is often used to mean "insubstantial or misleading language" (which is connected to the classical concerns about the use of rhetorical power for honorable ends). In this chapter, *rhetoric* means "the use of the best means of persuasion." We will discuss argument throughout the chapter and define the term on page 491.

Modern Concepts of Argument

In the twenty-first century, much attention has been paid to argument, at least partly because both mass media and education have extended their reaches. More communication and analyses of it from different points of view continue to provide new ways of thinking about arguments. Three important modern approaches are the *Toulmin method,* analyzing the effects of electronic communication, and various consensus-building strategies.

Toulmin's Method College composition students are often introduced to some concepts that have developed from the work of the British professor of philosophy Stephen Toulmin. Professor Toulmin's ideas about argument can be applied to almost any argument, no matter how it is constructed. Concepts important to the Toulmin method are *claim* and *qualified claim, grounds, warrants,* and *backings*.

Thinking Critically About Visuals

How Visual Arguments Influence Our Choices

Looking at these U.S. Army recruitment materials should help you understand warrants.

What is your reaction to the figure of Uncle Sam? How do you read the gesture he is making? At whom is he pointing? Who was the "you" he wanted? In 1917, who would Uncle Sam not have been recruiting? What are some assumptions, principles, beliefs—or warrants—that provide a foundation for the argument presented by this poster? What is the meaning or symbolism of the fact that Uncle Sam appears to be an older white man?

© Library of Congress

You already understand *claim* because *thesis, main point,* and *conclusion* are other ways to say it. You already understand *grounds* because it means *reasons, evidence, support, examples,* and *data.* You have established a thesis and provided support for it in most papers that you have written for this course.

What are the demographics in the images shown on the website? How do they compare to the 1917 poster? What does the idea of "Your Education Our Mission" suggest to you? While both this and the 1917 poster are recruitment devices, what different appeals do they make to potential enlistees?

Can you see some assumptions, principles, beliefs—or warrants—that are behind the approaches taken by the poster and by the website as they try to convince young people to enlist? See if you and your classmates found the same ones.

For additional examples of how visuals can be used to provoke, persuade, and argue, see Thinking Critically About Images on pages 2-1 to 2-8.

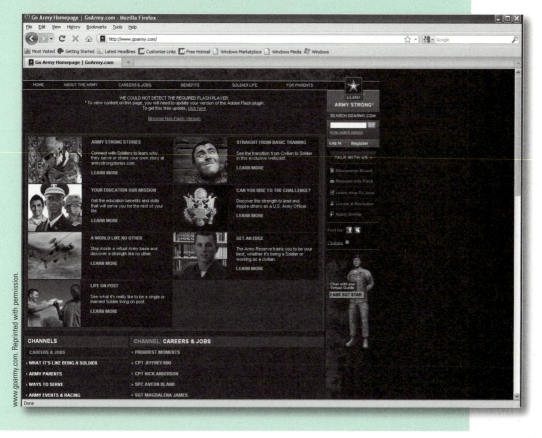

www.goarmy.com. Reprinted with permission.

As you improved your ability to develop a good thesis and studied Chapter 8's material on definition and classification, you were learning about qualified claims or qualifiers. A *qualified claim* is an accurately worded claim, one that establishes the category to be discussed. A qualified claim is not exaggerated or overly general. For example, you might not want to claim that "*Teenagers* should not be allowed to drive after midnight." Instead, you might claim that "People *under eighteen years* of age should not be allowed to drive after midnight." That way you would be acknowledging the probable differences in experience and maturity between a sixteen-year-old and an eighteen- or nineteen-year-old and showing that the overly general word *teenager* needs qualification. Properly qualified claims produce effective arguments.

Warrants are the assumptions, principles, premises, and beliefs that are the foundations of most arguments. This is an important concept to understand because warrants are not always stated. However, warrants provide the connection between a claim and its grounds, and they enable the acceptance or rejection of an argument. Here's a simple example:

Claim: People should brush and floss their teeth regularly.

Grounds: Dentists tell us that brushing and flossing will help prevent tooth decay and gum disease.

Warrants: People do not want their teeth to fall out. They do not want to have toothaches or ugly decayed teeth. People do not want drilling, fillings, and dentists' bills.

Backings are larger principles that support warrants. They are the foundations of the foundations. A backing for the warrants about brushing and flossing is the generally accepted principle of self-interest. People are concerned about their own health, appearance, and finances; people are concerned about situations that affect them. Therefore, the backing of the principle of self-interest supports the warrants about what people don't want, which support and connect the claim and grounds about dental hygiene.

This use of the word *warrant* is related to its use in law enforcement—a warrant for an arrest or a search warrant, which authorizes actions. The warrants of an argument are also related to the sources of beliefs (see Chapters 3 and 11). In addition, warrants are related to the premises used in deductive reasoning, which you will study later in this chapter.

Just as you need to understand the sources of your beliefs and those of others, you need to understand the warrants behind the arguments that you make and that people present to you. You need to recognize them when they are stated as part of an argument and search for them if they are not stated.

Argument and Electronic Media

Argument and Electronic Media   There is currently much speculation about the effects of electronic communication on arguments. Of course, different kinds of electronic technologies raise different questions. Obviously, podcasting transmits spoken arguments, and television uses both sound and visuals to produce its well-known impact on audiences. Computers do so many things that analysis is difficult—but exciting. Visuals, sounds, and texts can be combined in countless ways, so distinctions among written, pictorial, and spoken arguments are blurred.

Many characteristics of online communication can affect arguments. The movement of linking means that logical connections are not always made. The speed at which ideas are transmitted and the rapidity with which some information can change can cause confusion and raise questions about credibility. Many people tend to write more informally in email than on paper, and such informality can change the tone of an argument for better or for worse. The rapid transmission of email can quickly conclude an argument or cause it to go on longer.

On the other hand, many Internet texts are simply posted versions of printed material or have been composed in a traditional manner. You need to be aware of the ways in which electronic and written communications differ as well as the ways in which argumentative concepts operate similarly in various media.

More Links to the Thinking-Writing Model   Just as the concepts of classical rhetoric connect with components in the Thinking-Writing Model, so do the modern concepts. A claim, especially a qualified claim, clearly relates to defining a thesis. Grounds are important for generating and organizing ideas. Warrants and backing connect significantly with audience, purpose, and the writer. Writers need to understand their own assumptions and basic beliefs as they develop arguments in order to think critically about what they are presenting. Also, since assumptions and basic beliefs can differ in various communities, writers need to consider how the warrants beneath an argument might affect their audiences. Consensus-building approaches relate most obviously to reaching an audience but also pertain to purposes and to organizing ideas.

Achieving Mutual Understanding   Some people believe that the purpose of argument is to coerce or to "win." As we have seen in this book, though, critical thinkers strive to develop the most informed understanding, which

"I shall now punch a huge hole in your argument."

THINKING CRITICALLY ABOUT NEW MEDIA

Freedom of Speech on the Internet

The dramatic growth of new media has created new issues with respect to freedom of speech. Of course, even before the Internet, the guarantee of freedom of speech under the Constitution never meant that people could say *anything*. For example, you have never been permitted to yell "Fire" in a crowded theater because of the panic that might ensue. Nor is it legal to use wildly inflammatory language towards other people—"fighting words"—that could precipitate an altercation. And if you make false and unflattering allegations about a person or organization that are demonstrably false you can be sued for *libel* (written defamation) or *slander* (spoken defamation), or both. And, of course, there have been bans on content dealing with child pornography and other taboo subjects.

But the development of new media has introduced new battlegrounds where freedom of speech is being debated. For example, the Center for Democracy & Technology (CDT) <http://www.dct.org/> is an organization devoted to maximizing freedom of speech and minimizing censorship on the Internet to the greatest extent possible, as they explain in the following passage:

> Free speech has long been a hallmark of a healthy democracy and a free society. The Internet and new communications technologies have become unprecedented tools for expanding the ability for individuals to speak and receive information, participate in political and democratic processes, and share knowledge and ideas. Recognizing the potential of these technologies, courts have extended the highest level of First Amendment protection to the Internet medium. Online free expression also requires that private online service providers be protected from legal liability for content posted by users, so they will be willing to host that speech.

> CDT works to keep the Internet and communications technologies free of government censorship and content gatekeepers alike, and to extend the highest level of free speech protection afforded the Internet to all converged media. User choice and control over access to information are the key to protecting core First Amendment values while still addressing important social ills in the digital age. Through our advocacy, CDT seeks to maximize the ability of individuals to decide for themselves what they say, hear, publish, and access online.

There are others who believe that while freedom of expression is of paramount importance in a free democracy, this right must be balanced against threats to personal safety. For example, should sexual predators be permitted to create false Internet identities and try to lure children into inappropriate correspondence or even dangerous encounters in the real world? Should advertisers be allowed to use deceptive advertising to sell prescription drugs to both minors and adults alike? What about information related to your personal health: should insurance companies be able to gain access to this material which they might then use to raise your rates or deny you health coverage? The entire issue of consumer privacy is an issue also, as detailed profiles about each one of us—our demographics, the websites we visit, our buying patterns, our financial data, etc.—are available and often shared among organizations and businesses without our knowledge. One recent court judgment has ruled that Internet organizations like Craigslist.com on which people post advertisements, cannot be held responsible for the content of the ads themselves. For example, if people want to use these online venues to solicit sexual business or sell illegal pharmaceuticals, it is not up to the owners of the site to "police" these ads and prohibit or report them. (Despite this ruling, Craigslist recently decided to prohibit "adult content" in its publication.)

In addition to the Center for Democracy & Technology, which provides frequent updates on challenges to free speech online and elsewhere in society, there are other sites devoted to this complex issue, including:

- Electronic Frontier Foundation <www.eff.org> is a site that advocates for freedom of speech online and offers legal resources and information for people interested in pursuing these issues.
- *PCWorld.com* <www.pcworld.com> and *Wired* <www.wired.com> are consumer magazines about computing that frequently publish articles that go beyond the *content* of "free speech" online to the *technology* that allows for—and complicates—freedom of speech.

Sources: Excerpt from Center for Democracy & Technology (CDT) website (http://www.cdt.org/). Reprinted by permission.

Thinking-Writing Activity

FREEDOM OF SPEECH ON THE INTERNET

After exploring the Internet sites devoted to freedom of speech on the Internet, including those noted above, respond to the following questions:

1. Do you believe that existing laws concerning consumer rights, freedom of speech, and intellectual property (copyrights, performance licensing, etc.) are sufficient to cover what occurs on the Internet, or do we need stricter regulations to protect children, the elderly, consumers, and others? Explain the reasoning supporting your perspective.

(Continues)

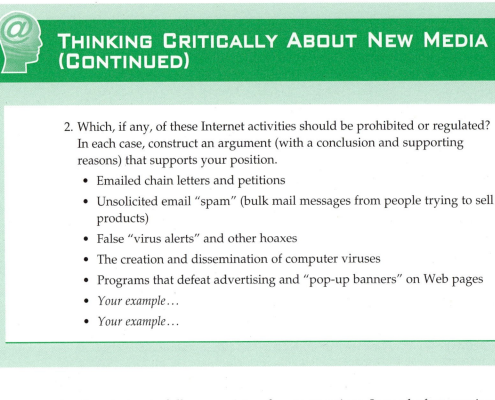

2. Which, if any, of these Internet activities should be prohibited or regulated? In each case, construct an argument (with a conclusion and supporting reasons) that supports your position.

- Emailed chain letters and petitions
- Unsolicited email "spam" (bulk mail messages from people trying to sell products)
- False "virus alerts" and other hoaxes
- The creation and dissemination of computer viruses
- Programs that defeat advertising and "pop-up banners" on Web pages
- *Your example…*
- *Your example…*

involves trying to fully appreciate other perspectives. Instead of attempting to prove others wrong, a more desirable purpose is to arrive at a clear and mutual understanding about the issue being discussed. Sometimes people are so far apart in their convictions that agreement cannot be reached and an impasse (or worse) occurs. At other times people "agree to disagree" and work around their differences; but if agreement does come, good feelings can result in progress, problem solving, or other desired achievements. By thinking critically, you can inspire others to think critically as well so that all parties are working together to achieve the clearest understanding rather than splintering into adversarial factions. In the cartoon on page 483, the man on the right seems to be pursuing conflict rather than mutual understanding. What are the disadvantages of such an approach? Can you think of some more constructive strategies that he could use?

Considering Other Points of View   People do not argue about things on which they agree, nor do they argue about concepts that are accepted as facts. For example, it's not likely that an argument would arise over the relative lengths of a meter and a yard. A measuring tape takes care of the question. However, people do argue about whether the United States should adopt the metric system. Arguments develop because people have different opinions about issues.

You should not ignore opposing points of view when you are making an argument. Sometimes, people will ignore other ideas and present one-sided cases—as in most advertisements, some sermons, many political statements, and attempts at pushing proposals through. But in reasoned arguments, you should address varying ideas in order to demonstrate your grasp of the issue and also to try to achieve mutual understanding and, if possible, consensus or agreement.

Guidelines for Addressing Other Points of View

1. *Restate the other claim to show that you understand it.* This is often easier to do in a face-to-face discussion than in writing, but it is important in any argument. Sometimes misunderstandings can be uncovered by this technique. Restatements can also lead to finding common ground. A restatement should be made in a nonjudgmental, respectful tone.

2. *Find areas of agreement, or common ground, at the outset of the argument.* This, too, is sometimes easier to do in a face-to-face discussion than in writing. It is a technique often used in negotiations and mediation. However, in a written argument, you should try whenever you can to establish common ground with those who have other beliefs about the issue that you are addressing. Often identifying warrants can lead parties to find areas of agreement. When people see that they agree about some parts of an issue, they can establish mutual respect and then examine their differing opinions carefully.

3. *Identify which differences are important and which are trivial.* This, too, is more easily done when people talk with each other, but it is also something that can be attempted in written argument. Here, too, identifying warrants sometimes clarifies the significance of some parts of an argument.

4. *Concede points that you cannot uphold.* Sometimes you will have to concede that some of your opponents' ideas are so strong that you cannot counter them, even if you do not agree with them.

5. *Compromise.* At times, accepting a middle position or a partial achievement of your purpose is better than arguing for its complete achievement.

6. *Rebut.* This means to refute or to present opposing evidence. Rebuttal often seems necessary. It is part of the debate tradition and is important in legal arguments, but it maintains adversarial positions. If you have to rebut an opposing point, do so courteously.

(Continues)

7. *Be sensitive to different argumentative philosophies.* Some cultures, some groups, and some individuals prefer indirect methods of argumentation while others want to get to the point quickly. Sometimes a direct approach is seen as rude or overly aggressive; sometimes an indirect approach is seen as weak, sneaky, or confusing. In the United States, directness is often considered as the best approach. If your audience is from a different culture, however, be sure that you understand that culture's argumentative style.

Thinking-Writing Activity

ESTABLISHING AGREEMENT

1. Find a classmate who disagrees with you about something—for example, the quality of a specific television show, a political principle, or a controversy at your college. Each of you should then write a brief statement about your position. Next, read each other's statements.

2. See if you can establish some areas of agreement. Can you identify warrants for your position and for your classmate's? Where might you compromise? Determine whether any differences are not important. Do either of you have to concede a point?

Analyzing the Audience   You learned long ago that you should speak and write differently to different audiences. You use one kind of vocabulary and tone with your friends and another with your grandparents. You write formally in a job application letter and informally in an email to your sister describing what you did last weekend.

The suggestions for completing every Writing Project in this book include some discussion of your audience because it is one of the major components of any writing situation and therefore is prominently featured in the Thinking-Writing Model. However, consideration of audience is especially important when you are writing an argumentative paper, particularly if you hope to effect some change or action. Also, remember that you may have more than one audience. Here are some questions to ask yourself about the audiences for any argument you write:

- Who is interested in this issue?
- What concerns do these interested people have?
- What is their level of education or expertise?
- What related issues interest them?
- How much time might they give to reading my argument?

- Who can do something about the situation?
- Who is opposed to my point of view?
- What are the opposing claims?
- What format, tone, or method of presentation will be effective with this audience?

Can you think of other questions to ask about audiences?

Going Too Far Paying attention to audiences does not mean telling an audience only what it wants to hear or manipulating ideas just to reach a certain audience. Some advertisers and politicians mislead audiences in such ways. Pandering to an audience is one of the ways in which rhetoric can be misused. Responsible writers and speakers accommodate their audiences honestly.

Recognizing Arguments

Two Friends Argue: Should Marijuana Be Legalized?

Consider the following dialogue about whether marijuana should be legalized. Have you participated in such exchanges? In what ways do dialogues like this differ from written argument? How do such dialogues provide a starting point for written arguments?

DENNIS: Have you read about the medical uses of marijuana—that people who have cancer, AIDS, and some other diseases might be helped by smoking? I think some doctors are prescribing it, and some states may be changing their laws. This might change people's thinking more than all those discussions about unenforced laws, unjust punishments, and victimless crimes that have been going on since my uncles were in college.

CAROLINE: Well, I agree that we need to think about drug laws. But I hope you agree that we have to be careful. Drugs pose a serious threat to the young people of our country. Look at all the people who are addicted to drugs, who have their lives ruined, and who often die at an early age of overdoses. And think of all the crimes people commit to support their drug habits. So I don't know if anything that's illegal now should be legalized...and the laws should be enforced.

DENNIS: That's ridiculous. Smoking marijuana is nothing like using drugs such as heroin or even cocaine. It follows that smoking marijuana should not be against the law if it's harmless and maybe even helpful to some sick people.

CAROLINE: I don't agree. Although marijuana may not be as dangerous as some other drugs, it does affect things like a driver's ability to judge distances. And smoking it surely isn't good for you. And I don't think that anything that is a threat to your health should be legal.

DENNIS: What about cigarettes and alcohol? We know that they are dangerous. Medical research has linked smoking cigarettes to lung cancer, emphysema, and heart disease. Alcohol damages the liver and also the brain. Has anyone ever proved that marijuana is a threat to our health? And even if it does turn out to be somewhat unhealthy, it's certainly not as dangerous as cigarettes and alcohol.

CAROLINE: That's a good point. But to tell you the truth, I'm not so sure that cigarettes and alcohol should be legal. And in any case, they are legal. The fact that cigarettes and alcohol are bad for your health is not reason to legalize another drug that can cause health problems.

DENNIS: Look—life is full of risks. We take chances every time we cross the street or climb into our cars. In fact, with all the irresponsible drivers on the road, driving could be a lot more hazardous to our health than any of the drugs around. Many of the foods we eat can kill. For example, red meat contributes to heart disease, and artificial sweeteners can cause cancer. The point is, if people want to take chances with their health, that's up to them. And many people in our society like to mellow out with marijuana. I read somewhere that over 70 percent of the people in the United States think that marijuana should be legalized.

CAROLINE: There is a big difference between letting people drive cars and letting them use dangerous drugs. Society has a responsibility to protect people from themselves. People often do things that are foolish if they are encouraged to or given the opportunity. Legalizing something like marijuana encourages people to use it, especially young people. It follows that many more people would use marijuana if it were legalized. It's like society saying "This is all right—go ahead and use it."

DENNIS: I still maintain that marijuana isn't dangerous. It's not addictive—like heroin is—and there is no evidence that it harms you. Consequently, anything that is harmless should be legal.

CAROLINE: Marijuana may not be physically addictive like heroin, but I think that it can be psychologically addictive because people tend to use more and more of it over time. I know a number of people who spend a lot of their time getting high. What about Carl? All he does is lie around and get high. This shows that smoking it over a period of time definitely affects your mind. Think about the people you know who smoke a lot—don't they seem to be floating in a dream world? How are they ever going to make anything of their lives? As far as I'm concerned, a pothead is like a zombie—living but dead.

DENNIS: Since you have had so little experience with marijuana, I don't think that you can offer an informed opinion on the subject. And anyway, if you do too much of anything, it can hurt you. Even something as healthy as exercise can cause problems if you do too much of it. But I sure don't see anything wrong with toking up with some friends at a party or even getting into a relaxed state by yourself. In fact, I find that I can even concentrate better on my school work after taking a little smoke.

CAROLINE: If you believe that, then marijuana really has damaged your brain. You're just trying to rationalize your drug habit. Smoking marijuana doesn't help you concentrate—it takes you away from reality. And I don't think that people can control it. Either you smoke and surrender control of your life, or you don't smoke because you want to retain control. There's nothing in between.

DENNIS: Let me point out something to you. Because marijuana is illegal, organized crime controls its distribution and makes all the money from it. If marijuana were legalized, the government could tax the sale of it—like cigarettes and alcohol—and use the money for some worthwhile purpose. For example, many states have legalized gambling and use the money to support education. In fact, the major tobacco companies have already copyrighted names for different marijuana brands—like "Acapulco Gold." Obviously they believe that marijuana will soon become legal.

CAROLINE: The fact that the government can make money out of something doesn't mean that they should legalize it. We could also legalize prostitution or muggings and then tax the proceeds. Also, even if the cigarette companies are prepared to sell marijuana, that doesn't mean that selling it makes sense. After all, they're the ones who are selling us cigarettes....

Can you think of other views on the subject of legalizing marijuana? Can you think of other subjects about which such dialogues are taking place now?

The previous discussion illustrates two people's engaging in dialogue, the systematic exchange of ideas. Discussing issues with others encourages you to be mentally active, to ask questions, to view issues from different perspectives, to develop reasons that support conclusions, and to write convincingly.

This chapter focuses on the last quality of thinking critically—supporting claims with reasons—because when we offer reasons to support a conclusion, we are presenting an argument, the essence of most college and business writing. An *argument* is a form of thinking in which certain statements (reasons or evidence) are offered to support another statement (a conclusion or a claim).

In the dialogue, Dennis presents the following argument for legalizing marijuana:

Reason: Marijuana might help some people who have serious diseases.

Reason: Marijuana isn't dangerous like heroin and cocaine.

Reason: Governments could tax the sale of marijuana as they do cigarettes and alcohol.

Claim: Marijuana should be legalized.

Expanding the definition of *argument*, we can define the main ideas that make up an argument. *Reasons, evidence,* or *grounds* are statements that support another statement (a conclusion, claim, or thesis), justify it, or make it more probable. The *claim, thesis,* or *conclusion* is a statement that explains, asserts, or predicts on the basis of statements (known as reasons) that are offered as evidence to support it.

The type of thinking that uses argument—presenting reasons to support conclusions—is known as *reasoning,* and it is a type of thinking explained throughout this book. We are continually trying to explain, justify, and predict through the process of reasoning, and often we must present such thinking in writing.

Of course, our reasoning—and that of others—is not always correct. The reasons someone offers may not really support the claim they are intended to, a conclusion may not really follow from the reasons stated, or the reasons may be questionable or wrong. These difficulties are illustrated in a number of the arguments contained in the previous discussion on marijuana.

Nevertheless, whenever we accept a conclusion as likely or true on the basis of certain reasons, or whenever we offer reasons to support a conclusion, we are using arguments—even if our reasoning is weak or faulty and needs improvement.

Let's return to the discussion about marijuana. After Dennis presents one argument, Caroline presents another, giving reasons that lead to a conclusion that conflicts with the one Dennis has offered.

Reason: Drugs pose a very serious threat to the young people of our country.

Reason: Many crimes are committed to support drug habits.

Claim: As a result, society has to have drug laws and enforce them to convince people of the seriousness of the situation.

Which of Dennis's or Caroline's arguments do you see as reasonable? Which seem weak or faulty?

English, like other languages, provides guidance in our efforts to identify reasons and conclusions. Certain key words, or cue words, signal that a reason is being offered to support a conclusion or that a conclusion is being drawn on the basis of certain reasons. After you read the following list, go back to the dialogue and see how and when Dennis and Caroline use these words.

The following are some commonly used cue words for reasons and conclusions. Of course, identifying reasons, claims, and conclusions involves more than looking for cue words. The words and phrases just listed do not always signal reasons and conclusions, and in many cases people present arguments without using cue words. Cue words, however, do alert us that an argument is being offered. Careful use of cue words helps us to write effective arguments.

Useful Words for Recognizing and Writing Arguments

Cue Words Signaling Reasons

since	in view of
for	first, second
because	in the first (second) place
as shown by	may be inferred from

as indicated by	may be deduced from
given that	may be derived from
assuming that	for the reason that

Cue Words Signaling Conclusions

therefore	then
thus	it follows that
hence	thereby showing
so	demonstrates that
(which) shows that	allows us to infer that
(which) proves that	suggests very strongly that
implies that	you see that
points to	leads me to believe that
as a result	allows us to deduce that
consequently	

Thinking-Writing Activity

ANALYZING A DIALOGUE

Write responses to the previous dialogue. Then share your responses with classmates and note where you agree and disagree.

1. Review the discussion and underline cue words that signal when Dennis and Caroline are giving reasons or announcing conclusions.

2. Identify one argument in the dialogue that you find convincing and one that seems unconvincing. Write your reasons for your opinions, referring to specific places in the dialogue.

In the first of the following articles, *Why We Must Ration Health Care,* the philosopher Peter Singer argues that rationing health care is unavoidable and that in fact we already do it—we just don't do it very well. The second article, *Rationing Medical Care: A Second Opinion* by Leonard Laster, the Chancellor of the University of Massachusetts Medical School, argues an opposing viewpoint. While Laster acknowledges the compelling reasoning in support of rationing, he contends that adopting a rationing policy might be a profound mistake based on even more compelling considerations. After reading each of the articles, respond thoughtfully to the questions that follow.

"Why We Must Ration Health Care"

by Peter Singer

In the current U.S. debate over health care reform, "rationing" has become a dirty word. Meeting last month with five governors, President Obama urged them to avoid using the term, apparently for fear of evoking the hostile response that sank the Clintons' attempt to achieve reform. In a *Wall Street Journal* op-ed published at the end of last year with the headline "Obama Will Ration Your Health Care," Sally Pipes, C.E.O. of the conservative Pacific Research Institute, described how in Britain the national health service does not pay for drugs that are regarded as not offering good value for money, and added, "Americans will not put up with such limits, nor will our elected representatives." And the Democratic chair of the Senate Finance Committee, Senator Max Baucus, told CNSNews in April, "There is no rationing of health care at all" in the proposed reform.

Health care is a scarce resource, and all scarce resources are rationed in one way or another. In the United States, most health care is privately financed, and so most rationing is by price: you get what you, or your employer, can afford to insure you for. But our current system of employer-financed health insurance exists only because the federal government encouraged it by making the premiums tax deductible. That is, in effect, a more than $200 billion government subsidy for health care. In the public sector, primarily Medicare, Medicaid and hospital emergency rooms, health care is rationed by long waits, high patient copayment requirements, low payments to doctors that discourage some from serving public patients and limits on payments to hospitals.

The case for explicit health care rationing in the United States starts with the difficulty of thinking of any other way in which we can continue to provide adequate health care to people on Medicaid and Medicare, let alone extend coverage to those who do not now have it. Health-insurance premiums have more than doubled in a decade, rising four times faster than wages. In May, Medicare's trustees warned that the program's biggest fund is heading for insolvency in just eight years. Health care now absorbs about one dollar in every six the nation spends, a figure that far exceeds the share spent by any other nation. According to the Congressional Budget Office, it is on track to double by 2035.

Rationing health care means getting value for the billions we are spending by setting limits on which treatments should be paid for from the public purse. If we ration we won't be writing blank checks to pharmaceutical companies for their patented drugs, nor paying for whatever procedures doctors choose to recommend. When public funds subsidize health care or provide it directly, it is crazy not to try to get value for money. The debate over health care reform in the United States should start from the premise that some form of health care rationing is both inescapable and desirable. Then we can ask, What is the best way to do it?

Last year Britain's National Institute for Health and Clinical Excellence gave a preliminary recommendation that the National Health Service should not offer Sutent for advanced kidney cancer. The institute, generally known as NICE, is a government-financed but independently run organization set up to provide national guidance on promoting good health and treating illness. The decision on Sutent did not, at first glance, appear difficult. NICE had set a general limit of £30,000, or about $49,000, on the cost of extending life for a year. Sutent, when used for advanced kidney cancer, cost more than that, and research suggested it offered only about six months extra life. But the British media leapt on the theme of penny-pinching bureaucrats sentencing sick people to death. The issue was then picked up by the U.S. news media and by those lobbying against health care reform in the United States. An article in the *New York Times* last December featured Bruce Hardy, a kidney-cancer patient whose wife, Joy, said, "It's hard to know that there is something out there that could help but they're saying you can't have it because of cost." Then she asked the classic question: "What price is life?"

5   There's no doubt that it's tough—politically, emotionally and ethically—to make a decision that means that someone will die sooner than they would have if the decision had gone the other way. But if we think badly of the British system of rationing health care, we should remind ourselves that the U.S. system also results in people going without life-saving treatment—it just does so less visibly. Pharmaceutical manufacturers often charge much more for drugs in the United States than they charge for the same drugs in Britain, where they know that a higher price would put the drug outside the cost-effectiveness limits set by NICE. American patients, even if they are covered by Medicare or Medicaid, often cannot afford the copayments for drugs. That's rationing too, by ability to pay.

A New York Times report on the high costs of some drugs illustrates the problem. Chuck Stauffer, an Oregon farmer, found that his prescription-drug insurance left him to pay $5,500 for his first 42 days of Temodar, a drug used to treat brain tumors, and $1,700 a month after that. For Medicare patients drug costs can be even higher, because Medicare can require a copayment of 25 percent of the cost of the drug. For Gleevec, a drug that is effective against some forms of leukemia and some gastrointestinal tumors, that one-quarter of the cost can run to $40,000 a year.

In Britain, everyone has health insurance. In the U.S., some 45 million do not, and nor are they entitled to any health care at all, unless they can get themselves to an emergency room. Hospitals are prohibited from turning away anyone who will be endangered by being refused treatment. But even in emergency rooms, people without health insurance may receive less health care than those with insurance. Joseph Doyle, a professor of economics at the Sloan School of Management at M.I.T., studied the records of people in Wisconsin who were injured in severe automobile accidents and had no choice but to go to the hospital. He estimated that those who had no health insurance received 20 percent less care and had a death rate 37 percent higher than those with health insurance. This difference held up even when those without health insurance were compared with those without automobile insurance, and with those on Medicaid—groups with whom they share some characteristics that might affect treatment. The lack of insurance seems to be what caused the greater number of deaths.

We readily relate to individuals who are harmed by a government agency's decision to limit the cost of health care. But we tend not to hear about—and thus don't identify with—the particular individuals who die in emergency rooms because they have no health insurance. This "identifiable victim" effect, well documented by psychologists, creates a dangerous bias in our thinking. Doyle's figures suggest that if those Wisconsin accident victims without health insurance had received equivalent care to those with it, the additional health care would have cost about $220,000 for each life saved. Those who died were on average around 30 years old and could have been expected to live for at least another 40 years; this means that had they survived their accidents, the cost per extra year of life would have been no more than $5,500—a small fraction of the $49,000 that NICE recommends the British National Health Service should be ready to pay to give a patient an extra year of life. If the U.S. system spent less on expensive treatments for those who, with or without the drugs, have at most a few months to live, it would be better able to save the lives of more people who, if they get the treatment they need, might live for several decades.

Estimates of the number of U.S. deaths caused annually by the absence of universal health insurance go as high as 20,000. One study concluded that in the age group 55 to 64 alone, more than 13,000 extra deaths a year may be attributed to the lack of insurance coverage. But the estimates vary because Americans without health insurance are more likely, for example, to smoke than Americans with health insurance, and sorting out the role that the lack of insurance plays is difficult. Richard Kronick, a professor at the School of Medicine at the University of California, San Diego, cautiously concludes from his own study that there is little evidence to suggest that extending health insurance to all Americans would have a large effect on the number of deaths in the United States. That doesn't mean that it wouldn't; we simply don't know if it would.

10   When a Washington Post journalist asked Daniel Zemel, a Washington rabbi, what he thought about federal agencies putting a dollar value on human life, the rabbi cited a Jewish teaching explaining that if you put one human life on one side of a scale, and you put the rest of the world on the other side, the scale is balanced equally. Perhaps that is how those who resist health care rationing think. But we already put a dollar value on human life. If we are going to have consumer-safety regulation at all, we need some idea of how much safety is worth buying. Like health care bureaucrats, consumer-safety bureaucrats sometimes decide that saving a human life is not worth the expense. Twenty years ago, the National Research Council, an arm of the National Academy of Sciences, examined a proposal for installing seat belts in all school buses. It estimated that doing so would save, on average, one life per year, at a cost of $40 million. After that, support for the proposal faded away. So why is it that those who accept that we put a price on life when it comes to consumer safety refuse to accept it when it comes to health care?

Of course, it's one thing to accept that there's a limit to how much we should spend to save a human life, and another to set that limit. The dollar value that bureaucrats place on a generic human life is intended to reflect social values, as revealed in our behavior. It is the answer to the question "How much are you willing to pay to save your life?"—except that, of course, if you asked that question of people who were facing death, they would be prepared to pay almost anything to save their lives. So instead, economists note how much people are prepared to pay to reduce the risk that they will die. How much will people pay for air bags in a car, for instance?

Once you know how much they will pay for a specified reduction in risk, you multiply the amount that people are willing to pay by how much the risk has been reduced, and then you know, or so the theory goes, what value people place on their lives. Suppose that there is a 1 in 100,000 chance that an air bag in my car will save my life, and that I would pay $50—but no more than that—for an air bag. Then it looks as if I value my life at $50 x 100,000, or $5 million.

The theory sounds good, but in practice it has problems. We are not good at taking account of differences between very small risks, so if we are asked how much we would pay to reduce a risk of dying from 1 in 1,000,000 to 1 in 10,000,000, we may give the same answer as we would if asked how much we would pay to reduce the risk from 1 in 500,000 to 1 in 10,000,000. Hence multiplying what we would pay to reduce the risk of death by the reduction in risk lends an apparent mathematical precision to the outcome of the calculation—the supposed value of a human life—that our intuitive responses to the questions cannot support. Nevertheless this approach to setting a value on a human life is at least closer to what we really believe—and to what we should believe—than dramatic pronouncements about the infinite value of every human life, or the suggestion that we cannot distinguish between the value of a single human life and the value of a million human lives, or even of the rest of the world. Though such feel-good claims may have some symbolic value in particular circumstances, to take them seriously and apply them—for instance, by leaving it to chance whether we save one life or a billion—would be deeply unethical.

As a first take, we might say that the good achieved by health care is the number of lives saved. But that is too crude. The death of a teenager is a greater tragedy than the death of an 85-year-old, and this should be reflected in our priorities. We can accommodate that difference by calculating the number of life-years saved, rather than simply the number of lives saved. If a teenager can be expected to live another 70 years, saving her life counts as a gain of 70 life-years, whereas if a person of 85 can be expected to live another 5 years, then saving the 85-year-old will count as a gain of only 5 life-years. That suggests that saving one teenager is equivalent to saving 14 85-year-olds. These are, of course, generic teenagers and generic 85-year-olds. It's easy to say, "What if the teenager is a violent criminal and the 85-year-old is still working productively?" But just as emergency rooms should leave criminal justice to the courts and treat assailants and victims alike, so decisions about the allocation of health care resources should be kept separate from judgments about the moral character or social value of individuals.

Health care does more than save lives: it also reduces pain and suffering. How can we compare saving a person's life with, say, making it possible for someone who was confined to bed to return to an active life? We can elicit people's values on that too. One common method is to describe medical conditions to people—let's say being a quadriplegic—and tell them that they can choose between 10 years in that condition or some smaller number of years without it. If most would prefer, say, 10 years as a quadriplegic to 4 years of nondisabled life, but would choose 6 years of nondisabled life over 10 with quadriplegia, but have difficulty deciding between 5 years of nondisabled life or 10 years with quadriplegia, then they are, in effect, assessing life with quadriplegia as half as good as nondisabled life. (These are hypothetical figures, chosen to keep the math simple, and not based on any actual surveys.) If that judgment represents a rough average across the population, we might conclude that restoring to nondisabled life two people who would otherwise be quadriplegics is equivalent in value to saving the life of one person, provided the life expectancies of all involved are similar.

15   This is the basis of the quality-adjusted life-year, or QALY, a unit designed to enable us to compare the benefits achieved by different forms of health care. The QALY has been used by economists working in health care for more than 30 years to compare the cost-effectiveness of a wide variety of medical procedures and, in some countries, as part of the process of deciding which medical treatments will be paid for with public money. If a reformed U.S. health care system explicitly accepted rationing, as I have argued it should, QALYs could play a similar role in the U.S.

Some will object that this discriminates against people with disabilities. If we return to the hypothetical assumption that a year with quadriplegia is valued at only half as much as a year without it, then a treatment that extends the lives of people without disabilities will be seen as providing twice the value of one that extends, for a similar period, the lives of quadriplegics. That clashes with the idea that all human lives are of equal value. The problem, however, does not lie with the concept of the quality-adjusted life-year, but with the judgment that, if faced with 10 years as a quadriplegic, one would prefer a shorter lifespan without a disability. Disability advocates might argue that such judgments, made by people without disabilities, merely reflect the ignorance and prejudice of people without disabilities when they think about people with disabilities. We should, they will very reasonably say, ask quadriplegics themselves to evaluate life with quadriplegia. If we do that, and we find that quadriplegics would not give up even one year of life as a quadriplegic in order to have their disability cured, then the QALY method does not justify giving preference to procedures that extend the lives of people without disabilities over procedures that extend the lives of people with disabilities.

This method of preserving our belief that everyone has an equal right to life is, however, a double-edged sword. If life with quadriplegia is as good as life without it, there is no health benefit to be gained by curing it. That implication, no doubt, would have been vigorously rejected by someone like Christopher Reeve, who, after being paralyzed in an accident, campaigned for more research into ways of overcoming spinal-cord injuries. Disability advocates, it seems, are forced to choose between insisting that extending their lives is just as important as extending the lives of people without disabilities, and seeking public support for research into a cure for their condition.

The QALY tells us to do what brings about the greatest health benefit, irrespective of where that benefit falls. Usually, for a given quantity of resources, we will do more good if we help those who are worst off, because they have the greatest unmet needs. But occasionally some conditions will be both very severe and very expensive to treat. A QALY approach may then lead us to give priority to helping others who are not so badly off and whose conditions are less expensive to treat. I don't find it unfair to give the same weight to the interests of those who are well off as we give to those who are much worse off, but if there is a social consensus that we should give priority to those who are worse off, we can modify the QALY approach so that it gives greater weight to benefits that accrue to those who are, on the QALY scale, worse off than others.

Whether decisions about allocating health care resources should take such personal circumstances into account isn't easy to decide. Not to do so makes the standard inflexible, but taking personal factors into account increases the scope for subjective—and prejudiced—judgments.

20   The QALY is not a perfect measure of the good obtained by health care, but its defenders can support it in the same way that Winston Churchill defended democracy as a form of government: it is the worst method of allocating health care, except for all the others. If it isn't possible to provide everyone with all beneficial treatments, what better way do we have of deciding what treatments people should get than by comparing the QALYs gained with the expense of the treatments?

Will Americans allow their government, either directly or through an independent agency like NICE, to decide which treatments are sufficiently cost-effective to be provided at public expense and which are not? They might, under two conditions: first, that the option of private health insurance remains available, and second, that they are able to see, in their own pocket, the full cost of not rationing health care.

Rationing public health care limits free choice if private health insurance is prohibited. But many countries combine free national health insurance with optional private insurance. Australia, where I've spent most of my life and raised a family, is one. The U.S. could do something similar. This would mean extending Medicare to the entire population, irrespective of age, but without Medicare's current policy that allows doctors wide latitude in prescribing treatments for eligible patients. Instead, Medicare for All, as we might call it, should refuse to pay where the cost per QALY is extremely high. (On the other hand, Medicare for All would not require more than a token copayment for drugs that are cost-effective.) The extension of Medicare could be financed by a small income-tax levy, for those who pay income tax—in Australia the levy is 1.5 percent of taxable income. (There's an extra 1 percent surcharge for those with high incomes and no private insurance. Those who earn too little to pay income tax would be carried at no cost to themselves.) Those who want to be sure of receiving every treatment that their own privately chosen physicians recommend, regardless of cost, would be free to opt out of Medicare for All as long as they can demonstrate that they have sufficient private health insurance to avoid becoming a burden on the community if they fall ill. Alternatively, they might remain in Medicare for All but take out supplementary insurance for health care that Medicare for All does not cover. Every American will have a right to a good standard of health care, but no one will have a right to unrationed health care. Those who opt for unrationed health care will know exactly how much it costs them.

One final comment. It is common for opponents of health care rationing to point to Canada and Britain as examples of where we might end up if we get "socialized medicine." On a blog on Fox News earlier this year, the conservative writer John Lott wrote, "Americans should ask Canadians and Brits—people who have long suffered from rationing—how happy they are with central government decisions on eliminating 'unnecessary' health care." There is no particular reason that the United States should copy the British or Canadian forms of universal coverage, rather than one of the different arrangements that have developed in other industrialized nations, some of which may be better. But as it happens, last year the Gallup organization did ask Canadians and Brits, and people in many different countries, if they have confidence in "health care or medical systems" in their country. In Canada, 73 percent answered this question affirmatively. Coincidentally, an identical percentage of Britons gave the same answer. In the United States, despite spending much more, per person, on health care, the figure was only 56 percent.

Questions for Reading Actively

1. Why does Singer believe that "rationing" has become a "dirty word" in the national debate over health care?

2. Why does Singer believe that the rationing of health care is inevitable and that it is better to acknowledge it and develop a rational policy regarding it, rather than pretend that it doesn't exist?

Questions for Thinking Critically

1. Singer contends that "If the U.S. system spent less on expensive treatments for those who, with or without the drugs, have at most a few months to live, it would be better able to save the lives of more people who, if they get the treatment they need, might live for several decades." Do you agree or disagree with this position? Why?

2. Explain the QALY (the "quality-adjusted-life-year") approach to evaluating how health care should be resourced. Do you think this approach makes sense? Why or why not?

Questions for Writing Thoughtfully

1. Singer contends that health care is already rationed because it is based on the level of health insurance we are able to afford. In the case of those receiving government supported health care (Medicare and Medicaid), which is paid for by your taxes, how much money should be spent to extend a patient's life for one year? Explain your reasoning in an essay using the Toulmin method.

2. How would you go about rationing health care if you were asked to by the President? Outline your plan in a short essay.

"Rationing Medical Care: A Second Opinion"

by Leonard Laster

After listening to economists, physicians and politicians, among others, Oregonians have concluded that they can no longer afford unlimited medical care. The only way they see to control the rising costs of such care is to ration it. They have legislated a rationing

Source: "Rationing Medical Care: A Second Opinion" by Leonard Laster. From *The Washington Post*, August 30, 1990. Copyright © 1990 Leonard Laster. Reprinted with permission.

system that has attracted national interest. It may turn out to be a trial run that could eventually affect all of us.

On the surface, the arguments for rationing seem reasonable. Each year, health care costs rise much faster than inflation. New procedures and technologies appear at a breakneck pace and jack up medical expenses. Large segments of the population, such as older people, increase in number and need more complex care. Yet as a nation, we have only a limited amount of money to spend on treating the sick.

By not recognizing this dilemma, by not realizing that we are, in fact, already rationing care and by not institutionalizing a fair and logical system for rationing, we fly in the face of common sense. We spend huge sums of money on individuals whose chances of benefiting are painfully small, such as elderly patients with only days or weeks to live, while depriving others, such as children and pregnant women, of care that could make a big difference at only a modest cost.

Despite the compelling power of the reasoning, I'm not ready to go ahead, and I don't believe that those who are ready fully understand what rationing implies. We have not given enough consideration to other alternatives. The financial problem is serious, but by accepting the concept of rationing we cross a moral divide from which there may be no return. It is no small step to decide that we will require physicians, nurses and their colleagues to adhere to a formula that spells out who is worth saving and who is not. We should move cautiously and try to avoid mistakes.

We've made some big mistakes in the past, especially in medical matters. In the early '70s, experts persuaded us to release the bulk of the mentally ill from the back wards of institutions. Lacking adequate community facilities, the patients ended up fending for themselves in a hostile environment, and as a result the mentally ill now make up a major segment of the street people, many of them suffering worse fates than they did in the institutions. We cannot reverse this mistake easily or quickly.

5   Let us not make another. We should learn much more about the implications of rationing before adopting it. Under rationing, we would undoubtedly decide not to fund expensive procedures, such as kidney dialysis or transplantation, for patients classified as too old. The British set the age limit for treatment of kidney failure at 55. In the abstract, such a decision may seem regrettable but unavoidable. Still, when the guidelines affect a real person—such as yourself or a close relative—views change briskly.

A friend of mine who taught English literature developed kidney failure at age 57. Because chronic dialysis was available to him, he was spared a sentence of early death and remained active for 10 more years, teaching and mentoring his grateful students. Was the money spent on giving this man 10 more years of productive life a waste? Did we really deprive some children of immunization against measles and polio because we spent the money prolonging the life of this teacher? Would rationing have been the more intelligent course?

Under rationing, major new ideas for medical treatment would be discouraged as too expensive and unnecessary. The problem is, what seems far-out and frivolous today could become commonplace and essential tomorrow. In the early '50s, one of my surgery professors developed a new technique for operating inside the human heart to repair defective or damaged valves. Early on, the procedure was very expensive and seemed to be just a futile technical exercise, but we paid for the development and evaluation costs, and today valvular surgery constitutes a routine treatment providing a long and useful life to heart patients of all ages.

Had rationing been in effect when the procedure was first proposed, in all likelihood it would have gone unfunded and left at the idea stage. By and large, rationing would narrow our horizons, inhibit creative imagination and vision, slow the progress of medicine and trap us within the limitations of today's knowledge and today's technology—a high price to pay.

Do we really have only a limited amount of money for medical care, and must we start rationing now? Obviously, we cannot allocate the bulk of our gross national product to medical care, and we must continue to improve the efficiency and effectiveness of the myriad activities we group under the phrase "health care system." But isn't it odd that even though we are resolved to spend $500 billion for the S&L bailout, when it comes to dealing with the far lesser costs of medical care, we grow mightily exercised, dig in our heels and turn to rationing?

10   Could it be that our preoccupation with the bottom line has reached the point of gross insensitivity to values that cannot be quantified or incorporated into a balance sheet? What kind of people will we become after we agree to toss sick human beings onto the trash heap because they aren't worth paying for? Are we really so impoverished financially and intellectually that we see no other way out? Possibly, but we ought to slow down some and get ourselves a second opinion.

Questions for Reading Actively

1. What arguments does Laster acknowledge that support the view that medical care should be rationed?

2. Laster contends that "rationing would narrow our horizons, inhibit creative imagination and vision, slow the progress of medicine and trap us within the limitations of today's knowledge and today's technology—a high price to pay." Why does Laster believe that rationing would lead to these undesirable consequences?

Question for Thinking Critically

1. Laster believes that "by accepting the concept of rationing we cross a moral divide from which there may be no return." What does Laster mean by saying this and what are the reasons that support this conclusion?

Question for Writing Thoughtfully

1. Based on your thoughtful analysis of both Singer's and Laster's sides of this issue, what is your informed conclusion regarding what ought to be done: to ration or not to ration? Describe the strongest arguments that support your point of view.

Arguments as Inferences

When you construct arguments, you are constructing views of the world by means of your ability to infer. As you saw in Chapter 11, inferring is a thinking process used to reason from what one already knows (or believes to be the case) to acquire new knowledge or beliefs. This is usually what you do when you construct arguments: work from reasons you know or believe to draw conclusions based on them.

Just as you can use inferences to make sense of different types of situations, you can also construct arguments for different purposes. As already noted, some people believe in using arguments to coerce or to "win." A more desirable goal is to use arguments to clarify issues, develop mutual understanding, and if possible, bring about agreement or consensus on the issue being discussed. Notice how you can work toward agreement when you construct arguments to do any of the following: decide, explain, predict, persuade.

Constructing Arguments to Decide

Reason: Throughout my life, I've always been interested in all kinds of electricity.

Reason: There are many attractive job opportunities in the field of electrical engineering.

Claim: Electrical engineering would be a good major for me.

Audience: Myself, my parents, my academic adviser, the scholarship office

Constructing Arguments to Explain

Reason: I was delayed leaving my house because my dog needed emergency walking.

Reason: There was an unexpected traffic jam caused by motorists slowing down to view an overturned chicken truck.

Claim: Therefore, I couldn't help being late for our appointment.

Audience: The person waiting for me

Constructing Arguments to Predict

Reason: Some people will always drive faster than the speed limit allows, no matter whether the limit is 55 or 65 mph.

Reason: Car accidents are more likely to occur at higher speeds.

Claim: A reinstated 65 mph speed limit will result in more accidents.

Audience: Legislators, voters, drivers

Constructing Arguments to Persuade

Reason: Chewing tobacco can lead to cancer of the mouth and throat.

Reason: Young people sometimes begin chewing tobacco because they see ads that feature sports heroes they admire doing it.

Claim: Ads for chewing tobacco should be banned.

Audience: Parents, voters, legislators, advertising agencies, media executives

Evaluating Arguments

To construct good arguments, you must be skilled at evaluating the effectiveness, or soundness, of arguments already constructed. You must investigate the components of an argument to determine the soundness of the argument as a whole.

1. How true are the reasons being offered to support the conclusion?
2. To what extent do the reasons support the conclusion, claim, or thesis—or to what extent does the conclusion follow from the reasons offered?

Truth: How True Are the Supporting Reasons?

The first aspect of an argument that you must evaluate is the truth of the reasons being used to support a conclusion. Ask yourself these questions:

- What specific evidence is the writer offering to illustrate each reason?
- Are any reasons consistent with my own experience?
- Are the reasons based on reliable sources?
- Are the reasons relevant to the subject of the argument?

You use these questions and others like them to analyze the reasons offered and to determine how true they seem to be. As you saw in Chapter 11, evaluating the kinds of beliefs used as reasons in arguments is a complex challenge.

Validity: Do the Reasons Support the Claim or Conclusion?

In addition to determining whether the reasons are true, evaluating arguments involves investigating the relationship between the reasons and the claim or the conclusion (which becomes the thesis of a piece of writing that argues a position on an issue).

When the reasons support the conclusion in such a way that the conclusion follows from them, you have a *valid argument*. If, however, the reasons do not support the conclusion—that is, if the conclusion does not follow from the reasons being offered—you have an *invalid argument*. Remember that the words *valid* and *true* do not have the same meaning. You must first evaluate the truth of a reason, then determine its validity.

One way to focus on the concept of *validity* is to assume that all the reasons in an argument are true, then try to determine how probable they make the conclusion. The following is an example of one type of valid argument.

Reason: Anything that is a threat to our health should not be legal.

Reason: Marijuana is a threat to our health.

Conclusion: Therefore, marijuana should not be legal.

This is a valid argument because if we assume that the reasons are true, its conclusion does necessarily follow from them.

Of course, we may not agree that either or both of the reasons are true; in that case, we would not agree with the conclusion. Nevertheless, the structure of the argument is valid. This particular form of thinking is known as *deduction*.

Here is a different type of argument:

Reason: As part of a project in my social science class, we selected one hundred students in the school to be interviewed. We took special steps to ensure that these students were representative of the student body as a whole (total students: 4,386). We asked the students whether they thought that the United States should actively try to overthrow foreign governments that it disapproves of. Of the one hundred students interviewed, eighty-eight said that the United States should definitely not be involved in such activities.

Conclusion: We can conclude that most students in this school believe that the United States should not be engaged in attempts to actively overthrow foreign governments that it disapproves of.

This is a persuasive argument because if we assume that the reason is true, that reason provides strong support for the conclusion. In this case, the key part of the reason is the statement that the one hundred students selected were representative of the entire student population at the school. To evaluate the truth of the reason, we might want to investigate the procedure used to select the one hundred students in order to determine whether this sample was in fact representative of all the students. (Notice that the conclusion carefully said "in this school." It did not imprecisely say "most students.")

This particular form of thinking is an example of *induction*.

Soundness: Is the Argument Both True and Valid?

When an argument includes both true reasons and a valid structure, the argument is considered sound. When an argument has either false reasons or an invalid structure, however, the argument is considered unsound.

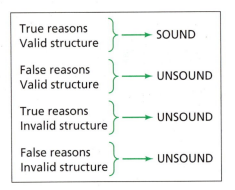

FIGURE 13.1
Sound and Unsound Arguments

Figure 13.1 reminds us that in terms of arguments, *truth* and *validity* are not identical concepts. An argument can have true reasons and an invalid structure or have false reasons and a valid structure. In both cases the argument is unsound. Consider the following argument:

Reason: Professor Davis believes that megadoses of vitamins can cure colds.

Reason: Davis is a professor of computer science.

Conclusion: Megadoses of vitamins can cure colds.

This argument is obviously not valid: even if we assume that the reasons are true, the conclusion does not follow. Professor Davis's expertise with computers does not provide her with special knowledge about nutrition and medicine. This invalid thinking is neither structurally nor factually acceptable. It is clearly not a sound argument. Now, consider this argument:

Reason: For a democracy to function most effectively, the citizens should be able to think critically about the major social and political issues.

Reason: Education plays a key role in developing critical thinking abilities.

Conclusion: Therefore, education plays a key role in ensuring that a democracy is functioning most effectively.

A good case could be made for the soundness of this argument because the reasons are persuasive and the argument structure is valid. Of course, someone might counter that one or both of the reasons are not completely true, which illustrates an important point about the arguments we construct and evaluate. Many of the arguments we encounter in life fall somewhere between complete soundness and complete unsoundness because often we are not sure if our reasons are completely true. Throughout this book, we have found that developing accurate beliefs is an ongoing process and that our beliefs are subject to clarification and revision. As a result, the conclusion of any argument can be only as certain as the reasons supporting the conclusion.

Forms of Argument

Arguments occur in many forms, but two major thinking methods—deduction and induction—provide the foundations for most arguments and also influence the organizational structure of arguments. They can be seen as (1) moving from general principles to specific applications and (2) moving from specific examples to general conclusions. Deduction and induction are seldom applied in "pure" or textbook

Thinking Critically About Visuals

Visual Persuasion

The images in this portfolio were created as persuasive rhetoric. To be effective, their creators kept in mind audience and purpose, and they also drew upon such rhetorical strategies as *ethos, logos,* and *pathos;* satire; awareness of audience; and a nuanced sense of the different types of meanings. The following "public service advertisements" (PSAs) work to *persuade* people to take a stand, to change a behavior, or to participate in community and civic life. Unlike other kinds of written arguments, an effective PSA has a very limited amount of time or space in which to make its point and has a great deal of competition for your attention. Each of the PSAs that follows draws upon strategies used by critical readers and thoughtful writers to communicate effective, brief, attention-getting persuasive arguments related to public health, community life, and educational issues to the broadest possible audience.

After looking and reading through this portfolio, create your own PSA that addresses a specific issue discussed in a reading elsewhere in this book. This can be done alone or as a collaborative project.

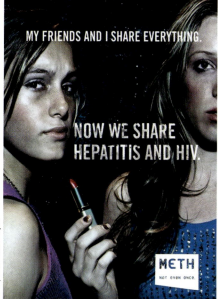

Courtesy of The Meth Project

Thinking Critically About the Image

1. Who is the target audience for this ad? What aspects of the ad make that apparent?
2. Does this advertisement rely on logos, ethos, or pathos—or some combination of these elements? Explain your answer, making reference to specific components of the ad.

"METH Not Even Once." is an ad from the Montana Meth Project. (Link to more of their ads through your text's website.)

WE ALL HAVE AIDS

IF ONE OF US DOES.

KNOW, PREVENT, CARE, CURE.

kNOw HIV/AIDS is a campaign of Viacom Inc. and the Kaiser Family Foundation.

Thinking Critically About the Image

1. This ad relies on the persuasive powers of celebrity to make its argument. Referring to Chapter 13, what kind of an appeal would this be classified as?

2. The text of this ad calls to mind the Three Musketeers' motto "All for one, and one for all!" What kind of message does this statement convey?

3. How is color used in this ad? For what effect do you think the creators of this ad were striving in their use of color?

Members of PETA (People for the Ethical Treatment of Animals) and Anima Naturalis protest naked at Catalunya Square in central Barcelona January 21, 2007. (Link to ads by PETA through your text's website.)

Thinking Critically About the Image

1. The demonstrators in this photo are using "shock value" as a tool of persuasion. Explain the emotional and ethical appeals this demonstration makes.

2. A "flash mob" is a large group of people who assemble suddenly in a public place, perform an unusual act—often dance routines—for a brief time, and then disperse (see examples on the text's website). How does what a flash mob does differ from what the people in this photo are doing?

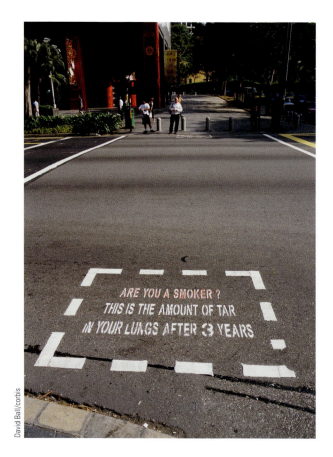

David Ball/corbis

Thinking Critically About the Image

1. Who is the audience for this message? Why is the statement made an argument? How does the placement of this message affect its potential impact?

2. The American Legacy Foundation's (ALF's) Truth Campaign also encourages people to not smoke. Visit your text's website to link to a video the ALF created. How does the video use parody to make its point? How does video's approach differ from that of the message in this photo?

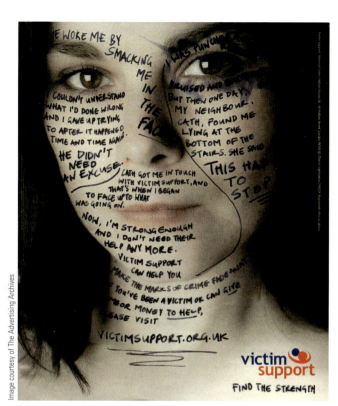

"Find the Strength" is a campaign ad from Victim Support, an independent charity for victims and witnesses of crime in England and Wales. (Link to more ads from this campaign through your text's website.)

Thinking Critically About the Image

1. Why is the type of print and placement of it significant in this ad? How does the smudged ink create a visual metaphor?

2. How is narrative used to create an argument in this ad?

CAUTION : CHILDREN AT WAR

Abolish the use of child soldiers worldwide. Children have the right to be children.

AMNESTY INTERNATIONAL

www.amnestyusa.org

Amnesty International ad to abolish the use of child soldiers worldwide

Thinking Critically About the Image

1. This ad was created using a familiar sign format. Why do you think the ad creator chose to use this style to convey the ad's message? Do you think someone would be more or less likely to consider the content of an ad like this seriously because of the format? Why is that?
2. The ad says, "Children have the right to be children." What does that mean? Does it mean something different in different cultures?
3. Look back at the photo of Iraqi boys playing with guns on p. 1–4. Compare the objective of the photojournalist who took the photo of the Iraqi boys with that of the ad creator who created the ad on this page. What differs in the message and tone they hope to communicate? How is this achieved visually?

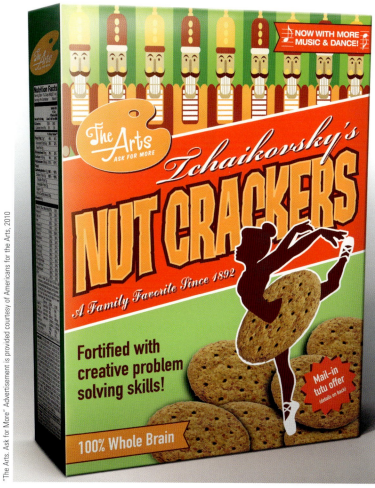

"The Arts. Ask for More." is a national arts education public awareness campaign put together by Americans for the Arts, the Ad Council, and the NAMM Foundation, as well as local, state, and national official campaign partners. (Link to more ads from this campaign through your text's website.)

Thinking Critically About the Image

1. Who is the target audience for this campaign, and how does it get that audience's attention?

2. Chapter 6 explores the ways in which effective writers use figurative language to craft their message. What specific figurative strategy is featured in this public service announcement? Why is this strategy persuasive?

Thinking Critically About the Image

1. How is an appeal to fear being used in this public service message? Why is its placement important?

2. Is drinking and driving a problem on your campus? Do you think a display like this would be effective at reducing the amount of drinking and driving among students?

ways in real-life arguments. Instead, they often are compressed or combined, so recognizing and analyzing their uses can sometimes be difficult. In fact, some teachers and students feel that studying them separately is more a mental exercise than a practical activity. However, as a critical thinker, a writer of arguments, and an analyst of arguments, you need to understand these principles.

Deductive Reasoning

The deductive argument is the one most commonly associated with the study of logic. Though it has a variety of valid forms, they all share one characteristic: if you accept the supporting reasons (also called *premises*) as true, you must also accept the conclusion as true. A *deductive argument* is an argument form in which one reasons from premises that are known or assumed to be true to a conclusion that necessarily follows from these premises. For example, consider the following famous deductive argument:

Reason/Premise: All persons are mortal.

Reason/Premise: Socrates is a person.

Conclusion: Therefore, Socrates is mortal.

In this example of *deductive reasoning,* accepting the premises of the argument as true means that the conclusion necessarily follows; it cannot be false. Many deductive arguments, like this one, are structured as *syllogisms,* an argument form that consists of two supporting premises and a conclusion. There are also, however, a large number of invalid deductive forms, one of which is illustrated in the following defective syllogism:

Reason/Premise: All persons are mortal.

Reason/Premise: Socrates is a person.

Conclusion: Therefore, all persons are Socrates.

This example is deliberately absurd, but people do shift terms in these ways and think things such as "all tall people should play basketball" just because basketball players are usually tall. Despite the variety of invalid deductive structures, once you become aware of the concept of *validity,* you should be able to detect invalidity.

One way to do this is through the application of a general rule. Whenever we reason by using the form illustrated by the valid Socrates syllogism, we are using the following argument structure:

Premise: All A (people) are B (mortal).

Premise: S is an A (Socrates is a person).

Conclusion: Therefore, S is B (Socrates is mortal).

This basic argument form is valid no matter what terms are included. For example:

Premise: All politicians are untrustworthy.

Premise: Bill White is a politician.

Conclusion: Therefore, Bill White is untrustworthy.

Notice again that with any valid deductive form, if we assume that the premises are true, we must accept the conclusion. Of course, in this case it is unlikely that the first premise is true.

Although we are not always aware of doing so, we use this basic type of reasoning whenever we apply a general rule. For instance:

Premise: All eight-year-old children should be in bed by 9:30 P.M.

Premise: You are an eight-year-old child.

Conclusion: Therefore, you should be in bed by 9:30 P.M.

Often we present this kind of reasoning in an abbreviated form called an *enthymeme*, which assumes the first premise: You should be in bed by 9:30 because you're an eight-year-old child; Bill White is a politician, so he's untrustworthy.

Describe an example from your own experience in which you use this deductive form, both as a syllogism and as an enthymeme.

Other Deductive Forms

Deductive arguments, or syllogisms and enthymemes, come in many other forms, most of which have been named by logicians. At some point in your college education, you should consider taking a course in critical thinking or logic to learn about as many kinds of reasoning as you can. This chapter provides only an introduction.

Affirming the Antecedent

Premise: If I have prepared thoroughly for the final exam, I will do well.

Premise: I prepared thoroughly for the exam.

Conclusion: Therefore, I will do well on the exam.

When we reason like this, we are using the following argument structure:

Premise: If A (I have prepared thoroughly), then B (I will do well).

Premise: A (I have prepared thoroughly).

Conclusion: Therefore, B (I will do well).

Like all valid deductive forms, this form is valid no matter what specific terms are included. For example:

Premise: If the Democrats register 20 million new voters, they will win the presidential election.

Premise: The Democrats have registered more than 20 million new voters.

Conclusion: Therefore, the Democrats will win the presidential election.

As with other valid argument forms, the conclusion will be true if the reasons are true. Although the second premise in this argument expresses information that can be verified, the first premise would be more difficult to establish.

Denying the Consequent

Premise: If Michael were a really good friend, he would lend me his car for the weekend.

Premise: Michael refuses to lend me his car for the weekend.

Conclusion: Therefore, Michael is not a really good friend.

When we reason in this fashion, we are using the following argument structure:

Premise: If A (Michael is a really good friend), then B (He will lend me his car).

Premise: Not B (He won't lend me his car).

Conclusion: Therefore, not A (He's not a really good friend).

Again, like other valid reasoning forms, this form is valid no matter what subject is being considered. As always, the truth of the premises must be evaluated.

Disjunctive Syllogism

Premise: Either I left my wallet on my dresser, or I have lost it.

Premise: The wallet is not on my dresser.

Conclusion: Therefore, I must have lost it.

When we reason in this way, we are using the following argument structure:

Premise: Either A (I left my wallet on my dresser) or B (I have lost it).

Premise: Not A (I didn't leave it on my dresser).

Conclusion: Therefore, B (I have lost it).

This valid reasoning form can be applied to any number of situations and still yield accurate results. For example:

Premise: Either your stomach trouble is caused by what you are eating, or it is caused by nervous tension.

Premise: You tell me that you have been very careful about your diet.

Conclusion: Therefore, your stomach trouble is caused by nervous tension.

To determine the accuracy of the conclusion, we must determine the accuracy of the premises. If they are true, then the conclusion must also be true.

Thinking-Writing Activity

EVALUATING DEDUCTIVE ARGUMENTS

Analyze the following brief arguments by completing these steps:

1. Summarize the reasons and conclusions given.
2. Identify which, if any, deductive argument forms are being used.
3. Evaluate the truth of the reasons that support the conclusion.

> For if the brain is a machine of ten billion nerve cells and the mind can somehow be explained as the summed activity of a finite number of chemical and electrical reactions, [then] boundaries limit the human prospect—we are biological and our souls cannot fly free.
>
> —Edward O. Wilson, *On Human Nature*

> The extreme vulnerability of a complex industrial society to intelligent, targeted terrorism by a very small number of people may prove the fatal challenge to which Western states have no adequate response. Counterforce alone will never suffice. The real challenge of the true terrorist is to the basic values of a society. If there is no commitment to shared values in Western society—and if none are imparted in our amoral institutions of higher learning—no increase in police and burglar alarms will suffice to preserve our society from the specter that haunts us—not a bomb from above but a gun from within.
>
> —James Billington, "The Gun Within"

> To fully believe in something, to truly understand something, one must be intimately acquainted with its opposite. One should not adopt a creed by default, because no alternative is known. Education should prepare students for the "real world" not by segregating them from evil but by urging full confrontation to test and modify the validity of the good.
>
> —Robert Baron, "In Defense of Teaching Racism, Sexism, and Fascism"

> The inescapable conclusion is that society secretly wants crime, needs crime, and gains definite satisfactions from the present mishandling of it! We condemn crime; we punish offenders for it; but we need it. The crime and punishment ritual is a part of our lives. We need crimes to wonder at, to enjoy vicariously, to discuss and speculate about, and to publicly deplore. We need criminals to identify ourselves with, to envy secretly, and to punish stoutly. They do for us the forbidden, illegal things we wish to do and, like scapegoats of old, they bear the burdens of our displaced guilt and punishment—"the iniquities of us all."
>
> —Karl Menninger, "The Crime of Punishment"

All of the preceding basic argument forms can be found not only in informal daily conversations but also at more formal levels of thinking. They appear in academic disciplines, in scientific inquiry, in debates on social issues, and so on. Many other argument forms—both deductive and inductive—also constitute human reasoning. By sharpening your understanding of these ways of thinking, you will be better able to make sense of the world by constructing and evaluating effective arguments.

Inductive Reasoning

The preceding section focused on deductive reasoning, an argument form in which one reasons from premises that are known or assumed to be true to a conclusion that follows necessarily from the premises. This section introduces *inductive reasoning,* an argument form in which one reasons from premises or instances that are known or assumed to be true to a conclusion that is supported by the premises but does not necessarily follow from them.

When you reason inductively, your premises, instances, or data provide evidence that makes it more or less probable (but not certain) that the conclusion is true. The following statements are examples of conclusions reached through inductive reasoning. As you read them, think about how the data might have been obtained and what arguments could be based on each statement.

1. A recent Gallup poll reported that 74 percent of the American public believe that abortion should remain legal.

2. On the average, a person with a college degree will earn over $830,000 more in his or her lifetime than a person with just a high school diploma.

3. The outbreak of food poisoning at the end-of-year school party was probably caused by the squid salad.

4. The devastating disease AIDS is caused by a particularly complex virus that may not be curable.

5. The solar system is probably the result of an enormous explosion—a "big bang"—that occurred billions of years ago.

Each of the first two statements is an example of inductive reasoning known as *empirical generalization*—a general statement about an entire group made on the basis of observing some members of the group. The final three statements are examples of *causal reasoning*—a form of inductive reasoning which claims that an event (or events) is the result of the occurrence of another event (or events).

Causal Reasoning

You were introduced to causal analysis in Chapter 10 and also to the fallacies that can result if causes are not analyzed logically. Review pages 351–355 to recall the characteristics of this pattern of induction.

Causal reasoning is the backbone of the natural and the social sciences. It is also central to the *scientific method,* which operates on the assumption that the world is constructed in a complex web of causal relationships that can be discovered through systematic investigation. You apply the scientific method in your science courses.

Empirical Generalization

An important tool used by both natural and social scientists is empirical generalization. Have you ever wondered how the major television and radio networks can predict election results hours before the polls close? These predictions are made possible by using *empirical generalization,* a form of inductive reasoning defined as "reasoning by examining a limited sample to reach a general conclusion based on that sample."

Network election predictions, as well as public opinion polls that are conducted throughout a political campaign, are based on interviews with a select number of people. Ideally, pollsters would interview everyone in the "target population" (in this case, voters), but doing this, of course, is hardly practical. Instead, they select a relatively small group of individuals from the target population, known as a "sample," who they have determined will adequately represent the group as a whole. Pollsters believe that they can then generalize the opinions of this smaller group to the target population.

There are three key criteria for evaluating inductive arguments:

- Is the sample known?
- Is the sample sufficient?
- Is the sample representative?

Is the Sample Known?   An inductive argument is only as strong as the sample on which it is based. For example, sample populations described in vague terms— such as "highly placed sources" or "many young people interviewed"—provide a treacherously weak foundation for generalizing to larger populations. In order for an inductive argument to be persuasive, the sample population should be explicitly known and clearly identified. Natural and social scientists take great care when selecting members of sample groups. They also make information on members of the sample groups available to outside investigators who may wish to evaluate and verify the results.

Is the Sample Sufficient?   The second criterion for evaluating inductive reasoning is to consider the size of the sample. It should be large enough to provide an accurate sense of the group as a whole. In the polling example discussed earlier, we would be concerned if only a few registered voters had been interviewed, and the results of the interviews were then generalized to a much larger population.

Overall, the larger the sample, the more reliable the inductive conclusions. Natural and social scientists have developed precise guidelines for determining the size of the sample needed to achieve reliable results. For example, poll results are often accompanied by a qualification such as "These results are subject to an error factor of ±3 percentage points." This means that if the sample reveals that 47 percent of those interviewed prefer candidate X, we can reliably state that 44 to 50 percent of the target population prefers candidate X. Because a sample is usually a small portion of the target population, we can rarely state that the two match each other exactly—there must always be some room for variation. The exceptions to this are situations in which the target population is completely homogeneous. For instance, tasting one cookie from a bag of cookies is usually enough to tell us whether or not the contents of the entire bag are stale.

Is the Sample Representative?   The third crucial element in effective inductive reasoning is the representativeness of the sample. If we are to generalize with confidence from the sample to the target population, we have to be sure the sample is similar in all relevant aspects to the larger group from which it is drawn. For instance, in the polling example, the sample population should reflect the same percentage of men and women, of Democrats and Republicans, of young and old, and so on, as exists in the target population. It is obvious that many characteristics—such as hair color, favorite food, and shoe size—are not relevant to the comparison. The better the sample reflects the target population in terms of relevant qualities, however, the better the accuracy of the generalizations. On the other hand, when the sample does not represent the target population—for example, if the election pollsters interviewed only females between the ages of thirty and thirty-five—the sample is termed *biased*, and any generalizations about the target population will be highly suspect.

How do we ensure that the sample is representative of the target population? One important device is *random selection*, a selection strategy in which every member of the target population has an equal chance of being included in the sample. For example, the various techniques used to select winning lottery tickets are supposed to be random—each ticket is supposed to have an equal chance of winning. In complex cases of inductive reasoning—such as polling—random selection is often combined with the confirmation that all the important categories in the population are adequately represented. For example, an election pollster would want to ensure that all significant geographical areas are included and then would randomly select individuals from within those areas to compose the sample.

Understanding the principles of empirical generalization is crucial to effective thinking because we are continually challenged to evaluate this form of inductive thinking in our lives. In addition, when writing about political or social issues, we often use the results of inductive investigations, so we should be able to determine their accuracy and relevance.

Thinking-Writing Activity

ANALYZING EMPIRICAL GENERALIZATION

Review the following examples of empirical generalizing. Select two and then evaluate the quality of the thinking by answering the following questions:

1. Is the sample known?
2. Is the sample sufficient?
3. Is the sample representative?
4. Do you believe that the conclusions are likely to be accurate? Why or why not?
5. What are some arguments that might be based on your answers?

In a study of a possible relationship between pornography and antisocial behavior, questionnaires went out to 7,500 psychiatrists and psychoanalysts whose listing in the directory of the American Psychological Association indicated clinical experience. Over 3,400 of these professionals responded. The result: 7.4 percent of the psychiatrists and psychologists had cases in which they were convinced that pornography was a causal factor in antisocial behavior, an additional 9.4 percent were suspicious, 3.2 percent did not commit themselves, and 80 percent said they had no cases in which a causal connection was suspected.

A survey by the Sleep Disorder Clinic of the VA hospital in La Jolla, California (involving more than one million people), revealed that people who sleep more than ten hours a night have a death rate 80 percent higher than those who sleep only seven or eight hours. Men who sleep fewer than four hours a night have a death rate 180 percent higher, and women with less [than four hours'] sleep have a rate 40 percent higher. This might be taken as indicating that too much and too little sleep cause death.

In a recent survey, twice as many doctors interviewed stated that if they were stranded on a desert island, they would prefer X Aspirin to Extra Strength Y. Being a general practitioner in a rural area has tremendous drawbacks— being on virtual 24-hour call 365 days a year, patients without financial means or insurance, low fees in the first place, inadequate facilities and assistance. Nevertheless, America's small-town G.P.s seem fairly content with their lot. According to a survey taken by *Country Doctor*, fully 50 percent wrote back that they "basically like being a rural G.P." Only 1 in 15 regretted that he or she had not specialized. Only 2 out of 20 rural general practitioners would trade places with their urban counterparts, given the chance. And only 1 in 30 would "choose some other line of work altogether."

More Fallacies: Forms of False Reasoning

As we pointed out in Chapter 10, certain forms of reasoning are not logical. These types of pseudoreasoning (false reasoning) are often termed *fallacies:* arguments that are not sound because of various errors in reasoning. Fallacious reasoning is sometimes used to influence others. It seeks to persuade not on the basis of sound arguments and critical thinking but rather on the basis of emotional and illogical factors. Sometimes fallacious reasoning is used inadvertently. However, it is always dangerous, so it is important to recognize it as well as to avoid using it. Detecting fallacious reasoning is a significant factor in evaluating sources of beliefs, the concept discussed in Chapter 11.

In Chapter 8, we explored the way in which we form concepts through the interactive process of generalizing (identifying the common qualities that define the boundaries of the concept) and interpreting (identifying examples of the concept). This process is similar to the process involved in constructing empirical generalizations as we seek to reach a general conclusion based on a limited number of examples and then apply this conclusion to other examples. Although generalizing and interpreting are useful in forming concepts, they also can lead to fallacious ways of thinking, including hasty generalization, sweeping generalization, false dilemma, begging the questions, and red herring.

Hasty Generalization

Consider the following examples of reasoning. Do you think the arguments are sound? Why or why not?

- My boyfriends have never shown any real concern for my feelings. My conclusion is that men are insensitive, selfish, and emotionally superficial.
- My mother always gets upset over insignificant things. This leads me to believe that women are very emotional.

In both of these cases, a general conclusion has been reached that is based on a very small sample. As a result, the reasons provide very weak support for the conclusions. It does not make good sense to generalize from one or a few individuals to all men or all women. The conclusion is *hasty* because the information is not adequate enough to justify the generalization.

Sweeping Generalization

Whereas the fallacy of hasty generalization deals with errors in the process of generalizing, the fallacy of *sweeping generalization* stems from difficulties in the process of interpreting. Consider the following examples of reasoning. Do you consider the arguments sound? Why or why not?

- Vigorous exercise contributes to overall good health. Therefore, vigorous exercise should be practiced by recent heart-attack victims, people who are out of shape, and women in the last month of pregnancy.

- People should be allowed to make their own decisions, providing that their actions do not harm other people. Therefore, people who are trying to commit suicide should be left alone to do as they please.

In both of these cases, generalizations that are true in most cases have been deliberately applied to examples that are clearly intended to be exceptions to the generalizations because of their special features. Of course, the use of a sweeping generalization motivates us to clarify the generalization, rephrasing it to exclude examples, like those given here, that have special features. For example, the first generalization could be reformulated as "Vigorous exercise contributes to the overall good health of most people *except* recent heart-attack victims, people who are out of shape, and women who are about to give birth." Sweeping generalizations become dangerous when they are accepted without critical analysis.

Examine the following examples of sweeping generalizations. In each case (a) explain why it is a sweeping generalization and (b) reformulate the statement to make it a legitimate generalization.

1. A college education stimulates you to develop as a person and prepares you for many professions. Therefore, all people should attend college, no matter what career interests them.

2. Drugs such as heroin and morphine are addictive and therefore qualify as dangerous drugs. This means that they should never be used, even as painkillers in medical situations.

3. Once criminals have served time for the crimes they have committed, they have paid their debt to society and should be permitted to work at any job they choose.

False Dilemma

The fallacy of the *false dilemma*—also known as the *either/or* fallacy and the *false dichotomy* fallacy—occurs when one is asked to choose between two extreme alternatives without being able to consider additional options. For example, we may say, "You're either for me or against me." Sometimes giving people only two choices on an issue makes sense ("If you decide to swim the English Channel, you'll either make it or you won't"). At other times, however, viewing a complicated situation in such extreme terms can result in a serious oversimplification.

The following statements are examples of false dilemmas. After analyzing the fallacy in each case, suggest different alternatives than those being presented.

Example: "Everyone in Germany is a National Socialist—the few outside the party are either lunatics or idiots." (Adolf Hitler, quoted by the *New York Times*, April 5, 1938)

Analysis: Hitler was saying that Germans who were not Nazis were lunatics or idiots. By limiting the classification of the population to these three categories, Hitler was simply ignoring all the people who did not qualify as Nazis, lunatics, or idiots.

1. "America—love it or leave it!"
2. "She loves me; she loves me not."
3. "Live free or die."
4. "If you're not part of the solution, you're part of the problem."
5. "If you know about a BMW, you either own one or you want to."

Begging the Questions

This fallacious approach presents a circular argument that restates the claim in different words and so "begs off," or sidesteps, the important questions involved.

Example: Tough antidrug laws reduce drug use by making usage a criminal act.

Analysis: This begs the question of the effectiveness of prohibiting a substance and of punishment for its use.

Red Herring

Here is another way of moving the discussion away from a basic issue. This colorful expression comes from an old practice of dragging a very dead fish on the ground in front of young hunting dogs to teach them to follow a scent.

Example: Speculating about whether the governor will be re-elected as you analyze the environmental impact of a proposed new highway.

Analysis: Who is governor may well affect legislation authorizing the highway, but this matter has little to do with analyzing environmental data.

Fallacies of Relevance

Many fallacious arguments try to gain support by appealing to factors that have little or nothing to do with the arguments. In these cases, false appeals substitute for sound reasoning and a critical examination of the issues. Such appeals are known as fallacies of *relevance*.

Appeal to Authority   In Chapters 3 and 8, we explored the ways in which we sometimes use various authorities to establish our beliefs or to prove our points. At that time, we noted that to serve as a basis for beliefs, authorities must have legitimate expertise in the area in which they are advising—for example, an experienced mechanic could diagnose your car's problem. However, people occasionally appeal to authorities who are not qualified to give an expert opinion. Consider the reasoning in the following advertisements. Do you think the arguments are sound? Why or why not?

- Hi. You've probably seen me out on the football field. After a hard day's work crushing halfbacks and sacking quarterbacks, I like to settle down with a cold, smooth Maltz beer.
- SONY. Ask anyone.
- Over 11 million women will read this ad. Only 16 will own the coat.

Each of these arguments is intended to persuade us of the value of a product through the appeal to various authorities. In the first case, the authority is a well-known sports figure; in the second, the authority is large numbers of people; in the third, the authority is a select few, so the appeal is to our desire to be exclusive ("snob appeal"). Unfortunately, none of these authorities offers legitimate expertise about the product. Football players are not beer experts, large numbers of people are often misled, and exclusive groups of people are frequently mistaken in their beliefs. To evaluate authorities properly, we have to ask:

What are the professional credentials on which the authorities' expertise is based?

Is their expertise in the area on which they are commenting?

Appeal to Pity   Consider the reasoning in the following arguments. Do you think the arguments are sound? Why or why not?

- I know that I haven't completed my term paper, but I really think that I should be excused. This has been a very difficult semester for me. I caught every kind of flu that came around. In addition, my brother has a drinking problem, and this has been very upsetting for me. Also, my dog died.
- I admit that my client embezzled money from the company, Your Honor. However, I would like to bring several facts to your attention. He is a family man with a wonderful wife and two terrific children. He is an important member of the community. He is active in his church, coaches a Little League baseball team, and has worked very hard to be a good person who cares about people. I think that you should take these things into consideration when handing down your sentence.

In each of these arguments, the reasons offered to support the conclusions may indeed be true, yet they are not relevant to the conclusion. Instead of providing evidence that supports the conclusion, the reasons are designed to make us feel sorry for the person involved and therefore to agree with the conclusion out of sympathy. Although these appeals can often be effective, the arguments are not sound. The validity of a conclusion can only be established by reasons that support and are relevant to the conclusion.

Appeal to Fear   Consider the reasoning in the following arguments. Do you consider the arguments sound? Why or why not?

- I don't think you deserve a raise. After all, there are many people who would be happy to have your job at the salary you are currently receiving. I would be happy to interview some of these people if you really think that you are underpaid.

- If you continue to disagree with my interpretation of *The Catcher in the Rye*, I'm afraid it may affect the grade on your paper.

In both of these arguments, the conclusions being suggested are supported by an appeal to fear, not by reasons that provide evidence for the conclusions. In the first case, the threat is that if you do not forgo your salary demands, your job may be in jeopardy. In the second case, the threat is that if you do not agree with the teacher's interpretation, you may receive a low grade. In neither instance are the real issues— Is a salary increase deserved? Is the student's interpretation legitimate?—being discussed. People who appeal to fear to support their conclusions are interested only in prevailing, regardless of which position might be more justified.

Appeal to Ignorance   Consider the reasoning in the following arguments. Do you find the arguments sound? Why or why not?

- You say that you don't believe in God. But can you prove that an omnipotent spirit doesn't exist? If not, then you have to accept the conclusion that it does in fact exist.

- Greco Tires are the best. No others have been proved better.

When this argument form is used, the person offering the conclusion is asking his or her opponent to *disprove* the conclusion. If the opponent is unable to do so, the conclusion is asserted to be true. This argument form is not valid because it is the task of the person proposing the argument to prove the conclusion. The fact that an opponent cannot disprove it offers no evidence that the conclusion is justified.

Appeal to Personal Attack   Consider the reasoning in the following arguments. Do you think the arguments are valid? Why or why not?

- Senator Smith's opinion about a tax cut is wrong. It's impossible to believe anything he says since he left his wife for that model.

- How can you have an intelligent opinion about abortion? You're not a woman, so this is a decision that you'll never have to make.

This argument form has been one of the fallacies most frequently used through the ages. Its effectiveness results from ignoring the issues of the argument and focusing instead on the qualities of the person presenting it. Trying to discredit the other person is an effort to discredit the argument—no matter what reasons are offered. This fallacy is also referred to as the *ad hominem* argument (which means drawing attention "to the man" rather than to the issue) and as *poisoning the well* (since the speaker is trying to ensure that any water drawn from the opponent's well will be regarded as undrinkable).

The effort to discredit can take two forms, as illustrated in the preceding examples. The fallacy can be *abusive* by directly attacking the credibility of an opponent. In addition, the fallacy can be *circumstantial* by claiming that a person's circumstances, not character, render his or her opinion so biased or uninformed that it cannot be treated seriously. Another example of the circumstantial form would be disregarding the views on nuclear-plant safety that were presented by an owner of a nuclear plant.

Appeal to Popular Opinion or the Bandwagon   You are probably familiar with this "everybody else is doing it" appeal. Children use it while trying to convince parents to allow questionable activities and purchases. However, it is not absent from adult situations. Political and advertising campaigns often use the result of surveys to influence voters or consumers:

- Awww, Dad, I really need a new iPod. Everyone else in my class has one! Puuuhhhleeeeze . . .

- 58 percent of registered voters surveyed say that they will vote for Green Party nominee Edward Norton next week. Let's all get to the polls to send a message to the incumbents that we support Norton and his proposals for change!

- Well-dressed women will want pin-striped suits for fall!

This appeal can be effective because even thoughtful adults gravitate toward fashions in clothing and home furnishings, and voters want to support the policies and candidates with whom they agree. A certain amount of conformity is essential to a stable society, but clear thinkers are aware of the attraction of a "bandwagon" before they jump on.

Analyzing well-known arguments to see how they use deduction, induction, evidence *(logos)*, *ethos*, *pathos*, appeals—and perhaps fallacious reasoning—is a challenging activity and one that can help you with your own arguments. Read the Declaration of Independence and the Declaration of Sentiments and Resolutions, which follow, and Martin Luther King Jr.'s speech, "I Have a Dream" (see pages 184–187 in Chapter 6). Then answer the questions that follow the readings.

Thinking-Writing Activity

ANALYZING FALLACIES

1. Find in advertisements, political statements, or other arguments that you have encountered, examples of two or three false appeals. Write a brief explanation of why you think the appeal is not warranted. Look for the following fallacies:

   - Appeal to authority
   - Appeal to pity
   - Appeal to fear
   - Appeal to ignorance
   - Appeal to personal attack
   - Appeal to popular opinion

2. Share the fallacies you have found with classmates and also examine the ones they have identified.

3. Write a few sentences explaining how you can avoid using fallacies in your own writing.

The Declaration of Independence

In Congress, July 4, 1776

The unanimous declaration of the thirteen United States of America When in the course of human events, it becomes necessary for one people to dissolve the political bands which have connected them with another, and to assume among the powers of the earth, the separate and equal station to which the Laws of Nature and of Nature's God entitle them, a decent respect to the opinions of mankind requires that they should declare the causes which impel them to the separation.

We hold these truths to be self-evident, that all men are created equal, that they are endowed by their Creator with certain unalienable rights, that among these are life, liberty and the pursuit of happiness. That to secure these rights, governments are instituted among men, deriving their just powers from the consent of the governed. That whenever any form of government becomes destructive of these ends, it is the right of the people to alter or to abolish it, and to institute new government, laying its foundation on such principles and organizing its powers in such form, as to them shall seem most likely to effect their safety and happiness. Prudence, indeed, will dictate that governments long established should not be changed for light and transient causes; and accordingly all experience hath shown, that mankind are more disposed to suffer, while evils are sufferable, than to right themselves by abolishing the forms to which they are accustomed. But when a long train of abuses and usurpations, pursuing invariably the same object evinces a design to reduce them under absolute despotism, it is their right, it is their duty, to throw off such government, and to provide new guards for their future security. Such has been the patient sufferance of these Colonies; and such is now the necessity which constrains them to alter their former systems of government. The history of the present King of Great Britain is a history of repeated injuries and usurpations, all having in direct object the establishment of an absolute tyranny over these States. To prove this, let facts be submitted to a candid world.

5   He has refused his assent to laws, the most wholesome and necessary for the public good.

He has forbidden his Governors to pass laws of immediate and pressing importance, unless suspended in their operation till his assent should be obtained; and when so suspended, he has utterly neglected to attend to them.

He has refused to pass other laws for the accommodation of large districts of people, unless those people would relinquish the right of representation in the Legislature, a right inestimable to them and formidable to tyrants only.

He has called together legislative bodies at places unusual, uncomfortable, and distant from the depository of their public records, for the sole purpose of fatiguing them into compliance with his measures.

He has dissolved representative houses repeatedly, for opposing with manly firmness his invasions on the rights of the people.

He has refused for a long time, after such dissolutions, to cause others to be elected; whereby the legislative powers, incapable of annihilation, have returned to the people at large for their exercise; the State remaining in the meantime exposed to all the dangers of invasion from without and convulsions within.

10   He has endeavoured to prevent the population of these States; for that purpose obstructing the laws of naturalization of foreigners; refusing to pass others to encourage their migration hither, and raising the conditions of new appropriations of lands.

He has obstructed the administration of justice, by refusing his assent to laws for establishing judiciary powers.

He has made judges dependent on his will alone, for the tenure of their offices, and the amount and payment of their salaries.

He has erected a multitude of new offices, and sent hither swarms of officers to harass our people, and eat out their substance.

He has kept among us, in times of peace, standing armies without the consent of our legislatures.

15   He has affected to render the military independent of and superior to the civil power.

He has combined with others to subject us to a jurisdiction foreign to our constitution, and unacknowledged by our laws; giving his assent to their acts of pretended legislation.

For quartering large bodies of armed troops among us.

For protecting them, by a mock trial, from punishment for any murders which they should commit on the inhabitants of these States.

For cutting off our trade with all parts of the world.

For imposing taxes on us without our consent.

20   For depriving us, in many cases, of the benefits of trial by jury.

For transporting us beyond seas to be tried for pretended offences.

For abolishing the free system of English laws in a neighbouring Province, establishing therein an arbitrary government, and enlarging its boundaries so as to render it at once an example and fit instrument for introducing the same absolute rule into these Colonies.

For taking away our Charters, abolishing our most valuable laws, and altering fundamentally the forms of our governments.

For suspending our own Legislatures, and declaring themselves invested with power to legislate for us in all cases whatsoever.

25   He has abdicated government here, by declaring us out of his protection and waging war against us.

He has plundered our seas, ravaged our coasts, burnt our towns, and destroyed the lives of our people.

He is at this time transporting large armies of foreign mercenaries to complete the works of death, desolation and tyranny, already begun with circumstances of cruelty and perfidy scarcely paralleled in the most barbarous ages, and totally unworthy the head of a civilized nation.

He has constrained our fellow citizens taken captive on the high seas to bear arms against their country, to become the executioners of their friends and brethren, or to fall themselves by their hands.

He has excited domestic insurrections amongst us, and has endeavoured to bring on the inhabitants of our frontiers, the merciless Indian savages, whose known rule of warfare, is an undistinguished destruction of all ages, sexes, and conditions.

30   In every stage of these oppressions we have petitioned for redress in the most humble terms: our repeated petitions have been answered only by repeated injury. A prince whose character is thus marked by every act which may define a tyrant is unfit to be the ruler of a free people.

Nor have we been wanting in attention to our British brethren. We have warned them from time to time of attempts by their legislature to extend an unwarrantable jurisdiction over us. We have reminded them of the circumstances of our emigration and settlement here. We have appealed to their native justice and magnanimity, and we have conjured them by the ties of our common kindred to disavow these usurpations, which would inevitably interrupt our connections and correspondence. They too have been deaf to the voice of justice and of consanguinity. We must, therefore, acquiesce in the necessity, which denounces our separation, and hold them, as we hold the rest of mankind, enemies in war, in peace friends.

We, therefore, the Representatives of the United States of America, in General Congress assembled, appealing to the Supreme Judge of the world for the rectitude of our intentions, do, in the name, and by the authority of the good people of these Colonies, solemnly publish and declare, That these United Colonies are, and of right ought to be Free and Independent States; that they are absolved from all allegiance to the British Crown, and that all political connection between them and the State of

Great Britain, is and ought to be totally dissolved; and that as Free and Independent States, they have full power to levy war, conclude peace, contract alliances, establish commerce, and to do all other acts and things which Independent States may of right do. And for the support of this declaration, with a firm reliance on the protection of Divine Providence, we mutually pledge to each other our lives, our fortunes, and our sacred honor.

Declaration of Sentiments and Resolutions

by Elizabeth Cady Stanton

A leading suffragist of the nineteenth century, Elizabeth Cady Stanton was born in Jamestown, New York. Her father was a judge, and while working as his assistant, Stanton became aware of the extent of male dominance in the eyes of the law. She married an abolitionist, in spite of her parents' concerns, and together they crusaded to change racial and gender inequities. She organized the first Women's Rights Convention in Seneca Falls, New York, in 1848. In 1851, she formed a working relationship with Susan B. Anthony that united them for the rest of their lives. Stanton ran for Congress in 1866 and cofounded *The Revolution,* a suffragist newspaper, in 1868. Today, she is revered by feminists as an early leader in the fight for equality.

When, in the course of human events, it becomes necessary for one person of the family of man to assume among the people of the earth a position different from that which they have hitherto occupied, but one to which the laws of nature and nature's God entitle them, a decent respect to the opinions of mankind requires that they should declare the causes that impel them to such a course.

We hold these truths to be self-evident: that all men and women are created equal; that they are endowed by their Creator with certain inalienable rights; that among these are life, liberty, and the pursuit of happiness; that to secure these rights governments are instituted, deriving their just powers from the consent of the governed. Whenever any form of government becomes destructive of these ends, it is the right of those who suffer from it to refuse allegiance to it, and to insist upon the institution of a new government, laying its foundation on such principles, and organizing its powers in such form, as to them shall seem most likely to effect their safety and happiness. Prudence, indeed, will dictate that governments long established should not be changed for light and transient causes; and accordingly all experience hath shown that mankind are more disposed to suffer, while evils are sufferable, than to right themselves by abolishing the forms to which they were accustomed. But when a long train of abuses and usurpations, pursuing invariably the same object evinces a design to reduce them under absolute despotism, it is their duty to throw off such government, and to provide new guards for their future security. Such has been the patient sufferance of the women under this government, and such is now the necessity which constrains them to demand the equal station to which they are entitled.

The history of mankind is a history of repeated injuries and usurpations on the part of man toward woman, having in direct object the establishment of an absolute tyranny over her. To prove this, let facts be submitted to a candid world.

He has never permitted her to exercise her inalienable right to the elective franchise.

5   He has compelled her to submit to laws, in the formation of which she had no voice.

He has withheld from her rights which are given to the most ignorant and degraded men—both natives and foreigners.

Having deprived her of this first right of a citizen, the elective franchise, thereby leaving her without representation in the halls of legislation, he has oppressed her on all sides.

He has made her, if married, in the eye of the law, civilly dead.

He has taken from her all right in property, even to the wages she earns.

10   He has made her, morally, an irresponsible being, as she can commit many crimes with impunity, provided they be done in the presence of her husband. In the covenant of marriage, she is compelled to promise obedience to her husband, he becoming, to all intents and purposes, her master—the law giving him power to deprive her of her liberty, and to administer chastisement.

He has so framed the laws of divorce, as to what shall be the proper causes, and in case of separation, to whom the guardianship of the children shall be given, as to be wholly regardless of the happiness of women—the law, in all cases, going upon a false supposition of the supremacy of man, and giving all power into his hands.

After depriving her of all rights as a married woman, if single, and the owner of property, he has taxed her to support a government which recognizes her only when her property can be made profitable to it.

He has monopolized nearly all the profitable employments, and from those she is permitted to follow, she receives but a scanty remuneration. He closes against her all the avenues to wealth and distinction which he considers most honorable to himself. As a teacher of theology, medicine, or law, she is not known.

He has denied her the facilities for obtaining a thorough education, all colleges being closed against her.

15   He allows her in Church, as well as State, but a subordinate position, claiming Apostolic authority for her exclusion from the ministry, and, with some exceptions, from any public participation in the affairs of the Church.

He has created a false public sentiment by giving to the world a different code of morals for men and women, by which moral delinquencies which exclude women from society are not only tolerated, but deemed of little account in man.

He has usurped the prerogative of Jehovah himself, claiming it as his right to assign for her a sphere of action, when that belongs to her conscience and to her God.

He has endeavored, in every way that he could, to destroy her confidence in her own powers, to lessen her self-respect, and to make her willing to lead a dependent and abject life.

Now, in view of this entire disfranchisement of one-half the people of this country, their social and religious degradation—in view of the unjust laws above mentioned, and because women do feel themselves aggrieved, oppressed, and fraudulently deprived of their most sacred rights, we insist that they have immediate admission to all the rights and privileges which belong to them as citizens of the United States.

20   In entering upon the great work before us, we anticipate no small amount of misconception, misrepresentation, and ridicule; but we shall use every instrumentality within our power to effect our object. We shall employ agents, circulate tracts, petition the State and National legislatures, and endeavor to enlist the pulpit and the press in our behalf. We hope this Convention will be followed by a series of Conventions embracing every part of the country.

Resolutions

WHEREAS, The great precept of nature is conceded to be, that "man shall pursue his own true and substantial happiness." Blackstone in his Commentaries remarks that this law of Nature being coeval with mankind, and dictated by God himself, is of course superior in obligation to any other. It is binding over all the globe, in all countries and at all times; no human laws are of any validity if contrary to this, and such of them as are valid, derive all their force and all their validity, and all their authority, mediately and immediately, from this original; therefore,

Resolved, That such laws as conflict, in any way, with the true and substantial happiness of woman, are contrary to the great precept of nature and of no validity, for this is "superior in obligation to any other."

Resolved, That all laws which prevent woman from occupying such a station in society as her conscience shall dictate, or which place her in a position inferior to that of man, are contrary to the great precept of nature, and therefore of no force or authority.

Resolved, That woman is man's equal—was intended to be so by the Creator, and the highest good of the race demands that she should be recognized as such.

25   *Resolved,* That the women of this country ought to be enlightened in regard to the laws under which they live, that they may no longer publish their degradation by declaring themselves satisfied with their present position, nor their ignorance, by asserting that they have all the rights they want.

Resolved, That inasmuch as man, while claiming for himself intellectual superiority, does accord to woman moral superiority for it is preeminently his duty to encourage her to speak and teach, as she has an opportunity, in all religious assemblies.

Resolved, That the same amount of virtue, delicacy, and refinement of behavior that is required of woman in the social state, should also be required of man, and the same transgressions should be visited with equal severity on both man and woman.

Resolved, That the objection of indelicacy and impropriety, which is so often brought against woman when she addresses a public audience, comes with a very ill-grace from those who encourage, by their attendance, her appearance on the stage, in the concert, or in feats of the circus.

Resolved, That woman has too long rested satisfied in the circumscribed limits which corrupt customs and a perverted application of the Scriptures have marked out for her, and that it is time she should move in the enlarged sphere which her great Creator has assigned her.

30   *Resolved,* That it is the duty of the women of this country to secure to themselves their sacred right to the elective franchise.

Resolved, That the equality of human rights results necessarily from the fact of the identity of the race in capabilities and responsibilities.

Resolved, therefore, That, being invested by the Creator with the same capabilities, and the same consciousness of responsibility for their exercise, it is demonstrably the right and duty of woman, equally with man, to promote every righteous cause by every righteous means; and especially in regard to the great subjects of morals and religion, it is self-evidently her right to participate with her brother in teaching them, both in private and in public, by writing and by speaking, by any instrumentalities proper to be used, and in any assemblies proper to be held; and this being a self-evident truth growing out of the divinely implanted principles of human nature, any custom or authority adverse to it, whether modern or wearing the hoary sanction of antiquity, is to be regarded as a self-evident falsehood, and at war with mankind.

[At the last session Lucretia Mott offered and spoke to the following resolution:]

Resolved, That the speedy success of our cause depends upon the zealous and untiring efforts of both men and women, for the overthrow of the monopoly of the pulpit, and for the securing to women an equal participation with men in the various trades, professions and commerce.

Questions for Reading Actively

1. What is the thesis of each of these arguments? Where is it stated in each of these arguments?

2. How does the Declaration of Independence use deduction and induction? Identify the premises and the conclusion in the second paragraph. Comment on the effectiveness of this deliberate use of these basic reasoning methods.

3. How does the Declaration of Sentiments and Resolutions use induction to support the central claim? What are the effects of its parallels with the Declaration of Independence?

Questions for Thinking Critically

1. In your library or on the Internet, locate a copy of Martin Luther King Jr.'s "Letter from Birmingham Jail." What differences in approach do you see between it and "I Have a Dream" (pages 184–187)? What about the tone or *ethos*? Can you identify the warrants and qualifiers in King's arguments?

2. How would you define *liberty* and *the pursuit of happiness*? Is it possible, in your current circumstances, to achieve either liberty or happiness? To what extent is the state responsible for guaranteeing *liberty* and *the pursuit of happiness*, according to your definition of both terms?

Question for Writing Thoughtfully

1. These political arguments address profound questions about human rights. What in these arguments could be applicable to arguments that you might write about academic or business issues? What might not be applicable? Explain in a short essay.

Deductive and Inductive Reasoning in Writing

As pointed out earlier in this chapter, writers and speakers seldom use deductive or inductive reasoning solely or purely. In their arguments, conclusions reached by induction become premises for deductions; statements that are premises are asserted but not demonstrated, as in the opening sentences of the Declaration of Independence. Deductively developed paragraphs interact with inductively developed ones, as in Gould's "Evolution as Fact and Theory" in Chapter 11.

However, deduction is used obviously when a definition or principle is established by the writer, and the point of the paper or paragraph is to claim that the subject being discussed fits the definition or demonstrates the principle. If the readers agree with the definition and also agree that the subject fits it, the claim is proved for whatever purpose the writer has. Political science, literature, philosophy, theology, psychology, and law are among the many fields that employ deductive arguments in this way.

Inductive reasoning is reflected in two ways in writing. One is structural. When a writer chooses to present instances of evidence first, leading readers to the claim presented as a conclusion, the paragraph or paper is organized inductively. Composition instructors tend to steer students away from using this technique to structure entire papers since great skill is needed to keep readers with the argument. The sections Organizing Ideas and Revising in the Writing Projects have asked you to think carefully about where you state your thesis or claim for this reason. It is usually more effective to use a deductively based structure.

A reflection of inductive reasoning that is often used in writing occurs when the writer makes a claim in a topic sentence or thesis statement, then simply exemplifies it. The writer is asking the readers to re-enact the inductive process that led him or her to make the claim. Notice how the list of evils alleged to have been committed by the British government functions this way in the Declaration of Independence. Notice how regularly you use this technique, and how often much of what you read uses it, too.

In addition, deduction often appears in the abbreviated form of the enthymeme (see page 508), and induction is commonly presented through the small sample of the example, the inference, and the anecdote. These practices are neither wrong nor fallacious. Writers cannot take the time or space to state all the premises of every deduction or to give multiple instances to support each idea. However, critical thinkers need to understand these reductions so that claims and evidence can be evaluated. Deduction and induction, the basic reasoning methods, are at work in various ways in what we write and read.

Writing Project: Arguing a Position on a Significant Issue

This chapter has emphasized the importance of the basic concepts and terminology connected with argument because reasoned argument leading to mutual understanding, consensus, or agreement is the foundation of a democratic society and also is often the key to success in personal, academic, and business activities.

Because so much college and professional writing is argumentative, this Writing Project asks you to concentrate on the two central elements of argument: establishing a clear thesis and providing sound evidence for it. In addition, you should be particularly careful to be logical, to avoid fallacious statements, to consider your audience, and to present yourself as a reasonable, well-informed proponent of your claims.

Write an essay in which you argue logically for a position on an issue that you consider significant. Use print sources, electronic sources, and—if possible—an interview with an informed individual to support your claims. Follow your instructor's directions regarding the number and range of sources, length of the paper, and academic format for citation of sources. Be sure to follow exactly the model in your handbook when you complete your paper in MLA, APA, or other appropriate format. Consult Chapter 14 and the appendix in this book.

On a page separate from your paper, identify the audience to whom you are addressing your argument and explain why members will benefit from understanding your position. Also, either within the paper or in an accompanying note, explain why this issue is important to you so that your classmates and instructor, as they help you revise your drafts, can be aware of the nature of your expertise and any possible biases.

 This chapter has included both readings and Thinking-Writing Activities that encourage you to think about argument. Be sure to reread what you wrote for those activities; you may be able to use some of the material for this Writing Project.

Begin by considering the key elements in the Thinking-Writing Model in Chapter 1 on pages 6–7.

The Writing Situation

Purpose   Your primary purpose is to write an argument that will persuade your intended audience to agree with your claim or thesis. As you work toward that goal, you will have to think critically about a subject that you care about and clarify or modify your view of it, which is another useful purpose.

Audience   The audience is a major concern in any argument. A successful writer understands the characteristics and attitudes of his or her audience. When you develop an argument, you must have a specific audience in mind. Although pandering dishonorably to the audience by distorting evidence or by using flattery is bad rhetoric, an arguer still should be aware of the makeup of the audience and accommodate its members' needs. Some factors to consider are knowledge (an expert audience needs less background than an uninformed one does), age (younger and older people often have different points of view), roles (people have various roles and respond differently as those roles change), relationships (an audience of peers can be approached differently than another kind of audience), and the emotional level of the issue and situation (a highly charged situation should be approached differently than a calm one would be).

Subject   Whenever you argue for a position about which you are concerned, you are addressing an important subject. In addition, the techniques of argument themselves constitute a subject that merits much attention because argument has such importance in people's lives.

Writer   If you have been using sources for other projects, you should be comfortable incorporating other people's ideas into your writing and documenting them appropriately. A new role for you may be that of the good rhetorician, the responsible arguer; if you use your developing critical thinking abilities, you will manage that role well.

The Writing Process

The following sections will guide you through the stages of generating, planning, drafting, and revising as you develop your argument.

Generating Ideas

- You may be involved with an issue because of your sex, ethnicity, or field of study or through some organization in which you participate. Or you may be concerned about a problem at your college, in your community, in your country, or elsewhere in the world. If so, you should have no problem deciding what to write about.

- If no issue comes quickly to mind, look around your campus and community to see what problems exist or what changes could be made.

- Be attentive to various print, broadcast, and online news outlets. Talk with friends, family members, and professors about significant issues.

- Think about questions in your areas of interest: your favorite college subjects, sports, entertainment, food, cars, the environment, architecture. Some of these questions may pertain to serious issues; some might be more lighthearted; many will merit a reasoned argument.

- Freewrite about one or two of your concerns. See how many issues or positions you can come up with in five minutes.

Defining a Focus   After selecting an issue to write about, draft a thesis statement that describes the position that you will argue. Be sure that the statement states your points accurately; it may be a complex sentence. Then share it with classmates to profit from their responses. Revise it on the basis of their feedback.

Organizing Ideas   Your argument should probably be set up in the traditional "no-fail" structure: introduction, thesis, evidence, handling of other views, summing up, conclusion/recommendation for action. However, you may be able to use some other arrangement effectively.

Notice how your material adapts itself to various thinking patterns. Use them firmly to clarify your points.

Select and place material from your sources carefully. Connect source material smoothly with your ideas by introducing and commenting on it.

Drafting   Begin with the easiest part to write, which for this paper might be the beginning since you have been thinking so much about your thesis and its context.

However, never get stymied by trying to compose a beginning. Draft sections in any order that works for you. You might want to draft the paragraphs that present your evidence, then consider what inductive or deductive methods you should use.

- Sometimes copying a draft or parts of it and revising one version while retaining another is productive. That way, if a revision is not satisfactory, you have preserved the earlier version.
- Sometimes writers need to start over by making a new file for a revised version.
- Sometimes it helps to scroll down or up and to rewrite a paragraph or section. Then you can use the better version and delete the weaker one.

Be sure to keep track of publication information for all sources. Note abbreviated titles, authors, and pages in your draft. Then, when you revise, you can cite the sources in the required format. Be sure to use quotation marks or indenting in your draft whenever you quote.

Principles for Writing Responsible Arguments

The following principles for writing responsible arguments are fundamental to the Western tradition of logical, structured argument. Always be sure to follow them as well as you can.

Principles for Writing Responsible Arguments

1. Formulate and qualify the thesis statement carefully. Place it purposefully. Use deductive and inductive approaches as appropriate to develop and support the thesis.

2. Provide a context for the thesis; give reasons for its importance. These might be warrants.

3. Provide sound evidence, or grounds, presented clearly and specifically.

4. Acknowledge and demonstrate understanding of other points of view. Grant validity to any point when it is justified. To strengthen your argument, refute courteously points with which you disagree.

5. Use the thinking/organizing patterns in Part Two. Arguments often rely on definitions. Causes of a situation and the effects of a proposal are often vital to an argument. Narratives and chronologies are often effective. Contrasts, comparisons, and analogies illuminate your points.

6. Don't use fallacious reasoning.

7. Be aware of your tone. You want to sound reasonable, thoughtful, and polite as you argue your points.

8. Remember that the conclusion to an argument is extremely important. Restate the thesis or claim with a suggestion, a call for action, a decision, or further thought.

Revising, Editing, and Proofreading   Use the Step-by-Step method in Chapter 6 on pages 169–171 to revise your essay and prepare a final draft.

Guidelines for Revising an Argument

❏ Is my claim clearly stated and adequately qualified?

❏ Do I provide adequate evidence to support the validity of my claim? Have I correctly cited and documented the sources of that evidence?

❏ Are any of my statements fallacious? Have I double-checked my argument for fallacies?

❏ Should I clearly state the warrants for my argument, or should I leave them unstated?

❏ Have I appropriately established my *ethos* (the impression my audience will have of me) and *pathos* (the effect my argument will have on my audience)?

❏ Have I considered, and included, other points of view? Does my argument clearly prove why my claims are more logical, sensible, useful, or appealing than the opposition's viewpoints?

Student Writing

Josephine Cimino's Writing Process

Part-time student Josephine Cimino makes use every day of critical thinking and problem-solving strategies. As a mother of two who also holds a full-time job, Cimino has multiple responsibilities that require her to make thoughtful decisions no matter how difficult or pressing the circumstances. Her reasoning abilities and careful, logical thinking are evident in the following argument. Although she recognized that the issue of cell phones in schools is not as obviously urgent as the human rights issues addressed by Elizabeth Cady Stanton and Martin Luther King Jr.—or as difficult and problematic as the issues of rape and alcohol abuse discussed in Chapter 12—Cimino chose an issue that was of close personal interest. This allows her to clearly establish her *ethos* (as a working parent) and to visualize a specific audience (other parents of school-age children). Josephine began with the exercise on page 504, Constructing Arguments to Persuade, as a way of structuring her thinking about this issue.

> Reason: For many working parents, cell phones allow them to keep track of their children's whereabouts and safety.
>
> Reason: Because of the increasing use of cell phones, there are very few public pay telephones available either on school grounds or at places like athletic fields where students go after school.
>
> Claim: Students should be allowed to carry cell phones on school grounds and during after-school activities.
>
> Audience: Other parents who might not be aware of current efforts to make cell phones illegal on school grounds.

Cellular Phones in Public Schools

by Josephine R. Cimino

As one half of a two-income domestic partnership, I find it very difficult to keep track of my son's, my husband's and my own activities. I can only imagine how much harder it is for families with more children. My husband's job requires him to travel, often out of state. As a very concerned and involved parent, I am left with the task of keeping track and assuring the safety of our child. My son is now in high school, and his day is filled with school, sports, and other extracurricular activities.

He went to a high school football game not too long ago, and I did not have to worry about him because one of his friend's parents was going to give him a ride home. When he got home, he said one of his other friends was caught using a cellular phone to call his parents to pick him up. Unfortunately, the assistant principal saw and confiscated the phone. The student was automatically suspended for ten days for violating Maryland law and school policy. I was so perturbed by this incident that I spoke with a school administrator, Mrs. Shenk, who stated she agreed that the law should be changed. In fact, she had given her daughter, a senior in high school, a cell phone to keep in her car. The administrator admitted that her daughter kept the cellular phone hidden at all times to avoid detection by other school administrators or teachers.

A law was enacted in Maryland in 1989 banning cellular phones and pagers from school grounds and school-related activities (Shen M3). According to a Montgomery County Public Schools regulation, if a student is caught using a cellular phone, the phone is confiscated, and the student is automatically suspended for ten days. In addition, for a second offense, the school is obliged to notify the police. Further, the student can also be expelled if the use of the cellphone was related to any criminal activity (Regulation). According to Shen, violation of the law is a misdemeanor, punishable by a fine of as much as $2500, and a maximum six-month imprisonment (M1).

Various news reports state that some educators and lawmakers have been opposed to the use of cellular phones on school grounds and at school-related activities due to the perception in the late 1980's and early 1990's that cellular phones were used for drug and other illegal activities. According to Mrs. Shenk, some educators and opponents of cellular phones think that cell phones will cause undue disruption in the schools because of the ringing of phones and kids talking on the phones inappropriately. She further states that another argument against cell phones is the possible loss or theft of cell phones by other students. Further, she states, cell phones can also distract students from their school-related activities and their studies.

I do not agree with the current Maryland law. I believe that this law has been surpassed by the electronic age and the availability of cellular phones. I believe that students in the middle schools and high schools should be allowed to carry cellular phones on school grounds and be allowed to use them before and after classes. Further, I believe that students should be allowed to carry and use cellular phones at school-related activities as long as the use is not related to something illegal.

The reasons for having cell phones available to students in schools are compelling. First of all, cell phones are a real time-saver for busy working parents with several children who need to be in several places. Parents do not have to wait around for activities to finish. The children can call when they are ready to be picked up, or to say that they are staying longer and need to be picked up later. Parents still spend an inordinate amount of time in their cars waiting for their children to finish their activities. If children are allowed to have cell phones, parents can use their time more productively. An example is my son's friend at the football game. His parents were probably doing errands or eating dinner, rather than waiting in the parking lot. They probably used their time for something they wanted or needed to do, other than just waiting for their son.

The availability and accessibility of regular pay phones in schools and on school grounds are sadly lacking. There is only one pay phone outside of my son's high school building, and there are no pay phones available near the football field, the basketball courts, or the soccer field. The school is often closed when games are played during the evening hours; therefore, the pay phones inside cannot be accessed. The students often have to wait in long lines to use the one pay phone available on school grounds to call their parents.

Another reason why students should be allowed to have cell phones is so parents can keep track of their children. Parents like me want to know what their children are doing at all times. I, for one, want to know where my son is so that I can be assured that everything is going the way it should. If he tells me he is going home with another child, I want to know for sure that this is what he is doing and that there are no hitches in the plans. I do not want him to be stranded somewhere because his plans fell apart. Parents should be able to call their children after school is over to confirm their schedules and activities.

Finally, students should be allowed to have cellular phones for safety reasons. With the current prevalence of abductions, kidnappings, and school violence, students should be allowed the safety net of having a cellular phone. It would be easy to dial 911 in case of an accident, or if the safety of the child was in question. Students should be able to call parents in case of a dead car battery after a school activity, or if a ride home fell through, or they are separated from friends during a football game. Numerous news reports said that some students were able to call their parents during the Columbine shooting in Colorado. Parents were assured that their children were still alive and able to talk to them about what was happening.

Incidents like the Columbine shooting and other reports of abductions and kidnappings on the way to and from school force parents to think of safety first and to minimize the consequences if a child is caught using the cell phone during school-related activities. Most parents would rather have their kids safe than take the risk of their being harmed.

Earlier this year, a bill was introduced unsuccessfully to change the current laws regulating cellular phones in public schools (Shen M1). However, on April 26, 2000, the School Board of Montgomery County gave the principals in all Montgomery County public schools the discretion of suspending students from one to ten days, instead of the previous automatic ten-day suspension (MCPS–Board). Obviously educators and school administrators agreed that the law needed changing by this revision of county policy. This is a good start, but is not enough to keep our children safe.

Parents, as advocates for the safety of children, should continue efforts to convince lawmakers to change the current law. Students should be allowed to use and carry cell phones in schools and during school activities under strict guidelines. If these guidelines are not followed, then those students should suffer the consequences. Students should not be punished for wanting to be safe and to be in contact with their parents. The safety of our children should be our foremost priority.

Works Cited

Montgomery County Public Schools. "Board Endorses Reduced Penalty for Use of Cellular Phones, Approves Non-Recommended Reductions to FY2001 Operating Budget Request." MCPS Media Announcement. Web. 26 Apr. 2000. <http// filemaker.mcps.k12.md.us>.

———. "Regulation—Portable Communication Devices COG-RA." Web. 26 Apr. 2000. <http//www.mcps.k12.md.us>.

Shen, Fern. "Rules on Cell Phones Decried." *Washington Post* 17 Feb. 2000: M11. Print.

Shenk, Susan. Personal interview. 2 January 2000.

Alternative Writing Project: The Pursuit of Happiness

Early women rights activists, including Elizabeth Cady Stanton, modeled much of their rhetoric, style, and evidence for their Declaration of Sentiments and Resolutions on the original American Declaration of Independence. Both documents assert—or warrant—that the "pursuit of happiness" is an "unalienable right." In a well-argued essay, define the concept of *happiness* as it relates to a specific aspect of your academic or professional life. Are you currently in that state of happiness, and if so, argue for its adoption by other students or others in your career field. Is there something or someone impeding your "unalienable right" to this specific kind of happiness? Argue, perhaps by drawing up a list of injustices as the framers of the Declaration of Independence did against King George, that this obstacle to your specific pursuit of happiness is unfair and unjust. Your final argument may draw upon as many of the rhetorical strategies and specific appeals to audience that appear in both of these Declarations.

CHAPTER 13   Summary

- The classical concepts of argument include *ethos,* the character of the speaker or writer; *pathos,* the effect on the audience; and *logos,* the logic and substance of an argument.

- In this chapter, *rhetoric* should be understood to mean the use of the best means of persuasion.

- Concepts important to the Toulmin method of argument are *claim* and *qualified claim, grounds, warrants,* and *backings.*

- When arguing, you should consider other points of view and strive to reach mutual understanding and, if possible, consensus or agreement.

- When considering your audience, you should be careful not to cross over the line into pandering.

- *Inferring* is a thinking process used to reason from what one already knows or believes to acquire new knowledge or beliefs.

- You can work toward agreement when you construct arguments to decide, explain, predict, or persuade.

- When an argument includes both *true* reasons and *valid* structure, the argument is considered *sound.*

- In a *deductive argument,* one reasons from premises that are known or assumed to be true to a conclusion that necessarily follows from these premises.

- A *syllogism* is an argument form that consists of two supporting premises and a conclusion; an *enthymeme* assumes the first premise.

- Types of syllogisms or enthymemes include affirming the antecedent, denying the consequent, and disjunctive syllogism.

- In an *inductive argument,* one reasons from premises or instances that are known or assumed to be true to a conclusion that is supported by the premises but does not necessarily follow from them.

- Causal reasoning is central to the scientific method used in the natural and social sciences.

- *Empirical generalization* is a form or inductive reasoning, which is defined as "reasoning by examining a limited sample to reach a general conclusion based on that sample."

- To evaluate inductive reasoning, you must determine if the sample is known, sufficient, and representative.

- Types of false reasoning, or fallacies, include: hasty generalization, sweeping generalizations, false dilemma, begging the question, red herring, and fallacies of relevance.

- Fallacies of relevance include appeals to authority, pity, fear, ignorance, personal attack, or popular opinion (or bandwagon).

Roger L. Wollenberg/UPI /Landov

All research begins with a question, a desire to know more about a particular subject. Sometimes, curiosity requires courage as well, especially when the research question might lead to difficult, challenging, even dangerous inquiry. Lawyer, journalist, and human-rights activist Samantha Power is devoted to bringing the worst humanitarian crimes of recent years to international attention, including the mid-1990s genocides in Rwanda (see student Chris Buxton-Smith's paper on the subject, p. 572) and Bosnia. How does research writing differ from other types of writing?

Writing About Investigations:
Thinking About Research

"If we would have new knowledge, we must get a whole world of new questions."

—Susanne K. Langer

Rewards of Research

When you work on your college research projects, you are participating in one of humanity's oldest and most productive efforts. You can easily come up with an endless list of scientific, technical, historical, and social investigations that have made our lives richer and safer. Conducting good research can also be rewarding for you. It can contribute to your success in college and, often, to your progress in a career. As you continue your studies, you will do several kinds of research, including retrieving and understanding what others have discovered, synthesizing and connecting others' discoveries, connecting others' discoveries with your own ideas, and formulating new concepts and theories yourself. Each of these activities is rewarding in itself, and each is also an important component in research as an extensive human activity.

Critical and creative thinking are parts of all aspects of research. The concepts discussed in every chapter of this book also pertain to research. As people seek information, they constantly deal with *perceptions, beliefs, perspectives, processes, causes, comparisons, contrasts, analogies, definitions,* and *arguments.* Research often involves *making decisions* and *problem solving.* Researchers present *reports, inferences,* and *judgments.*

In addition, like writing, research is often a recursive process rather than a linear one. One source will lead to another, new questions will arise, a creative insight will illuminate a topic, or a critical analysis will change the direction of a project.

This chapter introduces and explains strategies for using researched information in academic papers. An appendix to this book provides guidelines for using the Modern Language Association (MLA) documentation style and the American Psychological Association (APA) documentation style. Your instructor and your campus or local librarians can provide you with additional information.

Critical Thinking Focus: Deciding what information to look for, what to use, and how to present it

Writing Focus: Completing a research paper

Writing Project: A research project

539

Starting with Questions

Researchers begin with a question. Researchers are in pursuit of answers. Student researchers are often assigned a topic by their instructors, and asking questions about it is usually an effective approach because questions can help a researcher find a focus and can stimulate inquiry. Questions can help in various ways.

Questions That Identify Your Topic

If you are choosing your own topic, ask yourself questions:

- What interests me most within the guidelines for this project?
- What within the guidelines pertains to my college major or my future career?
- What affects my life or the lives of people close to me?
- What affects my community?
- What topics can I find material about in my college library and on the Internet?

Thinking-Writing Activity

DEVELOPING RESEARCH QUESTIONS

1. Identify a field of study that interests you. Then write two or three questions about specific issues in that field.

2. If you can, show your questions to a professor or graduate student in the field. Ask her or him if these questions have been answered or if researchers are still working on them.

3. Share your questions with classmates. See if they have additional questions that pertain to this field of study.

Questions That Focus Your Topic

After you have selected a broad topic, or if your instructor has assigned a topic, you can use questions to focus it into a manageable and interesting topic. (Notice how many of these questions use the thinking patterns discussed in previous chapters of this book.)

- What are the issues involved in a topic? How are they defined? (Chapter 8)
- What are some different perspectives on the issues? (Chapter 9)
- Who is the audience for my research?
- What did people believe about my topic in previous historical periods? (Chapter 11)

- How have theories about it changed? (Chapter 11)
- What caused it? (Chapter 10)
- What problems are connected with it? How might they be solved? (Chapter 12)
- What is my purpose for conducting this research?
- What are future concerns about it likely to be?

The specific question that you want to investigate can be called a *research question*.

Thinking-Writing Activity

IDENTIFYING RESEARCH QUESTIONS

1. In your own words, write the research question(s) that might have inspired some of the student or professional writers included in this book.

2. What strategies did these writers use to develop their research questions?

Searching for Information

Finding Electronic and Print Sources in the Library

You are probably accustomed to using an online search engine to connect you with all kinds of information. However, you should use the resources of your college's computer center or library to help you learn the best ways to use these resources. Most college libraries provide guides to their resources. Some instructors or departments require completion of a workbook or physical or online attendance at library orientation sessions. You should take every opportunity to improve your ability to use your college library and the Internet.

Your library uses computers in at least four ways to direct you to source material:

1. The library's holdings are *cataloged* via a computer program, so the best way for you to find books, articles, videos, and DVDs is to learn to use the terminals in your library.

2. Most college libraries subscribe to *databases* such as Expanded Academic ASAP and National Newspapers that contain whole texts of articles from newspapers, magazines, and specialized journals, so a good way for you to find solid information is to learn to use whatever service your library has. The library provides databases that cannot be accessed on most home computers.

3. Your library probably has a *collection of CD-ROMs* containing encyclopedias, books, poems, and visuals.

4. Computer terminals available to library patrons allow you to access the Internet and use various search engines to find an infinite variety of material.

Thinking-Writing Activity

LEARNING ABOUT YOUR LIBRARY

1. Go to your college or community library. Find out how to access its holdings and learn what Internet services it provides.

2. Write a paragraph explaining what your library can do for you and how to use its computers. Also, explain how you would go about obtaining print sources.

Primary and Secondary Sources

Researchers find valuable information in both *primary* and *secondary* sources. Primary sources include original documents such as letters, texts of speeches, or governmental resolutions; works of literature such as novels, stories, poems, plays, and autobiographies; and firsthand reports of experiments, observations, or interviews by the persons who conducted them. Secondary sources comment on other sources. Examples are literary criticism, biographies, studies of historical events, and any synthesis or analysis of other sources.

You should use primary sources as much as possible and try to compare secondary sources with the primary sources on which they comment to be sure that interpretations seem valid.

Collecting Information from Experts and from the Field

In addition to obtaining material from print and electronic sources, you can get information from people who have expertise on your subject. Also, you can go to places or events that are important to your research questions and conduct field research, where you observe and carefully document what goes on.

Interviews   Conducting an interview can be a valuable way to obtain information. Your creativity and critical abilities will be well used in an interview. Here are some guidelines for interviewing:

1. Identify the person with whom you wish to talk and then make an appointment with that person.

2. Carefully develop—and write out—the questions you will ask. You might want to email them to the interviewee ahead of time so that he or she will be able to prepare thorough responses.

3. Be careful as you record the interview. If you want to tape the interview, you must ask permission. If you are writing down the responses or keying them into a laptop computer, you must be sure to be accurate.

4. Do not take up too much of your interviewee's time, and—of course—give appropriate thanks.

5. Use and cite the material from an interview as you would any other source (see the MLA appendix, page 585 for guidelines). It should be effectively integrated into your paper where it works best to develop the points that you are making.

6. If you can, give your interviewee a draft of your paper to show how you have presented the material and be willing to heed suggestions if any are offered.

7. Provide the person interviewed with a copy of the completed paper and thank him or her again.

Questionnaires   Using questionnaires is another way to obtain information from people, but they are difficult to design well. If you want to gather information with a questionnaire, you should review the material on inductive reasoning and empirical generalization in Chapter 13 on pages 512–514. As a beginning researcher, you should ask only a few questions, perhaps no more than three or four.

Also, think about these concerns:

1. What exactly is the issue about which you want people's opinions? Define it very clearly.

2. How can you state questions to obtain unambiguous information? Sometimes "yes-no" or "two-way" questions are best since they elicit specific responses. However, sometimes yes-no questions are frustrating because people do not want to respond in such a limited way.

3. If you do not ask yes-no questions, how can you obtain possible responses in a small number of consistent categories that pertain to the information you want? Do you want choices? Do you want to construct a scale?

4. Can the responses be easily tabulated?

5. How many people can you poll in the time that you have and with the methods that you want to use? Will that group provide a representative sample appropriate for the scope of your project?

6. How will you use the results? How can you report them accurately, clearly identifying the characteristics and numbers of those who responded?

7. How can you use caution when drawing conclusions?

Questionnaires can be administered in several ways: by face-to-face polling; by mailing forms with a stamped, addressed return envelope; or by email. Practically speaking, a first attempt should focus on a small group—for example, asking the people on your block about a community issue or asking the students in one of your classes about a campus or political issue.

If you know someone experienced in questionnaire use—such as a social science professor, a public health researcher, or a journalism major—you might ask that person to help you craft your instrument. Also, test your questions on a few close friends or family members to see what kinds of answers you get. Then, after revising any questions that need adjusting, pose them to your selected group.

ONLINE RESOURCES
Additional Resources for Questionnaire Use
Visit the website for this text, accessed through **CengageBrain.com**, to find additional resources on questionnaires.

Field Research   Observations provide firsthand data and are often used in art history, sociology, education, environmental studies, medicine, and other branches of science. If you want to conduct field research, you should review Chapter 7 to remind yourself about factors that might affect your perceptions and Chapter 9 to recall different perspectives that you might take as an observer, either consciously or unconsciously. You should consider the following principles when you conduct an observation:

1. Identify a place, situation, or object that pertains to your research question.

2. Ask permission from an appropriate person if the site is reserved for use by a specific group such as a class, a club, or a religious assembly.

3. Select a good time to go to your observation site.

4. Do not become involved in any of the activities that you have come to observe.

5. Be as unobtrusive as possible. The presence of an observer often alters the dynamics of a situation.

6. If you are observing an object such as a painting, statue, building, or element of nature, try to study it at different times of day or under varying circumstances. In your write-up, accurately report the circumstances under which you made your observations.

7. Note your observations carefully.

8. Present your observations as objectively as possible. State any inferences and judgments carefully and separate them from your reporting of information obtained through your senses.

Thinking-Writing Activity

INTERVIEWS, QUESTIONNAIRES, AND OBSERVATIONS

1. Interview one of your instructors about using firsthand (or "primary") sources of information. Ask him or her about how observations, questionnaires, and interviews are used in his or her field. Ask how these instruments should be designed and what pitfalls to avoid.

2. Write a paragraph or two about what you have learned from the interview.

Using Information

Finding material is relatively easy. Dealing with it is the challenging part. You must evaluate the information that you have found, which involves active and critical reading. You must use critical thinking to select what you will use, and then save, copy, or take notes from it carefully. Writing your paper involves all the interrelated elements of the Thinking-Writing Model. In addition, you must integrate and cite source material in a prescribed academic format, which may at first seem difficult. Most important, you must present information accurately and honestly.

Evaluating Sources for a Research Project

All material found during research has to be evaluated. Sometimes evaluation is easy—a source may be so obviously good that you know you will use it, or it may be so clearly weak or irrelevant to your inquiry that you know you will not need it.

Here are some guidelines for deciding whether print and online material will be useful to you. These guidelines are an abbreviated version of the material in Chapter 11 on pages 393–395. Also, you may want to consult Chapters 3 and 11 to think again about some of the ways in which your beliefs have been formed since beliefs have a strong influence on evaluation.

These basic questions can help to judge information and sources:

1. *How reliable is the source?*
   - What kind of text is this? an editorial, a report, an advertisement?
   - Who is its intended audience? Is this audience important to the text's point of view?
   - When was it written? Is the date relevant to my research question?
   - Is it a primary or secondary source?

2. *How knowledgeable or experienced is the author?*
   - What credentials does the person who provided this information have?
   - If the person is not an expert, under what circumstances did she or he provide the information?

3. *What specific ideas are being presented?*
   - What is the main point, claim, or thesis?
   - What reasons or evidence support the information? Does anything about it seem false?
   - Does anything seem to have been left out?
   - Are interests, purposes, and intended audiences apparent?
   - If an argument is presented, can you identify its warrants?

THINKING CRITICALLY ABOUT NEW MEDIA

Evaluating Online Information

The Internet is an incredibly rich source of information on almost every subject that exists. But it's important to remember that information is not knowledge. Information doesn't become *knowledge* until we think critically about it. As a critical thinker, you should never accept information at face value without first establishing its accuracy, evaluating the credibility of the source, and determining the point of view or bias of the source. These are issues that we will explore throughout this book, but for now you can use the checklist on pages 547–548 to evaluate the information on the Internet—and other sources as well.

Before You Search

The first stage of evaluating Web sources should happen before you search the Internet! Ask yourself what you are looking for. If you don't know what you're looking for, you probably won't find it! You might want

narratives	arguments
facts	statistics
opinions	eyewitness reports
photographs or graphics	

Do you want new ideas, support for a position you already hold, or something entirely different? Once you decide, you will be better able to evaluate what you find on the Web.

Choose Sources Likely to Be Reliable

Ask yourself, "What sources (or what kinds of sources) would be most likely to give me the kind of reliable information I'm looking for?" Some sources are more likely than others to

be fair	lack hidden motives
be objective	show quality control

Sometimes a site's address (or uniform resource locator [URL]) suggests its reliability or its purpose. Sites ending in

- .edu indicate educational or research material
- .gov indicate government resources
- .com indicate commercial products or commercially sponsored sites
- .org usually indicate nonprofit organizations

"\\7,126\\ NAME" in a URL may indicate a personal home page without a recognized affiliation.

Keep these considerations in mind; don't just accept the opinion of the first sources you locate.

Checklist for Evaluating the Quality of Internet Resources

Criterion 1: Authority

❏ Is it clear who sponsors the page and what the sponsor's purpose is in maintaining the page? Is there a respected, well-known organizational affiliation?

❏ Is it clear who wrote the material and what the author's qualifications for writing on this topic are?

❏ Is there a way of verifying the legitimacy of the page's sponsor? In particular, is there a phone number or postal address to contact for more information? (An email address alone is not enough.)

❏ If the material is protected by copyright, is the name of the copyright holder given? Is there a date of page creation or version?

❏ *Beware!* Avoid anonymous sites and affiliations that you've never heard of or that can't be easily checked.

Criterion 2: Accuracy

❏ Are the sources for any factual information clearly listed so they can be verified by another source?

❏ Has the sponsor provided a link to outside sources (such as product reviews or reports filed with the Securities and Exchange Commission [SEC]) that can be used to verify the sponsor's claims?

❏ Is the information free of grammatical, spelling, and other typographical errors? (These kinds of errors not only indicate a lack of quality control but can actually produce inaccuracies in information.)

❏ Are statistical data in graphs and charts clearly labeled and easy to read?

❏ Does anyone monitor the accuracy of the information being published?

❏ *Beware!* Avoid unverifiable statistics and claims not supported by reasons and evidence.

Criterion 3: Objectivity

❏ For any given piece of information, is it clear what the sponsor's motivation is for providing it?

❏ Is the purported factual information clearly separated from any advertising or opinion content?

(Continues)

THINKING CRITICALLY ABOUT NEW MEDIA (CONTINUED)

❏ Is the point of view of the sponsor presented in a clear manner, with his or her arguments well supported?

❏ *Beware!* Avoid sites offering "information" in an effort to sell a product or service, as well as sites containing conflicts of interest, bias and one-sidedness, emotional language, and slanted tone.

Criterion 4: Currentness

❏ Are there dates on the page to indicate when the page was written, first placed on the Web, and last revised?

❏ Are there any other indications that the material is kept current?

❏ If material is presented in graphs or charts, is there a clear statement about when the data were gathered?

❏ Is there an indication that the page has been completed and is not still in the process of being developed?

❏ *Beware!* Avoid sites that lack any dates, sources, or references.

ONLINE RESOURCES
Guide to Critical Thinking About What You See on the Web
Visit the website for this text, accessed through **CengageBrain.com**, for a guide to critical thinking about what you see on the Web.

Thinking-Writing Activity

EVALUATING THE QUALITY OF TWO WEBSITES WITH CONTRASTING PERSPECTIVES ON AN ISSUE

1. Select an issue that plays an important role in our world today, such as global warming, genetically modified foods, the increasing use of drugs to treat children for attention-deficit hyperactivity disorder (ADHD), etc.

2. Locate two different websites that present contrasting views on the issue.

3. Evaluate each website using the checklist above.

4. Write a one-page summary of your informed view on the issue and explain the reasons and evidence that support your perspective.

Thinking Critically About Visuals

Is FactCheck.org a Reputable Source of Information?

Using the guidelines you just learned, how reliable would you say this site is? In addition to considering this screen capture, feel free to visit the website itself and see if you can find additional evidence of the site's reliability or lack thereof.

Thinking-Writing Activity

EVALUATING PRINT AND WEB SOURCES

1. After you have found a print source, ask the evaluative questions above and then write your answers.

2. Go to an Internet site and evaluate it according to the Web guidelines. Then write your answers.

3. Examine your answers to the previous two questions. How will they influence your possible use of these sources?

Moving from Questions to Thesis

The next step in your research is to move from your research questions to a thesis for your research paper. The guidelines for all of this book's Writing Projects include suggestions for identifying a focus and defining a thesis. Reviewing these suggestions will help you when you are writing a research paper.

Some research papers take an informative position; others are strongly argumentative. This distinction will depend on your purpose, the traditions of the discipline in which you are writing the paper, and your instructor's goals for the assignment. Be sure that you understand whether your instructor wants your paper to be informative or argumentative.

Thinking-Writing Activity

GOING FROM QUESTIONS TO THESIS

1. Select one of the questions that you wrote for the Thinking-Writing Activity: Developing Research Questions on page 540. Then find or imagine some answers to it. Next, write at least one thesis statement that answers it or makes a claim about an answer to it.

2. Look at the questions and statements that two or three of your classmates created for this Thinking-Writing Activity. Identify the statements that seem clearest and have the most potential to be developed into solid papers.

Understanding Plagiarism and Using Information Ethically

Plagiarism is presenting another person's ideas or words as your own. There are two good reasons not to plagiarize. The first is honesty. Most people do not want to be fakes; they want to be honest, and so they do not want to steal others' ideas and work without giving credit. The second is that plagiarism can bring severe penalties, both in college and at work.

In college writing, two kinds of plagiarism are possible. One is deliberate and dishonorable—the willful copying of all or part of another student's paper or all or part of a source. Buying a paper from a service is also plagiarism because a student who does this is taking credit for someone else's words, ideas, and effort.

The other kind of plagiarism is accidental and happens when a student does not know how to document properly. Once you understand that you must always signal where any material from a source begins and ends and that you must always make clear who said something and where it was said, you should be able to avoid accidental plagiarism. The sections in this chapter on Taking Notes, The Logic Behind Documentation Formats, and Tips on Avoiding Plagiarism will help.

A *fabrication* is a deliberately false or invented statement. It presents as true something that is made up or distorted, such as an event that did not happen, a statement that was not made, a misleading addition or omission of words or data, a listing of a source that was not used. Some writers are tempted to fabricate or falsify if they do not have real information that they need in order to make a point or create a desired effect. Yet readers must be able to trust the material that is presented in academic work and in responsible media.

Fabrication is different from making a mistake, which unfortunately almost everyone does occasionally, but not deliberately. A fabrication is different from a hypothesis or hypothetical example, which should be identified as such.

Guidelines for Avoiding Plagiarism

❏ Remember that all material from any source must be documented in some way. Downloaded items, websites, email, interviews, illustrations, DVDs, videos, films, broadcasts, lectures, books, articles—anything that is not drawn from your own experience, observation, or creativity— must be cited appropriately.

❏ Learn the different methods of citation used in various writing situations. In college, you may need to use different formats in papers written for different classes. These disciplinary formats are explained in guides to research and handbooks. At work, you will give credit to others as expected in your occupation. In writing done for community activities, you will probably cite information informally, just stating that a person, article, or report said something.

❏ Be sure to present quoted material (exact words) in quotation marks, indented, or in some other indicative way, depending on the format that you are using.

❏ Remember that copied-and-pasted material, paraphrases, summaries, and short extracts, even of less than a sentence, all must be cited. Other people's ideas must be documented as well as their exact words.

❏ Be sure to indicate in all drafts where source material is from so that you do not lose track of it as you revise and edit.

❏ Signal where material from others begins and where it ends. Learn to do this in a variety of ways, as appropriate to the writing situation.

❏ Take pride in presenting your own thinking and distinguish your ideas clearly from those of your sources.

❏ Be careful to capture all bibliographic material as you download, photocopy, and take notes so that you can easily provide documentation. Be sure to record authors' full names, exact titles, publication information, dates, page numbers, URLs, and other access items.

❏ Consult with your instructors and writing center tutors about citing sources when you are drafting your researched writing.

❏ When in doubt, cite.

Thinking-Writing Activity

PLAGIARISM IN THE NEWS

1. Read carefully your college's statements about plagiarism. Does your college have an honor code? If so, what does it say about plagiarism? Write a few sentences giving your responses to these statements.

2. Search for information about Stephen Glass, Jayson Blair, Janet Cook, James Frey, Stephen Ambrose, or Doris Kearns Goodwin. Find out what any of these writers are reported to have fabricated or plagiarized, what they said about their situations, and what happened to them.

3. What can college students learn from the experience of these professionals?

Share your responses to these questions with classmates and see how your ideas are similar or different.

Taking Notes

Although photocopying and downloading have made note-taking less necessary than it was in previous eras, researchers still need to have methods for deciding what to note, highlight, or underline; for accurately recording content and bibliographic information; and for integrating source material thoughtfully into their own written work.

Deciding When to Take Notes

Sometimes you can easily see that certain parts of an article, book, or website relate to your research question or working thesis. Naturally, in such cases, you will then note the material or photocopy, highlight, or download it. However, at other times, you may not be sure what to select from a source.

Your critical reading abilities will come into play here. Before you even think about taking notes, you should read an entire article. If you are consulting a book, read the whole book—if possible—or skim it, consult the index, and read the chapters that contain information related to your topic. Look for headings, topic sentences, chapter titles—all the elements that point out what the writer is discussing. As you read through, jot down page numbers or mark passages that strike you in some way, but you really should not take notes until you have a grasp of the entire piece.

After getting an overview of the work, you need to go back and select specific points that pertain to your question or thesis. If you're not sure how the material relates, note it! At this stage, you want too much information instead of too little. Highlighting and underlining are forms of note taking because you are choosing information.

Quoting and Paraphrasing

Another decision that you have to make while taking notes is when to quote (using exact words) or to paraphrase (restating). Highlighting and underlining are forms of quoting. There are only two rules:

1. When you quote, put all of the quoted material inside quotation marks in your notes so that you will never forget that these are the author's exact words. Then you will know that anything else in your notes that is not in quotation marks is paraphrased.

2. Be accurate.

The following are some guidelines for quoting:

- If the author has said something in a distinctive way, quote or highlight it.
- If the author has said something complicated and/or technical, quote or highlight it.
- If the author has said something controversial, quote or highlight it.
- When in doubt, quote the author's words in your notes. You can decide if you would rather paraphrase them later when you are writing your paper.
- If you know that you only want a summary of a source or an indication of what it says, paraphrase it.

Here are examples of a full note and the paraphrased version:

Quoted note: "A Kampala journalist named Michael Wakabi told me that Kampala has become a 'used culture.' The cars are used—they arrive from

Japan with broken power windows and air conditioning, so Ugandan drivers bake in the sun. Used furniture from Europe lines the streets in Kampala. The Ugandan Army occupies part of neighboring Congo with used tanks and aircraft from Ukraine. And the traditional Ugandan dress made from local cotton, called gomesi, is as rare as the mountain gorilla. To dress African, Ugandans have to have money."—Packer 58.

Paraphrased note: The economy of Uganda is ruined by exploitation—local industries and culture are almost extinct. Nothing is fabricated or produced in Uganda anymore; most consumer goods are rejects from Western countries. Because native Ugandan products are so rare, only wealthy Ugandans can have them.—Packer 58.

The author's full name and all publication information will be on a bibliography card or list (see pages 555–556).

Using Common Knowledge

It is usually not necessary to document information that is considered "common knowledge," or things that "everybody" knows. Common knowledge is often factual, such as the fact that hijacked planes piloted by terrorists crashed into the World Trade Center on September 11, 2001. Well-known sayings like "Haste makes waste" are usually not documented, nor are accepted concepts like consuming large amounts of high-calorie food will cause most people to gain weight. However, discussions of facts or well-known ideas are not common; they are produced by individuals and must be documented.

In addition, common knowledge is not universally common. Different cultures, different time periods, different academic disciplines, and different occupations all have their own common knowledge and often do not see ideas from other groups or eras as well known. Therefore, you need to be cautious about presenting something as common knowledge and perhaps consult with your instructor. If in doubt, document. It is better to overcite than to plagiarize.

Characteristics of Effective Note-Taking Systems

Good note-taking systems include:

- accuracy in recording material
- accuracy in recording full bibliographic information
- differentiation between quoted and paraphrased material
- indication of the source from which a specific note is taken
- indication of the section of a paper to which a specific note pertains
- capacity to rearrange notes to put material into the appropriate sections of a paper

The traditional technique of using note cards has all of these characteristics. Other methods can accomplish the same tasks, but researchers need to use care to separate noted items and to find a way to sort information in order to insert it in its logical place in the paper. If, like many students today, you only use note cards when you cannot photocopy or download a source, you need to think carefully about ways to develop a method that will provide you with the benefits of the note-card system.

The traditional system has two parts: a note card for each piece of information and a bibliographic card for every source.

Note Cards   Each note card contains only one item of information. The act of selecting specific items motivates you to think carefully about what *you* are looking for in order to present your ideas in the paper. Figure 14.1 shows an example of a note card.

You indicate clearly on the card whether the material is quoted by using quotation marks or whether it is paraphrased by not using the marks. You also briefly identify the source on the card and note the section or subtopic of your paper to which the information pertains. As you begin drafting, arrange the cards in groups according to the places in the paper where that information will be used. Citation of sources is easy because each card records its source.

Bibliographic Cards   A good note-taking system includes a set of bibliography cards (or a list), which provides the full publication information for each source. You arrange the cards alphabetically by author or title when preparing your Works Cited list.

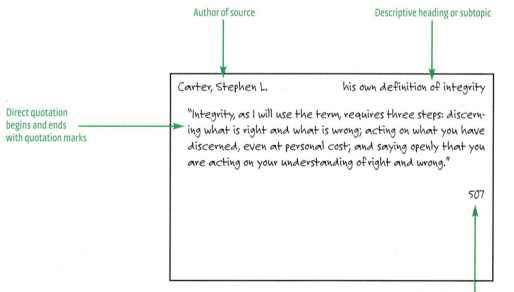

Author of source

Descriptive heading or subtopic

Carter, Stephen L.   his own definition of integrity

Direct quotation begins and ends with quotation marks

"Integrity, as I will use the term, requires three steps: discerning what is right and what is wrong; acting on what you have discerned, even at personal cost; and saying openly that you are acting on your understanding of right and wrong."

507

Page where quotation was found

FIGURE 14.1
Note Card

Carter, Stephen L. "The Insufficiency of Honesty."
Great Writing. Ed. Harvey S. Weiner and Nora Eisenberg.
3rd ed. San Francisco: McGraw, 2002. 507–512.

FIGURE 14.2
Bibliography Card

Figure 14.1 shows the bibliography card for the source of the quotation illustrated in Figure 14.2.

Look at the Works Cited list for one of the documented student papers in this book or consult your handbook. Then ask yourself: Is this source recorded in the MLA Works Cited–list format? Is it a book, a periodical, or an Internet source? Why will it be easy for this student to insert this source into her Works Cited list?

Using Your Computer to Take Notes   Computers can be used in many ways for note-taking. Simply by using a word-processing program, you can enter notes in appropriate files or under specific headings, and by pasting, copying, or using other combining methods, you can put the information into the part of your paper where you want it. You should double- or triple-space so that you can see items clearly, write changes interlinearly on printouts, and cut pages up to rearrange material. You can compile a Works Cited (MLA) or References (APA) list by using an alphabetizing program or simply by copying or pasting.

Thinking-Writing Activity

CREATING YOUR OWN NOTE-TAKING METHODS

1. If you have previously worked on research projects, write an explanation of your own note-taking and record-keeping processes. How do you use your computer to complete tasks? What do you do that is effective? What do you need to improve?

2. Share your system with your classmates and learn about their systems. Does a classmate have a technique that you would like to adopt?

Most students use combinations of note-taking and recording methods—card- or paper-based systems when necessary, electronic-based ones when possible. Probably the most unwieldy system—and one to avoid—is writing page after page of notes in a notebook, on both sides of the paper, without leaving spaces for notes to be annotated or cut apart and rearranged. You should avoid using any technique that does not allow you to review and organize material easily.

Thinking-Writing Activity

LEARNING ABOUT THE METHODS OF EXPERIENCED NOTE-TAKERS

1. Ask one of your instructors or a successful upper-division student how he or she takes notes, keeps records of sources, and arranges source material for use in a paper. Ask also about the advantages and disadvantages of the system.

2. Write a paragraph summarizing what you have learned. Then share what you have written with classmates and see what systems they have learned about.

Summarizing

You will often need to summarize what a source says, either as a way of taking notes or as a way of inserting information into your paper. Your critical reading abilities will serve you well when you write a summary. Here are some guidelines:

- A summary is by definition short. An article or book chapter might be summarized in five or six sentences.

- A summary presents major points, not introductory material or multiple examples. It might give one necessary example.

- A summary should state the main point or the thesis clearly, probably at the beginning.

- A summary does not include your commentary on or evaluation of the material. You can comment later as you introduce summarized material into your paper or after you have included it.

  Comment or evaluation: "This article discussed a major breakthrough...."

  Summary: "It says..."

  Comment or evaluation: "This book takes a stand that is no longer accepted...."

  Summary: "It claims..."

- Signal that you are presenting summarized material. One way to begin a summary is to state the main point. Signal words such as *The article says...He points out...* or *She concludes...* are helpful throughout a summary.

- Usually a summary paraphrases a source, but if you quote special words, graceful phrases, or entire sentences, be sure to use quotation marks.

- A summary is accurate.

The following is a professionally written summary of the article "Hospice Care or Assisted Suicide: A False Dichotomy," by John L. Miller.

In this paper, the author argues that making assisted suicide available is not a contradictory position to espousing hospice care. He draws on historical and political examples to explain the ethical basis for this assertion. By defining the issue at stake as one of personal autonomy (the loss or gain thereof), the author challenges the argument that making assisted suicide available leads to a slippery slope toward euthanasia, eugenics, or genocide. He asserts that narrowing choices by preventing people from seeking assistance in suicide is more likely to lead us down the slippery slope toward coercive medical and state intervention in our lives.

Thinking-Writing Activity

LEARNING TO SUMMARIZE

1. Write a four- or five-sentence summary of one of the sources that you evaluated for the Thinking-Writing Activity: Evaluating Print and Web Sources on page 550.

2. If you can, ask a classmate to read the source and then comment on whether your summary seems accurate.

Preparing an Annotated Bibliography

One technique that can help you evaluate your sources is writing an annotated bibliography. Your research librarian can show you annotated bibliographies about many subjects, either as books, as indexes, or online.

Sometimes instructors will ask students to create an annotated bibliography as a part of a research project. An *annotated bibliography* is a list of sources with a brief summary of and some evaluative comments about each one.

A student who was researching genocide in Rwanda made the entries shown in the example in Figure 14.3 on page 559. His instructor had required students to prepare an annotated bibliography of several sources before drafting their research papers.

Thinking-Writing Activity

CREATING AN ANNOTATED BIBLIOGRAPHY

1. Find three sources that pertain to one of the questions that you used in a previous Thinking-Writing Activity or to a paper that you are writing.

2. After you have read the sources carefully, create an annotated bibliography in which you list full bibliographic information. Also, summarize each source in one or two sentences and comment in one or two sentences about what each source's value would be in a paper about the subject.

Carter, Stephen. L. "Defending Our Neighbor." *Christianity Today*. Christianity Today International, Nov. 2004. Web. 15 Nov. 2005.

In this essay, Carter provides a very detailed definition of integrity and a thoughtful discussion of applications of the concept of integrity to difficult real-world situations.

These examples helped me see that I could connect the concept of integrity with the United States' and United Nations' lack of response to the atrocities in Rwanda. This essay will be central to my paper because I want to show that integrity demanded that they intervene.

United Nations General Assembly. "Convention on the Prevention and Punishment of The Crime of Genocide." 1948. Web. 15 Nov. 2005. <http://www.hrweb.org/legal/genocide.html>.

The 19 articles of this United Nations document state clearly that genocide is a political as well as a moral crime. It specifies genocidal acts, such as killing a group's members, aiming to destroy a group, preventing birth of or taking its children, and causing physical and mental harm that will prevent a group from maintaining its way of life.

This primary document provides valuable context and support for my paper's thesis. I will use it to show that in addition to the moral obligation to intervene in Rwanda, there was a contractual obligation as well.

FIGURE 14.3
Sample Annotated Bibliography Entries

Integrating Source Material

Research has often been described as an endless conversation. The formats in which academic work is presented reflect the metaphor of research as conversation by indicating who is saying what.

The most important point to remember is that *you* are the person presenting the information in your paper. You are, in effect, participating in a conversation with your sources and your readers. Your paper is not just a series of quotations and paraphrases from sources; instead, it is a presentation of your ideas about the issue and your thinking about what your sources have said.

Introducing Sources

An extension of the notion of research as conversation is seeing a research paper as analogous to a dignified television or radio talk show or a panel discussion about a current issue. Think of yourself as a talk-show host as you write a paper that uses source material. Just as the host sets up the discussion, you will provide a context and a clear purpose for presenting the material that you have found. Just as the host introduces each guest to the audience, you will select sources your audience will be interested in and respect. Just as the host helps the guests interact, you will point out the connections and oppositions between and among your sources. And just as the host wraps the show up, you will conclude your paper in an effective manner.

To be considerate of your audience, you will need to know how academic writers introduce a source into a paper. Here are some techniques:

- *Use the name of the author, especially a significant writer or scholar:*

  "Elizabeth Cady Stanton wrote that 'it is the duty of the women of this country to secure to themselves their sacred right to the elective franchise.'"

- *Use the name of the publication:*

  "A *New York Times* article provides guidelines for evaluating information found on the Web. It says…"

- *Establish a context:*

  "Students now receive much advice about how to decide whether information found on the Internet is likely to be good or useless. For example, an article in the *New York Times* provides a list of hints and warnings. This article says…"

- *Indicate your purpose for presenting the information.* This is part of the research conversation. You are talking about the source. In the following passage, a student has commented in his own voice both before and after paraphrasing from a source.

Student

Integrity is at the heart of my position on this situation. According to Stephen L. Carter in his essay "The Insufficiency of Honesty," integrity is much more than acting or appearing noble when dealing with a situation. He says that there are three steps in defining the degree of one's integrity. These are "discerning what is right and what is wrong; acting on what you have discerned, even at personal cost; and saying openly you are acting on your understanding of what is right and what is wrong" (507).

Source

Obviously the massacre of 800,000 innocent people is inherently wrong; having knowledge that a massacre of 800,000 people is about to occur is inherently wrong, and not acting on this legitimate intelligence is painfully misguided. It is completely devoid of any semblance of integrity.

Student

Establishing Your Voice

You will use your own voice in your research writing to fulfill several purposes. First, as just explained, you will always signal in some way that you are introducing source material into your paper. In addition, as the author of a paper, not just a complier of other people's ideas, you might

- *Comment on what sources say.* You should indicate your purpose for including the source material in the paper. You could express agreement or disagreement with particular sources. You might explain which sources you consider most important to the points you are making in the paper. Providing such commentary is an important part of your role as "host."
- *Synthesize what sources say.* You should discuss ways in which sources relate to each other. You might point out a chronological sequence of concepts or explain how theories differ from each other. You could show how sources agree.
- *Present your own thinking.* You have established a thesis for your paper, and, of course, you will present ideas to support it. You might explain why you agree with one source or a group of sources or why you differ from them all and have your own claim to put forth. You might present ideas that have come from your experiences, your observations, your interpretations, or your creative thinking.

You need to clarify when you are speaking in order to be credited for your ideas and comments, just as you must indicate when your sources are speaking so that proper credit is given to them.

Your voice should be easily identifiable as long as you have indicated where all source material begins and ends. Then everything else is either your commentary, your synthesis, or your own thinking. Often, you will want to use words or phrases to show that you are commenting—such as "Therefore," "A consideration of these concepts shows . . .," or "Another significant idea is . . ."

Choosing Point of View

If your instructor agrees, you could simply present some of your comments and ideas as first-person statements: "I want to suggest . . ."; "After analyzing these reports, I decided . . ."; "I believe . . ." However, there is an academic tradition that discourages the use of the first person singular pronoun (*I*) in order to suggest an objective and impersonal point of view. This tradition is stronger in some disciplines than in others. You should ask your instructors about the preferred pronoun use in research papers and also look at pronoun use in academic journals in the fields in which you are studying.

Also be careful about using *we*. Be sure you identify who "we" is—people sometimes use the word to mean society at large, the citizens of a particular country, or the readers of a particular newspaper or magazine. However, your readers should never have to assume. In addition, the second person (*you*) is rarely used in academic writing.

Thinking-Writing Activity

CLARIFYING WHO IS TALKING

1. Look at the student paper at the end of this chapter, at other documented papers in this book, or at a research paper in your handbook. Notice how the student writers introduce other people's ideas into their papers. Then write a paragraph about what you have observed. Quote some different ways in which these student writers bring sources into their papers.

2. Notice how the writers clarify what their own thinking is about the source material or about the point that the source is being used to support. Identify two specific places where student writers are speaking in their own voices.

Think about how this activity might help you to write your next documented paper and to avoid creating a paper that is just a string of quotations and paraphrases of others' ideas.

The Logic Behind Documentation

Reasons for Documentation

Two principles underlie academic documentation formats:

- Readers have to know *who* says something.
- Readers have to know *where* something is said.

All academic formats provide this information in logical systems whether they use parentheses, endnotes, or footnotes. Different disciplines use different formats, but they are all based on these two principles. Your handbook or guide to research will explain most of the formats, such as those adopted by the American Psychological

Association (APA), the Council of Science Editors (CSE), and the Modern Language Association (MLA). Also, these associations maintain websites on which you can find the most current format models. Guidelines to the MLA and APA styles are in this book's appendix.

Researchers clarify who said something and where it was said for a number of reasons:

- *To give credibility to a paper.* The strength or weakness of source materials helps readers judge the strength or weakness of a research project and its presentation.

- *To help readers and other researchers learn more.* Proper documentation can direct readers to sources so that they can find out more about a subject than what is presented in a paper.

- *To give credit where credit is due.* Research papers combine many people's ideas. Democracy tells us that each person is important. Giving appropriate credit shows respect for the human being who expressed the idea being used. Further, out of self-respect, researchers and writers want their own ideas to be credited to them just as much as they want to acknowledge others' ideas.

- *To observe the courtesies of conversation.* If research is a millennia-long conversation, the courtesies of conversation are in order. People take turns speaking during a conversation; sometimes points are recapped; often questions are asked and answered. It is usually important to know who is speaking in a conversation.

- *To avoid plagiarism.*

Thinking-Writing Activity

CITING AND PARAPHRASING

Students usually know that quoted material of a sentence or more must be documented. However, students sometimes have difficulty understanding that paraphrases and quotations of short, "apt phrases" must also be cited. Read the following passage that was written by Lynn Z. Bloom and appears on page 90 of the eighth edition of *The Essay Connection*, published by Houghton Mifflin in 2007:

> *Original passage:* "Narratives have as many purposes, as many plots, as many characters as there are people to write them. You have but to examine your life, your thoughts, your experiences, to find an unwritten library of narratives yet to tell."

(Continues)

Why is this use acceptable?

1. Lynn Bloom points out that all people have stories worth telling if they will just look into their lives and experiences where they will "find an unwritten library of narratives." (90)
   Why could this use be seen as plagiarism by some or as an error in punctuation by others? What do you think?

2. Each person's life can be seen as holding an unwritten library of narratives. (Bloom 90)
   Where do you see plagiarism here?

3. Storytelling may be one of the defining characteristics of the human species. Stories come in countless forms, and have been told in various ways by almost everybody who has ever lived. Indeed, narratives have as many purposes, as many plots, as many characters as there are people to tell them.

The Logic of MLA Style

The MLA system is used in this book because it is widely used in English classes and the humanities. To understand how it works, look at the paper at the end of this chapter or at a model in your handbook or guide to research.

1. First, note that at the end of a paper, there is a list of Works Cited, with the sources listed alphabetically according to *author,* or if no author is given, according to the *title* of the source. Full bibliographic information is given in this list so that it does not have to be provided in the parenthetical citations within the body of the paper.

2. Next, look at the places within the paper where sources are cited. Note that when material has been taken from a source, the last name or an abbreviated title under which it is listed in Works Cited is given—either when the material is introduced or in parentheses at the end of its use. The number of the page on which the material can be found is given in parentheses at the end of the quotation or paraphrase. The parentheses signal the end of the source material.

3. If a source does not have a page number, then a number cannot be given, so you must otherwise signal that use of the source has ended. Many online documents do not show page numbers, so you must be careful to indicate where your use of such a source ends.

Thinking-Writing Activity

EXPLAINING THE MLA SYSTEM

1. Look again at the documented paper in this chapter or in your handbook. Then write an explanation of how the MLA system works as illustrated in that paper. Explain the relationship between the Works Cited list and the parenthetical citations.

2. Next, explain the MLA system to a classmate. Then tell your classmate why you believe the reasons for documentation are important. See if she or he agrees.

Working Thoughtfully on Research Projects

Much of the work you do to produce a research paper is similar to what you do when you write from your own resources. However, research projects often involve some special steps and concerns, including scheduling a significant amount of time, planning your paper carefully, using a specified academic format, and, often, consulting with librarians and with your instructor.

Time

No one needs to tell you that you cannot just sit down and write up the results of a research project in a short hour spent at your keyboard. Reading, evaluating, selecting, noting, commenting on, and arranging material demands the use of critical and creative thinking processes that usually cannot be hurried.

Using a library can involve waiting for help from a librarian, learning to use the computerized catalog, searching the shelves for material, seeing interesting material that doesn't pertain to your paper, and, of course, having to read, evaluate, copy, take notes, and think about what you've found. College libraries are pleasant places where time is usually well spent—and where you will spend much time while working on a research project.

Deciding on the scope of a project, working though research questions, narrowing a topic, interviewing knowledgeable persons, and revising and qualifying a thesis all take time.

Therefore, you should make a schedule when you begin a research project. You must complete the project within the time frame that your instructor allows. Instructors usually give weeks or months for research projects, but it is amazing how quickly that time evaporates and how suddenly deadlines are staring you in the face. Start as soon as you are given the assignment. Block out time to work on it regularly. Be sure to follow any time line that your instructor establishes.

One instructor gives her students this checklist:

Research Project Checklist	Due Date	Date(s) Completed
Decide on focus	_____	_____
Develop research questions	_____	_____
Locate and evaluate sources (ongoing)	_____	_____
Select and read sources (ongoing)	_____	_____
Identify useful sources; take notes	_____	_____
Develop thesis	_____	_____
Develop working outline	_____	_____
Draft sections of paper	_____	_____
Conference with instructor	_____	_____
Draft(s) of complete paper	_____	_____
Peer review	_____	_____
Revise, edit, and proofread paper	_____	_____
Hand in completed paper and all required material	_____	_____

Remember that this checklist makes research seem more linear and less recursive than it usually is.

Planning and Outlining

Since research papers are often longer than essays or reports, planning and outlining are important steps. You will probably have to gather information before you can see what shape your paper will take, but as soon as you can, you will want to block out the sections of the paper and make a working outline (to be changed as the paper develops). If your instructor requires that a formal outline be submitted with your finished paper, look at the paper at the end of this chapter or consult your handbook for a model. Some word-processing programs include formal outlines in their formatting options, so your computer might help you create an outline.

Formats and Models

You must use an accepted academic documentation format when you write a research paper for a college class. You cannot be creative about documentation. You must follow the models exactly. You should also familiarize yourself with the style, design, and format your instructor requires for the presentation of your research paper.

Collaboration

The research conducted in business, at large laboratories, and by think tanks and professional organizations is often done by teams. Therefore, to give students this experience, some instructors may assign team projects in college classes. But even if the project that you will be working on will be an individual effort, other people can provide much help. You will want to work with your instructor, the librarians, computer experts, and your classmates as much as you can as you complete your research. See Chapter 6, pages 169–171 for using peer response groups as a revising strategy.

Writing Project: A Research Paper

This chapter emphasizes the reasoning behind many of the activities that occur while you are engaged in research. The Thinking-Writing Activities should help you find and use information. Be sure to reread what you wrote for those activities.

> Following all instructions given by your instructor, complete a research project and write a well-documented paper in which you report and discuss your findings.

Begin by considering the key elements in the Thinking-Writing Model in Chapter 1 on page 6–7.

The Writing Situation

Purpose   Your two major purposes for research are to learn as much as you can about your topic and then to present your thinking about your findings in an effective paper. Also, you can improve your ability to use your college library and the Internet. You can also become more skilled at using and better understanding academic formats. In addition, you will further develop your critical and creative thinking abilities as you apply almost every concept presented in this book to your research project.

As tempting as this "mental blender" approach to research might appear, there is at this time no substitute for research based on thoughtful exploration, effective planning, productive collaboration, and above all, critical thinking.

Audience   If your classmates are working on similar projects, they will be an excellent audience for your finished paper as well as for drafts. If your research topic is about a social or political issue, your audience might include people beyond your college. Perhaps you can find a way to share what you've learned at a community forum; in a newspaper, newsletter, or listserv; or on a website. Your instructor remains the audience who will judge how well you have shaped your research question, investigated possible answers, discussed what you have found, and documented your paper in the required academic format.

Subject   Obviously, you should be interested in the subject of your research so that your work will be a pleasure rather than a chore. If the subject is significant in your life or connected with one of your favorite academic fields, you should be able to think of a stimulating research question. If the subject has been assigned and, perhaps, is not among your interests, do everything you can to connect it to your interests. Ask questions about it, read as widely as you can, and consult websites. You will almost surely find issues within any subject that you can relate to your own concerns.

Writer   If you've already worked on research projects in previous classes, you should feel confident as you undertake this one, but you should be willing to improve your abilities throughout the entire process. Be your most efficient self by setting up a schedule, working steadily, and meeting all deadlines. Don't hesitate to ask for help from librarians, computer room staff, and your instructor.

Remember the talk-show analogy presented in this chapter: you are the host, in charge of the paper. Comment on what you discover during your investigation; present your own thinking and keep yourself in the paper as much as is appropriate to the subject, to the traditions of the discipline in which you are working, and to your assignment.

The Writing Process

Much of the material already presented in this chapter relates to generating ideas, finding a focus, and defining a thesis as you work on a research project. You should review it before you begin your paper.

Generating Ideas

- As you use the technique of asking questions about your subject, look again at the questions presented in Chapter 4 (pages 99–101). Apply as many of those questions as you can.

- Brainstorm and freewrite as you begin your research project, just as you would do when writing a paper from your own experience. "Talk to yourself" on paper about what you want to investigate and what you want to say about the topic.

- Use the thinking patterns discussed in Chapters 7 to 10 as ways to find ideas. Ask yourself about any processes involved in your subject. Describe important objects connected with it. Think about similarities and differences within it. Identify causal relationships. Define important terms. And be sure to write down what the thinking patterns show you.

- Before you decide on a limited focus, read widely about your subject. Consult encyclopedias and websites to get background information and ideas.

Defining a Thesis or Making a Claim   As you turn your research question (or questions) into a tentative thesis statement or claim, you need to be sure that your thesis or claim reflects the rhetorical purpose of your paper. Are you explaining, describing, or presenting different points of views? In that case, you will need to create a thesis statement. Or are you arguing for a specific position? For a researched argument, you will need to match and support a claim.

Notice how the documented student papers in Chapters 8 and 10 explain their topics. Notice how Joshua Bartlett's paper in Chapter 12 and the paper in Chapter 13 argue for specific changes. Notice how the paper in this chapter argues for a claim.

Draft more than one possible thesis statement or claim and then decide which one best serves your purposes. Remember that you may refocus your paper as you draft and revise it, so you should be open to reshaping your thesis statement or claim as you rework the paper.

Organizing Ideas   Research papers, are usually divided into logically distinguished sections. As you organize your paper, you need to think about how the material that you have found pertains to different aspects of the topic. And in an interactive process, as your research develops, the material you find will suggest different points that you may want to develop.

For example, if you are researching changes in beliefs about healthy diets, you might divide your paper chronologically or according to food groups, depending on what you decide to emphasize. If you are researching homelessness in a community in order to present an overview of it to an audience of relatively affluent young people, your paper might include almost equally developed sections on the estimated numbers of homeless people, the causes of homelessness, and the programs to help the homeless. If your purpose is to argue for improved programs, your paper might have a short introductory section on the numbers and causes and well-developed sections on various options for helping the homeless.

If you have used note cards and classified them according to the aspect of your topic to which they contribute, you can easily arrange and rearrange them as you incorporate information into your draft. If you have taken notes on your computer, you can print files and/or copy and organize. If you have assembled printouts and photocopies of articles and pages, you'll need to identify the parts of your paper where this information belongs and sort it appropriately. If you have a combination of downloaded material, photocopies, and written notes—which is likely—you will need to put them in logical piles or arrange them near your keyboard in a way that will help you to incorporate information and keep track of where every item came from.

Outlines are usually necessary planning tools for long research papers. You should draft working outlines several times during your research process. If your instructor requires a formal outline, you can write one at the end of your planning, after you have completed a draft or after you finish the paper. A formal outline will provide a good measure of the organization of your paper.

Drafting   Drafting a research paper differs from drafting a personal paper in one important way: you must remember to indicate within the draft where source material begins, where it ends, where it is from, and whether it is quoted or paraphrased. In a draft, citation formats and wordings of the signals that indicate a source do not have to be perfect. You can polish these up when you revise and edit, but to avoid accidental plagiarism, you must keep track of this material as you draft.

One decision you will have to make during drafting is whether to quote, paraphrase, or summarize source material. This is not always an easy choice. You do not want to quote too much, yet you do need to report what sources say. You should read documented papers and articles in your fields of interest in order to develop a sense of how experienced academic writers use their sources. Notice how these writers use short quotations, long quotations, paraphrases, and summaries.

The following are some guidelines for deciding what to quote, paraphrase, or summarize:

- You probably should quote if what a source has said is worded in a special way, is complicated or technical, or is controversial.

- If you are still learning about the field that your sources are discussing, you might need to quote more than an expert would.

- You should not use many long quoted passages. If you include a lot of lengthy quotations, you may end up compiling a small anthology instead of writing a paper.

- Remember that you do not have to quote whole sentences; often a few words will suffice. Example: In contrasting facts and theories, Stephen Jay Gould calls facts "the world's data" and theories "structures of ideas that explain and interpret facts." (page 419 in Chapter 11)

- You might want to quote fairly extensively in an early draft and then ask your classmates, writing center tutors, or instructor for help with shortening quotations and paraphrasing.

- *Paraphrasing,* or restating another's ideas in your own words, requires a good vocabulary and well-developed critical reading skills. Ask yourself as you are drafting: "Let's see. What is this source saying? How do these ideas help develop my paper?" Then write your answers and see how they might help you to incorporate the source into your paper.

- You use *summaries* to show the main points of an article, section, chapter, book, or Internet source. Remember to explain the significance of the summarized material.

Remember that you must always signal the beginning and end of source used, and cite appropriately, whether you are quoting, paraphrasing, or summarizing.

You should remain aware of your talk-show host role as you comment on what you have used from your sources. You will probably need to draft your statements several times as you reread your notes and sources and rethink what you want to say.

Revising, Editing, and Proofreading   Use the Step-by-Step Method in Chapter 6 on pages 169–171 to revise your essay and prepare a final draft.

Annotated Student Research Paper with Outline and Drafts

The paper on pages 574–582 was written for an English composition course that emphasizes exposition, argument, and research. A sequence of reading and writing assignments led up to the paper assignment. Students responded to each other's drafts during two peer review sessions. Chris Buxton-Smith describes how he thought about his writing situation and writing process.

Chris Buxton-Smith's Writing Situation

Purpose   Midway through the semester, our instructor gave us an assignment for which we were to choose one of several concepts and write an argument of at least six pages, using a minimum of four sources. The essay was to address a specific concept in order to argue for or against a particular act or position. Among the concepts were *masculinity, femininity, racism,* and *integrity,* as well as a whole slew of others that pertained to readings we had been assigned throughout the semester. The purpose was to demonstrate our understanding of the concept and our proficiency at writing a strong argumentation paper. After some thought, I saw that I might be able to choose a subject that, since my late teens, I had always wanted to write about: the Rwandan Genocide that left nearly a million ethnic Tutsis dead.

Audience   I identified my audience as my classmates, who could also be regarded as a portion of the general American public, most of whom were in the dark about the atrocities that occurred in 1994 in the African country of Rwanda. Many Americans had not been aware that a genocide was occurring, even under the watchful eye of the world press. In class, after a peer review, classmates were awed by the fact that such things could occur in this seemingly modern world where almost a million people were scratched from existence in only one hundred days, in spite of the potential of United States military power and the possibility of diplomacy by the United Nations. I wanted to open my audience's eyes.

Subject   When I started, I was torn between [writing on one of the suggested] concepts and [determining] how I could effectively apply one to a pertinent subject in which I had great interest. I knew I could take the easier route and write a straightforward essay addressing one of the concepts in a one-dimensional fashion. Instead, I chose a pair that had a number of controversial details to discuss. I opted for the concept of *integrity* and how it applied to the United States' and the United Nations' involvement, or lack thereof, in the Rwandan Genocide. In the end, I was able to connect the two in a way that met the demands of the assignment.

Writer   After reading about the situation that occurred in Rwanda in a book called *We Wish to Inform You That Tomorrow You Will be Killed with Your Families* by Phillip Gourevitch, I became haunted by the subject of modern-day mass genocide. I tried to write the paper in a state of sort of suspended ignorance in order to keep an open mind since I had already read the book on Rwanda, and I had preconceived emotions about the subject. When I began researching, I tried to check those emotions at the door and allow myself to remain open to a fresh perspective. But, in the end, my research reinvigorated my anger and confusion about how genocides still occur.

Chris's Writing Process

Brainstorming   The process I used to write this paper was relatively straightforward. Using techniques of which I had prior knowledge and new ones that I learned in class, I set about writing. The first step was to brainstorm. Using this technique, I was able to come up with numerous ideas, no matter the quality, and choose from among them a subject that I could combine with a concept given by our instructor. Even the most outlandish idea was not subject to disposal. I found brainstorming very helpful because I wrote down possible subjects to think about.

Finding a focus   After brainstorming for a while, I set about choosing a concept and subject. In choosing *integrity*, I found myself with a general concept that needed to be narrowed down to address a specific aspect or act of integrity. At first, I thought integrity would be difficult to write about; but in combination with the subject of Rwanda, everything began to come together.

Researching   My next steps, and perhaps the most important ones, were researching my subject and finding quality sources to use. Since I had two topics which I had to bring together, I needed to find sources about each and combine them. Using books, periodicals, and online resources, I was able to dredge up enough information in what I thought were legitimate sources.

Organizing   Generating a working outline was a very important step in my writing process. Since so much information is usually contained amidst the clutter of notes, I found it very helpful to filter out information and organize it in a fashion that was easily viewable when I sat down to write my first draft. Honestly, though, my outline was rather sparse because I found myself really getting into freewriting about the subject. Sometimes, when one has strong feelings about a subject, the words just flow. Eventually, I was able to trim my content down and develop clear paragraphs.

Drafting and revising   As I said, my drafting process consists of a lot of freewriting in confluence with my outline. I took the items in the outline, wrote topic sentences explaining them, and developed the paragraphs accordingly. Often, I found myself with too much content. So I tried to streamline each sentence, omitting redundant ideas. Oddly enough, this seemingly redundant material often proved valuable in later paragraphs when I thought I was stuck—but then saw that those points fit in.

Finishing   After a peer review session, I set about typing my final draft, using peer input combined with extra proofreading. I took into account everything I had learned about writing an argument and using sources. In addition, I added heartfelt conviction to a subject that I believe needed to be addressed.

Chris's Working Outline
Lest We Forget Rwanda
- I. Introduction/thesis
- II. Integrity
  - Integrity and Rwanda
  - Definition

III. Background
  - Conflict between the two ethnicities
  - Revolution and power struggle
  - Rise of Hutu power
IV. World awareness
  - Initially world not aware
  - America's stance on war and intervention
  - U.N. resolution
 V. Genocide
  - Definition of *genocide*
  - Goal of the Hutu government regarding Tutsis
  - U.N. and U.S. viewed conflict as a civil war
VI. Civil war
VII. Misinformation/ignoring intelligence
  - Hutu security official's fax
VIII. Intervention
 IX. Lack of morality/integrity
  X. Conclusion/thesis

Sample Annotated Research Paper

Chris Buxton-Smith "Lest We Forget About Rwanda"

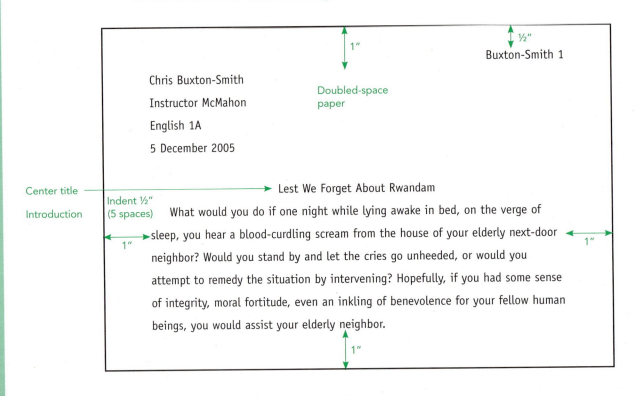

1"   ½"
Buxton-Smith 1

Chris Buxton-Smith

Instructor McMahon   Doubled-space
paper
English 1A

5 December 2005

Center title ——→   Lest We Forget About Rwandam

Introduction   Indent ½"
(5 spaces)   What would you do if one night while lying awake in bed, on the verge of

1"   sleep, you hear a blood-curdling scream from the house of your elderly next-door   1"

neighbor? Would you stand by and let the cries go unheeded, or would you

attempt to remedy the situation by intervening? Hopefully, if you had some sense

of integrity, moral fortitude, even an inkling of benevolence for your fellow human

beings, you would assist your elderly neighbor.

1"

Buxton-Smith 2

This comparison is a microcosm of a situation that occurred in the African country of Rwanda. According to Philip Gourevitch—author, journalist, and the editor of *The Paris Review,* "In Rwanda, in the course of 100 days in the spring and early summer of 1994, 800,000 people were put to death in the most unambiguous case of state-sponsored genocide in an attempt to exterminate a category of humanity, a people, since the Nazi Holocaust of the Jews of Europe" (*Triumph*). This massacre was one of the most expeditious and brutally efficient genocides in terms of the number of people that were killed in a relatively short period of time.

The question I must pose is: Should the United States and the United Nations have, as a matter of integrity, intervened in the situation? Understandably, many would say no. The U.S. is not the police force of the world, and the U.N. must adhere to a strict set of guidelines before it embarks on any peacekeeping mission. Many people feel that the two bodies must allow countries to carry out and conduct their own internal affairs whenever possible. I agree; but where do we draw the line that allows a nation to maintain its political sovereignty when its government sponsors the massacre of a portion of its own population? My answer is that America and the United Nations did, as a matter of integrity, have a moral obligation to intervene in the Rwandan massacre.

Integrity is at the heart of my position on this situation. Law professor and author Stephen L. Carter observes in his essay "The Insufficiency of Honesty" that integrity is more than acting nobly when dealing with a situation. He says that there are three steps in defining the degree of one's integrity. These are "discerning what is right and what is wrong; acting on what you have discerned, even at personal cost; and saying openly you are acting on your understanding of what is right and what is wrong" (507). Obviously the massacre of 800,000 innocent people is inherently wrong; having knowledge that a massacre of 800,000 people is about to occur is inherently wrong, and not acting on this legitimate intelligence is painfully misguided. It is completely devoid of any semblance of integrity.

Background information; source identified, quotation of four lines or fewer not indented.

Research question

Background information; preview of specific points

Statement of thesis or claim; answer to research question

Warrants

Page number given; essay source

Buxton-Smith 3

Background
information

In order to understand the birth of the complex conflict between the two native ethnic groups in Rwanda, the Hutus and the Tutsis, it is necessary to have some background on the matter. Rwanda is located in central Africa, surrounded by Burundi, the Democratic Republic of the Congo, Tanzania, and Uganda.

Before the Germans and then the Belgians colonized Rwanda, there was little racial distinction or tension between the two groups; what tension there was, was due to the disproportionate distribution of economic wealth and political power. Gourevitch explains: "Until the late 19th century, which is to say, until European colonization, Tutsis (the minority) represented the aristocratic upper classes; Hutus were the peasant masses." Then, when the Europeans arrived, they used the pre-existing socioeconomic situation as a skeleton for the new colonial government that was implemented. They "took this traditional structure and made it even more extreme and more polarized into an almost apartheid-like system. And ethnic identity cards were issued, and Tutsis were privileged for all things, and Hutus were really made into a very oppressed mass" (*Triumph*).

Rwanda gained independence from Belgium in 1962. Then, Gourevitch reports, a revolution occurred. After years of oppression, the Hutus finally gained power over the Tutsis. They took over the country's government institutions and infrastructure; this new-found power, coupled with resentment towards their Tutsi counterparts, began a new era of Hutu power movements. With this new era came the social oppression of the once powerful Tutsis. There was "...a Hutu dictatorship running through the '60s, the '70s, the '80s, and into the mid '90s. Throughout that period, there was systematic political violence used to maintain this Hutu power" (*Triumph*).

According to Gourevitch, this violence climaxed when the slaughter of the Tutsis began in 1994, after Hutu President Habyarimana was killed when his plane was apparently shot down. Habyarimana was engaged in peace talks sanctioned by the U.N. in order to establish a cease fire between the rival groups, which—it

Source quoted, paraphrased, and quoted; on-line source—no page numbers

Source worked into a sentence

Buxton-Smith 4

has been suggested—militant Hutu leaders did not want. These militant leaders incited the massacre by building ethnic hatred of the Tutsis and saying that the Tutsis had killed the president (*Triumph*).

Initially, the world was not well informed about the situation in Rwanda because conflicting stories from inside sources, chaos within the country, and biased intelligence from within the Hutu regime clouded the brutal reality of the situation. The United States and the United Nations had been aware of some escalating violence and tension between the groups, but they seem to have shrugged it off as a conflict limited to within the Rwandan border. They did not intervene.

America's involvement in international conflicts has long been the topic of heated bipartisan and civilian debate, ranging from general support for the "World Wars" to heavy protest against the Vietnam War. U.S. involvement in a sovereign nation's war with another country, or with a country's civil war, is drastically different from U.S. involvement in a government-sponsored genocide like the one that occurred in Rwanda. However, both America's stance on genocide and the action required when it is occurring are clear. On December 9, 1948, the U.S., as a member of the United Nations, adopted a resolution, specifically resolution 260 (III), which states as follows: "The contracting parties confirm that genocide, whether committed in time of peace or in time of war, is a crime under international law which they undertake to prevent and to punish" (United Nations). Not only did America and the U.N. have a moral obligation to assist with the situation in Rwanda; they had a contractual obligation as well.

As a result of the European Holocaust of the 1930s and 40s, the word *genocide* was coined; it means "'the destruction of a nation or of an ethnic group' and implies the existence of a coordinated plan aimed at total extermination" (Destexhe, quoting Raphael Lemkin). This describes the goal of the Hutu government, Gourevitch claims, especially officials with close ties to the recently

Source para-phrased and cited

Student writer synthesizing information that is generally accepted

Warrants

Source using a source

Buxton-Smith 5

assassinated president. With no evidence, they blamed Tutsi extremists for the assassination, using it as a rallying call for Hutu militias to take up arms against their Tutsi neighbors. For decades, intermittent massacres had been occurring at the hands of Hutu extremists with the full knowledge of the government. To the rest of the world, including the United States, this appeared to be nothing more than a decades-long power struggle between two ethnic parties vying for political control; in essence, a civil war (*Triumph*).

United Nations and United States foreign policy dictate that, unless crimes against humanity are being committed, it is a violation of a nation's sovereignty to intervene in a civil war. A civil war, according to The *American Heritage Dictionary of the English Language, Fourth Edition* is "1. A war between factions or regions of the same country. 2. A state of hostility or conflict between elements within an organization." This seemed like what was occurring in Rwanda, but in reality the Tutsis had no political power or influence; they had no representatives in the government because the rule was totalitarian under the Hutu party. However, "much of the reporting said, 'The civil war has been renewed in Rwanda.' But a civil war involves two or more armies fighting one another—a rebel army and a government army. And it means that soldiers fight soldiers. The objective is to defeat the other party" (Gourevitch *Triumph*). Under this premise, the United Nations and the United States did not intervene.

Unfortunately, the premise upon which the U.S. and the U.N. did not intervene was not simply a case of misinformation; rather, it was a case of ignoring viable intelligence from a legitimate source within the Hutu regime. Gourevitch reports that on January 14, 1994, a Hutu security advisor sent a fax to the United Nations intelligence office alerting U.N. officials to the situation he knew was about to occur. This Hutu official was in the upper echelon of the party and was aware that his government was about to sponsor a massacre against unarmed Tutsi civilians. The official stated in his fax that he been hired

[margin notes:]

Synthesis of material; source worked into sentence

Source paraphrased and cited

Buxton-Smith 6

by the now-deceased president's political party to train the Interahamawe, a Hutu power militia, in order to orchestrate the extermination of the Tutsis (*Triumph*). No one listened.

Only after the killings of a small contingent of Belgian U.N. peacekeepers and the identification of large arms caches, did the U.N. define the situation as genocide:

> By early June, the Secretary-General of the U.N.—and even, . . . the French Foreign Minister—had taken to describing the slaughter in Rwanda as "genocide." But the U.N. High Commissioner for Human Rights still favored the phrase "possible genocide," while the Clinton administration actually forbade unqualified use of the g-word. The official formulation approved by the White House was: "acts of genocide may have occurred." (Gourevitch *Genocide*)

The U.S., after suffering a recent humiliation in the peacekeeping mission of Somalia, chose not to intervene. In addition, officials may have wanted to appear "respectful" of a sovereign nation's boundaries and its affairs within those boundaries.

Not only was there no intervention by the U.S., but little attention was paid by the U.S. government to the genocide in Rwanda. In her Pulitzer Prize–winning book *"A Problem from Hell": America and the Age of Genocide,* Samantha Power states, "It is shocking to note that during the entire three months of the genocide, Clinton never assembled his top policy advisors to discuss the killings." Power offers this explanation: "Rwanda generated no sense of urgency and could safely be avoided by Clinton at no political cost" (366). America and the United Nations, a country and an organization built upon the idea of maintaining freedom and integrity in regards to the civilized world, chose to ignore the desperate cries for help from an African nation on the brink of disaster.

Material omitted (. . .)

Four lines or more quoted, indented; no quotation marks.

Buxton-Smith 7

Clearly, both the United States and the United Nations, in their failure to intervene, lacked any sense of integrity regarding the massacre in Rwanda; moral and lawful obligation deemed it necessary that action be taken. Because no action was taken, they subsequently violated standards and ethics upon which the frames of both bodies were built. Stephen L. Carter states this about the Rwanda situation in an article in *Christianity Today:*

> In cases of genocide, we often hear opponents of unilateral action say that it is up to the world community to act. But this argument touches only expediency, not morality. We can well imagine a war that is morally imperative even though every country in the world lines up against it. We can also imagine a war that is morally prohibited even though every country supports it. If protecting a people against the ravages of their own sovereign is indeed a matter of moral urgency, one cannot shirk it on the ground that others do not agree. ("Defending")

Summing up

It is true that the U.N. was created to be an organization where collective decisions lead to unified action in regards to world affairs; but when those collective decisions and their subsequent actions become mired in a political bog of allegiances and futile hopes of letting the situation run its course, action must be taken to preserve the sanctity of morality and the safety of the world. Carter again makes a poignant statement on the issue when he says that "the morality of humanitarian intervention has nothing to do with whether others agree that the action is appropriate" ("Defending").

Our country and our world now have the blood of over 800,000 innocent men, women, and children on their hands because people with bureaucratic allegiances and obligations could not see past the red tape hindering their views of the reality in the Rwanda situation. In 1848, the American philosopher and author Henry David Thoreau—angered by the Mexican War—wrote this about American integrity: "This American government,—what is it but a tradition, though a recent

Buxton-Smith 8

one, endeavoring to transmit itself unimpaired to posterity, but each instant
losing some of its integrity." The mistakes of the past should not cement
our reactions towards events of the future. In times of peril, we must not
let past actions cloud our response to imminent threats of human barbarity
and depravity.

Conclusion; restatement of the claim or thesis

As one nation and a part of one world, the United States cannot turn a deaf
ear to the cries of a people under duress. The United Nations and the United
States must remain vigilant towards maintaining the integrity of the rules and the
laws that they have established, through consistent enforcement of resolutions
like that of resolution 260 (III), lest we forget about those one hundred terrible
days in Rwanda.

Restatement of title

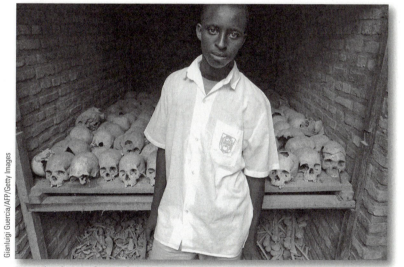

Gianluigi Guercia/AFP/Getty Images

Rwandan boy in front of skulls from Rwandans massacred during the genocide.

Electronic publication; simultaneous print publication

Article in print anthology

Electronic version of print dictionary

Online posting of television program

Book

Web site

Works Cited

Carter, Stephen. L. "Defending Our Neighbor." *Christianity Today.* Christianity Today International, Nov. 2004. Web. 15 Nov. 2005.

"Civil war." *The American Heritage Dictionary of the English Language.* 4th ed. Boston: Houghton, 2000. Web. 1 Dec. 2005.

Destexhe, Alain. *The Crime of Genocide.* 1995. Web. 15 Nov. 2005.

Gourevitch, Philip. Genocide in Rwanda as quoted in "Glimpses of Tyranny and Resistance" 2003. Web. 10 Nov. 2005.

———. *The Triumph of Evil.* 1996. Web. 10 Nov. 2005. "The Insufficiency of Honesty." *Great Writing.* Ed. Harvey S. Weiner and Nora Eisenberg. San Francisco: McGraw, 2002. 507–12. Print.

Power, Samantha. *A Problem from Hell: America and the Age of Genocide.* New York: Perennial, 2003. Print.

"Rwanda." *The Free Dictionary.* Farlex. Web. 1 Dec. 2005.

"The Rwandan Genocide through Photographs." *Rwanda.* Web. 1 Dec. 2005. <http://emileelime.tripod.com/id5.html>.

Thoreau, Henry David. *The Columbia World of Quotations.* New York: Columbia UP, 1996. Web. 20 Nov. 2005.

United Nations General Assembly. "Convention on the Prevention and Punishment of the Crime of Genocide." 1948. Web. 15 Nov. 2005. <http://www.hrweb.org/legal/genocide.html>.

CHAPTER 14 Summary

- Researchers use questions to help them identify and focus their topic.

- *Primary resources* include original documents, works of literature, and firsthand reports, observations, or interviews; *secondary resources* comment on other resources.

- When doing research, you can use electronic and print sources in the library, collect information from experts, or obtain data from the field through interviews, questionnaires, and field research.

- To evaluate sources for a research project, you should ask yourself: how reliable is the source? How knowledgeable or experienced is the author? and What specific ideas are being presented?

- To evaluate the reliability of a website, you need to determine its authority, accuracy, objectivity, and currency.

- *Plagiarism*, presenting another person's ideas or words as your own, is a serious offense. Avoid plagiarism by documenting your sources in your research paper thoroughly and accurately.

- *Quoting* is using someone's exact words; *paraphrasing* is restating an idea in your own words. Use quotation marks *only* for quotes, but credit the source for *both* quotes and paraphrased ideas. Information considered common knowledge does not require quotes or documentation.

- To keep track of your research and ensure proper documentation of your sources, take notes on your computer and/or on note cards, create an annotated bibliography, and summarize your findings.

- To successfully integrate source material into your research paper, be sure to introduce sources, establish your voice, and choose a point of view appropriate for your purpose and be consistent with it.

- Proper documentation is necessary to: give credibility to a paper, help readers and other researchers learn more, give credit where credit is due, observe the courtesies of conversation, and avoid plagiarism.

- Allow yourself enough time to plan, research, collaborate on, write, and format your paper properly.

Modern Language Association Style

Careful documentation and a complete works-cited list provide readers with full information on sources cited in the paper. (See The Logic of MLA Style, Chapter 14, pages 564–565 for information on in-text citations.)

To be useful to readers, citations must be clear and consistent. Therefore, very specific rules of documentation have been devised and must be applied.

Quick Reference

Using the following formats, begin preparing your works-cited entries as soon as you begin taking notes.

- A book by one author

  Author's last name, first name. *Book title.* Additional information. City of publication: Publishing company, publication date. Medium of publication.

- An article by one author

  Author's last name, first name. "Article title." *Periodical title* Date: inclusive pages. Medium of publication.

Citation Format

Most research writing in English and other humanities courses uses the documentation format described in the *MLA [Modern Language Association] Handbook for Writers of Research Papers,* seventh edition (New York: MLA, 2003). This documentation format, known as MLA style, is simple, clear, and widely accepted.

Accuracy and Completeness

Because works-cited entries direct readers to sources used in research writing, they must be as complete as possible and presented in a consistent and recognizable format. If the following guidelines do not cover a source you want to use, consult the *MLA Handbook,* your instructor, or a reference librarian.

What to Include in MLA Citations

MLA citations present information in an established order. When combining forms (to list a translation of a second edition, for example), follow these guidelines to determine the order of information:

1. *Author(s).* Use the name or names with the spelling and order shown on the title page of a book or on the first page of an article, without degrees, titles, or affiliations. If no author (individual or organization) is named, list the work by title in the works-cited entry.

2. *Title.* List titles from part to whole: the title of an essay (the part) before the book (the whole), the title of an article before the periodical title, an episode before the program, or a song before the compact disc. Use complete titles, including subtitles, no matter how long they are.

3. *Additional information.* In the order noted next, include any of the following information listed on the title page of the book or on the first page of an article: editor, translator, compiler, edition number, volume number, or name of series.

4. *Facts of publication.* For a book, find the publisher's name and the place of publication on the title page and the date of publication on the copyright page (immediately following the title page). Use the publisher's name in abbreviated form (numerous samples are present throughout the appendix), use the first city listed if more than one is given, and use the most recent date shown. When a city is outside the United States, include an abbreviation for the country, if necessary, for clarity. For a periodical, find the volume number, issue number, and date on the masthead (at the top of the first page of a newspaper or within the first few pages in a journal or magazine, often in combination with the table of contents).

5. *Page numbers.* When citing a part of a book or an article, provide inclusive page numbers without page abbreviations. Record inclusive page numbers from one to ninety-nine in full form (8–12, 33–39, 68–73); inclusive numbers of one hundred or higher require at least the last two digits and any other digits needed for clarity (100–02, 120–36, 193–206).

6. *Medium of publication.* MLA now requests that the medium of publication be included in citations: Print, Web, Film, DVD, and so on. For examples, see pp. 90, 288, 340, 380, 434, 474, 536, 582.

Format for MLA Works-Cited List

The MLA Works-Cited list follows these general formatting guidelines:

- Begin the first line of each entry at the left margin and indent subsequent lines one-half inch (five spaces).

- Invert the author's name so that it appears with the last name first (to alphabetize easily). If sources are coauthored, list additional authors' names in normal, first-last order.
- Italicize titles of full-length works. (MLA no longer recommends underlining in place of italicizing.)
- Separate major sections of entries (author, title, and publication information) with periods and one space, not two. When other forms of end punctuation are used (when titles end with question marks or exclamation points, for example), the period may be omitted.
- Double-space all entries; do not insert additional space between entries.

Annotations

Annotations are sometimes used to clarify for readers the value of sources or to provide additional information. Typically, these comments assess the quality of the source, describe the source's condition or availability, or provide additional clarification. In most student writing, annotations usually evaluate a source's value for the research project by highlighting its special features.

Present an annotation in one or more complete sentences. It follows the citation's closing period and retains the citation's indention pattern and line spacing, as in this sample.

> National Commission on Excellence in Education. *A Nation at Risk: The Imperative for Educational Reform.* Washington: GPO, 1983. Print. With its aggressively critical tone, this small publication by the NCEE launched the educational reform movement that is affecting our schools today.

Books

Book by one author

> Monmonier, Mark. *Rhumb Lines and Map Wars: A Social History of the Mercator Projection.* Chicago: U of Chicago P, 2004. Print.

(The letters *U* and *P,* without periods, abbreviate *University* and *Press.* Also note the medium consulted at the end of the entry, in this case *Print.*)

Book by two or more authors

Authors' names appear in the order in which they are presented on the title page, which may or may not be alphabetical. A comma follows the initial author's first name; second and third authors' names appear in normal order.

> Fainaru-Wada, Mark, and Lance Williams. *Game of Shadows: Barry Bonds, BALCO, and the Steroids Scandal That Rocked Professional Sports.* New York: Gotham, 2006. Print.

When a book has four or more authors, include only the first author's name in full form; substitute *et al.* (meaning "and others," not italicized) for the names of additional authors.

> McDaniel, Susan H., et al. *Family-Oriented Primary Care: A Manual for Medical Providers.* 2nd ed. New York: Springer, 2004. Print.

Book with no author   When no author is named, list the work by title. Alphabetize books listed by title using the first important word of the title, not the articles *a, an,* or *the.*

> *UPI Stylebook and Guide to Newswriting.* 4th ed. Sterling: Capital, 2004. Print.

Multiple works by the same author   When citing multiple works by the same author, present the first citation completely. Subsequent entries, alphabetized by title, are introduced by three hyphens and a period. Coauthored works require full names and are alphabetized after those with single authors.

> Ehrenreich, Barbara. *Bait and Switch: The (Futile) Pursuit of the American Dream.* New York: Metropolitan Books, 2005. Print.

> ---. *Nickel and Dimed: On (Not) Getting By in America.* New York: Holt, 2002. Print.

> Ehrenreich, Barbara, Elizabeth Hess, and Gloria Jacobs. *Re-Making Love: The Feminization of Sex.* Garden City: Anchor-Doubleday, 1986. Print.

(Notice that the publisher of the last selection includes a two-part name: the imprint and the major publisher; see "An Imprint," page 590, for an additional sample).

Books with an organization as author   When an organization is both the author and the publisher, present the name completely in the author position and use an abbreviation in the publisher position.

> American Psychological Association. *Publication Manual of the American Psychological Association.* 6th ed. Washington: APA, 2001. Print.

Edition other than the first   The edition number, noted on the title page, follows the title of the book. When a book also has an editor, translator, or compiler, the edition number follows that information. Edition numbers are presented in numeral-abbreviation form (2nd, 3rd, 4th).

> Bjelajac, David. *American Art: A Cultural History.* 2nd ed. Upper Saddle River: Prentice, 2004. Print.

Reprint   A reprint, a newly printed but unaltered version of a book, is identified as such on the title page or copyright page. The original publication date precedes the facts of publication, and the date of the reprinted edition follows the publisher's name.

> Joyce, James. *Ulysses.* 1992. Mineola: Dover, 2002. Print.

Multivolume work   A multivolume work may have one title, or it may have a comprehensive title for the complete work and separate titles for each volume. When you use the entire set of volumes, use the collective title and note the number of volumes. If volumes are published over several years, provide inclusive dates (2000–02); if the work is still in progress, include the earliest date, a hyphen, one space, and the closing period (1999– .).

The Norton Anthology of American Literature. Ed. Nina Baym. 6th ed. 5 vols. New York: Norton, 2002. Print.

To emphasize a single volume, first cite the volume as a separate book. Then add the volume number, the collection title, and the total number of volumes.

Ramazani, Jahan, Richard Ellman, and Robert O'Clair, eds. *Modern Poetry.* 3rd ed. New York: Norton, 2003. Print. Vol. 1 of *The Norton Anthology of Modern and Contemporary Poetry.*

Work in a collection

To cite a work in a collection, include the name of the selection's author, the title of the specific selection (appropriately punctuated), the collection title, publication facts, and the inclusive page numbers for the selection (without page abbreviations). To cite more than one selection from the collection, prepare separate citations (see Multiple Selections from the Same Collection, which follows).

Foster, Roy. "Something of Us Will Remain: Sebastian Barry and History." *Out of History: Essays on the Writings of Sebastian Barry.* Ed. Christina Hunt Mahony. Washington: Catholic U of America P, 2006. 183–97. Print.

Previously published work in a collection

To indicate that a selection has been previously published, begin the citation with original facts of publication. *Rpt.,* meaning "reprinted," begins the second part of the citation, which includes information about the source you have used.

Sloan, Gary. "Sleuthing Patriotic Slogans." *Alternet* 10 Apr. 2003. Rpt. in *The Thomson Reader: Conversations in Context.* Ed. Robert P. Yagelski. New York: Wadsworth, 2006. 323–26. Print.

Multiple selections from the same collection

To cite several selections from the same collection, prepare a citation for the complete work—beginning either with the editor's name or with the collection title. Additional references begin with the author of the individual selection and its title. However, instead of providing full publication information, include the editor's name or a shortened version of the title; provide inclusive page numbers for the selection. Notice that all citations are alphabetized.

Denman, Peter. "From Rhetoric to Narrative: The Poems of Sebastian Barry." Mahony 9–23.

Mahony, Christina Hunt, ed. *Out of History: Essays on the Writings of Sebastian Barry.* Washington: Catholic U of America P, 2006. Print.

Roche, Anthony. "Redressing the Irish Theatrical Landscape: Sebastian Barry's *The Only True History of Lizzie Finn.*" Mahony 147–65.

Article in an encyclopedia or other reference work

Use an author's name when it is available. If only initials are listed with the article, match them with the name from the list of contributors. Well-known reference books require no information other than the title, edition number (if any), and date.

Citations for less well-known or recently published reference works include full publication information. Page numbers are not needed when a reference work is arranged alphabetically.

> DeGregorio, William. "Zachary Taylor." *The Complete Book of U.S. Presidents.* 6th ed. New York: Gramercy, 2005. 175–86. Print.

(Because the articles on presidents are arranged chronologically, not alphabetically, page numbers are required.)

> Angermüller, Rudolph. "Salieri, Antonio." *The New Grove Dictionary of Music and Musicians.* 2001 ed. Print.

(This twenty-volume set is extremely well known and consequently needs no publication information.)

When no author's name or initials appear with an article, begin with the title, reproduced to match the pattern in the reference book. Other principles remain the same.

> "Socrates." *Encyclopedia of Ancient Greece.* Ed. Nigel Wilson. New York: Routledge, 2006. Print.

Work in a series The name of a series (a collection of books related to the same subject, genre, time period, and so on) is typically found on a book's title page and should be included at the end of the entry. Abbreviate the word *Series* (*Ser.*) if it is part of the series title.

> Yang, Gua-ja. *Contradictions.* Trans. Stephen Epstein and Kim Mi-Young. Ithaca: Cornell UP, 2005. Print. Cornell East Asia Ser.

When a volume in a series is numbered, include both the series name and the number, followed by a period.

> Audubon, John James. *The Audubon Reader.* New York: Knopf, 2006. Print. Everyman's Library 284.

Imprint An imprint is a specialized division of a larger publishing company. When an imprint name and a publisher name both appear on the title page, list them together (imprint name first), separated by a hyphen and no additional spaces.

> Atwood, Margaret. *The Tent.* New York: Talese-Doubleday, 2006. Print.

(Nan A. Talese is the imprint, which is shortened to *Talese*; Doubleday is the publisher.)

Translation A translator's name must always be included in a citation for a translated work because he or she prepared the version that you read. To emphasize the original work (the most common pattern), place the abbreviation *Trans.* (for "translated by," not italicized) and the translator's name after the title (but following editors' names, if the translator translated the entire work).

Allende, Isabel. *Zorro: A Novel*. Trans. Margaret Sayers Peden. New York: Harper, 2005. Print.

If selections within a collection are translated by different people, then each translator's name should follow the appropriate selection.

Freixis, Laura. "Absurd Ending." Trans. John R. King. *Short Stories in Spanish: New Penguin Parallel Texts*. Ed. John R. King. New York: Penguin, 2001. 143–62. Print.

(This citation indicates that John R. King was both translator and editor.)

Preface, introduction, foreword, epilogue, or afterword   To cite material that is separate from the primary text of a book, begin with the name of the person who wrote the separate material, an assigned title (if applicable) in quotation marks, a descriptive title for the part used (capitalized but not punctuated), the title of the book, the name of the book's author (introduced with *By*, not italicized), publication facts, and inclusive page numbers for the separate material. Note that most prefatory or introductory material is paged using lower-case roman numerals.

Updike, John. Introduction. *Walden*. By Henry David Thoreau. Ed. J. Lyndon Shanley. Princeton: Princeton UP, 2004, ix–xiii. Print.

Pamphlet   When a pamphlet contains clear and complete information, it is cited like a book. When information is missing, use these abbreviations: *N.p.* for "No place of publication," *n.p.* for "no publisher," *n.d.* for "no date," and *N. pag.* (with a space between the abbreviations) for "no page."

Depression and Spinal Cord Injury. Seattle: UW Medicine, 2005. N. pag. Print.

Dissertation   A citation for an unpublished dissertation begins with the author's name, the dissertation title in quotation marks, the abbreviation *Diss.* (not italicized), the name of the degree-granting school (with *University* abbreviated), and the date.

Wentland, Meghan Pontbriand. "Terrorists and Terrorism: Representations of Violence in 'Troubles' Fiction." Diss. Catholic U of America, 2004. Print.

A published dissertation is a book and should be presented as such. However, include dissertation information between the title and the facts of publication.

Sacred writings   A citation for a sacred writing follows a pattern similar to that of any other book, except information about its version and who translated it is should be included when available as well.

The Bhagavad Gita. Trans. and Intro. by Juan Mascaró. London: Rider & Co., 1970. Print.

The New Oxford Annotated Bible. Ed. Herbert G. May and Bruce M. Metzger. Rev. Expanded Edition. New York: Oxford UP, 1977. Print. Standard Version.

(This citation provides full information, highlighting a version other than the King James and the editorial work that it includes.)

Government-Civic Documents

Government
document

A citation for *Congressional Record* is exceedingly brief: the italicized and abbreviated title, *Cong. Rec.*, the date (presented in day-month-year order), and the page number. Page numbers used alone indicate Senate records; page numbers preceded by an *H* indicate records from the House of Representatives.

> *Cong. Rec.* 7 April 2006. 3380. Print.
>
> *Cong. Rec.* 6 April 2006. H1566. Print.

Government agency

Information to describe a government document is generally presented in this order: (1) country, state, province, or county; (2) government official, governing body, sponsoring department, commission, center, ministry, or agency; (3) office, bureau, or committee; (4) the title of the publication, italicized; (5) if appropriate, the author of the document, the number and session of Congress, the kind and number of the document; (6) the city of publication, the publisher, and the date.

When citing more than one work from the same government or agency, use three hyphens and a period to substitute for identical elements.

> United States. Cong. Senate. *Committee on Energy and Natural Resources.* 107th Cong., 2nd sess. 2002. Washington: GPO, 2003. Print.
>
> ---. Dept. of Education. *Alcohol, Other Drugs, and College: A Parent's Guide.* Washington: GPO, 2000. Print.
>
> ---. Dept. of Health and Human Services. *Steps to a Healthier US.* Washington: GPO, 2005. Print.

(The Government Printing Office, the publisher of most federal documents, is abbreviated to save space.)

Periodicals

Article in a monthly
magazine

To cite an article in a monthly magazine, include the author's name, the article's title in quotation marks, the magazine's name (italicized), the month (abbreviated) and year, the inclusive pages of the article (without page abbreviations), and the medium of publication.

> Teague, Matthew. "Double Blind: The Untold Story of How British Intelligence Infiltrated and Undermined the IRA." *The Atlantic* Apr. 2006: 53–62. Print.

(Note that the period comes before the closing quotation marks of the article's title, that one space [but no punctuation] separates the periodical title and the date, and that a colon separates the date and the pages.)

Article in a weekly magazine

A citation for an article in a weekly or biweekly magazine is identical to that for a monthly magazine, with one exception: the publication date is presented in more detailed form, in day-month-year order (with the month abbreviated).

> Conley, Kevin. "How High Can You Go? The Roller Coaster's New Golden Age." *The New Yorker* 30 Aug. 2005: 48–55. Print.

Article in a journal with continuous paging

A journal with continuous paging numbers issues sequentially for the entire year. For this kind of journal, place the volume and issue numbers after the journal title, identify the year in parentheses, follow it with a colon, list page numbers, and end with the medium of publication. Note that MLA no longer makes a distinction between journals continuously paged or not; include the volume and issue numbers for both.

> Fry, Prem S., and Dominique L. Debats. "Sources of Life Strengths as Predictors of Late-Life Mortality and Survivorship." *International Journal of Aging and Human Development* 62.1 (2006):303–34. Print.

Article in a journal with separate paging

For a journal that pages each issue separately, follow the volume number with a period and the issue number (without spaces). If no volume number is given, include the issue number alone.

> Brittan, Alice. "The Diarist, the Cryptographer, and *The English Patient*." *PMLA* 121.1 (2006): 200–13. Print.

Article in a newspaper

A citation for a newspaper resembles that for a magazine: it includes the author's name, article title (in quotation marks), newspaper title (italicized), the date (in day-month-year order, followed by a colon), inclusive pages, and medium of publication.

However, when a newspaper has editions (*morning, evening, national*), they must be identified. After the year, place a comma and describe the edition, abbreviating common words.

When sections of a newspaper are designated by letters, place the section letter with the page number, without a space (*A22, C3, F11*). If sections are indicated by numerals, place a comma after the date or edition (rather than a colon), include the abbreviation *sec.* (not italicized), the section number, a colon, a space, and the page number (*sec. 1: 22, sec. 3: 2, sec. 5: 17*).

> Callender, David. "Amid Scandals, Still No Sign of Campaign Reform." *Capital Times* [Madison] 15 Dec. 2005: A1. Print.

When an article continues in a later part of the paper, indicate the initial page, use a comma, and then add the subsequent page. If the article appears on more than three separated pages, list the initial page, followed by a plus sign (*22+, A17+, sec. 2: 9+*).

Weekly newspapers are cited just like daily newspapers.

Keefe-Feldman, Mike. "Heart of Noise." *Washington City Paper* 7 Apr. 2006: 311. Print.

Editorial   The citation for an editorial resembles that for a magazine or newspaper article, with one exception: the word *Editorial* (not italicized), with a period, follows the title of the essay.

Herbert, Bob. "George Bush's Trillion-Dollar War." Editorial. *New York Times* 23 Mar. 2006, natl. ed.: A25. Print.

Letter to the editor   Include the author's name, the word *Letter* (not italicized), the name of the publication (magazine, journal, or newspaper), and appropriate facts of publication. Do not record descriptive, attention-getting titles that publications, not authors, supply.

Alexie, Sherman. Letter. *Harper's* Dec. 2005: 6. Print.

Review   Begin with the author's name and the title of the review (if one is provided). The abbreviation *Rev. of* (not italicized) follows, publication information ends the citation, incorporating elements required for different kinds of sources.

Gleiberman, Owen. "The High Drama." Rev. of *Traffic*, dir. Steven Soderbergh. Perf. Benicio Del Toro, Catherine Zeta-Jones, Don Cheadle, and Michael Douglas. *Entertainment Weekly* 5 Jan. 2001: 45–46. Print.

Nonprint Sources

Lecture or speech   If you have difficulty finding the information to document nonprint sources clearly, ask your instructor or a librarian for help.

A citation for a formal lecture or speech includes the speaker's name, the title of the presentation (in quotation marks), the name of the lecture or speaker series (if applicable), the location of the speech (convention, meeting, university, library, meeting hall), the city, the date in day-month-year order, and the medium of delivery.

Courtright, Robert. "The Carpe Diem Poem." George Mason U, McLean. 11 Apr. 2006. Class Lecture.

Doyle, Roddy. "An Evening with Roddy Doyle." Seattle Arts and Lectures. Seattle.15 Nov. 2004. Lecture.

(For class lectures, provide as much of this information as possible: speaker, title of lecture in quotation marks, a descriptive title, the school, the city, and the date.)

Bush, George W. State of the Union Address. U.S. Capitol. 31 Jan. 2006. Address.

Work of art   When an artist titles his or her own work, include this information: artist's name; the title (italicized); the date of composition (if the year is unknown, write *N.d.*); the medium of composition; the museum, gallery, or collection where the work of art is housed; and the city (and country if needed for clarity).

> Cézanne, Paul. *Houses along a Road.* N.d. Oil on canvas. The Hermitage, St. Petersburg, Russia.

When an artist has not titled a work, use the title that art historians have given to it (not italicized), followed by a brief description of the work. The rest of the citation is the same.

> Madonna and Child with Cherubim. N.d. Bas-relief in marble. Vatican Library, Vatican City.

Map, graph, table, or chart A map, graph, table, or chart is treated like a book. If known, include the name of the author, artist, designer, scientist, person, or group responsible for the map, graph, table, or chart. Then include the title (italicized), followed by a separately punctuated descriptive title. Also include any other necessary information.

> Pope, C. Arden. *Children's Respiratory Hospital Admissions.* Graph.

Cartoon Begin with the cartoonist's name, the title of the cartoon in quotation marks, and the word *Cartoon* (not italicized), followed by a period. Then include the citation information required for the source and conclude with the medium of publication.

> Rees, David. "Get Your War On." Cartoon. *Rolling Stone* 11 Dec. 2003: 36. Print.

Film To cite a film as a complete work, include the title (italicized), the director (noted by the abbreviation *Dir.,* not italicized), the studio, and the date of release. If you include other people's contributions, do so after the director's name by using brief phrases (*Screenplay by, Original score by*) or abbreviations (*Perf.* for "performed by," *Prod.* for "produced by") to clarify their roles. Indicate a nonfilm format—VHS, DVD, or laserdisc—before the studio name. If a film is released by two studios, include both names, separated by a hyphen.

> *Ray*. Dir. Taylor Hackford. Perf. Jamie Foxx, Regina King. Universal Pictures, 2004. Film.

To emphasize the contribution of an individual (rather than the film as a whole), place the person's name first, followed by a comma and a descriptive title (beginning with a lowercase letter). The rest of the citation follows normal patterns.

> Allen, Woody, dir. *Anything Else*. Perf. Jason Biggs and Christina Ricci. Dream-Works SKG, 2003. Film.

> "Flunky File Clerk." *American Splendor*. Dir. Robert Pulcini and Shari Springer Berman. Perf. Paul Giamatti. HBO Video, 2003. DVD.

Television broadcast List a regular program by the title (italicized), the network (CBS, CNN, Fox), the local station (including both the call letters and the city, separated by a comma), the broadcast date (in day-month-year order), and the medium of reception.

Include other people's contributions after the program title, using brief phrases (*Written by, Hosted by*) or abbreviations (*Perf.* for "performed by," *Prod.* for "produced by") to clarify their roles.

> *The Sopranos*. Perf. James Gandolfini and Edie Falco. HBO. 15 Apr. 2006. Television.

To cite a single episode of an ongoing program, include the name of the episode in quotation marks before the program's title. Other elements are presented in the same order as used for a regular program.

> "Two Weeks Out." *The West Wing*. Perf. Alan Alda, Jimmy Smits, and Richard Schiff. NBC. WRC, Washington. 19 Mar. 2006. Television.

List special programs by title, followed by traditional descriptive information. If a special program is part of a series (for example, Hallmark Hall of Fame, Great Performances, or American Playhouse), include the series name without quotation marks or italics immediately preceding the name of the network.

> *The Sleeping Beauty*. Composed by Peter Ilich Tchaikovsky. Chor. Marius Petipa. Perf. Viviana Durante and Zoltan Solymosi. Great Performances. PBS. WFYI, Indianapolis. 24 Dec. 1995. Performance.

Radio broadcast A citation for a radio broadcast follows the same guidelines as those for a television broadcast.

> *The War of the Worlds*. CBS Radio. WCBS, New York. 30 Oct. 1938. Radio.

Recording A citation for a recording usually begins with the performer or composer, followed by the title of the recording (italicized except for titles using numerals for musical form, key, or number), the recording company, the copyright date, and the medium (such as *CD* for compact disc or *LP* for long-playing record).

> The Beatles. *Let It Be . . . Naked*. Capitol/Apple, 2003. CD.

> Davis, Miles. *The Cellar Door Sessions 1970*. 6 discs. Sony, 2005. CD.

To cite a single selection from a recording, include the selection title in quotation marks followed by the title of the complete recording. All else remains the same.

> Springsteen, Bruce. "Silver Palomino." *Devils and Dust*. Sony, 2005. CD.

To cite liner notes, the printed material that comes with many recordings, list the name of the writer and the description *Liner notes* (not italicized), followed by a period. The rest of the citation follows normal patterns.

MLA Style

> Kooper, Al. Liner notes. *Bob Dylan: No Direction Home: The Soundtrack [The Bootleg Series Vol. 7]*. 2 Discs. Sony, 2005. CD.

Interview A citation for a personally conducted interview includes the name of the person interviewed, the type of interview (personal or telephone), and the interview date.

> Heller, William. Personal interview. 5 Feb. 2006.

A citation for a broadcast or printed interview includes the name of the person interviewed, the descriptive title *Interview* (not italicized), and information necessary to describe the source.

> Holloway, Dave. Interview. *Larry King Live*. CNN. 11 Apr. 2006. Television.

Transcript A transcript of a program is presented according to the source of the original broadcast, with clarifying information provided.

> Adler, Margot. "Letters Offer Glimpse of Life in Nazi Labor Camps." *All Things Considered*. Natl. Public Radio. 7 Mar. 2006. Print. Transcript.

Questionnaire or survey A citation for a personally conducted questionnaire or survey begins with your name (since you are the author of the questions and compiler of the results) and then includes a descriptive title and the date (which may be inclusive) on which you gathered your information. For additional clarity, you may include information about the location of your work.

> Greene, Erika. Survey. Terre Haute: Indiana State U. 30 Jan. 2006. Print.

Electronic Sources

Businesses, organizations, government agencies, and publishers of all kinds have transferred many of their print-based documents to subscription databases, CD-ROMs, the Internet, online video broadcasts, and other electronic formats.

As you gather citation information for Internet and other electronic sources, you must be both resourceful and patient because the patterns of electronic publication are less consistent than those of traditional print publication. Your goal should be to gather the most complete set of data possible to describe each electronic source, following the patterns described in this section.

Online scholarly project or information database To cite an entire online scholarly project or information database, present available information in this order: the title of the project or database, italicized; the editor or compiler, if identified, introduced with the abbreviation *ed.* or *comp.* (not italicized); the version number, if applicable; the date of electronic posting or the date of the most recent update; the name of the sponsoring organization or institution, if identified; the medium of publication (Web); the date you accessed the site; and the electronic address (URL), in angle brackets. Note: Current MLA guidelines recommend that a URL be included in works-cited entries only when the reader probably cannot find the source without it or if your instructor requires one.

> *ProQuest.* 2006. ProQuest Company. Web. 10 Apr. 2006.

> *The Victorian Web.* Ed. George P. Landow. 2005. Brown U. Web. 11 Apr. 2006.

To cite a selected source—article, illustration, map, or other—from an online scholarly project or information database, begin with the name of the author (or artist, compiler, or editor) of the individual source, if appropriate; the title of the source, punctuated appropriately (quotation marks for articles, italics for charts, and so on); and print information if the source reproduces a print version. Continue the citation with the name of the online project or database and other required information. However, use the URL of the specific source, not the general address for the project or database, in angle brackets.

> Cody, David. "Queen Victoria." *Victorian Web.* 2005. Brown U. Web. 11 Sep. 2010. <http://www.victorianweb.org/vn/victor6.html>.

> Cooke, Bill. "Fatal Attraction." *Astronomy* 34.5 (2006): 46–52. *ProQuest.* 2006. ProQuest Company. Web. 20 Apr. 2006. <http://proquest.umi.com/pqdweb/>.

Website   To cite a website, including blogs, podcasts, and video, provide the name of the author, editor, or host, if any; the title of the site, italicized; the date of electronic posting or the date of the most recent update; the name of the organization or institution, if any, affiliated with the site; the medium of publication; the date you accessed the site; and the URL (if needed), in angle brackets. As the variety of online content, such as podcasts and v-casts, increases, new academic citation guidelines will be issued. For the purposes of your papers, it is most important that you provide your reader with enough information to locate and verify the site, and that you properly acknowledge any ideas or content that you find online.

> *ABA Law Student Division.* 5 Jan. 2002. American Bar Association. Web. 11 Jan. 2002.

> *UNICEF.* 7 Jan. 2002. United Nations. Web. 12 Jan. 2002.

> Atrios. "Unpopular President." *Escaton.* Web. 24 Apr. 2006. Weblog. <http:// atrios .blogstop.com.>

> ABC News. *The Afternote.* 22 Apr. 2006. Podcast. Web. 24 April 2006. <http:// abcnews.go.com/ThisWeek/>.

Online book   To cite an online book that has a corresponding print version, first prepare a standard citation describing the print version. Then provide additional information required for a scholarly project or information database, if applicable; the medium of publication; the date you accessed the site; and the specific URL of the book, not the general project or database, in angle brackets.

Tarkington, Booth. *Gentle Julia*. New York: Doubleday, 1922. *Project Gutenberg*. Apr. 2006. U of Illinois. Web. 26 Apr. 2006. <http://www.gutenberg.org/ etext/18259>.

Article in an online encyclopedia or reference source

To cite an online book that is available only in electronic form, provide the name of the author or editor; the title, italicized; the date of electronic posting or the date of the most recent update; the name of the sponsoring organization or institution, if provided; the medium of publication; the date you accessed the site; and the URL of the book, not the project or database, in angle brackets.

Buxhoeveden, Sophie. *The Life and Tragedy of Alexandra Feodorvna, Empress of Russia*. 2004. *Russian History Website*. Web. 20 Apr. 2006. <http://www .alexenderpalace.org/alexandra/>.

To cite an article from an online encyclopedia or reference source, provide the author of the entry, if there is one; the title of the entry exactly as it appears in the source ("Paige, Satchel"); the name of the reference work, italicized; the date of electronic posting or the date of the most recent update; the medium of publication; the date you accessed the site; and the URL for the specific article, not the general reference, in angle brackets.

Coney, Peter. "Plate Tectonics." *Encarta Online Encyclopedia*. 2006. Web. 4 Apr. 2006. <http://encarta.msn.com/encyclopedia_761554623/Plate_ Tectonics.html>.

Online government document

To cite an online version of a government document—book, report, proceedings, brochure, or other—first provide the information required for the print source. Then continue the citation with the information appropriate to the electronic source, whether it is a scholarly project, an information database, or a website.

United States. Cong. Budget Office. *China's Growing Demand for Oil and Its Impact on U.S. Petroleum Markets.* Washington: GPO, 2006. Cong. Budget Office. Web. 26 Apr. 2006. <http://www.cbo.gov/ftpdocs/71xx/doc7128/ 04-07-ChinaOil.pdf>.

Article in an online magazine

To cite an article in an online magazine, provide the name of the author, if appropriate; the title of the article, in quotation marks; the name of the magazine, italicized; the date of electronic publication or the date of the most recent update; the medium of publication; the date on which you accessed the article; and the URL of the specific article, not the general magazine site, in angle brackets.

O'Neill, Hugh. "You Say You Want a Resolution?" *Men's Health.com* 9 Jan. 2001. Web. 11 Jan. 2002. <http://www.menshealth.com/health/resolution.html>.

Article in an online journal

To cite an article in an online journal, provide the name of the author, if appropriate; the title of the article, in quotation marks; the name of the journal, italicized; the volume and issue number; the year of publication, in parentheses; the medium of publication; the date on which you accessed the article; and the URL of the specific article, not the general journal site, in angle brackets.

> Cramer, Kenneth M., and Lynn A. Perrault. "Effects of Predictability, Actual Controllability, and Awareness of Choice on Perceptions of Control." *Current Research in Social Psychology* 11.8 (2006). Web. 20 Apr. 2006. <http://www.uiowa.edu/%7Egrpproc/crisp/crisp.html>.

Article in an online newspaper

To cite an article in an online newspaper, provide the name of the author, if appropriate; the title of the article, in quotation marks; the name of the newspaper, italicized; the date of electronic publication or the date of the most recent update; the medium of publication; the date on which you accessed the article; and the URL of the specific article, not the general newspaper site, in angle brackets.

> Rodriguez, Cindy. "Amid Dispute, Plight of Illegal Workers Revisited." *Boston Globe* 9 Jan. 2001. Web. 10 Jan. 2002 <http://www.boston.com/dailyglobe2/010/nation/amid_dispute_plight_of_illegal_workers_revisited1.shtml>.

Online transcript of a lecture or speech

To cite the transcript of a lecture or speech, first provide the information required for a lecture or speech. Then include the word *Transcript*, not italicized; the date of electronic publication or the date of the most recent update; the medium of publication; the date on which you accessed the transcript; and the URL of the specific transcript, not the general site, in angle brackets.

> King, Martin Luther, Jr. Nobel Peace Prize Acceptance Speech. Nobel Prize Ceremony. Oslo, 10 Dec. 1964. Transcript. 2001. Web. 31 Jan. 2002. <http://www.stanford.edu/group/king>.

Work of art online

To cite a work of art online, provide the name of the artist, if known; the assigned title of the work of art, italicized, or the common name of the work of art, not italicized; a phrase describing the artistic medium; the museum, gallery, or collection where the work is housed; the city; the medium of publication; the date on which you accessed the work of art; and the URL of the specific work of art, not the general site, in angle brackets.

> Picasso, Pablo. *Les Demoiselles d'Avignon.* Oil on canvas. Museum of Modern Art. New York. Web. 30 June 2002. <http://www.moma.org/docs/collection/paintsculpt/C40.htm>.

Online map, graph, table, or chart

To cite a map, graph, table, or chart online, first provide the information required for the kind of visual element. Then continue the citation with the information appropriate to the electronic source, whether it is a scholarly project or an information database or a web site.

> "New York City Subway Route Map." Map. 5 Mar. 2000. New York City Subway Resources. Web. 9 Jan. 2002. <http://www.nycsubway.org/maps/route/>.

Online cartoon

To cite a cartoon online, provide the name of the cartoonist, if known; the assigned title of the cartoon, in quotation marks; the word *Cartoon,* not italicized; the source, italicized; the date of electronic publication or the date of the most recent update; the medium of publication; the date on which you accessed the cartoon; and the URL of the cartoon, not the general site, in angle brackets.

> Steiner, Peter. "Don't Anybody Move: This Is a Merger." Cartoon. *Cartoonbank.* 10 Jan. 2001. Web. 13 Jan. 2001. <k.com/cartoon_closeup.asp?/mscssid-52BGLVUGOU7S92MD000GPBQXMNAB6808>.

Online film or filmclip

To cite an online film or filmclip, first provide the information required for a film. Then include the name of your electronic source, italicized; the date of electronic publication or the date of the most recent update; the medium of publication; the date on which you accessed the film or filmclip; and the URL of the film or filmclip, not the general site, in angle brackets.

> *Reefer Madness.* Dir. Louis J. Gasnier. 1938. *The Sync.* 2000. 22 Apr. 2002. <http://www.thesync.com/ram/reefermadness.ram>.

Online transcript of a television or radio broadcast

To cite an online transcript of a television or radio broadcast, first provide the information required for a television or radio broadcast. Then include the word *Transcript,* not italicized; the medium of publication; the date on which you accessed the transcript; and the URL of the transcript, not the general site, in angle brackets.

> "Inside the World of Polygamy." *Larry King Live.* CNN, Washington. 15 Apr. 2006. Transcript. Web. 25 Apr. 2006. <http://transcripts.cnn.com/TRANSCRIPTS/0604/15/lkl.01.html>.

Online recording

To cite an online recording of previously released material, first provide the information required for a traditional recording. Then include the date of electronic publication or the date of the most recent update; the medium of publication; the date on which you accessed the recording; and the URL of the recording, not the general site, in angle brackets.

To cite an online recording that has not been previously released, provide the name of the recording artist; the title of the selection; and performance information such as concert locations and dates, recording studios, locations, or other relevant information. Then provide information about your source for the recording, whether a database or a website.

> Dylan, Bob. "Yea! Heavy and a Bottle of Bread." New York City, 11 Nov. 2002. Web. 20 Apr. 2006. <http://bobdylan.com/performances>.

CD-ROM sources

Because Internet sites provide researchers with more easily updated materials than do CD-ROMs, most libraries are phasing out CD-ROMs from their collections. However, you may still need to cite a CD-ROM source.

If a CD-ROM source reproduces material available in print form, begin the citation with full print information: author (or editor), title, and facts of publication. If the material is not available in print form, begin the citation with identifying information: author, if given; title, italicized; and the date of the material, if appropriate. Next, citations for both kinds of materials include the title of the publication, italicized; the description *CD-ROM*, not italicized; the city, if known, and name of the company that produced the CD-ROM; and the date of electronic publication.

> *The Baseball Encyclopedia: The Complete and Definitive Record of Major League Baseball.* CD-ROM. New York: Macmillan, 1996.

> Becklake, Sue. *All about Space.* Illus. Sebastian Quigley. CD-ROM. New York: Scholastic Reference, 1998.

Email interview

To cite an email interview, include the name of the person you interviewed; the phrase *Email interview,* not italicized; and the date of the email posting.

> Lublin, Robert. Email interview. 1 Mar. 2006.

Online posting

To cite an online posting to a forum or discussion group, provide the name of the author, if known; the official title of the posting, in quotation marks; or a descriptive title, without quotation marks; the phrase *Online posting,* not italicized; the date of electronic publication or the date of the most recent update; the name of the forum or discussion group; the medium of publication; the date on which you accessed the posting; and the URL of the posting, not the general forum or discussion site, in angle brackets.

> Bailey, Buddy. "What's Wrong with My Miniature Roses?" Online posting. 22 Apr. 2006. Miniature Roses Forum. Web. 26 Apr. 2006. <http://forums.gardenweb.com/forums/load/rosesmin/msg0422021712641.html?4>.

Creating a Works-Cited Page

Visit the website for this book for more information on creating a works-cited page.

American Psychological Association Style

In fields such as psychology, education, public health, and criminology, researchers follow the guidelines given in the *Publication Manual of the American Psychological Association,* sixth edition (Washington: APA, 2010) to document their work. Like MLA style, APA style encourages brevity in documentation, uses in-text parenthetical citations of sources, and limits the use of numbered notes and appended materials.

Paper Format

Title page Include a descriptive title, your name, and your affiliation (course or university), with two spaces between elements; center this information left to right and top to bottom. In the upper-right corner, include the first few words of the paper's title, followed by five spaces and the page number (without a page abbreviation). Two lines below, at the left margin, type the words *Running head* (not italicized), a colon, and a brief version of the title (no more than fifty letters and spaces) in all capital letters. The title page is always page 1.

Abstract On a separate page following the title page, type the label *Abstract* (capitalized but not italicized). Two lines below, include an unindented paragraph describing the major ideas in the paper; it should contain no more than 120 words.

Introduction Include a paragraph or series of paragraphs to define the topic, present the hypothesis (or thesis), explain the method of investigation, and state the theoretical implications (or context).

Body Incorporate a series of paragraphs to describe study procedures, results obtained, and interpretations of the findings.

In-text documentation In parentheses, include the author and date for summaries and paraphrases; include the author, date, and page number for quotations and facts.

List of sources Cite sources used in the paper in a listing titled "References."

Appendix Include related materials (charts, graphs, illustrations, and so on) that cannot be incorporated into the body of the paper.

Manuscript Format

Fonts Use any standard font with serifs (cross lines on the ends of individual letters). Sans serif fonts like Helvetica are used only for labeling illustrations, not for text.

Spacing Use italics to identify titles of complete, separately published works.

Margins All elements of the paper are double-spaced.

Paging Use one-inch margins at the top and bottom and on the left and right. Indent paragraphs five to seven spaces; indent long quotations five spaces.

Put the first two or three words of the title (no more than fifty letters and spaces) in the upper-right corner; after five spaces, include the page number without a page abbreviation.

Heading Whenever possible, use headings to label divisions and subdivisions of the paper.

Number style Express numbers one through nine (and zero) in words and all other numbers in numeral form.

Citation Format

The following samples illustrate a number of basic citation forms. If you are using other kinds of sources, consult the APA style guide.

Reference List Format

Book by one author Monmonier, M. (2004). *Rhumb lines and map wars: A social history of the Mercator Projection.* Chicago: University of Chicago Press.

(Use initials for the author's first name. After the author's name, place the publication date in parentheses, followed by a period. Capitalize only the first word of the title and of the subtitle and any proper nouns and proper adjectives. Spell out the names of university presses. For other publishers, retain only the words *Books* and *Press*.)

Book by two or more authors Fainaru-Wada, M., & Williams, L. (2006). *Game of shadows: Barry Bonds, BALCO, and the steroids scandal that rocked professional sports.* New York: Gotham.

(Invert the names of all authors. Insert an ampersand [&] before the last author's name.)

Book with an organization as author American Psychological Association. (2010). *Publication manual of the American Psychological Association* (6th ed.). Washington: Author.

(When the organization is also the publisher, use the word *Author* [not italicized] in the publisher position.)

Edition other than the first

Bjelajac, D. (2004). *American art: A cultural history* (2nd ed.). Upper Saddle River, NJ: Prentice Hall.

(Insert information about the edition in parentheses, following the title but before the period.)

Work in a collection

Foster, R. (2006). Something of us will remain: Sebastian Barry and history. In C. H. Mahony (Ed.), *Out of history: Essays on the writings of Sebastian Barry* (pp. 183–197). Washington: The Catholic University of America Press.

(Do not enclose the title of a short work in quotation marks. *In,* not italicized, introduces its source. Provide the editor's name, the abbreviation *Ed.* [capitalized, not italicized, and placed in parentheses] followed by a comma, the collection title, and inclusive page numbers for the short work [given in parentheses]. Abbreviate *pages.*)

Article in a monthly magazine

Teague M. (2006, April). Double blind: The untold story of how British intelligence infiltrated and undermined the IRA. *The Atlantic, 297,* 53–62.

(Give the year of publication followed by a comma and the month and day [if any]. When appropriate, follow the magazine title with a comma, one space, the volume number, and another comma [all italicized]. Do not use a page abbreviation.)

Article in a journal with separate paging

Brittan, A. (2006). The diarist, the cryptographer, and *The English Patient. PMLA: Publications of the Modern Language Association of America, 121*(1), 200–213.

(Italicize the name of the journal, the comma that follows it, and the volume number. The issue number [or numbers] in parentheses immediately follows the volume number; no space separates them; the issue number is *not* italicized. No abbreviation for pages accompanies the inclusive page numbers.)

Article in a newspaper

Callender, D. (2005, December 15). Amid scandals, still no sign of campaign reform. *The Capital Times* (Madison, Wisconsin), p. 1:1.

(Invert the date. Do not include information about the edition or section. When sections are indicated by letters, present them along with the page numbers with no intervening space.)

Lecture or speech

Doyle, R. (2004, November 15). *An evening with Roddy Doyle.* Lecture presented for Seattle Arts and Lectures. Seattle, Washington.

(Italicize the title of the speech. Follow the title with the name of the sponsoring organization and the location, separated by commas.)

Nonprint materials

Allen, W. (Director). (2003). *Anything else* [motion picture]. United States: Dream-Works SKG.

(List entries by the name of the most important contributor [director, producer, speaker, and so on]; note the specific role in full in parentheses following the name. Identify the medium [motion picture, slide show, tape recording] in brackets after the title. The country of origin precedes the name of the production company.)

Electronic Sources

Online scholarly project, information database, or website

Cody, D. (2005). Queen Victoria. Victorian Web. Providence: Brown University. Retrieved from http://www.victorianweb.org

(To cite an online scholarly project, information database, or professional website, include the author, if known, and the date in parentheses; the title of the source without special punctuation [followed by the date if there is no author]; the name of the project, database, or website; and a retrieval statement.)

Article in an online encyclopedia or reference source

Children in foster care. (2004). [Chart]. *Infoplease almanac.* Retrieved from http://www.infoplease.com/

(To cite an article from an online encyclopedia or reference source, provide the author of the entry, if there is one, and the date in parentheses; the title of the entry exactly as it appears in the source, without special punctuation [followed by the date if there is no author]; the type of medium in brackets [e.g., chart, figure, table]; the name of the reference work, italicized; and the retrieval statement.)

Article in an online magazine

Wheelright, J. (2001, January). Betting on designer genes. *Smithsonian, 31.* Retrieved from http://www.smithsonianmag.sr.edu/smithsonian/issues01/jan01/gene.html

(To cite an article in an online magazine, provide the name of the author, if appropriate; the date in parentheses; the title of the article; the name of the magazine and volume number, italicized; and the retrieval statement.)

Article in an online journal

Cramer, K., & Perrault, L. (2006). Effects of predictability, actual controllability, and awareness of choice on perceptions of control. *Current Research in Social Psychology, 11*(8). Retrieved from http://www.uiowa.edu/%7Egrpproc/crisp/crisp.html

(To cite an article in an online journal, provide the name of the author, if appropriate; the date in parentheses; the title of the article; the name of the journal and the volume number, italicized, and the issue number, not italicized; and the retrieval statement.)

Article in an online newspaper

Rodriguez, C. (2001, January 9). Amid dispute, plight of illegal workers revisited. *Boston Globe.* Retrieved from http://www.boston.com/dailyglobe2/010/nation/Amid_dispute_plight_of_illegal_workers_revisited1.html

(To cite an article in an online newspaper, provide the name of the author, if appropriate; the date of publication in parentheses; the title of the article; the name of the newspaper, italicized; and the retrieval statement.)

CD-ROM sources

Welmers, W. E. (2003). African languages. *The new Grolier multimedia encyclopedia*. Retrieved from Grolier database (Grolier, CD-ROM, 2003 release).

(To cite a CD-ROM source, provide the name of the author, if given; the release date; the title of the selection, without special punctuation; the CD-ROM title, italicized; and a special CD-ROM retrieval statement, which includes the publisher's name, without special punctuation, and, in parentheses, the name of the database; the description *CD-ROM,* not italicized; the release date; and an item number, if applicable.)

Online posting

Whinney, K. (2001, January 11). Discussion of *A clockwork orange.* [Online forum comment]. Book Lovers' Discussion. Retrieved from http://www .Whatamigoingtoread.com/book.asp?bookid56395

(To cite an online posting to a forum or discussion group, provide the name of the author, if known; the date of the posting; the official or descriptive title of the posting; a description of the message, in brackets; the name of the forum or discussion group; the phrase *Retrieved from,* not italicized; and the URL.)

Text Citation Format

One author

Greybowski (1995) noted that . . .

Or:

In a recent study at USC (Greybowski, 1995), participants were asked to . . .

Multiple authors: first citation

Cadrillo, Thurgood, Johnson, and Lawrence (1967) found in their evaluation . . .

Multiple authors: subsequent citations

Cadrillo et al. (1967) also discovered . . .

Corporate author: first citation

. . . a close connection between political interests and environmental issues (Council on Environmental Quality [CEQ], 1981).

Corporate author: subsequent citations

. . . in their additional work (CEQ, 1981).

Quotations Within the Text

First option

She stated, "The cultural awareness of a student depends, by implication, on the cultural awareness of the parents" (Hermann, 1984, p. 219).

Second option

Hermann (1984) added that "enrichment in our schools is costly and has little bearing on the later lives of the students" (pp. 230–231).

Third option

"A school's responsibility rests with providing solid educational skills, not with supplementing the cultural education of the uninterested," stated Hermann (1984) in her summary (p. 236).

Index

Thinking and Writing Journal

Thinking and Writing Journal

Thinking and Writing Journal

Thinking and Writing Journal

Thinking and Writing Journal

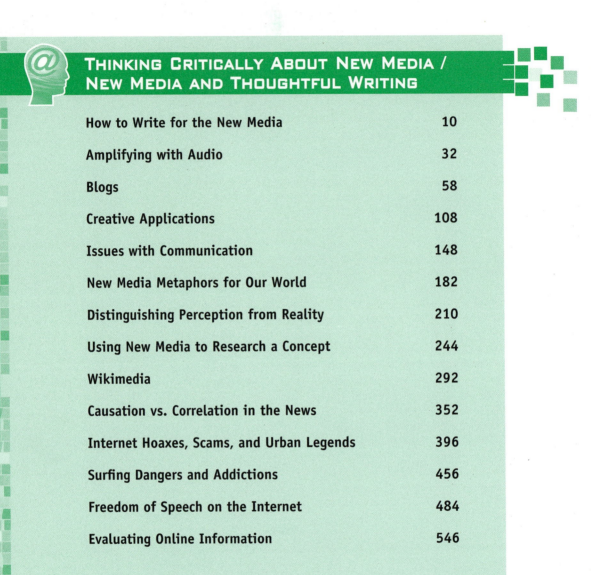

THINKING CRITICALLY ABOUT NEW MEDIA /
NEW MEDIA AND THOUGHTFUL WRITING